THE VICTORIA HISTORY
OF THE
COUNTIES OF ENGLAND

—

A HISTORY OF
STAFFORDSHIRE

VOLUME VI

THE VICTORIA HISTORY
OF THE
COUNTIES OF ENGLAND

EDITED BY C. R. ELRINGTON

THE UNIVERSITY OF LONDON
INSTITUTE OF
HISTORICAL RESEARCH

Oxford University Press, Walton Street, Oxford OX2 6DP

OXFORD   LONDON   GLASGOW
NEW YORK   TORONTO   MELBOURNE   WELLINGTON
KUALA LUMPUR   SINGAPORE   JAKARTA   HONG KONG   TOKYO
DELHI   BOMBAY   CALCUTTA   MADRAS   KARACHI
NAIROBI   DAR ES SALAAM   CAPE TOWN

© *University of London* 1979

ISBN 0 19 722733 3

PRINTED IN GREAT BRITAIN BY
ROBERT MACLEHOSE AND CO. LTD
PRINTERS TO THE UNIVERSITY OF GLASGOW

INSCRIBED TO THE

MEMORY OF HER LATE MAJESTY

QUEEN VICTORIA

WHO GRACIOUSLY GAVE THE TITLE TO

AND ACCEPTED THE DEDICATION

OF THIS HISTORY

The May cattle fair in Gaolgate Street, Stafford, *c.* 1890

A HISTORY OF THE COUNTY OF STAFFORD

STAFFORD

VOLUME VI

EDITED BY M. W. GREENSLADE AND D. A. JOHNSON

PUBLISHED FOR

THE INSTITUTE OF HISTORICAL RESEARCH

BY

OXFORD UNIVERSITY PRESS

1979

Distributed by Oxford University Press until 1 January 1982
thereafter by Dawsons of Pall Mall

CONTENTS OF VOLUME SIX

LIST OF ILLUSTRATIONS

Grateful acknowledgement is made to the following for permission to use material: Aerofilms Ltd.; the British Library Board; the Controller of H. M. Stationery Office; Highfield Photographics; Mr. J. S. Horne; the National Monuments Record; the Staffordshire County Council Museum Service; the Staffordshire County Council Planning Department; and the Trustees of the William Salt Library.

LIST OF ILLUSTRATIONS

LIST OF MAPS AND PLANS

All the maps and plans were drawn by K. J. Wass of the Department of Geography, University College, London, except for the church plans, which were drawn by A. P. Baggs. The elevation and plan of Stallington Grange was redrawn from J. Loch, *An Account of the Improvements on the Estates of the Marquess of Stafford* . . . (1820), plate XXVI, and the plan of new buildings for Beaudesert Home Farm from the original at the Staffordshire Record Office (D. 603, unlisted). The maps of Groundslow Fields farm were redrawn from two printed maps (Birmingham, 1844; copies at the William Salt Library, Stafford, 11/313/50). The map of Stafford in 1977 was drafted by M. W. Greenslade and is based on the Ordnance Survey with the sanction of the Controller of H.M. Stationery Office, Crown Copyright reserved. The plan of Stafford in 1610 is reproduced from the map of Staffordshire dated 1610 in J. Speed, *The Theatre of the Empire of Great Britaine* (1611). The plan of Stafford in 1835 was redrawn from the central portion of *Plan of Stafford from Actual Survey, 1835* (surveyed by John Wood and published by Leith & Smith, Edinburgh, n.d.). The map of Stafford in 1877 was redrawn from a map at the William Salt Library (M. 765), produced by the borough surveyor's office in December 1877. The elevation and plan of the Staffordshire General Infirmary by Benjamin Wyatt & Sons is reproduced from Staffordshire Views, ix. 30, at the William Salt Library. Thanks for permission to use material are rendered to the Marquess of Anglesey and the Trustees of the William Salt Library.

EDITORIAL NOTE

THIS volume is the eighth to appear in the Staffordshire set of the Victoria History of the Counties of England. Like its six immediate predecessors it has been produced by the Staffordshire Victoria History Committee, which represents a partnership between the University of London and the Local Authorities in Staffordshire. The nature of the partnership is described in the Editorial Note to Volume IV. Since 1974 the contributing authorities have been the Staffordshire County Council and the metropolitan boroughs of Dudley, Sandwell, Walsall, and Wolverhampton. The University of London wishes to express its thanks to them for their continued support and their generous and increased financial help. The individual members of the Staffordshire Committee are listed below on page xiv. In 1978 Dr. C. R. J. Currie resigned as Assistant County Editor to take up the post of Deputy Editor of the Victoria History of the Counties of England.

Of the many people and organizations who have helped in the preparation of the volume, several are acknowledged in the lists of illustrations and of maps and plans and in the footnotes to the articles where their help was given. Thanks are also offered to Mr. D. E. Almond, chief executive of Stafford Borough; Mr. J. F. Amery; Mrs. Joan Anslow; Mr. S. Barton, Staffordshire County Librarian, and his staff at the County Library Headquarters; Mr. D. R. Beard of Stoke-on-Trent Central Library; Mr. P. Butters; Mr. H. Dyson of Stafford Library and his staff, especially Miss M. S. Reid; Mr. C. Ecclestone of Stafford Museum; Mr. M. B. S. Exham, Registrar of Lichfield Diocese; the Earl of Harrowby and Miss Mairi Macdonald, formerly archivist at Sandon Hall; Mr. J. S. Horne; Miss Jane Isaac, assistant archivist at the Lichfield Joint Record Office; Mr. R. A. Lewis of the Staffordshire County Council Education Department; the Revd. J. D. McEvilly, archivist to the Archbishop of Birmingham; Mr. A. J. Mealey of Walsall Central Library; Mrs. P. J. Phelps of Tamworth Library; Mr. J. Rhodes of the Museum of Staffordshire Life at Shugborough; Mr. K. W. Sheridan of the Staffordshire County Council Planning Department; Mr. F. B. Stitt, Staffordshire County Archivist and William Salt Librarian, and his staff, especially Miss Beryl Daniels; and Mr. A. G. Taylor of the Staffordshire County Council Planning Department.

The structure and aims of the *Victoria History* as a whole are outlined in the *General Introduction* (1970).

LIST OF CLASSES OF DOCUMENTS
IN THE PUBLIC RECORD OFFICE
USED IN THIS VOLUME
WITH THEIR CLASS NUMBERS

NOTE ON ABBREVIATIONS

Among the abbreviations and short titles used the following, in addition to those listed in the Victoria History's *Handbook for Editor and Authors*, may require elucidation:

'Agric. Our Vital Ind.'	A series of articles in *Staffordshire Advertiser* under the general title 'Agriculture — "Our Vital Industry" ', written by 'Viator' until the issue of 31 August 1918 and thereafter by Neville Wood
B.R.L.	Birmingham Central Library, Reference Library
Bradley, *Charters*	*The Royal Charters and Letters Patent granted to the Burgesses of Stafford A.D. 1206–1828*, translated and annotated by John W. Bradley (Stafford, 1897)
Calvert, *Stafford*	C. Calvert, *History of Stafford, and Guide to the Neighbourhood* (Stafford, 1886)
Cherry, *Stafford*	J. L. Cherry, *Stafford in Olden Times* (Stafford, 1890)
City of London R.O.	City of London Record Office
Dewhirst & Nichols, *Map of Stafford* (1838)	*Map of the Borough of Stafford* (drawn by J. Dewhirst, published by Dewhirst & Nichols, 1838)
Erdeswick, *Staffs.*	S. Erdeswick, *A Survey of Staffordshire*, ed. T. Harwood (1844 edn.)
'Farming Interviews'	A series of articles under that general title by Neville Wood in *Staffordshire Advertiser*
G.R.O.	General Register Office, London
J.R.A.S.E.	Royal Agricultural Society of England, *Journal*
Keen, *Letter to Inhabitants of Stafford*	W. Keen, *A Letter to the Inhabitants of Stafford, containing some account of the trusts reposed in the Corporation, and of the charities given to the Borough* (Stafford [1828])
Kettle, 'Street-names'	Ann J. Kettle, 'The Early Street-names of Stafford', in the Stafford Historical and Civic Society's *Transactions* for 1974–6
L.J.R.O.	Lichfield Joint Record Office
Lich. Dioc. Regy.	Lichfield Diocesan Registry
Myers, *Staffs.*	J. Myers, *Staffordshire* (1945; part 61 of *The Land of Britain*, published by the Land Utilisation Survey of Britain)
N.S.J.F.S.	*North Staffordshire Journal of Field Studies*
Pevsner, *Staffs.*	N. Pevsner, *The Buildings of England: Staffordshire* (1974)
Pitt, *Staffs.*	W. Pitt, *A Topographical History of Staffordshire* (Newcastle-under-Lyme, 1817)
Plot, *Staffs.*	R. Plot, *The Natural History of Staffordshire* (Oxford, 1686)
Roxburgh, *Stafford*	A. L. P. Roxburgh, *Stafford* (Stafford, 1948)
S.H.C.	Staffordshire Record Society (formerly William Salt Archaeological Society), *Collections for a History of Staffordshire*
S.R.O.	Staffordshire Record Office
Salop. R.O.	Shropshire Record Office
Shaw, *Staffs.*	Stebbing Shaw, *The History and Antiquities of Staffordshire* (2 vols., 1798, 1801)
Speed, *Map of Staffs.* (1610)	'Stafford countie and towne with the ancient citie Lichfeild described . . . 1610', in John Speed, *The Theatre of the Empire of Great Britaine* (1611)
Stafford Libr.	Staffordshire County Libraries, Stafford Area Library
Staffs. Cath. Hist.	*Staffordshire Catholic History* (the Journal of the Staffordshire Catholic History Society)

NOTE ON ABBREVIATIONS

Staffs. County Mus.   Museum of Staffordshire Life, Shugborough

Sturgess, 'Agric. Staffs.'   R. W. Sturgess, 'The Response of Agriculture in Staffordshire to
                                       the Price Changes of the 19th Century' (Manchester University
                                       Ph.D. thesis, 1965)

T.B.A.S.   Birmingham and Midland Institute: Birmingham Archaeological
                                       Society, *Transactions and Proceedings*

T.N.S.F.C.   North Staffordshire Field Club, *Transactions*

T.O.S.S.   Old Stafford Society (later Stafford Historical and Civic Society),
                                       Transactions

T.S.H.C.S.   Stafford Historical and Civic Society, *Transactions*

W.S.L.   William Salt Library, Stafford

Wood, *Plan of Stafford* (1835)   *Plan of Stafford from Actual Survey, 1835* (surveyed by John
                                       Wood, published by Leith & Smith, Edinburgh)

Yates, *Map of Staffs.* (1775; 1799)   W. Yates, *A Map of the County of Stafford . . . Begun in the Year
                                       1769 and Finished in 1775* (1775; revised edition by W. Faden,
                                       1799)

ANALYSIS OF SOURCES

PRINTED IN

COLLECTIONS FOR A HISTORY OF STAFFORDSHIRE

(STAFFORDSHIRE RECORD SOCIETY)

AND USED IN THIS VOLUME

ANALYSIS OF SOURCES

MEDIEVAL AGRICULTURE

The Late 11th Century, p. 1. 1100 to 1350, p. 6 (the Fields, p. 12; the Landlords, p. 18; the Peasantry: Holdings, Status, and Rent, p. 24; the Peasantry: Farming, p. 30). The Later Middle Ages, p. 35 (Crisis, p. 35; Landlords and Peasants, p. 39; Farming, p. 43).

THE basic pattern of medieval settlement in the county was established by the 11th century.[1] It was concentrated in the south-east and east, especially in the valleys of the Trent, Tame, and Dove, in the central lowland, in particular along the river valleys, and in the south-west. The whole of the northern upland was thinly populated, notably the south Pennine fringe in the far north and north-east. Two areas in the centre of the county were conspicuously bare of settlement, an indication of the presence of Cannock and Needwood forests. The main manors of the important pre-Conquest landholders, which were often large and with numerous appendages, lay mostly along the river valleys of the south-east and centre and in a band extending west towards the Severn. This may reflect the main lines of Anglo-Saxon settlement of the county, dating back to the late 6th century. The later-settled, smaller, and unitary manors of the areas in between and the northern upland tended to be held by lesser men.[2]

THE LATE 11TH CENTURY

Domesday Book lists some 334 Staffordshire settlements, most of them small; 74 were without recorded inhabitants in 1086, 148 had fewer than 10, and only 16 had 30 or more. The county's total recorded population of about 3,000 varied in density from only 0·3 and 0·6 per square mile in, respectively, the Cannock forest and the north-eastern regions to 4·6 in the south-east.[3]

Both plough-lands and plough-teams are normally recorded in the Staffordshire Domesday. The latter, generally assumed to indicate actual working eight-ox ploughs, were thinly spread in Staffordshire compared with neighbouring counties to the south and east. This is particularly so throughout the whole of the north, the southern upland, and the area of Needwood forest, but even in the south-east, where teams were most numerous, the density reached only 1·6 per square mile.[4] Also, individual concentrations of arable were generally small, with three or fewer plough-teams in over half the settlements.

Plough-lands present greater problems of interpretation. It has been assumed that they represent a contemporary estimate of potential or once-cultivated arable. In that case the frequent excess of lands over teams which is characteristic of Staffordshire may show a recent regression of cultivation, with only a few exceptional cases where recent expansion had produced more teams than lands. It seems more likely, however, that plough-lands represent an attempt at a new fiscal re-assessment, using various

[1] Thanks are offered to Dr. E. Miller for reading and commenting on this article in draft.

[2] For a full discussion of the Staffordshire Domesday see P. Wheatley, 'Staffordshire', *Domesday Geography of Midland Eng.* ed. H. C. Darby and I. B. Terrett (1971 edn.), 163–216; *V.C.H. Staffs.* iv. 1–60. A comparison of Staffs. material with that of other counties is possible from *A New Historical Geography of Eng.* ed. H. C. Darby, 39–74.

[3] *Domesday Geog. Mid. Eng.* 171–5, 188; *V.C.H. Staffs.* iv. 20.

[4] *Domesday Geog. Mid. Eng.* 184–5.

local bases for the calculation.[5] Staffordshire's hidage, about 500, was low, but there were about 1,300 plough-lands.[6] For the estate of Burton abbey a possible correlation between hides and plough-lands has been traced, but a comparison with surveys drawn up by the abbey in the early 12th century suggests another line of approach. The *censarii*, or money-rent payers, who are recorded in significant numbers in the surveys, are not mentioned in Domesday Book, though they can hardly all have appeared since 1086. Domesday's record of the peasant population may therefore ignore some categories. The existence of the money-rent payers may, however, be reflected in the Domesday plough-lands, which seem to be based on the villein teams plus the teams of the *censarii*.[7]

Domesday's manorial values also present problems of interpretation. There is a frequent apparent lack of correlation between listed resources and values in particular cases and in addition a likelihood that values may reflect other forms of wealth such as pastoral farming. Staffordshire is a county of low values, with vills worth £2 or less characteristic of every hundred.[8] The average value per working team and per recorded person, which may show the uneven distribution of sources of wealth other than arable, is very much the same (about 9s. and 3s.) for the hundreds of Totmonslow in the north-east, Pirehill, covering the rest of the north and much of the central lowland, and Seisdon in the south-west. They are both higher for Offlow hundred, which includes the rich river valleys of the south-east, and the calculation, which can admittedly only give a rough indication, tends to emphasize for this early period the relative prosperity of the south-east, in which there may well have been a pastoral element. Some of the highest values per team in the county occur in the south-east: Alrewas, for example, had 8 teams and a value of £11 and Elford had 11 teams and a value of £12. Outside the south-east, Rocester (11 teams and a value of £8), Leek (6 teams and a value of £5), and Pattingham (3 teams and a value of £3) are outstanding examples of manors with a value that seems high in view of the listed resources.[9]

Domesday also notes mills, fisheries, meadow, and woodland. At least 50 mills are recorded, mainly scattered along the rivers and streams of the central lowland, the south-east, and the south-west, and worth for the most part a few shillings.[10] Three mills at Worfield (later Salop.) worth 40s. and a pair of mills at Drayton Bassett rendering 21s. are the most valuable recorded. The relationship between mill renders and manorial values is not clear, but even the small renders which are the norm are significant compared with the typically low Staffordshire values. Overall, however, it is the small number of mills which is a characteristic of the county. The record of a render of 4,000 eels from Meretown mill in Forton and references to the 1,500 eels issuing from the Trent at Alrewas and to a fishery at Worfield show the importance of fishing in the local economy.

Meadow was of vital importance in an economy where the provision of fodder for stock was a perennial problem. It was recorded in considerable acreages in the river valleys of the east and south-east, but in only small amounts in most of the rest of the county and very rarely in the north.[11]

Domesday notes stretches of woodland attached to about half the settlements described and makes it plain in several entries that it was for stock that woodland was chiefly valued.[12] The entries are given in a way that makes realistic estimates of area

[5] Sally P. J. Harvey, 'Domesday Book and Anglo-Norman Governance', *Trans. R.H.S.* 5th ser. xxv. 186 sqq.

[6] *Domesday Geog. Mid. Eng.* 183, 186.

[7] J. F. R. Walmsley, 'The "Censarii" of Burton Abbey and the Domesday Population', *N.S.J.F.S.* viii. 73–80.

[8] *V.C.H. Staffs.* iv. 11–12.

[9] Ibid. 39–40.

[10] For the rest of this para. see *Domesday Geog. Mid. Eng.* 204–7; *V.C.H. Staffs.* iv. 21.

[11] *Domesday Geog. Mid. Eng.* 199–201.

[12] For this para. see ibid. 194–9; *V.C.H. Staffs.* ii. 335; iv. 21.

impossible, and in any case they probably record only the woodland exploited by farmers. The first clear documentary references to the forests which covered much of the county date from the 12th century, but the woodland is certainly older, and indeed Domesday appears to refer to expanding royal forest in entries for the Kinver and Brewood areas. The presence of the forests of Cannock and Needwood, as has been noted above, is shown in the settlement pattern.

Domesday records a large number of settlements, about a fifth of the total, that were waste, with plough-lands estimated but without inhabitants, teams, mills, or other manorial resources. Most of those settlements lay in the northern uplands. The phenomenon has been attributed both to harrying by William I in 1069–70 and to the general poverty of the county.[13] In fact it seems likely that it was the richer lowlands that were ravaged. If so, the Domesday waste reflects colonization of marginal land in late Saxon times as a result of population pressure and subsequent migration into the more favourable lowlands after they had been depopulated by William.[14] It may also be that some settlements were listed as waste not because they were desolate but because they had been absorbed into other manors and were administered from them.[15]

The chief landholders of the immediate pre-Conquest period in addition to the king were the bishop of Lichfield and a small group of earls.[16] The endowment of Burton abbey included a number of properties donated by the wealthy Mercian thegn Wulfric Spot, whose will of c. 1000 reveals a large estate, including land in many counties, which was broken up on his death. Burton abbey suffered some losses in the pre-Conquest period but also achieved some consolidation of its estates overall and inside the county.[17] Similarly several of the 1086 properties of another pre-Conquest foundation, the collegiate church at Wolverhampton, date back to the original endowment.[18] In 1086 the chief landholders in addition to the king were the bishop of Chester, Burton abbey, and four barons, Henry de Ferrers, Robert de Stafford, William fitz Ansculf, and Roger, earl of Shrewsbury, whose estates together accounted for a good proportion of the county. Three of the baronial estates survived in the main through the Middle Ages, though the Ferrers estate, the honor of Tutbury, passed to the Crown as part of the duchy of Lancaster; the estate of Earl Roger did not long survive the Conquest. In 1086 a high proportion of the Staffordshire manors of all four barons were in the hands of under-tenants, and the ancestors of several prominent 12th-century Staffordshire families can be traced in the Domesday entries.[19]

The characteristic manorial division of land between demesne and tenant land was found in about two-thirds of the county's villages by 1086. Of the rest a very few had demesne only, and more possessed only peasant teams. Over the county as a whole about three-quarters of the teams were held by peasants, and peasant teams outnumbered demesne teams in most villages. Villages of divided lordship were rare. Demesnes were usually small, the great majority having three teams or less. Burton abbey had, in comparison with other Staffordshire landowners, a large area of demesne as opposed to tenant land, with 10½ demesne teams compared with 20½ of the peasantry. The bishop's 22 demesne teams compared with over 60 held by peasants, and the demesne of the large, scattered baronial estates tended to be even smaller in proportion.

[13] *Domesday Geog. Mid. Eng.* 202–4; *V.C.H. Staffs.* iv. 12–13.
[14] T. A. M. Bishop, 'The Norman Settlement of Yorks.' *Studies in Medieval Hist. Presented to F. M. Powicke*, ed. R. W. Hunt and others, 7; D. M. Palliser, *The Staffs. Landscape*, 58.
[15] See W. E. Wightman, *The Lacy Family in Eng. and Normandy 1066–1194*, 50–1, 53.
[16] *V.C.H. Staffs.* iv. 6 sqq. For changes in the style of the bishopric see ibid. iii. 2, 7 sqq.
[17] Ibid. iii. 200–1.
[18] Ibid. 321–2; C. R. Hart, *Early Charters of Northern Eng. and the N. Midlands*, 97–8.
[19] *V.C.H. Staffs.* iv. 26 sqq.; Sanders, *Eng. Baronies*, 148–9.

Earl Roger had 10 teams in demesne in the county, compared with 34 peasant teams; Robert de Stafford 6 compared with 45½.[20]

The Staffordshire Domesday divides the peasantry neatly into three categories, villeins (nearly 60 per cent), bordars (about 30 per cent) and slaves (about 8 per cent).[21] Villeins and bordars, usually assumed to be respectively villagers with holdings of a size large enough to support a family and smallholders or landless, are normally found together and in no regular proportions. The form of the Staffordshire entries suggests that bordars often shared village plough-teams with villeins. No standard level of plough-beasts amongst either category existed. At two extremes, both villeins and bordars occasionally appear without ploughs, while a single villein held a plough with a slave at Coton, in St. Mary's, Stafford. In general villeins probably held bigger shares in teams, while overall, if each team consisted of 8 oxen, most peasants probably had between 1 and 3 oxen.[22] Villein labour-rent, described in more detail for the Burton abbey estate in the early 12th century, is indicated in the entry for Drayton Bassett,[23] but otherwise Domesday is silent on peasant status and rent.

The third category of peasants, the slaves, were least numerous but were still a sizeable minority. They appear, usually in ones and twos, on manors throughout the county, though rarely in the north-east and with some concentration in the south-west. Most are apparently associated with demesnes, appearing on both large and small demesnes and on manors of lesser and greater lords. The bishop, for example, with a large number of slaves by Staffordshire standards, had 8 at Brewood, with 3 demesne plough-teams, but only 2 at Eccleshall, with 4 demesne plough-teams, and none at either Baswich (1 demesne plough) or Haywood in Colwich (2 demesne ploughs). Slaves are sometimes associated with the other peasants, as at Tittensor in Stone, where 8 villeins, 2 bordars, and a slave held 1½ plough.[24]

In 1086 the county was poor, backward, and thinly settled.[25] The north, especially the extreme north-east, was characterized by thinly-scattered and small settlements concentrated in the Dove and Manifold valleys. There were two manors in Ellastone, where 19 villeins and 9 bordars held 4½ ploughs between them (a high ratio of peasants to a team), but the settlements further north were very small, and several are described as waste or without teams. The demesnes were all small. There was one team each at Alstonefield (held of Earl Roger), Blore (held of Robert de Stafford), and Mayfield (in the hands of the king), though the bishop had 2 teams at Ellastone and Robert de Stafford 1½ with a slave (the latter rare in that part of the county). Recorded meadow consisted of 8 a. at Mayfield, 8 a. at Warslow (a member of Alstonefield), and 15 a. at Ellastone, and there was a little woodland on several manors. Values were low, £2 T.R.E. at Mayfield being the highest. Further west the population and plough-team density remained low, but there were more settlements, including a few of some size and value by the standards of the county. The high value of the royal manor of Leek, for example, has already been noted. Its listed resources include 12 plough-lands, 15 villeins and 13 bordars with 6 ploughs, 3 a. of meadow, and some woodland. To the south-west another royal manor, Penkhull in Stoke-upon-Trent, had 11 plough-lands, 2 teams in demesne, 8 teams held by 17 villeins and 6 bordars, and a 1086 value of £6. Smaller settlements were more numerous, for example a string of small manors in the north-west held in 1086 by thegns. Thus Gamel had land valued at 4s. at Balterley in Barthomley, no demesne team, but a villein and 3 bordars with half a team. He apparently had no demesne team on his manor at Talke in Audley, where

[20] V.C.H. Staffs. iv. 41–53, 58–9.
[21] Domesday Geog. Mid. Eng. 187.
[22] V.C.H. Staffs. iv. 18–19.
[23] Ibid. 40.
[24] Ibid. 41–2, 51.
[25] The next 5 paras. are based on the translation of the Staffs. Domesday printed ibid. 37–60.

there were 4 villeins with a plough, but he had one at Audley itself, where 4 villeins and 3 bordars shared another plough. Talke was valued at 3s., Audley at 10s. Talke and Audley had an acre of meadow each and Balterley ½ acre; all three also had some woodland.

Another thinly populated region was the southern upland, in particular the northern part, which was apparently more or less completely bare of settlement and was the heart of Cannock forest. To the east, however, Lichfield, the chief episcopal manor, was a settlement of some importance, described as having land for 73 ploughs. The bishop had there the second largest demesne in the county, 10 teams with 10 slaves. There were 42 villeins and 12 bordars with 21 ploughs. Five canons of Lichfield held a further 3 ploughs, and the manor had 35 a. of meadow, a large area of woodland, and two mills worth 4s. Numerous villages, some near by, some at a distance, are described as members or berewicks of Lichfield, and their 7 demesne ploughs, 25 peasant ploughs, meadows, and mill contributed to the Lichfield value of £15.

To the west of the southern upland there were several larger settlements, notably Wolverhampton and Sedgley. The former, held by the canons of Wolverhampton, was unusual for the county. There were more demesne than peasant plough-teams (10 to 9) and a group of 14 slaves on the demesne. The recorded peasant population was remarkable for the high proportion of bordars: there were 30, who shared the 9 ploughs with 6 villeins. Sedgley, a manor of William fitz Ansculf, was more typical of the larger manors in the county. William had there one demesne team and 3 slaves, while 45 villeins, a priest, and 2 bordars held 18 teams. In addition a certain Geoffrey held 2 hides of William, with one demesne plough, and 9 villeins held 2 ploughs. The main manor was valued at £10 and Geoffrey's part at £1.

The remainder of the county was more populous, except where woodland, notably Needwood forest, limited settlement. By the standards of the county villages were dense on the central lowland round Stafford and to the west, while the south-east was remarkable for a handful of prosperous settlements along the Trent and Tame, including Alrewas, valued at £11, and Elford and Clifton Campville, valued at £12 each. There were demesnes of 2 teams at Harlaston in Clifton Campville (with 2 slaves), Clifton itself (with 2 slaves), and Alrewas (with 1 slave), and of 3 teams at Elford. There were recorded peasant populations of over 20 at Harlaston (16 villeins and 5 bordars), Alrewas (20 villeins, 6 bordars, and a priest), Elford (24 villeins and 8 bordars), and Clifton (33 villeins, 7 bordars, and a priest). Several manors possessed extensive stretches of meadow, notably Clifton with 50 a. and Hopwas in Tamworth with 30 a. All five manors mentioned were in the hands of the king in 1086. Burton abbey's manors in the Trent valley were smaller. Further north, in the valley of the Dove, was the royal manor of Uttoxeter (worth £8), with 2 teams in demesne and 24 villeins and 11 bordars holding 11 ploughs. Henry de Ferrers's manor of Rolleston (worth £10) had 4 teams in demesne, with 18 villeins, 16 bordars, and a priest holding 14 teams. Like the Trent and Tame manors those in the Dove valley had extensive meadowland — 40 a. at Marchington in Hanbury, 50 a. at Fauld, also in Hanbury, and 50 a. at Rolleston — and there was also 'woodland for pasture'.

Two of the three Domesday towns were in that part of the county. Tamworth appears only through references to burgesses attached to the near-by manors of Wigginton in Tamworth and Drayton Bassett. No burgesses are mentioned in connexion with Tutbury, where 42 men lived in the borough from trade and rendered, with the market, £4 10s. This compares with the value of 24s. given for the manor with its 4 demesne ploughs, and with the £10 given for near-by Rolleston. The third borough, Stafford, presumably served in the main the relatively prosperous and numerous villages of the central lowland. It had connexions in the form of attached burgesses or messuages with a number of near-by villages, Creswell, Chebsey, Marston, and Bradley, and three others in the south-west of the county, Sheriffhales and Worfield (both later Salop.) and Upper Penn. All the chief landholders had messuages in the town.

1100 TO 1350

Staffordshire shared in the general expansion of agriculture in the 12th and 13th centuries. Its population increased and the characteristic tiny settlements of 1086 were replaced by sizeable villages. By 1300 the countryside was in some places overcrowded. The evidence for population increase does not allow a precise chronology or an accurate measurement of its scale, but the general trend is clear. Domesday records as having very few or no inhabitants a number of northern settlements — Betley, Audley, Talke, Endon in Leek, and Alstonefield — which later passed into the hands of the Audley family and were surveyed in 1308. In 1086 the largest were Audley and Alstonefield, including Warslow, each with seven recorded inhabitants. In 1308 there were over 100 tenants at Betley and Audley, over 70 at Alstonefield, over 40 at Talke, and nearly 30 at Endon.[26] A survey of the estates of the bishop of Coventry and Lichfield in 1298 shows a four- or five-fold increase on the manor of Eccleshall since 1086.[27] On his manor of Brewood 51 inhabitants were recorded in 1086; in 1298 there were about 30 free tenants and tenants of new lands, 29 tenants of burgages, 62 neifs, and 36 cottars.[28] His manors of Cannock and Rugeley had respectively 14 and 9 recorded inhabitants in 1086; in 1298 there were over 90 peasant tenants in each.[29] The Needwood forest area saw similar increases. King's Bromley had 15 peasants in 1086, over 80 in 1300.[30] At Barton-under-Needwood there were 27 in 1086 and well over 100 in 1327, by which date the population had probably declined slightly from an earlier peak.[31]

By the end of the 13th century the cultivated area too had expanded substantially. There are references to assart in the villages whose increased populations were noted above. At Alstonefield, for example, in 1308 48 tenants held at will tenements of between 1 a. and 30 a. of newly assarted land.[32] At King's Bromley in 1300 the free sokemen paid 12s. 1½d. for a piece of land newly appropriated from the waste and there were 30 'foreign' tenants of recently assarted land.[33] At Rugeley over half the tenants listed in 1298 held some assart.[34]

Assarting had begun much earlier. In the 12th century it was probably only sporadic and seems to have been particularly a feature of central and southern Staffordshire. The bishop may have been assarting in Cannock forest as early as the 1120s; in 1155 he secured from the king a grant of 1,500 a. assarted in the forest since 1135.[35] By 1130 there were assarts at Chillington in Brewood, Kingswinford, and Arley (later Worcs.).[36] The mid-12th-century record of the assart made by Siward the cobbler and Ailric Berley and of the assarts of Leofric and Ravekel on the manor of Brewood[37] is one of several references suggesting groups of assarts made by numerous individuals. There are indications of similar activity in Needwood and in the Trent valley in the 12th century.[38]

[26] *V.C.H. Staffs.* iv. 41, 47, 57; *S.H.C.* n.s. xi. 256–60, 263–6.

[27] P. and M. Spufford, *Eccleshall* (Keele, 1964), 11 (copy in W.S.L. Pamphs. *sub* Eccleshall).

[28] *V.C.H. Staffs.* iv. 41; S.R.O., D.(W.) 1734/J.2268, ff. 13v.–16.

[29] *V.C.H. Staffs.* iv. 39–40, 57; S.R.O., D.(W.) 1734/J.2268, ff. 20v.–22v.

[30] *V.C.H. Staffs.* iv. 39; *S.H.C.* 1911, 258–9.

[31] *V.C.H. Staffs.* iv. 39; S.C. 11/602.

[32] *S.H.C.* n.s. xi. 258.   [33] *S.H.C.* 1911, 259.

[34] S.R.O., D.(W.) 1734/J.2268, ff. 20v.–21v.

[35] *V.C.H. Staffs.* ii. 337, 342.

[36] *S.H.C.* i. 2.   [37] Ibid. iii(1), 182.

[38] Ibid. 1937, pp. 9, 19, 27; ibid. 4th ser. iv, p. 77; below, p. 7.

It was probably speeded by the advent of the Cistercians. Their first Staffordshire house, Radmore, founded in Cannock forest *c.* 1145, soon moved to Warwickshire. Croxden, the most southerly of the three which survived, was established on the fertile land between the Churnet and the Dove in 1179. Dieulacres was founded near Leek in 1214 and Hulton on the site of an existing settlement near Stoke-upon-Trent in 1223.[39]

For the 13th century, especially the later part, there is evidence of assarting by lords and peasants on a considerable scale throughout the county. At Sedgley, already a large settlement in 1086, rents of assarts in 1273 totalled £5 10s. 9d., a quarter as much as from free and customary rents.[40] At the other end of the county the men of Wolstanton and Newcastle held 127 a. of assart in 1298.[41] It was not always a peaceful process, as in many cases the expansion of one man's land through assarting was at the expense of the rights of others, in particular of their common pasture rights. In 1293 Robert de Bromley brought a case against Walter de Beysin, alleging the unlawful impounding of fourteen oxen at Ashley. Walter claimed that he had acted lawfully as the oxen should not have been on common pasture, but Robert won the case after producing a deed to which he, Walter, and John de Eyton were parties; it stated that each could approve, assart, and build in Ashley waste without impediment by the others.[42] A similar agreement is described in 1302 in the course of a dispute at Hilderstone between Robert de Hugeford and John de Pulton.[43] Peasant tenants often objected to assarts, and in many cases drove their beasts on to the crops grown on land which they claimed had always been common pasture. Typical was the dispute at Clifton Campville between Geoffrey de Campville and the men of Newton Solney (Derb.) who, it was claimed in 1284, 'came with many and divers beasts and trampled down the oats'. The dispute flared up again in 1300 when it was claimed that the men of Newton had rescued by force seventy pigs, oxen, and cows impounded by Geoffrey's servants. In 1306, after two later episodes, Geoffrey alleged that £300 worth of damage had been done to his wheat, rye, and oats.[44]

Staffordshire's extensive woodland was eroded by farmers looking both for pastures for their stock and for potential arable. Much of the woodland was royal forest and thus protected by forest law, which presented a restraint to expansion. The New Forest, north of Stafford, and Brewood forest, west of Cannock, were, however, disafforested in John's reign.[45] Cannock and Kinver remained forest, but there was considerable expansion of farming in and around them. The royal officials found it impossible to prevent assarting by land-hungry peasants and lords. Instead their policy was to keep track of assarters and to collect fines and rents. The policy proved highly profitable. The surviving records of forest eyres in the later 13th century list payments made by scores of people from villages in and around the forest who were presented for assarting. Many assarts were small, often single acres and half acres, but, overall, substantial areas were involved. At the Cannock eyre in 1286 at least 485 a. were presented as new assart and purpresture. The offenders came mostly from the villages of the southern part of the forest. Typical was Henry de Hethe, who fined 8s. 6d. for 2 a. of new assart enclosed with a ditch and low hedge and already winter-sown twice and spring-sown three times.[46] Needwood was not a royal forest but was held by the Ferrers family as part of the honor of Tutbury. Grants of land by them made assarting possible as early as the mid 12th century and particularly in the 13th century.[47]

[39] *V.C.H. Staffs.* iii. 225–6, 230, 235.
[40] *S.H.C.* 1911, 154.
[41] Ibid. 243.
[42] Ibid. vi(1), 225.
[43] Ibid. vii(1), 101.
[44] Ibid. vi(1), 132–3; vii(1), 74, 169.
[45] *V.C.H. Staffs.* ii. 337, 348.
[46] E 32/188 mm. 16 sqq., partly calendared in *S.H.C.* v(1), 170–5.
[47] *V.C.H. Staffs.* ii. 349.

The emergence of many small towns and the increasing number of markets and fairs in the 13th and earlier 14th centuries testify to the growth of local trade in Staffordshire, presumably largely in agricultural produce and livestock, to the demand for the services of specialist craftsmen, and to the ambition of local lords. At least 41 places had fairs and 44 markets by 1500, most of them granted in the 13th century. By 1350 there were at least 21 boroughs. In some cases the grant probably merely enfranchised an already established town. It seems likely, for example, that Burton was already a trading centre when a market was granted in 1200; burgage tenure is recorded there in the late 12th century. Often, however, a lord anxious to raise his receipts attempted to establish a market in what was simply a village. Several attempts failed and many markets established by the early 14th century no longer existed in 1500.[48] Newborough in Hanbury, founded by Robert de Ferrers, earl of Derby, on his manor of Agardsley in 1263, is an example of an unsuccessful foundation. The only sign of urban activity visible in the accounts of the manor of Agardsley in 1313–14 is the rent of 101 burgages (£7 11s. 8d.). In contrast, near-by Uttoxeter, north of Needwood forest and on the Dove, was better sited for trade; in 1313–14 £9 rent of 145 burgages and 32½ stalls is recorded, £14 13s. 4d. for the tolls of the market and the port-moot, and £4 for the farm of the common oven. Further down the Dove at Tutbury there were more burgages (216 with 17 stalls, rented for £11 4s. 6d.), and the urban income included £4 18s. toll of the barony, £2 10s. from the common oven, £2 2s. 1¼d. toll of markets and fairs, and £1 11s. 7d. toll of ale.[49] Urban development in the county, however, remained limited in the Middle Ages. The three Domesday boroughs, Tutbury, Stafford, and Tamworth, remained small by national standards.

TABLE: DEMESNE PLOUGH-TEAMS ON EPISCOPAL AND BURTON ABBEY MANORS 1086 AND c. 1307

The Bishop			Burton Abbey		
	1086	1307–8		1086	1306–7
Baswich	1	2	Stretton	1	3
Haywood	2	5	Abbots Bromley	1	8
Brewood	3	4	Burton	2	2
Eccleshall	4	7	Shobnall	0	3

Sources: *V.C.H. Staffs.* iv. 41–4; (the Bishop) E 358/13; (Burton Abbey) S.R.O., D.(W.) 1734/2/3/112a; Walmsley, 'Estate of Burton Abbey', 187. The information for Stretton is dated 1306 and that for the other 3 places 1307.

The basic pattern of settlement in medieval Staffordshire, already established in 1086, was not radically altered by the expansion of the following two centuries. The largest arable demesnes on the estates of the richer landowners in the county still lay in the central lowlands. In 1298 the bishop had 849 a. at Eccleshall, 488½ a. at Haywood, and 406 a. at Brewood.[50] The earl of Lancaster's large demesnes in the Dove valley included 420 a. at Uttoxeter and 334 a. at Tutbury and Rolleston.[51] Burton abbey, the richest religious house in the county, had c. 730 a. at Abbots Bromley and c. 500 a. on its manors near Burton.[52] The demesnes had grown considerably since 1086; the table provides a comparison of numbers of demesne plough-teams in the early 14th century with those recorded in Domesday for manors on the estates of Burton abbey and the bishop. At Haywood, scene of the greatest increase on the bishop's estates, the

[48] D. M. Palliser and A. C. Pinnock, 'Markets of Medieval Staffs.' *N.S.J.F.S.* xi. 50–2, 58 (which includes Dudley (Worcs.), here omitted); Palliser, 'Boroughs of Medieval Staffs.' ibid. xii. 70 (with the omission here of Dudley); J. F. R. Walmsley, 'The Estate of Burton Abbey from the 11th to the 14th centuries' (Birmingham Univ. Ph.D. thesis, 1972), chap. 9.

[49] *V.C.H. Staffs.* ii. 349; D.L. 29/1/3.

[50] S.R.O., D.(W.) 1734/J.2268, ff. 13v., 16, 22v.–23.

[51] D.L. 29/1/3. [52] S.R.O., D.(W.) 1734/2/3/112a.

1298 survey describes some 76 a. of demesne as 'once woodland' and 28½ a. as 'newly assarted'.[53]

Even at their maximum such demesnes were not large compared with those found in more prosperous counties. Inquisitions *post mortem* suggest that Staffordshire demesnes were in general small. There was a demesne of 5 carucates at Alton in 1327[54] and several of 3 carucates, for example on the manor of Stafford in 1308,[55] but most of those described in late-13th- and early-14th-century inquisitions were of 2 carucates or less.[56]

The river valleys of central Staffordshire had the valuable asset of natural, rich meadows. Many were noted in Domesday, and their value and importance stand out in later estate surveys. The earl of Lancaster had 42 a. at Barton-under-Needwood in the Trent valley and over 80 a. at Tutbury on the Dove in 1313–14. At Barton 11 a. of meadow was leased at nearly 2s. an acre, while the arable demesne was leased at only 10d. an acre.[57] At Wychnor in Tatenhill in 1355 60 a. of demesne meadow was valued at 1s. an acre, 160 a. of arable at only 2d. an acre.[58] In 1298 the bishop had 65 a. of meadow at Haywood, where the Sow joins the Trent, almost 32 a. at Baswich, and almost 52 a. at Longdon.[59]

Though the largest arable demesnes were found in the central lowland and the south of the county, arable farming was practised wherever there were farmers. Substantial arable demesnes by Staffordshire standards were found in the most favourable northern sites. In 1327 the Verduns, whose 5-carucate demesne at Alton has already been noted, had 120 a. at Wootton and 120 a. at Stanton, both in Ellastone.[60] In the north-west the Audleys had 2 carucates at Audley in 1308,[61] and there were 218½ a. sown at Keele in 1312.[62] In the north, however, the emphasis was on pastoral farming. The limited arable demesnes of many northern manors contrast with their extensive and highly valued pastures. At Audley in 1308, 2 carucates of arable demesne were valued at £4 a year but the park at £5 a year, a value probably largely reflecting the pastures it contained. Five acres of meadow was valued at 10s. a year. At Endon there was no arable demesne, but Old Park was valued at £8 a year. At Alstonefield 61 a. of arable demesne was said to be worth £1 6s. 3d. a year, but 5 a. of meadow was valued at 15s. a year and there was pasture worth £4 a year.[63]

Sheep-farming and cattle-farming were both important in the economy of the north. Here were sited five of the six Staffordshire religious houses which appear in Pegolotti's list of English and Scots wool-producing houses. Their appearance suggests that by the later 13th century they were producing wool for export. Pegolotti estimated that the three Cistercian houses, Croxden, Dieulacres, and Hulton, could supply annually 30, 20, and 8 sacks of wool.[64] At a conservative reckoning of 240 fleeces to the sack, the figures indicate a flock of at least 7,200 sheep for Croxden and at least 4,800 for Dieulacres, large by Midland standards but much smaller than those of the richest English wool-producing houses; moreover, some at least of the wool probably came in the form of tithes and *collecta*.[65] The most expensive Staffordshire wool was that from Croxden, which Pegolotti valued at between 21 and 11 marks a sack on the Flemish market; the value of the wool of other Staffordshire houses was between 16 and 8½ marks a sack. Staffordshire, however, was never amongst the foremost wool-producing counties: Pegolotti valued the best English wool at 28 marks a sack.[66]

[53] S.R.O., D.(W.) 1734/J.2268, f. 23.
[54] *S.H.C.* 1913, 13.   [55] Ibid. 1911, 297.
[56] See e.g. ibid. 137, 157, 242, 262, 318, 320, 375.
[57] D.L. 29/1/3.   [58] *S.H.C.* 1913, 158.
[59] S.R.O., D.(W.) 1734/J.2268, ff. 1, 23, 25.
[60] *S.H.C.* 1913, 14.   [61] *S.H.C.* N.S. xi. 263.
[62] E 358/19 m. 36.

[63] *S.H.C.* N.S. xi. 256–7, 263.
[64] Francesco Balducci Pegolotti, *La Pratica della Mercatura*, ed. A. Evans, 261. For the date of the list see e.g. Eileen Power, *Wool Trade in Eng. Medieval Hist.* 22.
[65] See e.g. J. M. Wagstaff, 'Economy of Dieulacres Abbey, 1214–1539', *N.S.J.F.S.* x. 92.
[66] Pegolotti, *Pratica della Mercatura*, 261, 267–8.

The Cistercians were also raising cattle. In 1252 Dieulacres was guaranteed pasture for 200 in summer beyond the Churnet after a dispute with Hulton over pastures.[67] There was a tannery at Hulton in the late 13th century, and the abbey claimed that 300 sheep were stolen from Normacot in Stone in 1265 and 40 cattle from Mixon in Leek at about the same time.[68] Such disputes were perhaps a consequence of more extensive stock-rearing on the northern pastures.

Pegolotti listed two other wool-producing religious houses in north Staffordshire, Rocester and Trentham, both Augustinian. He estimated that each could produce about 10 sacks for sale, that is, the wool of about 2,400 sheep.[69] Tutbury priory had sheep at Mayfield and claimed in 1325 that 376 sheep and 100 lambs, with 47 cattle, were stolen in 1322.[70] The Templars had 260 sheep and nearly 30 cattle at Keele in 1308.[71] Among lay lords stock-farming on northern manors were Ralph, Lord Stafford, with nearly 100 cattle, excluding oxen, and 360 sheep at Madeley in 1349, and the Audleys, who had a vaccary at Alstonefield in 1308.[72]

Stock-rearing was important further south, on the rich grasslands of the central lowland and Needwood forest and on the extensive heaths of Cannock forest. The herds of cows on the Burton abbey manors in the early 12th century were large for the period. The largest, according to one survey, was at Leigh and consisted of 23 cows, 2 bulls, and 11 calves; there were 39 cattle, excluding oxen, at Branston and 36 at Wetmore, both in Burton-upon-Trent, and 28 at Burton itself.[73] The early development of cattle farming in the county is also suggested by the existence of two royal vaccaries in 1129–30.[74] In the early 14th century Sir Robert de Holland, lord of Yoxall, had a large dairy herd in Needwood, with nearly 40 cows in 1327.[75] There were substantial dairy herds on the bishop's manors in central Staffordshire at the end of the 13th century. The largest, at Haywood, consisted of 90 cattle. There were 45 at Brewood and smaller herds at Baswich, Eccleshall, and Longdon.[76] A lawsuit in 1320 may indicate that Staffordshire cattle were already sold outside the county. John of Trysull, near Wolverhampton, sued William of Suddington for 12 marks, part of £20, the price of 40 oxen sold to William a few years earlier at Ombersley (Worcs.).[77]

Burton abbey was, according to Pegolotti, the second largest wool-producing house in Staffordshire, with an annual production of 25 sacks. Sheep are mentioned only at Whiston in Penkridge in the early-12th-century surveys, and it is not clear when the abbey expanded its flocks. The bishop had flocks of a few hundred sheep on his manors of Longdon, Brewood, Haywood, and Baswich, about 2,300 altogether in the early 14th century.[78] In 1341 local juries declared sheep-farming to be the chief business of the inhabitants of Stafford and Newcastle.[79] The most highly taxed resident of Stafford in 1332–3, Robert le Rotour,[80] dealt in wool. He brought a case against the executors of Philip Noell, lord of Seighford, in 1319, alleging unjust detention of 3 sacks, 4 stones of wool worth £30.[81] Another Stafford man, Roger Wryde, sued the rectors of Mavesyn Ridware and Draycott-in-the-Moors in 1341 for 8 marks and a sack of wool worth 10 marks, perhaps another indication of a local wool trade.[82]

The early-12th-century surveys of the estates of Burton abbey mention small herds

---

[67] *S.H.C.* N.S. ix. 357.
[68] *V.C.H. Staffs.* iii. 236; *S.H.C.* iv(1), 158; v(1), 121. For a 1246 agreement between Trentham and Hulton confirming pasture for 400 head to each house see *S.H.C.* xi. 306.
[69] Pegolotti, *Pratica della Mercatura*, 267–8.
[70] *S.H.C.* x(1), 61.
[71] E 358/18 m. 4.
[72] S.R.O., D.641/1/2/30; *S.H.C.* N.S. xi. 257, recording also a second vaccary, held by a tenant, at Quarnford in Alstonefield.

[73] *S.H.C.* 1916, 212, 215, 219, 226. See also R. Lennard, *Rural Eng. 1086–1135*, 264–5.
[74] *S.H.C.* i. 1.
[75] D.L. 29/367/6126. See also S.C. 6/1147/24.
[76] E 358/13.
[77] *S.H.C.* ix(1), 83.
[78] E 358/13.
[79] *Inq. Non.* (Rec. Com.), 131.
[80] *S.H.C.* x(1), 81.
[81] Ibid. ix(1), 74.
[82] Ibid. xi. 109.

of goats and pigs at Leigh and a large herd of pigs (nearly 130) at Burton.[83] Goats are rarely mentioned in the Middle Ages, though the bishop had a herd at Beaudesert in Longdon in the late 15th century.[84] Pigs, on the other hand, were always numerous in the county. They seem to have been particularly common in the stock of peasants. Robert de Holland, however, had 40 at Yoxall in 1323, and the earl of Lancaster 30 in Needwood forest in 1313–14.[85] Needwood also provided grazing for horses. The earl of Lancaster had over 40 in the forest in 1313–14 and over 100 in 1327.[86]

In spite of the erosion of woodland by assarters and the royal disafforestations, Staffordshire remained well wooded. Its remaining forests, Needwood, Cannock, and Kinver, gave a distinctive character to agriculture in the county. Tenements in or

DRAWING ON A COPY OF A GRANT BY THE EARL OF DERBY OF PASTURE AND PANNAGE IN NEEDWOOD FOREST, 1253

near the forests often carried with them extensive pasture rights. For example, a tenant in Huntington in Cannock claimed common pasture in 1,000 a. of wood and 1,000 a. of pasture in Cannock in 1333.[87] In 1281 a tenement in Walsall carried pasture rights in 500 a. of wood and waste at Stonnall in Shenstone.[88] A holding at Tipton included 100 a. of wood, 200 a. of pasture, and 20 a. of meadow in 1279.[89] The large demesne stock owned by lords with forest manors, such as the bishops, the earls of Lancaster, and the lords of Yoxall, has been noted. The earls of Lancaster further exploited Needwood by the sale of the agistment of several fenced parks inside the forest, whose rich grassland was ideal for the summer fattening of beasts for slaughter and sale. In 1313–14, in Tutbury ward, summer agistment in Castlehay was worth

[83] Ibid. 1916, 212, 226.
[84] S.R.O., D.(W.) 1734/3/2/3, m. 6. Goats were sometimes excluded from common pastures, e.g. at Shenstone in the late 13th century: E 32/188 m. 13d.
[85] S.C. 6/1147/24; D.L. 29/1/3.
[86] D.L. 29/1/3; D.L. 29/367/6126.
[87] S.H.C. xi. 45.
[88] Ibid. vi(1), 149–50.
[89] Ibid. 96.

£5 3s., in Stockley Park £1 5s. 4d., and in Hanbury Park £3 2s. Agistment and sale of pasture in all five wards fetched nearly £27 for the earl that year. Branches cut specially or taken from trees blown down or felled were used to supplement winter feed for stock, and sales, with wood, were worth over £60 to the earl in 1313–14. Other forest resources sold included nuts, honey, and small birds, as well as timber and bark. The bark of limes, used to make 'baston ropes', was particularly prized.[90]

Cannock forest, too, provided extensive pasture for the stock of lords and peasants. In addition there was, by the late 13th century, some small-scale industrial development. The surnames and occupational descriptions of those presented at forest eyres for industrial offences such as charcoal-burning and agricultural offences such as assarting suggest a wide diffusion of crafts using forest resources and the absence of a rigid separation of industry and agriculture. In 1286 two charcoal-burners were working at a hearth illegally set up by Richard de Whiston in his wood of Wyrley. Four other charcoal-burners were presented at the same eyre. Simon Jordan of Walsall and Richard the bloomer of Bentley were presented for having forges. Among the many men presented for offences against the wood were William the turner of Saredon in Shareshill, William Carpenter of Longdon, Richard the cooper, and Thomas Smith, and amongst the many assarters were Richard the arrowsmith, Robert the roper, and William Carpenter at Walsall.[91] At an eyre in 1271 there were many presentments, especially of forest officers, for taking and selling timber. William Cardon was said to have had a cart and two horses carrying wood and timber (*buscam et meremium*) from Alrewas Hay to Lichfield and elsewhere. With the connivance of another forester three men and a woman had been working in the same hay burning birch, lime, and other trees and selling the ashes for use in dyeing cloth. The forester was said to have taken either 16d. or 18d. a week from them.[92]

In the bishop's chase of Cannock an iron mine at Rugeley was worth £2 in 1310–11.[93] There was also coal-mining at Longdon; the impression is of small-scale but significant activity, seasonal and fluctuating sharply in volume from year to year. In the early 14th century the value to the bishop of the mines on the manor ranged from £5 15s. in 1310–11 to 8s. 4d. in 1313–14. In 1305–6 six men paid at the rate of 6d. per week per pick for varying lengths of time; 6d. an acre was a normal annual assart rent on the manor at that date. Typical was Richard Herdman, who paid 18s. for two picks for eighteen weeks and 4s. 6d. for one pick for the next nine weeks.[94] At the same period the bishop's foresters were making regular presentments for wood offences at the manorial courts of Cannock and Rugeley.[95]

The nature and scale of forest industry at this period is difficult to gauge. It seems, however, that crafts using wood as raw material and industries using wood fuel were diffused, though small-scale. They complemented an agriculture where the emphasis was on pastoral farming with its more limited demands on labour than in arable areas, and where there was a proliferation of tenants of only a few arable acres.

The Fields

Staffordshire lies on the northern boundary of the traditional open-field region of England. H. L. Gray's line defining the area of the two- and three-field system passes through the county, separating, roughly, the northern upland and south Pennine

[90] D.L. 29/1/3. See also Jean R. Birrell, 'Forest Economy of Honour of Tutbury in 14th and 15th centuries', *Univ. of Birmingham Hist. Jnl.* viii. 114 sqq.

[91] E 32/188 mm. 12d., 13, 18d.

[92] E 32/184 m. 9, partly calendared in *S.H.C.* v(1), 150–1.

[93] L.J.R.O., D.30/N 16.

[94] S.R.O., D.(W.) 1734/J.2057.

[95] S.R.O., D.(W.) 1734/2/1/175.

fringe from the central lowland and southern parts.[96] Recent work has tended increasingly to blur the distinction between the 'open' and 'inclosed' regions of England, as more evidence has been found of open fields in the north and west and of inclosures and 'irregularities' in the traditional open-field area. It is not surprising, therefore, to find that, though Gray's line is not without its significance for Staffordshire, open fields existed to the north of it. Gray himself quoted the examples of Madeley, more or less on his dividing line, and Leek, further north on the Moorlands. An inquisition at Madeley in 1337 declared that of 180 a. of arable demesne, 120 were sown every year while 60 lay fallow and in common. At Leek a holding lay in the west, north, and east fields.[97] Open fields have been described as typical of the nucleated villages in the east of the north-eastern uplands, such as Butterton, in Mayfield, and Wetton,[98] and there is evidence of them in the 14th century at Newcastle and at Endon in Leek.[99]

It seems likely, however, that in the northern villages and hamlets the open fields were always small and that much of the arable lay outside them. The evidence for the 13th and 14th centuries is fragmentary. Many peasant holdings are described in the surviving court rolls for Keele, Endon, Horton, and Tunstall. They give an impression of holdings which were typically part open and part inclosed. At Keele, for example, there were 'two lands in the field called Bradley' in 1368 and '2½ selions lying in divers fields' in 1374; more typical, however, is a transaction of 1388 which concerned 'one piece of land called Wenslond, inclosed', and 'one field called Stounelowe'.[1] At Endon fields called Endon field, Orchard, and Sydhalgh, in which several tenants held small pieces of land, can be distinguished, but many pieces of land there, as in other villages on the manor, seem to have been inclosed. Some transactions concerned pieces of land distinguished by names which include the elements 'ridding' or 'hurst', suggesting assarts.[2]

Open fields were probably larger and more predominant in manors in the centre and south of the county. A three-field system is indicated in the 14th century in inquisitions for manors throughout the county, for example at Maer in the north-west, at Essington in Bushbury in the southern upland, at Norbury in the central lowland, and at Wigginton in the Trent valley.[3] The names winter and Lent, or wheat and Lent, fields are used at Coppenhall in Penkridge (1367) and at Bradley, near Stafford (1483).[4] Some 15th-century demesne leases at Himley consisted of equal numbers of selions in each of three fields.[5] The pasture rights attached to a tenement at Elford are described in detail in 1332. They consisted of common pasture in 200 a. for two years after the corn had been harvested until it was resown, and in the third year, during the fallow, for the whole year; pasture in 60 a. of meadow every year after the hay was cut and carried until Lady Day; pasture in 30 a. of wood for two years from Michaelmas to Martinmas for hogs, and from Martinmas to Lady Day for all cattle, extended in the third year to Michaelmas in the case of cattle.[6]

Although three-field villages seem to have been widespread in the county, the systems were often far from simple. In many villages much land lay outside the three fields. In Cannock and Rugeley there were three open fields which seem to have been cropping units, Halseyfield, Greystones, and Calughill at Cannock, Upfield, Churchfield, and Hoddesley at Rugeley. Many holdings described in the 14th- and 15th-

[96] H. L. Gray, *Eng. Field Systems*, frontispiece and p. 63. See also C. S. and C. S. Orwin, *The Open Fields* (1967 edn.).

[97] Gray, *Eng. Field Systems*, 497–8. For a translation of the Madeley inquisition see *S.H.C.* 1913, 61–2.

[98] F. J. Johnson, 'The Settlement Pattern of North-East Staffs.' (Univ. of Wales M.A. thesis, 1965), chap. 3.

[99] *V.C.H. Staffs.* viii. 49; see below.

[1] Univ. of Keele, Sneyd MSS. S.2422, S.2424, S.2463.

[2] S.R.O., D.(W.) 1490/3, rott. 2–3; /6, rott. 6d.–7.

[3] *S.H.C.* 1913, 66, 76, 87, 128.

[4] S.R.O., D.641/1/4A/10; /4A/19, rot. 3d.

[5] S.R.O., D.593/0/3/3, rot. 6.

[6] *S.H.C.* xi. 20–1.

century court rolls consisted of pieces of more or less equal size in each of the three fields,[7] and the frequent cases of animals straying in growing crops give the impression that each sown field was devoted solely to either a spring or a winter crop. Many holdings also contained land outside the three fields. A typical Cannock holding, described in 1419, consisted of 2 a. in Halseyfield, 2 a. in Greystones, 3 a. in Calughill, and 2 a. in Colletriding.[8] Another, described in 1356, consisted of a few butts in each of the three fields and a butt in Burghaleridding.[9] The names of the land outside the open fields, as in the two examples quoted, often suggest assarts. Cannock and Rugeley were forest villages which had grown rapidly since the 11th century. A case in 1465 at Rugeley points to one difference between the inclosed land and open fields. The tenant of Watcroft alleged damage by stray animals to his crop of rye, barley, and oats, all three apparently growing together in the croft.[10]

In many villages inside the main open-field area there were elements of an open-field system, but with little regularity. Abbots Bromley illustrates the complexity and irregularity which can be detected in many Staffordshire villages. The abbot of Burton's demesne is described in an early-14th-century survey.[11] It lay in various named places, some large (Holegrene contained $114\frac{1}{2}$ a. 7 p.), some small (Andrewfield contained 7 a. 12 p.). Several fields are named, some of them fairly big (Oldfield had over 40 a.). There was also a croft, Sotecroft, containing $88\frac{1}{2}$ a. 1 r. Various pieces of land were grouped into three roughly equal sections for cropping. Pieces of Cockhurst (about 60 a. in all) and Bentiley (about 100 a.) lay in all three. A 1416 rental[12] describes or names each holding. The word 'field' is used about a dozen times in Bromley itself and eight times in the hamlet of Hurst. Some fields were large and contained many small pieces of the land of several tenants, ranging in size from a rood to several acres. Hayfield contained at least 19 parcels, totalling about 25 a.; the parcels included 2 a. in a close, a further complexity. Some fields were small and held by one tenant, for example $4\frac{1}{2}$ a. called Lucyfield and 4 a. $2\frac{1}{2}$ r. called Sharpsbydfield. Thus individual holdings consisted both of pieces in larger fields, presumably open in the sense that the various component pieces were unfenced, and of complete fields which may well have been inclosed. Many other named pieces of land are recorded in the rental; it is not clear whether they were parts of open fields or inclosed, or to what extent they were subject to common cropping and pasturing routines.

A rental of the manor of Uttoxeter in 1414 seems to indicate a similar situation.[13] Holdings are described as lying in many different, named places, some of which were inclosed, some parts of larger fields. Thus one man held Cooksfield, which contained 20 a.; two tenants held an acre each in Wilkfield; a fourth held 6 a. 'in a certain close'.

The arable demesne of the lord of the manor was sometimes wholly separate from the holdings of the peasant tenants, sometimes intermixed. The demesne of John de Heronville at Wednesbury seems to have consisted entirely of pieces, many very small, intermixed with peasant strips in the open fields. A description of his widow's dower made in 1315 lists over 150 selions and several butts, lying in groups of between two and twelve.[14] On many manors at least part of the demesne lay in open-field strips, for example on the Basset manor of Pattingham and the Somerville manor at Alrewas in the early 14th century.[15] There was often, however, some consolidation. A survey of the manor of Keele in 1331 differentiated between 120 a. of arable demesne in severalty and 40 a. lying in the open fields.[16]

7 See e.g. S.R.O., D.(W.) 1734/2/1/176, rot. 7.
8 Ibid. rot. 33.   9 Ibid. /175, rot. 23.
10 Ibid. /178, rot. 143Ad.
11 S.R.O., D.(W.) 1734/2/3/112a, ff. 4v.–5.
12 Ibid. /2/3/1.
14 S.H.C. 1911, 321–2.
15 S.R.O., D.(W.) 1807/1 and 2; S.R.O., D.(W.) 0/3/9.
16 B.L. Cott. MS. Nero E. VI, f. 168.
13 D.L. 42/4.

Detailed descriptions survive of the demesne on two large estates *c.* 1300, that of the bishop in 1298 and that of Burton abbey in 1307.[17] By then the demesne was partly consolidated on both estates, though unevenly so between manors. On all the manors it lay in many pieces, called fields, furlongs, ridings, hursts, crofts, or, especially at or near Burton, flats. Some of the pieces may have lain in larger fields but, if so, the administrators did not regard that as important enough to record.

The Burton abbey demesne at Stretton was fragmented. It included a number of typical open-field furlongs, each named, made up of several selions and adding up to several acres. The smallest, Pesefurlong, consisted of 12 selions containing 4 a. 1 r. 28¾ p. The largest, Clayfurlong, comprised nearly 16 a. in one part and nearly 3 in another. The few selions whose area is recorded varied in size from less than ½ rood to over 2 roods. The demesne also contained both larger pieces, such as Elond, 17¾ a., and many small pieces, such as the 4 butts which comprised a nook of 38 perches. At near-by Shobnall, where the demesne seems to have been a post-Domesday creation, there were much larger consolidated blocks, for example 63 a. in Hallestude and 50 a. 3½ r. in Schawe.

The bishop's demesne at Eccleshall contained some very large stretches of land, such as the 235 a. of the new field of Ruyl. A total of 840 a. of demesne on the manor lay in nine places, seven of them called fields. In contrast, at Baswich much of the demesne consisted of pieces of between 3 a. and 20 a. in furlongs, lying, presumably, in larger open fields.

There are indications of considerable flexibility in cropping on both estates. The surveys group the various parts of the demesne on each manor into three sections, described as 'seasons' on the bishop's estate and with their crops indicated on the Burton abbey estate. The three sections are often uneven in size and may well not have been permanent. At Longdon in 1298, for example, the three 'seasons' were of 23, 46, and 57 acres. Early-14th-century accounts for Longdon[18] imply that spring-sown crops usually occupied a larger area than winter crops, and suggest a flexible approach to cropping. In 1304–5 Markeodok field, part of the first 'season' in the 1298 survey, was sown partly with winter-sown *mixtum* (wheat and rye) and partly with spring-sown barley. Gattemor, not mentioned in 1298, was sown with wheat, *mixtum*, and oats. In 1305–6 Beadlesfield was sown with wheat, peas, and oats. Gallfield, whose 46 acres constituted a whole season in 1298, was, however, sown only with oats and peas in 1304–5. On the home manor of Burton abbey two 'flats' were divided between different 'seasons' in 1307. One was part rye and part fallow, the second was part wheat and part oats.

The extreme fragmentation of the Heronville demesne at Wednesbury in 1314 was probably less typical of demesne at that date than of peasant holdings in open-field villages. Significantly, a peasant holding recently incorporated into the demesne at Eccleshall in 1298 consisted of 11 a. ½ r. lying 'in various parcels in the fields', in contrast to the large blocks which comprised the rest of the demesne. A 14th-century terrier of a peasant holding at Streethay in St. Michael's, Lichfield, shows extreme fragmentation in a holding consisting of over 70 selions or other small pieces of land lying a few at a time (at most 4) in six fields.[19] At near-by Alrewas in 1332 one half-virgate with its meadow lay in 17 different pieces and in 1347 another lay in 12 pieces in nine places.[20]

Many lords and some lesser men had the advantage of holding at least part of their

[17] For this and the next 3 paras. see, unless otherwise stated, S.R.O., D.(W.) 1734/J.2268; D.(W.) 1734/2/3/112a.

[18] S.R.O., D.(W.) 1734/J.2057.

[19] Ibid. /J.2269.

[20] S.R.O., D.(W.) 0/3/15, rot. 3d; /33, rot. 7.

pasture and meadow in severalty. The 1298 survey of the bishop's estate carefully distinguishes between several and common pasture. The latter lay in extensive tracts, often of some hundreds of acres; the former usually consisted of much smaller pieces, though there was a block of 280 a. newly inclosed at Rugeley. The meadow, not described as several, often lay in small pieces in a number of places; at Baswich there was just over 30 a. in nine pieces. The survey includes a rare record of the meadow attached to customary peasant tenements. Amounts were small, usually an acre or two. At Baswich, for example, 22 half-virgaters with arable holdings of 10 or 11 a. held between 1 a. and 3 a. of meadow each.

Stretches of meadow usually lay separate from the arable fields. On some manors, however, a considerable degree of intermingling of meadow and arable can be detected. At Alrewas there were pieces of meadow in arable fields and vice versa, though most meadow lay separately. There was a rood of meadow in Southfield in 1317, and ½ a. of arable in Oldfield was described in 1347 as having meadow in the middle and at the heads.[21] Conversely in 1259 there was ½ a. of arable in the meadow called Mucleholm, located between the arable of two other tenants. Close proximity, at the very least, is suggested by a case brought to the manorial court in 1346 alleging unjust ploughing of a piece of meadow.[22] Intermingling was not unique to Alrewas. At Abbots Bromley c. 1300 there was 5 a. 1 r. of arable in Brereley meadow next to another piece of arable, and parts of the Burton abbey arable demesne at Shobnall and Stretton were called 'holms', a word meaning meadow.[23] The age or degree of permanence of these juxtapositions is not revealed.

The open-field system, with intermingling of tenants' land and a complex system of obligations and rights, presented many problems for those involved. The 14th- and 15th-century court rolls of several Staffordshire open-field manors record frequent disputes over rights, duties, and abuses and the attempts made to solve them both by adjudicating in individual cases and by the formulation and declaration of custom in ordinances, sometimes called by-laws.[24] Boundaries were disputed and sometimes the exact location of a piece of land proved difficult to establish. In 1329 a tenant at Alrewas paid 4d. for an inquiry into the location of her lands, and later that year there was an inquiry into the location of a dole and a rood.[25] In 1352 an inquiry was ordered to discover whether an acre of land ploughed and sown by one tenant was his daughter's, as he claimed, or was part of the adjoining strip of another tenant. In 1325 a Burton abbey tenant at Horninglow was accused of augmenting his own holding by ploughing three furrows of his neighbour's land.[26]

The arable fields had to be fenced at certain times of the year to protect the growing corn and thrown open to stock once the harvest was gathered in. In some cases a last date for closure was agreed and recorded in the manor court together with penalties for offences. At the manor court of Alrewas, for example, in February 1350/1 it was agreed that the date for fencing the sown field at Orgreave that year should be Lady Day. Fines of 2d. or 4d. for leaving one or two gaps were levied from three offenders.[27] Lady Day was agreed as the date for spring fencing at Haywood in 1413[28] and at Hammerwich in St. Michael's, Lichfield, in 1421;[29] the date for fencing the winter field was to be Martinmas at Haywood and Christmas at Hammerwich. Similar rules were laid down on other Staffordshire manors, and courts can be seen ordering

21 S.R.O., D.(W.) o/3/8, rot. 1; /33, rot. 12.
22 *S.H.C.* N.S. x(1), 265; S.R.O., D.(W.) o/3/32, rot. 9.
23 *S.H.C.* 1937, p. 91; S.R.O., D.(W.) 1734/2/3/112a.
24 For the use of the word 'by-law' see e.g. S.R.O., D.(W.) o/3/18, rot. 7.
25 Ibid. /13, rott. 2, 4.
26 Ibid. /40, rot. 6; S.R.O., D.(W.) 1734/2/1/101a, m. 9.
27 S.R.O., D.(W.) o/3/38, rott. 5d., 6d.
28 S.R.O., D.(W.) 1734/2/1/428, rot. 3d.
29 Ibid. /379, rot. 6d.

the erection of fences and the closure of gaps at a variety of dates in spring and summer.[30]

In the autumn there was a temptation to put animals into the fields before the harvest was complete. The earliest surviving court rolls for the county record amercements for selling and carrying away fences and hedges 'before the statutory time' at Alrewas,[31] and there were frequent limitations on or prohibitions of tethering animals in sown fields. At Billington in Bradley in 1481 it was ordained that no one should keep cattle in the grain fields until the open time except on his own land or with the permission of the other tenants.[32] At Alrewas it was agreed in August 1334 that no one should pasture cattle or tether affers in the stubble until the last sheaf was carried and that no one should put animals in the hay field until the last cock of hay was brought in. The by-law was to last for the year. At a court in September fourteen offenders were presented, some of whom had offended with one beast only, others with several. John Adam, for example, was amerced 40d. twice for 160 sheep, Nicholas of Alrewas 6d. for 6 cows. The lord of the manor was presented for 20 cows.[33]

The meadows had to be protected as carefully as the arable fields. The normal practice was to close them in the spring to protect the new grass, and the date was usually either Candlemas or Lady Day.[34] The 'customary' dates were not always unanimously accepted. At Alrewas in 1338 a group of men, alleged to have let cattle trespass in a meadow, claimed that it should have been open until Lady Day. An inquiry supported the plaintiff, a canon of Lichfield cathedral, and perhaps a powerful local figure, and declared that throughout the manor meadow was closed from Candlemas until the hay was carried.[35] There were also disputes about the status of meadow associated with the fallow field, and again uncertainty about custom is revealed. In 1338 the Alrewas hayward, accused of poor custody of a piece of meadow by Oldfield, defended himself by claiming that the meadow was common when Oldfield lay fallow. A jury, however, declared that the meadow ought to be mown every year, whether Oldfield was fallow or sown.[36]

The harvest brought many problems, in particular the prevention of theft, and was the subject of frequent by-laws. A set agreed at Alrewas in 1342 covers most of the points which recur on this and other manors.[37] It forbade the theft of corn at night in the autumn and the harbouring of thieves and prohibited the carriage of corn after sunset and the giving of sheaves as payment in the fields. Gleaning was forbidden to those who could earn ½d. a day with food, presumably in an attempt to encourage labour at harvest, when it was always short. Peas and beans were to be picked only by their owners or by the poor under the supervision of the hayward. The regulations were to be effective for one year only.

At Alrewas the clerk of the court usually noted the assent of the lord and community to the ordinances; on the manors of Burton abbey and of the Stafford family the starker 'it is ordained . . .' was preferred. On the Burton abbey manors in the 14th century the penalties were paid to the lord, occasionally 'without any grace'.[38] At Alrewas in the mid 14th century fines were paid half to the lord, half to the church.[39] Fines were variable but tended to be high compared with the run of manorial court amercements.

[30] See e.g. D.L. 30/111/1662; S.R.O., D.641/1/4A/18, rott. 2, 4–5; S.R.O., D.(W.) 1490/6, rot. 39; T. Pape, *Medieval Newcastle-under-Lyme*, 152.
[31] *S.H.C.* N.S. x(i), 267, 269.
[32] S.R.O., D.641/1/4A/18, rot. 2d.
[33] S.R.O., D.(W.) 0/3/18, rott. 6 and 7.
[34] S.R.O., D.(W.) 1734/2/1/428, rot. 3d.

[35] S.R.O., D.(W.) 0/3/22, rot. 5.   [36] Ibid. rot. 8.
[37] Ibid. /27, rot. 9. See also S.R.O., D.(W.) 1734/2/1/101b, m. 22; /102, rot. 21; /103, rot. 6.
[38] S.R.O., D.(W.) 1734/2/1/102, rot. 21.
[39] S.R.O., D.(W.) 0/3/27, rot. 9 (described as a specifically 15th-century practice by W. O. Ault, *Open Field Farming in Medieval Eng.* 63).

The Landlords

The administration of the estates of the great landlords is better documented than the management of peasant holdings and there are detailed estate surveys for the county. There are, however, few ministers' accounts, the documents which are most informative about landlord farming, for the period before the Black Death. Many of those which survive are for isolated and exceptional years, and thus of limited use. Also they come from only a handful of estates, in particular large estates such as those of the bishop and the earl of Lancaster. A list of Staffordshire landowners drawn up in 1337 names over a hundred families with property valued at between £5 and £100.[40] Little or nothing is known about demesne agriculture and estate management on most of their estates. It seems unlikely that farming techniques differed very much from small to large landlords but estate management may well have done so.

A landlord had to decide whether to entrust his manors or demesnes to 'farmers' for an agreed rent or to keep them in hand and administer them directly. The practice of farming was widespread in the 12th century, and probably earlier,[41] and Burton abbey was no exception. There are indications in Domesday that some of its manors were farmed in the late 11th century, particularly those more distant from the abbey, and farms are more clearly indicated and described in two surveys of the abbey's estates made in 1114–15 and c. 1126–7.[42] About 1126–7 nine Staffordshire manors or pairs of manors were farmed for cash rents. The farmers were sometimes single individuals, such as Nawen at Whiston in Penkridge, who had held the land in 1086, sometimes pairs, in one case a group. Abbots Bromley was held by the men of the vill in 1114–15 and by a priest and four men, all tenants of the abbey, c. 1126–7, which was perhaps only a different description of the same arrangement. The two farmed manors close to the abbey, Branston and Winshill, were held by Edric, a monk. Farms were either for a period of years, for example 20 at Abbots Bromley and 16 at Leigh c. 1126–7, or for a life or lives. Life tenures could become hereditary; the manor of Okeover, held c. 1126–7 by Orm, was later granted to his son in fee farm.[43] Even in the case of the farmed manors the abbot was not a remote *rentier* lord, as some interest beyond the collection of the annual rent was generally maintained. Thus the wood at Abbots Bromley was excepted from the farm, and at Leigh the abbey retained the right to have a dairy-farm and a pig-farm.

Several manors, including most of those close to the abbey, seem to have been kept in hand and administered directly in the early 12th century. That method of estate management became more attractive towards the end of the 12th and in the 13th century, and was adopted widely as leases of manors and demesnes fell in. The change in attitude can be attributed to a number of factors, in particular the stimulus of growing demand for agricultural produce and rising prices. The latter rendered farming more profitable and encouraged landlords to seek ways of increasing their incomes. The abbots of Burton reacted to the changed conditions by expanding direct demesne cultivation, and other landlords in the county presumably did the same. There was widespread direct cultivation by the late 13th century, but there is little evidence when it started. Even on the Burton estate the chronology is obscure. It has been suggested that direct cultivation was a 13th-century phenomenon, after the policy of demesne

[40] S.C. 12/1/32, quoted and discussed in R. H. Hilton, *The Eng. Peasantry in the Later Middle Ages*, 216 sqq.
[41] E. Miller, 'England in the 12th and 13th Centuries: an Economic Contrast?' *Ec.H.R.* 2nd ser. xxiv. 1–14.
[42] Lennard, *Rural Eng.* 93, 176–7; Walmsley, 'Estate of Burton Abbey', 43–4, 115–18. The surveys are printed in

S.H.C. 1916, 212 sqq., and discussed by J. H. Round, 'The Burton Abbey Surveys', *E.H.R.* xx. 275–89 (reprinted in *S.H.C.* N.S. ix. 271–89); Lennard, *Rural Eng.* 357 sqq.; Walmsley, 'Estate of Burton Abbey', chap. 3.
[43] *S.H.C.* 1937, p. 13. The family is discussed in Walmsley, 'Estate of Burton Abbey', 103 sqq.

leasing and the farming of manors had reached its peak *c.* 1200.[44] There was some direct demesne cultivation at the end of the 13th century on manors and estates as diverse as those of Burton abbey, the bishop, the Templars at Keele, the earl of Lancaster, the Hollands of Yoxall, the Bassets at Pattingham, and the Somervilles at Alrewas.[45]

Despite the paucity of ministers' accounts it is possible to gain some idea of demesne agriculture in the county. The early-12th-century Burton surveys record stock and plough-teams on the abbey manors. The importance of dairy farming has already been noted, as have the abbot's goats at Leigh, sheep at Whiston, and pigs at Burton itself. About 1114–15 there were two plough-teams, suggesting demesnes of modest size, at Leigh, Burton, Branston, Wetmore, Winshill, and Stretton, three at Stapenhill, and one at Abbots Bromley. The classic eight-ox plough-team was in use in each case. There were a few *animalia otiosa*, now usually assumed to be oxen not in use as draught animals, on each of the four manors with herds of cattle (Burton, Branston, Leigh, and Wetmore), and one or two horses on all the manors with plough-teams. A mare at Burton was said to be for harrowing, but the horses were presumably chiefly used for carting. At Burton, however, oxen, despite their slowness in such work, were kept for carting, two for lime and two for wood. There was a stud of some 70 horses and 3 Spanish asses at Burton.[46] There were many changes on the estate by the end of the 13th century, but that level and type of provision of draught animals, that is eight-ox teams and a couple of horses for harrowing and carting, was still the norm there and elsewhere throughout the county.

The abbey's arable demesne increased in size between 1086 and the early 12th century, and more markedly by the end of the 13th century. There were 10½ teams on the six manors close to the abbey in 1086 and one each at Abbots Bromley and Leigh. About 1114–15 there were 13 teams on the Burton group of manors, one at Abbots Bromley, and two at Leigh. The 1307 survey is incomplete, but it shows marked increases at Abbots Bromley (7 extra teams) and Burton (3 extra teams at Shobnall) and a smaller increase at Stretton (1 extra team).[47] The 13th century has been described as a period of 'general acquisitiveness' for the abbey and there had no doubt also been assarting. Shobnall had the advantage of relative safety from flooding, not unimportant to Burton abbey with its Trent valley site.[48] There was a similar expansion on the episcopal estate. The number of demesne ploughs on the manors of Brewood, Baswich, Haywood, and Eccleshall increased from 10 in 1086 to 18 in 1307.[49]

There were by the early 14th century, however, signs of a withdrawal from direct demesne cultivation which foreshadowed the wholesale withdrawal later in the century. In some cases whole demesnes had been leased, in others the demesne was being eroded by leases of small pieces of land. On the Audley manor of Alstonefield the whole demesne was farmed out in 1308.[50] On the Lancastrian estate the withdrawal was almost complete by 1313–14. The arable demesnes at Agardsley, Barton, Marchington, and Uttoxeter were farmed, the leases granted sufficiently long ago to be in need of revision. At Tutbury 120 out of 334 a. were in hand but had recently been leased. The meadows at Tutbury, Barton, and Marchington were in hand in 1313–14, but by 1322 only a small amount of meadow was retained and all the arable was leased.[51]

[44] Walmsley, 'Estate of Burton Abbey', 121.
[45] For Alrewas see e.g. S.R.O., D.(W.) 0/3/18, rott. 5d., 7. For the rest see below.
[46] There is a puzzling reference to 95 mares at Whiston in the earlier survey: *S.H.C.* 1916, 228.
[47] Walmsley, 'Estate of Burton Abbey', 181 sqq.
[48] Ibid. 196–7, 199 sqq.

[49] The number of plough-teams is recorded in the accounts for 1307–8 (E 358/13), when the bishop's temporalities were seized by the king. The demesne acreage is given in the 1298 survey (S.R.O., D.(W.) 1734/J.2268), and there was roughly 100 a. per plough-team of 1307.
[50] *S.H.C.* N.S. xi. 257.
[51] D.L. 29/1/3; S.C. 6/1146/11.

On the Burton abbey estate direct cultivation remained on a larger scale. At least 100 a. of demesne at Abbots Bromley had been leased by the early 14th century, but on the manors near the abbey, and possibly at Abbots Bromley too, direct farming with the use of labour services continued.[52] Similarly on the Basset manor of Pattingham there were a few leases of small pieces of demesne, but direct cultivation continued on the remainder.[53]

Wheat, rye, barley, and oats were grown, also peas and, occasionally, beans and vetch. The two winter-sown crops, wheat and rye, were sometimes grown mixed, and barley and oats were grown mixed as dredge. Spring-sown crops, especially oats, were important on many demesnes. An early indication of the importance of oats is contained in the record of the re-sowing of the bishop's demesnes in 1242 when the estate was in the king's hands. Whereas wheat, rye, oats, barley, and beans were sown on episcopal manors in Warwickshire, oats were the sole crop at Haywood, Baswich, Brewood, and Eccleshall.[54] Wheat, rye, barley, and peas were also grown on those four manors in 1307–8, when there are accounts for two successive harvests.[55] Oats, however, were the chief crop overall and on every manor. In 1307 nearly 712 quarters of oats were harvested, only 362 quarters of wheat. Spring-sown crops were important elsewhere. At Tutbury in 1313–14 nearly 60 a. was sown with barley, oats, and peas compared with 32 a. devoted to wheat. At Yoxall, in the 1323 harvest, oats were more than twice as important as wheat. The predominance of spring-sown crops was not, however, universal. The 1307 survey of the Burton abbey estate describes some 260 a. as under winter-sown crops and some 206 a. as under spring-sown crops, largely oats. A few early-14th-century accounts for Keele suggest that wheat and oats were grown there in roughly equal proportions. Of other crops peas were occasionally grown in significant amounts. At Tutbury in 1313–14 24 of the 92 a. sown were devoted to peas, and at Yoxall in 1324 over 30 of 173 a. At Eccleshall in 1307–8 peas were more important than barley or rye, and at Haywood they were more important than rye. Beans were grown on the Burton abbey demesne and at Yoxall, but seem to have been less common. These nitrogenous crops were becoming more important on demesnes throughout the country and may have benefited soils otherwise cropped repeatedly with cereals. Peas seem to have been usually used as a supplementary food for stock, in liveries to farm servants, or as a small-scale cash crop. At Eccleshall in 1307–8, for example, over 36 of 50 quarters harvested were sold.

The few surviving accounts suggest that cereal production for the market was of only limited importance in Staffordshire. On the bishop's manors much of the harvest was consumed on the estate in the form of liveries to servants, fodder for stock, and seed corn. That accounted for most of the rye and mixed corn, with Baswich supplying other manors as necessary. Livestock consumed large quantities of oats and a little was included in liveries to servants. Estate consumption often amounted to a third of the harvest, and seed corn to a little less, leaving a relatively small proportion of the harvest to be sold.

There is a little evidence about crop yields, but almost all for single isolated years. The yield from seed on the bishop's manors for the harvests of 1307 and 1308 was extremely poor; just over 3:1 for wheat at Haywood is the best recorded. Oats yielded only just over 1:1 at Haywood. Equally poor yields for oats and only slightly higher

---

[52] For leases of demesne at Abbots Bromley see Walmsley, 'Estate of Burton Abbey', 188 sqq. Direct cultivation on the group of manors near Burton is shown by court rolls of the 1320s: S.R.O., D.(W.) 1734/2/1/101a and b.
[53] S.R.O., D.(W.) 1807/1 and 2.
[54] Cal. Lib. 1240–5, 110–11.

[55] Unless otherwise stated the rest of this para. and the following 5 paras. are based on E 358/13; E 358/18 m. 4 (Keele Jan. 1307/8 – Jan. 1308/9); E 358/19 m. 36 (Keele Dec. 1311 – Jan. 1313/14); D.L. 29/1/3 (Tutbury 1313–14); S.C. 6/1147/24 (Yoxall 1323–4); L.J.R.O., D.30/N 1 (Baswich 1312–13).

yields for peas, barley, rye, and wheat are recorded for Haywood and the other manors. At Keele in 1313 the wheat yield seems to have been higher, just over 5:1, but it was just over 2:1 in 1314. Oats yielded about 2:1 in 1313 and just over 1:1 in 1314. Sowing rates at Keele were low, but generally in line with the recommendations of a 13th-century agricultural treatise, the anonymous 'Husbandry'.[56] Wheat was sown at 2 bushels an acre in 1312 and 1314 and at about 2¾ bushels in 1313. Oats were sown at 4 bushels an acre in 1312 and 1313. Slightly higher rates are recorded for Tutbury in 1313–14 and Yoxall in 1323–4.

Seed corn seems generally to have been taken from the previous harvest, but occasionally it was purchased, as recommended by the author of another 13th-century treatise, Walter of Henley.[57] At Yoxall in 1323–4 7 quarters of wheat were bought 'pro semine mutando' but the remaining 50 quarters came from the manor.

Eight-ox plough-teams, standard on the heavy soils of the Midlands, were found at Keele and on manors in south and central Staffordshire. Occasionally the number of oxen fell slightly below what was necessary, as if, even on the demesnes of big estates, oxen were in short supply. At Yoxall in 1323–4 three horses were bought for ploughing and carting, but the chief plough-beast was everywhere the ox, with horses normally reserved for tasks such as harrowing or carting, where their greater speed or strength was useful. Horses not only cost more but also needed more and better food. They were fed a daily ration of oats, usually 1 bushel, throughout the winter. Oxen too needed feeding in the winter, but not on that scale. At Eccleshall in 1307–8 the 54 oxen consumed rather less oats (57 qr. 4 bu.) than the 5 cart-horses (58 qr. 1 bu.). As with oxen the number of horses seems to have been kept to a minimum, and hiring was often necessary to complete specific tasks such as harrowing.

Ploughs were the chief pieces of equipment, followed by wagons and carts.[58] All were constructed basically from wood, but ploughs had iron parts, principally share, coulter, and 'feet', and some wagons and carts were strengthened with iron bindings. Iron 'feet', costing between 1½d. and 3d. each in the earlier 14th century, shares (between 4d. and 7d.), or pieces of iron and steel, were often bought, and local carpenters and smiths were employed to repair or construct the ploughs.

The better carts and wagons were bound with iron, but even on demesnes some were apparently made entirely of wood.[59] As with ploughs, some parts of the carts and harness were bought, some made on the demesne. At Baswich in 1312–13 a horse collar was bought for 6d. and two halters were made from hemp. At Longdon in 1308–9 a halter was bought for 1d. Wooden yokes for plough oxen were usually made on the demesne. Cart bodies were often specially repaired for the autumn and heavy harvest work; a 'long' body was specified at Baswich in 1312–13 in this context. Muck-carts are also mentioned, for example at Yoxall in 1323–4.

The cost of maintaining ploughs and carts, especially the iron parts, was a regular and significant charge on the demesnes. The 'cost of ploughs' at Baswich in 1312–13 was 10s. 6½d. and the 'cost of carts' 8s. 6d. At Longdon in 1307–8 the cost of clouts, nails, a collar, cord, tallow, grease, a pair of wheels, and other necessities for the wagon and carts, fitting axles, and shoeing the cart-horses, came to 19s. 1d. A smith at Baswich in 1312–13 contracted to shoe two cart-horses for the year for 3s., and another at Yoxall in 1323–4 to shoe three affers 'in all their feet' for 3s. 8¾d.

[56] Dorothea Oschinsky, *Walter of Henley and other Treatises on Estate Management and Accounting*, 443.

[57] Ibid. 174–5, 325.

[58] Unless otherwise stated the rest of this section is based on 5 sets of accounts: E 358/13; S.C. 6/1147/24; S.R.O., D.(W.) 1734/J.2057 (Longdon 1304–14); S.R.O., D.641/2/30 (Madeley 1349–50); L.J.R.O., D.30/N 1.

[59] On 5 manors on the episcopal estate in 1307–8 8 iron-bound carts, 3 iron-bound wagons, and a wagon without iron were listed.

Some demesne inventories include harrows, sometimes strengthened with iron. Buying seven pieces of iron (4*d*. each) and fitting them to two harrows cost 3*s*. 9½*d*. at Madeley in 1349–50. A wooden harrow at Yoxall in 1323–4 was said to be for oxen, but this was probably unusual.

Other implements included shovels or spades, forks (muck forks and three-pronged forks are specifically mentioned), axes, 'cropping-hooks', and 'weed hooks'. There was a wooden threshing-floor at Yoxall in 1323–4. A list of purchases at Longdon in 1304–5 — an axe (8*d*.), a basket (4*d*.), a 'bill' (5*d*.), a pickaxe (8*d*.), a cropping-hook (4*d*.), and a seed-basket (3*d*.) — gives some idea of the costs of minor items. The iron for two shovels and two forks cost a further 4*d*.

The labour needs of the estates were met from a number of sources. In the early 14th century labour services were still performed, there was some wage labour, and each demesne had a core of full-time servants (*famuli*). Seasonal services were all that remained in Staffordshire at that period, and by no means all those due were performed. Commutation took place both as a permanent arrangement on individual peasant holdings and on an annual basis by arrangement with all the customary tenants. For example, a cottage at Branston previously held for 8*d*. a year with three boon-works in autumn was taken in 1315 for 18*d*. a year and a hen at Christmas.[60] There could be difficulties in extracting all the services that remained. The Burton abbey court-rolls for the early 14th century record frequent amercements of individuals and groups of tenants for non-performance of services.[61] On the bishop's estate ploughing, hay-making, harvesting, and carting services were performed, but there, as elsewhere, they were supplementary to other types of labour. At Baswich in 1312–13 40 a. was harvested by customary labour, 99 a. by wage labour. At Longdon in 1304–6 the customary tenants harvested 38 a. with 114 'works', each accounting for a third of an acre, while wage labour was used for the remaining 44 a. At Tutbury in 1313–14 the services of the burgesses and of some Scropton (Derb.) bondsmen were commuted, but the services of 16 Scropton customary tenants and 26 from Rolleston were used to mow 83¼ a. of meadow.[62] Seasonal services were also used at Alrewas in the early 14th century. At Keele they seem to have been commuted by 1308.[63]

Wage labour was used in various ways. Harvesters at Longdon in 1305–6 were paid 4½*d*. an acre. Threshing and winnowing were usually done by piecework, though some was done by the *famuli*. The rates varied a little from year to year, threshing being always more highly paid than winnowing, and work with wheat and rye more highly paid than with beans, peas, barley, and oats. Hoeing and haymaking were also done by wage labour, in the latter case usually supplementary to labour services.

The *famuli* included the teams of ploughmen, the *fugatores* who drove the oxen and the better-paid *tenatores* who guided the ploughs, and carters, dairymaids or dairymen, and shepherds. Often there was a woman to make pottage for the *famuli* and sometimes a lad. In general there was a high degree of uniformity between estates and between Staffordshire and other counties in the division of work between the *famuli* and the type of payment. Wages consisted of liveries in cash and kind, the latter principally rye and wheat, and were carefully graded according to the job. At Baswich in 1312–13 the carter and the two *tenatores* each received 4*s*. a year with a quarter of corn every 12 weeks, the two *fugatores* 3*s*. each and a quarter every 12 weeks, and the woman 3*s*. and a quarter every 16 weeks. The shepherd was paid 1½ quarter of corn

[60] S.R.O., D.(W.) 1734/2/3/112a, f. 52. For a detailed list of sale of works see S.C. 6/1147/24.
[61] See e.g. S.R.O., D.(W.) 1734/2/101a, m. 6; /101b, m. 11.
[62] D.L. 29/1/3.
[63] S.R.O., D.(W.) 0/3/20, rot. 1d.; /27, rot. 10; E 358/18 m. 4; E 358/19 m. 36.

for 18 weeks' work. At Keele in 1312 cash payments were higher, 5s. a year for *tenatores* and 4s. for *fugatores*, but the corn allowance of the *fugatores* was lower, a quarter every 13 weeks.

The demesnes were essentially mixed-farming enterprises, and most had cattle, sheep, and pigs as well as arable. Cattle were important in the county and both cattle-rearing and dairying can be seen. In 1307–8 there were mixed herds at Haywood, Brewood, and Baswich. The largest, at Haywood, consisted of a bull, 45 cows, 27 young cattle, and 17 calves. There were 13 steers at Longdon and a dairy herd of 2 bulls and 24 cows at Eccleshall. At Madeley in the north-west of the county the herd consisted of 2 bulls, 46 cows, and 47 steers in 1349.[64] There was a mixed herd of cows, steers, and calves at Yoxall in 1323–4. At Haywood the large herd merited two dairymen and also a lad to look after the steers. Cows were often leased with their calves, some-times to the dairyman. At Baswich in 1312–13 thirteen were leased for 4s. 6d. each. Cattle were kept not only for milk but also as draught animals (6 bullocks at Haywood were re-designated oxen in the account of 1308) and for meat (4 cows and a bull from Longdon were supplied to the bishop's larder in 1305).

The flocks on the bishop's estate were organized on a manorial basis, with close co-operation between shepherds. In 1307–8 there were several hundred sheep on each manor, with the largest flock, over 700, at Haywood, the bishop's chief stock-rearing manor. In that year the flocks at Longdon and Baswich were specialized wool-producing flocks consisting almost entirely of wethers, the castrated males which produced heavier fleeces. Elsewhere the flocks were mixed, although wethers were always important. At Brewood, for example, the flock was made up of 8 rams, 161 ewes, 256 wethers, 112 hoggasters (sheep in their second year), and 140 lambs. The absence of a series of accounts makes it difficult to get an idea of flock management. The chief surviving account, that for 1307–8, is exceptional since the estate was then in the hands of the king and nearly all the livestock was sold off before the year was out. One or two points of interest emerge, however. As well as transfers of sheep between the Staffordshire manors there were purchases from outside and transfers from episcopal manors else-where. In 1304 the Longdon flock was replenished with 10 sheep bought at Stafford and 20 bought in Shropshire, the former costing 2s. 0½d. each, the latter 1s. 10½d. each. In 1312–13 189 sheep and 6 lambs were transferred to Baswich from Prees (Salop.). The wool was sold to London merchants who sometimes came to the estate in the course of their negotiations. In 1307–8 Haywood was used as a collecting centre for the Staffordshire and Shropshire manors, and nearly 2,000 fleeces were assembled, 1,611 of them from Staffordshire. Together they amounted to over 8 sacks, sold at *c.* £8 a sack. Recorded fleece weights included *c.* 1⅔ lb. (an average of 186 fleeces) at Longdon in 1304–5 and *c.* 1⅓ lb. (an average of 171 fleeces) at Baswich in 1312–13, typical weights for the Midlands at the time.

The flocks received the type of care normal on demesnes throughout the country. Milk and ale were bought for the lambs, and they were fed oats and a little wheat. Grease, tar, and verdigris were applied against disease, which nevertheless took a heavy toll, especially of the young. In 1307–8 72 out of 200 hoggasters died at Haywood, and 33 out of 112 at Brewood. The lambing rate was low and, combined with disease, presented formidable problems to stockmasters attempting to build up flocks. At Eccleshall in 1307–8 220 ewes produced only 170 lambs, 64 of which failed to survive a year.

Hens and geese were also kept on demesnes. A detailed account was rendered for

---

[64] S.R.O., D.641/1/2/30.

a flock of hens at Baswich in 1312–13. Ten hens and a cock produced 18 chickens, of which 4 died and 6 were caponized. Ten hens were sold for 1*d*. each. The eggs are not mentioned, but they and the capons were presumably destined for the lord's larder. There were swans at Eccleshall, Longdon, and Yoxall, though it is not clear to what extent they were ornamental, to what extent reared for food. They were sufficiently highly considered to be fed oats in the winter. Nearly 5 quarters of oats were bought for 21 swans at Longdon in 1309–10. At Yoxall in 1323–4 foxes took 5 swans in winter and 5 others were sold with 8 cygnets for £1 8*s*. 8*d*.

The Peasantry: Holdings, Status, and Rent

In most villages peasant holdings accounted for more land than the lord's demesne, and in some there was no demesne at all. Despite considerable variations in size, apparent in the earliest records, peasant farms generally possessed the same basic components. First there was the arable, usually up to a maximum of 30–40 a., but occasionally larger. It could be composed of pieces of land in the open fields, enclosed plots, or a mixture of both. It was vital to the peasant farm, as it produced the main crop, cereals grown for consumption or sale. The farm generally included other elements, chief among them a share in the village meadows and rights on the village pastures. Other rights, varying to some extent from place to place but vital to the peasant economy, included the right to take wood for fuel and fencing.

The surveys of Burton abbey's estates made in 1114–15 and *c*. 1126–7 throw light on certain aspects of peasant economy and society in Staffordshire for the first time and reveal some changes taking place between the two dates. They describe a peasantry apparently fairly well provided with land, though unequally so. There were three main groups, the *censarii*, or money-rent payers, the *villani*, or villeins, whose rent was predominantly in labour, and the *cotseti*, cottars, smallholders whose rent was also usually in labour. The surveys are early evidence of the existence of a basic distinction between peasants with holdings large enough to provide a living for a family and those whose income from their few acres was likely to be regularly supplemented from other sources, including, perhaps, labour on the larger holdings.[65] *Censarii* typically held two bovates, sometimes less but often more, sometimes considerably more. Most villeins held two bovates, but some only one.

The numbers and importance of villeins and *censarii* varied from manor to manor. At Leigh in 1114–15 the 12 villeins were all two-bovaters and outnumbered the 9 money-rent payers. The latter, however, held more land, 42 bovates in all. At Winshill, in contrast, there were only 10 villeins holding for labour rent (11 if one smallholder is included), compared with 15 money-rent payers (including one described as a villein). Of the labour-rent paying villeins 4, described as 'full villeins', had two bovates each, while 6 'half-villeins' had only one each. Their 14 bovates compared with the 38 held for cash. On several of the abbey's smaller and more distant manors, such as Ilam and Okeover, no villeins are recorded. Throughout the estate, it has been calculated, over half the area of substantial holdings was held for cash rents.[66]

On several manors near the abbey there were also a few *bovarii*, between 2 and 5 on each manor, tenants of one or two bovates for services. Although there is only an approximate relation between their numbers and demesne ploughs, it seems likely that they were full-time servants of the demesne, or their descendants, settled on holdings and assuming some of the hallmarks of customary tenants.[67]

[65] Lennard, *Rural Eng*. 357.   [66] Ibid. 376.   [67] Walmsley, 'Estate of Burton Abbey', 64 sqq.

The *censarii* often owed some services in addition to their money rent. Those included lending ploughs and wagons for work on the demesne, reaping, carrying, helping with the hunt, and, occasionally, messenger service and attendance at the shire court and wapentake. The services of the villeins were heavier and usually included week-work. About 1126–7 the 8 villeins at Burton, each a two-bovater, had to work two days a week and to perform other services, including ploughing twice a year and a further ½ a. in Lent, reaping in August, and carting. They had to put their animals in the lord's fold. Customary payments included 2 hens at Christmas and pannage. The services of villeins on the other manors were based on those at Burton, but with some variations. Villeins with one bovate usually worked only one day a week on the demesne but performed similar services. The *cotseti* usually worked one day only, though some paid money rent or other types of service. A cottar at Burton, for example, held a house for four weeks' service, two in summer and two in Lent.

The services were not heavy for the type of estate and the period. Heavier week-work was widely found on the estates of Benedictine abbeys in other counties in the 12th century.[68] There are indications that the importance of villeinage and labour services declined slightly between 1114–15 and *c*. 1126–7. By the later date there were fewer villeins on eleven manors for which the comparison can be made (101 compared with 108), and more *censarii* (100 compared with 83). The number of bovates held by villeins had decreased from 216 to 196, whereas the number of bovates held by *censarii* had increased from 231 to 272.[69] On individual holdings changes from labour- to money-rent are more common than vice versa. Villeins disappeared altogether from the manor of Abbots Bromley, some ten miles from the abbey, west of Needwood forest. In 1114–15 there were five villeins with two bovates each and labour services and customary payments, whereas by *c*. 1126–7 all the bovates were held for money rent. It seems likely that the change is connected with the situation of the manor in the forest, where assarting and associated freedom were significant. Recent cultivation of waste land may account for part of the increase in land held for money rent on some other manors.[70]

Smallholders were nowhere numerous except on the manor of Burton, and it seems likely that here they were in fact inhabitants of what was already becoming a small town. The surveys may in fact present too simple a picture of landholding on the estate. A substantial tenant at Branston was said in 1114–15 to have seven sub-tenants, and there may have been others unrecorded.

There is no comparable source of information about peasant holdings, status, and rent until 1298 when the survey of the bishop's estate describes in detail seven manors containing well over twice that number of villages and hamlets and nearly a thousand tenants.[71] The listed peasant tenants ranged from substantial freemen with 50, 60, or more acres, appearing alongside the bishop's military tenants, to smallholders with an acre or two or less. The core of the tenants, both free and unfree (*nativi*), held standard holdings, which were usually recorded in acres and were equated for rent and services with a virgate, a half-virgate, or a nook (quarter-virgate). In some cases the holdings in each group were similar in size, in others they varied considerably. At Baswich 22 unfree holdings, held as half-virgates, each contained 10 a. or 11 a. of arable and a small amount of meadow and paid 2s. a year with services. In addition two nooks, the size of which is not given, paid 12d. and half the services of a half-

[68] Lennard, *Rural Eng.* 378–87. For a ref. to labour services in the Staffs. Domesday see ibid. 370–1.
[69] Walmsley, 'Estate of Burton Abbey', 60.
[70] Ibid. 62.

[71] For this and the following 2 paras. see S.R.O., D.(W.) 1734/J.2268, discussed in Hilton, *Eng. Peasantry in Later Middle Ages*, 229–30; Spufford, *Eccleshall*, 12–18.

virgate. In contrast, at Brewood tenements held as half-virgates varied in size from 12 a. to 26 a. and nooks from 7 a. to 20 a. In each case most holdings were in a range well inside the two extremes; most half-virgates were between 16 a. and 24 a., most nooks between 10 a. and 12 a. The average acreage was at the lower end of the half-virgate range — just over 17 a. Over the estate as a whole most unfree tenants' holdings were reckoned as half-virgates — perhaps between two-thirds and three-quarters. A few, at least 10 per cent, held full virgates, the rest less than half a virgate.

The high proportion of smallholders, tenants of 5 a. or less, is one of the features of the estate. The number and proportion varied from manor to manor. Nearly two-thirds of the tenants at Cannock, which, like near-by Rugeley, had no unfree tenants, were smallholders; at Haywood and Baswich about a third were smallholders. Over the estate as a whole about 40 per cent of the tenants held 5 a. or less. There is some overlap in the lists, and some smallholders may have held land elsewhere; but the high percentage remains significant, since many smallholders could not have made a living from their holding alone.

Many held a few acres of assart, often listed under a heading such as 'new lands'. Among manors where smallholders of assart land were most numerous were the two forest manors of Rugeley and Cannock. On the former there was one substantial free tenant, 22 sokemen, mostly holding nooks, 60 tenants of 'new lands', mostly holding a few acres, and 15 cottars.

A high proportion of smallholders was characteristic elsewhere in the county in the early 14th century. On the Audley estate in the north-west of the county about half the tenants were in that class. On the Lancastrian manor of Barton-under-Needwood in 1327 there was a similarly large proportion of smallholders.[72]

A rental of the Burton abbey manors of Horninglow and Stretton in 1286 seems at first sight to describe a peasantry much better provided with land.[73] Only 3 of the 21 tenants at Horninglow were smallholders, and only 4 of the 29 at Stretton. The proportions may, however, be misleading. A separate section lists tenants of assart at Stretton in 1289–90. A note of four cottagers who had been tenants of the late Henry de Stretton, a freeholder, indicates the existence of sub-tenants not otherwise mentioned in the rental. On the other hand, the evidence of land transactions in the late-13th-century court rolls at Burton abbey suggests that many peasants had standard holdings: of the transactions recorded between 1280 and 1303 45 per cent involved holdings of 1 virgate or more and 25 per cent 1 bovate.[74]

A high proportion of free tenants was another characteristic of the county c. 1300. Free tenants accounted for some 40–50 per cent of the total on three estates, those of Tutbury priory (40 per cent), the Audleys (42 per cent), and the bishop (51 per cent).[75] Court rolls from the Burton abbey manors c. 1300, however, suggest a substantial proportion of unfree tenure.[76] The 1286 rental of Horninglow and Stretton records a high proportion of unfree tenants on both manors — three-quarters at Horninglow (tenants in villeinage) and even more at Stretton (neifs). There was certainly no typical manorial pattern in the county. On the Staffordshire part of the honor of Tutbury, for example, there was no villeinage in the early 14th century at Uttoxeter, Tutbury, or Agardsley, all manors in which boroughs had been created, but there

[72] Hilton, *Eng. Peasantry in Later Middle Ages*, 229.
[73] S.R.O., D.(W.) 1734/J.2049.
[74] J. F. R. Walmsley, 'Peasantry of Burton Abbey in the 13th Century', *N.S.J.F.S.* xii. 54.
[75] Hilton, *Eng. Peasantry in Later Middle Ages*, 227.
[76] The terminology used c. 1300 for unfree tenants varies from estate to estate and, indeed, from document to

document. Thus the term 'neif' was preferred on the Burton abbey estate and on the bishop's estate (though aid was 'of customary tenants' in the 1307–8 confiscation accounts) while on the honor of Tutbury the word used was 'bondsman'. As far as possible the terminology of the documents has been followed.

were many unfree tenants at Marchington, Rolleston, and Barton. At Barton a 1327 rental describes just over a quarter of the tenants of Barton itself as bondsmen, but it records only two bond tenants in the rest of the manor, which included several hamlets in Needwood such as Tatenhill, Callingwood, and Dunstall.[77] There was an entirely free population at Adam de Brompton's manor of Church Eaton in 1315, but only customary tenants on the manors of Lapley priory in 1339.[78]

It has been suggested that the reasons for the comparatively slight incidence of unfree tenure in Staffordshire by the early 14th century included the relative lack of importance in the county of old and highly organized estates, the extensive recent settlement of waste land and forest, and the increase of population. The latter developments were also likely to produce a high proportion of smallholdings.[79]

Villein rent on the Burton abbey manors in the early 12th century has been described above. In the absence of similar evidence for other estates, it is impossible to say how typical the Burton manors were at that date, though villeinage was likely to be as heavy a burden on the manors of the county's richest and oldest Benedictine house as anywhere. There is much evidence for the nature of villein obligations in the county at the end of the 13th century. The 1307 survey of the Burton abbey estates describes in detail the services at Burton and the near-by manors.[80] Week-work had disappeared. In addition to a cash rent of 2s., the virgater at Burton had to perform certain ploughing, haymaking, weeding, reaping, and carting services, none very heavy. He had, for example, to plough twice in winter and twice in Lent with his own beasts and without food. On the third day of the harvest boon-work, called the 'metebene', he had to find two men, whose work he supervised, while the abbey provided two loaves of bread, one of rye and one of wheat, a gallon of ale or cider, and a large dish of beef or pork. For the first two days, and any days required after the third, the boon was without food or with cheese or herring instead of meat. The virgater had to find a man for the hunt for three days, though this service was in 1307 commuted for $1\frac{1}{2}d.$, and to care for hound pups until they were a year old if he were in a position to do so. He was liable to a number of customary dues: aid, called 'stud', at Michaelmas, merchet and a fine to put his son to letters, pannage (recently commuted to 4d. at Martinmas), a hen at Christmas and 20 eggs at Easter, 'buryord' (2d.), and 'hayord' ($2\frac{1}{2}d.$). Sales of pigs, male horses, and beehives were controlled and taxed.

Virgaters at Branston, Stretton, Horninglow, Wetmore, Winshill, and Stapenhill had to perform similar services.[81] There was a higher cash rent, 3s., at Winshill and Branston, and the services at Winshill included harrowing in Lent. At Stapenhill, on the death of an unfree tenant, the abbot took two oxen, a male horse if there was one, and a mare.

The longer and more precisely defined list of customary dues is, like the disappearance of week-work, a marked change since the early 12th century. The evidence from other estates suggests that the absence of week-work combined with heavy customary payments was characteristic of the county c. 1300. On the bishop's estates services varied from manor to manor.[82] The heaviest were at Haywood, where some neifs had to perform a limited amount of week-work, 2 days a week for 15 weeks from mid June to Michaelmas. Other neifs on the same manor were liable only to specified haymaking and harvest services. Both groups owed numerous other services, including carting, ploughing, and mill works, and were liable to payments such as pannage and

[77] S.C. 11/602.
[78] Hilton, *Eng. Peasantry in Later Middle Ages*, 227–8.
[79] Ibid. 228–9.
[80] S.R.O., D.(W.) 1734/2/3/112a, f. 9. For a discussion
of villeins' obligations as set out in the survey see *N.S.J.F.S.* xii. 52–4.
[81] S.R.O., D.(W.) 1734/2/3/112a, ff. 10v.–12.
[82] S.R.O., D.(W.) 1734/J.2268.

merchet. In some cases services were adapted to the local conditions of each manor and the particular needs of the estate, for example nut-collecting at Haywood and Brewood, and carting services linking the manors. Carting services were heavy; Eccleshall virgaters had to carry millstones to the mills at Eccleshall and Bishop's Offley in Adbaston, corn, malt, and oats to Haywood and Brewood, salt from 'Wich', and timber for new houses and for ploughs, harrows, mills, and bays, as well as bringing in the hay and corn. Some free tenants were liable to seasonal services, usually carrying and haymaking, occasionally hunting, and some cottars were liable to hay-making, harvesting, and other services, including, on the manor of Longdon, driving cattle to Haywood, Brewood, Tachbrook (Warws.), and Sawley (Derb.).

At Haywood the cash rent of a half-virgater was 1s. 6d., and services, not including customary payments such as pannage, were valued at considerably more, well over 7s. for those working two days a week for part of the year, nearly 5s. for the rest. Elsewhere on the estate, services were usually valued at about the same as the cash rent, for example 3s. or 4s. in cash for a virgate at Eccleshall with services valued at about 3s. 6d. Brewood was exceptional, with a higher cash rent of 4s. for a half-virgate and services valued at less than 2s.

The services of virgaters at Barton on the estate of the earl of Lancaster were described in the 1327 rental.[83] Again there were seasonal services only, heavy carting services, and liability to various dues. Together the services were valued at considerably more than the cash rent of 3s.

The scanty evidence for the rest of the county suggests that the services on those three estates, held respectively by a Benedictine abbey, a bishop, and an earl, and including manors in the best arable regions of the county, were not surpassed elsewhere. Lighter seasonal services were found on the estates of a smaller Benedictine house, Farewell priory, in the early 14th century. For some half-virgaters on the priory's estate at Chorley they included washing and shearing the prioress's sheep.[84]

Customary dues and payments seem to have been heavy throughout the county on manors of both greater and lesser lords. Heriots and *principalia*, not always clearly distinguished in practice, were widely found and onerous. On the death of a virgater in Barton, according to the 1327 rental, the lord took the best beast and all brass pots, iron-bound carts and wagons, beehives, uncut woollen cloths, affers and male foals, male and female pigs, whole bacons, and money if there was any.[85] There was a similar liability on the bishop's manors, except that the unfree tenants could sometimes retain one sow or half their herd of pigs.[86] At Wednesbury in the early 14th century John de Heronville claimed half his customary tenants' pigs, a boar, all male colts, an iron-bound cart, uncut cloths, and whole hams.[87] On the Lapley priory manors the claim was more modest, the best beast and male horses and pigs.[88]

Evidence from court rolls suggests that the claims as set out in rentals were tempered in practice but that heriot was a heavy burden throughout the county. The normal practice seems to have been for the lord to take certain animals: thus in 1328 on the death of a bovater at Burton the abbot took two mares as mortuary and heriot, and in 1329 on the death of another Burton villein he took a mare, an ox, and a cow.[89] Levies of goods are also recorded. On the death of a virgater at Rolleston in 1342, for example, the lord took an ox worth 6s., a cart worth 2s., two bowls worth 6d., and a brass pot worth 18d., all sold to the heir.[90] At Alrewas a few small cash heriots are recorded in

[83] S.C. 11/602.
[84] S.R.O., D.(W.) 1734/J.2034.
[85] S.C. 11/602.
[86] S.R.O., D.(W.) 1734/J.2268.
[87] *S.H.C.* ix(1), 18.
[88] *S.H.C.* 1913, 70.
[89] S.R.O., D.(W.) 1734/2/1/101b, mm. 18, 34.
[90] D.L. 30/109/1618, ct. held on St. Valentine's day 16 Edw. III.

the court rolls of the late 13th century.[91] In the earlier 14th century the lord normally took the best beast and, increasingly, certain other animals or pieces of equipment which 'pertained to him by custom'. A garment was taken on the death of the landless and of some smallholders.[92]

Many other customary payments mentioned in rentals were not valued, since they were at the will of the lord. Merchet on the Burton manors in the early 14th century was usually a few shillings.[93] A dozen women were fined 5s. 4d. each for leyrwite in 1328, and their villages were amerced for concealing the offences.[94] 'Stud' on six Burton manors in 1326 came to £33.[95] A tenant who put his son to letters without licence was fined 6s. 8d. in 1328.[96] In the 1307 survey heriot was recorded for only one Staffordshire manor, Stapenhill, but it was apparently collected on the other manors near Burton.[97]

Customary payments added significantly to peasant rent. Their arbitrary incidence and nature makes it difficult to estimate what they meant to a typical virgater, although some idea of their weight on certain holdings over a period of years can be gained. When William the Blower of Branston, a virgater, died in 1297, the lord took 2 oxen and a mare, and William's son, Stephen, paid £1 6s. 8d. to inherit. Stephen died in 1301. The heriot due was an ox, a cow, and a mare, but his widow, Felice, bought it out for 12s. She also fined 6s. 8d. to take the holding until the heir came of age. In 1303 Robert Palfreyman paid 6s. 8d. to marry Felice and hold the virgate until the heir came of age, when Robert was to keep ¼ virgate. In 1316 Adam de Naunton, husband of Alice, daughter of Stephen and Felice, fined 30s. to have the holding for life. On his death in 1321 the heriot was a mare with a foal. Alice kept the land.[98] Thus five beasts and £4 2s. were taken from the holding between 1297 and 1321. In a similar case at Stretton heriot of two oxen and a mare and payments totalling £8 in entry fines to the land and for permission to marry a female tenant can be traced between 1311 and 1317.[99] Arrangements were often made for heavy cash fines to be paid in instalments. One of the entry fines mentioned above was to be paid in three 2-mark instalments, and a 5-mark entry fine at Horninglow in 1310 was to be paid in three parts, £1 at Michaelmas, £1 at Martinmas, and £1 6s. 8d. at Candlemas.[1] There were heavy customary payments elsewhere. Aid was high on many manors. Over £13 was collected from the bond tenants of Rolleston, Marchington, and Barton in 1313–14, and over £16 from four episcopal manors (Baswich, Brewood, Eccleshall, and Haywood) in 1307–8.[2] At Alrewas a wide range of dues was exacted, some of them high. For example, it was the custom for the lord to select his reeve from two men put forward by the customary tenants, and the fines from the 'unsuccessful' candidate to be quit of the office could be as high as 5s. or 6s. 8d.[3]

Income from the exercise of lordship was substantial in the county. It amounted to well over a third of the total revenue on the estates of the bishop and the earl of Lancaster, and to about a fifth on the lesser estates of Tutbury priory and the Verduns.[4] It seems likely that seigneurial dues were a particularly attractive source of income to lords in a county where arable demesne agriculture was relatively undeveloped and there were few labour services. It is also likely that they were deliberately exploited in the 13th century, a time when most lords were attempting to increase estate income.

[91] S.H.C. 1910, 120.
[92] See e.g. S.R.O., D.(W.) o/3/9, rot. 11; /12, rott. 7, 8; /15, rot. 5; /22, rot. 8d.
[93] S.R.O., D.(W.) 1734/2/1/101a, m. 5; /101b, mm. 8, 33.
[94] Ibid. /101b, mm. 25–6.
[95] Ibid. m. 7.
[96] Ibid. m. 24.
[97] S.R.O., D.(W.) 1734/2/3/112a.

[98] Ibid. ff. 33v., 36, 37v., 54, 59.
[99] Ibid. ff. 48, 52v., 56v.–57 (holding of Rob. son of Reynold). For a similar case at Horninglow see ff. 31v., 58v.
[1] Ibid. f. 47v.
[2] D.L. 29/1/3; E 358/13.
[3] S.R.O., D.(W.) o/3/9, rot. 1; /15, rot. 1.
[4] Hilton, Eng. Peasantry in Later Middle Ages, 232–3.

The development did not pass unnoticed by their tenants. At Abbots Bromley there were complaints about new customs regarding strays in 1228, and in 1236 villein services were refused by tenants after an arbitrary tallage had been levied in three consecutive years.[5] The detailed records of John de Heronville's claims to many customary payments and obligations at Wednesbury are due to the fact that his tenants resisted them, claiming the privilege of ancient demesne.[6] Peasants protested against increased exactions at Tettenhall, another ancient demesne manor; on the estate of the dean of Wolverhampton; and, no doubt, elsewhere.[7]

It must be remembered, however, that villeinage existed alongside a high incidence of free tenure. A variety of historical and geographical factors had produced considerable variations in manorial structure by the end of the 13th century. Thus on the bishop's estates there existed such contrasting manors as Haywood, a 'typical' manor, with a substantial core of unfree tenants, some performing heavy seasonal services on the demesne, and Cannock and Rugeley, in the forest, with little or no arable demesne, no villeinage, and a high proportion of smallholders with assart land.

The Peasantry: Farming

Peasant farming is poorly documented. Surviving manorial records concentrate on landlord farming and on the peasantry merely as tenants and providers of labour. They contain enough information, however, to make possible a partial and impressionistic picture of the peasants as farmers. This section discusses peasant farming c. 1300, although it is sometimes necessary to use evidence from the 14th and 15th centuries.

Descriptions of peasant messuages, curtilages, crofts, and gardens are infrequent, but some typical features can be seen. Barns are the farm buildings most often referred to. Detailed records of the cost of two-, three-, and four-bay barns on customary tenements on the duchy of Lancaster estate in the 1440s throw light on their construction and the type of labour used. The main part of £6 9s. 2d. spent on a three-bay barn at Rolleston in 1444–5 consisted of daily wages of 5d. to two carpenters and 4d. to another for a total of 152 days' work on the chief timbers (£2 19s. 2d.) and 1s. a day to 15 tenants for a total of 30 days' carting the timber from the forest to the tenement with their own beasts, carts, and wagons (£1 10s.). A roofer and his mate were paid 7d. a day for 9 days' work using straw bought locally. Cutting, carting, and preparing material for the walls cost 4s., 2,600 lath nails were bought for 2s. 6d., and other wood for such items as laths, spurs, and studs was cut, sawn, and carted for 10s. 6d. Stones for footings for posts were prepared and carted for 2s. 8d., and bread, ale, and meat were bought for tenants helping with the barn's erection. In 1445–6 16s. 1d. was spent on further carpentry and iron-work, chiefly on a large and a small door and windows.[8]

That type of construction and the use of a mixture of skilled, semi-skilled, and tenant labour seems to have been typical. A house of three bays is mentioned at Haywood in 1409, and another with a lower chamber and a kitchen at Cannock in 1413.[9] There are occasional indications that peasants employed specialists on their own buildings: a contract to thatch with straw a peasant house at Burton was allegedly broken in 1327, and John de Ideshale of Rugeley was described as a thatcher in 1357.[10]

Vegetables and fruit were grown in crofts and gardens. There were vegetables, including leeks, and apples in a close at Alrewas in 1332, and beans in a garden there in 1352.[11]

[5] N.S.J.F.S. xii. 49–50; S.H.C. v(1), 65–6.
[6] S.H.C. ix(1), 17–18.
[7] Hilton, Eng. Peasantry in Later Middle Ages, 237 sqq.
[8] D.L. 29/370/6184, 6186, and 6189.
[9] S.R.O., D.(W.) 1734/2/1/427, rot. 24d.; /176, rot 3.
[10] Ibid. /101b, m. 11; /175, rot. 27.
[11] S.R.O., D.(W.) 0/3/16, rot. 1; /39, rot. 7d.

On their holdings in the arable fields, peasants grew all four main cereals, wheat, rye, barley, and oats. Sometimes the two former or the two latter were sown mixed as maslin or dredge, crops with a reputation for being safer in precarious conditions. Peas were widely found as field crops by 1300, and, increasingly, beans. The relative importance of those and other crops is difficult to gauge from the evidence which survives. In some parts of the county oats were probably the predominant crop, for example on thin soils assarted in the late 13th century in Cannock forest. At a regard in 1262 all but ½ a. of 17 a. presented as illegally assarted and sown had carried 2 or 4 crops of oats only; the ½ a. had been sown once with rye and once with oats. In 1272 19 of 28 small assarts presented had carried equal numbers of crops of oats and a winter-sown crop, the rest mostly or solely oats.[12] In the high, limestone north-east 25 neifs of Tutbury priory at Wetton paid a commuted work-rent in oats in 1294,[13] and the rent of the mills at Alton, a little further south, was paid largely in oats and oat-malt in 1339.[14] In the more sheltered and fertile north-west the chief crop in the multure of the mill at Newcastle in the early 14th century was also oats.[15] The same is true at that date of the multure at Lichfield, where spring crops, predominantly oats, regularly amounted to twice as much as the winter-sown crops of wheat and maslin.[16]

In the relatively unspecialized economy of the period, however, most peasants probably grew as wide a range of crops as they could, even in the north of the county: a tithe disputed at Balterley in 1352 included wheat, rye, barley, oats, beans, and peas, and a tenant at Keele had wheat, rye, and oats on his land in 1374.[17] The crop forfeited by a felon of Forebridge in Castle Church in 1481 consisted of rye worth 7s. and barley worth 5s.[18] In the southern half of the county vetch is occasionally recorded, for example near Burton in 1367, and there were 'flaxlands' at Cannock in the mid 14th century.[19] Peas and beans were sufficiently well established to merit special harvest regulations on the Burton abbey manors in 1325 and at Alrewas in 1342,[20] but the main crops were the four cereals. Probably wheat and oats predominated, but three references to peasant crops at Alrewas in the 1330s and 1340s demonstrate the danger of generalizing. One peasant possessed seed corn consisting of 2 strikes of rye and 2 of oats; a second died leaving 4 strikes of wheat sown; a third alleged damage to his crop of oats and dredge in one year and to his rye the year after.[21] The record of tithe at Abbots Bromley in 1419–20 suggests some concentration by the peasants on the more profitable crops of wheat and barley. Those accounted for about three-quarters of the total harvest; oats were considerably less important and rye insignificant.[22]

At the end of the 13th century peasants were probably ploughing chiefly with oxen. Horses, more expensive to buy and keep, were generally used for carting. Those who owned cart-horses sometimes hired them to those who had none or not enough, and that sometimes led to disputes. Thus the owner of a mare hired to take a load from Alrewas to Leicester in 1352 claimed that the animal had been injured.[23] The more substantial peasants often owned several draught animals, and some were very well endowed. At Burton in 1328 the presentments for strays included offences with both small and large numbers: 2, 3, and 12 (twice) affers, 2 horses (twice), and 2 and 4 oxen. There is no reason, of course, to suppose that those represented the whole of

[12] E 32/184 m. 8; /187 m. 3. See also ibid. /184 m. 10 and v.; /188 mm. 16–17v.

[13] *S.H.C.* 4th ser. iv, p. 224.

[14] *S.H.C.* 1913, 79.

[15] Jean R. Birrell, 'The Honour of Tutbury in the 14th and 15th Centuries' (Birm. Univ. M.A. thesis, 1962), 16.

[16] E 358/13; L.J.R.O., D.30/N 12–13.

[17] *S.H.C.* xiii. 51; Univ. of Keele, Sneyd MSS. S.2424–5 (tenement of Thos. Budde).

[18] S.R.O., D.641/1/4A/19, rot. 1.

[19] S.R.O., D.(W.) 1734/2/1/102, rot. 16; /175, rot. 29A.

[20] Ibid. /101, m. 11; S.R.O., D.(W.) o/3/27, rot. 9.

[21] S.R.O., D.(W.) o/3/15, rot. 5; /32, rot. 8; /33, rot. 11d.; /34, rot. 4d.

[22] S.R.O., D.(W.) 1734/3/3/2.

[23] S.R.O., D.(W.) o/3/39, rot. 9d. See also ibid. /27, rot. 3d. For a rare ref. to the use of a horse for ploughing see Univ. of Keele, Sneyd MS. S.2424.

their owners' stock.[24] Heriots on the Burton abbey estate, as has been mentioned, often included both oxen and horses, sometimes two of each.[25]

A plough and a cart were the chief items of farm equipment regularly appearing in lists of peasant goods, and they were probably regarded as essential equipment for virgaters.[26] Iron parts or bindings increased both their cost and efficiency. A 'share-beam' and 'plough-beam' were valued at 1½d. in Alrewas in 1345 and a cart body was bought there for 8d. in 1347; a wheel was valued at 6d. at Rugeley in 1368.[27] An iron-bound cart at Rolleston in 1399 was valued at 10s., and a pair of plough irons at Rugeley in 1356 at 40d.[28]

The services of specialist craftsmen were necessary for iron-working and were probably common with largely wooden equipment such as ploughs and carts. Trans-actions with smiths are recorded from time to time.[29] Henry the cartwright, of Burton, was alleged in 1325 to have made a cart with wood other than that provided, and in 1327 to have made for the abbot a pair of wheels not worth the agreed price.[30] The surname Plowright appears at Burton in 1326.[31]

A harrow, again sometimes strengthened with iron, was another major piece of equipment.[32] Mattocks, forks, sickles, and axes were also in common use; they were listed in inventories, taken as security, borrowed, and stolen.[33] An axe (securis) unjustly detained at Cannock in 1368 was valued at 8d., the same price as a double-edged axe (bisacutum) borrowed at Alrewas in 1346.[34] A winnowing-fan was valued at 2d. at Alrewas in 1347.[35]

There is a little evidence about peasant farming techniques. The type of equipment discussed is in itself a guide. Double ploughing with fallowing was common practice. It was specified in a lease between peasants at Alrewas in 1333 that the lessee and his heirs were to fallow, plough, and replough the land at their own cost.[36] Both marl and dung were put on the land. Marlpits are often mentioned, though in their role as landmarks or hazards to the unwary traveller. Dung was precious enough to be stolen; fifty cartloads stolen at Alrewas in 1332 were valued at 5s.[37]

Cattle, sheep, pigs, hens, and geese, as well as draught animals, were found on peasant holdings, and the better off were likely to have a few of each. An Alrewas virgater accused of letting 20 sheep stray in 1331 had a cow, a mare, 2 colts, a foal, a sow, and 9 piglets at the time of his death in 1338.[38] It is, however, difficult to estimate the average size of peasant herds and flocks, as most references mention only some of their animals, those taken as heriot, for example, those let stray, or those worried by dogs. Such evidence gives merely an impression of the type of animals commonly owned by peasants and of minimum herd and flock sizes. By the early 14th century some peasants had built up fairly large flocks or herds. There were flocks of 80, 100, and 160 sheep at Alrewas at that time, though flocks of 10 or 20 were probably much more common.[39] Herds of cows were smaller, and a man with 6 at Alrewas in 1333[40] was probably unusually well endowed. The cow was often the animal provided as heriot

[24] S.R.O., D.(W.) 1734/2/1/101b, m. 20.
[25] Ibid. /101a, m. 5; /101b, mm. 9, 11.
[26] The entrant to a virgate at Burton 'habet diem ad habendum unam carucam et j carectam cum decet ad statum suum': ibid. /103, rot. 49.
[27] S.R.O., D.(W.) o/3/32, rot. 1d.; /33, rot. 9; D.(W.) 1734/2/1/175, rot. 38d.
[28] D.L. 30/110/1646 rot. 1; S.R.O., D.(W.) 1734/2/1/175, rot. 23. Plough irons were sometimes listed alone: D.(W.) 1734/2/1/103, rot. 52. See also D.(W.) o/3/15, rot. 3d., for a plough with iron parts and D.(W.) 1734/2/1/102, rot. 17, for a 'bound' cart.
[29] See e.g. S.R.O., D.(W.) 1734/2/1/102, rot. 9.
[30] Ibid. /101a, m. 4; /101b, m. 11.
[31] Ibid. /101b, m. 10.
[32] S.R.O., D.(W.) o/3/32, rot. 1d.; D.(W.) 1734/2/1/103, rot. 52.
[33] S.R.O., D.(W.) 1734/2/1/101b, m. 1; /175, rott. 12, 23, 40; S.R.O., D.(W.) o/3/15, rot. 3d.
[34] S.R.O., D.(W.) 1734/2/1/175, rot. 37; D.(W.) o/3/32, rot. 11.
[35] S.R.O., D.(W.) o/3/33, attachment to rot. 11d.
[36] Ibid. /18, rot. 1. [37] Ibid. /15, rot. 7.
[38] Ibid. rot. 1; /22, rot. 8d. (Ric. Mably).
[39] Ibid. /15, rot. 1; /16, rot. 4; /18, rott. 5d., 7.
[40] Ibid. /18, rot. 7.

at Alrewas by smallholders and landless tenants who apparently had no oxen.[41] A smallholder at Winshill who died in 1312 owned a cow and 6 sheep.[42] Pigs were important for Staffordshire peasants and were widely owned. Herds of 6 or 8 were common on the Burton abbey manors, where herds of 12 and 15 are also mentioned.[43] Hens are rarely mentioned, except as fines or rents, but geese frequently occur. Gaggles of 5, 7, 8, 12 (three times), 14 (twice), 16, 20, and 24 strayed on the abbey manors in 1328.[44]

Animals were often leased by one peasant to another for short periods. Three cases illustrate the practice. Eleven ewes were handed over for 3 years in 1325 at Alrewas; the lessee was to look after them in return for half the fleeces and lambs. A cow was leased for 6 years for half the issue on the same manor in 1334.[45] At Winshill in 1327 a sow was leased for 2 years for half the issue.[46]

There was also by the early 14th century a peasant market in animals, often recorded only as a result of disputes taken to the manor court. Failure to make full payment was the most common complaint but not the only one. Thomas Gyn of Alrewas, who bought 13 sheep from two brothers in 1328 and found that they all died from murrain, brought a case against the brothers. They claimed successfully, however, that the sheep were sound and healthy when they were sold, and Thomas was amerced for a false claim.[47] The constraint on villein sales of certain animals on some manors was at least sometimes enforced; six people who sold male foals without licence were amerced at Rolleston in 1339.[48]

Ownership of animals was made plain by distinguishing marks.[49] Animals were often in the care of the village herdsman paid by contributions from the villagers.[50] Herdsmen were frequently presented at the manor court for poor custody of the animals in their care or for letting them stray and cause damage. In 1326, for example, the common herdsman of Stapenhill was amerced 3d. for letting the beasts of the whole village stray.[51]

It is characteristic of peasant economy that the main labour of cultivating the holdings is provided by the family. By the 13th century, however, there was some hired labour among the peasantry. There were Staffordshire holdings big enough to need more labour than even a large family could supply, and many smallholders presumably supplemented the income from their holding. In addition some families were small, and there were also seasonal fluctuations in the amount of labour needed. Hired labour was needed at harvest time and one of the purposes of the Alrewas gleaning by-laws of 1342 was to maintain a supply of labourers. Leaving the manor to work outside at that time of year was also prohibited, and offenders were amerced for doing so.[52] Evidence of agreements between peasants is provided by cases brought to the manor court when things went wrong. Thus on the Burton estates in 1328 William Mancorneys successfully claimed that 14d. of his stipend for seven days' work in the autumn was still unpaid, and Robert Mancorneys made a similar successful claim about his stipend of 5s.[53] Men were hired at other busy periods, for example for ploughing and for particular jobs such as carting. A man at Alrewas brought two cases against his employer in 1346 alleging non-payment for ploughing a dole of land

[41] See e.g. the long list of heriots in 1349: ibid. /36, rot. 1 and d.
[42] S.R.O., D.(W.) 1734/2/3/112a, f. 50.
[43] S.R.O., D.(W.) 1734/2/1/101a, m. 7; /101b, mm. 10, 23.
[44] Ibid. /101b, mm. 20–2.
[45] S.R.O., D.(W.) 0/3/12, rot. 6; /18, rot. 6.
[46] S.R.O., D.(W.) 1734/2/1/101b, m. 10.

[47] S.R.O., D.(W.) 0/3/9, rott. 9, 11.
[48] D.L. 30/109/1615 rot. 4d.; above, p. 27.
[49] S.R.O., D.(W.) 0/3/33, rot. 2d.; D.(W.) 1807/21; D.(W.) 1734/2/1/427, rot. 4d.
[50] S.R.O., D.(W.) 0/3/9, rot. 11; /33, rott. 2, 4d.
[51] S.R.O., D.(W.) 1734/2/1/101b, m. 5.
[52] Ibid. /103, rot. 15; /175, rot. 45.
[53] Ibid. /101b, mm. 18, 25.

(2d.) and carrying timber from 'Ridware' to Orgreave in Alrewas (3d.).[54] A case in 1390 reveals a longer contract of employment and the ill-feeling which could arise between master and man. Henry Adcock of Alrewas was amerced for expelling John of Egginton from his service from 1 August to 11 November, causing him a loss estimated at £1, and for failing to pay him 9s. for looking after some sheep. At the same court John successfully defended himself against charges of poor custody of Henry's sheep and of pulling down fencing in Henry's garden and the 'evespolles' of his house, but he was amerced 3d. for damage to Henry's beans.[55]

Though the use of hired labour on peasant holdings was common, it remained limited, and holdings were essentially family affairs, worked by the tenants. Holdings were often surrendered by those who were unable to cope, in particular the old. Thus a father at Alrewas handed over his land to his son in 1269 on the understanding that he would retain a bed in the house and a third of the corn and would pay a third of the rent.[56] A younger brother took over a holding at Stretton in 1295 because of the poverty and *inbecillitas* of his elder brother.[57] Such surrenders were not always confined to the family. Robert son of Walter handed over his holding at Burton to William by the Fleet for life in 1316, retaining only a messuage, a croft, ½ a. of arable, and 3 r. of meadow and receiving from William an annual allowance of two quarters of mixed wheat and rye. In 1321 William was licensed to cultivate for six years Richard Gossip's bovate, paying him a third of the produce, Richard remaining responsible for services.[58]

The replacement, even if only temporary, of incompetent tenants was encouraged by the manorial administration. In 1296, for example, a bovate at Stretton was taken into the lord's hands because its tenant did not cultivate it, and was leased to another.[59] In such circumstances it was not uncommon for the enterprising to acquire holdings temporarily or permanently. Between 1294 and 1308 William of Branston acquired two bovates in Winshill surrendered in quick succession by Adam Walrand because of poverty, as well as a third, to which he had the right through his mother, on the death of its tenant. On William's death his wife fined for the two bovates formerly Adam's until their son came of age, and for the third for life.[60]

A significant degree of fluidity in peasant landholding can be seen by the end of the 13th century. As well as the type of transaction described above there were numerous sales and leases of peasant land. On the Burton abbey manors c. 1300 most such transactions were sales of virgate or bovate holdings. Many merely passed from one member of a family to another, but a significant proportion, as far as one can tell, changed family.[61]

The abbot of Burton attempted to control leases and sales of customary land, and amercements for leasing without licence to villeins or free men were common in the early 14th century on the abbey estates. At a court in 1328 two Burton men were amerced for unlicensed leases and four from Branston for unlicensed leases to free men.[62] On the Somerville manor at Alrewas sales and leases are recorded in the late 13th century, but it is not until the 14th century that sales become common. Most involve small pieces of land, often only roods and selions. Many transactions are clearly between members of one family, but many, apparently, are not. The activities of a late-13th-century tenant, Roger Wytemay, who appears successively as lessor of 2 a. for 6 crops, 1 a. for 6 crops, ½ r. of meadow for 8 crops or years, a piece of land for 20

54 S.R.O., D.(W.) 0/3/32, rot. 11. See also ibid. /27, rot. 3; /32, rot. 12; /40, rot. 1d.
55 Ibid. /85, rot. 4 and d.
56 S.H.C. 1910, 94.
57 S.R.O., D.(W.) 1734/2/3/112a, f. 30v.
58 Ibid. ff. 53, 59.
59 Ibid. f. 32v.
60 Ibid. ff. 30v., 45v., 47.
61 Walmsley, 'Estate of Burton Abbey', 234.
62 S.R.O., D.(W.) 1734/2/1/101b, m. 18.

years, and $\frac{1}{2}$ a. for 6 crops, seem typical in the size of the pieces of land involved and the length of terms.[63] Rents on leases between peasants were in both cash and kind. A rent in beans at Alrewas is mentioned in 1347, and a lease of 4 a. at Stapenhill in 1328 was for half the crop.[64]

In those circumstances a few peasants were able to accumulate large holdings which the expanding market for agricultural produce in the 13th century made profitable. A peasant on the Burton abbey estate held three virgates at his death in 1302, another held two in 1314, and there were several three-bovate holdings.[65] At Barton in 1327 one bond tenant held 2 virgates and 40 a., another held $1\frac{1}{2}$ virgates, a cottage, and about 70 a.[66]

Such accumulation remained, however, exceptional. Most holdings passed from one tenant to the next according to customary inheritance rules and were more or less untouched by permanent alienations. The normal practice was for the eldest son to inherit. At Alrewas, however, 'borough English', by which the heir was the youngest son, prevailed.[67] In 1351, for example, an elder brother agreed to look after his younger brother, then ten years old, and his land. In 1348 two sisters inherited jointly some new land which was held freely, but half an acre of land of 'base tenure' was taken by the younger alone. In 1350 the son of a younger daughter was said to have a greater right to a tenement than his aunt, the elder daughter.[68]

In practice many heirs did not inherit on their fathers' death because widows held their dead husbands' tenements for life. On the Burton abbey manors at the end of the 13th century widows customarily held only until the heir came of age, though in practice they seem often to have died in possession.[69] It was possible for women to manage tenements alone. A virgater at Stretton surrendered his holding to his daughter in 1296 on the understanding that she would care for him, and it was 1298 before she married and her husband fined for the holding and agreed to care for her father.[70] Widows often remained unmarried and in possession of their holdings for many years or until death. In 1306 a widow at Horninglow fined for a messuage, a virgate, and 4 a. of forland of her late husband's holding for eleven years until the heir came of age and for another $2\frac{3}{4}$ a. for life. In 1318 she was licensed to hold and cultivate the virgate for a further eight years.[71] Many widows remarried, however, and held their tenements jointly with their new husbands, though retaining their rights if they lived the longer. The customs governing the rights of widows, widowers, and their children to customary land, at a period when remarriage was common, were complex, and often the subject of dispute, despite frequent attempts at careful definition.[72]

THE LATER MIDDLE AGES

Crisis

The 14th and 15th centuries have been seen as a period of more or less unrelieved decline, rooted in the over-expansion of the previous period, or as a time of crisis, readjustment, and growth on a healthier basis. Many of the signs of crisis in the 14th century can be seen in Staffordshire, as well as long-lasting depression, but there are also signs of adaptation to changed conditions.

[63] *S.H.C.* 1910, 95–6, 103, 125, 127.
[64] S.R.O., D.(W.) o/3/33, rot. 5d.; D.(W.) 1734/2/1/101b, m. 23. See also D.(W.) o/3/32, rott. 3, 6, 11.
[65] S.R.O., D.(W.) 1734/2/3/112a, ff. 37, 51v., and, for 3-bovate holdings, 28v., 30v., 32, 34v., 35.
[66] S.C. 11/602.
[67] *S.H.C.* 1910, 136.
[68] S.R.O., D.(W.) o/3/34, rot. 9d.; /38, rott. 4d., 7d. See also *S.H.C.* 1910, 136.
[69] See e.g. S.R.O., D.(W.) 1734/2/3/112a, ff. 28v., 29, 36v.
[70] Ibid. ff. 32, 34v.
[71] Ibid. ff. 44v., 58.
[72] See e.g. ibid. f. 28; S.R.O., D.(W.) o/3/23, rot. 2.

There are indications of extreme pressure on resources by the early 14th century. The high proportion of smallholders on manors throughout the county has been mentioned above. The persistent demand for land meant that assarting continued in some parts of the county. High entry fines testify to the strong demand, and new and recent assarts are widely mentioned in the records. At Longdon, for example, a manor with access to Cannock forest, over 60 a. of assart paid rent for the first time in 1308–9, and 32 a. at Cannock itself in the same year.[73] Entry fines were generally 10s. an acre, although it seems likely that at Longdon, as at Eccleshall, some of the expansion may have been on to poor land unlikely to give high returns to arable farmers.[74] Similarly assarting continued on the Lancastrian manors in and near Needwood. At Uttoxeter over 150 a. was assarted between 1314 and 1322, and there were numerous small assarts on the manors of Barton and Marchington.[75] At Pattingham fines of 8s., 10s., and 13s. 4d. an acre were charged on small assarts in 1314.[76] High entry fines were also often charged on transfers of old land. Entry fines of over £24 were collected at Marchington in 1313–14. Two, three, and four marks were paid for bovates on the Burton abbey manors, and 6s. 8d. on small pieces of land at Pattingham (1½ a. and ½ a.) in 1312 and 1313.[77]

It may, however, be questioned whether the high fines were in practice collected, as many accounting officers accumulated arrears heavy enough to suggest more than the normal difficulties of rent collection. Reeves on the five Lancastrian manors in Staffordshire owed nearly £90 at Michaelmas 1313, and at Longdon arrears in the early 14th century were consistently high, usually well over £50, often much nearer £100.[78] Peasant poverty frequently prevented the collection of fines or forced the surrender of holdings, and there are ominous mentions of peasants without land or stock. It seems that a particular conjuncture of circumstances made peasant poverty acute and widespread in the early 14th century. The Burton abbey court rolls for the late 13th and early 14th centuries record a trickle of surrenders of holdings because of destitution, fines excused because of poverty, and heriots waived because there were no animals. Often the very poor were cottagers such as the tenant of a cottage and a croft at Wetmore on whose death in 1307 the abbot had nothing 'because he was poor'. Tenants of standard holdings also were reduced to this plight. Another tenant who died in 1307 leaving no stock from which heriot could be levied was Robert Emmot of Stapenhill, a bovater. In both cases the sons who inherited were apparently able to raise cash entry fines for the holdings, 6s. and 16s. respectively.[79]

The famine which swept Europe from 1315 to 1317 affected Staffordshire. The Croxden chronicle describes 1316 as a year 'memorable for dearness, famine, disease, and death'.[80] The Burton abbey court rolls show a noticeable increase in 1316 and 1317 in the number of cases where no heriot could be levied; now virgaters were among those who had no animals left at the time of their death.[81] Some of the abbey's tenants starved. In 1317 a Branston virgater, Alice, widow of William of Appleby, died of hunger (*oppressa fame interiit*). So did Robert Bouchett, a Horninglow bovater. Another tenant at Branston, Margery, wife of Nicholas of Branston, also died of hunger 'so they [the people of Branston] say'.[82]

On the Lancastrian manors in Staffordshire some assarting continued in the early

[73] S.R.O., D.(W.) 1734/J.2057; L.J.R.O., D.30/N 10.
[74] Spufford, *Eccleshall*, 17.
[75] D.L. 29/1/3; S.C. 6/1146/11.
[76] S.R.O., D.(W.) 1807/2.
[77] S.R.O., D.(W.) 1734/2/3/112a, ff. 28v., 33, 44; D.(W.) 1807/1 and 2

[78] D.L. 29/1/3; S.R.O., D.(W.) 1734/J.2057; L.J.R.O., D.30/N 15; E 358/13.
[79] S.R.O., D.(W.) 1734/2/3/112a, f. 45.
[80] C. Lynam, *Abbey of St. Mary, Croxden*, chronicle, p. vii.
[81] S.R.O., D.(W.) 1734/2/3/112a, ff. 54 sqq.
[82] Ibid. ff. 55v., 56v.

14th century but other land was being abandoned and some rents were falling. In 1313–14 over 600 a. of land at Uttoxeter and Marchington were either out of use or had their rent reduced by 2d. or 4d. an acre. By the 1320s a much larger area had been abandoned there and on the other manors. The accounts of 1322 listed as derelict 58 messuages, over 1,800 a. of arable, 40 cottages, 14½ virgates, 20 bovates, and 37 a. of meadow in Barton, Rolleston, Marchington, and Uttoxeter and numerous empty burgages and shops in Tutbury. The abandoned land included substantial amounts of demesne at Rolleston and Uttoxeter, bovates and virgates, presumably from the old land of the manors, and many acres which probably included assarts. The 'decay' is usually recorded in stages, as if it were the result of developments over several years. At Marchington, for example, the sum of the first 'decay' was £2 17s. 8d., of the second £11 11s. 10¾d., and of the third £7 3s. 10d. The accountants offered lengthy explanations for the decline in rent income. The tenants had left, it was declared, both because of their poverty and because of the poor quality of the land; some were dead and no new tenants could be found to take the land even as pasture. Lack of demand for pasture was blamed on the scarcity of stock, both because of murrain and because of the depredations at the time of Thomas of Lancaster's rebellion.[83]

There was a similar decay in 1323–4 on the manor of Yoxall, also in the king's hands after the rebellion.[84] The king's army had marched into that part of Staffordshire in 1322 and had inflicted some damage,[85] but that can only have been a minor aggravation of a serious situation. Other parts of the county also suffered. In 1319 the Croxden chronicle records 'a plague or murrain of animals unseen and unheard of hitherto' in which the abbey sustained losses valued at 200 marks.[86] At Keele land was lying out of use in the 1320s and the familiar explanations were offered: poverty had forced tenants to flee, the land was not wanted as pasture because there were too few animals, and it was too infertile to bring back into use as arable.[87] This evidence lends credibility to the statement in an inquisition *post mortem* of 1339 that 240 a. of demesne at Alton lay uncultivated because it could not be leased nor the herbage sold because pasture was abundant, and that the tenants were poor and destitute. There was more waste land at Stanton in Ellastone and Bradley in the Moors.[88]

A Barton rental of 1327 suggests some recovery. Five cottages, half a virgate, and 90 a. of land are listed as derelict, compared with 19 messuages, 28 cottages, 14½ virgates, and 180 a. in 1322. Amendments to the rental suggest that it soon proved possible to find tenants for more of the decayed tenements.[89]

There is evidence therefore of a considerable malaise in Staffordshire in the early 14th century, and it seems that the widespread murrain and famine of 1315–17 and the 1320s had affected the county badly. It was thus a troubled countryside, though one probably somewhat recovered from an earlier trough, that felt the impact of the Black Death and later attacks of plague. The Black Death reached Staffordshire in the spring of 1349 and spread throughout the county. By the end of the year pestilence was being blamed for difficulties in collecting the full manorial income in villages as scattered as Wootton in Ellastone in the north-east, Ashley and Gerrard's Bromley in Eccleshall in the west, and Great Wyrley in Cannock.[90]

At Alrewas the court rolls suggest that mortality was at its height for about four months in the spring and early summer of 1349. Nearly 60 deaths are recorded in May, over 70 in June, about 50 in July, and about 12 in August. The figures compare

[83] Birrell, 'Honour of Tutbury', 50 sqq.
[84] S.C. 6/1147/24.
[85] J. R. Maddicott, *Thomas of Lancaster*, 309–11.
[86] Lynam, *Croxden*, chronicle, p. vii.

[87] S.C. 6/1146/11 m. 3; E 358/16 mm. 8–9.
[88] *S.H.C.* 1913, 77, 79.
[89] S.C. 11/602.
[90] *S.H.C.* 1913, 131–3, 136.

with 2 or 3 deaths recorded for each of the earlier and later months of 1349. It may be significant that nearly a third of those who died were landless and that over a fifth were cottagers or smallholders.[91] Alrewas was a populous manor where a little sporadic and small-scale assarting had continued throughout the earlier 14th century; a few tenements had been temporarily in hand but there had been an active land market. Despite the large number of deaths in 1349 few tenements were empty at the end of the year: only 13 were listed as in hand at the December court.[92] Most tenements were quickly claimed by an heir, though often by one who was under age or more distant a relative than usual. Some tenements changed hands more than once in the course of the year: for example, part of the tenement of Henry Ward, who died in May, passed first to his widow Alice, then, on her death in June, to their twelve-year-old son, John, who was placed in the custody of his nearest relative until he came of age.[93] The impact of the Black Death seems, in the short term at least, to have been limited at Alrewas. Certainly the court rolls suggest that the manorial administration coped adequately with the increased business of collecting heriot on the death of tenants or landless persons.

By the end of the 14th century there was land lying out of use, old arable leased as pasture, and ruinous farm-buildings in villages throughout the county. In some villages the decay was severe early in the century and was followed by marked, though still partial, recovery. Elsewhere it seems to have been a feature of the later 14th century. The Black Death and the second serious outbreak of plague in 1361 both left their mark. A tenement at Pattingham was said in 1357 to have 'lain empty and ruinous since the time of the pestilence'. At Whittington, in the manor of Longdon, arrears of £12 in 1365 were said to date from 1361, and at Tutbury in 1370 seven untenanted shops were said to have lain empty since 'the first pestilence'. Similarly it was stated in the 1370s that certain labour services due to Farewell priory had not been performed since 1349.[94] It is clear, however, that plague was not the sole cause of agrarian problems in the 14th century.

The abandonment of land and holdings was widespread and the results were similar on many manors. At Pattingham in the 1360s entry fines were reduced or waived for tenants taking uncultivated land or agreeing to repair ruinous buildings. At Whittington in 1366 many tenements were in hand or let at reduced rates. Only £1 10s. of the £6 due as aid from the neifs of Longdon and Whittington could be collected, and only 8s. of the 18s. 6d. due for pannage. Rents worth £7 12s. 1½d. were decayed at Walsall in 1388–9. At Barton in 1370–1 most of the demesne was leased at £1 14s. 7¾d., a reduction of £2 12s. 6d. Old decayed tenements were re-leased at will for £1 5s. 11d. and the herbage of 15 abandoned acres fetched 1s. 8d. Rents of £1 6s. 8d. were allowed on tenements in hand, and £2 13s. 9d. of the charge of £4 17s. 4d. for tallage and £1 0s. 4d. for views was excused because of the poverty of the tenants. A very bad murrain (*maxima morina*) of cattle was blamed for low rents at Marchington in the 1370s.[95]

Further north the evidence is fragmentary, but it is clear that some manors were affected. There were decays of rent and abandoned holdings late in the 14th century on several Stafford family manors, Stafford itself, Madeley, Barlaston, Tittensor in Stone, and Norton-in-the-Moors. In most cases, however, they were not serious. None is recorded in three accounts of the 1360s and 1370s for the Audley manors of Tunstall

91 S.R.O., D.(W.) 0/3/35–7.   92 Ibid. /37, rot. 5.   6/988/14; L.J.R.O., D.30/G 4.
93 Ibid. /35, rot. 6d.; /36, rot. 1.   95 S.R.O., D.(W.) 1807/25 and 27; D.(W.) 1734/J.2057;
94 S.R.O., D.(W.) 1807/22; D.(W.) 1734/J.2057; S.C.   B.L. Eg. Roll 8467; S.C. 6/988/14.

and Chesterton.[96] It is possible that the effects of the crisis and population decline were more marked in some of the populous manors of the south and centre of the county. The region of the greatest concentration of villages known to have been deserted after the mid 14th century was the south-east. At least 18 desertions dating from the mid 14th to the mid 16th centuries took place, and the figure may have been as high as 50.[97]

Landlords and Peasants

The altered conditions of the 14th and 15th centuries presented new problems and opportunities for landlords and peasants and led to changes in their relationship. For the peasantry the relaxation of the pressure on land opened the way to changes in the nature and size of peasant holdings and to changes in the terms of tenure and rent.

The number of smallholders and of the near-landless in the county fell, although there remained a relatively high proportion of smallholders. At Barton, for example, nearly half the tenants in 1327 were smallholders, but only just over a third in 1414.[98] At Abbots Bromley in 1416 about a quarter of the tenants held 5 a. or less.[99]

Some peasants were able to accumulate large holdings, which typically consisted of more than one customary holding with fragments of other land, often including old assart and demesne, acquired at different times.[1] At Barton in 1414 Ralph Leysing held 2 virgates, John Pennyfather and John Glyn the elder each held 1½ virgate, and John London held 3 messuages with 3 virgates and 2 half-virgates. Each also held a number of small pieces of land. John Glyn the elder, for example, also held an acre and 2 separate half-acres of arable, 2 r. of waste, 2 a. of waste, another 2 a. of waste, and a cottage, for an annual rent of 16s. 8d. John London also held 22 a. in 13 pieces, a plot, a path, and 3 cottages for an annual rent of £2 3s. 5¼d.

A few large, composite holdings of this type were common on many manors by the late 14th century. Holdings of a virgate or a bovate with an acre or two of assart or demesne were, however, more numerous. At Marchington in 1414 all 17 bond tenants held 2 bovates each, while at Rolleston 27 of the 28 bond tenants were full virgaters. About a dozen of the latter also held 1, 2, or at most 3 a. of land at will.

In the long run peasant rent fell, but it was a slow and uncertain process. Rent was determined by other factors than simple supply and demand, and there was no steady, over-all decline with the decline of population and of demand. Land leased by the acre, such as assart or demesne, was most responsive to changes in demand, and in general its rent fell more rapidly and significantly. At Tutbury the demesne was leased at 1s. an acre in 1313–14. By 1370 most of it, 211½ a., was leased at 10d. an acre and the rest, 60 a., at 6d. The rent of the 211½ a. had fallen to 6½d. an acre by 1440. At Uttoxeter most of the demesne was leased at 10d. an acre in 1313–14, 2d. an acre less than formerly. In 1414 nearly 100 a. remained at 10d. but about 140 a. was leased for less, most of it at 6d. an acre or less. At Marchington over 120 a. of land which had earlier fallen out of use was leased at between 1½d. and 3½d. an acre in 1370.[2]

Rents on customary holdings, however, were often maintained at more or less their old levels well into the 15th century. At Barton, for example, the rent of each of 19

[96] S.R.O., D.641/1/2/38; /41, rott. 1–2, 4–5; 'Court Rolls of Manor of Tunstall', ed. J. C. Wedgwood, *T.N.S.F.C.* lix. 58–61, 73–8, 83–6.

[97] P. V. Bate and D. M. Palliser, 'Suspected Lost Village Sites in Staffs.' *Trans. S. Staffs. Arch. & Hist. Soc.* xii. 31–6.

[98] S.C. 11/602; D.L. 42/4.

[99] S.R.O., D.(W.) 1734/2/3/1.

[1] For the next 2 paras. see D.L. 42/4.

[2] D.L. 29/1/3 (1313–14); S.C. 6/988/14 (1370–1); D.L. 42/4 (1414); D.L. 29/369/6179 (1440–1).

virgates was 3s. in cash with works valued at 5s. 2d. according to rentals of 1327 and 1414, with the rent of 11 half-virgates *pro rata*.[3]

On the Burton abbey manors rents of standard holdings in the late 14th century are remarkably uneven. Services were retained in some cases and commuted or lost in others, but that does not explain why virgates were rented for as little as 2s. a year or as much as 13s. 4d. and half-virgates for anything from 1s. to 11s.[4] Presumably individual bargains had been struck between lord and tenant, with the old high rents retained in some cases but with drastic reductions in others.

Entry fines too varied greatly, though the high fines often charged in the early 14th century seem to have disappeared. At Alrewas in the 1360s, for example, 6s. 8d., 12s., 13s. 4d., and £1 were charged on entry to virgates. At Burton in 1367 entry fines of £1 and 6s. 8d. were paid for two virgates while the fine on a third was condoned on condition that the tenement was rebuilt.[5]

Such concessions were widely made in the later 14th century and the 15th century to encourage tenants to repair or improve tenements which had suffered neglect. At Haywood in 1413 a tenant who took a messuage and half a virgate for 1s. agreed to build a barn within a year at his own cost except for the timber.[6] Exhortations to repair and maintain holdings were common in the late 14th century. On the Burton abbey manors tenants unable to maintain holdings were apparently forced into surrender, and named individuals or the community at large were ordered to take responsibility for the cultivation of empty holdings.[7] A more positive policy of rent concessions in return for repairs was common in the 15th century. At Pattingham, where in the 1430s and 1440s ruinous tenements were a serious embarrassment to the lord, as many as fourteen men were presented for the offence at one court in 1438. Substantial sums were allowed to tenants to subsidize repairs; in 1446, for example, the rent on a half-virgate was reduced from 9s. 8d. to 9s. and an immediate allowance of 9s. 8d. made to the entrant.[8]

There were various subsidies for improvements to customary holdings on the duchy of Lancaster manors, particularly in the 1440s. In 1444–6, for example, £7 5s. 2d. was provided towards the cost of a three-bay barn at Rolleston and 16s. 9d. for a two-bay barn at Marchington. In 1448–9 16s. 8d. was spent on a four-bay barn at Marchington which had decayed when in hand before a new tenant was found.[9]

A mixture of poverty and resistance on the part of the peasantry made many customary payments impossible to collect in full in the later Middle Ages. That was in spite of an apparently deliberate exploitation of such dues on some manors in the later 14th century, when they probably seemed particularly attractive to lords and officers as rent income fell. Their incidence and history varied greatly between manors, and no clear chronology of their decline emerges. Tallage, for example, was often virtually abandoned in the later 14th century but was in some cases collected almost in full up to the end of the 15th century. At Marchington, where tallage had been £4 at the beginning of the 14th century, it could not be levied at all in 1370–1 because of the poverty of the bond tenants, and only 5s. was collected in 1400 and throughout the 15th century. At Barton tallage had been reduced by half by 1370–1, and it never proved possible to reimpose the full charge. At Rolleston, however, a few miles away on the same estate, nearly all of the full tallage of £4 2s. 6d. was apparently collected throughout the 15th century.[10] On the Audley estate substantial though reduced tallage

[3] S.C. 11/602; D.L. 42/4.
[4] See e.g. S.R.O., D.(W.) 1734/2/1/102, rott. 11–21.
[5] S.R.O., D.(W.) 0/3/52, rott. 2, 6; D.(W.) 1734/2/102, rott. 17, 18.
[6] S.R.O., D.(W.) 1734/2/1/428, rot. 2.
[7] See e.g. ibid. /102, rott. 14, 19; /103, rott. 4d., 8d.
[8] S.R.O., D.(W.) 1807/69 and 73.
[9] D.L. 29/370/6184, 6186, and 6189.
[10] D.L. 29/1/3; S.C. 6/988/14 and 16.

was still being collected in the late 15th century: £3 at Audley, £4 14s. 4d. at Tunstall, where it had been £7 in the late 14th century, and £1 18s. 5½d. at Horton. 'Stud', due every third year, was also still collected, £3 10s. at Audley and £8 at Tunstall, where it had been £12 in the late 14th century.[11] At Sedgley, a manor with a high proportion of customary tenants, tallage of over £7 was collected in the late 15th century. A small part of the rent due (8s.) was, however, successfully refused by the tenants.[12]

Similarly heriot and *principalia* continued to be a heavy burden on some manors. Two oxen, a horse, and a mare were taken on the death of a virgater at Burton in 1392, and an ox worth 8s., two poor horses (2s. 6d.), a piglet (5d.), and a pot (1s.) at Patting-ham in 1436.[13] Their incidence seems, however, to have become more sporadic in the 15th century.

At Pattingham marriage fines of 6s. 8d. were common in the decades after the Black Death, and marriage fines of 13s. 4d. were charged on the Burton abbey estate, for example in 1368 and 1380.[14] At Alrewas one of the two nominees for the post of reeve fined 6s. 8d. in 1353 and 10s. in 1360 to be quit once the lord had made his choice, and in 1359 amercements of 2s. were imposed on four men who had put their sons to letters.[15]

Resistance to the lord's monopoly of milling led to frequent amercements. A dozen tenants at a time were amerced at Pattingham in the 1380s, and on the Burton abbey estate there seems to have been widespread refusal to use the abbey's mill in 1367 and 1368.[16] The failure to pay certain dues and perform surviving services frequently caused trouble on the abbey's estate. Many customary holdings still carried the obligation to perform limited carrying, haymaking, harvest, or ploughing services, though those seem to have diminished since the beginning of the 14th century. At a court at Stretton in 1367, for example, nine men and a woman were amerced 2d. each for arrears with their autumn services.[17] Evidence of the unpopularity of labour services comes from other estates, and it is clear that resistance had some effect. At a Farewell priory court of 1372 it was alleged that one tenant's reaping and hoeing services were in arrears 'since the first pestilence' and another's for twenty years.[18] Surviving services were more often commuted, but they were not therefore easier to collect. At Walsall it was claimed in 1418 that the customary tenants had been refusing certain dues of that type for over sixteen years, and the matter was referred to the lord's council. At Sedgley, however, £7 for sale of works was charged to customary tenants in the late 15th century.[19]

For the lords the situation was aggravated by the mobility of the peasant population. This was not new, but in the course of the 14th century the movement of peasants became a particular problem because of the shortage of tenants and labour. At Pattingham fourteen men were presented in 1337 for living away from the manor and were ordered to return,[20] and presentments were frequent for the rest of the century.[21] In most cases there was little that lords could do to prevent movement or to recover lost tenants. Some tenants, however, paid a tax of a few pence a year to live away from the manor, thus maintaining rights and the possibility of return, and others paid for

[11] S.C. 6/988/2, rott. 1, 4 and d. (1469–70); *T.N.S.F.C.* lix. 58, 84. 'Stud', as a regular payment, seems a Staffs. feature: above, p. 27; N. Neilson, 'Customary Rents', *Oxford Studies in Social and Legal Hist.* ed. P. Vinogradoff, ii. 97–8.

[12] S.R.O., D.593/0/3/3, m. 3.

[13] S.R.O., D.(W.) 1734/2/1/103, rot. 52; D.(W.) 1807/68.

[14] See e.g. S.R.O., D.(W.) 1807/26; D.(W.) 1734/2/1/102, rot. 19; /103, rot. 3.

[15] S.R.O., D.(W.) 0/3/41, rot. 1; /50, rot. 1; /51, rot. 1.

[16] S.R.O., D.(W.) 1807/31 and 33; D.(W.) 1734/2/1/102, rott. 17, 18d., 19.

[17] S.R.O., D.(W.) 1734/2/1/102, rot. 11.

[18] L.J.R.O., D.30/G 4.

[19] B.L. Eg. Roll 8503; S.R.O., D.593/0/3/3, m. 3.

[20] S.R.O., D.(W.) 1807/3.

[21] See e.g. ibid. /22.

the right to leave. Flight was not always safe. A neif from Pattingham living illegally at Upper Arley (later Worcs.) was caught at Kidderminster fair in 1356.[22]

Many who left settled in neighbouring counties, often in small towns such as Kidderminster, Droitwich, or Bridgnorth. Some went further afield. In the later 14th century there were Staffordshire peasants in Herefordshire and Oxfordshire and at Stamford, Leicester, and Lincoln.[23]

Landlords' income from rents was thus eroded in a number of ways in the later Middle Ages, and there is little evidence of significant recovery. On the duchy of Lancaster estate rent receipts in 1370–1 were at least 10 per cent lower on each manor than in 1313–14. By the end of the century there had been some recovery, but the position described in 1414 was gradually eroded in the ensuing decades; at Barton, for example, rent receipts had fallen by some 9 per cent by 1440–1. After that there seems to have been a slight increase, then some stability, though certain receipts continued to fall. The farm of the corn mills of Tutbury, Marchington, Uttoxeter, and Barton, worth just over £40 in 1400–1, fell to £30 in 1473 and to just over £20 in 1475.[24] On the bishop's manor of Eccleshall rent income in the 1470s was in general about a third less than it had been at the end of the 13th century.[25] Comparisons of rent income over a long period must, however, be treated with caution.

Direct cultivation of the demesne, generally adopted by income-conscious landlords in the 13th century, had declined by the 14th century. A number of Staffordshire demesnes were in the hands of tenants by the early 14th century, although some direct cultivation continued. It persisted into the second half of the century, though on a reduced scale, on estates of different size and type of lordship, such as those of the bishop,[26] Burton abbey,[27] the Staffords,[28] Ralph, Lord Basset (d. 1390),[29] the Hospitallers,[30] and Farewell priory.[31] Though on the Farewell estate it continued well into the 15th century, direct demesne cultivation was rare in the county by 1400. It is usually difficult to discover the date of the first demesne leases. On many manors the first complete or substantial leases were preceded by leases of small amounts. Court rolls of the Burton abbey manors in the 1390s reveal what was probably a typical arrangement, occasional leases of an acre or two of demesne with continued direct cultivation of the rest. Though landlords in general chose leasing as the best solution to the problem of demesne administration at a time of uncertain markets and labour problems, they were frequently reluctant to part with their entire demesnes. The earl of Stafford retained a home farm at Stafford in the 15th century.[32] Some stock and pastures were often retained when the arable was leased. Burton abbey continued to keep sheep well into the 15th century. In a lease of the manor of Branston in 1431 two sheepfolds, a croft, and some meadow were reserved for the abbot.[33] The bishop kept horses, cattle, sheep, goats, and pigs on his manors of Haywood and Beaudesert throughout the 15th century. Twenty sheep in Beaudesert in 1473 were 'for the household of the lord'. The number of cattle fluctuated.[34] The earls and dukes of Lancaster kept a stable at Tutbury throughout the Middle Ages, using the forest pastures of Needwood.[35]

Many different types of lease are found. At Walsall in the 1380s and 1390s, for example, there were many leases of small and large pieces of demesne for terms as

[22] S.R.O., D.(W.) 1807/21.

[23] Ibid. /22 and 28; S.R.O., D.(W.) 1734/2/1/103, rott. 23, 36.

[24] Birrell, 'Honour of Tutbury', 78 sqq.

[25] Spufford, *Eccleshall*, 20.

[26] See e.g. S.R.O., D.(W.) 1734/2/1/426, rot. 2 and d.; D.(W.) 1734/J.2057 (Whittington 1365–6).

[27] See e.g. S.R.O., D.(W.) 1734/2/1/103, rott. 3–4, 8–9.

[28] See e.g. S.R.O., D.641/1/4A/10 (Hyde 1367–8).

[29] See e.g. B.L. Eg. Roll 8467.

[30] See e.g. Univ. of Keele, Sneyd MSS. S.2420–1.

[31] See e.g. S.R.O., D.(W.) 1734/2/1/378; D.(W.) 1734/3/3/34; D.(W.) 1734/J.2037.

[32] S.C. 6/988/12.

[33] *S.H.C.* 1937, p. 164.

[34] S.R.O., D.(W.) 1734/3/2/3, especially rott. 6 and 11.

[35] *V.C.H. Staffs.* ii. 355.

short as one year or as long as twenty years. Most were for between five and seven years, and the names of the lessees suggest that they were mostly local peasant tenants. Two or three men often joined together, as did John Spurrier, Robert Shelfield, and Robert Edingale, who took 10 a. of arable for nine years in 1397–8 for an annual rent of 6s. 8d. Spurrier also held a pasture with some meadow and a close for twenty years at a rent of £1 10s.[36] In contrast, at Keele between at least 1391 and 1394 the entire demesne was held by the bailiff, John del Nabbe, for £2 10s.,[37] and leases of whole demesnes were normal on the Stafford family's estate. In 1396–7, for example, the demesne arable, meadow, and pasture and the chief messuage of Barlaston was held on a twelve-year lease by John Wylacroft for £5 6s. 8d.[38]

Those examples from the late 14th century illustrate the features of leases throughout the next hundred years. No single type became predominant. Demesne servants recur as lessees. On the Dudley estate in 1489–90 the lessee of the demesne at Prestwood was Thomas Bradley, the rent collector, who paid £4 13s. 4d., with an additional 8s. 4d. for a pasture.[39] Individual tenants continued to hold large demesnes but often there were several lessees. At Bradley the whole demesne was leased to Hugh Stanford, rent collector at Stafford, for £2 in 1400–1, but it was divided between several tenants later in the century.[40] In 1489–90 there were two or more demesne lessees on the manors of Sedgley, Dudley, Rowley Somery, and Himley.[41] The arable demesnes at Barton, Marchington, and Uttoxeter were largely held in small pieces by local tenants. On the other hand 211½ a. at Tutbury was consistently leased to one or two tenants or to a small group of lessees for terms of years until the late 15th century, when it was divided among individual lessees. The meadow was leased in blocks of various sizes; the 30-a. Obholme was usually leased to one or two men or to a small group of lessees.[42]

Some demesne lessees were gentry. Sir John Bagot, for example, held a grange at Haywood for £5 6s. 8d. in 1474.[43] In general, however, they were local peasants, some operating on a large scale. Typical were Richard Holland, John Pennyfather, John London, and John Hopkinson, all of Barton, who together leased 40 a. of the demesne meadow and a sheepfold in 1410 on a ten-year lease. At least two of them also held small pieces of arable demesne. John Hopkinson was a prosperous free tenant with 2½ virgates, 2 cottages, and some 70 a., and the others were among the better-off bond tenants.[44]

Leases including stock were also occasionally granted in the 15th century. At Branston the demesne lease in 1431 included 8 oxen and 200 ewes. One of the two lessees was a butcher, John Blount. Eight oxen, a sow, four piglets, and a small boar were leased with the demesne at Perton in Tettenhall in 1423.[45]

The situation remained fluid, with the lessees and the type of lease changing frequently. The demesnes presented opportunities to many tenants for an expansion of their farms, and the fluctuating rents on both small and large leases testify to the real bargaining that took place, in contrast to the steadier customary rents found on some manors.

Farming

Although the great landlords of Staffordshire tended to withdraw from direct demesne cultivation during the course of the 14th century, it persisted in a few places.

[36] B.L. Eg. Roll 8476.
[37] Univ. of Keele, Sneyd MS. S.2475.
[38] S.R.O., D.641/1/2/38.
[39] S.R.O., D.593/0/3/4, rot. 5.
[40] S.R.O., D.641/1/2/41, rot. 1; S.R.O., D.(W.) 1721/1/8, rot. 15.
[41] S.R.O., D.593/0/3/3, rott. 2–3, 5d., 6.
[42] See e.g. D.L. 29/368/6166; D.L. 29/369/6179; D.L. 29/370/6190; D.L. 29/373/6212.
[43] S.R.O., D.(W.) 1734/2/1/428, rot. 5d.
[44] D.L. 29/368/6166; D.L. 42/4.
[45] S.H.C. 1937, p. 164; S.R.O., D.593/A/2/10/12.

The earl of Stafford maintained his demesne on Stafford manor, and an account of 1437–8 presents a picture of landlord farming then.[46] The demesne arable supplied 137 quarters of corn (wheat, oats, and a little rye) for the household, and barley, the largest crop, for the market; 193 quarters of the latter were sold, with 13 quarters of peas. There were some full-time demesne servants. Other wage labour was extensively used; it was organized and paid for in various ways, and a flexible system had developed for its use. Piece-work was widespread and was used for most of the threshing and winnowing, for cutting and spreading grass, and for some reaping. Much of the field work, including harvesting and haymaking but not cutting and spreading the grass, was done by workers hired and paid by the day. So was much of the carting. There was also a little contract work. Some men and women appear to have acted as small-scale entrepreneurs, bringing gangs to perform certain tasks for which all, apparently, received the same pay. Women were employed in various capacities, often in lighter or less skilled jobs which seem to have been reserved largely or exclusively for them. Threshing, for example, was done by men, but winnowing by women. Gathering and binding corn and hoeing were women's work. Reaping, though mostly a man's job, was occasionally done by women. Agnes Togood, for example, harvested two flats of peas and, with her companions (*sociis suis*), reaped oats by piece-work for a total sum of 8*s.* 7*d.* She earned a further 4*d.* for spreading demesne hay. The job of shearing the sheep and wrapping the fleeces was also done by women. Like men, women were hired and paid by the day, by piece-work, and by contract. It is possible that they worked in the fields rather more widely than at first appears, among the numerous 'people' (*persones*, as opposed to men and women, *homines* and *mulieres*) employed for certain jobs.

Wage rates were considerably higher than in the early 14th century. On Stafford manor in 1437–8 4*d.* a quarter was paid for threshing wheat and rye, compared with 2*d.* a quarter at Baswich in 1312–13; 2*d.* a quarter was paid for threshing oats and barley, compared with 1*d.* or 1½*d.* a quarter in 1312–13.[47] The rate for winnowing had risen from 1*d.* for 4 or 6 quarters in 1312–13 to 1*d.* for only 3 quarters. In 1437–8 1*s.* a day was paid to men bringing in the hay in their own carts; 8*d.*, 4*d.*, and 2*d.* a day, usually with food, was paid for other work connected with haymaking and the harvest. Most of the haymaking was done by gangs of people working at the low daily rate of 1*d.* or 1½*d.* a head, probably a survival of boon works.

The main period of wage increases in Staffordshire as elsewhere was the 14th century. At Chesterton in Wolstanton in 1374–5 the rates for threshing and winnowing were already as high as those noted at Stafford in 1437–8.[48] At Farewell in 1378 the rate for threshing was 3*d.* a quarter for all types of corn, and at Abbots Bromley in 1415–16 it was 8*d.* for 3 quarters, and for winnowing 1*d.* for 3 quarters.[49] Women winnowers at Farewell in 1375–6 were paid 2*d.* a day.[50] At Walsall in 1388–9 1*s.* 6*d.* a day was paid for the hire of carts at haymaking, 7*d.* a day for cutting grass, and 4*d.* a day for spreading it and for forking hay on to carts.[51]

The labourers on the Stafford demesne in 1437–8 were often provided with food and drink in addition to their cash wages. It included ale, either bought locally or brewed on the demesne, meat, some of it supplied by Mathew Butcher of Stafford, cheese, some of it bought in Stafford market, bread, and salt. The demesne thus had a marked effect on the local economy. In 1437–8 £10 7*s.* 8*d.* in cash was paid for wage labour

[46] S.C. 6/988/12, which, unless otherwise stated, covers this and the following para.
[47] For the Baswich figures see L.J.R.O., D.30/N 1.
[48] *T.N.S.F.C.* lix. 75.
[49] S.R.O., D.(W.) 1734/J.2037; D.(W.) 1734/3/3/1.
[50] S.R.O., D.(W.) 1734/J.2035. [51] B.L. Eg. Roll 8467.

on the arable and meadows, a sum which represented seasonal employment for many people. At haymaking alone, for example, in addition to the gangs already mentioned, four men with their companions were hired to cut the grass, two with their companions to spread it, and eight more to cart the hay to Stafford castle and its barn. Numerous other jobs provided further work on the manor; seven men were employed for a total of 22 days on fencing alone in 1437–8. Over 200 quarters of corn was put on the local market, and a number of purchases were made locally to supply the home farm. They included 18 cart-clouts and 6 wain-clouts bought from Richard Glover of Stafford, and various other items as well as the food and drink mentioned.

As already seen, most demesnes were in the hands of lessees in the later Middle Ages, and some surviving leases provide details of farming practice. When the demesne was leased at Perton in 1423, it had been sown with 3 quarters of wheat, 2 quarters of rye, 6 quarters of barley, 7 quarters 6 pecks of peas, and 5 quarters 3 pecks of oats, and was to be returned at the end of the nine-year term similarly sown. As much land as was reasonable in the fallow field was to be left fallowed and refallowed (*warectata et rewarectata*) for sowing with wheat and rye in the following year. The equipment handed over included a plough, price 2s. 8d., and 2 harrows, price 2s., and the chief buildings were two barns and a shippon.[52]

It is clear that the later Middle Ages was not simply a period of stagnation. In contrast with the decays and reductions, there were small-scale initiatives by peasants and flourishing pasture farming. Fifteenth-century manorial accounts and court rolls record not only minor rent increases but also grants of licences to peasants to build sheep-pens, to extend tenements, and to inclose.[53] Licensed inclosures were often of small pieces of land, but there were also some larger grants. In 1430, for example, a tenant at Barton took 80 a. with the right to inclose, at a rent increased from 13s. 4d. to £1.[54] Many inclosures were unlicensed, and presentments for illegal inclosure were common in manorial courts.[55] The offenders included greater as well as lesser men. Amongst those presented at Haywood in the early 14th century, alongside peasant tenants, was a knight, Thomas de Gresley. His offence was typical: he had inclosed several pieces of pasture and meadow which should have been open all or part of the year.[56] Grass inclosures were widespread in the 15th century, and there was a significant increase in the proportion of grassland mentioned in final concords from *c.* 1440.[57]

Though some of the large-scale enterprises of the great landlords were cut back in the later Middle Ages, animal husbandry remained an essential part of the economy of the gentry and peasants. There are indeed signs of an increased emphasis on stock-farming. Frequent disputes arose over animals pasturing on the county's extensive grasslands. Flocks of up to several hundred sheep are frequently mentioned. In 1389 Robert Swynfen claimed that the dogs of John Wylde, a Lichfield butcher, worried 100 sheep at Wall in St. Michael's, Lichfield, so badly that 60 died. In the same year Sir Thomas de Arden alleged the theft of 120 sheep at Elford by two men, one from Lichfield, the other from Alrewas.[58] In 1403 Simon Calton alleged that 90 sheep bought from John Dey of Waterfall and guaranteed sound were 'putrid and corrupt'.[59] In 1418 John Basset of Waterfall claimed that 60 lambs had been worried by the dogs of William Blore, husbandman of Grindon.[60] In 1428 two gentlemen, Richard Grey

[52] S.R.O., D.593/A/2/10/12.
[53] See e.g. a 1440–1 account for the duchy of Lancaster manors (D.L. 29/369/6179), a 1443–4 account for the episcopal manors (S.R.O., D.(W.) 1734/3/2/1), and a Farewell rental *c.* 1429–30 (S.R.O., D.(W.) 1734/J.2051).
[54] D.L. 29/369/6179.   [55] See e.g. D.L. 30/111/1669.
[56] S.R.O., D.(W.) 1734/2/1/428, rot. 1. See also ibid.

/427, rot. 29d.
[57] E. M. Yates, 'Enclosure and the Rise of Grassland Farming in Staffs.' *N.S.J.F.S.* xiv. 52; Frances G. Davenport, 'Agricultural Changes of the 15th Century', *Quarterly Jnl. of Economics*, xi. 208.
[58] *S.H.C.* xv. 18, 20.
[59] Ibid. 107.   [60] Ibid. xvii. 61.

and John Wilford, sued Hugh Shepherd of Oakley, a drover, for the theft at Oakley of 600 sheep worth £40.[61] Other thefts included that of 300 sheep and 60 lambs from a close at Morwhale in Streethay, in St. Michael's, Lichfield, in 1398, 100 sheep by two Handsworth men in 1403, 200 from a close at Elmhurst in St. Chad's, Lichfield, by two husbandmen in 1416, and 100 from Wigginton in 1425.[62] Cattle were less vulnerable to dogs, although Thomas Botheby of Uttoxeter claimed in 1416 that he had suffered £5 worth of damage when his herd of 37 was chased by dogs.[63] They were, however, equally attractive targets for thieves. Thus 40 were stolen at Church Eaton in 1387, 20, with 6 pigs and 100 sheep, at Eccleshall and Millmeece in 1390, and 24 at Marchington in 1464.[64] Such cases doubtless involved less than their owners' total stock.

Sheep, cattle, and pigs were frequently the subject of cases which came before the manorial courts in the later Middle Ages. In 1367 there were cases of trespass with 120 and 60 sheep, 24 and 21 cattle, and 18 pigs at Hyde in Coppenhall;[65] again the beasts are unlikely to represent the whole of their owners' stock. Trespasses with 100 and 400 sheep are recorded on the Burton abbey manors late in the 14th century; in Needwood forest in 1420 one man was amerced for overcharging the pasture of Yoxall ward with 140 sheep and another for the same offence in Barton ward with 240 sheep for sale.[66]

Connexions with the local towns are often revealed. In 1351 a tenant at Alrewas claimed 2 marks from Robert de Coton of Tamworth for wool sold to him, and in 1352 Thomas the taverner, of Lichfield, was amerced for trespass at Alrewas with 36 cattle.[67] In 1355 Hugh le Verrer of Lichfield sued Richard atte Syke over the care of Hugh's sheep on the manors of Cannock and Rugeley.[68] A stray beast seized at Haywood in 1406 was claimed by a Birmingham man.[69] Birmingham in fact was developing as a cattle market in the later Middle Ages, serving south Staffordshire and other areas. In 1403 its lord, William de Birmingham, alleged evasion of tolls on cattle and other goods bought and sold at his market and fairs by John Ryngesley of Tipton and several customary tenants of Wednesbury. William claimed that the men of Wednesbury had refused to pay toll on 60 oxen, 60 steers, and 60 cows at markets and 40 head of each at fairs.[70] Stafford seems to have had a cattle market by the 15th century.[71]

There are indications of pressure on the common pastures from local tenants and others, and on some manors regulations for the use of common pastures appear and presentments for overcharging became frequent. At Church Eaton, for example, it was ordered in 1481 that nobody should overcharge the common pasture with cattle for sale.[72] Overcharging is recorded on manors throughout the county, including Madeley and Horton in the north[73] and Cannock and Rugeley further south.[74] On the duchy manors in the Needwood forest area presentments were made from early in the 15th century but do not become frequent until later. Sometimes the offenders had exceeded a stint; more often they had no rights in the pastures. Often the animals were being reared for sale, and the offenders came from many manors, including Scropton (Derb.) and Burton.[75]

[61] *S.H.C.* xvii. 118.   [62] Ibid. xv. 89, 108; xvii. 59, 109.
[63] Ibid. xvii. 56.
[64] Ibid. xv. 4, 24; D.L. 30/111/1676 rot. 2d.
[65] S.R.O., D.641/1/4A/10.
[66] S.R.O., D.(W.) 1734/2/1/103, rott. 49, 53; D.L. 30/110/1659, woodmote at Byrkley 16 June 1420.
[67] S.R.O., D.(W.) 0/3/38, rot. 7; /39, rot. 4d.
[68] S.R.O., D.(W.) 1734/2/1/175, rot. 22.
[69] Ibid. /427, rot. 18d.

[70] *S.H.C.* xv. 107, 110.
[71] See p. 213.
[72] S.R.O., D.641/1/4A/18, rot. 5 and d.
[73] For Madeley see e.g. S.R.O., D.641/1/4A/16, rot. 4; /20, rot. 4. For Horton see e.g. D.(W.) 1490/6, rot. 57.
[74] S.R.O., D.(W.) 1734/2/1/178, rot. 143A.
[75] See e.g. D.L. 30/110/1659, view at Uttoxeter 26 Oct. 1419 and woodmote at Byrkley 16 June 1420; D.L. 30/111/1669, courts at Barton and Rolleston Oct. 1443.

The demand for the rich pastures of Needwood forest is shown by the continued high values of leases of the demesne pasture in the forest throughout the later Middle Ages, often in marked contrast to income from other resources. Considerable trouble was taken to maintain the fencing and gates of the parks in each ward. The agistment or herbage of the parks and other inclosures was usually leased for terms of years, and the lessees presumably collected fees from local stock-farmers who put their animals in the parks. Dues for pasture and pannage were usually worth well over £40 during the 15th century, compared with £38 in 1313–14 and about £35 in the 1370s. The value of leases fluctuated during the 15th century, reaching almost £49 in 1427–8, declining to less than £35 in 1460–1, and rising to just under £46 in 1475–6. Low receipts in the 1480s were due to an increase in the number of deer and the consequent exclusion of cattle.[76]

A set of detailed accounts for 1440–1 lists the animals agisted in several parks.[77] Annual fees ranged from 1s. 6d. for horses to 2d., 3d., and 4d. for pigs. Many animals were agisted for six months at a reduced fee, perhaps being fattened in the summer for slaughter or sale. In 1440–1 £10 15s. 1d. was collected for the pannage of 784 pigs, £2 5s. 6d. for the agistment of 81 cattle, and £3 14s. 9d. for the pasture of 68 horses. A further £32 came from other pasture leases, so that there were probably something like twice as many animals again on those pastures. The duchy's pastures apparently supported stock-rearing on a scale considerably beyond that possible on the common pastures of the villages in and around the forest, and stock-rearing seems in general to have prospered in the 15th century. The lessees of the duchy's pastures were often duchy officials. Thus in 1462 William Aleyn, bailiff of Uttoxeter manor and collector of Uttoxeter ward, took a lease of pastures in Needwood for twelve years at an annual rent of £9 13s. 4d., and the collector of Barton ward, Thomas Smith of Elford, yeoman, held the herbage of three parks in Needwood in 1475–6 for £5 16s. 8d.[78]

Hundreds of cartloads of branches were cut to supplement grass in some years and were sold at prices varying from one part of the forest to another. In 1417–18 branches from Yoxall ward were sold for 7d. a cartload, while those from one park in Tutbury ward fetched as much as 1s. Over 400 loads were cut in four wards and sold for over £15.[79] The practice seems to have dwindled in importance during the 15th century for reasons which are obscure but may have included a desire to conserve woodland, and sales were increasingly confined to the branches of trees blown down or felled for other purposes.

Sporadic sales of timber continued in the 15th century. In 1442 for example, the right to cut underwood, branches, and wood in Uttoxeter ward for three years was sold for £31 13s. 4d.[80] There were also regular small sales of wood. Oak barks fetched about 10d. a tree in the early 15th century, and sales were worth nearly £2 a year to the duchy. There were occasional small sales of honey and wax (for example, 2 gallons of honey at 8d. a gallon and 3 lb. of wax at 7d. a lb. in Tutbury ward in 1440–1), and of swarms of bees (10d. for a 'brik' in Marchington ward in 1440–1).[81] Bird traps were worth a few pence a year in Barton ward, and customary payments continued to be made for nuts. The alabaster deposits in Tutbury ward were used for the duchy's own building works, and a little alabaster was regularly sold.

There were also many animals on the woodland pastures of the bishop's manors in the 15th century, including the horses, cattle, sheep, and goats of the bishop himself

[76] Jean R. Birrell, 'Forest Economy of Honour of Tutbury in 14th and 15th Centuries', *Univ. of Birmingham Hist. Jnl.* viii. 120–1.
[77] D.L. 29/369/6179.
[78] D.L. 29/371/6197; D.L. 29/370/6192.
[79] D.L. 29/368/6166. Sales are recorded in most ward accounts at that period.
[80] D.L. 29/370/6184.
[81] D.L. 29/369/6179.

and those of his servants.[82] Tenant stock was more numerous. In the parks at Beaudesert in 1461–2, for example, 95 pigs were pannaged.[83] There, as in Needwood forest, branches were cut to provide winter fodder for stock; oak, ash, and elm are mentioned in 1463–4.[84] At Beaudesert and Haywood there were regular sales of trees and bark.[85] Bird traps in Haywood park were leased for small sums throughout the 15th century, four of them fetching 15s. in 1461–2.[86] At Brewood herbage and pannage in the park was worth £10 in 1478–9.[87]

The main woodland of the bishop's estate was, however, Cannock Chase. Oak, holly, birch, and hazel are specified, and saplings, timber, underwood, fencing wood, and fuel are distinguished. There a more varied type of development, already visible in the 13th century, continued. The result was a diversified peasant economy. At Rugeley the poll-tax returns of 1381 list a barker, a cooper, a bowyer, three stringers, twelve cutlers, and a grinder.[88] The court rolls of Cannock and Rugeley provide further evidence of woodland crafts among the peasantry, directly by occupational descriptions and indirectly by surname evidence, which, though no longer reliable as a guide to occupation, can be taken to indicate the local presence of the crafts concerned. As well as the usual woodland craft-surnames such as Sawyer, Carpenter, Hewster, and Barker, there are Bowyers, Fletchers, and Stringers.[89]

[82] See e.g. S.R.O., D.(W.) 1734/3/2/3, rot. 6.
[83] Ibid. /2, rot. 3d.
[84] Ibid. rot. 10d.
[85] S.R.O., D.(W.) 1734/3/2/1 and 2.
[86] Ibid. /2, rot. 8.
[87] Ibid. /3, rot. 47d.
[88] *S.H.C.* xvii. 186–8. A Wm. the cutler was taxed at Rugeley in 1327, and a Fletcher and a Cutler in 1332–3: ibid. vii(1), 237; x(1), 120.
[89] See e.g. S.R.O., D.(W.) 1734/2/1/176, rott. 1–9.

AGRICULTURE 1500 TO 1793

Inclosure, p. 51. Arable Farming, p. 58. Grassland and Stock, p. 68. Agrarian Economy and Society, p. 78 (1500–1640, p. 78; 1640–1740, p. 82; 1740–1793, p. 86).

THE period from the early 16th century to the formation of the Board of Agriculture in 1793 saw many changes in agrarian practice and in the structure of landholding.[1] The dominant feature of the period was the progress of inclosure. At the end of the 15th century and during the 16th century inclosures caused sporadic outbursts of violence by those who felt that their commoning rights were in danger; the hedge-breaking movement, however, was of less significance in Staffordshire than in some of the east Midland counties. On the whole the inclosure of the open fields proceeded peacefully and the movement accelerated during the 17th century. In 1698 Celia Fiennes found Staffordshire a county of inclosures.[2] Parliamentary inclosure from the beginning of the 18th century was mainly concerned with the inclosure of commons and wastes. Leland c. 1540 found the south of the county 'reasonably well wooded and pastured, but not very apt to bear good corn, as a ground full of heath and fern in many places'.[3] In 1637 the county justices described Staffordshire as consisting for the most part of barren land, 'one fourth part being heath and waste and another fourth being chases and parks; it also abounds with poor people'.[4] The semi-colonized state of the county with its abundance of rough pasture helped to make the transition from open fields to inclosed farms an easy one. The period saw the continued progress of encroachments on the waste, especially by poor cottagers, a development which was to prove a serious social problem at the end of the 18th century when the large-scale inclosure of the wastes began. A notable characteristic of the period was the shifting cultivation of the waste. It is likely that a substantial increase in the arable acreage resulted when the practice was as its height in the 17th century,[5] and the Staffordshire agronomist William Pitt was impressed by the 'evident marks of a cultivation far more extended than anything known in modern times'.[6] The permanent improvement of the commons and wastes, however, had to await the advances in draining techniques in the 19th century.

Staffordshire in the early modern period was predominantly a county of mixed farming. The increasing conversion from tillage to pasture, however, even within the open fields, led to a certain amount of specialization, notably the rise of dairying in the lower Trent valley in the 17th century. By the later 18th century the county fell into three clearly-defined farming regions. In the Moorlands, where the farmers were said in the 1790s to be 'scandalously backward, ignorant, selfish, and bigoted',[7] grassland farming prevailed, with a general emphasis on stock-rearing and some concentration on dairying. The heavy lands of the western marls and the Trent valley were an area of corn- and dairy-farming, while the light lands in the south were a region of sheep-and-corn farming.[8] In spite of the continued importance of grass-farming, there is

---

[1] Thanks are offered to Dr. Joan Thirsk for reading and commenting on this article in draft.
[2] Celia Fiennes, *Journeys*, ed. C. Morris, 166, 169, 174.
[3] Leland, *Itin.* ed. Toulmin Smith, ii. 99.
[4] *Cal. S.P. Dom.* 1636–7, 408.
[5] *Agrarian Hist. of Eng. and Wales*, iv, ed. Joan Thirsk,

100.
[6] W. Pitt, *General View of Agric. of County of Stafford* (1796 edn.), 233. The 1796 edn. has been used throughout this article.
[7] Ibid. 56.
[8] Sturgess, 'Agric. Staffs.' 40.

evidence that grain production increased considerably in the second half of the period. After the disastrous English harvest of 1527 grain had to be imported into Staffordshire from neighbouring counties,[9] and in 1649 Walter Blith included Staffordshire in the 'woodlands, who before enclosure were wont to be relieved by the fielden with corn of all sorts'.[10] In 1766, however, Richard Whitworth claimed that 'immense quantities' of grain were carried from Staffordshire to Woore (Salop.) and Sandbach (Ches.) 'in order to go to Manchester for home consumption and to Liverpool for exportation'.[11] The farmers of Staffordshire seem to have been responsive to the demands of new markets, especially in the later 18th century with the growth in demand from Birmingham and the Black Country and from the Potteries.

The chief criteria used by one writer to assess an agricultural revolution between 1560 and 1690 are 'the floating of water meadows, the substitution of up-and-down husbandry for permanent tillage and permanent grass or for shifting cultivation, the introduction of new fallow crops and selected grasses, marsh drainage, manuring, and stock-breeding'.[12] All can be traced in Staffordshire agrarian practice and were described by Robert Plot in the first contemporary description of the farming regions and practices of the county in the 1680s.[13] Whether those new practices were sufficiently widespread to constitute an agricultural revolution is debatable, though throughout the period there were many individual farmers who were interested in improved techniques. A more self-conscious concern with 'improvement' came in the later 18th century, particularly in the south of the county. William Marshall, perhaps the soundest of the new breed of agricultural economists,[14] managed a farm at Statfold for Samuel Pipe Wolferstan between 1784 and 1786 and said of the district: 'except in Yorkshire, I have found the spirit of improvement nowhere so high.'[15] The surviving evidence supports Marshall's view, echoed by Pitt, that the leaders of improvement in the county were the landed gentlemen, farming a proportion of their own estates, and the more substantial tenant-farmers.[16]

The dissolution of the monasteries and the redistribution of monastic lands brought about far-reaching and long-lasting changes in the structure of landowning in Staffordshire. In 1669 Sir Simon Degge wrote, though probably with some exaggeration: 'in sixty years . . . one half (I believe) of the lands in Staffordshire have changed their owners; not so much, as of old they were wont, by marriage, as by purchase.'[17] Monastic lands, often combined with commercial or industrial fortunes, frequently led to the establishment of substantial new estates, and it is possible to trace the fortunes of some of those estates and their tenants. More efficient estate management, often by professional agents and stewards, led to the replacement of leases for lives by short leases and rack-renting to ensure that rents kept pace with rising land values. The introduction of tenancy agreements and farming covenants shows a growing concern to improve the value of estates by the closer supervision of the farming practices of tenants. A characteristic of Staffordshire agriculture, clearly revealed by probate inventories, was the part-time nature of agrarian activity over much of the county in the 16th and 17th centuries; extensive commons and woodlands and the possibilities of

[9] R. W. Heinze, *Proclamations of the Tudor Kings*, 101 and n.

[10] W. Blith, *The Eng. Improver* (1649 edn.), 40.

[11] R. Whitworth, *The Advantages of Inland Navigation* (1766), 33.

[12] E. Kerridge, *The Agric. Revolution*, 40.

[13] For a discussion of Plot's work in that connexion see J. Myres, 'Dr. Plot and Land Utilisation in Staffs.' *T.N.S.F.C.* lxxxiii. 58–73.

[14] J. D. Chambers and G. E. Mingay, *The Agric. Revo-*lution, *1750–1880*, 73.

[15] W. Marshall, *The Rural Economy of the Midland Counties* (1796 edn.), i. 83; ii, pp. xix–xxii. The 1796 edn. has been used throughout this article. For his employment by Pipe Wolferstan see S.R.O., D.1527/8, 29 and 30 Sept., 17 and 25 Oct. 1783; /9, 9 and 16 May 1784; /10, 10 Jan., 7 Feb., 17 June 1785; /11, 7 May 1786.

[16] Marshall, *Rural Econ.* i. 141; Pitt, *Agric. Staffs.* 17.

[17] Erdeswick, *Staffs.* p. lv.

part-time industrial and commercial employment attracted an army of immigrants.[18] It is possible that the spread of inclosure and the more efficient management of estates, resulting in the rise of rents and the amalgamation of holdings, brought about some changes in the structure of agrarian society in the county, but the small farmer remained important in the pattern of farming throughout the period.[19]

INCLOSURE

Inclosure of open fields and commons had began in Staffordshire long before the 16th century and was to continue steadily throughout the period. The term covers a great variety of practices from piecemeal encroachments on the waste to large-scale conversion of arable to pasture, from holdings in severalty within the open fields and pastures to complete inclosure of the fields. It will also be used here to describe arrangements for the temporary cultivation of commons and waste.

The term is associated with the popular agitation and widespread hedge-breaking which took place during the 16th century.[20] It has been argued that the agitation against inclosure was the result of the threat to common rights represented by inclosure of the commons or inclosure of strips within the common fields and meadows. The diminishing of the waste and the growth of population meant that common rights were under increasing pressure. There was also fear of depopulation from large-scale conversion from arable to pasture and the engrossing of holdings. The pressure leading to inclosure was equally strong: farmers wished to increase the scale of their undertakings, especially the amount of their livestock, and there was a desire to alter systems of husbandry, to introduce new crops and rotations, and to use land in a more flexible manner. The history of inclosure in Staffordshire in the early modern period illustrates all those factors, and the county had its share of inclosure disputes in the 16th century. It was, however, spared widespread hedge-breaking and agricultural revolt and was exempted from most of the statutes against inclosure. That may have been due to the predominantly pastoral nature of farming in the county, but even in the fielden districts of Staffordshire inclosure did not arouse as much passion as in the counties of the east Midlands.

The principle laid down in 1236 by the Statute of Merton, that manorial lords could improve the waste so long as they left enough commons for their free tenants, was still accepted in the 16th century. Thus the duke of Buckingham inclosed Forebridge waste in Castle Church c. 1512, and when in 1555 the hedges were broken by some of the inhabitants of Forebridge alleging obstruction, it was stated that at the time of the inclosure the duke had left sufficient common for the tenants.[21] In 1566 John Browne, lord of the manor of Warslow, was accused by one of his tenants of unjust inclosure. Browne claimed that in the 1540s his predecessor, Vincent Mundye, had licensed his poor tenants and cottagers to inclose and till a portion of the waste but had left enough common for the rest of the tenants. He added that his accuser made 'his outward show thereby that he would be a commonwealth man, and put down inclosures, whereas in truth he seeketh to destroy tillage and the increase of corn'.[22]

Tenants were often quick to take action if they feared that licensed inclosures of the

[18] *Agrarian Hist. Eng. and Wales*, iv. 106–7; below, p. 82.

[19] For a discussion of this subject see G. E. Mingay, *Enclosure and the Small Farmer in the Age of the Industrial Revolution*.

[20] For a recent discussion of this subject see *Agrarian Hist. Eng. and Wales*, iv. 200–55.

[21] *V.C.H. Staffs.* v. 94, which, following its source, states that the inclosure was by Lord Stafford. In 1512 the lord of the manor of Forebridge was Edward Stafford, 3rd duke of Buckingham (d. 1521).

[22] *S.H.C.* N.S. ix. 111–13.

waste by their lord would interfere with their commoning rights. In 1567 seventeen of Lord Paget's tenants complained of encroachments and inclosures in Cannock Chase and the projected inclosure of Woodhay.[23] In 1580 and 1581 several of Lord Paget's inclosures on the Chase, which he claimed had been kept in severalty and inclosed for the preservation of timber for a long time, were broken, the hedges burnt, and common rights re-established by the grazing of flocks of sheep.[24] In 1600 protests were made against similar inclosures in the area in Bentley, Cheslyn, Ogley, Gailey, Teddesley, and Alrewas hays.[25] An early example of violent action to protect common rights against inclosure by the lord of the manor was the throwing down of hedges on Crakemarsh by the inhabitants of Uttoxeter. The inclosures had been made by Sir John Delves at the beginning of the reign of Edward IV; the hedges were afterwards re-erected and guarded by Delves's servants. His heir, Sir James Blount, reopened the inclosures, but Blount's heir, Sir Robert Sheffield, renewed the inclosures and in 1502–3 his tenants brought an action against him.[26] It was not always easy to enforce legal decrees against inclosure; for example, Thomas Lane was attached in 1630 for contempt of an order of 1577 which prohibited inclosure of part of Bentley Hay and protected the common rights of the tenants.[27] Sometimes lawsuits resulted in compromises: in 1670 a draft agreement dividing Cheslyn Hay was drawn up between Robert Leveson and the freeholders and copyholders of Great and Little Saredon in Shareshill and Great Wyrley in Cannock in order to avoid further lawsuits concerning rights of common in grounds inclosed by Leveson.[28]

In some areas commons and wastes had formerly been so plentiful that there had been no need to define the boundaries of each manor's waste until, in the 16th century, the spread of inclosure and increasing pressure on the commons led to disputes between neighbouring manors throughout the county. In 1528 inclosures by the inhabitants of one village in the parish of Tatenhill, Wychnor, resulted in violent resistance by the inhabitants of another village, Barton-under-Needwood, to increased pressure on the commons;[29] in 1534 a similar dispute over intercommoning between the inhabitants of Whitgreave and those of Great Bridgeford in Seighford led to accusations and counter-accusations of inclosure going back to the end of the 15th century;[30] and in 1569 Sir Edward Littleton was ordered to open his inclosures on Teddesley Hay after protests from the earl of Oxford, lord of the manor of Acton Trussell and Bednall.[31] There were similar disputes over Mayfield common in 1566[32] and Morridge waste in Ipstones in the late 17th century. In the latter case Walter Aston was accused of excessive inclosure and the overburdening of the waste with cottages;[33] his accuser, Thomas Holinshed of Ashenhurst, had also been making inclosures on Morridge.[34] The temporary cultivation of the waste, usually a peaceful procedure,[35] could cause disputes when it threatened intercommoning rights as on Knightley Hay in Gnosall in 1543–4[36] and on Ilam Moor in 1542 and 1551.[37] Cannock Chase was shared commoning for several manors and in the later 17th century was subject to extensive shifting cultivation; the temporary inclosures were, however, opposed and pulled down by the inhabitants of Longdon, who kept large flocks of sheep on the common.[38]

[23] S.R.O., D.(W.) 1734/2/5/15a. See also *S.H.C.* N.S. x(1), 167.

[24] S.R.O., D.(W.) 1734/1/3/30. For a detailed analysis of the riots see C. J. Harrison, 'Social and Economic Hist. of Cannock and Rugeley, 1546–1597' (Univ. of Keele Ph.D. thesis, 1974), 158, 168–82, 195.

[25] B.R.L. 328854.

[26] D.L. 3/6 ff. 581, 587.

[27] *S.H.C.* 1931, 67.

[28] W.S.L., M.214.

[29] D.L. 1/4 ff. 40–1; D.L. 1/6 f. 78. See also *S.H.C.* N.S.

x(1), 115–19.

[30] *S.H.C.* 1912, 69–70.

[31] S.R.O., D.(W.) 1734/1/3/6; D.260/M/E/429/32.

[32] *S.H.C.* 1926, 93–4.

[33] B.L. Add. Ch. 46823; see also W.S.L., H.M. Aston 23.

[34] B.L. Add. MSS. 36664, f. 180; 36665, f. 64v.

[35] See p. 56.

[36] *V.C.H. Staffs.* iv. 113.

[37] *S.H.C.* 1912, 144, 181–7.

[38] E 134/34 Chas. II Mich./10.

The most bitterly resented attempts at inclosure were those in the surviving forest areas where commoning rights were highly valued. Inclosures of the hays of Cannock forest by the hereditary keepers in the later 16th century were strongly contested by the commoners,[39] and there was similar resistance to the inclosure of Iverley Wood in Kinver forest at the beginning of the 17th century.[40] Even more bitterly opposed were the plans to disafforest Needwood during the 17th and 18th centuries. Nineteen neighbouring manors and townships claimed commoning rights in the forest,[41] and in 1559 they were said to be damaging the surviving timber, 'what with the number of cottages builded in the borders of the forest and daily felling the wood, and then the sheep coming after and destroying the spring'.[42] Unstinted common rights in the forest were all the more valued since the keepers of the Needwood parks had, before 1559, been increasing the agistment charges in the parks.[43] In 1637 the inclosure of Uttoxeter ward was greeted by riots, and in 1654, when it was decided to divide and sell the whole forest, the commoners protested that to do so would make thousands of the poor homeless and impoverish the whole county.[44] There were serious riots in 1659 when the partition of the forest was attempted, and later attempts at inclosure were strongly resisted by the commoners, though not with violence. Needwood was finally disafforested and inclosed under an Act of 1801.[45]

Permanent conversion of arable to pasture, the most contentious sort of inclosure in the 16th century, was not a major problem in Staffordshire. There seem to have been few large graziers in the county and wool was produced by numerous small farmers.[46] The Staffordshire returns to the 1517 inquiry, though possibly incomplete, show that since 1489 only 488 a. had been inclosed, 406 a. of which involved conversion of arable to pasture.[47] Several of the recorded inclosures were for deer-parks, though later many of the parks in the county were converted to pasture or cultivated.[48] The imparking movement gained fresh momentum in the 18th century and then involved extensive inclosure and the obliteration of villages such as Chillington in Brewood and Shugborough in Colwich.[49] During the 16th and early 17th centuries there are some cases of pastures thrown open by villagers and some complaints of depopulation. In 1535 the hedges around 200 a. of pasture called Clare Heyes in Enville belonging to Sir Giles Strangeways were broken,[50] and in 1544 men of Cannock threw open pastures and meadows inclosed by Ralph Bostock and Thomas Alport.[51] After an arbitration in 1529 Thomas Leveson was ordered to open his inclosures in the common fields of Wolverhampton and deprived of his right of common for a year.[52] In several cases it seems that inclosed pastures which had been quietly enjoyed in severalty for many years were thrown open when increased population led to the re-establishment of extinct common rights.[53] At the beginning of the 17th century in Tutbury 'the rich sort of cottagers having store of cattle' petitioned against the long-keeping in severalty of three ancient inclosures.[54] At Sandon, at the end of the 16th century, Hugh Erdeswick and his son Sampson were said to be inclosing large amounts of waste and portions of the open fields and to be converting arable to pasture. This had involved some depopulation and indeed led eventually to the desertion of the village of Great Sandon. The

[39] V.C.H. Staffs. ii. 343; above, p. 52.
[40] V.C.H. Staffs. ii. 348.
[41] B.L. Add. MS. 31917; see last folios for burns or marks of the townships.
[42] D.L. 42/109 f. 19.
[43] See p. 69.
[44] V.C.H. Staffs. ii. 352; Cal. S.P. Dom. 1655, 31–2.
[45] V.C.H. Staffs. ii. 353–4.
[46] P. J. Bowden, Wool Trade in Tudor and Stuart Eng. 81.
[47] S.H.C. 1931, 65.
[48] V.C.H. Staffs. xvii. 184; S.R.O., D.593/B/1/9/1; /B/

1/22/1/2; S.R.O., D.(W.) 1734/1/3/42, mm. 24, 34; R. Blome, Britannia (1673), 202. For the exploitation of the Needwood parks at the end of the 17th century see S.R.O., D.(W.) 1721/3/256, pp. 167, 171, 173–4.
[49] V.C.H. Staffs. v. 29; S.R.O., D.590/363 and 368; S.H.C. 4th ser. vi. 86–110.
[50] S.H.C. N.S. x(1), 141–3.
[51] V.C.H. Staffs. v. 60.
[52] S.R.O., D.593/E/1/2.
[53] S.H.C. 1912, 197–200; S.H.C. N.S. ix. 219–20.
[54] D.L. 44/957.

people of Sandon much resented that the Erdeswicks had 'fraudulently, against all Christianity, left out certain small parcels of their ground to the intent to claim common in your poor orators' land, nothing more coveting than the extreme destruction of your poor orators and the having of the whole manor to theirselves, whereby (as the prophet sayeth) they may live alone upon the earth'.[55] In 1635 it was said that William Brooke had depopulated Haselour and kept cattle there,[56] but in general depopulating inclosure was not a serious problem in Staffordshire.

Much inclosure took place without arousing violent opposition. It was in this period that most of the open arable land was inclosed, either piecemeal by exchange, or by agreement between the tenants, often on terms that would have caused riots elsewhere. Where there were only a few freeholders inclosure was a simple matter and came early, as at Packington in Weeford, where the land of the three freeholders was inclosed by 1536.[57] At Fenton Culvert in 1540 the five freeholders decided to divide and inclose all their lands, meadows, and pastures not yet inclosed.[58] In 1585 the inhabitants of Salt and Enson decided to keep their open fields in severalty both in winter and summer, thus extinguishing common rights and removing all obstacles to inclosure.[59] The open fields of Tunstall were inclosed by agreement in 1613[60] and those of Upper Penn in 1686.[61] In 1714 the copyholders of Mere and Forton petitioned the lord of the manor for a general inclosure, 'by reason of the great damages your tenants and we sustain, all the neighbouring fields being in a manner inclosed'.[62] The tenants of Marston agreed in 1757 to allow their landlord, Thomas Giffard, to divide and allot their arable fields and common pastures,[63] and in 1770 the arable fields of Alrewas were divided by two surveyors.[64] Occasionally, however, opposition to a general inclosure had to be overcome. Rowland Firth, who had large flocks of sheep, was said to be hindering the tenants of Over Stonnall in Shenstone from inclosing their field ground in 1634.[65] In 1699 a group of freeholders agreed to evict from their lands 'a certain number of men called sheep-masters' if they continued to oppose the inclosure of the open fields of Lichfield.[66]

Usually there survives no direct record of the inclosure of open-field manors, and the fact of inclosure can be deduced only from casual references[67] and the disappearance of the names of the open fields from the records.[68] In the nucleated villages of north-east Staffordshire the movement to inclose the open fields gained momentum from the late 16th century, and by 1700 many villages were virtually inclosed. Inclosure was a gradual process and led to a fragmentary farm pattern, each tenant having closes in the various open fields; only in Blore and Okeover, both deserted villages associated with imparking, was there a different pattern, with land divided into large blocks.[69] In other areas of the county too inclosure of the arable was a gradual process as tenants consolidated their holdings by exchange and purchase and then inclosed. Between 1559 and 1568 John Skrymsher, lord of the manor of Mere and Forton, was licensing piecemeal inclosures of arable and pasture, a century and a half before the manor was totally inclosed.[70] Complicated exchanges of land were taking place in 1655 between

[55] W.S.L., H.M. Chetwynd 67/1–3; P. V. Bate and D. M. Palliser, 'Suspected Lost Village Sites in Staffs.' *Trans. S. Staffs. Arch. & Hist. Soc.* xii. 36.
[56] S.P. 16/287 f. 40.
[57] S.R.O., D.(W.) 1810, f. 305.
[58] *V.C.H. Staffs.* viii. 217.
[59] W.S.L., H.M. Chetwynd 83.
[60] *V.C.H. Staffs.* viii. 98.
[61] S.R.O., D.593/B/1/17/10.
[62] S.R.O., D.(W.) 1788, P.17, B.1.
[63] S.R.O., D.590/289.
[64] S.R.O., D.(W.) 1851/1/1/35.
[65] E 134/10 Chas I. East./47 m. 5v.
[66] S.R.O., D.661/1/82.

[67] e.g. W.S.L., S.MS. 326/1 (inclosure of common fields at Longdon before 1571); S.R.O., D.547/M/1/165 (Hanbury, Marchington, Newborough, Draycott, Stubby Lane and Moreton, Woodend, Fauld, and Coton described in 1647 as inclosed); *V.C.H. Staffs.* v. 126 (Rodbaston stated in 1674 to have been inclosed within living memory).
[68] See *S.H.C.* 1931, 70–2, 79–82.
[69] F. J. Johnson, 'Settlement Pattern of North-East Staffs.' (Univ. of Wales M.A. thesis, 1965), 163–5.
[70] F. A. Twemlow, 'Hist. of Mere and Forton' (TS. in W.S.L.), ii. 23–4. See also *V.C.H. Staffs.* v. 38 (Brewood), 94 (Castle Church); W.S.L., H.M. Chetwynd 88–9 (Hopton); B.L. Add. MS. 31917 (Fauld); W.S.L., S.D. Pearson 827 (Alrewas).

tenants of Penkridge Deanery manor;[71] such exchanges had resulted by the end of the 17th century in complete confusion of landholding in Penkridge: 'the tenants of the several lords both freeholders, copyholders, and leaseholders have interchanged and inclosed the lands both of demesne of my lord and the other lords and their own freehold and copyhold lands . . . without the privity of the several lords and without any surrenders in court or deeds of freeholders amongst themselves.'[72] The records of exchanges in the 18th century emphasize the convenience and possibilities of improvement resulting from the consolidation and inclosure of arable land, as at Shenstone in 1772[73] and Whittington, near Lichfield, in 1776.[74] It has been calculated that nearly 50,000 a. of open field was inclosed in Staffordshire during the 18th century,[75] and contemporary writers were in no doubt as to the advantages of inclosure. Marshall wrote that 'common field husbandry, of this, as well as of other districts, is inconvenient and unproductive'.[76] William Bourne of Elford, while admitting that inclosure sometimes injured the small farmers, described in 1794 the great improvements following the inclosure of Elford by Act in 1765;[77] it was the first open-field village in Staffordshire to be inclosed by Act of Parliament.[78]

Notable in the early modern landscape of the county were the pasture closes within the common fields. They resulted from various arrangements, often eccentric, designed to secure an adequate amount of grazing, either communal or private. Occasionally an agreement would be made between a lord and his tenants to inclose completely all their pasture lands. Thus in 1575 Richard Brooke of Lapley and Wheaton Aston and his tenants agreed to take in severalty and inclose and keep inclosed all their meadows, and also to inclose within the open fields enough land for one beast-grass for each half 'ware' of arable land.[79] Sometimes open pastures were walled or fenced for the protection of stock and were still used in common:[80] at Alrewas some of the closes of freeholders were inclosed all the year round, while some were Lammas lands and had to be thrown open at Michaelmas.[81] At Shareshill the town meadows were inclosed in 1647, and it was agreed that they should be held in severalty by rotation among the tenants year by year.[82] Sometimes the establishment of pasture closes involved a reduction of arable land, as at Rolleston in the early 17th century, where the tenants were given permission to inclose part of their arable holdings in the town fields, 'in so much as they had little or no several grounds, either pasture or meadow, to depasture either oxen or horses to plough their land or give them milk . . . or to get hay to winter the same'.[83] Sometimes, with the increasing toleration of changing land-use, inclosed pastures were put under the plough.[84]

The permanent, wholesale inclosure of rough commons and waste was a complicated and often expensive procedure, and from 1719 many thousand acres of common were inclosed by Act of Parliament.[85] The advantages of the systematic inclosure of the commons and wastes were clearly seen by the end of the 18th century,[86] and the last great advance into the waste came at the beginning of the 19th century with the improvement of draining techniques. During the preceding centuries, however, inroads had been made. The pressure of increasing population was relieved by the

[71] S.R.O., D.260/M/E/429/13.
[72] Ibid. /33, letter from Hen. Parslow to Brooke Bridges, 6 Dec. 1698 (wrongly endorsed 1798).
[73] W.S.L., M. 389.
[74] S.R.O., D.661/8/1/3/8.
[75] S.H.C. 1931, 79.
[76] Marshall, *Rural Econ.* ii. 208.
[77] Pitt, *Agric. Staffs.* 41.   [78] S.H.C. 1941, 14.
[79] W.S.L., M. 283. See also S.H.C. 1938, 144 (Mayfield, c. 1560); S.R.O., D.(W.) 1784/2 (Shenstone, 1637).

[80] *S.H.C.* 1910, 63–4 (Wetton, c. 1542).
[81] W.S.L., S.D. Pearson 707.
[82] S.R.O., D.260/M/E/429/14.
[83] D.L. 44/930. See also D.L. 1/4 f. 41.
[84] e.g. S.R.O., D.(W.) 1810, ff. 255–62 (Bradley, 1542); W.S.L., M. 408 (Stretton, 1604); 'Tunstall Manor Court Rolls', *T.N.S.F.C.* lxiii. 78 (Tunstall, 1610); S.R.O., D.(W.) 1851/1/1/35 (Alrewas, 1621). And see below, p. 56.
[85] *S.H.C.* 1931, 90–3.
[86] Pitt, *Agric. Staffs.* 109–10.

piecemeal taking in of the waste, and throughout the period there are numerous references to small encroachments[87] and to the mushrooming of cottages on the waste.[88] The preamble to the Ipstones Inclosure Act of 1777 stated that, besides the usual benefits, inclosure would 'put a stop to many encroachments that are every day making upon the common by people who have no right to them and will keep many bad people out of the neighbourhood'.[89] In north-east Staffordshire the 16th and 17th centuries saw the continued steady spread of settlement into the waste, notably on Alstonefield Frith, where by the mid 16th century scattered farms were distributed up the tributary valleys of the Manifold, and where the later infilling of settlement on the waste between the valleys resulted in smaller, poorer holdings.[90] In many of the villages of the north-east there is a clear division between open-field nucleated settlement on the fertile limestone and dispersed settlement on the shales and grit, poorer land which had been open moorland in the Middle Ages and was inclosed for pasture or arable in the early modern period.[91]

Wherever there was a plentiful supply of commons, it became an increasingly frequent practice during the later 16th and the 17th centuries to inclose and cultivate parts of the waste for a few years and then to allow the plots to revert to common once more.[92] The decision to break up the commons was usually the result of amicable agreement between the commoners and the manorial lord. It caused disputes only when the inclosures were unlicensed,[93] when the tenants failed to pay what the lord considered a reasonable increase in rent or tithes for improving the land,[94] or when the common rights of neighbouring manors were threatened.[95] Sometimes the lord was over-enthusiastic: in 1796 it was recalled that Viscount Chetwynd, lord of the manor of Brereton in Rugeley, had proposed to take in the whole of Brereton Hill for the free-holders, 'but they would not accept it, thinking it uneasy to plough and not worth taking in'.[96] Usually such inclosures were welcomed, especially as it was recognized that ploughing benefited the subsequent pasture,[97] and in some cases the temporary inclosures prepared the land for the more regular routine of cultivation by alternate husbandry.[98] It has been said that such inclosures 'acted as a safety valve, ensuring an adequate supply of arable as population rose'.[99] Occasionally philanthropy was the stated reason for inclosure: when part of Haywood park was sown with corn in the 1590s it was 'for the relief of the poor inhabitants of the townships thereabouts',[1] and in 1737 30 a. on Cannock Chase was inclosed and the rents were used for the repair and improvement of the Cannock waterworks.[2]

The size of such inclosures, the length of time they were cultivated, and the terms of the agreements for shifting cultivation varied greatly. In 1551 an octogenarian asserted that within his memory all of Ilam Moor had been ploughed,[3] and in 1597 it was

[87] e.g. W.S.L., S.MS. 335(ii) (Chartley, 1526–7); W.S.L., M. 540 (Dieulacres, 1542); S.R.O., D.(W.) 1734/2/3/J. 2029 (Cannock, 1570); W.S.L., S.MS. 326/1 (Longdon, 1571).

[88] e.g. *S.H.C.* 1936, 216–17 (Rowley Regis, 1556); D.L. 42/109 f. 19 (Needwood, 1559); W.S.L., S.MS. 326/1 (Longdon, 1571); S.R.O., D.(W.) 1734/2/3/37 (Cannock Wood, late 16th cent.); B.L. Add. MS. 24822, f. 63v. (Pelsall and Hatherton, 1652); Add. MS. 36664, ff. 175–7 (Bradnop, 1687); S.R.O., D.593/H/14/1/4, ff. 39v., 40v. (Over Penn and Nether Penn, 1712–15); D.593/ G/2/1/30 (Trentham, Kingswood, Northwood, Cocknage, and Blurton, 1715–16); *V.C.H. Staffs.* xvii. 28 (West Bromwich, 17th and 18th cents.), 183 (Walsall, 17th and 18th cents.). And see below, p. 82.

[89] S.R.O., D.554/160.

[90] Johnson, 'NE. Staffs.' 168, 171, 173–4.

[91] Ibid. 123, 125–6, 131, 140–4. See also *S.H.C.* 1938,

143–4.

[92] For the cultivation of these inclosures see below, pp. 59–60.

[93] e.g. W.S.L., H.M. Chetwynd 74, great court of Salt and Ingestre, 1582; S.R.O., D.(W.) 1734/2/1/331 (Cannock and Rugeley, 1616); D.260/M/E/429/5 (Penkridge, 1661).

[94] e.g. E 134/40 and 41 Eliz. I Mich./34 mm. 4, 7v.; S.R.O., D.260/M/E/429/32.

[95] e.g. *S.H.C.* n.s. x(1), 132; *S.H.C.* 1912, 169–70; W.S.L., H.M. Chetwynd 38.

[96] W.S.L. 41/8/45.

[97] E 134/19 Chas. I East./1; /34 Chas. II Mich./10 m. 12v.

[98] *Agrarian Hist. Eng. and Wales*, iv. 100. [99] Ibid.

[1] E 134/38 and 39 Eliz. I Mich./12 m. 3. See also *S.H.C.* n.s. ix. 111–12.

[2] White, *Dir. Staffs.* (1834), 486; *V.C.H. Staffs.* v. 52.

[3] *S.H.C.* 1912, 186.

stated that the Aldridge part of Sutton Coldfield waste had been sown for eight years at a time for the past fifty years.[4] On Morridge the length of time during which the inclosures were cultivated seems to have depended on the fertility of the soil,[5] while at Great Barr waste land was allowed to be cultivated for four years only, after which it was given at least seven years to recover.[6] In the early 17th century the townships claiming common in Iverley Wood were taking one or two crops of corn and then laying their commons open again.[7] The most detailed records of shifting cultivation are for the area around Cannock Chase. Temporary cultivation of the waste was apparently an accepted practice at Huntington by 1629.[8] In 1657 inclosures on Micklewood Heath in Penkridge were laid open after three crops;[9] land in the same part of the heath was still being inclosed for cultivation in 1684.[10] The freeholders of Penkridge allowed three men to plough Quarry Heath for five years in 1657, and the rent was used for charitable purposes.[11] In 1662 Gailey Hay was cultivated by agreement for five years, the commoners paying every seventh sheaf to the lords and the lords maintaining the fences around the inclosure.[12] In 1692, by a further agreement, the hay was inclosed for seven years, the commoners paying a tenth sheaf and maintaining their own fences;[13] it was apparently the last such inclosure before the Act of Inclosure in 1773.[14] In the later 17th century Teddesley Hay was being tilled for five years in every fourteen, with the Littleton family taking a sixth part of the grain, but there too cultivation ceased in the early 18th century.[15] In 1676 it was found that 80 a. had been ploughed on Penkridge Heath, 12 a. on Quarry Pit Heath, and 16 a. on Dunston Heath, the last by poor men who asked to pay the 4d. or 6d. an acre which was the usual rent for common ground, rather than 'any sheaf or part of the corn'.[16] At Hatherton in 1666 part of the common was being cultivated for five years out of twelve.[17] Also in 1666 the inhabitants of Little Wyrley in Norton Canes agreed to take four crops from a piece of the waste which was to be divided into one-acre holdings; they were to pay the lord 6d. an acre and a tenth of every crop, 'provided there be visible ridge and reine'.[18] One of the last such agreements was a division of the Over Stonnall commons between the lord of the manor and the commoners in 1717; the freeholders were at liberty to plough their portions during the following seventeen years.[19] Temporary cultivation of the waste presumably resulted in a considerable increase in grain production during the 16th and 17th centuries,[20] although it is difficult from the surviving records to obtain an accurate idea of the extent of the practice. Pitt noticed that 'most of our commons and waste lands have on them evident marks of the plough' and deduced that 'probably the land was cropped as long as it would bear it, and then left to nature'. He was, however, only partly correct in his attribution of this extensive cultivation to the period before the Civil War.[21] Indeed, shortly before Pitt made his survey Young found that 600 a. of Sutton Coldfield waste, on either side of the county boundary, was still being cultivated for short periods.[22]

---

[4] E 134/39 and 40 Eliz. I Mich./21 m. 8.
[5] E 134/40 and 41 Eliz. I Mich./24 mm. 4–7v.
[6] J. T. Gould, *Men of Aldridge* (Bloxwich, 1957), 55.
[7] E 134/19 Chas. I East./1.
[8] S.R.O., D.260/M/E/429/16.
[9] Ibid. /18.
[10] W.S.L., M. 22.
[11] S.R.O., D.260/M/E/429/32.
[12] Ibid. /36.
[13] S.R.O., D.260/M/T/4/53.
[14] S.R.O., D.260/M/E/429/36; /M/T/4/53.
[15] S.R.O., D.260/M/E/429/35; /M/T/5/130.

[16] S.R.O., D.260/M/E/429/32.
[17] S.R.O., D.260/M/PV/1, 5 Feb. 1665/6.
[18] S.R.O., D.978/12.
[19] W.S.L., S.D. Pearson 744. See also S.R.O., D.593/H/14/1/4, f. 3v.
[20] *Agrarian Hist. Eng. and Wales*, iv. 100.
[21] Pitt, *Agric. Staffs.* 233.
[22] *Tours in Eng. and Wales by Arthur Young: selected from the Annals of Agric.* (London Sch. of Economics, Reprints of Scarce Tracts in Economic and Political Science, no. 14, 1932), 264–5; Shaw, *Staffs.* ii. 105, for cultivation of 'Colfield' in 1665.

ARABLE FARMING

In general arable farming throughout the period was subordinate to animal husbandry, and fodder crops were grown predominantly to meet the needs of stock, with little excess for the market. There were, however, considerable regional differences in arable farming within the county and considerable changes in the amount of land under tillage and in the methods of arable farming.

Little change was possible on the poor soils of the north, and any changes in arable practice there had only begun by the later 18th century. Those soils, as Plot commented, 'with the best helps are fit indeed only for oats and barley'.[23] In 1801 the vicar of Biddulph reported that 'this is not a corn country', and the curate of Meerbrook in Leek that 'beans, peas, and turnips are strangers in our neighbourhood'.[24] On the other hand the vicar of Cheddleton reported a rapid increase in the amount of wheat, barley, and turnips grown in the parish within the previous seventeen years or so.[25]

On the clay soils of central Staffordshire there was an increase in the amount of land under tillage, particularly in the 16th and 17th centuries, and probably in response to increasing population. Portions of the waste were cultivated for short periods, and alternate husbandry, the breaking-up of pasture and meadow for a few years at a time,[26] seems to have been widely adopted. The fertility of both permanent and temporary arable was increased by heavy manuring, and according to Plot the area, particularly the rich clay lands around Needwood, produced 'as good hard-corn [wheat and rye], peas, beans, etc. as any in the south, though not so much'.[27] The fielden country in the south-east and south-west of the county was more markedly a mixed farming district, and arable crops were heavier and more varied. It is on those lighter soils that there is evidence in the 18th century of the spread of the Norfolk system, a four- or five-course rotation pivoting on a turnip fallow.[28]

As has already been shown,[29] most of the open fields had disappeared by the late 18th century, through either wholesale or piecemeal inclosure. In addition, the system of open-field husbandry had been modified by the addition of new and smaller fields, either permanently or temporarily under cultivation, or by the increased practice of alternate husbandry along with the establishment of pasture leys within the common fields.[30] The possible complexity of farming arrangements in surviving open-field manors can be seen in the Shenstone area. At Shenstone the court rolls between 1628 and 1640 mention seven open fields. Only two of them, however, were permanent; the others were temporary breaks on poorer soils. In neighbouring villages there was the same system of permanent open fields with temporary joint inclosures alongside; in each village the field pattern varied according to the geological conditions.[31] Equally complex arrangements have been traced in the north-east of the county, though in most villages piecemeal inclosure was well under way by the 17th century.[32] A survey of Wootton in Ellastone in 1547 shows five open fields and many small inclosed crofts and pastures, with the proportion of open to inclosed land approximately 5:1.[33] Calton, which was slightly behind its neighbours in the progress of inclosure, consisted

[23] Plot, *Staffs.* 109.
[24] *S.H.C.* 1950–1, 237.
[25] Ibid. 233.
[26] On this system of husbandry, variously called alternate, convertible, 'up-and-down', and 'field-grass' husbandry and also 'ley farming', see Kerridge, *Agric. Revolution*, 181–221.
[27] Plot, *Staffs.* 109.
[28] Sturgess, 'Agric. Staffs.' 22–3.

[29] See pp. 54–5.
[30] See p. 60.
[31] R. E. Hebden, 'Development of the settlement pattern and farming in the Shenstone area, prior to the general enclosure movement', *Trans. Lichfield & S. Staffs. Arch. & Hist. Soc.* iii. 33–9. But see *V.C.H. Staffs.* xvii. 180–2 for arrangements in Walsall par.
[32] Johnson, 'NE. Staffs.' *passim*; above, p. 54.
[33] Johnson, 'NE. Staffs.' 146–7.

in the early 17th century of two large open fields, totalling 400 a., surrounded by 26 closes totalling only 27 a.[34] Such evidence supports Gray's conclusion that, outside the Trent valley, Staffordshire seems to have been a county tending to show irregularities in its open fields characteristic of forest areas rather than the orderliness of two- and three-field systems.[35]

The usual course of husbandry on open fields was two years under cultivation and the third year fallow. The fields, however many there were, were arranged in three groups. Thus in 1653 the manor court of Hatherton arranged the fallows for the next six years: '1654 Royall and Showcroft, for the year 1655 Ucroft and Gammon Field, for the year 1656 Hill Field, and so successively according to the custom.'[36] In 1601–2 four fields at Hopton were cultivated as three: 'the said three fields time out of mind have been sowed with corn in form following: i.e. every of them or some part of them in every two years one after the other and in the third year lieth fresh.'[37] Plot describes the usual method of open-field cultivation of clay soils in the late 17th century. The fallow was ploughed first at the end of March or the beginning of April; then in the middle of June it was manured with dung and the manure ploughed in; it was ploughed again at the end of August to kill the weeds, and ploughed finally and sown with wheat at Michaelmas. The second crop was peas or beans, or both; 'for these they plough at Candlemas and sow in the decrease of the moon'.[38] Such three-course rotation was followed in the earlier 18th century at Leigh, where the open fields were sown with wheat after the fallow and then with beans and vetches and sometimes oats as well; there were, however, more flexible rotations in many small inclosures and temporary breaks.[39] According to Marshall, writing towards the end of the 18th century, the common-field rotation in the south-east of the county was fallow, wheat or barley, then pulse or oats, though 'of late years clover has been substituted, in some instances, in place of beans; and, in others, turnips have been sown, on the fallow, for barley; the last, however, is a practice which has not gained an established footing.'[40] Marshall was probably right to say that 'common-field husbandry, of this as well as of other districts, is inconvenient and unproductive';[41] there was, however, some flexibility and experiment within the system. Thus the fallow fields at Alrewas were sown with peas for the first time in 1621,[42] though, as was laid down in 1702, most of the owners of land in the fields had to agree to any sowing in a fallow year.[43] In 1661 twenty of Sir Edward Bagot's tenants at Abbots Bromley requested permission to sow that year's fallow field.[44]

Temporary cultivation of the waste, which was usually a joint enterprise,[45] required different management. The land needed careful preparation and heavy manuring. Plot reports that according to most opinions the best way to treat such land was to dig up the turf and burn it in May, then to lay lime before ploughing at Michaelmas for sowing the following spring, although in the Moorlands the land was sometimes limed for three or four years before ploughing; another method, practised at Ipstones, involved frequent harrowing.[46] In 1598 one acre of land inclosed out of Morridge was said to cost £4 in lime and muck before it was fit to bear crops.[47] Plot recommended 4 loads or 16 quarters of lime for each acre[48] but at Little Wyrley in 1666 it was agreed to lay 10 quarters of lime on every acre of newly inclosed waste, 'for the present benefit

[34] Ibid. 128–30.
[35] H. L. Gray, *Eng. Field Systems*, 87–8.
[36] S.R.O., D.260/M/PV/1, 14 July 1653; Harrison, 'Cannock and Rugeley', 72.
[37] W.S.L., H.M. Chetwynd 58B. [38] Plot, *Staffs*. 340–1.
[39] W.S.L. 95–97/31, e.g. the tithe accounts of Edw. Blurton.
[40] Marshall, *Rural Econ*. ii. 205. [41] Ibid. 208.
[42] S.R.O., D.783/1/1/1, p. 77.
[43] S.R.O., D.(W.) 0/3, 26 Oct. 1702.
[44] S.R.O., D.(W.) 1721/3/170.
[45] See pp. 56–7. [46] Plot, *Staffs*. 344.
[47] E 134/40 and 41 Eliz. I Mich./34 m. 7.
[48] Plot, *Staffs*. 343.

of corn and future good to posterity'.[49] The quality of crops obtained depended on the nature of the land and the sort of preparation: the first crops from Morridge were said to be very coarse.[50] According to Plot the sequence of crops on heathy land was usually rye, barley, peas, oats, and oats again, after which the inclosures were thrown open. In the Moorlands they could get four crops: barley, oats, rye, and oats.[51]

Most of the land thus reclaimed was only temporarily cultivated, but some of the better land was more regularly cultivated as part of a routine of alternate husbandry. The spread of more flexible land-use is characteristic of the period. Exhausted arable was laid down to grass to regain its fertility, and pasture and meadow were cropped for a few years and then allowed to rest again. Alternate husbandry could be carried out within the open-field system. At Alrewas in 1621 the tenants decided to crop part of the pasture land of the manor,[52] and there are similar examples of joint cultivation of pasture at Leigh in the 18th century.[53] The practice was, however, as Plot says,[54] more usually associated with single proprietors. Light soils, if well mucked, would produce rye, buckwheat, and oats for three years, but if marl and lime were used the land could be cropped for six years at a time in a rotation of wheat, barley, peas, wheat, barley, and oats, with, on occasion, three additional crops of beans or vetches before being laid down to grass. The heavier clay soils, if marled, could produce eight or nine crops, but if a heavy marl was used the land had to be prepared for grass by the use of lime and manure.

Early evidence of the tillage of pasture can be found in inclosure disputes: in 1526 3 a. of a 14-a. pasture in Gnosall was sown,[55] in 1542 at Ilam 100 a. of pasture was under corn,[56] and in the same year barley and flax were being grown in a pasture at Bradley near Stafford.[57] In 1572 William Greene of Wolverhampton claimed that he had spent much money on a pasture leased from Thomas Leveson and had sown part of it.[58] In leases of pasture closes at Adbaston in 1670 provision was made for the payment of tithes if any crops were taken from the ground.[59] On the Trentham estate in the early 17th century pasture land was under the plough,[60] and in the early 1630s meadow land was producing crops of oats and barley.[61] In 1689, however, George Plaxton, the Leveson-Gower agent, complained that the practice was being abused: 'land that stands in need of improvement by ploughing, liming and mucking [is] not heeded, and only the best pasture ground [is] brought under tillage.'[62] On the Dyott estate at Freeford as elsewhere in the county in the late 17th century extra rent was charged for ploughing up pasture.[63] In the 1680s Gregory King surveyed land at Pipe Hall which was to be broken up, and he also indicated land which was not ploughable.[64] At Streethay Richard Pyott took three crops of wheat and barley from Marchalls Close between 1711 and 1713. In 1703 and 1708 the close produced hay, and in 1709, 1710, and 1724 it was under flax.[65]

From the 17th century short cropping rotations followed by grass were increasingly stipulated in leases. In 1610 pastures in Burslem were leased for 21 years but it was stipulated that the lessees should not plough the land after 14 years unless they manured it well and did not till it for more than 3 years.[66] It was noted on a list of improved leases for the estates of the Dyotts of Freeford in 1632 that the tenants were at liberty

[49] S.R.O., D.978/12.
[50] E 134/40 and 41 Eliz. I Mich./34 m. 4.
[51] Plot, *Staffs.* 343–4.
[52] S.R.O., D.(W.) 1851/1/1/35.
[53] W.S.L. 94–97/31; S.R.O., D.795/23. Land newly under arable was not tithable until the seventh year, and the rector kept careful note of the tillage.
[54] Plot, *Staffs.* 341.
[55] *S.H.C.* 1912, 23.
[56] Ibid. 144.
[57] S.R.O., D.(W.) 1810, ff. 255–62.
[58] *S.H.C.* 1926, 132–3.
[59] W.S.L. 26/6/1/22.
[60] S.R.O., D.593/G/2/1/7.
[61] S.R.O., D.593/G/2/1/12, 14, 15.
[62] S.R.O., D.593/L/1/8.
[63] S.R.O., D.1042/1, e.g. Lady Day 1683.
[64] S.R.O., D.150/37/301 a and b.
[65] W.S.L., S.MS. 431.
[66] *T.N.S.F.C.* lxiii. 78, 83.

to plough for the first 15 years of 21-year leases but that they were not to plough during the last 6 years and were to take only one crop of oats from the land.[67] More usually leases imposed penalties for ploughing up pasture without permission.[68] A lease of meadow at Streethay in 1727 allowed the cultivation of part of the land for three years and provided that mud taken off the land should be put on the ploughed area.[69] The terms of leases of land in the Eccleshall area made by the Pershall family commonly restricted tenants to ploughing only a third of the arable in any year, or at least to ploughing only a third in the last four years of the lease, under penalty of heavy extra rents.[70]

In the later 18th century farming covenants in leases made by landlords who were interested in improved husbandry became more and more detailed with regard to the management of arable. Prohibitions on ploughing during the last few years of a lease became common, often with the stipulation that the land should be laid down with clover seed.[71] A lease of Lees farm in Castle Church in 1753 allowed only four crops, which had to be followed by four years under grass;[72] Richard Whitworth in his leases at Adbaston and Offley Park also allowed no more than four crops from each tillage, which would 'keep the said lands in good heart, plight, and condition, not mowing, ploughing, or tilling the same out of heart or beyond the usual course of husbandry'.[73] In letting Enson Moor farm in 1764 Thomas Giffard allowed only three crops from newly ploughed land, 'unless one be turnips and then only four before it is sown with clover'; the land was to rest at least two years before being broken up again.[74] On the Sneyd estates at Keele a lease in 1749 allowed three crops in six years.[75] A survey of the estate in the early 1770s recommended that some pasture which had been under tillage should not be ploughed at all in future; some other land, with careful management, could be tilled for short periods followed by longer periods under grass. In at least one case a turnip fallow was recommended.[76] Leases on the Bill estates in north-east Staffordshire in the 1750s and 1760s contained only stipulations about manure and penalties for breaking up pasture without permission, but in the 1780s they regulated the amount of land to be under tillage at one time and limited cultivation to three crops. In 1793 John Bill went even further in laying down husbandry practice in a lease: 'a reasonable agreement to be made with respect to the tillage, as I think two crops of corn together and then clover or turnips or fallow, is as much as that land will bear to keep it in good condition.'[77]

More general information on crop rotations on inclosed land can be obtained from agricultural writers in the later 18th century. From them it is clear that the difference between the management of light and heavy soil was becoming marked. Much of the heavy land was under 'Midland Grass', a rotation of six or seven years under grass, followed by oats, wheat, and barley, or some variation of this alternate system: at Dunstall in 1790 Thomas Miller kept land under clover and burnet for four, six, or even ten years, followed by oats, wheat, turnips, and barley.[78] On the lighter soils of the south the Norfolk system was spreading fast.[79] Arthur Young, an ardent advocate of the Norfolk system and not always an unbiased observer, visited south-east Staffordshire

[67] S.R.O., D.661/21/1/1, f. 4.
[68] e.g. B.R.L. 337128; W.S.L., S.D. 190/33.
[69] W.S.L., S.MS. 431.
[70] P. and M. Spufford, *Eccleshall* (Keele, 1964), 34–5.
[71] e.g. B.R.L. 277055; S.R.O., D.661/21/3/1, f. 174v.; D.661/11/2/1, notes on leases, 1752–4; S.R.O., D.(W.) 1788/Box F.1/Cradock, memo. of lease, 11 Nov. 1760.
[72] *V.C.H. Staffs.* v. 95.
[73] W.S.L. 26/6/2/22, Whitworth/Warren, 1768, Whitworth/Hand, 1775.

[74] S.R.O., D.590/820, list of covenants. See ibid. /541 for date of lease.
[75] Univ. of Keele, Sneyd MS. S. 1616.
[76] Ibid. S. 1634.
[77] S.R.O., D.554/51, esp. 'proposals for letting Lodge Farm, 30 Jan. 1793'.
[78] Marshall, *Rural Econ.* i. 184; P. Bassano, 'On the advantages of introducing grasses in a course of arable crops', *Annals of Agric.* xiv. 6.
[79] Sturgess, 'Agric. Staffs.' 29.

in 1768, and from his description of farms around Stone, Rugeley, and Shenstone differences in rotations are clear. On the sandy loams around Stone he found two rotations: fallow, wheat, oats, barley, clover for two or three years, oats, and beans, 'a vile, as well as strange, course', and fallow, wheat, oats, barley, turnips, barley, and clover, 'which is almost as odd as the other'. On the mixed soils around Rugeley there were three main courses: fallow, wheat, barley, and barley; fallow, wheat, oats, and clover for three years; fallow, barley, turnips, and barley. On the light soils around Shenstone rotations were nearer the Norfolk system, and the cultivation of turnips for the winter fattening of sheep was of great importance; there the main course was turnips, barley, barley, clover for two or three years, sometimes followed by wheat and oats.[80] Marshall reported that turnips were cultivated in the district around his farm at Statfold by a few advanced farmers, but that it did not enter into ordinary practice: 'at present, not one acre in a hundred . . . is subjected to turnip culture.'[81] West of the Tame, however, the turnip formed the basis of husbandry, though the 'proper management' of the crop was new. Marshall had heard that hoeing of turnips had been introduced within the previous twenty years by hoers brought from Norfolk by the Marquess Townshend, and Lord Harrowby was told in 1779 of a novel horse-hoe for turnips in use near Stafford.[82] The cultivation and hoeing of turnips was said to have fattened thousands of sheep at Shenstone and in 1773 caused an increase in the tithes.[83] The turnip fallow was, as Marshall realized, suited to only a small part of the county, though it apparently enjoyed a certain vogue towards the end of the century. A tenant at Chillington presented a bill of £13 6s. 6d. for a turnip fallow on a 7-a. field as part of a claim for compensation for improvement in 1767,[84] and in 1770 one of John Bill's tenants at Farley in Alton asked leave to make a turnip fallow on one of his fields 'which he would eat with sheep and lay it down the year after with proper seeds'.[85] The clay lands of central and northern Staffordshire were not suitable for turnip-growing and had to wait for the draining advances of the 19th century. There the fallow was retained as a recuperative and cleaning break.[86] William Tompson, who leased Forge farm at Abbots Bromley from 1768 to 1815 and had 110 a. of arable, worked out 'a regular mode of fallow' in 1792. He grouped his fields into five and followed a rotation of fallow, wheat, beans or barley or oats, seeds or oats, and seeds.[87]

There are a few details in Plot's *Natural History* of local eccentricities in the tools of arable husbandry: thus he found at Brereton an instrument designed to clear ground like a mattock, while Mr. Ashmore of Tamworth and Mr. Fernyhough at Fradswell in Colwich were using ploughs of their own invention.[88] Soon afterwards Sir Simon Degge noted that 'there is ploughs used in this country made for ploughing steep hillsides, that will turn the earth all one way, go they backward or forward', but he was unable to describe them; he also tells of Mr. Coleman of Cannock 'who wasted his estate in finding a way to make a wagon to go itself'.[89] Probably there was little change in the implements used on smaller farms until the end of the period, except in their cost:[90] a plough cost 6d. in the 16th century[91] and 14s. or 21s. in 1768.[92] In the later 18th century, however, new implements were gradually introduced, especially on

[80] A. Young, *Six Months' Tour through North of Eng.* (1770), iii. 313–14, 323–4.

[81] Marshall, *Rural Econ.* i. 203.

[82] Ibid. 204; Sandon Hall, Harrowby doc. 67, p. 45. Marshall's statement (turnip-hoeing 'has not been established . . . more, perhaps, than twenty years') also occurs in the 1790 edn. of his book (i. 254).

[83] H. Sanders, *Hist. and Antiquities of Shenstone* (1794), 331–2.

[84] S.R.O., D.590/810/1–2.

[85] S.R.O., D.554/91.   [86] Sturgess, 'Agric. Staffs.' 23.

[87] W. B. Mercer, 'William Tompson: a Record of Georgian Farming', *Jnl. of Min. of Agric.* xlv. 1127 (based on W.S.L. 43/1–7/54).

[88] Plot, *Staffs.* 344, 352.

[89] Ibid. (copy in W.S.L. with transcript of annotations by Sir Simon Degge), 352, 354.

[90] J. E. C. Peters, *Development of Farm Buildings in Western Lowland Staffs. up to 1880*, 187.

[91] S.R.O., D.(W.) 1734/2/2/32.

[92] Young, *Six Months' Tour through North of Eng.* iii. 322, 332.

larger farms. In 1785–6 Pitt made and used a simple drill-plough of his own design for drilling peas and beans; he claimed then that the only other drill-ploughs to have reached Staffordshire were 'complicated, expensive, and unfit for general use'.[93] A few years later, however, he noted two types of drill-plough in use in the county (neither of them his own), both of which worked well. One variety was sold by Joseph Cornforth of Bushbury, who also made winnowing machines.[94] Many tools were probably still made or repaired by local craftsmen. Marshall found that some of the larger farmers had blacksmiths' shops on their farms used by visiting smiths, but he had never seen a wheelwright's shop on a farm.[95]

Oxen seem to have retained their popularity as draught animals with wealthier farmers and where there was sufficient fodder to maintain them; they were, however, coming to be rivalled by the horse, especially on the lighter lands of the south. In the Alrewas area between 1558 and 1601 oxen are listed in just under half of the seventy-five surviving probate inventories, while horses, usually mares, occur in practically every list.[96] In inventories of the Lichfield and Sedgley districts in the late 16th and the 17th centuries horses are even more commonly found than oxen, probably because their owners were often engaged in only part-time agricultural work.[97] Many horses bred and sold in central Staffordshire were apparently destined for the plough.[98] Edward James of Kinvaston dealt in both horses and oxen. In the 1690s and 1700s he sold several yokes of oxen at fairs at Stafford and Albrighton (Salop.) at prices ranging from £9 19s. to £14 15s.;[99] at Alrewas in the later 16th century oxen had been valued at between £1 and 30s. each.[1] At Freeford in the 1730s oxen were being bought for about £5 each and fat oxen were sold, presumably to local butchers, for £10 each.[2] Plot reported that in many parts of the county oxen were preferred as plough-beasts because their carcasses could always be sold profitably.[3] In 1768 Young found that around Shenstone the number of ox-teams was decreasing.[4] Marshall, on the other hand, worked in an area where the heavy horse was the traditional draught animal; there, he noted, 'superior managers' were beginning to work a few ox-teams.[5]

The time and amount of ploughing depended on the crop.[6] Particular attention was paid to the preparation of the fallow. One method was pinfallowing, which Marshall called 'the forte of the Midland farmer' and of which he disapproved.[7] He gave the following account of it:

He breaks up his wheat stubble, in autumn or winter, and, having crossed it, in the spring, immediately sets about harrowing it, in order 'to get the twitch to the top'; which done, he gathers it up into lands, sows his barley, reharrows, and having got some more twitch to the surface, the fallow is completed. In this way, nine-tenths of the inclosed lands of the district have been, and still continue to be, laid down to grass.

In the later 18th century some innovatory practices were being introduced. Hoeing of turnips began c. 1770,[8] and Marshall mentions that drilling was being tried by a few farmers and that Major Bowles of Elmhurst had originated the practice of employing a woman to follow the plough and pick up weeds.[9] Care was taken in the preparation and choice of seed. Plot had found seed being steeped in brine and even mixed with soot

[93] *Annals of Agric.* iii. 191; v. 91–2.
[94] Pitt, *Agric. Staffs.* 38.
[95] Marshall, *Rural Econ.* ii. 88.
[96] S.R.O., D.783/5/2/2/1–75. The inventories cover Alrewas, Fradley, Edingale, King's Bromley, and Mavesyn Ridware.
[97] *S.H.C.* 4th ser. v. 21; J. S. Roper, 'Sedgley Probate Inventories, 1614–1787' (TS. in W.S.L.).
[98] *Agrarian Hist. Eng. and Wales,* iv. 192; below, p. 77.

[99] W.S.L., H.M. 27/2.
[1] S.R.O., D.783/5/2/2/1–75.
[2] S.R.O., D.661/21/3/1.
[3] Plot, *Staffs.* 352.
[4] Young, *Six Months' Tour through North of Eng.* iii. 327.
[5] Marshall, *Rural Econ.* i. 99–100.
[6] See p. 66.
[7] Marshall, *Rural Econ.* ii. 28.
[8] See p. 62.
[9] Marshall, *Rural Econ.* i. 158, 161.

and had noticed the practice of obtaining seed from different sorts of soils: 'upon this account it is, that in the southern parts of the county, they sometimes send for their seed wheat out of the Moorlands . . . and so do the Moorlands out of the south.'[10] The prevalence of the practice surprised Marshall, but he heard that it was becoming less fashionable.[11]

Manure, as has been shown above, played a most important part in the arable husbandry of the county, especially in the preparation of land under temporary or alternate cultivation.[12] Dung, marl, and lime were the principal manures and figure frequently in farming accounts,[13] but other materials, such as soot,[14] night-soil,[15] drift sand,[16] and pigeon droppings,[17] occur. In the Moorlands peat was cut, dried, and burnt, and the ashes, called 'ess', were used as manure.[18] The use of different manures was doubtless hallowed by long practice (Marshall thought that in many cases the use of marl was due to fashion rather than effectiveness)[19] but there is some evidence of experimentation. James Whitehall, rector of Checkley 1620–45, had heard from his father that the cost of liming could be recovered in four years, but he found that shale marl proved more effective on one of his fields.[20] Animal dung was the main manure in open-field manors, but other manures were also used on open-field strips: at Alrewas in 1700 Thomas Smith was allowed 10s. a year for three years by his landlord to buy lime for 'several parcels of plough-land lying dispersed in the fields of Alrewas',[21] and at Tunstall in 1604 land was leased with the right to dig for and apply marl.[22] From the 17th century many leases contained provisions that all dung produced was to be used on the property and that, at the end of the tenancy, all dung was to be left behind.[23] From at least 1771 leases on the Dartmouth estate at Sandwell in West Bromwich stipulated that for every load of hay or straw sold the tenant should bring to the farm 'one wagon load of good rotten dung'.[24] Muck is often valued in probate inventories; the term 'upmuck' occurs in several Lichfield inventories, always with a high valuation, and refers to the muck piled in heaps in the field ready for spreading and ploughing in.[25] According to Sir Simon Degge a rule of husbandry in Staffordshire was:[26]

> Be it wet or be it dry
> Spread your muck, and let it lie.

Young found that the farmers around Shenstone made a compost of dung with earth and 'ditch stuff',[27] and Marshall discovered that dung was very highly valued in his area, probably because of the demand from the market-gardeners around Tamworth.[28]

Plot described five different sorts of marl used by farmers in the county for manuring arable and grassland.[29] It was said that Staffordshire farmers preferred soft blue marl for arable and grey marl for pasture.[30] Marshall thought very little of the red marl, which was used in great quantities, since he found it low in calcareous content;[31] Young, however, described it as an excellent manure and stated that it was used around

[10] Plot, *Staffs.* 348, 350.
[11] Marshall, *Rural Econ.* ii. 194.
[12] See p. 59.
[13] See e.g. S.R.O., D.661/21/4/1, ff. 2–3v.
[14] Wm. Tompson of Abbots Bromley bought soot from a Uttoxeter sweep at 6d. a strike: *Jnl. Min. of Agric.* xlv. 1129.
[15] Plot, *Staffs.* 346. Ric. Pyott cleared over 1,000 loads of mud out of the 'Great Moat' in 1704 to put on his land: W.S.L., S.MS. 431.
[16] Plot, *Staffs.* 346.
[17] S.R.O., D.(W.) 1851/1/1/22, 22 Mar. 1691/2.
[18] Plot, *Staffs.* 115.
[19] Marshall, *Rural Econ.* i. 154.
[20] W.S.L., H.M. 308/40, f. 20.
[21] S.R.O., D.(W.) 1851/1/1/22, 2 Feb. 1699/1700.

[22] *T.N.S.F.C.* lxiii. 59.
[23] Sturgess, 'Agric. Staffs.' 324–5.
[24] Ibid. App. 4, p. 37; S.R.O., D.564/3/2/12, lease of Fryer's Park farm, 1771.
[25] *S.H.C.* 4th ser. v. 22.
[26] Plot, *Staffs.* (copy in W.S.L. with Degge annotations), 340.
[27] Young, *Six Months' Tour through North of Eng.* iii. 326.
[28] Marshall, *Rural Econ.* i. 147–8. The farmers of Shenstone fetched dung from Lichfield and Walsall: Sanders, *Shenstone*, 333.
[29] Plot, *Staffs.* 119–20.
[30] *The Complete Farmer, or a General Dictionary of Husbandry* (1766).
[31] Marshall, *Rural Econ.* i. 152.

Shenstone at the rate of 60 three-horse-cart loads an acre.[32] A lease of a farm in Castle Church in 1753 stipulated 200 tumbril-loads of marl an acre,[33] while a husbandry covenant made at the leasing of Toft farm at Trentham in 1782 allowed 20s. an acre for every acre marled with 180 loads of marl during the first four years of the tenancy.[34]

Camden describes the use of lime in the Dove valley in the late 16th century, and as already seen it was a popular manure in the 17th century.[35] In the later 18th century Marshall says that the fallow was dressed with lime, since farmers thought that it 'mellowed' the soil while in tillage and 'sweetened' the grass when the soil was laid down to pasture.[36] One of the first things that Pitt did when he took New House farm at Pendeford in 1780 was to build a limekiln by the Staffordshire and Worcestershire Canal where it ran through the farm; during the next three years he burnt 1,200 quarters of lime to dress his arable.[37] On the Dyott estate at Freeford wagon-loads of lime were regularly fetched from Hay Head in Walsall in the 1760s and the annual bill was about £12 to £13;[38] at Shenstone lime was used to improve the yield of arable land but was said to be costly at 25s. a wagon-load;[39] William Tompson of Abbots Bromley fetched his lime from Burton-upon-Trent at 11d. a horse-load.[40] According to Young the usual application around Shenstone was 8 quarters to an acre at a cost of 36s. an acre.[41]

Throughout the period the main crops produced were still wheat, oats, barley, and rye, with the proportions varying according to local conditions and needs but with oats, closely rivalled by barley, probably predominating over the county as a whole. Most of the crops produced were consumed by the farmer and his stock and any surplus was disposed of locally. Some new crops were introduced, mainly fodder crops such as turnips, clover, and other grasses,[42] and towards the end of the period there was an increase in the production of potatoes and in market-gardening generally to meet the needs of the new industrial areas.

Several varieties of wheat are found in the county. Plot mentions white-flaxen wheat, red wheat, double-eared wheat, and Poland (or cone) wheat.[43] In 1700 Edward James was buying, usually at Lichfield, red seed-wheat at 3s. 10d. a strike and white seed-wheat at 3s. 7d. a strike.[44] Red wheat was preferred on heavier soils;[45] Marshall found that it was the most common in his district but that other varieties, including Essex Dun, were being introduced.[46] At Forge farm William Tompson grew white wheat, and there is also mention of the Dunstable and Essex Dun varieties.[47] Plot found that Poland wheat was to be sown at Hilderstone in 1682;[48] according to Marshall it had been grown in his district but was no longer used there.[49] Red and white wheat were often sown together, and a wheat and rye mixture (muncorn, blendcorn, or maslin) was common.[50] Wheat was usually sown in the autumn, though Marshall found that spring wheat, sown in April, was being grown successfully.[51] There is very little detailed evidence about yields and prices for wheat or for other crops. Plot says that 2 strikes of red or white wheat an acre yielded 20 strikes;[52] a century later William Tompson

[32] Young, *Six Months' Tour through North of Eng.* iii. 325–6. The excellent marl found at Shenstone was said to have been 'greatly serviceable in the improvements made': Sanders, *Shenstone*, 332.
[33] *V.C.H. Staffs.* v. 95.   [34] S.R.O., D.593/L/1/18.
[35] Camden, *Brit.* (1586), 328; ibid. (1610), 587; above, pp. 59, 64.
[36] Marshall, *Rural Econ.* i. 148.
[37] W. Pitt, 'Particulars of the New House farm, Pendeford, Staffs.' *Annals of Agric.* xlii. 204–5.
[38] S.R.O., D.661/21/6/1. In 1679 on the Trentham estate lime was being bought at 1s. 2d. a load: S.R.O., D.593/F/2/18.
[39] Sanders, *Shenstone*, 332.
[40] *Jnl. Min. of Agric.* xlv. 1129.

[41] Young, *Six Months' Tour through North of Eng.* iii. 326; above, p. 62. See also *V.C.H. Staffs.* ii. 193.
[42] See pp. 70–1.   [43] Plot, *Staffs.* 205–6, 347.
[44] W.S.L., H.M. 27/2, Sept. 1700.
[45] *The Complete Farmer*; Plot, *Staffs.* 340.
[46] Marshall, *Rural Econ.* i. 182.
[47] *Jnl. Min. of Agric.* xlv. 1127.
[48] Plot, *Staffs.* 206.
[49] Marshall, *Rural Econ.* i. 183.
[50] Plot, *Staffs.* 341, 347; S.R.O., D.593/F/2/18 (muncorn sold at 2s. 8d. a strike, 1679); /19 (maslin, 1679); W.S.L., H.M. 27/2, 1697; W.S.L., S.MS. 431, e.g. 1722–4 where mixed crops of wheat and rye are valued at £3 an acre; S.R.O., D.661/21/3/1, /6/1, sales of blendcorn, 1732–72.
[51] Marshall, *Rural Econ.* i. 183.   [52] Plot, *Staffs.* 340.

sowed $2\frac{1}{4}$ strikes an acre for a yield averaging $14\frac{1}{2}$ strikes.[53] In 1546 wheat at Pillaton farm in Penkridge was valued at 5s. a quarter.[54] The valuations which Richard Pyott of Streethay put on his wheat crops in the early 18th century averaged £3 to £4 an acre,[55] rather higher than the £2 5s. or £2 10s. an acre valuation given in Lichfield inventories in the mid 17th century.[56] At Lichfield in 1667 white wheat was valued at 3s. 8d. a strike and red wheat at 3s. 4d. a strike;[57] between 1760 and 1795 prices obtained for wheat from Forge farm ranged from 4s. to 8s. a strike.[58] The rise in wheat prices in the later 18th century is reflected in the prices of loads of wheat sold from the Dyott estate at Freeford: in 1745 two loads were sold for £19; in 1771–2 one load fetched £23 15s.[59] By the late 18th century any surplus wheat was sold to the millers who supplied the industrial towns.[60]

Oats were the main crop of the Moorlands and were there used for bread; elsewhere they were grown as a fodder crop. Plot lists several varieties: red (found in the Moorlands), white, and black; he also saw naked oats at Burton-upon-Trent.[61] In the later 18th century William Tompson was growing Scotch grey, white Dutch, Polish, red, and black oats at Abbots Bromley.[62] In the 1690s the bailiff at Norbury bought white seed-oats from Knighton at 1s. 9d. a strike and accepted Polish seed-oats in part-payment of rent;[63] red oats and Polish oats were being sold from the Dyott estate in the 1760s.[64] Marshall mentions the Dutch oat and the Poland oat, and says that the latter, 'which was the favourite', was going out of fashion.[65] Oats were sown in spring, after one ploughing; Young and Marshall give roughly the same yield of 2 strikes an acre producing 24 strikes, but William Tompson sowed 4 strikes an acre and in 1775 recorded a yield of 30 strikes an acre.[66] Richard Pyott, who often sowed oats and peas together, valued his oat crops between 1710 and 1727 at prices ranging from £1 10s. to £3 10s. an acre;[67] William Tompson obtained between 2s. and 3s. a strike for his oats.[68] Between 1742 and 1761 an average of nearly 300 strikes of oats a year was sold from the Dyott estate.[69] As Marshall points out, however, in spite of the large quantities of oats grown little was sold off the farms, except to local inns for horse fodder.[70]

Barley was also a popular crop, used for bread, malt, and fodder. Plot mentions as the main varieties long-eared barley (said by Marshall to have been introduced to his Statfold area in the mid 18th century)[71] and sprat barley, while some naked (or French) barley, a survivor from Celtic times, was also sown.[72] Between the late 17th and late 18th centuries barley yielded about ten-fold, but sowing rates were reduced. According to Plot a sowing of 3 strikes of barley an acre yielded 30 strikes;[73] Young gives a yield of 20 strikes from a sowing of 2 strikes an acre[74] and Marshall 16 to 18 strikes from $1\frac{1}{2}$ strike an acre.[75] Richard Pyott, who grew more barley than any other crop, set an average valuation of £3 an acre on his crops produced between 1710 and 1725,[76] and at Fulfen in 1707 barley was valued at 2s. a strike.[77] Any surplus was bought by local maltsters. Increasing quantities of barley were sold from Freeford in the 18th century, reaching an average of 903 strikes a year between 1744 and 1761.[78]

[53] *Jnl. Min. of Agric.* xlv. 1127–8.
[54] S.R.O., D.260/M/E/429/22.
[55] W.S.L., S.MS. 431.
[56] *S.H.C.* 4th ser. v, e.g. nos. 38, 62, 72.
[57] Ibid. no. 89. [58] *Jnl. Min. of Agric.* xlv. 1128.
[59] S.R.O., D.661/21/3/1; /6/1.
[60] Marshall, *Rural Econ.* i. 188.
[61] Plot, *Staffs.* 204–5, 347.
[62] *Jnl. Min. of Agric.* xlv. 1128.
[63] Univ. of Keele, Sneyd MS. S.1873, pp. 74, 216.
[64] S.R.O., D.661/21/6/1.
[65] Marshall, *Rural Econ.* i. 193.
[66] Ibid. 194; Young, *Six Months' Tour through North of Eng.* iii. 324; *Jnl. Min. of Agric.* xlv. 1128.

[67] W.S.L., S.MS. 431.
[68] *Jnl. Min. of Agric.* xlv. 1128.
[69] S.R.O., D.661/21/3/1.
[70] Marshall, *Rural Econ.* i. 194.
[71] Ibid. 189. According to Plot this variety was suited to rank soil: Plot, *Staffs.* 342.
[72] Plot, *Staffs.* 205, 347; R. Trow-Smith, *Eng. Husbandry*, 121.
[73] Plot, *Staffs.* 342.
[74] Young, *Six Months' Tour through North of Eng.* iii. 324.
[75] Marshall, *Rural Econ.* i. 192.
[76] W.S.L., S.MS. 431.
[77] S.R.O., D.661/21/4/1, f. 8.
[78] Ibid. /21/3/1.

Rye, often mixed with wheat,[79] was grown throughout the county until the later 18th century; it was especially suited to the gravelly, dry soils of the Cannock hills and was a regular crop in the Moorlands.[80] It was used for bread and occurs in probate inventories, but there is little evidence that any surpluses were marketed.[81] Young reports a yield rate of 1:15 around Shenstone,[82] and at the beginning of the 18th century Richard Pyott valued his small quantities of rye at between £3 and £4 an acre.[83]

Peas were a regular fodder crop and occur frequently, often with beans on the heavier soils, and sometimes with oats or vetches.[84] There were many different varieties: Plot mentions white and grey peas, also 'the white rouncival, the big-brended pea, and the early ripe pea'; he says that Matthew Philips of Coton in Milwich had cultivated the garden rouncival with great success and that it was grown in the open fields of that parish.[85] In the late 17th and early 18th centuries Edward James purchased seed of beans, white peas, and brended peas,[86] and on the Dyott estate at Freeford white, blue, marrow, and hog peas were grown in the 18th century and small quantities sold, often for seed.[87] According to Plot peas sown on clay soil yielded five-fold and beans six-fold.[88]

Hemp and flax were, according to Plot, grown in small quantities throughout the county,[89] and in the mid 1690s Robert Sharrock described Staffordshire as exemplary in growing the two crops.[90] Production appears to have increased in the late 17th and early 18th centuries in order to supply the material for domestic weavers.[91] Richard Pyott leased part of his lands at 45s.–50s. an acre for the cultivation of flax, and in 1707 the 25 a. or so that was under flax was valued at £55 15s.[92] Edward James seems to have been leasing land for the same purpose in 1703.[93] In the later 18th century the growth of the two crops was being encouraged by government bounties.[94] They were, however, thought to impoverish soil; many leases contained prohibitions against the sowing of flax, rape, and cole-seed, and in 1741 David Martin, tenant of a farm on the Chillington estate, was given notice to quit for abuse of land because he had sown many acres with flax seed.[95]

Buckwheat (or French Wheat) was sown on barren lands in the late 17th century, often mixed with barley, and was used for making bread. One strike an acre yielded sixty-fold.[96] In the late 18th century it was grown for fodder or to be ploughed under as manure.[97]

Hops were being grown at Norbury in the 1680s.[98] In the late 17th century the cultivation of fruit trees was a fashionable hobby among Staffordshire gentlemen, and Plot was particularly impressed by a cherry plantation at Packington and by the variety of fruit trees in the garden of Rowland Okeover of Okeover.[99] Tettenhall was well known for pears, and there were large apple-orchards at Upper Arley (later Worcs.), which were, however, in decline by the later 18th century.[1] According to Pitt, Staffordshire farmers lacked interest in commercial fruit-growing.[2] Over most of the county

[79] See p. 65.
[80] *Agrarian Hist. Eng. and Wales*, iv. 169; Harrison, 'Cannock and Rugeley', 73; Plot, *Staffs.* 343–4; Pitt, *Agric. Staffs.* 52.
[81] e.g. *S.H.C.* 4th ser. v. 22; S.R.O., D.783/5/2/2/14 and 20; *V.C.H. Staffs.* xvii. 27, 183, 279. Rye from Beaudesert was sold at Lichfield in 1561 (S.R.O., D.(W.) 1734/3/3/48, f. 2v.), and small quantities were sold from the Dyott estate in 1711–13 and 1732–4 (S.R.O., D.661/21/3/1).
[82] Young, *Six Months' Tour through North of Eng.* iii. 325.
[83] W.S.L., S.MS. 431, 1711–13.
[84] *S.H.C.* 4th ser. v. 22; W.S.L., S.MS. 431; W.S.L. 94–96/31; Univ. of Keele, Sneyd MS. S.186/3.
[85] Plot, *Staffs.* 204, 347.
[86] W.S.L., H.M. 27/2, e.g. Apr. 1695, Mar. 1698/9, Mar. 1707/8.
[87] S.R.O., D.661/21/3/1; /6/1.　　[88] Plot, *Staffs.* 341.

[89] Ibid. 347. See also *V.C.H. Staffs.* xvii. 28, 183.
[90] R. Sharrock, *An Improvement to the Art of Gardening* (1694), 43–4.
[91] Joan Thirsk, '17th-cent. Agric. and Social Change', *Ag.H.R.* xviii (Supplement), 171.
[92] W.S.L., S.MS. 431.
[93] W.S.L., H.M. 27/2.
[94] S.R.O., Q/SO 18, e.g. ff. 149–50, 174v.–176, 199–200; 19, e.g. ff. 8v.–9, 49–50, 96v.–97v.
[95] Sturgess, 'Agric. Staffs.' 324; S.R.O., D.590/560.
[96] Plot, *Staffs.* 205, 345.
[97] Pitt, *Agric. Staffs.* 52–3.
[98] Univ. of Keele, Sneyd MS. S.1597.
[99] Plot, *Staffs.* 227. See also S.R.O., D.649/5; D.1527/5, 27 Mar., 17 May 1780.
[1] Plot, *Staffs.* 226; Pitt, *Agric. Staffs.* 88.
[2] Pitt, *Agric. Staffs.* 89.

vegetables were grown in gardens or on small pieces of land,[3] but the growth of the new industrial areas caused an increase in the commercial production of potatoes and cabbages in the later 18th century. The Potteries were supplied with potatoes by the Moorlands, and in 1792 part of Dilhorne Heath was manured and sown with potatoes; according to Pitt the potato was the main support of Moorland cottagers.[4] In the south of the county potatoes and cabbages were produced for Birmingham and the surrounding industrial district, and market-gardening became well established around Tamworth and Lichfield.[5]

The planting of timber grew in popularity during the 18th century, and Pitt describes a number of finely timbered estates, the best, in his opinion, being Blithfield and Chillington.[6] Profits from timber felled at Chillington in 1760 amounted to £978 19s., and there were further heavy fellings in the 1790s, when Cowper was celebrating the sowing of groves of oaks in the park.[7] One of the best known plantations was at Fisher-wick; in 1779 the earl of Donegall planted 25 a. of oaks there and was awarded a medal for having planted the greatest number of oaks in the country that year.[8] At Tamworth large quantities of garden quick-set were cultivated for the Birmingham market and for inclosure hedges, while coppices at Hopwas supplied wood for stakes, brooms, and crates for the packaging of pottery.[9]

GRASSLAND AND STOCK

Staffordshire was throughout the period predominantly a pastoral region with arable farming playing a supporting role to stock husbandry. Over much of the county grazing land was abundant, and there was rich meadow along the banks of the rivers. Good pasture was highly valued and its fertility was maintained by manuring; alternate husbandry too helped to improve the quality of grassland.[10] There is early evidence of the floating of meadows and, from the later 17th century, of the improvement of poor pasture land by the use of primitive draining techniques. Fodder crops for winter feeding were increasingly important, and the period saw the spread of turnip cultivation. A high valuation was set on good hay, and new grass crops, notably clover, were successfully introduced. Store sheep and cattle were bred in the hill-farming districts of the north for fattening on the richer lands of the south, and Staffordshire was noted for the fineness of its wool. An important development of the period was the growth of dairy specialization along the banks of the Dove and the Trent, centring on Uttoxeter. There was also some horse-breeding in central Staffordshire.

Grazing was provided by the aftermath of meadows, by the stubble and fallow of cornfields, by open or inclosed pastures,[11] and by rough pasture on heaths and wastes and in forests. The nature of pasturing arrangements depended on the progress of inclosure, and the value set upon commoning rights varied in different areas. Commoning rights in forests were jealously guarded. During the 16th century large flocks of sheep were kept in Iverley Wood in Kinver forest by the inhabitants of the surrounding townships,[12] and in the early 17th century 39 villages and townships claimed common in

[3] Small amounts of potatoes were tithed at Leigh in the 18th century (W.S.L. 95/31, 97/31), and potatoes and carrots at Baswich (W.S.L., S.MS. 429/iii, f. 11v.).

[4] Pitt, *Agric. Staffs.* 57, 129.

[5] Ibid. 53–4; Sturgess, 'Agric. Staffs.' 363; *Tours in Eng. and Wales by Arthur Young*, 141, 260; Marshall, *Rural Econ.* i. 197–203.

[6] Pitt, *Agric. Staffs.* 92–7. See also *V.C.H. Staffs.* xvii. 29.

[7] P. J. Doyle, 'The Giffards of Chillington, a Catholic Landed Family, 1642–1861' (Durham Univ. M.A. thesis, 1968), 346–9; *Poetical Works of William Cowper*, ed. H. S. Milford (1926 edn.), 397.

[8] Pitt, *Agric. Staffs.* 95–6; Shaw, *Staffs.* i. 370.

[9] Marshall, *Rural Econ.* i. 52–3, 73.

[10] See p. 60.

[11] See p. 55, for inclosure of pasture and pasture leys.

[12] E 134/18 Chas. I East./1.

Cannock Chase and large numbers of sheep were grazed there.[13] Free commoning for cattle in Needwood forest was vital for several of the 19 townships which claimed common rights. William Humberston, a senior official of the duchy of Lancaster, reported in 1559 that 'the town of Tutbury, the manors of Rolleston, Barton, and Marchington consist much in tillage and have not sufficient meadow and pasture either to keep milch kine for the furniture of their house or else for to keep their plough oxen for maintenance of their tillage'; in addition, prices for agistment of cattle in the forest parks had been increased by the keepers.[14] In areas where commoning was in short supply or where the existing commons were under pressure from an increase in the number of livestock, existing stinting regulations were severely enforced or new ones imposed.[15] At Lichfield, for example, heavy fines were being imposed by the burgess court in the early 18th century on sheep-masters who were accused of eating up the commons with their sheep and refusing to report the size of their flocks to the other commoners.[16] Even in open-field manors, however, sufficient pasturage and winter feed were usually available in the form of pasture leys within the arable fields and individual pasture closes and doles of meadow.[17] Where extra grass was available on such manors money could be made by agisting extra cattle. On the Trentham estate in the early 17th century animals were summered at 15s. each,[18] and at Alrewas a century later the bailiff charged £1 2s. or £1 3s. for each cow.[19] At Freeford in the early 18th century regular sums came from agisting animals on grass or on straw,[20] and William Tompson at Abbots Bromley charged 2s. a week for summer agistment on clover and 9d. to 1s. a week for winter agistment on stubble.[21]

There were two kinds of meadows: dry upland meadows which consisted of the best pasture shut up for hay,[22] and natural water-meadows along the river banks. The latter, which lay under water during the winter and were drained in the spring,[23] or were temporarily inundated by spring floods, were highly valued. The meadows of the Dove, often flooded in April, were probably the most valuable in Staffordshire: Leland noted the 'wonderful pastures' there, and common sayings were 'in April Dove's flood is worth a king's good' and 'as rich as Dove'.[24] At Coton-in-the-Clay in Hanbury in 1616 meadow land was valued at 11s. an acre, while arable holdings were valued at 8s. an acre;[25] in the 1790s the Dove lands were rented at nearly 40s. an acre.[26] Artificial watering of meadows is found as early as 1564 at Draycott-in-the-Moors, where water was diverted from the Blithe through a hollow trough into trenches cut in the neighbouring meadows.[27] In 1587 Thomas Congreve paid for a timber frame for a dam at Hatherton 'at Christbreedge meadow where the stream is turned'.[28] In the mid 17th century a meadow in Tutbury called the Trenches was described as 'environed with the river Dove and the new stream of water which was lately cut from the river Dove'.[29] Plot describes how at Drayton Bassett Lord Weymouth had increased the value of his

[13] S.R.O., D.(W.) 1734/2/5/1r.
[14] D.L. 42/109, ff. 14, 18, 54; and see above, p. 53.
[15] e.g. S.R.O., D.(W.) 1734/2/3/123 (Cannock Chase, 1605); W.S.L. 29/4/6/46 (Mavesyn Ridware, 1691); W.S.L., H.M. Chetwynd 83 (Ingestre and Salt, 1585); S.R.O., D.(W.) o/3/192, 30 Sept. 1699 (Edingale), 26 Oct. 1702 (Alrewas).
[16] S.R.O., D.661/16/9.
[17] e.g. S.R.O., D.(W.) 1851/1/1/22 (Alrewas); D.(W.) 1721/1/1, f. 65 (Tittensor); D.(W.) 1765/27 (Acton Trussell and Bednall). See D.L. 42/109-11 for distribution of arable, pasture, and meadow in townships in the honor of Tutbury in 1559. And see above, p. 55.
[18] S.R.O., D.593/G/2/1/7.
[19] S.R.O., D.(W.) 1851/1/1/22.
[20] S.R.O., D.661/21/3/1.

[21] Jnl. Min. of Agric. xlv. 1127.
[22] e.g. W.S.L. 95/31, for quantities of upland hay from inclosed pasture crofts at Leigh.
[23] S.R.O., D.(W.) 1765/23, 16 Sept. 1575.
[24] Leland, Itin. ed. Toulmin Smith, v. 19; Camden, Brit. (1610), 587; Plot, Staffs. 108; Pitt, Agric. Staffs. 69.
[25] B.L. Add. MS. 31917, ff. 45, 46v.
[26] Pitt, Agric. Staffs. 70.
[27] S.H.C. 1926, 66-9. See Agrarian Hist. Eng. and Wales, iv. 180-2, for general account of floating of meadows.
[28] S.R.O., D.1057, Congreve family and commonplace book 1585-1611, f. 9v.
[29] E 317/44 Staffs. f. 13. See also B.R.L. 297298, for 'floated meadow' in West Bromwich, 1650.

meadows by irrigation from 3s. to 30s. an acre.[30] In 1785 Marshall found a large stone in one of the meadows at Statfold:[31]

One of the labourers, an intelligent man, says that it has been the soal of a floodgate, for floating the meadow upward: namely, penning up the water, in times of flood, by means of a dam and floodgate, across the bottom of the meadow, or flat, to be watered.

According to the labourer that method of damming floodwaters had not been used for some twenty years.[32] At Tamworth Marshall was shown a meadow efficiently watered by a system of floodgates, sluices, and floats which had cost 40s. to 50s.[33]

Under-draining was another means of improving boggy and water-logged pasture ground, and although the main advances in draining were to come in the 19th century,[34] attempts were made to tackle the problem in the 17th and 18th centuries. According to Plot a Mr. Astley of Tamhorn was making drains which consisted of trenches lined with pebbles, filled in with faggots, and covered with soil, and a Mr. Sylvester of Weeford had invented an instrument to make similar drains without trenching.[35] There is evidence of the spread and improvement of under-draining in the later 18th century. Marshall found that around Statfold there had in the past been a primitive form of under-draining with three alder poles arranged to form a pipe[36] but that the method had been superseded in the 1750s by one learnt from some soughers from the Moorlands. Their methods were observed and copied by an enterprising labourer known as 'old Samuel Cleverdyche', according to Marshall 'a genius of the first cast', who was responsible for draining the main farms in the area. His method, as described by Marshall, is similar to that noted by Plot: trenches some 30 inches deep were lined with wood or pebbles, which were then covered with stiff clods of clay, loose earth, and turf.[37] Turf drains, which consisted of trenches covered with an arch of inverted turf, had also recently been introduced into Marshall's district by William Moore of Thorpe Constantine and had spread into Leicestershire.[38]

Meadow land not only provided rich grazing but also hay for winter feeding. In 1633 the demesne meadows at Trentham produced 95 loads,[39] and in the early 18th century Richard Pyott at Streethay was producing on average between 30 and 40 loads a year which he usually valued at £1 a load.[40] It was for Pyott's own use, though occasionally he sold or gave away loads. In time of scarcity it could fetch high prices: it was said that in April 1741, when fodder was very scarce, Mr. Hollinshed of Ashenhurst in Leek sold 200 tons of hay at £4 a ton within ten days.[41]

Although clover is not mentioned by Plot it may already have been grown in the county: Andrew Yarranton, a propagandist for the introduction of clover, promised in the early 1660s to arrange for supplies of seed for sale in twenty-nine west Midland towns, including Kinver, Dudley, Tamworth, Lichfield, Walsall, and Wolverhampton.[42] In the late 17th century Sir Simon Degge noted that 'they make a great improvement in this country by sowing clover, which they sow with their barley. It is of great benefit to them in the southern part of this country, where they are scarce of meadowing.' He himself had grown clover at Blythebridge in Kingstone.[43] It was being grown at Norbury in 1687 in large quantities. In January 1688/9 John Partington bought 249 lb.

[30] Plot, *Staffs.* 356–7. See also *Tours in Eng. and Wales by Arthur Young*, 271.
[31] Marshall, *Rural Econ.* ii. 53, 56.
[32] Ibid. 54.
[33] Ibid. 86.
[34] See pp. 97–9.
[35] Plot, *Staffs.* 356.
[36] That was apparently the method used at Weeford in the late 17th century: Plot, *Staffs.* 356.
[37] Marshall, *Rural Econ.* i. 139–41; ii. 220–8. See also Sanders, *Shenstone*, 331; Pitt, *Agric. Staffs.* 18–19.
[38] Marshall, *Rural Econ.* i. 141–2; T. Wright, *Formation and Management of Floated Meadows* (Northampton, 1808), 159, describing the turf drain and stating that 'an instance of this may be seen at Trentham Park, Staffs.'
[39] S.R.O., D.593/G/2/1/8.
[40] W.S.L., S.MS. 431.
[41] J. Sleigh, *Hist. of Leek* (1883 edn.), 108.
[42] A. Yarranton, *The Improvement improved, by a second edition of The Great Improvement of Lands by Clover* (1663), 44–6.
[43] Plot, *Staffs.* (copy in W.S.L. with Degge annotations), 353.

of clover seed.[44] Richard Pyott grew clover on his meadows for the first time in 1689,[45] and in 1693 Edward James was buying clover seed at 3*d.* a lb.[46] Clover was being grown on the Dyott estate at Freeford in the early 18th century; in 1709 seed was bought at 5*d.* a lb.[47] It was grown in increasing quantities at Leigh from the 1720s.[48] In the late 18th century a sowing of 10 lb. an acre of red clover was said to be usual.[49]

In the late 18th century William Tompson grew clover, rye-grass, and seeds at Abbots Bromley.[50] The Dyotts' bailiff was buying rye-grass seed in 1707,[51] and rye-grass was tithed at Leigh from the late 1720s.[52] Pitt's story that one of his uncles, still living in the 1790s, was the first to cultivate rye-grass in Staffordshire cannot therefore be accepted, though he was doubtless correct in saying that the demand for clover seed had increased a hundred-fold during the 18th century.[53] Another fodder crop to grow in popularity during that century was the turnip. Sir Simon Degge noted that the black soil of the north, manured with burnt turf, produced excellent turnips,[54] and turnips are mentioned in the Norbury accounts in 1694[55] and in Richard Pyott's accounts in 1719.[56] They were being grown at Fulfen in 1708,[57] and in small quantities, and not always successfully, at Leigh from the 1720s.[58] At the end of the period Lord Harrowby was experimenting with fattening his sheep and cattle at Sandon on turnips and was told that he could sell his crop at between £2 and £3 an acre.[59] The soils of the county were not, however, generally suited for their large-scale cultivation.[60]

The oldest breed of sheep known in the county was the black-nosed Moorland sheep, described by Plot.[61] It was a tough, coarse-woolled breed, well-suited to barren heaths and commons; at the end of the 18th century it was still found on the gritstones of the west Moorlands and on Cannock Chase.[62] The most important rule in sheep-farming was for the purchaser to buy stock for fattening from poorer soils than his own, and store sheep raised on the North Staffordshire hills would be sold to lowland farmers for finishing. In the 1560s Walter Barbour of Flashbrook in Adbaston bought 154 sheep at Newcastle-under-Lyme on the understanding that they were of a hardy breed, raised on hard soil. He found that they were in fact bred 'in a fruitful soil of Wales', and they deteriorated so much on the poor grazing of Flashbrook Heath that he had to sell his cattle and put the sheep in his best pasture.[63] A superior white-faced, polled variety of sheep was found on the limestones of the Moorlands; it produced good combing wool and was probably the most widespread breed in the county by the 18th century.[64] There was some experimenting in the later 18th century: Sir Edward Littleton at Teddesley was improving the Cannock Heath breed by crossing with Ross Ryeland rams, and Richard Dyott at Freeford was breeding New Leicesters.[65] At Thorpe Constantine William Moore, a disciple of Robert Bakewell, was one of the leading ram-breeders in the Midlands.[66]

Marshall describes how ewes were brought south from the hills of Shropshire, Staffordshire, and Derbyshire and, after they had reared their lambs and been fattened, were sold to the butchers or kept for another year for a further stock of lambs; the

[44] Univ. of Keele, Sneyd MS. S.1864.
[45] W.S.L., S.MS. 431.
[46] W.S.L., H.M. 27/2.
[47] S.R.O., D.661/21/2/2, f. 70v. See ibid. /21/3/1, for regular purchases of clover seed 1732–62.
[48] W.S.L. 94–97/31.
[49] Sandon Hall, Harrowby docs. 67, p. 34; 73, p. 1.
[50] *Jnl. Min. of Agric.* xlv. 1128.
[51] S.R.O., D.661/21/4/1/, f. 3.
[52] W.S.L. 95/31.
[53] Pitt, *Agric. Staffs.* 232.
[54] Plot, *Staffs.* (copy in W.S.L. with Degge annotations), 345.
[55] Univ. of Keele, Sneyd MS. S.1873, p. 346.

[56] W.S.L., S.MS. 431. See also W.S.L., M.512.
[57] S.R.O., D.661/21/4/1, f. 3. See ibid. /21/6/1, for purchases of seed 1762–72. See also Pitt, *Agric. Staffs.* 48.
[58] W.S.L. 98/31, e.g. Jas. Ashenhurst, 1727.
[59] Sandon Hall, Harrowby docs. 67, p. 9; 68, p. 11.
[60] See pp. 61–2 for introduction of turnip fallow.
[61] Plot, *Staffs.* 109, 257.
[62] J. Aikin, *Description of country from 30 to 40 miles round Manchester* (1795), 102; Pitt, *Agric. Staffs.* 136.
[63] *S.H.C.* N.S. ix. 93–4.
[64] Plot, *Staffs.* 257; Aikin, *Country round Manchester*, 102.
[65] Pitt, *Agric. Staffs.* 137, 142.
[66] Marshall, *Rural Econ.* i. 342.

lambs were driven into Worcestershire or the lowlands of Shropshire for fattening, with the dealers bringing back another supply of ewes from the Shropshire fairs.[67] On the Dyott estate in the 18th century wethers were sold early in the year and ewes and lambs were sold in the early autumn after shearing.[68] In the later 17th century the main sheep-markets in the county were apparently Newcastle-under-Lyme, Leek, and Uttoxeter in the north and Lichfield and Tamworth in the south.[69] In the 1670s and 1680s the bailiff at Trentham bought sheep at fairs at Newcastle, Stone, Stafford, and Albrighton, and travelled to Dovedale and into Derbyshire to find store sheep.[70] A few years later Edward James of Kinvaston was buying sheep at Cannock, Newport, Stone, and Eccleshall fairs.[71] In the later 18th century Lord Harrowby was obtaining sheep from Wales for fattening at Sandon.[72] Large numbers of sheep were then being sold at Tamworth and Fazeley fairs.[73]

Staffordshire sheep fattened on the rich river pastures were said to produce the sweetest mutton in England,[74] and they were also valued for their fine 'March' wool, surpassed in quality throughout the 16th and 17th centuries only by Herefordshire wool.[75] With the decline in quality of Cotswold wool in the later 16th and early 17th centuries much of the Staffordshire wool was bought by London dealers for West Country clothiers and later for the Essex clothiers, particularly those of Coggeshall and Dedham. A typical stapler of the later 16th century was Richard Baynes, who dealt almost entirely in the 'March' wool of Shropshire and Staffordshire.[76] Some of his dealings were with wealthy graziers, as in 1588 when he bought 600 stone of wool from a Wolverhampton dealer, Thomas Huntbache, who was acting for Sir Walter Leveson;[77] but most of his purchases were from small men and weighed less than 10 or 20 stone.[78] 'March' wool was not easy to collect: 'the parcelles be so smale where such wooles growe and aske so large tyme in gatheringe.'[79] In the later 17th century the short, fine wool went to Warwickshire and Gloucestershire and the longer, coarser wool to Lancashire and Yorkshire.[80] Marshall found that wool was bought by local dealers and sorted, some of it going to Leicestershire and Northamptonshire and the rest to more distant manufactories; in recent years Yorkshire manufacturers had been dealing directly with the growers.[81]

Sheep were kept all over the county. In areas where there was rich pasture and meadow they were subordinate to cattle and only a few were kept, especially with the rise of dairy farming. Where, however, there was abundant rough grazing on commons and heath there were large numbers of sheep. Flocks of between 300 and 600 were not uncommon on farms in the Moorlands in the 16th and early 17th centuries,[82] and large flocks were kept on the edge of forests and heaths. In the 1570s several flocks of 140 sheep or more were kept in Iverley Wood,[83] and in the early 17th century flocks of a similar size were being grazed in Cannock Chase.[84] At the end of the 16th century about 7,000 sheep were commoned there each winter, many in small flocks of 20 or less.[85] Even in the south-east of the county, where dairying was growing in importance, most farmers kept small flocks. Sheep are mentioned in 57 out of the 75 surviving probate inventories of yeoman farmers in the Alrewas area between 1558 and 1601, and although sheep were clearly less important there than cattle, the average flock numbered some

[67] Marshall, *Rural Econ.* i. 332–3. See S.R.O., D.661/21/5/4, f. 6v., note of 1746: 'Brierley had 8s. when he went with the sheep into Shropshire'.
[68] S.R.O., D.661/21/3/1.
[69] R. Blome, *Britannia* (1673), 204–5.
[70] S.R.O., D.593/F/2/18, 23, 25. [71] W.S.L., H.M. 27/2.
[72] Sandon Hall, Harrowby doc. 67, p. 33.
[73] Marshall, *Rural Econ.* ii. 21, 24–5.
[74] Blome, *Britannia*, 202.
[75] P. J. Bowden, *Wool Trade in Tudor and Stuart Eng.* 30.

[76] Ibid. 58, 64, 81. [77] Req. 2/175/19.
[78] Bowden, *Wool Trade in Tudor and Stuart Eng.* 81.
[79] Ibid. [80] Plot, *Staffs.* 258.
[81] Marshall, *Rural Econ.* i. 405.
[82] *Agrarian Hist. Eng. and Wales*, iv. 102 (citing evidence from probate inventories).
[83] E 134/18 Chas. I East./1.
[84] E 134/34 Chas. II Mich./10.
[85] Harrison, 'Cannock and Rugeley', 103–6 (based on S.R.O., D.(W.) 1734/2/1/264, ff. 8–13; /298, ff. 9–14).

20 sheep.[86] Probate inventories of the Lichfield district between 1568 and 1680 reveal a similar pattern. By the later 17th century some farmers around Lichfield kept only cattle. Where sheep are mentioned, however, the flocks are usually larger than those at Alrewas: in 1658 200 sheep belonging to John Quinton of Wall were valued at £36, and in 1670 Thomas Webb of Hammerwich had a flock valued at £42.[87] There were complaints that sheep-masters were abusing rights of common at Lichfield at the end of the 17th century,[88] and flocks in that area were apparently getting larger. At Street-hay in the early 18th century Richard Pyott kept a flock of some 50 sheep, which he usually valued at between £20 and £30, under half the valuation which he put on his cattle.[89] An important feature of agrarian history in some parts of the county before the Industrial Revolution was the combination of part-time agricultural work with other activities.[90] At Lichfield many tradesmen and professional men kept small flocks in the 16th and 17th centuries,[91] and the same thing happened at Stafford.[92] Around Sedgley in the 17th century farming was combined with metal-working: in 1649 a locksmith owned a flock of 39 sheep, and in 1688 an Ettingshall nailer had a quarter share in 18 sheep.[93]

The Trentham estate accounts and the accounts of Edward James of Kinvaston and of John Partington, the Skrymsher bailiff at Norbury, indicate the importance of sheep in central and western Staffordshire in the late 17th century. At Trentham 120 sheep were sheared in 1679, and in 1680 27 stone of wool was sold at 9s. a stone; in 1682 the demesne cattle on the estate were valued at £27 11s. 2d., while in 1682–3 the total value of cattle and sheep was £136 3s. 11d.[94] Between 1694 and 1710 Edward James's flock fluctuated in size. In 1699 he sheared 24 sheep and obtained 3 stone of wool; in 1703 he had a flock of 126 sheep and lambs, 83 of which he was grazing on Gailey Hay; in 1696 he sold the 4 stone of wool which he obtained from 40 sheep and 18 lambs at 11s. 6d. a stone.[95] John Partington maintained a flock of over 200 sheep at Norbury, and between 1687 and 1690 he recorded its movements. In May he sheared the feeding sheep and at the end of the month put out the lambs to wean; in early June he washed and sheared the rest of the sheep; in July he sheared the lambs; in October some of the flock was sold and replacements were bought in; from January to October the sheep were moved around between pastures and arable fields on the estate.[96]

In the 18th century the most detailed evidence on sheep-farming comes from a tithe book (1716–45) of the parish of Baswich and from the accounts of the Dyott estate at Freeford. Baswich, on the edge of Cannock Chase, was in a predominantly sheep-farming area. In 1716 the 40 tithe-payers of Brocton and Walton sheared 1,771 sheep and paid tithes on 477 lambs; there were three flocks of 100 or more sheep, eleven of between 50 and 100, eleven of between 25 and 50, and fifteen of between 9 and 25, figures which conform to the general Staffordshire pattern of relatively small-scale stock-farming. The largest flock in 1716 was that of William Cowper, who sheared 160 sheep; the size of Cowper's flock varied between 220 in 1724 and 80 in 1727. Cowper was later rivalled by J. Lycett, who began with a flock of 60 sheep in 1731 and built it up to 316 in 1735, the largest flock recorded in the tithe book. The vicar had difficulties with parishioners who moved their sheep from pasture to pasture, often to avoid paying tithes. In 1740 a Mr. Gnosal sent 40 of his sheep to Mavesyn

[86] S.R.O., D.783/5/2/2/1–75. The largest flock was that of John Gilbert, who died in 1591 and had 120 sheep: ibid. /67.
[87] S.H.C. 4th ser. v. 20–1.
[88] S.R.O., D.661/1/82.
[89] W.S.L., S.MS. 431.
[90] See pp. 82, 86. And see p. 117.
[91] S.H.C. 4th ser. v. 19.
[92] M. Rowlands, 'Houses and people in Stafford at the end of the 17th cent.' T.S.H.C.S. 1965–7, 49, 51, 54.
[93] J. S. Roper, 'Sedgley Probate Inventories, 1614–1787' (TS. in W.S.L.), 4, 85.
[94] S.R.O., D.593/F/2/18, 20, 27, 28.
[95] W.S.L., H.M. 27/2.
[96] Univ. of Keele, Sneyd MS. S.1597.

Ridware at Michaelmas, brought them to Walton for three weeks after Lady Day, and then sheared them just over the parish boundary.[97]

A large flock was kept on the Dyott estate at Freeford in the 18th century. By the 1790s the estate of some 800 a. specialized in sheep-breeding and there was a flock of 250 breeding ewes, fed on 70 a. of turnips and rearing 300 lambs. According to Pitt annual sales of sheep and wool averaged £650.[98] There are accounts, not always continuous, from 1732 to 1771 giving details of sheep sheared and sold, and profits from sales of wool. They are for a period when the estate was probably less specialized than it was in Pitt's day, and before the improvements and breeding experiments of Richard Dyott,[99] but they show that sheep-farming was the main activity on the estate. On average nearly 400 sheep were sheared each year and about £30 worth of wool sold at 10s. a stone; lamb's wool was sold separately at between 5d. and 7d. a pound. The largest profits probably came from the sale of fat sheep, for there were regular sales of wethers early in the year and of ewes and lambs in the autumn; between 1762 and 1772 an average of 103 sheep were being sold each year.[1]

In the 1620s Gervase Markham thought that the cattle bred in Staffordshire and Derbyshire were among the best in England,[2] and, according to Sir Simon Degge, 'both moorlands and woodlands produce as goodly cattle, large and fair spread, as Lancashire itself, and, the graziers say, will feed better'.[3] The main breed of cattle found in the county was the Staffordshire longhorn. These animals have been described as 'black-haired, with large white horns tipped with black, square stately bodies, and short legs . . . especially good for tallow, hide, and horn but also . . . good milkers and . . . strong in labour'.[4] In the late 18th century John Aikin considered the long-horned cattle found on the limestone hills of the Moorlands to be of a good size and form and superior to breeds found in the south of the county.[5] Marshall, on the other hand, found Staffordshire cows better adapted to grazing than to the dairy, but in general 'too light in their carcasses to be elegible, either as dairy or as grazing stock'; there was a better breed on the banks of the Trent which was probably a mixture of the Staffordshire and Derbyshire breeds.[6] At the end of the 18th century a gradual improvement was taking place in the breeds of cattle. At Blithfield Pitt saw 'a good many Scotch bullocks', as well as some fine oxen of Lord Bagot's own breed, and Richard Dyott of Freeford was buying heifers from John Princep, the experimental breeder at Croxall, just over the Derbyshire border.[7]

Before the growth of dairy-farming cattle were bred for the plough or the butcher. The county was celebrated for its fine oxen, which were bought by graziers from as far away as Buckinghamshire.[8] Store cattle were raised in the Moorland hills for fattening on the river pastures and the clay soils of central Staffordshire. As Plot pointed out: 'if amongst the mountains of the Moorlands, much more can they breed and feed cattle too in the rich meadows that adorn the banks of Trent, Blithe, Tene, Churnet, Hamps, and Manifold . . . and more especially still upon the famous Dove-bank, esteemed by many the best feeding land of England.' Needwood forest also provided rich pasture for fattening cattle.[9] In the 18th century the usual winter feed of cattle in the Burton area was supplemented by grain, fresh from the vats of the Burton breweries. It was said that this feed, costing 4d. a bushel, could fatten a lean cow

[97] W.S.L., S.MS. 429/iii.
[98] Pitt, *Agric. Staffs.* 142–3.
[99] See p. 71.
[1] S.R.O., D.661/21/3/1; /6/1.
[2] *Agrarian Hist. Eng. and Wales*, iv. 103.
[3] Erdeswick, *Staffs.* 3.
[4] *Agrarian Hist. Eng. and Wales*, iv. 186. For the product

of a fat ox in 1608 see S.R.O., D.260/M/F/1/5, f. 83.
[5] Aikin, *Country round Manchester*, 103.
[6] Marshall, *Rural Econ.* i. 290.
[7] Pitt, *Agric. Staffs.* 133–4.
[8] Joan Thirsk, 'Horn and Thorn in Staffs.: the economy of a pastoral county', *N.S.J.F.S.* ix. 6; Plot, *Staffs.* 107.
[9] Plot, *Staffs.* 107.

in four to six months.[10] Cows were always on the move on Staffordshire roads.[11] In 1530 Welsh drovers who were taking some 35 'oxen kine' belonging to Lord Ferrers from Wales to Chartley caused a riot when they pastured them overnight in the cornfields at Haywood.[12] In the 1560s Lord Stafford was obtaining cattle both from the Moorlands and from Wales.[13] Thomas Congreve of Stretton sold a yoke of fat oxen at Wolverhampton market in 1606, and in 1607 his son-in-law came from Powick (Worcs.) to buy store cattle at Newcastle fair.[14] In the 1630s cattle fed at Trentham were being sent on to Lilleshall (Salop.), and later in the 17th century the bailiff at Trentham was buying cattle at Middlewich (Ches.), Cheadle, Leek, Newcastle, Hilderstone, and Ashbourne (Derb.).[15] Around the turn of the century Edward James of Kinvaston bought or sold cattle at Stafford, Abbots Bromley, Rugeley, Eccleshall, Newcastle, and Brewood, and at Wellington and Albrighton (both Salop.).[16] In the later 17th century the main cattle markets in the north were at Newcastle, Leek, and Uttoxeter, and in the south at Wolverhampton and Tamworth.[17] By the 1780s there was a large fair at Fazeley where fat cows were purchased by butchers from Birmingham, Wolverhampton, and other manufacturing towns, and bulls were bought up 'chiefly for the collieries'.[18] In 1780 a Trentham farmer estimated his profit on cattle bought for fattening in May and sold before winter to be between £3 and £4 a beast.[19]

The importance of cattle in the county's agriculture can be seen in the efforts made by the county authorities in the late 1740s to prevent cattle-plague spreading into Staffordshire from the neighbouring counties to the east. An open letter to the farmers of Staffordshire in 1747 warned of the dangers of the plague's advancing across the barrier of the Trent: 'this and the counties beyond it to the west and north-west that supply the southern parts of the nation with young cattle must soon be great sufferers.'[20] During 1747 the bridges and fords across the Dove and Trent were guarded and inspectors appointed to prevent infected cattle being brought to Tamworth, Burton, and Fazeley fairs and markets.[21] By early 1748, however, the plague had reached the county, and at Easter the sale of cattle at Tamworth, Uttoxeter, Stafford, and Leek fairs was prohibited; in October Wolverhampton cattle market was closed, and that was followed by an order closing all cattle markets and fairs within the county.[22] Every effort was made, by the appointment of dozens of inspectors, to isolate outbreaks of the plague and prevent the sale of infected meat.[23] In March 1749 the constable of Pirehill South submitted a bill for his expenses in posting notices at infected places and his 'expenses, horse-hire and trouble for 6 weeks in going to inspect several infected places, such as Marston, Shallowford, Hardiwick, Stoke, and Stone, and to give orders as far as I could to prevent the distemper from spreading which I hope has had a good effect, particularly in Stone where the distemper was but in one place and is entirely ceased'.[24] Most areas in the county appear to have been infected, and compensation for the killing of distempered cattle was still being paid in 1751.[25]

Dairying for more than home consumption and local markets seems to have developed late in Staffordshire. It has been suggested that that might have been because of the

[10] Marshall, *Rural Econ.* i. 300–1.
[11] *N.S.J.F.S.* ix. 10.
[12] *S.H.C.* n.s. x(1), 104.
[13] W.S.L., M.561(ii), p. 7.
[14] S.R.O., D.1057, Congreve family and commonplace book 1585–1611, ff. 68, 79v.
[15] S.R.O., D.593/F/2/18, 19, 20, 25, 28; /G/2/1/8.
[16] W.S.L., H.M. 27/2.
[17] Blome, *Britannia*, 201, 205–6.
[18] Marshall, *Rural Econ.* ii. 21–2.
[19] Sandon Hall, Harrowby doc. 67, p. 27.
[20] *Letter to the Gentlemen, Farmers and Graziers in the*

County of Stafford; concerning the mortality or plague among the horned cattle (Birmingham, 1747; copy in W.S.L. Pamphs. *sub* Agriculture).
[21] S.R.O., Q/SO 14, ff. 216, 222, 230, 234v., 237; *Aris's Birmingham Gaz.* 25 May 1747. The churchwardens of Dilhorne bought 'a prayer for the cattle' in 1746–7: S.R.O., D.5/A/PC/2.
[22] S.R.O., Q/SM 1 and 2.
[23] S.R.O., Q/SO 14, ff. 241v., 252v., 255, 261, 264, 277; Q/SBe/17/13.
[24] S.R.O., Q/SBe/17/6.
[25] S.R.O., Q/SM 2.

satisfactory links already established with butchers and graziers.[26] At the beginning of the 17th century it was the butchers and curriers of Tutbury who opposed inclosure there.[27] Yet it has been argued that at the same period at Rolleston the rising cost of herbage in the Needwood parks led to the conversion of arable to pasture in order to support larger herds and the change to dairy specialization: 'the sure produce of their dairies, which now became their principal object, more than counterbalanced the risk attending the culture of their grain.'[28] Probate inventories show the emergence of dairying. Large numbers of cattle were kept in the Alrewas area in the later 16th century, but cheese or dairy equipment is mentioned in only four inventories between 1558 and 1601.[29] In and around Lichfield a century later many cows were kept and inventories mention cheese, butter, dairies, and dairying equipment.[30] John Smyth of Timore in St. Michael's, Lichfield, who died in 1675, had 24 cows and calves and possessed churns, sieves, cheese vats and presses, milk pans, and butter pots; he left 22 cheeses valued at £1.[31] Thomas Neale of Whittington, who died in 1667, had a herd of 15 cows and a dairy-house which contained equipment for separating cream from milk. There are many similar examples.[32] Inventories also show farmers in the Eccleshall area concentrating on dairy-farming in the later 17th century.[33] Cow-houses to provide shelter for dairy cattle survive in central Staffordshire apparently from the 17th century.[34] According to Plot the rich pastures and river meadows of the north-east were producing great quantities of butter and cheese in the late 17th century which were being bought at Uttoxeter market by the agents of London cheesemongers.[35] The butter was sold in marked pots supplied by the potters of Burslem and Stoke, and in 1675 men at Onecote, Alstonefield, Cheadle, Horton, and Norton-in-the-Moors were charged with selling butter in unmarked pots.[36] In the mid 18th century considerable amounts of Staffordshire cheese, hard-pressed and friable in texture, were being sent to London.[37] William Tompson of Abbots Bromley got together a small dairy herd of 12 to 15 cattle in 1786 and began making cheese. His cows produced on average $2\frac{1}{2}$ cwt. of cheese each which he sold for about 38s. a cwt.[38] Young, in 1768, recorded a slightly higher yield of 3 cwt. a cow for the area around Stone, but a lower price of 27s. a cwt.[39] An even better yield was achieved by Thomas Miller of Dunstall who, in Pitt's opinion, had the largest and best dairy in the county in the 1790s. In 1790 he kept about 70 milch-cows and produced some 12 tons of cheese (a yield of almost $3\frac{1}{2}$ cwt. a cow), which he sold for about 33s. a cwt.[40]

As with sheep-farming, the general impression is of a multitude of small producers and very few large herds. Around Alrewas in the later 16th century the average size of herd was about twelve.[41] Similar numbers were kept in the Lichfield area in the 17th century, though there the average covers gentlemen farmers who kept larger herds and small tradesmen who kept one or two animals for milk.[42] The same pattern is found around Sedgley, where some locksmiths and nailers kept as many as 7 or 10 cows.[43] At Trentham in 1679 there was an estate herd of 67 cattle, consisting of 3 fat oxen, 4 bulls, 13 stirks, 32 heifers, and 15 calves.[44] There were 75 cattle on the Skrymsher estate at

[26] Agrarian Hist. Eng. and Wales, iv. 103.
[27] D.L. 44/957.
[28] Sir Oswald Mosley, Hist. of Castle, Priory, and Town of Tutbury (1832), 163. And see above, p. 69.
[29] S.R.O., D.783/5/2/2/48, 63, 69, 72.
[30] S.H.C. 4th ser. v. 20–1.   [31] Ibid. 239–40.
[32] Ibid. 167–8. See also ibid. 81–5, 105–12, 125.
[33] P. and M. Spufford, Eccleshall (Keele, 1964), 30–1. For dairying at Madeley in the 17th century see Madeley, ed. J. Kennedy (Keele, 1970), 33–5.
[34] J. E. C. Peters, Development of Farm Buildings in Western Lowland Staffs. 131–2.

[35] Plot, Staffs. 108.
[36] Ibid.; S.R.O., Q/SR, Trans. 1675.
[37] V. Cheke, Story of Cheese-Making in Britain, 15, 115.
[38] Jnl. Min. of Agric. xlv. 1126.
[39] Young, Six Months' Tour through North of Eng. iii. 315.
[40] Pitt, Agric. Staffs. 134; Annals of Agric. xiv. 6, 10; xv. 266.
[41] S.R.O., D.783/5/2/2/1–75. See also Madeley, 33.
[42] S.H.C. 4th ser. v. 20–1.
[43] Roper, 'Sedgley Probate Inventories, 1614–1787', 4, 5, 31, 99, 102.
[44] S.R.O., D.593/F/2/19.

Norbury in 1689.[45] Richard Pyott kept a herd of between 9 and 19 cattle at Streethay in the early 18th century which he valued at between £35 and £60; in his valuations he sometimes distinguishes between feeding and milking cows.[46] Leigh in the 18th century was a parish of small farmers where cattle were the most important stock kept but where the herds seldom reached double figures; in 1717 the 100 or so tithe-payers shared just over 200 cows and their calves.[47] The Blurtons were one of the most substantial families of farmers in the parish and the size of their herd varied from 27 in 1738 to 46 in 1750.[48]

Horse-breeding and horse-dealing supplemented sheep- and cattle-farming, especially in central Staffordshire.[49] Such activity was an incidental part of mixed farming and was on a small scale. Mares were kept for work and were also used for breeding, the foals being sold as yearlings or broken in and sold as two- or three-year olds.[50] The probate inventories of small farmers in the late 16th and the 17th centuries frequently mention one or two mares and their colts or fillies.[51] Richard Pyott's stock of horses varied between 13, valued at £74, in 1713 and 5, valued at £40, in 1727; he was probably breeding and selling horses on a small scale.[52] Edward James of Kinvaston also bred horses, and he dealt in them at Penkridge, Stafford, Rugeley, Walsall, Eccleshall, Lichfield, and Albrighton fairs.[53] Penkridge was the most notable horse-fair in the county. Horses were being sold at Penkridge fair by 1522, and by 1598 they were the only merchandise.[54] Buyers came from the neighbouring counties and from Nottinghamshire and Yorkshire,[55] and in the 1720s Defoe described it as 'the greatest horse-fair in the world, for horses of value, and especially those we call saddle-horses'.[56] Transactions at other horse-fairs in the county were on a smaller scale: the tolls of Brewood and Eccleshall fairs in the 17th century show that the buyers and sellers came only short distances and usually bought, sold, or exchanged only one animal each.[57]

Pigs were also kept on a small scale, mainly for the larder, though larger numbers were kept in forest areas where they could be cheaply fattened.[58] Edward James bred pigs in a small way and sold or killed most of them in autumn.[59] Staffordshire was noted for its hygienic and economical system of pig-feeding;[60] Marshall saw a fattening sty at Fisherwick which had running water through it.[61]

Poultry were widely kept as a useful source of food; hens, ducks, and occasionally turkeys are found in inventories and accounts, and also geese where there was abundant commoning.[62] An Ettingshall locksmith who died in 1658 left 15 geese,[63] but at Alrewas in 1702 the commoners were limited to two old geese and one gander.[64] Many farmers kept bees, sometimes on a large scale: Anthony Ellison of Wall, who died in 1654, had nine stalls of bees in his garden, numerous old hives, and £1 worth of stalls leased out to other men, and Plot found John Whitehall of Pipe Ridware, 'a most intelligent bee-master', experimenting with hives.[65]

[45] Univ. of Keele, Sneyd MS. S.186/3.
[46] W.S.L., S.MS. 431.
[47] W.S.L., 93/31.
[48] Ibid. 95–97/31.
[49] Agrarian Hist. Eng. and Wales, iv. 105; D.L. 4/85/62.
[50] Spufford, Eccleshall, 32.
[51] S.R.O., D.783/5/2/2/1–75; S.H.C. 4th ser. v. 21–2.
[52] W.S.L., S.MS. 431.
[53] W.S.L., H.M. 27/2.
[54] V.C.H. Staffs. v. 129.
[55] B.L. Eg. MS. 3008, ff. 2–22.
[56] D. Defoe, Tour thro' the Whole Island of Gt. Brit. ed. G. D. H. Cole, ii. 477.
[57] S.R.O., D.590/435/1–3; Spufford, Eccleshall, 32.
[58] Agrarian Hist. Eng. and Wales, iv. 104; S.H.C. 4th ser.

v. 22; S.R.O., D.783/5/2/2/1–75; S.R.O., D.593/F/2/19; W.S.L., S.MS. 431; D.L. 42/109, f. 19v.
[59] W.S.L., H.M. 27/2.
[60] N.S.J.F.S. ix. 7. See S.R.O., D.260/M/F/1/5, ff. 4v., 7v., for a description of a palatial hen-house and swine-cote built at Reynolds Hall in Walsall in 1588.
[61] Marshall, Rural Econ. i. 330–1.
[62] L.J.R.O., inventory of Rob. Ryder (will proved 13 Apr. 1580); S.H.C. 4th ser. v. 22; S.R.O., D.783/5/2/2/ 1–75; W.S.L., H.M. 27/2.
[63] Roper, 'Sedgley Probate Inventories, 1614–1787', 28.
[64] S.R.O., D. (W.) 0/3/192, 26 Oct. 1702.
[65] S.H.C. 4th ser. v. 22; Plot, Staffs. 386. For further refs. to bee-keeping in Staffs. see Trans. Lichfield & S. Staffs. Arch. & Hist. Soc. iv. 51.

AGRARIAN ECONOMY AND SOCIETY

The period saw great changes in the size and distribution of estates within the county and in the social structure of landowning. The changing role of the landlord in the agricultural history of the county can be traced in developments in methods of estate management and in the introduction of new renting and leasing policies. Staffordshire remained a county where much farming was on a small scale, carried on by small tenant-farmers and, for the first half of the period at least, by part-time agriculturalists. Detailed evidence on many aspects of agrarian economy and society is lacking, especially for much of the 16th century, so that any generalizations on development during this period must necessarily be of a tentative nature.

1500–1640

Sir Simon Degge, in claiming in 1669 that the ownership of half the land in Staffordshire had changed during the preceding sixty years,[66] was probably exaggerating. Nonetheless the 16th and earlier 17th century saw considerable changes in the structure of landowning in the county. The Crown, as landowner, was not very important in the agrarian economy of the county. Its main estates were the forests, which were less valuable than they had been in the Middle Ages as a source of revenue, though efforts were made to increase the profits from sales of timber in the early 17th century.[67] Cannock and Kinver ceased to be of any importance as royal forests, and the keepers of the various hays came to treat their bailiwicks as normal landed estates.[68] Needwood forest was more important, and attempts by the Crown to 'improve' it by disafforestation and inclosure were vigorously resisted.[69] Leases of the Needwood parks, which contained valuable pasture, were used by the Crown as a source of reward and favour to officials and members of the local nobility and gentry.[70] The execution of the duke of Buckingham in 1521 removed a dominating aristocratic influence from the county, and a century later the estates of the Talbot earls of Shrewsbury were dismembered.[71]

The distribution of monastic lands among lay landowners caused a widespread change in the structure of landholding in the county. There was often a scramble to obtain desirable monastic sites and manors, especially those close to the estates of the prospective purchasers. In 1536 Sir Simon Harcourt asked Cromwell for Ranton priory, 'as it adjoins such small lands as I have in that country'; although Lord Stafford was also begging for the lease of it ('it is within four miles of my house and reaches my park pale'), it was Harcourt who was leased the site on the dissolution of the house.[72] Thomas Giffard of Stretton and Edward Littleton of Pillaton competed for Brewood priory; and in 1539 the site and certain pastures in Brewood, valued at £7 9s. 1d. a year, were sold to Giffard for £134 1s. 8d.[73] The lands of St. Thomas's priory near Stafford were acquired by Rowland Lee, bishop of Coventry and Lichfield, to provide for his Fowler nephews.[74] An attempt was made to secure Hulton abbey for the Audley family, but the site and neighbouring lands passed instead to Sir Edward Aston in 1543.[75] Sometimes monastic property was secured by newcomers to the county such as William Crompton, a London mercer, who bought the site of Stone priory.[76] Sometimes it was held for some years by Crown agents before being acquired by local men:

---

[66] See p. 50.
[67] V.C.H. Staffs. ii. 348, 352, 357.
[68] Ibid. 343, 348.
[69] See p. 53.
[70] V.C.H. Staffs. ii. 352–3, 355, 358.

[71] L. Stone, Crisis of the Aristocracy, 1558–1641, 253.
[72] V.C.H. Staffs. iii. 254.
[73] Ibid. 222.
[74] Ibid. 266.
[75] Ibid. 237.
[76] Ibid. 246.

Dieulacres was held for the Crown by Edward, earl of Derby, formerly steward of the abbey, until 1552 when the site and neighbouring property was granted to Sir Ralph Bagnall, son of a former mayor of Newcastle-under-Lyme.[77] Some monastic property in Staffordshire changed hands several times in the years after dissolution; Degge used the fact to buttress his argument that the malign influence of monastic lands was 'a worm' in the estates of Staffordshire gentry.[78]

Degge's biased account ignored the fact that monastic property was the basis of several new, substantial, and long-lasting estates. James Leveson of Wolverhampton, who had begun a policy of systematic land purchase in south Staffordshire from 1528, acquired between 1537 and 1540 more than 20,000 a. which had belonged to Trentham priory, Stone priory, and the Shropshire houses of Lilleshall and Wombridge; he and his family also bought or leased considerable property from Wolverhampton collegiate church.[79] In 1545 Sir William Sneyd bought the Hospitallers' manor of Keele from the Crown and made it the basis of a substantial estate in north-east Staffordshire; he purchased a further 15,000 a. from the Audley family between 1553 and 1561.[80] In 1611 the Sneyds also acquired the manor of Hulton from the Astons.[81] Another substantial Staffordshire estate, that of the Paget family, was acquired in the 1540s at the expense of the Church. In 1546 the bishop of Coventry and Lichfield was compelled to surrender a large block of property in central Staffordshire, including the manors of Haywood, Baswich, Longdon, Cannock, and Rugeley, to the king for the benefit of Sir William Paget; Paget also acquired Abbots Bromley and Burton from the estates of the dissolved college of Burton, and the manor of Farewell and the property of the chantry of St. Radegund from the dean and chapter of Lichfield cathedral.[82]

Degge bewailed the ruin of the old gentry and the coming of the new men who had risen from trade and the professions to claim gentility.[83] He relied heavily on malicious gossip for his accounts of social changes in the county and he exaggerated the speed of the changes, but he made his point. The legal profession provided several new county families, including the Skrymshers of Norbury, the Dyotts of Freeford, the Ansons of Shugborough, and the Littletons of Pillaton, while the fortunes of the Pyotts of Streethay, the Levesons of Wolverhampton, and the Sneyds of Keele were made in trade.[84] The rapid change in landownership resulted in a great increase in the number of claims to gentility made to the College of Arms; in 1583 200 families in Staffordshire were called at the visitation of heralds to prove their claims and 47 of the claims were rejected.[85] As well as those families which were new to the county and rose quickly to claim gentility, many yeoman families had prospered and were consolidating substantial estates. Often the line between gentlemen and yeomen was blurred and was determined by attitudes and way of life rather than by landed property. According to Degge, Thomas Scott of Great Barr was 'the owner of a pretty gentleman's estate, but may justly be accounted the prince of yeomanry', one of the tests of his yeoman status being that he was not ashamed to put his hand to the plough to encourage his servants.[86] Yeomen were probably distinguished by an active interest in farming as well as in the rent roll, but they could be as concerned as the gentry about the ancestry of their families. Robert Rider of West Bromwich, whose will was proved in 1580, expressed in it a wish that his son would retain his land 'in the name wherein it hath remained

[77] Ibid. 233–4; M. J. C. Fisher, *Dieulacres Abbey* (Leek, 1969), 58 (copy in W.S.L. Pamphs. *sub* Leek).
[78] Erdeswick, *Staffs.* pp. lvi–lvii.
[79] J. R. Wordie, 'A Great Landed Estate in the 18th Century: aspects of management on the Leveson-Gower properties, 1691–1833' (Reading Univ. Ph.D. thesis, 1967), 26; *V.C.H. Staffs.* iii. 325–8.
[80] *Agrarian Hist. Eng. and Wales*, iv. 342; *S.H.C.* xii(1),
213; xiii. 211–12.
[81] *V.C.H. Staffs.* viii. 249.
[82] Ibid. iii. 51–2, 166–7; *S.H.C.* 1937, 188.
[83] Erdeswick, *Staffs.* pp. lv–lix.
[84] Ibid. p. lviii; *V.C.H. Staffs.* iv. 157; *N.S.J.F.S.* ii. 15–16; Shaw, *Staffs.* i. 363.
[85] Stone, *Crisis of the Aristocracy*, 67.
[86] Shaw, *Staffs.* ii. 104.

many hundred years as by old and ancient deeds it doth and may appear'—unless he could get a good price for it.[87] Rider's son, Simon, kept a commonplace book, his 'Hypomnema', one of several family and commonplace books which have survived for the period, filled with details of family history, leases, legal procedures, evidences of landownership, and records of agricultural activities.[88] The new class of prosperous county gentlemen and yeomen built themselves substantial and comfortable houses, of which Haughton Hall and Woodroffe's at Marchington are good examples.[89]

Detailed evidence on estate management is lacking for the period but what evidence survives suggests that Staffordshire conformed to the national pattern. Aristocratic and ecclesiastical landlords appear to have been content to rely on traditional methods of management, notably the granting of long leases in return for high entry fines, and to have been little interested in demesne farming, except to supply their households.[90] The middle rank of landowners appear to have been more progressive and more concerned to obtain a share of rising agricultural profits by inclosing and encouraging inclosure[91] and by their leasing policies. The most numerous class of tenants held their land by copyhold tenure, and on the larger estates and under old-fashioned management, as on the Paget estate, copyhold of inheritance, with its security of tenure, fixed rents, heriots, and fines, survived.[92] Copyhold tenure caused many legal disputes, especially when land changed hands frequently and tenants attempted to claim that their holdings were freehold.[93] From at least the beginning of the 17th century there seems to have been a growing market in copyhold land, with copyholders leasing out their land;[94] at Sedgley in 1613 it was said to be the custom that copyholders could lease their holdings for up to three years without licence of the lord of the manor.[95] More progressive landlords were increasingly converting copyhold to leasehold and attempting to manipulate leases so that rents would keep pace with rising prices.[96] Detailed surveys were often a preliminary to increased rents. Monastic lands were surveyed while in royal hands: in 1542 the valuations of the royal surveyors were noted on a rental of the lands of Dieulacres abbey.[97] Sometimes surveys were made by new landlords anxious to discover the value of their acquisitions: the Paget estates were surveyed in 1549 and in the early 1570s.[98] In the later 16th century leases were usually for 21 years or for three lives.[99] Long, beneficial leases brought an initial high return to the landlord in entry fines but saddled him with low rents for long periods. In the late 16th and early 17th centuries many landlords attempted to change to a system of rack-renting, that is, short leases and full economic rents. A survey in 1599 of the estates of Sir Walter Leveson showed that his Staffordshire estates were leased for 21 years or three lives at uneconomic rents. The surveyor worked out the rack-rents for the property; Thomas Crompton, for example, held 200 a. at Hounds Cheadle for three lives at a rent of £5 13s., while the rack-rent was estimated at £21 18s. 4d. a year.[1] As leases on the Leveson estate fell in during the early 17th century rack-rents were introduced.[2] Beneficial leases were, however, generally preferred by tenants, in spite of high fines and the uncertainty of the duration of leases for lives. In 1608 the

---

[87] L.J.R.O., will of Rob. Ryder of West Bromwich, proved 13 Apr. 1580.

[88] W.S.L., S.MS. 336. See also e.g. S.R.O., D.1057, Congreve family and commonplace book; D.260/M/F/1/5 (Persehouse memoranda book).

[89] Agrarian Hist. Eng. and Wales, iv. 719, 738–9.

[90] See e.g. B.R.L. 347137 (acct. roll of receiver of Viscount Lisle, 1544–5); W.S.L., M.561(ii) (Lord Stafford's estate accts. 1562–4); V.C.H. Staffs. iii. 52–3, 166–7, 170–1.

[91] See pp. 51–5.

[92] S.H.C. 4th ser. vi. 96.

[93] See e.g. S.H.C. 1926, 78–9, 95.

[94] e.g. T.N.S.F.C. lxiii. 78–9.

[95] B.R.L. 337360.

[96] For a general discussion of this topic see Stone, Crisis of the Aristocracy, 307–22.

[97] W.S.L., M.540. See also B.L. Add. MS. 25297, ff. 3–16v. (survey of Norton-in-the-Moors in 1577 by Chris. Poyton).

[98] S.R.O., D.(W.) 1734/2/3/60–2, 112b; W.S.L., S.MS. 326/1. See also Burton Public Libr, Anglesey MS. 1944 (memo. of various matters of estate policy to be decided or investigated on Burton estates).

[99] See e.g. S.R.O., D.593/H/14/1/1.

[1] Ibid.

[2] Ibid. /G/2/1/22.

earl of Shrewsbury attempted to persuade his Staffordshire tenants to accept immediate rent increases in return for a promise of a reduction of fines in the future, but most refused outright. When the surveyor pointed out to them that they held their land on lease with fines of up to £80, they replied that they 'had rather smart one year than every year'.[3] In Staffordshire, as elsewhere, many rents doubled during the period, the biggest increases taking place between 1590 and the early 1620s. In some areas, however, there were significant variations.[4] The rentals of the Burton family of Coton and Fauld in Hanbury in the early 17th century reveal a vigorous market in meadows on the banks of the Dove, with very short leases resulting in large and frequent rent increases.[5] In the Cannock area rents remained stable, possibly because exploitation of the waste was proving more profitable.[6]

The social structure of Staffordshire at this period exhibits all the features of a predominantly pastoral economy.[7] It has been estimated from the 1666 Hearth Tax returns that 'well-to-do yeomen and gentry with houses of five or more hearths represented between 2½ and 6 per cent of the population in the county, depending on the district, whereas in Leicestershire these more substantial dwellings represented between 6 and 8 per cent of the total'.[8] Nor was the gentry class evenly distributed throughout the county. Over much of Staffordshire the population lived in small and scattered hamlets instead of compact villages containing a mixture of different classes. In the forest areas, in particular, many of the communities consisted entirely of poor and middling peasants.[9] The fact that, for the most part, the classes were not so intermixed or so economically dependent on each other as in arable areas, and that much agricultural activity was on a small scale and based on family labour, with plenty of opportunities for supplementing agricultural work, gives the agrarian history of the county its own peculiar character. The abundance of commoning and the part-time nature of much pastoral husbandry meant that an increasing population could be supported without the poverty and hardship found in the arable areas. There was a large class of husbandmen living comfortably on holdings of between 30 a. and 100 a. which, with common rights, provided grazing and fodder crops for small herds of cattle and flocks of sheep, with swine and poultry to supplement the family's diet. At Wetton the average size of holding was 38 a., such holdings were usually run by family labour, though one farm of 62 a. employed a farm labourer.[10] At Hounds Cheadle in 1599 there was the one holding of 200 a., while the other five holdings averaged 57 a.;[11] at Weston-under-Lizard in the mid 17th century one tenant held 112 a., and another twelve had average holdings of 50 a.[12] The prosperity of such small farmers depended on sufficient commoning: at Rolleston in the early 17th century one 'reeves thing' of 20 a. of arable land was insufficient to maintain a family without cheap pasturing.[13]

Some idea of the economics of small-scale animal husbandry can be obtained from probate inventories. Seventy-five inventories survive of the property of farmers in the Alrewas area, whose wills were proved between 1558 and 1601.[14] The testators ranged from William Whytting of Fradley who had a cow, a horse, and 8 sheep and whose property was valued at £5 9s. 10d., to John Gilbert, also of Fradley, who had 44 cattle, 120 sheep, and 8 horses and whose property was valued at £179 16s.[15] The average valuation of property was about £28; usually the value of stock made up over two-thirds of the total value of the estate, while on average tools of husbandry were valued at £1.

[3] Stone, *Crisis of the Aristocracy*, 316.
[4] *Agrarian Hist. Eng. and Wales*, iv. 292.
[5] B.L. Add. MS. 31917.
[6] Harrison, 'Cannock and Rugeley', 42–4.
[7] *N.S.J.F.S.* ix. 1–16.
[8] Ibid. 6.
[9] Ibid. 3, 4, 6.
[10] Johnson, 'NE. Staffs.' 107.
[11] S.R.O., D.593/H/14/1/1.
[12] *V.C.H. Staffs.* iv. 173.
[13] D.L. 44/930.
[14] S.R.O., D.783/5/2/2/1–75.
[15] Ibid. /67 and 75.

The wealthier husbandmen could supplement their income by hiring out stock to those who had common rights but few cattle or sheep. George Syncockes of West Bromwich, whose property was valued in 1577 at £71, had 21 cattle and over 50 sheep out on hire when he drew up his will.[16]

Frequent references to the building of cottages on the waste reveal the pressure of increasing population.[17] The forest areas, in particular, had to support numerous immigrants; William Humberston noted in 1559 how the cottagers were encroaching on the borders of Needwood.[18] Most of these cottagers had very small holdings of land, though cottage holdings of 11 a., or even 30 a., were found in Kinver forest.[19] The existence of poor cottagers was often the reason for the temporary cultivation of the waste: in the 1540s cottagers on the manor of Warslow were given permission to inclose and sow the waste around their cottages.[20] The inhabitants of the cottages were often farm labourers who, with the crofts around their cottages and with their common rights, could keep a few animals.[21] There were, however, also many opportunities for part-time, non-agricultural work to help support not only the poor cottagers but also the husbandmen and poorer yeomen. In the south there was the manufacture of small metal articles, especially nails and locks; in the north there was pottery and mining; and the forest areas provided opportunities for wood-working, tanning and the leather trades, iron-working, and alabaster digging. All could easily be combined with small-scale pastoral husbandry. There was a great demand for inns and ale-houses to accommodate the drovers passing through the county, and inn-keeping was another occupation which could be combined with farming.[22]

Little evidence survives about the wages and conditions of farm labourers who lived in. In the late 16th century John Persehouse of Reynolds Hall in Walsall paid yearly wages of 40s. to male farm labourers and 16s. to females; he also employed casual labour during harvest at 8d. a day.[23] At the same period Thomas Congreve, who lived first at Little Saredon and then at Stretton, employed a head servant in husbandry, a miller, and other farm servants. Between 1591 and 1606 he paid his millers 40s. to 46s. 8d. a year and his farm servants between 23s. 4d. and 50s. 8d. a year. In 1596 he hired William Newall as a husbandman: 'his wage must be yearly 40s. and a frieze coat this year—he demanded a blue coat but I did not grant it.'[24]

1640–1740

More detailed evidence on estate management and farming activities survives for the century which opened with the Civil War. The century was not, in general, an easy time for tenant-farmers. For landlords, 'improvement' still meant a larger rent-roll rather than the encouragement of better farming techniques by their tenants. Higher rents, more efficient estate management, and the acceleration of inclosure led to the failure of many small tenant-farmers whose holdings were amalgamated into larger farms.[25] In the mid 17th century small-scale farming could still be successfully combined with industrial and other activities, but increasingly from the end of that

[16] L.J.R.O., will and inventory of George Syncockes of West Bromwich (will proved 16 Dec. 1577).
[17] e.g. S.R.O., D.(W.) 1748/M.119 (Whitmore); W.S.L., S.MS. 326/1 (Longdon); B.L. Add. MS. 25297, ff. 5v.–6v. (Norton-in-the-Moors); D.L. 43/21/5A (Marchington).
[18] D.L. 42/109, f. 19.
[19] *Agrarian Hist. Eng. and Wales*, iv. 403.
[20] *S.H.C.* n.s. ix. 111–12.
[21] For a first-hand account of the summer-time routine in 1598 of a labourer with a small pasture croft at Walsall Wood see *S.H.C.* 1935, 163. See also *Agrarian Hist. Eng.*

and Wales, iv. 455, for a labourer hiring out his horse by the day at Sedgley.
[22] Marie B. Rowlands, *Masters and Men*, 2 sqq.; *N.S.J.F.S.* ix. 8–11; *S.H.C.* 4th ser. v. 18–21; *V.C.H. Staffs.* ii. 239–40; S.R.O., D.(W.) 1734/1/3/30.
[23] S.R.O., D.260/M/F/1/5, ff. 3v., 22.
[24] S.R.O., D.1057, Congreve family and commonplace book, ff. 9, 24, 35, 67, 72 and v., 92, 110.
[25] For a general discussion of the topic see G. E. Mingay, *Enclosure and the Small Farmer in the Age of the Industrial Revolution*, 31–2.

century industry was becoming a full-time occupation and the part-time agricultural-ists began to disappear. The mushrooming of cottages continued, but the cottagers were little more than squatters on the waste, an embarrassment to landlords and tenant-farmers and often listed as beggars in rentals. Nationally the period was a difficult one for agriculture; there were only short intervals of prosperity, in the last years of the 17th century and the late 1720s, separated by long stretches of acute depression before the beginnings of general recovery in the 1740s. Staffordshire farmers suffered during the years of low prices and heavy taxation: in 1690 George Plaxton found it difficult to collect rents at Trentham ('all the tenants plead poverty and deadness of markets'),[26] and in 1734 Lord Dartmouth's agent wrote from Sandwell: 'I never knew money so scarce amongst your lordship's tenants since I was concerned.'[27]

Changes in estate management and the upward rise in rents are well illustrated by the history of the Leveson (later Leveson-Gower) estates in North Staffordshire and Shropshire. After the racking-up of rents at the end of the 16th century there was a pause until the 1670s when a vigorous re-leasing policy began; in North Staffordshire, however, the new policy did not take effect until the 1680s since Dame Catherine Leveson had sold many 21-year leases in the early 1660s.[28] Heavy fines, usually equivalent to 20 years' rent, were taken in the 1680s on new leases for three lives, but this policy of granting long leases mortgaged the future and the estate suffered from slack management, shown in mounting arrears of rent.[29] In 1690 Plaxton reported to Sir John Leveson-Gower that some of the Trentham tenants had paid no rent for seven years, and wrote: 'I could make vast improvements upon some part of your estate if you would be at the charges.'[30] Plaxton[31] was the family's chief agent from 1691 to 1720 and imposed a system of estate management which was, in several ways, in advance of its time for efficiency. He attempted to modify the existing system of tenant-bailiffs by superimposing on it a structure of under-agents, each responsible for a major block of property. The under-agents were responsible for supervising the bailiffs, inspecting farms, and reporting to the chief agent on possible rent increases and improvements.[32] As leases fell in, Plaxton reversed previous leasing policies and let at will only. Rack-renting enhanced the importance of the agent since it required careful supervision. Plaxton's main object was to prevent dilapidations, with the result that leasing conditions, other than those relating to the maintenance of buildings, tended to be negative.[33] In 1718 a farm at Hill Chorlton in Eccleshall, which Plaxton noted as 'much impoverished by bad husbandry and ill-management by the former tenants', was let for £45 a year, the tenant paying all taxes, though the landlord under-took to build a new farm-house and repair all the old buildings in return for a £5 increase in the rent.[34] In 1710 the Trentham rent-collector accounted for £1,367 18s. in rent but estimated that the lands on lease were worth another £661 a year; he noted, however, that his estimates were based on observation and common acceptance rather than an exact survey.[35] A detailed survey by Thomas Burton was begun in 1713 and confirmed Plaxton's belief that the estates were under-rented. In 1716 he reported: 'Mr. Burton has almost finished the survey of Trentham manor and demesnes, much land set for nothing, for example Jo. Liversage has 87 acres of good land for £14 a year, and the rest like him in proportion at Blurton, Newstead and in Trentham.'[36]

[26] S.R.O., D.593/L/1/8.
[27] S.R.O., D.(W.) 1778/V/1210, Thos. Scott to Lord Dartmouth, 30 Jan. 1733/4.
[28] Wordie, 'Great Landed Estate', 38.
[29] Ibid. 40–1, 296–7.
[30] S.R.O., D.593/L/1/8.
[31] For biographical details see Wordie, 'Great Landed Estate', 50.

[32] Ibid. 54–5.
[33] Ibid. 57–60, 361–2, 365.
[34] S.R.O., D.593/H/14/1/4, f. 18.
[35] Ibid. /G/2/1/29.
[36] Ibid. /H/14/1/4 (enclosure, Geo. Plaxton to Lord Trentham, 16 Apr. 1716); J. R. Wordie, 'Social Change on the Leveson-Gower Estates, 1714–1832', Ec. H.R. 2nd ser. xxvii. 595–6.

Between 1720 and 1742 Plaxton's rack-renting policy was maintained, and under his successor, Thomas Tibbett, the Trentham agent became the controlling agent of the whole estate; in 1737 an estate agent's office was built in the grounds of Trentham Hall.[37] Rents continued to rise, but an increasing amount was spent by the landlord on repairs to farm property and in the 1730s Lord Gower encouraged the inclosure of Cocknage Banks and Blurton Common.[38] The upward movement of rents can be traced on one of the Trentham properties, an estate of 290 a. at Newstead in Trentham. In 1578 there were two holdings, each paying 15s. 10d. a year rent; in 1599 the holdings, described as each consisting of 20 beast-pastures, 8 days' math meadow, and arable land for 20 strikes of seed, paid rent of 31s. 8d. a year on leases for three lives. In 1691 one holding paid £10 a year rent under a surviving lease for lives and the other was divided between father and son, each paying an economic rent of £15 a year. By 1730 the rent of the second holding had risen to £46 a year; that of the first was still £10, but by 1747 it had advanced to £50 a year. In 1750 the holdings were amalgamated into one farm, paying a rent of £100 a year.[39]

Policies similar to those of Plaxton were being followed by William Sneyd on the family estates around Keele. Sneyd cleared the estate of debts incurred during the Civil War and restored the family fortunes by efficient estate management. In 1694 he defended himself against charges of meanness by explaining his methods:

I am censured by near relations to be covetous, though they cannot justly charge me to be immoderately penurious. I was desirous to live in a mean and to increase my estate for the benefit of my posterity by increasing my rents. When leases expired I would not renew but kept my tenants upon a reasonable and easy rack, allowing those that were ancient tenants above a third part of the yearly value of their livings, most of them holding for lives upon an old rent, so that I have much increased my rents, treble to what I found them.

He was also buying land to consolidate his estates: he paid usually 20 years' purchase on copyhold land and 10 years' purchase after one life and 8 years' purchase after two lives on leasehold land held for lives.[40] Other landlords were equally set on 'improving' their rents at this period. In the 1660s Walter Chetwynd of Ingestre estimated that land which had yielded £1,081 in rents at the time of his father's marriage in 1632 would yield nearly double that sum at improved rents; in 1669 he persuaded five of his tenants at Mitton to agree to an increase of their combined rents from £95 10s. a year to £129 a year.[41] On the Paget estates at the end of the 17th century long leases in return for high entry fines and small reserved rents were being abandoned in favour of a system of rack-renting, under which no entry fines were paid but the rents were 'full and improved'.[42]

A full survey was usually necessary to discover economic rents, and many Staffordshire estates were efficiently surveyed in the early 18th century. The surveyors were sometimes local men. In 1714 Henry Rathbone wrote from Lichfield to Lord Dartmouth's Sandwell agent:[43]

My lord did speak to me the other day to inquire out one to survey the estate and make a map of it. And I have spoken to one Mr. Matlock in our town who is a good surveyor and draws a map well. And if his lordship pleases he will do it for 4d. per acre and says if he does not give his lordship entire satisfaction, he will have nothing for doing it. He keeps a great writing-school and would be glad to take the opportunity of surveying the estate a week before and in the Christmas holidays.

The Giffard family estate in the west of the county, which totalled approximately

[37] Wordie, 'Great Landed Estate', 67–75.
[38] Ibid. 70–4; S.R.O., D.593/L/1/7.
[39] S.R.O., D.593/G/2/1/1 and 28–9; /G/2/2/8; /G/2/3/17, 21, 23; /G/2/5/1; /H/14/1/1.
[40] Univ. of Keele, Sneyd MS. S.1833.
[41] S.R.O., D.649/5.   [42] S.R.O., D.(W.) 1734/3/2/32.
[43] S.R.O., D.(W.) 1778/V/1209, Hen. Rathbone to Fra. Mauries, 15 Nov. 1714.

9,400 a. and had been built up mainly during the 16th and 17th centuries, was surveyed in the 1720s;[44] the result was that rents which totalled £2,039 in 1716 had risen to £2,310 by 1747.[45] On that estate 'forehand rents' were paid,[46] a practice whereby the tenant agreed to pay six months' rent in advance. It astonished Marshall, who found that it was still the practice at the end of the 18th century 'in the interior parts of Staffordshire'.[47] In 1724 a survey of the estates of the Bagot family of Blithfield, 6,742 a. in the east of the county, estimated the value of the rents at £2,907, which was £614 more than was actually being paid.[48]

Similar methods were being used by smaller landlords to increase their income from rents. Between 1591 when Richard Pyott, a London alderman, bought the manor of Streethay, and 1723, when his grandson, Richard, bought two closes of pasture, the Pyott family assembled a considerable estate (694 a. in 1632) at Streethay, Lichfield, and Curborough.[49] The lands were surveyed in 1632 and the rents valued at £574 a year or £658 'upon improvement'. The account book which Richard Pyott kept between 1688 and 1727 reveals a vigorous and varied leasing policy and considerable rent increases in the 1720s. Between 1688 and 1713 his income from rents varied between just over £400 and about £480 a year, depending on the amount of land that he kept in hand. In 1713 he settled £100 worth of lands on his son, the improved value of which he estimated in 1722 to be worth £140. The lands which he retained himself were bringing him £383 in rents in 1722, but he estimated them to be worth £515 on improvement. Apparently it was not easy to increase rents as much as he would have liked, since in 1726 his income from rents was only £402. In the same area the Dyott family owned lands at Freeford, Fulfen, Lichfield, Streethay, Whittington, and Elford; the leased portion of the estate brought in rents of £309 in 1678, rising to £405 in 1684.[50] The rise in rents continued on the estate during the early 18th century,[51] though, like Richard Pyott, Richard Dyott tended to over-estimate the value of his lands. In 1728 he held in hand 450 a. at Freeford, which had been rented at 7s. 3d. an acre; he estimated the land to be worth 14s. an acre, but by 1746 his valuation had dropped to 12s. 6d. an acre.[52]

In his leases Richard Dyott occasionally charged a higher rent for the first few years of the term and stipulated that the land was not to be ploughed during the last three years of the lease.[53] Attempts by landlords to dictate farming practices to their tenants by detailed leasing conditions were, however, rare as yet.[54] Tenants were usually made responsible for dues and taxes and for repairs to buildings and fences, and provision was often made for the payment of extra rent if pasture land was brought under the plough; occasionally tenants were encouraged to manure their land by being given permission to dig for marl or by being allowed a reduction in rent for the purchase of lime.[55] It is difficult to know how strictly leasing agreements were enforced. It seems that in practice satisfactory tenants had considerable security of tenure, and that, even in the absence of detailed farming covenants, they attempted to improve their land. In 1661 William Southall, a tenant of Lord Brooke at Penkridge, asked for a 21-year lease of some property, which he had been improving by inclosure and other means, at a rent no

[44] S.R.O., D.590/349; /614.
[45] Ibid. /600.
[46] Ibid. /614.
[47] Marshall, *Rural Econ.* i. 20.
[48] S.R.O., D.(W.) 1721/3/260, final pages.
[49] W.S.L., S.MS. 431. For the Pyott family see Shaw, *Staffs.* i. 363–4.
[50] S.R.O., D.1042/1. In 1646 the family's lands had been valued by a parl. cttee. at £250 a year: D.661/1/33.
[51] S.R.O., D.1042/1; D.661/21/3/1, f. 191.

[52] S.R.O., D.1042/1. For contrasting accounts of the demesne land at Freeford in the mid 17th and the late 18th centuries see Shaw, *Staffs.* i. 360.
[53] S.R.O., D.661/21/3/1, f. 154v.
[54] See W.S.L., S.D. 190/33, for unusually detailed leasing conditions for a farm at Ipstones in 1657.
[55] e.g. B.L. Add. Ch. 46568 (Cheadle, 1654); W.S.L. 26/6/1/22 (Adbaston, 1662–73); S.R.O., D.(W.) 1851/1/1/22 (Alrewas, 1700); S.R.O., D.(W.) 1788, P.17, B.2 (Aqualate, 1715).

higher than its value before improvement, since 'it is hard I should pay for improvement before I have made up my charge'.[56] Southall leased out his own land at Great Saredon by the year and stipulated that the tenant should leave no crops sown on the land and remove no dung at the end of the term.[57]

Some landlords were beginning to show more interest in the profits to be gained from demesne farming, though it was not until the mid 18th century that home farms began to be showpieces of advanced agricultural techniques. During the 17th century part of the manor of Trentham was farmed directly for the Leveson family by a bailiff who was also responsible for supervising the demesne tenants.[58] On the manor of Norbury, which according to a survey in 1668 contained 1,241 a., 734 a. was farmed for the Skrymsher family by bailiffs.[59] The 450 a. of the Dyott home farm at Freeford made an average annual profit of about £213 between 1732 and 1740 from the sale of stock, wool, and surplus grain.[60] Richard Pyott farmed part of his estate at Streethay; between 1707 and 1727 he had an average of 27 a. under cultivation, as well as pasture and meadow. He made yearly valuations of his stock and grain, and the total average valuation between those dates was £264, stock accounting for about 53 per cent of the total.[61]

The accounts of Edward James of Kinvaston between 1692 and 1710 illustrate the farming life of a substantial yeoman whose dealings in stock took him regularly to the markets and fairs in his district.[62] The activities of smaller tenant-farmers can be traced in the tithe books of Leigh; the parish contained very small farms and there is little evidence of the consolidation of holdings during the early 18th century.[63]

The combination of farming with other trades continued. In the south of the county it was easy for yeomen and husbandmen to engage in metal-working as a side-line. Probate inventories for the Sedgley area in the later 17th century still show men describing themselves indifferently as yeomen, husbandmen, nailers, or locksmiths, who left substantial amounts of stock and grain, often valued at between a quarter and a half of the total inventory, and also shop tools and supplies of metal.[64]

The inhabitants of the cottages which still continued to encroach on the wastes and forests[65] probably supplied much of the casual day-labour which is found recorded in many farming accounts of the period. At Trentham in the later 17th century men were paid 1s. a day for the corn harvest and 8d. a day for haymaking, ploughing, and hedging; women were paid 8d. a day for the corn harvest and 5d. a day for haymaking.[66] At Kinvaston Edward James used casual labourers, mainly women, for marling, hoeing, clodding, and weeding, and at harvest time. He also hired several farm servants by the year, paying them their wages quarterly: in 1708 he was employing three men at £3 10s. or £3 12s. a year and three women at £1 14s. or £1 16s. a year.[67]

1740–1793

These years were, in general, prosperous ones for farmers, with a rise in prices from 1750 which more than compensated for rising rents. As has been shown above,

[56] S.R.O., D.260/M/E/429/32. [57] Ibid. /15.
[58] S.R.O., D.593/F/2/18–31; /G/2/1/8–18. For a survey of the Trentham demesnes in 1704 see ibid. /H/14/1/4, ff. 5v.–6.
[59] Univ. of Keele, Sneyd MS. S.1597.
[60] S.R.O., D.661/21/3/1, ff. 122 sqq.
[61] W.S.L., S.MS. 431.
[62] W.S.L., H.M. 27/2. [63] W.S.L. 93–97/31.
[64] Roper, 'Sedgley Probate Inventories, 1614–1787'; V.C.H. Staffs. ii. 239–40.

[65] e.g. S.R.O., D.(W.) 1750 (Madeley Holme, 1655); W.S.L. 55/58/52 (Gnosall, 1669); E 134/34 Chas. II Mich./10 m. 9d. (Cannock Chase, 1683); S.R.O., D.(W.) 1721/3/256, p. 174 (Hanbury Park in Needwood forest, 1684); B.L. Add. MS. 36664, ff. 175–6 (Bradnop, 1687); S.R.O., D.593/G/2/1/30 (Trentham, 1715–16); B.R.L. 338952 (Great Barr, 1725).
[66] S.R.O., D.593/F/2/19 and 25.
[67] W.S.L., H.M. 27/2. See S.R.O., D.661/16/13, for an indenture of a husbandry apprentice, 1729.

they saw the beginnings of experiments in improving breeds of livestock and the spread of new techniques in arable farming. Landlords began to be interested in more than an 'improved' rental and attempted to improve the farming techniques of their tenants by more detailed farming covenants and by example. When building the Sandon home farm in 1783 Lord Harrowby visited various model dairies, including those of the duke of Chandos and Lord Hillsborough.[68] Sir Edward Littleton's experiments in sheep-breeding at Teddesley were copied by his tenants,[69] and in the north of the county, at Dilhorne, John Holliday, by his 'unwearied exertions and successful efforts in improving the face of a wide country', showed the advantages that could come from inclosing waste.[70] Marshall, when he went to live at Statfold in 1784, found 'the spirit of improvement' high, and he, like Pitt, believed that the most ardent improvers came from the class of owner-occupiers and large tenants.[71] According to Pitt there was 'not perhaps a more useful or respectable set of men in the county than the proprietors of 200 or 300 acres of land, who farm it themselves'.[72] Marshall found that Midland farmers were eager to acquire new ideas: 'a German prince is probably less respected, in the environs of his residence, than Mr. Princep is, in the neighbourhood of Croxall.'[73] Marshall and Pitt were, perhaps, sometimes over-optimistic about the progress of improvement, just as Young, with his disparaging remarks on crop rotations in the county, failed to appreciate the problems of farming on heavy soils. During these years, however, changes in estate management and farming practice were beginning, and enlightened landlords were attempting to create suitable conditions for improvement by their tenants.

The cost of acquiring estates rose. In the early 18th century land in Staffordshire was apparently never sold under 20 years' purchase.[74] In 1749 Admiral Anson offered 25 years' purchase for an estate at Knightley in Gnosall, even though the tenants were poor and rents had been twice increased during the previous forty years.[75] In 1769 an estate at Eccleshall was valued at between 30 and 40 years' purchase,[76] and in 1779 an estate of 1,392 a. at Throwley in Ilam, with rents and woodland valued at £921 a year, was offered for sale at 28 years' purchase.[77] According to Marshall 30 years' purchase, on a fair rental, was thought to be a good price.[78] In special circumstances land could change hands at a much higher price. Between 1749 and 1809 Sir Edward Littleton added 1,911 a. to the 6,524 a. he had inherited, accumulated around Penkridge by his family since the beginning of the 16th century. He consolidated his estate by buying out the smaller freeholders in Penkridge parish, and he had to pay an average of £27 an acre, more than the usual 25 to 30 years' purchase for leased property.[79]

Rents also began a steep upward rise. Marshall found that farm-land was rented at a maximum of 20s. an acre, whereas thirty or forty years previously the best quality inclosed land had fetched only 12s. to 15s. an acre. Around Tamworth rich ground suitable for market-gardening was let for as much as £3 to £4 an acre.[80] According to Young the average rent in the east of the county was 14s. an acre for arable and 20s. for grass, though good grass could reach 30s. an acre in dairying areas.[81] William Tompson took on Forge farm at Abbots Bromley in 1768. The farm, 168 a. of heavy clay, was let at £95 a year in 1768, a rent of 11s. 4d. an acre; in 1786 the rent was increased to £120 a year, or just over 14s. an acre.[82] Rents were also rising in the Moorlands, and it has

[68] Sandon Hall, Harrowby doc. 72, p. 12.
[69] Pitt, *Agric. Staffs.* 137.
[70] W.S.L., M.148.
[71] Marshall, *Rural Econ.* i. 82–3.
[72] Pitt, *Agric. Staffs.* 17.
[73] Marshall, *Rural Econ.* i. 15.
[74] S.R.O., D.(W.) 1778/V/1206.
[75] B.L. Add. MS. 15955, ff. 87–8.

[76] S.R.O., D.(W.) 1788, P.24, B.3.
[77] W.S.L. 120/40.
[78] Marshall, *Rural Econ.* i. 16.
[79] Sturgess, 'Agric. Staffs.' 202, 207–9.
[80] Marshall, *Rural Econ.* i. 17.
[81] Young, *Six Months' Tour through North of Eng.* iii. 315, 323–4.
[82] *Jnl. Min. of Agric.* xlv. 1125.

been estimated that on the Bill estates in the north-east of the county rents increased by almost 66 per cent between 1780 and 1815.[83] At Trentham the total of farm rents rose from £1,621 in 1730 to £2,019 in 1760, and by 1787 had reached £3,726.[84]

On the Giffard estate around Brewood the total of rents increased from £2,932 in 1758 to £4,806 in 1775.[85] The greatest increases began in 1770 after an extensive survey in the late 1760s,[86] probably by an efficient surveyor called Weston who also surveyed the Sneyd estates and other estates in the north of the county.[87] The survey valued Giffard properties at Chillington and Blackladies, both in Brewood, and High Onn in Church Eaton at an average of 10s. an acre, according to the nature of the soil and the efficiency of the tenant. One farm was valued at 12s. 10d. an acre: 'the tenant upon this farm has great merit in the management of his lands which in great measure occasions the difference of value that appears between his grounds and those adjoining to them.'[88] In some cases rents were nearly doubled as a result of the survey and the increases were put into effect in stages over the next few years. Most tenants were prepared to accept the increases, though several submitted claims for allowances for improvements.[89] The smaller tenants were the most affected, and it was noted that one, whose rent was to be increased from £14 to £26, 'complains of being in a bad state of health, is 66, and hopes Mr. Giffard will not raise the rent during her life'.[90] At Chillington the average size of farm in 1770 was 145 a.; of the 19 tenants, 4 held farms of over 200 a., 8 farms of between 100 a. and 200 a., and 7 farms of less than 100 a.[91] Small farms were becoming uneconomic and the surveyor wrote of one: 'farms like this under 60 acres will not bear the same proportion of value being placed upon them as a large one, unless occupied by people in trade, the articles of housekeeping upon these small premises being nearly as expensive as upon a farm of double their consequence.'[92]

There were constant changes in the size of farms on the Giffard estates in the 1760s; holdings were amalgamated or divided, and by 1763 a new farm at Enson Moor in Marston had been created from portions of each of the old farms.[93] In general it seems that farms throughout the county were being consolidated.[94] The more substantial tenants held larger acreages, and although many smallholdings survived, probably still in many cases in the hands of part-time farmers, small farmers were finding it difficult to manage on farms of under 100 a.[95] On the Leveson-Gower estates the number of farms of over 200 a. increased, and, whereas in 1720 the average size of the larger farms was 80 a., by 1760 it was over 100 a.[96] The New House farm at Pendeford, which Pitt leased from 1780 to 1804, was some 230 a.[97] In 1790 Thomas Miller's leasehold farm at Dunstall was even larger, some 700 a.[98]

By the end of the 18th century there was still a great variety of leasing practices in the county. Young found leases for terms from 7 to 21 years as well as for 2 and 3 lives.[99] Leases for lives were beginning to disappear and be replaced by shorter terms or annual agreements; where farms were difficult to let, however, landlords might still grant a long lease.[1] Tenants sometimes demanded a long lease, especially when

[83] N.S.J.F.S. i. 81–2.
[84] Wordie, 'Great Landed Estate', 260, 265, 274.
[85] S.R.O., D.590/601.
[86] Ibid. /352 and 806–8.
[87] Univ. of Keele, Sneyd MS. S.1634; W.S.L. 120–122/40.
[88] S.R.O., D.590/352; /806, p. 8.
[89] Ibid. /352; /810/4 and 11.
[90] Ibid. /810/4.
[91] Ibid. /352.
[92] Ibid. /806, p. 7.
[93] Ibid. /601.
[94] See G. E. Mingay, 'The size of farms in the 18th

cent.' Ec. H.R. 2nd ser. xiv. 481–2, for figures for Bagot and Giffard estates 1722–68.
[95] In the south of the county many small farmers were supplementing their income by engaging in carrying trades: Aris's Birmingham Gaz. 9 Dec. 1754.
[96] Ec. H.R. 2nd ser. xxvii. 596–7; Pitt, Agric. Staffs. 23. See also V.C.H. Staffs. iv. 173 (Weston-under-Lizard); S.R.O., D.(W.) 1788, P.17, B.5 (Forton and Chetwynd); W.S.L. 120/40 (Throwley).
[97] Annals of Agric. xlii. 204–9.
[98] Ibid. xiv. 5.
[99] Young, Six Months' Tour through North of Eng. iii. 317.
[1] N.S.J.F.S. i. 81.

they intended to make expensive improvements,[2] though many landlords were willing to make allowances for improvements when revaluing farms.[3] In 1776 a tenant of Sir Edward Littleton was allowed a rent reduction of £42 for building at his own expense a cow-house, wagon-house, granary, brew-house, and pigsties.[4] Long leases were generally regarded as an obstacle to improvement and the more progressive landlords preferred to let at will. In 1779 it was said of an estate at Grindon: 'the leases will burden the purchaser with many inconveniences, particularly as the present mode of occupation is, in general, exceeding bad and while those leases continue no improvement in husbandry, draining, etc. can be set about.'[5] At Trentham George Plaxton's policy of letting at will was continued during the 18th century,[6] and at Teddesley Sir Edward Littleton put his farms at will as soon as leases fell in.[7]

Concern for the condition of leased land was shown in the terms of leases and tenancy agreements.[8] In 1775 Earl Gower agreed to pay £200 towards the cost of a new farm-house on New Park farm in Trentham, and in 1782 he agreed to let Toft farm in Trentham on the understanding that the tenant would make improvements and would be compensated if he gave up the tenancy before he had 'reaped a reasonable benefit' from his improvements.[9] Tenancy agreements were still mainly negative, concerned to prevent excessive ploughing, removal of dung, or the growth of impoverishing crops;[10] some, however, were beginning to approach the later cropping covenants, and surveyors occasionally recommended the imposition of different crop rotations.[11] In the north the Bill family was experimenting with leasing covenants in the 1780s and 1790s,[12] and at Teddesley Sir Edward Littleton was exerting increasing control over cropping after 1770 by means of tenancy agreements.[13] On the Dartmouth estate at Sandwell, however, the imposition of a four-course rotation by covenant was delayed until the end of the century because of opposition from the tenants.[14]

There is a little evidence on farm profits, apart from the generalized information given by Young and Pitt.[15] On the Trentham home farm sales of estate produce rose from £338 in 1760 to £417 in 1787.[16] In 1790 Thomas Miller estimated that his 700-a. tenant-farm at Dunstall brought him an annual net profit of some £110.[17] The profits to be gained by a medium-sized tenant-farmer can be traced in William Tompson's accounts for his 168-a. Forge farm, Abbots Bromley, between 1768 and 1815. In the mid 1770s, when he was unmarried and living with his brother on the neighbouring Town farm, Tompson was making an average annual profit of £90 from Forge farm; in the early 1790s, when he was living there and his rent had been increased from £95 to £120 a year, his profit was nearly £60 a year.[18]

Apart from his rent, William Tompson's largest item of expenditure was wages; labour cost him between £90 and £95 a year. He employed several types of labour: living-in farm servants, regular day-labourers, cottage labourers, and seasonal casual workers.[19] Marshall gave the wages of farm servants as £7 or £8 a year for a man and 3 guineas for a woman.[20] His figures are supported by the wages paid in 1790 by Thomas Miller, who employed 11 living-in farm servants. The 3 men were paid £8 a year each, the 4 boys and the 4 maids £3 each; Miller estimated that their board cost him a further

[2] S.R.O., D.590/806, pp. 7, 8.
[3] Sturgess, 'Agric. Staffs.' 213; S.R.O., D.593/L/1/8 and 18.
[4] Sturgess, 'Agric. Staffs.' 213.
[5] W.S.L. 121/40.
[6] Wordie, 'Great Landed Estate', 82.
[7] Sturgess, 'Agric. Staffs.' 212–13.
[8] Ibid. 217; Wordie, 'Great Landed Estate', 387.
[9] S.R.O., D.593/L/1/8 and 18.
[10] e.g. S.R.O., D.590/487–8 and 508; D.564/3/2/12;

B.R.L. 277055; V.C.H. Staffs. v. 95.
[11] Univ. of Keele, Sneyd MS. S.1634.
[12] S.R.O., D.554/51, 59, 91a.
[13] Sturgess, 'Agric. Staffs.' 214–15.   [14] Ibid. 324.
[15] Young, Six Months' Tour through North of Eng. iii. 316–20, 327–31; Pitt, Agric. Staffs. 33–5.
[16] Wordie, 'Great Landed Estate', 265, 274.
[17] Annals of Agric. xv. 269–70, correcting ibid. xiv. 7–11.
[18] Jnl. Min. of Agric. xlv. 1132.   [19] Ibid. 1129–32.
[20] Marshall, Rural Econ. i. 97–8.

£60 a year (£12 for each man and £6 for each boy or maid).[21] Regular day-labourers were usually paid 1s. a day during the period, with an allowance for beer. In 1778 Tompson hired a labourer for a year at 1s. a day, with an allowance of 1d. a day in winter and 2d. a day in summer for beer.[22] William Moore of Thorpe Constantine filled a gallon bottle with beer for each of his workmen every day of the year.[23] Marshall could not understand how a farm labourer could support a large family on a wage of no more than 7s. a week. 'Old George Barwell, who has brought up five or six sons and daughters', enlightened him: 'He has frequently been "hard put to it." He has some-times barely had *bread* for his children: not a morsel for himself! having often made a dinner off *raw hog peas*: saying, that he has taken a handful of peas, and ate them with as much satisfaction as, in general, he has eaten better dinners . . . closing his remarks with the trite maxim—breathed out with an involuntary sigh—"Ay, no man knows what he can do, till he's put to it." '[24] Cottagers with some land and a few animals were better off; Tompson kept accounts with several cottagers in which payments for labour were set against charges for rent, agistment of cattle, wheat, and beans.[25] Much farm work was seasonal, and casual labour, including women and children, was employed by the day, or, during harvest, at piece-rates.[26] In the early 1780s Pitt paid the women who pulled and trimmed his turnips 2½d. a cartload.[27] Some labour was supplied by itinerant farm workers from the Moorlands, where dairying and the rearing of store sheep and cattle left workers free to move south for the corn harvest. As Marshall noted, 'the wheat is much of it cut by itinerants, who are termed "peakrils" and "low country men", namely men, and some women, from the Peak of Derbyshire, and the Moorlands of Staffordshire.'[28]

[21] *Annals of Agric.* xv. 269.
[22] *Jnl. Min. of Agric.* xlv. 1129.
[23] Marshall, *Rural Econ.* ii. 45.
[24] Ibid. 197.   [25] *Jnl. Min. of Agric.* xlv. 1131.
[26] Ibid. 1129–30; Marshall, *Rural Econ.* i. 165–7; Sandon Hall, Harrowby docs. 67, pp. 30, 47; 72, p. 34.
[27] W. Pitt, 'On Storing Turnips', *Annals of Agric.* iii. 132.
[28] Marshall, *Rural Econ.* i. 165.

AGRICULTURE 1793 TO 1875

Improvers and Improvement, p. 93. Arable Farming, p. 102. Grassland Management, p. 109. Stock-farming, p. 110. Agrarian Economy and Society, p. 115.

IN Staffordshire as in the rest of England this period saw great fluctuations in the fortunes of agriculture.[1] Between 1793 and 1815 the rising prices caused by the French wars produced a phase of relative prosperity for farmers and landlords, with increased receipts and higher rents. From *c.* 1816 to the middle of the century, however, prices tended to fall. The resultant difficulties for agriculture were nevertheless variable in their effects on different parts of the county. Since its produce was already diverse and there were ready markets in the industrial towns, Staffordshire was perhaps less hard hit than other counties. The county's freeholders petitioned parliament in 1816 to reduce taxation and public expenditure, and there were three further petitions in 1820 and one in 1821, the worst years of the depression; but many more petitions were received from other areas.[2] From 1851 onwards Staffordshire shared in the general recovery with the advent of high farming.

During the period farming in Staffordshire became steadily less self-contained. Canals and railways improved marketing opportunities and enabled feed and fertilizers to be imported from elsewhere. Many local landlords had industrial and urban property which provided capital for agriculture. The growth of brick- and tile-making in the Potteries and in south Staffordshire made better and cheaper materials available for buildings and drainage, while the manufacture of agricultural machinery developed round Wolverhampton,[3] replacing the making of tools on the farm or by the local blacksmith.

During the depression after 1815 corn prices fell further than those of livestock and livestock products, and from the 1850s the differential between grain and livestock prices widened.[4] Hence farmers had a strong incentive to shift from grain sales to livestock production and to convert arable, especially of poor quality, to permanent grass. The desirability of conversion to pasture had been recognized by land-agents as early as the 1790s and they continued to advocate it.[5] By the late 1860s pasture land in north Staffordshire was worth 60 per cent more than it would have been as arable.[6] Early in the period, however, most of the county was still under the plough; William Pitt estimated that 600,000 a. was cultivated, of which 500,000 a. was arable, though much of that was rotation grass.[7] There were, however, already marked regional variations in the proportion of land in arable and in pasture. The Moorlands were predominantly under grass: thus in 1805 72 per cent of Rushton James township in Leek,

[1] In this article extensive use has been made of material collected by the late J. G. Jenkins. Thanks are offered to Professor F. M. L. Thompson for reading and commenting on the article in draft.

[2] *C.J.* lxxi. 265; *Rep. Cttee. on Agric.* H.C. 236, pp. 1–2 (1822), v; *Rep. Sel. Cttee. on Agric.* H.C. 612, pp. 521–33 (1833), v.

[3] *V.C.H. Staffs.* ii. 144–5.

[4] Sturgess, 'Agric. Staffs.' 62–4.

[5] J. R. Wordie, 'A Great Landed Estate in the Eighteenth Century: aspects of management on the Leveson-Gower properties, 1691–1833' (Reading Univ. Ph.D. thesis, 1967), 408–9; S.R.O., D.603 (unlisted), Hodson corresp., CE 421, Hodson to Sanderson, 29 Feb., 22 Apr. 1816; S.R.O., D.641/5/E(C)/21, 27 Aug. 1834; [R. S. Ford], *How is the Farmer to Live?* (Stone, 1846), 3 (copy in D.641/5/E(C)/27); *Staffs. Advertiser*, 13 Jan. 1844.

[6] H. Evershed, 'The Agriculture of Staffs.' *J.R.A.S.E.* 2nd ser. v. 269.

[7] W. Pitt, *General View of Agric. of County of Stafford* (1796 edn.), 11, 162. The 1796 edn. has been used in this article unless otherwise stated.

and 80 per cent of Horton Hay, were pasture and meadow.[8] Elsewhere in north Staffordshire half the farmland was often in permanent grass.[9] If Pitt's figures are to be believed, the south of the county was overwhelmingly arable.

Probably before the end of the French wars, however, Lord Bradford's conditions for letting farms provided for the compulsory laying down of land to pasture.[10] After the wars such a clause was frequently included in agreements and leases on other estates.[11] It was not always effective; on the Fitzherbert family's estate at Swynnerton, for instance, most farms seem still to have been 60 to 80 per cent arable in the 1830s and 1840s, and in some cases the farmer apparently ignored the requirement to lay down land to grass.[12] It was often in his short-term interest to carry on growing corn.[13] Nevertheless by c. 1840 grassland exceeded arable in most of north Staffordshire and roughly equalled it in much of the rest; only in the south-west, in parts of the area west of Stafford, and round Tamworth was more than 60 per cent of farm-land regularly arable.[14] Yet in 1850 it was thought that more than half the county's cultivated land was under the plough.[15] Conversion to pasture continued more rapidly in the 1850s and 1860s, especially in the north, where landlords took a more active interest in the process.[16] By 1875 367,013 a. (62 per cent of the cultivated area of the county) was under permanent grass; of this, 274,060 a. (46 per cent of the cultivated area) was pasture.[17]

By 1875 inclosure had been virtually completed. Most open fields had been inclosed by 1793; the rest, of which the last to be inclosed were at Warslow and Lower Elkstone in Alstonefield in 1839, were mainly relics covering small areas.[18] More important was the inclosure of pasture and waste. Pitt estimated that 30,000 a. was inclosed between 1794 and 1817;[19] the most important single inclosure was that of Needwood forest from 1805.[20] Between 1795 and 1841 there were 39 private inclosure Acts for commons, and between 1848 and 1870 10 further awards under the general inclosure Acts,[21] besides private inclosures without Act.[22] Much of Cannock Chase was inclosed, in the earlier 19th century by E. J. Littleton (later Lord Hatherton) and in the 1860s by the 2nd marquess of Anglesey.[23]

Marketing opportunities greatly improved. In the 1790s there were 24 towns with weekly markets, but those at Cannock and Betley were in abeyance and those at Rugeley, Tutbury, Abbots Bromley, and Brewood were unimportant; others, especially Wolverhampton, attracted a wide range of agricultural produce. Most of the towns had fairs, and there were other fairs in small places.[24] In 1810 there were apparently 95 fairs in 29 places,[25] and in 1818 127 fairs at 35 places, many being noted for cattle.[26] By 1848 there were monthly or fortnightly cattle markets at Lichfield, Uttoxeter, Burton, Stone, and Hanley, and 156 fairs at 43 towns and villages, some held once or twice a year, others, like those at Fazeley, held monthly.[27] Several had come to special-

[8] S.R.O., D.(W.) 1761, box 1, valuation of Horton Hay estate 1805; box 8, valuation of Rushton James and New Town.
[9] Sturgess, 'Agric. Staffs.' 367.
[10] S.R.O., D.1287/2/1, conditions for letting estates of Rt. Hon. Orlando Lord Bradford in Staffs. and Salop.
[11] S.R.O., D.641/5/E(L)/3 and 4; D.952/2/2/3; D.1213/4; D.(W.) 1781, bdle. K, 'Wolseley estate 1826' (recte 1825).
[12] S.R.O., D.641/5/E(L)/3 and 4.
[13] S.R.O., D.603 (unlisted), Hodson corresp., CE 421, Hodson to Sanderson, 29 Feb. 1816.
[14] A. D. M. Phillips, 'A Study of Farming Practices and Soil Types in Staffs. around 1840', N.S.J.F.S. xiii. 39.
[15] J. Caird, Eng. Agric. in 1850-1 (1852 edn.), 229.
[16] Sturgess, 'Agric. Staffs.' 381-2.
[17] Myers, Staffs. 637.

[18] S.H.C. 1931, 93-6; 1941, 15; S.R.O., Q/RDc 24.
[19] Pitt, Staffs. pt. ii. 20.
[20] S.H.C. 1941, 17.   [21] Ibid. 18-19.
[22] e.g. W.S.L. 11/313/50; S.R.O., D.641/5/E(L)/4, 4 July 1800; /E(C)/30, 30 May 1851.
[23] Sturgess, 'Agric. Staffs.' 230-1; J.R.A.S.E. 2nd ser. v. 294, 302.
[24] Pitt, Agric. Staffs. 2-3, 166.
[25] F. W. Hackwood, Staffs. Customs, Superstitions, and Folklore (Lichfield, 1924), 98-9, confusing Holy Cross in Clent (Worcs., formerly Staffs.) with Hoar Cross in Yoxall.
[26] Parson and Bradshaw, Dir. Staffs. (1818), pt. i, pp. ccxxxvii-ccxxxix.
[27] Staffs. Almanack for 1848 (Stafford, n.d. but 1847), 32-3, including Holy Cross (by then in Worcs. and therefore excluded from totals here).

ize in cheese.[28] Also notable was Rugeley great horse fair, held in May and June, the chief horse fair in the kingdom; many horses were bought for export.[29] In the earlier 19th century Walsall market was a noted centre of the pig trade.[30] The railways probably provided increasing opportunities for sales outside the county, but by the mid 1840s they had caused a lowering of prices for local grain and meat, which had formerly been dearer than elsewhere owing to the county's inland position.[31]

IMPROVERS AND IMPROVEMENT

Characteristic of the period was a growing interest in more scientific farming and the dissemination of new ideas and methods. In the late 18th century the most prominent improvers were prosperous tenants and yeoman owner-occupiers, whose capital, education, and opportunities for travel encouraged them to take an interest in new methods and to experiment.[32] During the French wars, however, agriculture became fashionable among large landowners. By 1817 several of the local nobility and gentry, including Earl Talbot at Ingestre, the earl of Bradford at Weston-under-Lizard, Lord Anson (son-in-law of Coke of Holkham) at Shugborough, Sir John Wrottesley at Wrottesley, Sir George Pigot at Patshull, Sir Robert Lawley at Canwell, Sir John Fletcher Boughey at Aqualate in Forton, and George Tollet at Betley, had established model home farms on which up-to-date husbandry was practised and new breeds were tried.[33] Such interest persisted; Lord Talbot (d. 1849) continued to be noted for his enthusiasm for farming, as was the 1st Lord Hatherton (d. 1863).[34] A writer in 1851 ascribed the improvements in agriculture to the large landowners, whose estates were 'a sort of school'.[35] By the 1860s it could be said that 'perhaps nowhere in England have the example and patronage of the great proprietors had a greater and more beneficial influence on agriculture than in the case of the great Staffordshire landowners'.[36] Improvements begun on home farms were disseminated among the tenants by means of leasing covenants and allowances; sometimes tenants were obliged to spend a minimum proportion of the rental on improvements.[37] The landlords' agents supervised the details of tenant farming more closely.

The period saw the rise of professional land-agents, of whom the economist James Loch, general agent 1812–55 to the Leveson-Gowers, was perhaps the most distinguished.[38] John Bright, the steward of E. J. Littleton (later Lord Hatherton) 1831–59, was noted as an inventor of farm machinery.[39] The agents were from varied backgrounds. Loch had been a lawyer; R. S. Ford, agent to Thomas Fitzherbert of Swynnerton 1828–50, had been an exemplary farmer on the Leveson-Gowers' Trentham estate;[40] John Aylmer, one of the Pagets' most energetic agents in the early 19th century, was an admiral on the active list.[41] On the other hand Harvey Wyatt, agent to the Ansons from 1827 to c. 1869, was the son of his predecessor, himself a surveyor, and had received a professional training under Coke of Holkham's steward Francis Blaikie.[42] Several agents acted for more than one landowner and thus helped to diffuse ideas and

[28] See p. 113.
[29] *Staffs. Advertiser*, 25 May 1844.
[30] *V.C.H. Staffs.* xvii. 187.
[31] *Staffs. Advertiser*, 21 June 1845.
[32] W. Marshall, *The Rural Economy of the Midland Counties* (1796 edn.), i. 82–5.
[33] Pitt, *Staffs.* pt. ii. 87–98.   [34] Caird, *Eng. Agric.* 230.
[35] White, *Dir. Staffs.* (1851), 53.
[36] *J.R.A.S.E.* 2nd ser. v. 287.
[37] S.R.O., D.641/5/E(L)/2, conditions for letting Skeath House farm; D.1213/4, leases of 8 Jan. 1836 and 30 Nov.

1844.
[38] Wordie, 'Great Landed Estate', 114, 129; *D.N.B.*
[39] Sturgess, 'Agric. Staffs.' 225–6; Caird, *Eng. Agric.* 243.
[40] S.R.O., D.641/5/E(C)/19, 22 Mar. 1828; /30, 9 Dec. 1850; J. Loch, *Account of Improvements on Estates of Marquess of Stafford in Staffs. and Salop.* (1820), 72–4.
[41] S.R.O., D.603 (unlisted), Hodson corresp., CE 278, 298, 314–16; *London Kal. for 1812*, 161; *Royal Kal. for 1819*, 144.
[42] *Rep. Sel. Cttee. on Agric.* 521; *J.R.A.S.E.* 2nd ser. v. 286; S.R.O., D.615/E(F)/4/11 and 21; /E(F)/7–8.

techniques. Wyatt by 1833 had been agent to four different landlords;[43] in 1846 Thomas Turnor of Abbots Bromley was agent to Lord Bagot, Bagot's brother the bishop of Bath and Wells, Sir Watkyn Williams Wynne, and Ralph Sneyd of Keele.[44] Agencies often became hereditary.[45]

From the earlier 19th century the improvement of agriculture was aided by, and reflected in, the formation of agricultural societies on both a county and a more local scale. There were two waves of such foundations; the first began c. 1800 and the second in the later 1830s. In 1800 a Staffordshire Agricultural Society was founded; the first president, Richard Dyott, was appointed by the Board of Agriculture. It met at Lichfield and drew its support mainly from south Staffordshire.[46] In 1812 it was apparently absorbed by a new Staffordshire General Agricultural Society, with the same secretary and with Earl Talbot as president.[47] Societies with a more local emphasis included the Newcastle-under-Lyme and Pottery Agricultural Society, founded in 1800 for an area 12 miles around Newcastle,[48] and the Moorland Agricultural Society, which existed by 1803 when it met at Cellarhead fair.[49] The Newcastle society was the most ambitious, at first meeting twice a year and offering prizes for a variety of crops and for improvements including the floating of meadows, drainage, manuring, and marling.[50] The others in practice confined themselves to an annual meeting and show with prizes for stock and for long-serving and fecund labourers.[51] By 1814 the Newcastle society awarded prizes merely for good husbandry and long service.[52]

The early societies were short lived. Nothing further is known of the Moorland society.[53] The Newcastle society still existed in 1817; the Staffordshire General dissolved apparently c. 1826.[54] In 1836 a Staffordshire Agricultural Association was founded with wider objects, including the encouragement of better breeding and feeding of stock, improved and scientific methods of cultivation, and the good conduct of farm labourers. The earl of Lichfield and several lesser landowners were among the founders.[55] It too failed to survive, but several others for more limited areas or purposes were soon founded. The most important were the Lichfield (later Lichfield and Midland Counties) Agricultural Society, founded in 1838, and the North Staffordshire Agricultural Society, which was founded in 1843 and became the Staffordshire Agricultural Society in 1854.[56] Both held shows to encourage improvements in crops, stock, and husbandry techniques; innovations in implements assumed a new importance.[57] As was later noted, such shows gave farmers the opportunity to test implements before buying them.[58] Their value in disseminating ideas is indicated by the fact that 1,923 people visited the North Staffordshire's first show in 1844.[59] The North Staffordshire divided its region into eight districts in which local meetings were held, and established a circulating library for members.[60]

[43] Rep. Sel. Cttee. on Agric. 521.
[44] S.R.O., D.641/5/E(C)/27, 9 May 1846.
[45] J.R.A.S.E. 2nd ser. v. 288.
[46] Rules of Staffs. Agric. Soc. instituted in 1800 (copy in S.R.O., D.661/20/9); Staffs. Advertiser, 26 Apr., 6 Sept. 1800, 11 July 1801, 7 and 14 Aug. 1802, 13 Aug. 1803.
[47] Staffs. Advertiser, 12 June, 19 and 26 Sept. 1812, 24 and 31 July 1813.
[48] Rules of Newcastle-under-Lyme and Pottery Agric. Soc. (copy in Newcastle Boro. Libr.).
[49] Staffs. Advertiser, 13 Aug. 1803.
[50] Ibid. 8 Aug. 1801, 13 Mar. 1802, 19 Feb. 1803; Rules of Newcastle-under-Lyme and Pottery Agric. Soc.
[51] Staffs. Advertiser, 26 Apr. 1800, 14 Aug. 1802, 13 Aug. 1803.
[52] Staffs. Gaz. and Newcastle & Pottery Advertiser, 1 Nov. 1814.
[53] It is not given in a national list of 1810: K. Hudson,

Patriotism with Profit, 130–3.
[54] Pitt, Staffs. pt. ii. 100; Staffs. Advertiser, 25 June 1825. No meeting of the Staffs. Gen. Agric. Soc. is recorded in Staffs. Advertiser for 1826.
[55] Staffs. Advertiser, 12 Dec. 1835, 30 Jan. 1836.
[56] Ibid. 3 Nov. 1838, 21 Sept. 1839, 9 Dec. 1843, 13 Jan., 28 Sept. 1844; Rep. of Staffs. Agric. Soc. for 1854, 7 (copy in W.S.L. Pamphs. sub Staffs. Agric. Soc.).
[57] Rules and Regulations of the Lichfield and Midland Counties Agric. Soc. for 1846 (copy in W.S.L. Pamphs. sub Staffs. Agric. Soc.); Rep. of N. Staffs. Agric. Soc. for 1847 (copy ibid. sub Agric.); Staffs. Advertiser, 28 Sept. 1844.
[58] Staffs. Advertiser, 28 Sept. 1861 (chairman's speech to Cheadle Agric. Soc.).
[59] S.R.O., D.641/5/E(C)/25, 1 Oct. 1844.
[60] Staffs. Advertiser, 14 Dec. 1844; White, Dir. Staffs. (1851), 53.

The large landowners were prominent supporters of the societies,[61] and some also founded local farming clubs to encourage emulation and to diffuse new ideas among their tenants and neighbours. Such a club was founded by the tenants on the Leveson-Gower estates, with Loch's encouragement, in 1813.[62] Earl Talbot had established a sheep show at Ingestre by 1828,[63] Sir Edward Vavasour founded a society for Draycott-in-the-Moors in 1838–9, and Lord Harrowby one for Sandon and Marston in 1839.[64] Similar clubs were set up at Burton by 1841, at Tamworth in 1843, at Lichfield and Rugeley by 1844, at Cannock (by Lord Hatherton) in 1845, and at Keele c. 1851.[65]

Other societies were set up to foster some special interest. The Rugeley Agricultural Society was formed in 1837 to improve the breeding and feeding of cattle.[66] In 1853 the growing interest in plant nutrition and artificial manures gave birth to the Tamworth Agricultural Chemistry Society, which appointed a consultant chemist to protect members against dealers' frauds.[67]

Most of the societies hoped to help farmers by encouraging technical improvement rather than by seeking legislative protection for agriculture. The scrutiny of legislation was, however, among the objects of the Staffordshire Agricultural Association, which in 1836 petitioned parliament for an inquiry into the distressed state of agriculture.[68] During the agitation preceding the repeal of the Corn Laws local Agricultural Protection Societies were set up to oppose repeal and to counter the propaganda of the Anti-Corn-Law League. Such societies were established at Tamworth in 1839 and at Stafford, Lichfield, and Wolverhampton in 1844.[69] In 1866 a Staffordshire Chamber of Agriculture was established to put more general pressure on parliament and government in the agricultural interest.[70]

The period also saw the beginnings of formal agricultural education in the county. In 1841 R. S. Ford proposed an agricultural school for the poor at Swynnerton.[71] The county's first agricultural school, however, was founded c. 1849 at Ipstones by the incumbent, John Sneyd; it was apparently an extension of the existing free school, and it held a plot of land which was cultivated by the boys.[72] By 1850 Lord Hatherton had established a training scheme at Teddesley for about 30 boys aged between 10 and 14, who were paid 6d. a day for light work under the supervision of an experienced labourer.[73]

Important improvements included not only new crops, better breeding stock, and more effective techniques of cultivation, but also the use of new and more intensively and scientifically applied manures. Attention was given to permanent improvements, especially to drainage, to better farm buildings, and to the enlargement of fields to assist cultivation. On arable farms machinery became more common.

The main manures at the beginning of the period were dung, marl, and lime.[74] Dung remained essential; leases prohibited its sale from the farm.[75] Sometimes they also specified minimum quantities to be applied: at Swynnerton between 1819 and 1824 from 8 to 14 tons to the acre, and elsewhere throughout the period 10 to 15 cubic yards

[61] S.R.O., D.641/5/E/(C)/24, 5 Dec. 1843; /25, paper between letters of 3 and 15 July 1844; *Staffs. Advertiser*, 13 Jan., 28 Sept. 1844.

[62] Wordie, 'Great Landed Estate', 417; S.R.O., D.593/K/1/5/2, Loch to Stafford, 11 Apr., Loch to Gower, 15 June, and Duncalfe to Stafford, 22 June 1813.

[63] S.R.O., D.240/U/474, 18 June 1828.

[64] *Staffs. Advertiser*, 22 Dec. 1838, 12 Oct. 1844, 4 Oct. 1856.

[65] Ibid. 13 Jan., 3 Feb., 5 Oct. 1844, 24 Sept. 1859; S.R.O., D.603 (unlisted), Burton Establishment accts. 30 Sept. 1840–31 Dec. 1843, Dec. Qr. 1841; Sturgess, 'Agric. Staffs.' 155, 251, 556; *V.C.H. Staffs.* v. 60.

[66] P. J. Doyle, 'The Giffards of Chillington, a Catholic Landed Family, 1642–1861' (Durham Univ. M.A. thesis, 1968), 324.

[67] *Staffs. Advertiser*, 5 Aug. 1854, p. 7.

[68] Ibid. 30 Jan. 1836; *C.J.* xci. 297.

[69] *Staffs. Advertiser*, 3, 10, and 17 Feb. 1844.

[70] Ibid. 29 Dec. 1866.

[71] S.R.O., D.641/5/E(C)/23, paper headed 'Agricultural Schools'.

[72] *Staffs. Advertiser*, 7 Dec. 1850; White, *Dir. Staffs.* (1834), 750; (1851), 779; *P.O. Dir. Staffs.* (1850; 1854).

[73] Caird, *Eng. Agric.* 232.

[74] See p. 64.

[75] See p. 109.

to the acre. Slightly more was usually required on arable than on grass.[76] At Croxden Abbey farm in the 1860s 15 tons to the acre was laid on swedes and 20 on cabbages.[77] New methods of application were tried in the 1850s and 1860s; Lord Hatherton ordered a mechanical muck-spreader in 1857,[78] and on some farms systems of pipes or channels were built to convey liquid manure to the land.[79] In 1850 Lord Hatherton used dung for wheat and swedes, although other progressive light-land farmers were using artificials for roots and keeping dung for the seeds.[80] The latter system was gaining ground in the late 1860s, but dung was still applied to roots and corn as well as grass.[81] Marl, on the other hand, ceased to be used on heavy land. In 1802 the Newcastle-under-Lyme and Pottery Agricultural Society offered premiums for marling.[82] Intensive marling was prescribed on the Chartley estate about that time.[83] It became clear, however, that further marling merely made soils harder to work. For that reason, and because of the loss of land to marl-pits, Loch forbade marling at Trentham from 1813.[84] By 1850 it was 'almost abandoned' in Staffordshire.[85]

Lime continued in general use. On estates in all regions of the county covenants required its application, sometimes as an alternative to dung.[86] By the end of the 18th century the county's main sources of limestone, Caldon Low in the north and Walsall and Rushall in the south, were connected to the canal system[87] and could send lime cheaply to most areas. From at least 1799 Blithfield home farm purchased large quantities from south Staffordshire suppliers.[88] Rates of application increased from a common $1\frac{1}{2}$–$2\frac{1}{2}$ tons an acre in the 1790s to 3–5 tons an acre by the late 1860s,[89] although 5 tons was occasionally required in agreements early in the period.[90]

The use of other artificial or purchased manures besides lime greatly increased, particularly in the mid 19th century. Manures in use near towns in the 1790s included night-soil, bone shavings, and other refuse.[91] On Lord Bradford's estate in 1802 manures recommended for labourers' gardens included hogmuck, vegetable leaves, soot, ashes, soap-suds, floor-sweepings, and weeds.[92] Bones were extensively used around Walsall in 1809, at a rate of 80 bushels to the acre on fallows.[93] Bone manure became common in more rural areas by the 1830s.[94] Peruvian guano too spread rapidly in the 1840s. A farmer at Seisdon was said to have been the first to use it.[95] A guano allowance for a tenant was proposed at Swynnerton in 1843;[96] it was certainly used there in 1844,[97] at Chillington by 1846,[98] and at Beaudesert by 1847.[99] In 1850 a mixture of 3–4 cwt. of bones and 20 bushels of guano an acre was used on turnips at Drayton Bassett. A farmer at Wolgarston in Penkridge was making superphosphate of lime from boiled bones and mixing it with guano for sale to other farmers. Lord Hatherton was adding salt and ashes to the mixture for use on swedes.[1] At the same

[76] S.R.O., D.641/5/E(L)/2, conditions for letting Skeath House farm; /3, agreements of 25 Mar. 1819, 1 Dec. 1822, 25 Mar. and 22 Sept. 1824; /4, 25 Mar. 1822, 11 Dec. 1823; D.590/497; D.593/I/2/13; D.(W.) 1813/31, /34, /36; D.1287/2/1, conditions for letting estates in Staffs. and Salop.   [77] *J.R.A.S.E.* 2nd ser. v. 275–6.
[78] *Staffs. Advertiser*, 23 May 1857.
[79] Ibid. 29 Nov. 1856; below, p. 110.
[80] Caird, *Eng. Agric.* 234, 240–1, 247.
[81] *J.R.A.S.E.* 2nd ser. v. 275–6, 281–2, 288, 291.
[82] *Staffs. Advertiser*, 19 Feb. 1803.
[83] Sturgess, 'Agric. Staffs.' 384.
[84] S.R.O., D.593/K/1/5/2, Loch to Clarke, 25 Oct., and to Woolfe and to Townsend, 15 Nov. 1813; Loch, *Acct. of Improvements*, 190.   [85] Caird, *Eng. Agric.* 229.
[86] S.R.O., D.240/K, bdle. A, agreements 1829–44; D.590/497; D.593/I/2/13; D.641/5/E(L)/3, 25 Mar. 1819; /2, conditions for letting Skeath House farm; D.1213/4, leases of 2 Dec. 1845, 30 Jan. 1865; D.(W.) 1761, box 1, Rushton leases, lease of 29 July 1797, and Horton Hay

deeds, agreements of 1813; box 2, Rushton leases, agreements of 1812; box 12, lease of 2 Feb. 1791; D.(W.) 1813/31.
[87] *V.C.H. Staffs.* ii. 194, 196, 291–3; xvii. 168, 191–2.
[88] S.R.O., D.(W.) 1721/3/165, 1st bdle., acct. bks. 1799–1800, 1802–3, 1806–7, Husbandry; /166b, acct. bks. 1813–18, Husbandry.
[89] Sturgess, 'Agric. Staffs.' 336; *J.R.A.S.E.* 2nd ser. v. 273.
[90] W.S.L., D.1798/371, Hodson to Collins, 10 Jan. 1804, and conditions for letting . . . lands of Hinton's Char. 4 Dec. 1820.   [91] Sturgess, 'Agric. Staffs.' 334.
[92] S.R.O., D.1287/2/1, 'Weston Christmas 1802'.
[93] Sturgess, 'Agric. Staffs.' 332.
[94] e.g. S.R.O., D.641/5/E(C)/19, 27 June 1829; /21, 5 Mar. 1834, 5 Aug. 1836.
[95] White, *Dir. Staffs.* (1851), 209.
[96] S.R.O., D.641/5/E(L)/4, lease of Row farm, 27 Dec. 1843.   [97] Ibid. /E(C)/25, 4 Oct. 1844.
[98] Doyle, 'Giffards', 327.
[99] S.R.O., D.603 (unlisted), 'B.D.F. 1847'.
[1] Caird, *Eng. Agric.* 236, 241, 247.

time farmers on Lord Harrowby's estate were being encouraged to use bones and guano.[2] Bones were in general use on pasture land, at 3–4 cwt. an acre, by the late 1860s; they were preferred to guano, though that was still widely used.[3] Nitrate of soda was used at Beaudesert by 1854[4] and on grass at Croxden Abbey farm in the late 1860s.[5] By the 1850s specially prepared manures for particular crops were available; thus at Beaudesert in 1855 2 tons of bean manure and 1 ton of vetch manure were bought at Birmingham.[6] In 1853 experiments were made at Fisherwick with various combinations of flesh manure, guano, salt, shoddy, dissolved bone, and a commercial turnip manure; ten plots of turnips were used for testing, and the commercial manure proved best.[7] Near the Black Country town manure was probably used increasingly in mid-century, as on the Sandwell estate in the 1850s.[8] By the late 1860s it was said to affect the farming of that part of the county considerably, obviating artificial manures.[9]

Landlords encouraged tenants to manure intensively by means of allowances. Allowances against rent for the purchase of lime were already given in the 1790s,[10] but both these and the direct provision of lime by the landlord became more popular in the depression years after 1815.[11] At Trentham, for example, it was seen as an alternative to a permanent lowering of rents.[12] Allowances and subsidies were extended to other manures besides lime: to bone manure at Swynnerton and Maer in the 1830s,[13] to guano at Ashley in 1848.[14] On the other hand the tenant was sometimes charged interest on manures bought by the landlord.[15]

In the earlier and mid 19th century progress in drainage permitted more varied cropping of heavy land, particularly the growing of root crops,[16] and improved the herbage on pasture. In 1812 drainage on the Branston estate in Burton-upon-Trent was considered to have increased the rental value by 10s. an acre; in 1814 land there 'which for years would not suffer a hoof to go upon it without sinking half a yard deep is now as sound in the most rainy weather as the turnpike road'.[17] In the 1790s field drains were simply trenches cut 3 feet deep and filled with layers of heather, pebbles, and inverted turf.[18] In the next twenty years, however, locally manufactured drainage tiles came into use; much drainage was done, more effectively and cheaply than before, especially as the duty on drainage tiles was repealed in 1815 through the efforts of Sir John Wrottesley of Wrottesley.[19] On the Trentham estate between 1812 and 1820 136,000 yards of underground drains and 127,000 yards of ditches were dug.[20] By 1833 much capital had been expended by landlords and tenants in the county on drainage, though often wasted through poor maintenance.[21] By the mid 1840s drainage pipes were beginning to replace tiles.[22]

In the earlier 19th century the cost of drainage was normally divided between landlord and tenant, the landlord providing tiles and the tenant laying them.[23] In 1810 at

[2] F. M. Reid, 'Economic and Social Aspects of Land-ownership in the 19th Century' (Oxford Univ. B.Litt. thesis, 1956), 56.   [3] *J.R.A.S.E.* 2nd ser. v. 274–6, 281.
[4] S.R.O., D.603 (unlisted), Beaudesert Farm Accts. 1854 and 1855, Beaudesert Farm Accts. 1854, cash acct., 26 May 1854.   [5] *J.R.A.S.E.* 2nd ser. v. 277.
[6] D.603 (unlisted), Beaudesert Farm Accts. 1854 and 1855, bdle. of receipts 1855, bill 15 Mar. 1855.
[7] *J.R.A.S.E.* xvi(1), 88–9.
[8] Sturgess, 'Agric. Staffs.' 99.
[9] *J.R.A.S.E.* 2nd ser. v. 292–3.
[10] e.g. S.R.O., D.(W.) 1761, box 12, Rushton leases, lease to John Shufflebotham, 25 Mar. 1797.
[11] e.g. S.R.O., D.641/5/E(L)/3, agreements of 24 Mar. 1820, 6 Mar. 1828, and lease of 12 Feb. 1830; /4, agreements of 18 Nov. 1835, 17 Dec. 1841; D.(W.) 1781, bdle. K, 'Wolseley estate 1826'.
[12] Wordie, 'Great Landed Estate', 425–6.

[13] S.R.O., D.641/5/E(C)/21, 5 Mar. 1834; D.1213/4, lease of 4 Jan. 1839.
[14] S.R.O., D.1213/4, lease of 29 Mar. 1848.
[15] Sturgess, 'Agric. Staffs.' 217; S.R.O., D.641/5/E(C)/21, 5 Aug. 1836; D.952/2/3/21, p. 46.   [16] See p. 105.
[17] S.R.O., D.603 (unlisted), Hodson corresp., CE 421, Hodson to Aylmer, 30 Aug. 1812, 2 Mar. 1814.
[18] Pitt, *Agric. Staffs.* 111.
[19] Pitt, *Staffs.* pt. ii. 61, 85–6; *D.N.B. sub* Wrottesley; 55 Geo. III, c. 176.
[20] Loch, *Acct. of Improvements*, 195–6.
[21] *Rep. Sel. Cttee. on Agric.* 521.
[22] [Ford], *How is the Farmer to Live?* 1–2.
[23] Sturgess, 'Agric. Staffs.' 452; Caird, *Eng. Agric.* 230; S.R.O., D.603 (unlisted), Hodson corresp., CE 421, Hodson to Sanderson, n.d. but between letters of 28 Nov. 1816 and 28 Feb. 1817; D.641/5/E(L)/3, 17 Apr. 1828; /E(C)/19, 25 Feb. 1829.

Swynnerton, and about the same time on Lord Bradford's estates, agreements began to require the tenant to drain.[24] Sometimes allowances were made, as for manures.[25] Increasingly, however, the landlord took over the full responsibility for drainage. In the early 19th century he often made the main drains on the estate, but his interest in underdraining was merely supervisory, as at Keele, Teddesley, Trentham, and Burton, where in 1814 12,417 yards of ditching had been completed but only 2,636 yards of

FARM HOUSE and OFFICES at STALLINGTON GRANGE
erected 1811-13

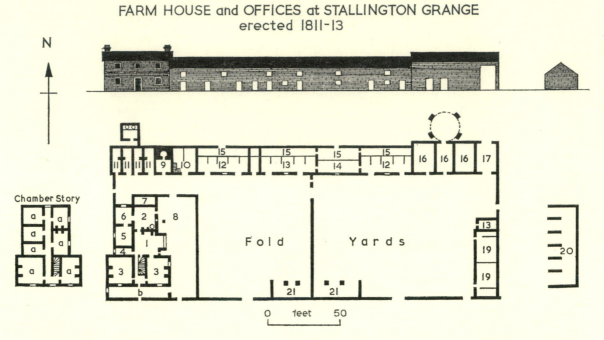

House: 1 *Kitchen*; 2 *Back kitchen*; 3 *Parlours*; 4 *Pantry*; 5 *Dairy*; 6 *Scullery*; 7 *Coal-house*; 8 *Back-yard*; a *Bed-chambers*; b *Passage*; Buildings: 9 *Bake-house*; 10 *Hackney stable*; 11 *Pig-styes*; 12 *Tyings for 20 cows*; 13 *Tyings for 10 cows, granary over*; 14 *Calf-house*; 15 *Straw-bin and feeding-way*; 16 *Barn*; 17 *Lock-up house and drift-way*; 18 *Tool house*; 19 *Stables*; 20 *Waggon-shed*; 21 *Open sheds for cattle*.

common soughing and 953 yards of deep soughing.[26] Under leases of 1813 at Horton Hay the landlord was to drain at the tenant's request, the tenant finding materials.[27] Where the landlord agreed to pay for the drains the tenant was required to pay interest on the outlay: $7\frac{1}{2}$ per cent, for example, on the Teddesley estate in 1809,[28] and 7 per cent at Beech Cliff, Swynnerton, in 1824.[29]

Provision of drainage by landlords became commoner towards the middle of the century, and it was then that most of the effective draining was done.[30] From 1844 Lord Hatherton took full responsibility for draining on his estate,[31] and in the late 1840s Sir Robert Peel did the same at Drayton Bassett, charging the tenants 4 to 5 per cent.[32] At Little Aston in Shenstone E. S. Parker Jervis charged a tenant 5 per cent for drainage done with tiles and pipes in 1847 and 1848.[33] Drainage expenditure on the Keele estate reached a peak in 1851.[34] The 2nd earl of Harrowby (d. 1882) spent five times as much to the acre on drainage as the 1st earl (d. 1847); interest was charged to the tenants.[35] Between 1854 and 1869 *c.* 7,000 a. was drained on Lord Lichfield's estate.[36] The rates charged by landlords were by then generally lower than the $6\frac{1}{2}$ per

[24] S.R.O., D.641/5/E(L)/2, agreements of 1810; Sturgess, 'Agric. Staffs.' 464.
[25] S.R.O., D.641/5/E(L)/3, 24 Mar. 1820; D.952/2/3/22, p. 24 (Weston Farm, 1868).
[26] Sturgess, 'Agric. Staffs.' 453; S.R.O., D.603 (unlisted), Hodson corresp., CE 421, Hodson to Uxbridge, 8 Sept. 1814. The Derbs. figures are excluded here.
[27] S.R.O., D.(W.) 1761, box 1, Horton Hay deeds, leases of 1813.

[28] Sturgess, 'Agric. Staffs.' 217.
[29] S.R.O., D.641/5/E(L)/3, 22 Sept. 1824.
[30] Sturgess, 'Agric. Staffs.' 455-7. [31] Ibid. 239.
[32] Caird, *Eng. Agric.* 245; N. Gash, *Sir Robert Peel*, 679.
[33] W.S.L. 11/27/2/50, 'Additions and Alterations of the Little Aston estate rental February 1849'.
[34] Sturgess, 'Agric. Staffs.' 158.
[35] Reid, 'Landownership', 39, 62, 71.
[36] *J.R.A.S.E.* 2nd ser. v. 308.

cent demanded by government on the drainage loans made available from 1846.[37] In the first year of the government's scheme the duke of Sutherland seems to have been the only Staffordshire landowner to use it; he took £20,000 for land in Staffordshire and Shropshire and another £15,000 for 10,776 a. in Staffordshire alone.[38] Between 1847

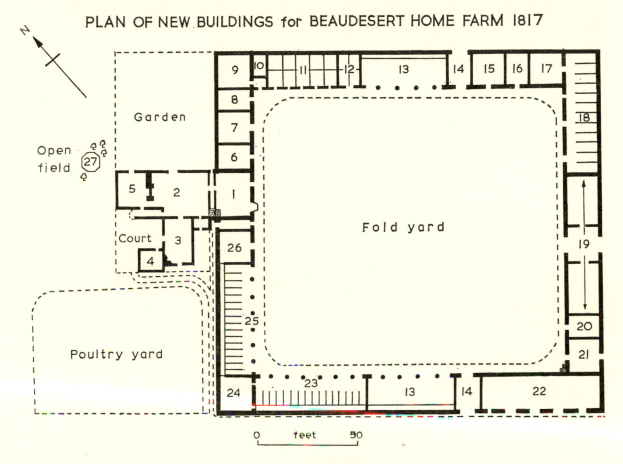

PLAN OF NEW BUILDINGS for BEAUDESERT HOME FARM 1817

1 *Bailiff's room*; 2 *Kitchen*; 3 *Servants' kitchen*; 4 *Cellar*; 5 *New scullery*; 6 *Hackney stable*; 7 *Sick cattle*; 8 *Boiling house*; 9 *Potato house*; 10 *Cistern*; 11 *Piggery*; 12 *Breeding styes*; 13 *Open shed*; 14 *Gateway*; 15 *Slaughter house*; 16 *Fasting house*; 17 *House for gearing*; 18 *Stable*; 19 *Barn*; 20 *Bull house*; 21 *Implements*; 22 *Cart shed with granary over*; 23 *Feeding shed*; 24 *Hay house*; 25 *Dairy cows*; 26 *Calf house*; 27 *Dairy*.

and 1868 Staffordshire landowners borrowed £152,485 from the government or improvement companies, probably mainly for drainage.[39] By the late 1860s large areas had been drained, and what remained to be done was mainly on small estates. The draining under government schemes, however, had not been done well, and on some heavy clays the land had had to be re-drained at a shallower depth by the owners.[40]

There was much modernization and replacement of farm buildings throughout the period, though large-scale rebuilding generally did not take place until the mid 19th century. The chief development on large farms was the integration of buildings to form a **U** or courtyard plan on three or four sides of a foldyard. Such arrangements became fashionable from the late 18th century.[41] On very large farmsteads there might be more than one foldyard, as in some of the extravagant complexes built on the Trentham estate in 1811–13.[42] Much of the new building reflected the shift to stock farming after the French wars. On the Pagets' estates between 1814 and *c.* 1830, for example,

[37] Public Money Drainage Act, 9 & 10 Vic. c. 101.
[38] *Returns Drainage Loans*, H.C. 146, p. 1 (1847), xxxiv.
[39] Sturgess, 'Agric. Staffs.' 455–6.
[40] *J.R.A.S.E.* 2nd ser. v. 306–7.

[41] J. E. C. Peters, *Development of Farm Buildings in Western Lowland Staffs. up to 1880*, 52; Pitt, *Agric. Staffs.* 19 and plates facing pp. 19, 20, 22.
[42] Loch, *Acct. of Improvements*, plates 22, 23, 26.

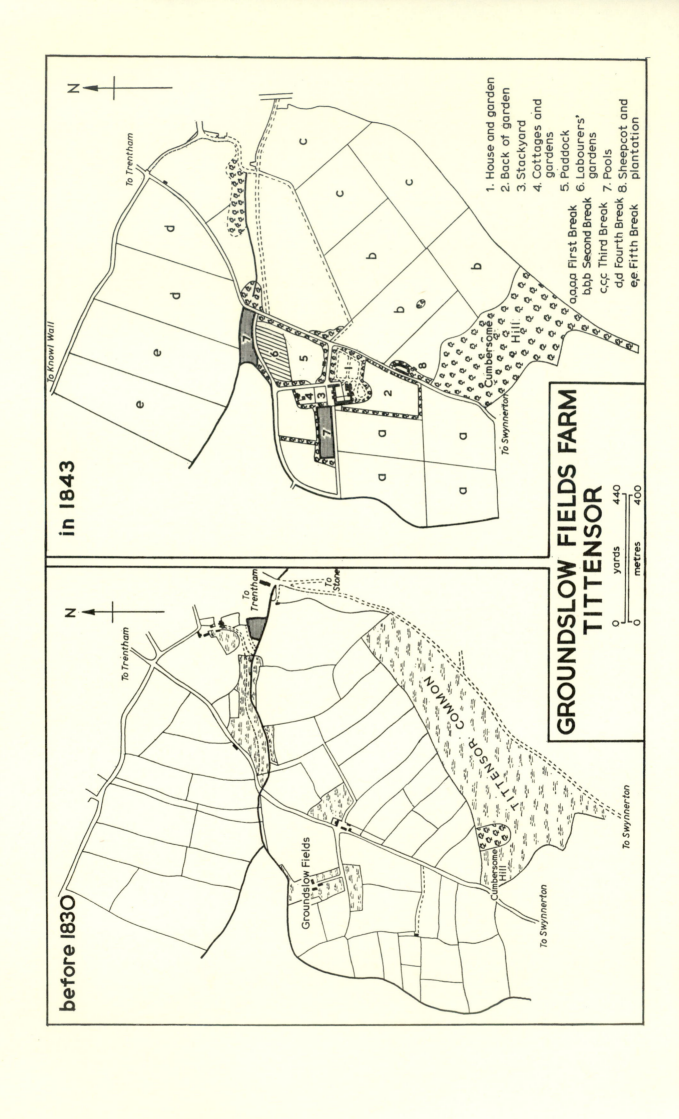

before 1830

N

To Trentham

To Trentham

To Stone

Groundslow Fields

Cumbersome Hill

TITTENSOR COMMON

To Swynnerton

To Swynnerton

in 1843

N

To Trentham

To Knowl Wall

To Swynnerton

Cumbersome Hill

Cumbersome Hill

**GROUNDSLOW FIELDS FARM
TITTENSOR**

1. House and garden
2. Back of garden
3. Stackyard
4. Cottages and gardens
5. Paddock
6. Labourers' gardens
7. Pools
8. Sheepcot and plantation

a,a,aa First Break
b,b Second Break
c,c,c Third Break
d,d Fourth Break
e,e Fifth Break

yards   0   440
metres   0   400

new buildings usually included extra cow-houses and sometimes fodder houses; barns were seldom rebuilt except as part of a general replacement, and the new barns were relatively small, of three bays only, with one threshing-floor.[43] Winnowing-machines helped to reduce the space needed for threshing.[44] Nevertheless a few large barns were still built.[45] Some new barns were designed for machine threshing, and old barns were adapted for that purpose.[46] As the 19th century advanced more rooms for feed preparation,[47] such as turnip-houses, mixing-houses, and boiling-houses, were required. They housed the cutters, pulpers, and steaming and boiling machinery. They might be attached to the cow-house where their products were consumed, or form part of the barn.[48] By the late 1860s the estate of Ralph Sneyd at Keele was particularly noted for its fixed steam-engines and improved machinery;[49] the farmsteads built there in the 1850s included hay-, turnip-, straw-, corn-, and steaming-houses, implement sheds, and liquid-manure tanks.[50] In 1850 Sir James Caird stated that Staffordshire farm buildings were the best he had yet seen,[51] and in the late 1860s they were compared favourably with those in arable counties.[52]

The cost of building tended to rise. Pitt's designs for farms in the 1790s allowed for a variation in expenditure of £2 to £10 an acre, including the cost of the farm-house.[53] In 1815 an estimate presented to Lord Uxbridge for new farm buildings at Haywood Park allowed for £2 15s. an acre.[54] In the 1860s £11 an acre was spent on farm buildings at Carmountside farm at Hulton on the Sneyd estate.[55]

The rise in building costs was paralleled by a shift in responsibility for buildings from the tenant to the landlord. Early in the period the landlord customarily put the farm in repair at the tenant's entry; the tenant then maintained it, the landlord finding materials, usually timber, tiles, and bricks.[56] A similar policy was also applied to new buildings, as on the Paget estates, where the landlord paid for materials, the tenant for labour.[57] By 1850, however, new buildings were generally the landlord's responsibility.[58] Accordingly a landlord's expenditure on buildings in the earlier 19th century was often low. Between 1798 and 1808 and between 1813 and 1818 repairs to tenants' buildings on Lord Bagot's estate were never more than 8·5 per cent of expenditure, and often less than 1 per cent.[59] Similar low figures are found on the Keele, Chillington, and Sandwell estates in the earlier 19th century.[60] On a few estates where there was an improving landlord investment in buildings was much higher, as at Trentham under the 2nd marquess of Stafford in the 1810s, Teddesley under Sir Edward Littleton and the 1st Lord Hatherton, and Ingestre under the 1st Earl Talbot.[61] In the 1850s and 1860s rebuilding was more general, and expenditure reached a peak on several estates, as at Keele, Chillington, and Sandon.[62] Several landowners borrowed money from the government or improvement companies for rebuilding farms.[63]

Other permanent improvements encouraged by landlords included the grubbing-up of hedges and rearrangement of fields to ease cultivation, the construction and

[43] S.R.O., D.603 (unlisted), Hodson notes and memoranda, plans and estimates for buildings, c. 1815–30.
[44] Peters, *Farm Buildings*, 72.   [45] Ibid. 69, 73, 76.
[46] Ibid. 87–9.   [47] See p. 114.
[48] Peters, *Farm Buildings*, 153, 165–72.
[49] *J.R.A.S.E.* 2nd ser. v. 303.
[50] Sturgess, 'Agric. Staffs.' 156–7.
[51] Caird, *Eng. Agric.* 232.   [52] *J.R.A.S.E.* 2nd ser. v. 303.
[53] Pitt, *Agric. Staffs.* plates facing pp. 19, 20, 22.
[54] S.R.O., D.603 (unlisted), Hodson corresp., CE 421, Hodson to Uxbridge, 6 Mar. 1815.
[55] Sturgess, 'Agric. Staffs.' 489.
[56] Pitt, *Agric. Staffs.* 22; S.R.O., D.240/K, bdle. A, agreements 1829–44; D.590/497; D.641/5/E(L)/2, conditions for letting Skeath House farm; D.661/8/1/1/3;

D.952/2/2/3 and 4; D.1287/2/1, conditions for letting estates in Staffs. and Salop.; D.(W.) 1761, box 1, Horton Hay deeds, leases of 1813.
[57] S.R.O., D.603 (unlisted), Hodson memos., plans and estimates for buildings, valuation of sundry buildings agreed to by Lord Uxbridge, Aug. 1814; plan for Mr. W. Higgott's buildings at Branston, [1814]; estimate for Higgott's buildings, 17 June 1814; plan of Mr. John Page's buildings at Stretton, 17 June 1814.
[58] Caird, *Eng. Agric.* 232.
[59] S.R.O., D.(W.) 1721/3/165, 1st bdle., acct. bks. 1798–1808; /166b, acct. bks. 1813–18.
[60] Sturgess, 'Agric. Staffs.' 468, 474–5.   [61] Ibid. 466–8.
[62] Ibid. 474, 478; Reid, 'Landownership', 39, 71.
[63] Sturgess, 'Agric. Staffs.' 471, 474.

straightening of farm roads, and the central siting of buildings. At Trentham Loch encouraged tenants to amalgamate and regularize fields, eliminated useless lanes, and built new roads.[64] At Groundslow Fields, Tittensor, farmed by William Lewis, the Leveson-Gowers' agent at Trentham,[65] the farm layout was completely altered between 1830 and 1843. The 56 irregular fields were reduced to 15 straight-fenced fields of 10 a. to 25 a., cultivated in five roughly equal 'breaks'. The farmstead was rebuilt, the roads were straightened, and new tracks were laid out; gardens were provided for the labourers.[66] By 1850 there had been a further rearrangement into eight fields cultivated on a four-course.[67] At Brancote, Tixall, the farmer had gone even further, removing almost all fences to form four 100-a. fields. In some areas, however, especially round Trentham, small fields were still a nuisance.[68] George Monckton of Stretton Hall in Penkridge, who in 1847 was advocating removal of hedges, also recommended centralizing farmsteads; a gain of at least 5s. an acre could be expected.[69] In the late 1860s Staffordshire farm buildings were said to be generally more central than those in arable counties.[70]

As has been seen, there was a gradual shift to the landlord of responsibility for permanent improvements. Sometimes tenants were willing to invest large sums in improvements; on several estates in the earlier 19th century there were tenants who spent hundreds or even thousands of pounds on drainage, seeding, buildings, or manures.[71] The absence of compensation for improvements, however, discouraged such expenditure. In the late 1860s Staffordshire tenants generally still had no security that they would be reimbursed for real improvements.[72] In 1872 the Land Tenure Committee of the Staffordshire Chamber of Agriculture proposed a system of compensation. The tenant was to receive the cost of bones and lime used on arable in the last four years of his tenancy and on grass in the last seven; a share in the cost of oil-cake, linseed, malt dust, or other purchased feed consumed in the last two years; the value of fixtures; and the value of drains laid in the last ten years.[73] In 1875 it was said to be the custom in south Staffordshire for the outgoing tenant to receive two-thirds of the value of linseed or cotton cake consumed in the last year, and one-third of that consumed in the penultimate year.[74]

Probably, however, it was not adventurous tenants but the more general involvement of landlords in the improvement of tenanted farms in the mid 19th century which brought about the 'great levelling up' in the agriculture of the county and deprived model farms like Brancote of their eminence.[75] That was the period of high farming, when techniques and improvements long practised on the best farms became widespread.

ARABLE FARMING

Most of the cultivated land in the county was arable in the late 18th century, and by 1816 the proportion had been increased by war-time ploughing of newly inclosed waste.[76] Three main arable regions, each with distinct farming systems, are discernible: the light sandy or gravelly soils of the south and parts of the north-west; the clays and marls of central Staffordshire; and the Moorlands. The urban growth of the Potteries

[64] Loch, *Acct. of Improvements*, 178–9, 212.
[65] White, *Dir. Staffs.* (1834), 681; (1851), 369.
[66] W.S.L. 11/313/50.
[67] Caird, *Eng. Agric.* 235.   [68] Ibid. 230, 233–4.
[69] G. Monckton, *A Treatise on Deep Draining; to which is added a few Words on the Food of Plants, the Potato Disease, Indian Cholera &c.* (Wolverhampton, 1847), 3–4 (copy in W.S.L. Pamphs. *sub* Agriculture).
[70] *J.R.A.S.E.* 2nd ser. v. 303.

[71] Sturgess, 'Agric. Staffs.' 252, 450–2; S.R.O., D.641/5/E(C)/25, 15 Nov., 6 Dec. 1844; /27, 3 Sept. 1846.
[72] *J.R.A.S.E.* 2nd ser. v. 301.
[73] Staffs. Chamber of Agric. *Rep. of Land Tenure Cttee. 1872* (copy in S.R.O., D.590/592).
[74] J. B. Lawes, 'On the Valuation of Unexhausted Manures', *J.R.A.S.E.* 2nd ser. xi. 29–30.
[75] Ibid. v. 287; Caird, *Eng. Agric.* 233–4.
[76] Pitt, *Staffs.* pt. ii. 20; above, p. 91.

and Black Country also resulted in the development of intensive farming systems and market-gardening around them.

The light soils, sufficiently well-drained for the growing of turnips and the avoidance of wasteful bare fallows, were and remained the most profitable for corn-growing and had proportionately the greatest area of arable.[77] It was claimed in the 1790s that the Norfolk rotation of turnips, barley, clover, and wheat was generally employed on those soils. In fact, however, the crop returns of 1801 show that while turnips were extensively grown in some light-land parishes and the barley acreage was important, only a few farmers adhered to a strict four-course. It had apparently made most progress in the south-west, especially at Trysull. Some farmers used rotations based on the Norfolk system but allowed the clover to lie for more than one year; others used rotations omitting wheat.[78] By the end of the French wars the home farms of Lord Talbot at Ingestre and Lord Anson at Shugborough provided large-scale examples of the Norfolk system in practice.[79] Landlords were beginning to enforce the four-course in tenancy agreements where the soil was suitable, and not only in the south of the county. Strict Norfolk rotations occur in leases on Lord Talbot's estate in Salt and Enson in St. Mary's, Stafford, in 1813 and on Thomas Twemlow's estate at Tyrley in 1817.[80] James Loch required it on light land at Trentham in 1813.[81] Lord Bradford imposed a four-course on his tenantry probably before 1815, but allowed a summer fallow instead of turnips.[82] In 1809 Sir Edward Littleton may have imposed the same conditions at Drayton in Penkridge.[83] The imposition of the four-course sometimes, however, developed in stages. On the Fitzherbert estate at Swynnerton agreements of 1810 required that not more than one straw crop be grown in succession and that one-third of the arable be vetches, turnips, or seeds. An agreement of 1812 forbade more than a quarter of the arable to be wheat or less than a quarter turnips. Once in 1816, and regularly from 1819, the full Norfolk system was imposed.[84] A strict four-course also occurs on the Dyott estate at Freeford in 1829 and 1845.[85]

Yet the four-course did not become universal on the lighter soils. Tenants often neglected cropping covenants. Pitt noted: 'Sometimes systems of cropping are inserted, but little attended to, if the tenant be supposed going on well.'[86] On Lord Talbot's estate in St. Mary's, Stafford, in 1814–15 most farms, including the one let on a strict four-course in 1813, were not cultivated under that system.[87] Landlords were also willing to modify the four-course. The 1st Lord Hatherton substituted oats for wheat in the course on all newly inclosed land.[88] Agreements allowed the alternative of a rotation in the same order as the four-course, but with longer leys, to continue.[89] In the late 1830s and 1840s there was a straightforward four-course in many light-land parishes, but it was more usual to allow the clover to lie two years. At Adbaston and Cannock bare fallows remained part of the course.[90] In 1850 on Sir Robert Peel's estate at Drayton Bassett the light land was normally managed on a four-course, but the grass often lay a second year.[91] In the later 1860s a six-course rotation of turnips, barley, seeds, seeds, oats, and wheat was common on light lands.[92]

[77] N.S.J.F.S. xiii. 27, 39, 43.
[78] Pitt, Agric. Staffs. 76, 78–9; S.H.C. 1950–1, 234–42.
[79] Pitt, Staffs. pt. ii. 88–90, 92–4.
[80] S.R.O., D.641/5/E(L)/2, conditions for letting Skeath House farm; D.952/2/2/3.
[81] S.R.O., D.593/K/1/5/2, Loch to W. Ford, 15 Nov. 1813.
[82] S.R.O., D.1287/2/1, conditions for letting estates in Staffs. and Salop.
[83] Sturgess, 'Agric. Staffs.' 216; S.R.O., D.260/M/E/2, p. 290.
[84] S.R.O., D.641/5/E(L)/2, agreements of 1810 and

agreement with Stych, 16 Apr. 1812; /3, agreement with G. Bates, 25 Mar. 1819, and misc. papers within, and later agreements.
[85] S.R.O., D.661/8/1/1/3–4.
[86] Pitt, Agric. Staffs. (1813 edn.), 39.
[87] Sturgess, 'Agric. Staffs.' 326; S.R.O., D.240/E/365.
[88] Sturgess, 'Agric. Staffs.' 251.
[89] S.R.O., D.590/497; D.1213/4, lease of 8 Jan. 1836; D.(W.) 1813/34–6.
[90] N.S.J.F.S. xiii. 42, 46.
[91] Caird, Eng. Agric. 247–8.
[92] J.R.A.S.E. 2nd ser. v. 288.

Before a regular rotation could be introduced on light land a preparatory course of cultivation might be necessary. A lease of a farm at Swynnerton in 1820 specified a six-year preliminary rotation, followed by the four-course on turnip-growing land.[93] When Lord Hatherton inclosed Calf Heath in Hatherton in 1858 he planned a five-year initial rotation of fallow, turnips, turnips, oats, and seeds, with heavy manuring, followed by the four-course.[94]

Light-land farming was based on an integration of arable farming with stock-fattening, since the root crops and rotation grasses both formed an intrinsic part of the arable rotation and served as fodder for stock. Cropping covenants sometimes specifically required roots to be consumed in the fields by sheep folded on the arable, as at Rickerscote in Castle Church in 1820, Tyrley in 1830, or Chillington in the 1840s.[95] More common was a simple prohibition of the sale of the green crops, already found on the Leveson-Gower estates in south Staffordshire in 1789,[96] and occurring in leases on the Monckton estate at Brewood from 1810,[97] Lord Talbot's estate in 1813,[98] on the Dyott estate at Freeford by 1829,[99] and the Maer Hall estate in 1865.[1] The fodder crops made it possible to keep more stock, to obtain more manure, and thus to achieve higher yields. By the 1840s wheat yields were generally, though not invariably, higher on light than on heavy lands, especially in the south.[2] Moreover the stock enterprise provided a hedge against fluctuating wheat prices, and price reductions were least damaging on light soils.[3]

On the heavy and poorly drained claylands of the east, west, and north-west of the county, however, root crops could not always be grown and bare fallows had to be retained. In the 1790s the rotation commonly followed on the heaviest soils was fallow, wheat, oats, and finally a ley of clover, trefoil, and rye-grass for one, two, or more years. On slightly more friable soils a rotation of fallow, wheat, beans or peas, barley or oats, and then seeds was found.[4] Barley was less common than on the light soils; often more than half the grain crop was wheat.[5]

It was apparently considered in the late 18th century that crop-rotation was less important on heavy lands, since they were less easily exhausted by bad rotations and less easily improved by good ones.[6] Thus c. 1800 cropping covenants rarely indicated a strict order of arable crops; they merely forbade more than three corn crops in a course and laid down a minimum period for temporary grass.[7]

By the end of the French wars attempts were being made to impose stricter rotations on tenants of heavy-land farms. In 1811 a tenant on the Paget estate round Burton-upon-Trent was evicted apparently for taking three white crops in succession, and in 1816 the 'system laid down' seems to have involved alternating white and green crops.[8] On the marquess of Stafford's Trentham estate Loch imposed stricter rotations apparently from 1813; the tenants were to follow a four-course of fallow, wheat, clover, and oats, or preferably a six-course of fallow, wheat, clover or turnips, oats or barley, turnips or beans, and oats, barley, or early wheat. Part of the 'bean' crop might be potatoes if well manured.[9] In 1815 he sent a circular stressing that the rotations were

[93] S.R.O., D.641/5/E(L)/3, 10 Mar. 1820.
[94] S.R.O., D.260/M/F/5/26/79, 10 Nov. 1858.
[95] W.S.L., D.1798/371, conditions for letting lands of Hinton's Char. 4 Dec. 1820; S.R.O., D.590/497; D.952/2/2/4; D.(W.) 1813/35, blank forms for agreements on Giffard estate.
[96] S.R.O., D.593/I/2/13.
[97] S.R.O., D.(W.) 1813/31, /34–6.
[98] S.R.O., D.641/5/E(L)/2, conditions for letting Skeath House farm.
[99] S.R.O., D.661/8/1/1/3.
[1] S.R.O., D.1213/4, lease of 30 Jan. 1865.

[2] N.S.J.F.S. xiii. 43.
[3] Rep. Sel. Cttee. on Agric. 527, 531.
[4] Pitt, Agric. Staffs. 76.
[5] S.H.C. 1950–1, 236, 238.
[6] Wordie, 'Great Landed Estate', 402.
[7] Sturgess, 'Agric. Staffs.' 372–4.
[8] S.R.O., D.603 (unlisted), Hodson corresp., CE 278, Aylmer to Hodson, 2 Oct. 1811; CE 421, Hodson to Sanderson, 5 Mar. 1816.
[9] S.R.O., D.593/K/1/5/2, Loch to Clarke, 25 Oct. and 15 Nov., to Townsend, to Woolfe, and to W. Ford, 15 Nov., and to R. S. Ford, 18 Nov. 1813.

to be followed as closely on stiff as on light soils.[10] Tenancy agreements from at least 1819 forbade the taking of two corn crops in succession.[11] In the 1820s R. S. Ford was advocating Loch's rotations to the tenants of the Swynnerton estate.[12] The attempt to use beans to reduce the frequency of fallow met with little success at Trentham, where the acreage under beans increased only from 1 per cent in 1820–1 to 2 per cent in 1850–1.[13] It was stated in 1817 that beans were widely grown on strong soils, especially west of Stafford, a typical rotation being fallow, wheat, beans, barley or oats, then seeds for one or more years.[14] About 1840, however, beans rarely covered more than 15 per cent of the arable on heavy land.[15]

In Staffordshire as elsewhere tenants on heavy land were reluctant to take a green crop in alternate years, since the corn crop paid the rent. The exhaustion caused by successive cropping with corn thus remained a problem well into the 1830s.[16] On a farm on the Wolseley family's estate in 1825, for example, 49 per cent of the land had been under corn at the previous harvest, and on several fields one corn crop was following another.[17] Wheat yields on the clays fell in the 1820s.[18] Bare fallows were still ubiquitous *c.* 1840,[19] and in the 1840s and 1850s agricultural societies still offered prizes for them.[20] In the late 1860s common rotations included: on poor clays, wheat, seeds for two or three years, then wheat or oats; on better soils, seeds for several years, oats, wheat, beans, then wheat, or fallow, wheat, barley, beans, wheat.[21] Some progress had been made towards solving the fallow problem. Nearly half the heavy-land areas in which farmers replied to the Tithe Commissioners' questionnaires *c.* 1840 had 40 per cent or more of their arable under green crops of some kind.[22] In 1851 Harvey Wyatt recommended growing peas before a fallow and replacing most of the latter by a green crop.[23] Drainage might permit turnips to be grown, as on the Keele estate by the 1850s;[24] in the Needwood forest area in the 1860s turnips were grown on all but the heaviest fallows.[25] The solution to the heavy-land farmer's difficulties, however, lay in converting arable to pasture and shifting the emphasis from corn. By the 1860s the arable was often primarily a source of fodder in a predominantly dairy farm.[26]

In the Moorlands such subordination of arable to pasture was already overwhelming in the 1790s. Oats were the predominant or even the sole crop.[27] A typical rotation was that described at Horton in 1805: 'The tenants here seem to have a custom of ploughing up their pasture, once in about eight or ten years, take 2 or 3 crops of oats, stating that the land will not bear wheat or barley, and lay it down to pasture . . . without sowing any sort of grass seeds whatever, but leave it to nature to throw up spontaneous produce which is to be pasturing for the cows.'[28] Such was still the practice at Grindon and Ilam *c.* 1840.[29] Leases in the late 18th century forbade more than three crops in a course and limited the area to be ploughed.[30]

Immediately before and during the French wars the arable area in parts of the

[10] Wordie, 'Great Landed Estate', 403.
[11] S.R.O., D.593/K/3/6/1.
[12] A Practical Farmer [R. S. Ford], *Hints and Observations on the Management of Arable Land* (Stone, 1828), 26–7. For purpose and authorship see S.R.O., D.641/5/E(C)/19, 24 July 1828.
[13] R. W. Sturgess, 'The Agric. Revolution on the Eng. Clays', *Ag. H.R.* xiv (2), 108.
[14] Pitt, *Staffs.* pt. ii. 29.
[15] *N.S.J.F.S.* xiii. 42.
[16] Practical Farmer, *Arable Land*, 22–3; *Staffs. Advertiser*, 26 Oct. 1833.
[17] S.R.O., D.(W.) 1781, bdle. K, valuation of farm of Sampson Sherratt, 1825.
[18] *Rep. Sel. Cttee. on Agric.* 522.

[19] *N.S.J.F.S.* xiii. 42.
[20] *Staffs. Advertiser*, 12 Oct. 1844, 4 Oct. 1856.
[21] *J.R.A.S.E.* 2nd ser. v. 272–3.
[22] *N.S.J.F.S.* xiii. 45.
[23] *Staffs. Advertiser*, 4 Oct. 1851.
[24] Ibid. 29 Nov. 1856.
[25] *J.R.A.S.E.* 2nd ser. v. 285.
[26] Ibid. 272–82.
[27] *S.H.C.* 1950–1, 234.
[28] S.R.O., D.(W.) 1761, box 1, valuation of Horton Hay estate 1805, Jas. Myatt's farm.
[29] *N.S.J.F.S.* xiii. 45.
[30] Sturgess, 'Agric. Staffs.' 409; above, p. 61; S.R.O., D.(W.) 1761, box 12, Rushton leases, 2 Feb. 1791, 25 Mar., 29 July 1797.

Moorlands increased and crops were diversified.[31] Potatoes were widely grown by cottagers in gritstone areas. In 1801 the quantity of grain grown around Cheddleton was said to have much increased in the previous seventeen years; wheat, barley, and turnips had been introduced. In 1811 at Alton Abbey Swedish and common turnips, potatoes, cabbages, and vetches were cultivated. At Rushton James in Leek the maximum permitted proportion of farm-land under arable rose from 12·1 per cent in a lease of 1797 to between 12·3 and 22·1 per cent in agreements of 1812 and to between 15·9 and 35·4 per cent in agreements of 1822 and 1826. In 1805 the estate was 21 per cent arable. At Horton Hay the average arable then covered 14 per cent of farm-land; the maximum permitted averaged 14·6 per cent in 1813 and 16·9 per cent in 1822 and 1826. Elsewhere, however, there may have been a contraction in the arable after 1815. The earlier expansion sometimes diverted manure from grassland, and on the Bill family's estates in Alton parish the use of manure on arable was restricted by 1815. At Rushton and Horton from 1822 all dung was to be laid on the grassland. In the 1830s further attempts were made round Alton to increase arable production with fodder crops and improved drainage; in the 1860s some farms there had about one-third of the land under the plough, growing rape and turnips as well as oats. Nevertheless oats remained predominant further north.

The urban growth of the Potteries and the Black Country produced special types of arable farming, either market-gardening or intensive corn cropping using town manure, though sometimes famers turned to cow-keeping and fattening.[32] In 1800 the Black Country parishes of Tipton, Sedgley, Rowley Regis, and Kingswinford had large areas under wheat, with higher yields than the surrounding countryside. Barley and rye were grown in some of them.[33] In West Bromwich in the 1830s good crops of wheat were grown on both unbroken and reclaimed land, and some oats were produced.[34] Some wheat was still grown at Tipton in the 1840s.[35] Rotations were irregular. On Lord Dartmouth's estate in West Bromwich the four-course was never imposed.[36] The prohibition, elsewhere general, on selling straw and hay was lifted, provided sufficient manure was restored.[37] In the 1850s a tenant was growing white straw crops in consecutive years, selling straw and buying town manure.[38] A like system was followed at Darlaston in the 1840s.[39] Market-gardening was then developing at Harborne,[40] while the heat of underground fires in abandoned collieries near Dudley permitted the raising of early potatoes for the London market.[41] A combination of good soil and ready markets encouraged a similar growth of gardening round Tamworth and Lichfield. In 1818 plentiful crops of early peas, and turnips and potatoes, were grown there, and by the early 1830s 'immense quantities' of onions and carrots for Birmingham, Walsall, and Wolverhampton. The area was 'the garden of the county'.[42] Potato ground would let at a better price than most neighbouring farm-land, as the potato was the staple of the poor.[43] In 1845 there were 68 market-gardeners in Lichfield and Tamworth.[44] In the early 1860s the Tamworth gardeners were using dry

[31] This para. is based on N.S.J.F.S. i. 80–1, 83–4; xiii. 42; S.H.C. 1950–1, 233; Sturgess, 'Agric. Staffs.' 413; B. Webb, 'The Parish of Sheen, Staffs.' Annals of Dioc. of Lichfield (1859), 24; S.R.O., D.(W.) 1761, box 1, valuation of Horton Hay estate 1805, and Horton Hay deeds, leases and agreements; box 2, Rushton leases; box 8, Rushton leases, and estate valuation 1805.
[32] See p. 112.
[33] Bodl. MS. Top. Gen. b. 51, f. 14.
[34] J. Reeves, Hist. and Topography of West Bromwich and its Vicinity (n.d. but preface dated 1836), 95.
[35] 1st Rep. Com. Midland Mining, S. Staffs. [508], p. 51, H.C. (1843), xiii.

[36] Sturgess, 'Agric. Staffs.' 324.
[37] Ibid. 91.
[38] Ibid. 99.
[39] N.S.J.F.S. xiii. 45.
[40] Ibid.
[41] 1st Rep. Com. Midland Mining, S. Staffs. p. v.
[42] Parson and Bradshaw, Dir. Staffs. (1818), pt. i, p. cl; White, Dir. Staffs. (1834), 64; Staffs. Advertiser, 26 Oct. 1833.
[43] J. T. Law, The Poor Man's Garden, or a few brief rules for regulating Allotments of Land to the Poor, for Potatoe Gardens (3rd edn. 1830), 5, 8–9.
[44] Sturgess, 'Agric. Staffs.' 363.

sewage and sweepings from Birmingham as manure.[45] Similar influences were at work elsewhere. In 1834 it was stated that the light soil at Wombourn was noted for the production of early vegetables and that 'extensive garden and nursery grounds' had long been cultivated there.[46] The produce presumably supplied the near-by Black Country towns. The spread of potato growing in the western Moorlands from the early 19th century is likewise attributable to the expanding market provided by the Potteries.[47]

Attention was being given from the early 19th century to the introduction of new root crops. Pitt made no mention of swedes in the 1790s, but in 1817 he stated that they were 'a favourite'. He himself was one of the first to try cultivating mangolds, on his farm at Pendeford, but by 1817 they had sunk into disrepute because they were thought to paralyze the cattle that ate them.[48] The 1st Lord Hatherton later encouraged his tenants by means of prizes to adopt mangolds instead of turnips.[49] By the late 1860s swedes and mangolds were the principal root crops.[50] An alternative fodder crop was the cabbage. It was widely cultivated in the late 18th century and was regarded as good for milking-cows and for sheep, but it was less often grown in the early 19th century because of the spread of swedes. To some extent the crops were complementary, since cabbages did best on heavy soils too wet for swedes.[51] By the 1860s the qualities of cabbage as fodder were again appreciated and its cultivation was 'greatly extending'.[52] In the early 19th century potatoes were also grown as fodder, especially for fattening pigs. Potatoes for sale were mainly supplied by cottagers and smallholders, but some were grown by farmers.[53] They were, however, thought to exhaust the soil, and leases severely restricted their acreage.[54]

Other crops, also grown but often prohibited or restricted, were hemp, flax, and rape. In the early 19th century a maximum of 1 a. was common in leases,[55] but smaller allowances or absolute prohibitions are recorded down to the middle of the century.[56] Appreciable quantities of flax were grown in the early 1870s, the maximum area under the crop being 194 a. in 1871.[57] In 1828 a farmer at Mitton near Penkridge was experimenting with hops.[58] Fruit seems to have been of little importance in the county, though Enville was noted for its black cherries[59] and in the late 1860s damsons were grown at Wootton and surrounding parishes for sale 'in distant markets'.[60]

Improved techniques of cultivation and the use of machinery on arable farms spread gradually. Oxen were little used for ploughing by the 1790s.[61] Sir Edward Littleton (d. 1812), however, championed them for other draught purposes.[62] They were still occasionally used, especially for harrowing, until at least 1850.[63] Normally, however, horses were thought more economical; the double, two-furrow plough, which required four horses and two men, and the single-wheeled plough, with two horses and one man, were both widespread in the 1790s.[64] Between 1796 and 1804 a

[45] R. J. Battersby, 'Development of Market Gardening in Eng. 1850–1914' (London Univ. Ph.D. thesis, 1960), 11.
[46] White, *Dir. Staffs.* (1834), 292.
[47] Sturgess, 'Agric. Staffs.' 417; Pitt, *Staffs.* pt. ii. 60.
[48] Pitt, *Staffs.* pt. ii. 41.
[49] Sturgess, 'Agric. Staffs.' 251.
[50] *J.R.A.S.E.* 2nd ser. v. 273.
[51] Pitt, *Agric. Staffs.* 53–4; Pitt, *Staffs.* pt. ii. 41.
[52] *J.R.A.S.E.* 2nd ser. v. 273.
[53] S.R.O., D.(W.) 1721/3/165, 1st bdle., acct. bk. 1802, Promiscuous; Pitt, *Staffs.* pt. ii. 41.
[54] S.R.O., D.240/K, bdle. A; D.952/2/2/3–4; D.1213/4, 29 Mar. 1848; D.(W.) 1813/31, /34, /36.
[55] Pitt, *Staffs.* pt. ii. 37.
[56] S.R.O., D.240/K, bdle. A; D.590/497; D.641/5/E(L)/2, conditions for letting Skeath House farm; D.952/2/2/4;

D.(W.) 1813/35, blank forms, and /36.
[57] Myers, *Staffs.* 599.
[58] *Staffs. Advertiser*, 8 Nov. 1828.
[59] White, *Dir. Staffs.* (1834), 256; (1851), 175.
[60] *J.R.A.S.E.* 2nd ser. v. 311.
[61] Pitt, *Agric. Staffs.* 149.
[62] Ibid. 150.
[63] *Staffs. Advertiser*, 1796–1800, farm-stock sale advertisements (22 per cent listing ox-harrows); ibid. 17 Apr. 1819, stock sale at Hilderstone Old Hall; S.R.O., D.641/5/E(A)/2/4, stock at 31 July 1815; /5, cash acct. 30 Dec. 1816; D.603 (unlisted), Hodson memos., misc. bdle., catalogue of stock sale at Tamhorn Park 1828; Peters, *Farm Buildings*, 112; W.S.L., Sale Cats. D/1/18, lots 79–84, 122–4; Caird, *Eng. Agric.* 242.
[64] Pitt, *Agric. Staffs.* 37; *Staffs. Advertiser*, 1796–1800, farm stock-sale adverts.

few of the gentry who were farming light soils introduced the Norfolk plough, with two horses pulling abreast,[65] and at a meeting of the Staffordshire Agricultural Society in 1802 Thomas Anson of Shugborough offered prizes for its use.[66] In 1813 two-horse Scotch ploughs were being used on heavy land also, as on the Paget estates at Burton[67] and the marquess of Stafford's at Trentham.[68] By 1819 Trentham covenants required tenants to plough and harrow with two horses abreast.[69] Loch instituted ploughing matches to encourage the use of fewer horses.[70] By 1821 the two-horse plough was apparently in use at Milwich.[71] It was required at Swynnerton by 1829.[72] Yet in 1838 on Sir Edward Vavasour's estate at Draycott-in-the-Moors, and in 1850 on Sir Robert Peel's at Drayton Bassett, the continued use of three or more horses in line, with two ploughmen, was criticized by visiting experts.[73] Ploughing with three or four horses was still common on strong land in the later 1860s.[74] Subsoil ploughing, which required eight to twelve horses, was tried on Sir Robert Peel's home farm in 1840. After further trials by a farmer at Lynn in Shenstone it was recommended where the surface was retentive but the subsoil not too clayey.[75] The 1st Lord Hatherton also tried it on newly inclosed land, without success.[76] It is not clear how far it was generally adopted, though in the late 1860s good loams might be ploughed to a depth of 10 inches.[77] In 1857 Lord Hatherton also tried a steam plough, apparently the first in Staffordshire, on his estate.[78] Steam ploughs were used on new inclosures on Cannock Chase in the 1860s.[79]

Another improvement was the spread of drill husbandry. In the early 1790s Pitt knew of only some twelve farms using seed-drills, half of them near his farm at Pendeford.[80] By 1817 wheat was often drilled in, and drilling-machines were made at Ettingshall.[81] On Lord Uxbridge's Burton estate, though there were still no corn-drills in 1814, bean-drills were used by then, and in 1812 the tenants had been encouraged to drill turnips. They were so convinced of the benefits of drilling that 'they would not have broadcast turnips another year if seed and labour was found them for nothing'.[82] In 1813 Lord Talbot required a tenant to use drills when sowing beans and peas.[83] Loch encouraged turnip-drilling on Lord Stafford's estates and noted in 1820 that the tenants had rapidly adopted it.[84] Tenants on an estate at Rickerscote in Castle Church were required in 1820 to drill their bean crops.[85] There were turnip- and bean-drills on Swynnerton Hall farm in 1826, and in 1828 the agent urged the tenants to drill root crops and beans.[86] Drilling seed in rows saved labour, since horse-hoes could be used between them. The use of horse-hoes and scufflers thus spread in association with drilling.[87] Nevertheless drilling and horse-hoeing did not become universal. In the late 1860s corn was not horse-hoed on heavy land and was often sown broadcast by choice.[88]

[65] W. Marshall, *Review of Reps. to Board of Agric. from Midland Dist. of Eng.* (York, 1815), 38.

[66] *Staffs. Advertiser*, 7 Aug. 1802.

[67] S.R.O., D.603 (unlisted), Hodson corresp., CE 421, memo. on petition of Thos. Page, 19 Apr. 1813, and Hodson to Williams, 25 Mar. 1814.

[68] S.R.O., D.593/K/1/5/2, Loch to Rennie, 7 June 1813.

[69] S.R.O., D.593/K/3/6/1.

[70] Loch, *Acct. of Improvements*, 188; plate facing p. 144 below.

[71] S.R.O., D.(W.) 1826/43, Feb. 1821.

[72] S.R.O., D.641/5/E(C)/19, 12 Mar. 1829.

[73] *Staffs. Advertiser*, 28 Dec. 1838; Caird, *Eng. Agric.* 250-1.

[74] *J.R.A.S.E.* 2nd ser. v. 272, 275.

[75] *Staffs. Advertiser*, 20 Jan. 1844.

[76] Sturgess, 'Agric. Staffs.' 251.

[77] *J.R.A.S.E.* 2nd ser. v. 272. For a subsoil plough at Chillington in 1861 see Doyle, 'Giffards', 329.

[78] *Staffs. Advertiser*, 21 Mar. 1857.

[79] Sturgess, 'Agric. Staffs.' 277; *J.R.A.S.E.* 2nd ser. v. 294-5.

[80] Pitt, *Agric. Staffs.* 58.   [81] Pitt, *Staffs.* pt. ii. 27, 32.

[82] S.R.O., D.603 (unlisted), Hodson corresp., CE 421, Hodson to Aylmer, 30 Aug. 1812, 24 Mar. 1814.

[83] S.R.O., D.641/5/E(L)/2, conditions for letting Skeath House farm.

[84] Wordie, 'Great Landed Estate,' 414; Loch, *Acct. of Improvements*, 186.

[85] W.S.L., D.1798/371, conditions for letting lands of Hinton's Char. 4 Dec. 1820.

[86] S.R.O., D.641/5/E(A)/2/10, verso of first leaf; Practical Farmer, *Arable Land*, 24-6.

[87] *Staffs. Advertiser*, 27 Feb. 1796, stock sale at Drayton Manor; ibid. 10 Mar. 1798, stock sale at Dunnimeer, Tamworth; Wordie, 'Great Landed Estate,' 414; S.R.O., D.641/5/E(A)/2/10, verso of first leaf; D.603 (unlisted), Hodson memos., misc. bdle., catalogue of stock sale at Tamhorn Park 1828; W.S.L., Sale Cats. D/1/18.

[88] *J.R.A.S.E.* 2nd ser. v. 273.

Besides improved techniques of cultivation, harvesting and threshing machinery was often introduced on arable farms. About one farm in seven had a winnowing-machine by 1800.[89] Threshing-machines were then still rare but became commoner in the early 19th century. They were made at Brewood by 1817; the manufacturer had a portable machine which was hired by farmers throughout the county. Almost all the farms built on the Trentham estate c. 1813–20 included threshing-machines, a few of them steam-powered. Lord Uxbridge's agents were having them made for his Burton tenants in 1813, and one was installed at Tamhorn Park farm about then.[90] Stationary threshing-machines were not used in the area west of Stafford until after 1820.[91] By the late 1860s threshing-machines were very common, and reaping-machines becoming universal.[92]

GRASSLAND MANAGEMENT

As has been seen, the period was marked by a gradual conversion of arable to permanent pasture, particularly on the northern and eastern heavy soils. Grassland management, which was already a marked feature of Staffordshire agriculture in the 18th century, thus grew steadily in importance.

On most farms early in the period meadow, and often permanent pasture, were strictly delimited, and tenants were forbidden to plough them on pain of penalty rents. Such restrictions continued.[93] Especially on the heavy lands, meadow often formed a high proportion — between a quarter and a half — of the total permanent grass, since hay was the principal source of winter feed.[94] This restricted the available summer pasture and hence the numbers of stock that could be kept.[95] Leases also prohibited the sale of hay and dung,[96] but the prohibition could not stop farmers using all manure on the arable; the consequent exhaustion of meadow-land might lead to a further extension of its area, as apparently happened on the Chartley estate between 1809 and 1855.[97] In the 1790s William Leigh of Rushall Hall introduced the novel requirement that tenants use all the dung on the turf; the results were beneficial.[98] On the Leveson-Gower estates by 1789, and on several other estates by the early 19th century, covenants restricted the mowing of meadows, usually to once a year, and required their regular manuring, commonly every second year but sometimes annually.[99] By the 1840s the excess of meadow on heavy lands was less common.[1] Moreover the increased use of artificial fertilizers enabled grassland to be mowed twice a year without damage and with higher yields. Thus in 1844 R. S. Ford at Swynnerton wrote: 'Having in July dressed my clover grounds with guano, I have now a fine second crop of clover and rye-grass . . . which I am mowing for my horses and cattle in the stalls.'[2]

[89] *Staffs. Advertiser*, 1796–1800, farm-stock sale adverts. (14 per cent listing winnowing-machine or machine fan).
[90] Pitt, *Staffs.* pt. ii. 26–7; S.R.O., D.603 (unlisted), Hodson corresp., CE 317, Aylmer to Hodson, 20 May 1813; ibid. Hodson memos., misc. bdle., catalogue of stock sale at Tamhorn Park 1828; Wordie, 'Great Landed Estate', 414.
[91] Peters, *Farm Buildings*, 9.
[92] *J.R.A.S.E.* 2nd ser. v. 303, 309.
[93] Pitt, *Agric. Staffs.* 30; S.R.O., D.593/I/2/13, agreements of 1789; D.661/8/1/1/3–4; D.240/K, bdle. A, agreements 1829–44; D.641/5/E(L)/2, conditions for letting Skeath House farm; D.952/2/2/3–4; D.1287/2/1 conditions for letting estates in Staffs. and Salop.; D.1213/4, leases and agreements to 1865; D.(W.) 1761, box 1, lease of 29 July 1797, and Horton Hay deeds, leases of 1813 and agreements of 1822 and 1826; D.(W.) 1813/31; /34; /35, blank forms; Sturgess, 'Agric. Staffs.' App. p. 38.

[94] Sturgess, 'Agric. Staffs.' 374; S.R.O., D.641/5/E(S)/10, valuation of Swynnerton estate 1809; D.952/2/5/2–5; D.1213/3/1, survey of Maer Hall estate 1796; D.(W.) 1761, box 8, valuation of Rushton James and New Town 1805; D.(W.) 1813/25/4, sale partics. of High Onn, Whiston, and Broomhall estates 1863; D.(W.) 1813/34; /35, 20 Nov. 1849.
[95] Sturgess, 'Agric. Staffs.' 374–5.
[96] Pitt, *Agric. Staffs.* 30.
[97] Sturgess, 'Agric. Staffs.' 375–6.
[98] Pitt, *Agric. Staffs.* 30.
[99] S.R.O., D.593/I/2/13, agreements of 1789; D.(W.) 1761, box 1, Horton Hay deeds, leases of 1813; box 2, Rushton leases of 1812; D.(W.) 1813/31; /34; /35, blank forms; D.641/5/E(L)/2, Swynnerton agreements 1811–12 and conditions for letting Skeath House farm; /E(L)/3, 1 Dec. 1822; D.952/2/2/3–4; D.1213/4, lease of 30 Jan. 1865; Sturgess, 'Agric. Staffs.' App. p. 38.
[1] *N.S.J.F.S.* xiii. 47.
[2] S.R.O., D.641/5/E(C)/25, 4 Oct. 1844.

Sometimes leases exempted the tenant from manuring meadow if it were properly irrigated.[3] Pitt noted that in the 20 years to 1817 irrigation had been extensively adopted in various parts of the county, and that at Ingestre some of Lord Talbot's irrigated meadows produced two crops of hay a year.[4] At Blithfield between 1800 and 1807 Lord Bagot spent from £3 12s. to £8 8s. a year in watering meadows.[5] In 1802 the Newcastle-under-Lyme and Pottery Agricultural Society offered premiums for floating meadows.[6] Watering was sometimes included among permanent improvements which leases required tenants to undertake.[7] Water-meadows needed careful maintenance, including the annual cleansing of gutters.[8] Such cleansing was sometimes required in leases.[9] In the 1860s it was alleged that an Act had been passed in the early 19th century to improve the meadows of the Penk by irrigation but that the scheme proved uneconomic.[10] In the 1860s, however, there were still many artificial water-meadows along the main streams of the county. At Thorpe Hall in Thorpe Constantine and at farms at Acton Trussell and Teddesley the irrigation system conveyed liquid manure from the farmyards to the land.[11]

The seeds used on grassland in the county varied according to its function. For rotation grassland red and white clover, trefoil, and rye-grass were normal in the 1790s. Less common grasses were burnet, lucerne, and rib-grass; sainfoin had fallen out of use.[12] Seeding ratios varied during the period but showed no marked tendency to increase. Pitt stated in 1817 that from 10 to 20 lb. of clovers and trefoil and from a peck to half a bushel of rye-grass were sown to the acre.[13] Leases sometimes specified seeding ratios; at Horton Hay in 1813 as little as 7 lb. of clover to the acre was required, but normally the specification remained within Pitt's limits.[14] In the 1860s a progressive farmer at Penkridge was seeding with 1 bushel of rye-grass and 12 lb. of mixed clovers, including alsike. He sowed red and white clovers in alternate courses.[15] Rye-grass and clover were often used for laying land down to permanent pasture, but by the 1840s local writers condemned the practice and recommended mixtures of a broader range of seeds suited to the type of soil.[16] In the late 1860s a common mixture was 1 quarter to the acre of Yorkshire hay-seeds, with 6 lb. white clover, 3 lb. alsike, 2 lb. trefoil, 1 lb. cow-grass, 2 lb. rib-grass, and 1 peck Italian rye-grass.[17]

STOCK-FARMING

Stock-farming, like arable farming, was subject to regional distinctions. The lighter lands in the south, where root crops augmented winter fodder, were characterized by a variable stock-keeping, with some cattle-rearing, dairying, and fattening, but with the emphasis on sheep. On the northern heavy lands there was a steady growth of dairying. In the Moorlands cattle-rearing was prominent, while dairying too developed, especially in limestone areas. Dairying also grew on the edge of towns. Stocking rates

---

[3] S.R.O., D.641/5/E(L)/3, 22 Sept. 1824; D.(W) 1813/31; /35, blank forms; D.952/2/2/3.
[4] Pitt, *Staffs.* pt. ii. 86, 89.
[5] S.R.O., D.(W.) 1721/3/165, 1st bdle., acct. bks. 1800–7, Husbandry.
[6] *Staffs. Advertiser*, 19 Feb. 1803.
[7] S.R.O., D.593/I/2/13, lease of 9 Feb. 1789 to Jas. Poynor of Great Wyrley; D.1213/4, lease of 8 Jan. 1836.
[8] Pitt, *Staffs.* pt. ii. 63.
[9] S.R.O., D.641/5/E(L)/2, conditions for letting Skeath House farm; /3, 20 Mar. 1827.
[10] *J.R.A.S.E.* 2nd ser. v. 298. The Act has not been identified but may be the Penkridge, Cannock, Berkswich, and Teddesley Inclosure Act, 1814, 54 Geo. III, c. 50

(Local and Personal, not printed).
[11] *J.R.A.S.E.* 2nd ser. v. 300.
[12] Pitt, *Agric. Staffs.* 79–80.   [13] Pitt, *Staffs.* pt. ii. 50–1.
[14] S.R.O., D.(W.) 1761, box 1, Horton Hay deeds, leases of 1813 and agreements of 1822 and 1826; D.(W.) 1813/31; /34; /36; D.641/5/E(L)/2, conditions for letting Skeath House farm; D.952/2/2/4; D.1213/4, lease of 8 Apr. 1850; W.S.L., D.1798/371, Hodson to Collins, 10 Jan. 1804, and conditions for letting lands of Hinton's Char. 4 Dec. 1820.
[15] *J.R.A.S.E.* 2nd ser. v. 291.
[16] *Staffs. Advertiser*, 13 Jan. 1844; [Ford], *How is the Farmer to Live?* 5.
[17] *J.R.A.S.E.* 2nd ser. v. 274.

were highest on the light lands,[18] because the greater winter keep from roots outweighed the lower proportion of grass.

In the 1790s sheep were widely kept on the waste lands in the south, west, and north of the county; each area had its own breed.[19] On cultivated ground they were less important than cattle. In the late 1790s about two-fifths of farmers kept them, while almost all kept cattle; those who kept sheep usually had two or fewer sheep for every head of cattle, and only a few had substantially more. Most, though not all, large-scale sheep enterprises, with more than 100 sheep, were in the south.[20] About 1840 it was still true that more sheep were kept in the south.[21] In 1850 all Peel's tenants at Drayton Bassett kept them.[22] Numbers of sheep in the county fell from c. 186,700 in 1800 to c. 120,000 in 1837, but rose again to 365,945 in 1868; in 1875 there were 316,800.[23]

The Cannock Heath sheep, a short-woolled Down breed, became the predominant breed on the light lands. Sir Edward Littleton's crossings with Ross rams improved both the meat and the wool.[24] The breed was slow to mature, but by 1850 early maturity was achieved by crossing a Cannock ram with a Leicester ewe and continuing the cross with a Cannock ram, as on Peel's estate at Drayton. The improvements to the breed produced a much heavier fleece. The Cannock became an accepted variant of the Shropshire breed and spread across the county, replacing shorter-woolled types. By 1876 it was general.[25]

Other breeds had been tried. In the late 18th and early 19th centuries some Derbyshire, Dorset, and Cotswold flocks were kept,[26] and in 1816 119 Norfolk ewes were bought for Swynnerton Hall farm.[27] George Tollet of Betley, who was living at Swynnerton in 1794, experimented with Merinos, crossed them with Ryelands and Southdowns, and showed some at the sheep-shearing at Holkham (Norf.) in 1805.[28] There were also fashions for other close-woolled breeds: for Ryelands c. 1800[29] and for Southdowns from the 1810s. The 1st Lord Hatherton kept up to 2,000 Southdowns until at least 1850.[30] Still more persistent were the long-woolled Leicesters, which were common in the 1790s.[31] They were said to be better adapted than the Southdowns to rich pastures[32] and were therefore kept, for example, at Trentham in 1820.[33] Lord Talbot, on the other hand, who kept a flock of Leicesters at Ingestre, eventually abandoned them because the land had become too rich for a breeding flock.[34] By the late 1860s the Leicesters, either pure-bred or crossed with Cotswolds or Lincolns, had emerged as the dominant Moorland breed, replacing the native Limestones.[35]

By the 1790s the demand for lamb as well as mutton from the industrial areas of the county encouraged farmers to keep flying flocks. Ewes were bought in at Michaelmas and put to the ram; the lambs were sold off in spring and the ewes a few months later.[36] Even when a permanent flock was kept many more animals might be bought and sold during the year: thus at Peatswood, Tyrley, in 1818–20 Thomas Twemlow was apparently buying wethers in the winter and selling them off fat the next year.[37] On Peel's

[18] N.S.J.F.S. xiii. 48.
[19] Pitt, Agric. Staffs. 136–41; above, p. 71.
[20] Staffs. Advertiser, 1796–1800, farm-stock sale adverts.
[21] N.S.J.F.S. xiii. 44.
[22] Caird, Eng. Agric. 249.
[23] Sturgess, 'Agric. Staffs.' 328–9; Agric. Returns G.B. [C. 1303], p. 81, H.C. (1875), lxxix.
[24] [T. H. Horne], The Complete Grazier (4th edn. 1816), 11; Pitt, Agric. Staffs. 137; above, p. 71.
[25] Sturgess, 'Agric. Staffs.' 328–9; Caird, Eng. Agric. 250; J.R.A.S.E. 2nd ser. v. 306.
[26] Pitt, Agric. Staffs. 144–5; Staffs. Advertiser, 27 Feb. 1796, 18 Feb. 1797, 16 Mar. 1799, 28 Mar. 1803.
[27] S.R.O., D.641/5/E(A)/2/4.
[28] Pitt, Agric. Staffs. 194–5; R. A. C. Parker, Coke of Norfolk: a Financial and Agricultural Study 1707–1842, 120.
[29] Staffs. Advertiser, 14 Jan., 18 Feb. 1797, 21 Apr. 1798, 16 Mar., 9 Nov. 1799, 8 Mar. 1800 (bis), 5 and 12 Mar. 1803; Pitt, Staffs. pt. ii. 96.
[30] Pitt, Staffs. pt. ii. 72, 94–6; S.R.O., D.952/2/3/7; D.641/5/E(A)/2/4–7 and 10, stocktakings; W.S.L., Sale Cat. D/1/18; Sturgess, 'Agric. Staffs.' 247; Caird, Eng. Agric. 242.
[31] Pitt, Agric. Staffs. 142.
[32] Pitt, Staffs. pt. ii. 73.
[33] Wordie, 'Great Landed Estate,' 408.
[34] Farmer's Mag. 2nd ser. xix. 3.
[35] J.R.A.S.E. 2nd ser. v. 313.
[36] Pitt, Agric. Staffs. 145.
[37] S.R.O., D.952/2/3/7.

estate at Drayton Bassett in 1850 some farmers sold off fat hoggets at 12 to 15 months but others fattened them a second year.[38] In the late 1860s on the Moorlands lambs had to be sold off each autumn because of the shortage of winter keep; on the other hand one model tenant on light land at Penkridge sold only a quarter of the flock each year.[39] Purchased foodstuffs were used to fatten sheep by the 1850s. In 1851 the use of rape cake was said to be spreading round Stafford; oilcake, carrots, and grains were also used.[40] On Croxden Abbey farm in the late 1860s the winter pasture was supplemented by the use of cake.[41]

The Moorlands had long been noted as a source of store cattle for richer pastures in the south;[42] in the 1860s shortage of winter keep still forced an annual autumn sale of surplus stock.[43] Rearing was also practised elsewhere in the county; in the 1840s it was important in the area west and north of Cannock Chase.[44] In the 1860s dairy farmers throughout the county usually reared replacements on the farm.[45]

In the 1790s Staffordshire was no longer 'considerably a feeding county'. Nevertheless some larger farmers fattened cattle, chiefly heifers and cows. Part-fed cattle were sold to drovers for the London market. Stall-feeding was practised in winter; feeds included turnips, grains, and cabbages, while linseed-oil cake was 'a good deal used'.[46] At Blithfield £25 8s. 4d. was spent on oilcake in 1805.[47] In 1816–17 Lord Anson was winter-fattening 60 cattle for sale at Smithfield, and about the same time Lord Talbot at Ingestre was fattening oxen on hay, turnips, and some oilcake.[48] By 1850 Lord Hatherton was stall-feeding bullocks in summer as well as winter on turnips, swedes, and mangolds, with 3 to 7 lb. oilcake or corn daily.[49] A similar system of fattening was pursued in light-land districts in the 1860s, with mangolds, chaff, and malt dust, or turnips, chaff, and oilcake.[50] There was apparently more emphasis on cattle-fattening in such districts from the mid 1860s.[51]

The chief development in cattle-farming, however, was the spread of dairying. In the years around 1800, though most farms had some dairy cattle[52] and the best dairy was said to be at Dunstall near Wolverhampton,[53] the principal dairying area was still between Trent and Dove.[54] By c. 1840, with the extension of permanent pasture, dairying predominated across north Staffordshire and was also widespread among mixed livestock enterprises further south.[55] By the late 1860s dairying 'is carried on more or less in almost every part of Staffordshire. It is the mainstay of its farming, except on the small extent of land which is too light for grass'.[56] It expanded round towns to supply the demand there for milk; it was important near Newcastle, for example, c. 1840.[57] In the Black Country by 1860 the 'land uninvaded by the other industries is mostly in small holdings used as pasture, which is highly profitable owing to the large demand . . . for milk'. Coal-tip wastes were rich in valuable salts and produced good pasture. The barren cows were fattened and sold to local butchers.[58] Cows were kept in the towns themselves and probably stall-fed on purchased foodstuffs; in 1851 there were 7 cow-keepers in Walsall, 7 in Bilston, and 20 in Wolverhampton.[59]

[38] Caird, *Eng. Agric.* 250.
[39] *J.R.A.S.E.* 2nd ser. v. 291, 313.
[40] *Staffs. Advertiser*, 1 Feb., 5 Apr. 1851.
[41] *J.R.A.S.E.* 2nd ser. v. 278.
[42] See p. 74.
[43] *J.R.A.S.E.* 2nd ser. v. 313.
[44] *N.S.J.F.S.* xiii. 44.
[45] *J.R.A.S.E.* 2nd ser. v. 270.
[46] Pitt, *Agric. Staffs.* 83–4.
[47] S.R.O., D.(W.) 1721/3/165, 1st bdle., acct. bk. 1805, Promiscuous.
[48] Pitt, *Staffs.* pt. ii. 90, 93–4.
[49] Caird, *Eng. Agric.* 242.

[50] *J.R.A.S.E.* 2nd ser. v. 291, 293.
[51] Sturgess, 'Agric. Staffs.' 346.
[52] *Staffs. Advertiser*, 1796–1800, farm-stock sale adverts.
[53] Pitt, *Agric. Staffs.* 134.
[54] Above, p. 76; *S.H.C.* 1950–1, 242; S.R.O., D.603 (unlisted), Hodson corresp., CE 421, Hodson to [Lord Graves], attached to letters of 16 and 22 Apr. 1816.
[55] *N.S.J.F.S.* xiii. 44, 48.
[56] *J.R.A.S.E.* 2nd ser. v. 269.
[57] *N.S.J.F.S.* xiii. 48.
[58] *Rep. Com. State of Popular Educ. in Eng.* vol. ii [2794-II], pp. 250–1, H.C. (1861), xxi(2).
[59] White, *Dir. Staffs.* (1851), 117, 148, 658.

There was apparently a condensed-milk factory near Eccleshall *c.* 1840, and in 1850 a farmer (apparently at Tixall) was manufacturing evaporated milk.[60]

In rural areas, however, the principal object of dairying remained cheese-making.[61] There were two types: Cheshire in the west and north-west, and Derbyshire in the north and east.[62] The Derbyshire cheeses were smaller. On the Drayton Bassett estate in 1850 a 25 lb. weight was preferred, and in the 1860s cheeses were commonly about that size, although heavier cheeses of 50–150 lb. were also made in eastern Staffordshire.[63] Cheddar cheese was made at Leigh by 1870.[64] Dairying was generally a seasonal activity, the peak period being the early summer when pastures were at their best. Cheese-making continued until November; and the winter's milk was used for suckling and butter-making. In the 1860s, however, some farmers made cheese all the year round.[65] It was either disposed of directly to cheese factors who carried it to London, or sold at weekly markets or seasonal fairs.[66] Uttoxeter fair was important for cheese early in the period.[67] Holy Cross in Clent (later Worcs.) had two cheese fairs by 1818, when Lichfield and Walsall fairs were also noted for cheese.[68] Burton fair was important by 1825, while new cheese fairs were established at Leek in the earlier 1820s, Stafford in 1838 and Stone in 1840.[69]

Such new or expanding fairs reflect the rising output of dairy produce, and there is some evidence that stocking densities also increased, especially on heavy land. In the Moorlands they were sometimes high early in the period. At Horton Hay in 1805, on an estate already predominantly in grass, there were on average tyings for 18 cows to every 100 a.,[70] the same figure as at Butterton, a limestone dairying district, in 1870.[71] Further south, however, relatively fewer cattle were kept in the late 18th and early 19th centuries. A farm at Swynnerton in 1799 had 5·45 cows to every 100 a.;[72] on the Wolseley family's estate in 1825 two farms had tyings for 6·5 and 8 cows respectively to every 100 a.[73] Those farms were still mainly arable, but by *c.* 1840 the shift to pasture had increased cattle stocking rates on heavy land to 7·5–11·5 to every 100 a.[74] In the mid 19th century they probably increased faster; at Chillington home farm, for instance, the dairy herd more than doubled between 1842 and 1858.[75] The cattle plague of 1865–6 was severe at least in north Staffordshire, but its effects seem to have been temporary.[76]

It was the increased use of purchased winter fodder by dairy farms that made possible the larger herds found from the 1850s onwards. George Vernon of Milwich, who in 1827 was foddering cattle with hay and straw only,[77] was probably typical of his period. In 1846 R. S. Ford noted that linseed cake, which was much cheaper than hay, 'has long been extensively and successfully used in stall-feeding by the best light-land farmers. But amongst dairy farmers and on strong soils, where from want of turnips its use is most indicated, it has been very little tried'. He recommended 6 lb. of cake a day for each cow. The use of upland hay might thus almost be superseded, and the

[60] 'Agric. Our Vital Ind.' 26 May 1917; Caird, *Eng. Agric.* 234–5.

[61] *N.S.J.F.S.* xiii. 48; *J.R.A.S.E.* 2nd ser. v. 269.

[62] Sturgess, 'Agric. Staffs.' 44.

[63] Caird, *Eng. Agric.* 249; *J.R.A.S.E.* 2nd ser. v. 270–1.

[64] W.S.L., Sale Cat. F/5/26.

[65] *J.R.A.S.E.* 2nd ser. v. 270–1; A. Henstock, 'Cheese Manufacture and Marketing in Derb. and N. Staffs. 1670–1870', *Derb. Arch. Jnl.* lxxxix. 36.

[66] *Derb. Arch. Jnl.* lxxxix. 38, 44–5.

[67] *Univ. Brit. Dir.* iv. 651.

[68] Parson and Bradshaw, *Dir. Staffs.* (1818), pt. i, pp. ccxxxvii–ccxxxix.

[69] Sturgess, 'Agric. Staffs.' 432–3; White, *Dir. Staffs.*

(1834), 700; (1851), 359; below, p. 215.

[70] S.R.O., D.(W.) 1761, box 1, valuation of Horton Hay estate 1805.

[71] Sturgess, 'Agric. Staffs.' 414.

[72] S.R.O., D.641/5/E(L)/2, 2 Feb. 1799, Thos. Robinson's agreement.

[73] S.R.O., D.(W.) 1781, bdle. K, particulars and valuation of lands in occupation of Ric. Wenlock, and of Sampson Sherratt's farm.

[74] *N.S.J.F.S.* xiii. 48.

[75] Doyle, 'Giffards', 315.

[76] R. Perren, 'The Cattle Plague in N. Staffs. 1865–67' (unpublished TS. in possession of Dr. Perren of Aberdeen Univ.), pp. 3–4, 7, 11.

[77] S.R.O., D.(W.) 1826/41, 1, 9, 25 Apr. 1827.

land devoted to making it, usually some of the best turf on the farm, might be added to the summer pasture.[78] Feeding with oilcake spread rapidly. It was being used by tenants at Swynnerton in the mid 1840s[79] and extensively at Beaudesert home farm by at least 1847.[80] By the late 1860s cake was in general use in dairy areas; the best farmers gave it in summer as well as winter. Grains were also a common foodstuff.[81] Brewers' grains spread from the immediate vicinity of Burton;[82] by the 1840s maize was beginning to be used;[83] rice meal occurs by the 1860s.[84] Fodder purchases were still rising fast in the late 1860s and early 1870s, as on the Twemlow estate at Tyrley and T. Carrington Smith's farm at Admaston in Blithfield.[85] On the Moorlands, however, despite the use of purchased feeds, winter fodder remained scarce and dairymen bought in cattle to milk during the summer only.[86]

As more and more farmers favoured stall-feeding with purchased and prepared feeds, more equipment and machinery was needed on the dairy farm. A handful of farmers in the late 18th century had straw-engines, and occasionally bean- or oat-mills.[87] Turnip-cutters apparently came into general use in the 1830s.[88] In 1833 the machinery at Shugborough Park farm included 4 turnip-cutters and 2 chaff-engines.[89] By the late 1860s there were root-pulpers and chaff-cutters on almost all dairy farms; on many estates steam-engines and mills for grinding and crushing had been installed.[90] On large farms from c. 1830 steaming or boiling equipment was sometimes installed,[91] but by the late 1860s boiling and steaming were going out of fashion in favour of pulping and mixing.[92] Mowing-machines were by then much reducing the cost of hay-making.[93]

In the 1790s the leading breed of cattle was a local longhorn.[94] It was gradually replaced by the shorthorn. Sir John Wrottesley kept shorthorns by 1817,[95] and Lord Lichfield had a herd in the early 1830s.[96] In 1838 a visiting expert recommended shorthorns, which were 'increasingly in demand', to Sir Edward Vavasour's tenants at Draycott-in-the-Moors.[97] In 1850 at Drayton Bassett the longhorn was giving way to the improved shorthorn, which matured earlier and fattened more heavily.[98] By the late 1860s the longhorn was almost extinct; most farmers kept shorthorns with a high proportion of pedigree blood.[99] There had been experiments with Channel Island cattle; some were being kept at Trentham in 1820,[1] some at Audley Cross, Tyrley, in 1834,[2] and a few at Chillington in the 1850s.[3] At Trentham, however, most of the milch kine were of Yorkshire breeds.[4]

Several landowners experimented with beef breeds. The 2nd Lord Bagot continued to build up the family's herd of Scotch oxen; between 1800 and 1807 £1,385 11s. was laid out on them.[5] He also bought a few Herefords in 1804, 1805, and 1808.[6] Lord

[78] [Ford], *How is the Farmer to Live?* 5–6.
[79] S.R.O., D.641/5/E(C)/26, Nov. 1845, memoranda; /28, 13 Apr. 1847.
[80] S.R.O., D.603 (unlisted), 'B.D.F. 1847', cash acct.
[81] *J.R.A.S.E.* 2nd ser. v. 270–7, 304.
[82] Sturgess, 'Agric. Staffs.' 389.
[83] S.R.O., D.603 (unlisted), 'B.D.F. 1847'; D.641/5/E(C) /26, 13 Aug. 1847.
[84] *J.R.A.S.E.* 2nd ser. v. 280; S.R.O., D.952/2/3/12, 8 July 1874.
[85] S.R.O., D.952/2/3/10–11; T. Carrington Smith, *Story of a Staffs. Farm* (Stafford, 1909 edn.), 34 (copy in W.S.L.).
[86] *J.R.A.S.E.* 2nd ser. v. 313.
[87] *Staffs. Advertiser*, 27 Feb., 12 Mar., 3 Dec. 1796, 15 Mar., 15 Nov. (*bis*) 1800, farm-stock sale adverts.
[88] Peters, *Farm Buildings*, 167.
[89] W.S.L., Sale Cat. D/1/18.
[90] *J.R.A.S.E.* 2nd ser. v. 303.

[91] Peters, *Farm Buildings*, 168; S.R.O., D.641/5/E(C)/25, 6 Dec. 1844; *Staffs. Advertiser*, 29 Nov. 1856; Caird, *Eng. Agric.* 235.
[92] *J.R.A.S.E.* 2nd ser. v. 303.
[93] Ibid. 309.
[94] Pitt, *Agric. Staffs.* 130.
[95] Pitt, *Staffs.* pt. ii. 95.
[96] W.S.L., Sale Cat. D/1/18.
[97] *Staffs. Advertiser*, 22 Dec. 1838.
[98] Caird, *Eng. Agric.* 249.
[99] *J.R.A.S.E.* 2nd ser. v. 269–70.
[1] Loch, *Acct. of Improvements*, App. p. 70.
[2] *Staffs. Advertiser*, 8 Mar. 1834.
[3] Doyle, 'Giffards', 315.
[4] Loch, *Acct. of Improvements*, App. p. 70.
[5] Above, p. 74; S.R.O., D.(W.) 1721/3/165, 1st bdle., acct. bks. 1800–7, Cattle and Sheep.
[6] S.R.O., D.(W.) 1721/3/165, 1st bdle., acct. bks. 1804–5, 1808, Cattle and Sheep; 1805, Promiscuous.

Talbot from the early 19th century to the 1840s was a prominent breeder of Herefords.[7] In 1817 Pitt noted several herds of Devons, sometimes kept as dairy cattle, at Weston Park, at Aqualate, and at Betley, as well as at Shugborough, where they had replaced pedigree longhorns; Sir George Pigot at Patshull kept Galloways.[8] In 1820 E. J. Littleton (later Lord Hatherton) had a mixed herd of longhorns, Devons, Herefords, and Durhams at Teddesley. In 1844–5 the Durhams were destroyed by rinderpest, and by 1850 Hatherton was concentrating on Herefords, which fattened better.[9] There were buffalo oxen at Shugborough in 1833.[10]

Pigs were widely kept in the county in the late 1790s, but in small herds.[11] Throughout the period they were normally an adjunct to the dairy, since they converted its refuse into a saleable product. They were also consumers of poor-grade meal and potatoes.[12] In 1850, however, 200 pigs kept at Brancote farm, Tixall, were folded on clover and roots, like sheep.[13] Early in the period the most popular pig was a cross between a large 'slouch-eared' breed and a smaller dwarf breed; they were killed after one or two years at 300 to 400 lb. weight. Larger animals had by then gone out of fashion.[14] The trend to smaller hogs continued; thus 30 pigs killed by George Vernon at his farm at Leigh between 1799 and 1806 averaged 299·6 lb., but 37 which he killed at his next farm at Milwich between 1812 and 1824 averaged 246 lb.[15] A new breed was the Tamworth pig.[16] It seems to have been a variant of the Berkshire breed, crossed with imported wild stock in the early 19th century.[17] Tamworths soon became popular, but by 1860 they were reported to be falling out of favour.[18] In 1834 the stock on a farm at Audley Cross, Tyrley, included several half-bred Chinese pigs.[19] In the late 1860s 'every mixture of white, black, and rusty-haired pigs' was kept; most store pigs came from Shropshire, and large bacon-hogs were again in favour.[20] In 1875 there were 50,820 pigs in the county.[21]

AGRARIAN ECONOMY AND SOCIETY

By the 1790s Staffordshire was a county dominated by large proprietors. Pitt could name 'six noblemen and two commoners within the county whose estates exceed £8,000 per annum'.[22] Large estates grew during the period. The Littletons' Teddesley estate increased from 8,310 a. in 1812 to 11,298 a. in 1863; the Leveson-Gowers' Trentham estate from 7,332 a. in 1809 to 10,507 a. in 1857; the Sneyds' Keele estate by 2,972 a. between 1829 and 1869.[23] The first earl of Harrowby (d. 1847) bought 679 a. in Staffordshire; the second (d. 1882) acquired a further 1,972 a. net.[24]

The object of such purchases was generally to round off the estate as a compact block, partly to make farming easier but partly to provide the landowner with a firmer basis for his social position and to avert intrusion on his land. Outlying plots were sold.[25] As a result the concentration of ownership increased. By 1873 31 per cent of the county

[7] Pitt, *Staffs.* pt. ii. 90; *Farmer's Mag.* 2nd ser. xix. 2–3.
[8] Pitt, *Staffs.* pt. ii. 93–7.
[9] Sturgess, 'Agric. Staffs.' 248; Caird, *Eng. Agric.* 242.
[10] W.S.L., Sale Cat. D/1/18.
[11] *Staffs. Advertiser*, 1796–1800, farm-stock sale adverts.
[12] Pitt, *Agric. Staffs.* 54, 151; Caird, *Eng. Agric.* 249; *J.R.A.S.E.* 2nd ser. v. 277–9, 306; Sturgess, 'Agric. Staffs.' 100.
[13] Caird, *Eng. Agric.* 234.
[14] Pitt, *Agric. Staffs.* 151.
[15] S.R.O., D.(W.) 1826/39, /43.
[16] See plate facing p. 129.
[17] A. F. Cheese, 'The Origin of the Tamworth Pig', *Friends of Shugborough Park Farm Newsletter* [no. 2,

1976], 5–7 (copy in W.S.L.).
[18] H. R. Davidson, *Production and Marketing of Pigs* (1953 edn.), 328.
[19] *Staffs. Advertiser*, 8 Mar. 1834.
[20] *J.R.A.S.E.* 2nd ser. v. 306.
[21] *Agric. Returns G.B.* [C. 1303], p. 81, H.C. (1875), lxxix.
[22] Pitt, *Agric. Staffs.* 16.
[23] Sturgess, 'Agric. Staffs.' 537–8.
[24] Reid, 'Landownership', 16–19, 48–53.
[25] Sturgess, 'Agric. Staffs' 538; Peters, *Farm Buildings*, 11; S.R.O., D.603 (unlisted), Hodson corresp., CE 421, Hodson to Uxbridge, 15 June 1814, 11 Jan. 1815; Hodson to (?)Sanderson, mid-Mar. 1817; D.641/E(C)/20, 30 Apr., 2 May, 20 July 1832, 18 Jan., 20 Mar., 1 Oct. 1833.

was owned by 6 peers and 2 commoners each with over 10,000 a.; Lord Lichfield, who had the largest estate, owned 21,433 a. The proportion of such very large estates was well above the national average. A further 17 per cent was covered by 26 estates of 3,000–10,000 a.; 9 of them were owned by peers and one by the duchy of Lancaster.[26]

Land prices in Staffordshire were high in relation to rental value. In 1796 the Maer Hall estate was valued at 27 years' purchase.[27] Thirty years' purchase was a more typical valuation c. 1830. In 1833 land was again falling to 27 years' purchase, except in the Lichfield market-gardening area where 30 years' purchase could still be obtained. Land was then worth more years' purchase in Staffordshire than in almost any other county, owing to the 'great mass of unemployed capital'.[28] On the one hand great landowners were willing to pay high, sometimes uneconomic, prices for convenient properties. In 1833 the duke of Sutherland's Trentham agent thought a convenient farm worth buying if it would pay $2\frac{1}{2}$ per cent on the purchase money,[29] while in the late 1830s and early 1840s Ralph Sneyd of Keele bought land at from 32 to 40 years' purchase, which was locally thought acceptable.[30] On the other hand manufacturers were investing in country estates. In Smethwick small estates were bought up by Birmingham and Black Country business and professional men;[31] in the north of the county the Twemlows are an example of successful pottery manufacturers who set themselves up as country squires.[32]

At the other extreme from the great estates were small properties of less than 100 a., which were unusually numerous in Staffordshire, occupying 16 per cent of the county in 1873.[33] That was partly no doubt the result of urbanization. There were, however, many small freeholds on Cannock Chase[34] and on parts of the Moorlands. In Upper Elkstone c. 1840, for example, the duke of Devonshire owned 143 a., another owner 141 a., and the rest was in 23 small freeholds of under 100 a.[35] Sheen c. 1859 was mainly owned by small freeholders who were said to be heavily mortgaged.[36]

Similarly the size of farms varied. On some estates, particularly in the south, fairly large farms were common early in the 19th century. On the Giffard estates in Brewood and neighbouring parishes in 1810 the median farm was over 100 a.; there were 9 farms over 300 a. and only 6 between 50 a. and 100 a. Yet there were also 26 holdings of between 5 a. and 50 a. and many cottage holdings.[37] On Lord Talbot's estate at Hopton in St. Mary's, Stafford, in 1815 there were as many farms over 200 a. as between 20 a. and 100 a., although the median was below 20 a.[38] Further north, as at Trentham and Swynnerton in 1809, there was the same variety, but with fewer large farms.[39] Small farms were probably most significant in the Moorlands. In 1820 E. J. Littleton noted that Moorland farmers were very poor compared with his own tenants.[40] In the Moorlands c. 1840 farms between 10 a. and 100 a. were six times as numerous as those over 100 a., and almost 22 times as numerous as those over 200 a.[41]

The size of farms, however, tended to grow. James Loch at Trentham was criticized for his 'great rage for uniting farms and turning adrift honest farmers',[42] and in fact the number of farms over 200 a. on the estate rose from 7 in 1809 to 13 in 1833.[43]

[26] *Returns of Owners of Land 1873, vol. ii* [C. 1097–1], H.C. (1874), lxxii; F. M. L. Thompson, *Eng. Landed Society in the 19th Century*, 32, 114. The leading 8 landowners were not of the same families as the 8 dominant in the 1790s.
[27] S.R.O., D.1213/3/1. [28] *Rep. Sel. Cttee. on Agric.* 528–9.
[29] S.R.O., D.641/5/E(C)/20, 18 Jan. 1833.
[30] Sturgess, 'Agric. Staffs.' 142.
[31] *V.C.H. Staffs.* xvii. 100–6.
[32] F. R. Twemlow, *The Twemlows: their Wives and their Homes* (Wolverhampton, priv. print. 1910), 37, 41–2, 44, 57.
[33] Thompson, *Eng. Landed Soc.* 117.

[34] *J.R.A.S.E.* 2nd ser. v. 295.
[35] F. J. Johnson, 'Settlement Pattern of North-East Staffs.' (Univ. of Wales M.A. thesis, 1964), 324.
[36] *Annals of Dioc. of Lichfield* (1859), 24.
[37] S.R.O., D.590/354. [38] S.R.O., D.240/E/193.
[39] Wordie, 'Great Landed Estate', App. IV; S.R.O., D.641/5/E(S)/10.
[40] Sturgess, 'Agric. Staffs.' 348.
[41] Johnson, 'NE. Staffs.' 205–339.
[42] T. Bakewell, *Remarks on a Publication by Jas. Loch* (Stone, 1820), 136–7.
[43] Wordie, 'Great Landed Estate', App. IV.

The same trend can be seen on other estates until the 1870s.[44] Landlords and agents favoured the large tenant with capital.[45] In the county as a whole the number of farmers fell from 7,430 in 1831 to 6,515 in 1841 and 6,508 in 1851.[46] Nevertheless even in the late 1860s the average farm in Staffordshire was only 44 a.; dairy farms were rarely above 200 a. and light-land arable farms rarely over 300 a.[47]

The low average illustrates the widespread persistence of smallholding. At Trentham the number of holdings under 20 a. rose from 351 in 1809 to 571 in 1833.[48] In 1835 the holdings of 36 out of Lord Anglesey's 46 tenants at Abbots Bromley, and 178 out of 257 at Burton-upon-Trent, were assessed at less than £10 rent, an indication that they were probably very small.[49] In 1850 there was in Staffordshire 'a large class of tenants with small holdings and little capital, chiefly on the stiff clay soils', who were said to be worse off than farm labourers.[50] In the late 1860s an observer noted many small dairy holdings along roadsides in Needwood forest.[51] In the Moorlands part-time farming re-emerged; on the limestone very high rents could be paid by men who worked in the copper mines or limestone quarries while the family looked after the dairy.[52] On the gritstone parts of Alstonefield parish further west quarrying, coal-mining, and domestic silk-weaving and button-making augmented the income from the holding.[53]

Regional differences in farm sizes were accompanied by differences in the degree of dependence on hired labour. In 1831 more than half the farms in more than three-quarters of the parishes and townships in the southern arable area employed non-family workers. On the Moorlands such a dependence on hired labour was found in less than a third of the villages, though the limestone dairymen used more hired labour than those in gritstone areas. In the rest of the county about a third of the parishes and townships had more than half their farms using only family labour.[54]

As has been seen, in the 18th century landlords were beginning to replace long leases of farms by annual agreements.[55] The process continued during the French wars. Sometimes the transition was gradual, a phase of short leases being interposed. Thus on the Leveson-Gower estates leases of from 3 to 7 years were granted round Wolverhampton between 1789 and 1792, although long leases, made earlier, still prevailed at Trentham. From 1804 the latter were bought up from the tenants. Loch introduced annual tenancies on the estate as leases fell in, and found that this encouraged tenants to improve their farms.[56] On the Antrobus family's estates at Rushton James and Horton there was still one life-lease in 1805, while some tenants held from year to year, but most farms were on 14-year leases expiring in 1806. In 1812 and 1813 seven-year leases were granted, but by the 1820s all farms were held on yearly agreements.[57] Such a gradual transition may have been general in the Moorlands.[58] Elsewhere yearly tenancies became normal in the early 19th century.[59] Though tenants still demanded leases occasionally,[60] yearly agreements proved popular, since leases provided less protection against falling prices and farms were more often revalued than under a yearly system. Yearly tenure remained general in the 1860s.[61]

[44] Sturgess, 'Agric. Staffs.' 338, 390. [45] e.g. ibid. 155.
[46] *Census* (1831–51). [47] *J.R.A.S.E.* 2nd ser. v. 315.
[48] Wordie, 'Great Landed Estate,' App. IV.
[49] S.R.O., D.603 (unlisted), Rentals, folder, Bromley Pagets rental to 5 Apr. 1835. [50] Caird, *Eng. Agric.* 232.
[51] *J.R.A.S.E.* 2nd ser. v. 295. [52] Ibid. 311.
[53] Johnson, 'NE. Staffs.' 312–13.
[54] Sturgess, 'Agric. Staffs.' 341–2, 381, 414. [55] See p. 88.
[56] S.R.O., D.593/I/2/13; Wordie, 'Great Landed Estate', 109; Loch, *Acct. of Improvements*, 176–7; R. Perren, 'Effects of Agricultural Depression on the Eng. Estates of the Dukes of Sutherland, 1870–1900' (Univ. of Nott.

Ph.D. thesis, 1967), 158.
[57] S.R.O., D.(W.) 1761, box 1, valuation of Horton Hay estate 1805; Horton Hay deeds, leases and agreements; box 2, Rushton deeds, leases and agreements; box 8, valuation of Rushton James and New Town.
[58] *N.S.J.F.S.* i. 81.
[59] S.R.O., D.1287/2/1, conditions for letting estates in Staffs. and Salop.; D.240/K, bdle. A, printed forms; D.641/5/E(L)/2, conditions for letting Skeath House farm; D.(W.) 1813/31; Reid, 'Landownership', 23.
[60] e.g. S.R.O., D.641/5/E(C)/19, 25 Feb., 12 Mar. 1829.
[61] Caird, *Eng. Agric.* 231; *J.R.A.S.E.* 2nd ser. v. 301.

The usual term of entry was Lady Day. The incoming tenant was allowed to prepare the land beforehand for planting, usually from 1 November. The outgoing tenant was to preserve the clover and meadows for his successor from dates varying between October and 2 February; in return he could consume hay and straw on the farm, and occupy a boozy (or held-over) pasture, until 1 May.[62] His successor paid him for hay, straw, and manure on the farm, for grass seed, and for tillage of fallow; they divided the wheat crop, the incomer taking half when it was a brush crop and one-third when it was a fallow crop.[63]

In the 1790s Pitt estimated that farm rents in the county averaged below 20s. an acre but remarked that they varied between 10s. and 30s. according to the 'staple and condition' of farms.[64] Indeed local variations in rental value for those reasons were always more significant than chronological fluctuations. On the Maer Hall estate, for example, a 1796 survey gave valuations averaging 32s. 7d. an acre, but varying from 20s. to 80s. on individual farms.[65] Meadow was generally worth more than pasture, and pasture than arable.[66] Nevertheless fluctuations in rent were considerable. During the French wars rents were repeatedly revalued; in 1817 Pitt estimated that they ranged from 30s. to £2 or £3 an acre.[67] Estate rentals show that there were large increases. At Horton Hay, on poor land, the rental rose by 140 per cent between 1805 and 1813.[68] Rents there averaged 12s. 11½d. an acre in 1805 and 27s. 8d. in leases of 1813.[69] At Trentham rents in 1815 were about 146 per cent above the level of 1794.[70] At Swynnerton the assessed rental reached a peak in 1813 at 135 per cent above the 1793 level.[71] At Chartley a general revaluation in 1810 raised rents by 42 per cent,[72] while on the Sandon estate received rents increased from 16s. 4½d. an acre in 1798–1802 to 26s. 9d. an acre in 1813–17.[73]

The fall in prices of farm produce after the French wars inevitably brought a fall in rentals. In 1833 it was claimed that the rent of clay land had fallen by 5s. an acre since 1819 to between 12s. and 18s. The reductions had mainly taken place between 1819 and 1822. There was generally a 20 per cent reduction, which was too indiscriminate, since small clay-land arable farmers were hardest hit. There was less difference between the profitability of pasture and good arable than between that of good and poor arable. Reductions on large estates were greater than those on small, since large landowners could better afford to make them.[74] By 1850 many landowners, especially on cold clays, were thought to be heavily embarrassed.[75]

Landlords' reaction to the pressures to reduce rents varied considerably. At Trentham Loch responded by increasing estate expenditure, and up to 1821 the nominal rental rose. From 1821, however, half each tenant's rent was made to vary according to the price of corn, and by 1824 the assessed rental had fallen by 22½ per cent.[76] At Sandon the 1st earl of Harrowby refused a general reduction but made concessions to individual tenants; the largest reductions were on the largest farms. The nominal rental was higher from the mid 1830s to the mid 1840s than in the mid 1810s. In the crisis of 1849–51 the 2nd earl had to reduce rents by 10 per cent; he gave a 10 per cent

[62] S.R.O., D.593/I/2/13; D.240/K, bdle. A; D.661/8/1/1/3; D.952/2/2/3–4; D.1287/2/1, conditions for letting estates in Staffs. and Salop.; D.641/5/E(L)/2, conditions for letting Skeath House farm; D.590/497; D.1213/4, 8 Jan. 1836, 29 Mar. 1848, 30 Jan. 1865; D.(W.) 1813/31; /35, blank forms; /36.
[63] Rep. Sel. Cttee. on Agric. Customs, H.C. 461, pp. 128–33 (1847–8), viii.
[64] Pitt, Agric. Staffs. 26.
[65] S.R.O., D.1213/3/1.
[66] e.g. S.R.O., D.952/2/5/2–4; J.R.A.S.E. 2nd ser. v. 269.

[67] Pitt, Staffs. pt. ii. 24.
[68] S.R.O., D.(W.) 1761, box 1, Horton Hay rentals.
[69] Ibid., box 1, valuation of Horton Hay estate 1805; Horton Hay deeds, leases.
[70] Wordie, 'Great Landed Estate', App. III, graph 3.
[71] S.R.O., D.641/5/E(R)/1/3–5.
[72] Sturgess, 'Agric. Staffs.' 505.
[73] Reid, 'Landownership', 31.
[74] Rep. Sel. Cttee. on Agric. 528.
[75] Caird, Eng. Agric. 231.
[76] Wordie, 'Great Landed Estate', 120–1, 425–6, and App. III, graph 3.

manure allowance as well.[77] On the Pagets' estates there was apparently little or no fall in the rental after the French wars, but enormous arrears were allowed to accumulate.[78] On the Anson estates the rents were much reduced in 1819–20, and less so in the mid 1830s and late 1840s, but all the reductions were temporary.[79] On the Teddesley, Ingestre, and Swynnerton estates large and enduring cuts were made. At Teddesley in 1816 rents were cut 15 per cent below the 1813 level, and again by 10 per cent in 1821 and a further 10 per cent in 1835.[80] At Ingestre rents fell by 10 per cent between 1816 and 1821; there was a further 15 per cent cut in 1822, another of 3½ per cent in 1835 (recovered in 1837), and another in 1844; another, of 25 per cent, was proposed in 1850.[81] At Swynnerton the rental remained high until 1818, but median rents in agreements of 1822–4 were 21 per cent lower than those of 1818–20. The receipts from rents in the later 1830s and the 1840s seem to have been usually less than 60 per cent of those in 1811–15. Despite the reductions many tenants left the estate; in Beech hamlet most of the tenants residing in 1828–35 had left by 1839.[82] By 1850 it was estimated that rents in the county were down to 26s. or 28s. an acre, less than in 1817 but still far above the levels of the 1790s.[83]

During the prosperous period from the 1850s to the mid 1870s rents generally rose, on most estates by about 10 per cent but sometimes, as at Trentham and Sandon, by as much as 25 to 30 per cent. The chronology of the changes varied; at Trentham and Teddesley some farmers were again in difficulties in the early 1870s, and abatements were made in 1871. Outright competition for farms was generally discouraged in the county while rents were rising; landlords preferred to ensure that tenants were competent and had adequate capital.[84]

In the 1790s labourers' wage-rates varied according to locality, the highest being paid near manufacturing towns.[85] Moreover during the early 19th century and again in the 1860s wages were generally lower in the south, though the difference between the north and the south was less marked in the 1830s.[86] The daily wage in the 1790s varied from 1s. to 1s. 6d. with beer, or in summer 1s. with meat, drink, and carriage of a load of coals. Wages had risen by 10 per cent in the early 1790s, supposedly because farmers had to compete for labour with canal companies. For more skilled work piece-rates enabled a good workman to earn 2s. or more a day with beer. Threshing was paid at 4d. a bushel for wheat, 2d. a bushel for barley, and 1½d. a bushel for oats; mowing at 2s. an acre; and reaping wheat at 5s. an acre with dinner. The hours were long, in winter from dawn to dusk and in summer from 6 a.m. to 6 p.m. During harvest work began when the dew had evaporated and ended at nightfall.[87] Wages rose considerably during the French wars and fell thereafter. At Blithfield Hall the cost of monthly-paid labourers rose from £238 4s. 8d. in 1798 to £531 5s. 6d. in 1805; by 1818 it was down to £277 11s. 7d., though that partly reflected a reduction in numbers employed.[88] Wages paid to individual labourers on the same farm might vary greatly. At Swynnerton Hall in 1811, for instance, men's daily wages ranged from 1s. to 3s. 6d., the commonest

[77] Reid, 'Landownership', 31–3, 55.
[78] S.R.O., D.603 (unlisted), Rentals; ibid., Hodson notes and memoranda, Staffs. rentals.
[79] Sturgess, 'Agric. Staffs.' 505–6.
[80] Caird, *Eng. Agric.* 231.
[81] Ibid.; Sturgess, 'Agric. Staffs.' 495; S.R.O., D.240/U/468, 28 Mar. 1822; /481, 7 May 1835; D.641/5/E(C)/25, 22 Nov. 1844.
[82] S.R.O., D.641/5/E(R)/1/5; /E(L)/2–4; /E(C)/21, 27 Aug. 1834, 29 May, 16 Dec. 1835, 27 May, 27 Nov. 1836; /22, 26 May, 1 Dec. 1837, 31 May, 26 July 1839; /23, 29 May 1840; /25, 31 May 1844; /26, 31 Jan., 30 May 1845; /27,

29 May, 27 Nov. 1846; /28, 28 May 1847; /29, 2 June, 29 Nov. 1849.
[83] Caird, *Eng. Agric.* 231.
[84] Reid, 'Landownership', 74; Sturgess, 'Agric. Staffs.' 103, 174, 278, 293, 509–12; Perren, 'Agric. Depression', 251–2, 430; *J.R.A.S.E.* 2nd ser. v. 311.
[85] Pitt, *Agric. Staffs.* 155.
[86] Sturgess, 'Agric. Staffs.' 60.
[87] Pitt, *Agric. Staffs.* 155–6.
[88] S.R.O., D.(W.) 1721/3/165, 1st bdle., acct. bks., Husbandry Labourers; /166b, acct. bks., Husbandry Labourers.

rate being 2s. 4d.; boys received 6d.[89] At Alton daily wages were 2s. 6d. from 1807 to 1816, 2s. from 1816 to 1821, and 1s. 9d. from 1822 to 1824.[90] In 1833 it was stated that wages in the county had fallen from 13s. a week in wartime to 10s. with beer worth 1s.[91] Piece-rates also fell. At Hilderstone Hall in 1818 and 1819 William Vernon paid his workers 6d. to 8d. a thrave for threshing wheat; at Milwich in 1831 he paid only 5½d.[92] Yet the labourer was allegedly more prosperous in the 1830s, since corn prices, and those of other commodities except meat, had fallen more than wages. Cottages were better furnished and families better clothed. The cottage usually had a good garden, especially on large estates; labourers were better off renting from head land-lords than from tenant farmers.[93] Staffordshire suffered little from the labourers' riots of 1830–1, though there was incendiarism at Himley in January 1831.[94]

In the 1830s and 1840s there was a movement to provide labourers with allotments. As early as 1802 Lord Bradford had encouraged gardening at Weston-under-Lizard, providing advice on cultivation and offering premiums for tidiness and efficiency.[95] In 1830 a writer recommended a comprehensive scheme of allotment gardens at Lich-field; 10 roods would supply one family, and 75 a. would suffice to feed all the city's poor with potatoes. He had received applications for garden ground from 180 families, of whom 40 had no regular work.[96] At Groundslow Fields, Tittensor, gardens were laid out for the labourers between 1830 and 1843.[97] In 1833 cottagers at Swynnerton were applying to the landlord for allotments to keep a cow each, while in 1841 the agent proposed a scheme for garden holdings.[98] By 1850 garden allotments on Sir Robert Peel's estates were let at 1s. a rood in the country and 1s. 6d. near Tamworth.[99] The 1st earl of Harrowby also established an allotment scheme, exempting tenants from land tax, rates, and levies but making tenure conditional on a high standard of personal morality.[1] By the late 1860s Lord Lichfield also was letting 45 smallholdings of 4 a. to 7 a. to his most industrious labourers.[2] In 1873 there were 33,672 cottagers in the county who cultivated less than an acre each, occupying over 4,000 acres.[3]

In 1850 the wages of agricultural labourers were still only 9s. to 10s. a week, although they could earn more from piece-work, which was very common.[4] From the 1850s, however, wage-rates rose again. At Beaudesert in 1855 the normal rate was 2s. 2d. a day, though many received less.[5] In the 1860s wages in the county rose from 12s. or 12s. 6d. to 13s. a week; by 1872 they had reached 14s. 6d.[6] There were still local vari-ations: workers on Teddesley home farm, for example, normally received less than those at Aqualate in Forton.[7] In the late 1860s piece-rates were still normal for mowing and reaping: for wheat 10s. to 20s. an acre, for barley and oats 9s. an acre if stacked and 3s. to 6s. if not. Threshing rates were lower than in 1831, at 5d. a thrave for wheat. Much of the harvest work was done by migrants from the Peak District or by Irishmen from the towns. A gallon of beer an acre was provided at harvest, in addition to the usual quart a day all the year round; beer 'oils creaking wheels and prevents rust'. Where food also was provided labourers were willing to work longer hours. On dairy-

[89] S.R.O., D.641/5/E(A)/2/2, labourers' work acct., ff. 1–2, 13v.–14, 26v.–27, 31v.–32.
[90] N.S.J.F.S. i. 83.   [91] Rep. Sel. Cttee. on Agric. 525.
[92] S.R.O., D.(W.) 1826/41.
[93] Rep. Sel. Cttee. on Agric. 526.
[94] E. Richards, 'Capt. Swing in the West Midlands', International Rev. of Social Hist. xix (1), 86–99.
[95] S.R.O., D.1287/2/1, 'Weston Christmas 1802'.
[96] Law, Poor Man's Garden, 7, 15.
[97] W.S.L. 11/313/50.
[98] S.R.O., D.641/5/E(C)/20, 14 Nov. 1833; /23, c. Aug. 1841, note on allotment system.
[99] Caird, Eng. Agric. 251.

[1] Reid, 'Landownership', 25; 2nd Rep. Com. Employ-ment Children, Young Persons and Women in Agric. 1867 [4202–I], p. 90, H.C. (1868–9), xiii.
[2] J.R.A.S.E. 2nd ser. v. 296.
[3] J. Bateman, Great Landowners of Great Britain and Ireland (1883), 509.
[4] Caird, Eng. Agric. 232.
[5] S.R.O., D.603 (unlisted), Beaudesert Farm Accts. 1854 and 1855, daily reps. of labourers.
[6] A. L. Bowley, 'Statistics of Wages in the U.K. during the last 100 years, part I, Agric. Wages', Jnl. Royal Statistical Soc. lxi. 705.
[7] Sturgess, 'Agric. Staffs.' App. pp. 35–6.

farms dairymaids received £18 to £22 a year, their assistants £8 to £14, and milkers 14*s.* a week. Statute fairs for hiring labour were still held at Burton, Uttoxeter, Tamworth, and Fazeley.[8]

Rents of labourers' cottages varied from 10*s.* to £3 a year in 1833 and were about £3 10*s.* a year in 1850.[9] By the late 1870s, however, cottages were often provided free.[10] The standard of accommodation remained low. About 1867 a survey of cottages in 63 parishes in the poor-law unions of Cheadle, Stafford, and Stone, and the Staffordshire part of the Ashbourne and Uttoxeter unions showed that only 213 had 3 bedrooms; 1,572 had 2 bedrooms, and 596, of which 212 were occupied by families with three or more children, had but one bedroom.[11] The labourer's earnings were sometimes supplemented by those of his wife and children. In 1867 the Staffordshire Chamber of Agriculture objected to any legislation to restrict female labour, claiming that it would harm both employers and employees. It resolved, however, that no child under 8 should be employed for wages, that none between 8 and 10 should be employed without a certificate of a certain amount of school attendance each year, and that none between 11 and 13 should be employed without a certificate of having passed an examination. By then few women were employed on farms in the county; in 1861 there had been only 412 female agricultural labourers. Boys, however, left school young to work on farms, some as early as 9, but more often at about 10 or 11 years.[12]

[8] *J.R.A.S.E.* 2nd ser. v. 308–9.
[9] *Rep. Sel. Cttee. on Agric.* 535; Caird, *Eng. Agric.* 232.
[10] *Agric. Interests Com.: Digest and App. . . . with Reps. . . .*
[C.2778–ii], pp. 322–4, H.C. (1881), xvi.
[11] *2nd Rep. Com. Emp. Children and Women, 1867,* 91–3.
[12] Ibid. 84, 86, 88–90.

AGRICULTURE 1875 TO 1975

Arable Farming, p. 125. Grassland and Stock, p. 129. Agrarian Economy and Society, p. 137. Agricultural Education, p. 147.

THE late 1870s, in Staffordshire as in England generally, marked the beginning of a long period during which agriculture was exposed to the full force of foreign competition and was often held by contemporaries to be in depression.[1] The period was one of low or falling rents and prices and of declining employment. Farmers were compelled to reduce costs and to alter their methods to produce those goods whose prices were least affected by imports. Those constraints persisted until the outbreak of the Second World War, though the First World War gave a brief respite.

The beginning of the period of adjustment is difficult to pinpoint: on some estates rents were falling from 1870, on others they declined only from the late 1870s.[2] The weather in the 1870s was frequently unfavourable. In 1877 floods of the Trent at Trentham were said to have destroyed the hay crop six times since 1865.[3] The wet summer of 1879 was disastrous in many places, though not universally.[4] Successive wet years caused widespread losses of stock from liver rot.[5] Farmers themselves disagreed about the date when the depression began. Lord Dartmouth's agent, while recognizing that there had been difficulties for some years, thought 1879 'disastrous'.[6] Richard Dyott of Freeford held that the depression began only in 1878,[7] but his agent considered the neighbourhood to have suffered from c. 1875.[8] The weather was generally blamed.[9] More than one farmer added dear and poor labour and high rates as further causes.[10] While low prices were also a grievance,[11] farmers disagreed about the effects of foreign competition, especially on light-land farming. Dyott thought that producers of good meat had not been affected,[12] and his agent admitted that wheat was the only article in which foreign competition was damaging.[13] At first, indeed, it appeared that dairy-farmers were hardest hit by imports.[14] By the early 1890s, however, it became clear that in Staffordshire as elsewhere, though arable farms had suffered, stock farmers had gained from the low prices of animal feed.[15]

Since so much land was already permanent pasture by 1875,[16] the long-term effects of foreign competition on Staffordshire agriculture were not generally severe, and rents fell less than elsewhere. The farmers' reaction to their problems was to continue the changes which had already been taking place before 1875. Even more land was laid

[1] In this article extensive use has been made of material collected by the late J. G. Jenkins. Thanks are offered to Professor F. M. L. Thompson for reading and commenting on the article in draft.

[2] See pp. 119, 141–2.

[3] R. Perren, 'Effects of Agricultural Depression on the Eng. Estates of the Dukes of Sutherland, 1870–1900' (Univ. of Nott. Ph.D. thesis, 1967), 57–8.

[4] Staffs. Advertiser, 2 Aug. 1879.

[5] F. Dun, 'Rep. on Liver Rot', J.R.A.S.E. 2nd ser. xvii. 182.

[6] S.R.O., D.564/8/1/17, Thynne to Dartmouth, 2 Oct. 1879.

[7] Mins. of Evidence before Com. Agric., vol ii [C. 3096], p. 651, H.C. (1881), xvii.

[8] Ibid. p. 184.

[9] Ibid. pp. 184, 642; Staffs. Advertiser, 26 July 1879; S.R.O., D.564/8/1/17, Thynne to Dartmouth, 2 Oct. 1879; Agric. Interests Com.: Digest and App.... with Reps. [C. 2778–II], pp. 269–72, H.C. (1881), xvi.

[10] Agric. Interests Com.: Digest (1881), pp. 270–1; Mins. of Evid. Com. Agric. ii (1881), p. 184.

[11] Staffs. Advertiser, 26 July 1879; S.R.O., D.564/8/1/17, Thynne to Dartmouth, 2 Oct. 1879.

[12] Mins. of Evid. Com. Agric. ii (1881), p. 649.

[13] Ibid. p. 185.

[14] Ibid. p. 192.

[15] Mins. of Evidence before Com. Agric. Depression [C. 7400–I], pp. 232, 279, H.C. (1894), xvi(1).

[16] See p. 92.

down to grass, and farmers relied more and more on cattle-farming, especially dairying, using imported foodstuffs; liquid milk sales replaced home production of cheese. The changes permitted a more economical use of labour.

The First World War temporarily interrupted those trends. Staffordshire played its part in the campaign to increase arable production, encouraged by the establishment of a county War Agricultural Committee in 1915[17] and by the higher prices guaranteed by legislation from 1917.[18] When price control was abandoned after the war, previous trends reasserted themselves.[19] The only arable farmers to benefit from government intervention in the 1920s were sugar-beet producers. From the 1930s, however, renewed government action in the form of guaranteed prices, import quotas, and regulated marketing arrangements[20] began to affect cropping and to increase arable production. The tendency became much more marked with the emergency measures of the Second World War and the continued support for agriculture provided under post-war legislation. The return to protection gave rise in Staffordshire as elsewhere to renewed prosperity for farmers, to a permanent reversion of much land to arable farming, to improvements in buildings and equipment, and to greatly increased output of both crops and animal products. The relationships of landlord and tenant were also regulated.

The increase of livestock numbers from the late 19th century, and of crop production from the Second World War, took place despite a marked fall in the area of cultivated land. Perhaps partly because of continued inclosure of waste, the area under crops and grass rose from 593,584 a., or $81\frac{1}{2}$ per cent of the county, in 1875 to a peak of 606,583 a., or 83 per cent of the county, in 1889. From that time it steadily declined to some 509,000 a., less than 70 per cent of the county, in 1973.[21] Most of the reduction was caused by loss of land to urban expansion.

The growth of towns posed special problems for farmers in urban areas, particularly between the World Wars. In the Black Country sulphuric acid from the atmosphere entered the soil and soured the pastures; clover would not grow, farmers could not afford lime, and there was further deterioration.[22] Smoke damaged crops: a Great Barr farmer complained as early as 1917 that barley would not grow well because of the smoke from Birmingham; another in Aldridge in 1919 had given up beans for the same reason.[23] Smoke pollution also caused trouble on the duke of Sutherland's Trentham estate in the late 19th century, while mining subsidence damaged farm drains.[24] In the late 1930s ribbon development, for example in the Aldridge area, impeded farmers' access to their land and exposed crops to damage by dogs and children and to theft.[25] Sheep were seldom kept near towns because of worrying by dogs, which also stole poultry and eggs.[26] Threats of compulsory purchase discouraged efficient farming and the use of fertilizers, while sometimes land for development was taken from several adjacent farms and made each uneconomic. New roads, too, by splitting up farms discouraged proper rotations.[27] Labour was also a problem: it was difficult to persuade agricultural labourers to work long hours on the farm.[28] Arable crops had to be hoed unnecessarily because of complaints from neighbouring householders about weeds.[29] Until the Second World War those difficulties encouraged concentration on

[17] S.R.O., Staffs. War Agric. Cttee. Mins. 1915–20, f. 1.
[18] K. A. H. Murray, *Hist. of Second World War: Agric.* 8.
[19] 'Farming Interviews', 3 Dec. 1927.
[20] Murray, *Agric.* 26–37.
[21] *Agric. Returns G.B.* Up to 9,488 a. of the apparent reduction was due to reclassification of smallholdings in 1967–8: ibid. 1968–9, table 63 A, notes. The title of the annual agric. statistics has changed several times since the returns began in 1866, but for simplicity the form *Agric.*

Returns G.B. has been used.
[22] I. Davies, 'Agric. of the West Midland Conurbation' (Birmingham Univ. M.A. thesis, 1953), 48.
[23] 'Agric. Our Vital Ind.' 18 Aug. 1917, 25 Jan. 1919.
[24] Perren, 'Agric. Depression', 252.
[25] Davies, 'Agric. of W. Midland Conurbation', 80.
[26] Ibid. 161, 163, 165; Myers, *Staffs.* 592.
[27] Davies, 'Agric. of W. Midland Conurbation', 171–6.
[28] Ibid. 170.
[29] Ibid. 166–7.

dairy-farming in both the Potteries and the south Staffordshire conurbation; the trend was evident by the First World War in the Black Country. The shortage of imported feed in the Second World War forced a return to mixed farming, at least in the Black Country.[30] In the early 1970s a variety of farming systems was practised there.[31] Part-time farming was widespread in the conurbation after the Second World War.[32]

The growing mechanization of farming in the 20th century affected both arable farms and dairy-farms in Staffordshire, particularly during and after the Second World War. There was a great increase in the number both of milking-machines[33] and of planting, harvesting, and spraying machinery,[34] and a corresponding reduction in the number of farm workers.[35] Tractors almost entirely replaced horses. In the First World War tractors were essential for rapid ploughing of grassland to grow arable crops. The county War Agricultural Committee acquired tractors, which were made available for the work; in March 1917 there were only five[36] but by April 1917 at least 23 more had been supplied and government departments had offered the committee at least forty-six.[37] Between October 1917 and November 1918 the committee received applications for petrol allowances for at least 51 tractors on farms in the county.[38] In 1942 there were 1,809 tractors, in 1944 2,607, in 1950 5,588, and in 1954 7,571. Horses used for agricultural purposes, on the other hand, declined from 13,030 in 1939 to 8,474 in 1949 and 1,639 in 1958.[39] Stationary power supplies on farms also improved, petrol and electric engines replacing steam-engines. In 1917–18 some 200 applications for fuel for petrol engines were received by the War Agricultural Committee.[40] By 1942 there were 3,599 petrol engines and oil-engines on farms, by 1944 3,678, and by 1950 5,089. By 1954 the number of petrol engines was falling; they were apparently being replaced by electric engines, which increased in number from 3,017 in 1950 to 4,479 in 1954.[41] By the early 1940s 31 per cent of farms in Staffordshire had an electricity supply, and 95 per cent of those were connected to the mains.[42]

Farmers could mitigate the difficulties caused by low or falling prices in the depression years by forming co-operatives to sell their products and to buy fertilizers and feed without the interposition of a middleman. Lord Dartmouth's agent suggested this in 1879,[43] but though dairy-farmers established cheese factories from the 1870s and associations for milk-selling from the 1890s[44] general co-operatives did not become popular until the First World War. In 1914 a meeting of 8 farmers at Brewood established the Wolverhampton and District Farmers' Association. It grew rapidly; by the end of 1916 there were 108 members and sales had increased twelvefold. It bought a grinding-mill in Wolverhampton in 1916–17, and by 1918 it had a milk factory.[45] In 1916 the Penkridge Farmers' Auction Ltd. was established; it held regular stock sales at Penkridge.[46] Similar auctions were established at Meir and Stone, which by August 1918 had merged as the North Staffordshire Farmers' Association.[47] In 1919 the Wolverhampton and North Staffordshire associations, the Penkridge Auction, and a similar association at Tamworth merged as Staffordshire Farmers Ltd., with 1,126

[30] Davies, 'Agric. of W. Midland Conurbation', 226–7; below, p. 133; *Agric. Returns G.B.* 1915, pp. 50–1 (Bilston div.); *Staffs. County Council Development Plan 1951: Survey Rep. and Analysis*, 127.
[31] e.g. *V.C.H. Staffs.* xvii. 184.
[32] Davies, 'Agric. of W. Midland Conurbation', 204.
[33] See p. 133.
[34] See p. 128; *Agric. Returns G.B.* 1939–44, 1950, 1954; Min. of Agric. *Agric. in West Midlands*, 18.
[35] See p. 144.
[36] S.R.O., War Agric. Cttee. Mins. 1915–20, 17 Mar. 1917.
[37] Ibid. 29 Dec. 1916, 5 and 26 May, 30 June, 11 Aug., 6 and 15 Sept., 6 Oct., 22 Dec. 1917, 17 Apr. 1918.

[38] Ibid. 6 Oct. 1917–3 Oct. 1918.
[39] *Agric. Returns G.B.* 1939–44, 1950, 1954, 1958.
[40] S.R.O., War Agric. Cttee. Mins. 1915–20, 6 Oct. 1917–3 Oct. 1918.
[41] *Agric. Returns G.B.* 1939–44, 1950, 1954.
[42] *Min. of Agric. and Fisheries, Nat. Farm Survey of Eng. and Wales (1941–1943)* (1946), 107.
[43] S.R.O., D.564/8/1/17, Thynne to Dartmouth, 2 Oct. 1879.
[44] See p. 132.
[45] *Staffs. Advertiser*, 28 Apr. 1917, 27 July 1918.
[46] Ibid. 27 May 1916 sqq.
[47] Ibid. 31 Aug. 1918. None of these co-operative auctions appears in *Kelly's Dir. Staffs.* (1916).

members; receipts from the first year's sales amounted to £305,744. The society had difficulties in the depression after 1921 and was obliged to give up auctions, meat-trading, and small dairies. In the 1930s, however, sales and membership greatly increased. The society incorporated Derbyshire Farmers Ltd. in 1942 and Shropshire Farmers Ltd. in 1950, when an engineering department was opened at Cannock. From 1957 the firm distributed a full range of tractors and implements. In 1975 there were 9,000 members, and sales of £27,000,000.[48]

ARABLE FARMING

From the mid 1870s until 1939 the importance of arable farming in Staffordshire declined, apart from a brief recovery as a result of government action during the First World War. Arable acreage fell from 226,566 a. in 1875 to 150,554 a. in 1915, rose to 185,432 a. in 1918 (far less than the government's requirement), and fell again to 114,184 a. in 1938.[49] In 1915 only the Lichfield and Brownhills, the Wolverhampton, and the Kingswinford and Wordsley petty sessional districts had more than half their land under the plough; while the Cheadle, Uttoxeter, and Leek districts, covering the Moorlands, had less than 10 per cent arable.[50] By 1939 only in the extreme south-west was arable more important than dairying.[51] Moreover in the late 19th century even the predominantly arable areas of south Staffordshire saw a shift from the production of cash crops to the growth of fodder for fattening livestock,[52] following the lead given by dairying areas in the mid 19th century.[53] Where sheep were kept the changed emphasis at first encouraged the continuation of the Norfolk four-course, since at least on light land more animals could be supported on an arable system than on permanent pasture.[54] On Lord Lichfield's estates, both in Alrewas and on heavy land north-west of Stafford, a four- or five-course rotation was required until the early 20th century, the four-course becoming gradually commoner.[55] Elsewhere traditional rotations and restrictions were sometimes abandoned, and landlords ceased to impose them in leases. In 1881 six of sixteen Staffordshire farmers giving evidence to the Royal Commission on Agriculture had no cropping covenants in their leases. Others, who had covenants, ignored them.[56] On the Bill family's estate in Alton parish cropping covenants were deleted in 1888.[57] By 1877 the prohibition of the sale of straw on the Giffard estates round Chillington had been abandoned; half the proceeds of such sales were to be spent on animal food.[58] Specialist rotations continued to develop round towns, where the increasing horse population provided manure and where night-soil too was available. In Handsworth and Harborne a two-course rotation of potatoes and wheat had emerged by the end of the century.[59] By 1918 south-east Staffordshire was largely engaged in potato-growing for the urban market.[60] In 1928 one farm had as much as 200 a. under potatoes.[61] By then a three-course rotation of corn, seeds, and potatoes or other roots may have been typical of potato-growing farms.[62] Yet a four-course

[48] Ex inf. Staffs. Farmers Ltd. (1976).
[49] These and later figures for acreages in the county are based on *Agric. Returns G.B.* unless otherwise stated. For government ploughing-up requirements for the 1918 harvest see S.R.O., War Agric. Cttee. Mins. 1915–20, Exec. Cttee. 16 June 1917, p. 5.
[50] *Agric. Returns G.B.* 1915, p. 50.
[51] Myers, *Staffs.* 593–4.
[52] Sturgess, 'Agric. Staffs.' 300–1.
[53] See p. 105.
[54] Sturgess, 'Agric. Staffs.' 354; *Agric. Interests Com.: Digest* (1881), p. 270.

[55] S.R.O., D.615/E(L)/1/2, 19, 26, 29, 61–2, 77, 85–6, 96; /E(L)/6/6–8, 11, 13, 20, 22, 46, 50, 66, 69–70, 72, 74, 92.
[56] *Agric. Interests Com.: Digest* (1881), p. 295.
[57] Sturgess, 'Agric. Staffs.' 423.
[58] Ibid. 368.
[59] Ibid. 362–3.
[60] *Bd. of Agric. and Fisheries: Wages and Conditions of Employment in Agric.* [Cmd. 25], pp. 307–19, H.C. (1919), ix.
[61] 'Farming Interviews', 11 Feb. 1928.
[62] Ibid. 17 Dec. 1927, 28 Jan., 21 Apr., 26 May 1928.

rotation was still said to be usual in Staffordshire.[63] Certainly most farmers, even when their arable acreage was very small, continued after the First World War to grow a wide variety of crops; monoculture, or even more than two successive corn crops, was unusual.[64] In the late 1930s the four-course was still perhaps the commonest rotation in the south, centre, and west of the county, but longer or shorter courses, or no systematic rotation, were also found.[65]

There were, however, some changes in the balance of cropping. Wheat acreage declined from 60,092 a. in 1868 to 25,532 a. in 1916; it rose again under the government's ploughing-up campaign to 37,378 a. in 1919 but fell to 13,559 a. in 1931. As a result of the guaranteed minimum price under the Wheat Act, 1932,[66] the acreage increased again to 26,022 in 1939.[67] It was then more or less evenly distributed, but was absent in the north-east and on Cannock Chase and was most important on the light soils of the south.[68] Barley declined more markedly from 32,660 a. in 1870 to 1,698 a. in 1939; it became concentrated almost exclusively on the light soils.[69] The area under oats, which were grown more easily than barley on heavy and moorland soils, fluctuated; it increased at the expense of barley to 37,522 a. in 1900, declined to 34,686 a. in 1916, reached a peak of 51,000 a. in 1918, and then fell again to 21,255 a. in 1939. The acreage under turnips and swedes also declined, especially in the years around 1900 and in the 1920s and 1930s. At first turnips and swedes were partly replaced by mangolds, but those too were less often grown in the 1920s. From the mid 1920s sugar beet became an important alternative root crop. A few pioneer farmers planted beet in the 1923–4 season;[70] one of them, Thomas Baxter of Freeford, became in 1924 chairman of the Sugar Beet Growers' Committee of the National Farmers' Union. Although his attempt to secure the establishment of a sugar-beet factory in Staffordshire failed, beet-growing was encouraged by the opening of factories at Kidderminster (Worcs.) in 1925 and Alscott in Wrockwardine (Salop.) in 1926.[71] The acreage, negligible until 1923, increased to 284 a. in 1925, 1,392 a. in 1926, 3,476 a. in 1927, and 5,730 a. in 1930. Sugar beet occupied 3,974 a. in 1939. The most important root by then was the potato, covering 10,539 a. Maize was grown at Thorpe Constantine in 1934.[72] The proportion of arable occupied by rotation grass for hay was well above the national average in 1938, reflecting the emphasis on livestock in the county's farming.[73]

It was claimed in 1881 that railways and foreign competition had ruined the market-gardening trade round Lichfield.[74] Yet the area of market-gardens doubled between 1872 and 1896, though the county's relative importance in market-garden produce declined. The main increase in acreage had taken place in the 1870s.[75] By 1891 there were specialist fruit-markets in Wolverhampton and Birmingham.[76] In the earlier 20th century the main market-garden area was still round Lichfield and Tamworth; market-gardeners moved out of the cities because of pollution.[77] Some vegetables were important elsewhere. F. R. Twemlow apparently grew carrots at Peatswood in Tyrley from 1883,[78] while a farmer at Ashley was growing carrots c. 1938, and by 1951 that area was noted for the crop.[79] In the south-western arable area broccoli and cauliflowers

63 'Farming Interviews', 28 Jan. 1928.
64 Ibid. 10 Dec. 1927–16 June 1928, especially 26 May 1928; 'Agric. Our Vital Ind.' 5 May–6 Oct. 1917, 21 Sept. 1918–18 Oct. 1919.
65 Myers, Staffs. 620–9.
66 22 & 23 Geo. V, c. 24.
67 Myers, Staffs. 595–6.
68 Ibid. 595.
69 Ibid. 597.
70 Agric. Returns G.B. 1924.
71 Ibid. 1925 (1), pp. 50–1; 1927 (1), pp. 6–7; R. A. Pepperall, Biography of Sir Thomas Baxter (Wells, 1950), 89–90.
72 Staffs. County Mus., photograph 41/3/9/76.
73 Myers, Staffs. 598.
74 Mins. of Evid. Com. Agric. ii (1881), pp. 187, 192.
75 R. J. Battersby, 'Development of Market Gardening in Eng. 1850–1914' (London Univ. Ph.D. thesis, 1960), 47 and App. 1.
76 Ibid. 135.
77 Myers, Staffs. 599; Davies, 'Agric. of W. Midland Conurbation', 227.
78 S.R.O., D.952/2/3/14, farm accts. 29 Dec. 1883 sqq.; /15–16.
79 Myers, Staffs. 621; Staffs. County Council Development Plan 1951: Survey Rep. and Analysis, 126.

were grown in the early 20th century. The seed farms of Edward Webb & Sons at Kinver were established in the late 1870s, covering 1,200 a., and were enlarged to 1,500 a. between 1904 and 1908.[80]

TABLE I: ACREAGE OF PRINCIPAL CROPS 1916–19

	1916	1917	1918	1919
Wheat	25,532	25,322	41,891	37,378
Barley	9,852	11,383	10,515	12,111
Oats	34,646	38,850	50,873	45,330
Mixed Corn[a]			2,479	2,321
Potatoes	10,998	12,386	15,895	11,745
Turnips	13,302	14,607	14,336	16,214
Mangolds	8,466	8,743	9,409	9,806
Sugar Beet	0	0	5	0
Cabbage	1,547	802	1,206	1,304
Other Vegetables	946	936	934	1,139

Source: *Agric. Returns G.B.*

[a] Figures are not available before 1918.

TABLE II: ACREAGE OF PRINCIPAL CROPS 1939–45

	1939	1940	1941	1942	1943	1944	1945
Wheat	26,022	28,123	34,519	40,501	55,889	48,662	35,599
Barley	1,698	3,765	5,025	4,989	5,373	6,884	9,162
Oats	21,255	39,028	44,700	48,615	39,680	43,071	46,110
Mixed Corn	453	4,979	17,929	14,914	19,203	16,170	16,226
Potatoes	10,539	12,547	18,713	23,628	23,285	24,775	25,612
Turnips	4,584	5,830	7,496	8,960	8,752	8,191	7,906
Mangolds	4,327	4,811	5,850	6,382	7,372	8,222	8,454
Sugar Beet	3,974	3,845	3,495	3,813	3,436	3,587	3,444
Cabbage	2,140	2,266	4,340	4,262	5,197	4,896	4,715
Other Vegetables	2,845	3,111	3,386	3,524	3,453	4,302	4,257

Source: *Agric. Returns G.B.*

The ploughing-up campaign of the Second World War resulted in a much greater increase in Staffordshire's arable acreage than had that of the First; it affected almost all important crops including cereals, cabbages, potatoes, and other roots (see Tables I and II). After the war government subsidies under the Agriculture Act, 1947,[81]

[80] *Wages and Conditions of Emp. in Agric.* 307; *Kelly's Dir. Staffs.* (1880; 1904; 1908).

[81] 10 & 11 Geo. VI, c. 48.

prevented much reversion of arable to pasture; a fall in arable area between the mid 1940s and the mid 1950s is largely accounted for by loss of farm-land to other uses. From 1960 arable increased both absolutely and in proportion to permanent grass. In 1972 218,521 a. (44·7 per cent of cultivated land) was under the plough, a higher proportion than at any time since at least 1866. Post-war cropping trends are shown in Table III. The most noticeable change, more marked in Staffordshire than in the

TABLE III: AVERAGE ACREAGES OF PRINCIPAL CROPS AFTER THE SECOND WORLD WAR

	1946–50	1951–5	1956–60	1961–5	1966–70	1970–3
Wheat	35,373	36,890	35,018	29,280	29,699	31,894
Barley	8,244	9,257	18,866	58,915	75,016	71,318
Oats	34,164	25,305	20,465	8,085	7,015	6,622
Mixed Corn	22,115	26,861	11,550	3,316	3,951	2,976
Potatoes	24,872	18,209	15,169	11,920	11,876	11,475
Turnips and Swedes[a]	5,434	4,065	2,578	1,408	915	895
Mangolds	7,093	5,077	3,145	1,720	581	374
Sugar Beet	3,116	4,906	4,342	4,504	3,728	5,517
Kale	4,032	4,496	5,248	3,660	2,471	2,206
Cabbage and Kohl Rabi				510	218	190
Vegetables for Human Consumption	4,025	3,192	3,051	3,062	2,780	3,016
Clover and Rotation Grass	68,675	74,484	86,241	87,958	74,097	75,349
Lucerne		384	267	151		348

Source: *Agric. Returns G.B.*

[a] Including fodder beet from 1952.

country as a whole, was the replacement of oats and mixed corn by barley, which by the 1970s occupied more than half the tillage land.[82] The change presumably reflects the declining importance of horses and the growth of intensive stock-feeding on barley, but was partly caused by the introduction of higher-yielding barley varieties.[83] The yield of barley in Staffordshire increased from 18·7 cwt. an acre in 1941–50 to 32·3 cwt. in 1973. That of oats also increased from 17·6 to 32·3 cwt. an acre in the same period, and that of wheat from 19·6 to 37·3 cwt. In most years barley yields were above the national average, oat and wheat yields below it.

The expansion of corn-farming was accompanied by greater use of machinery. There were, for example, 115 combine-harvesters in 1950, 288 in 1954, and over 1,000 in 1968; four grain driers in 1950 and 34 in 1954. In the 1960s on-the-floor grain-drying increased in popularity.[84]

The cropping figures also imply a widespread abandonment of traditional rotations

[82] *Agric. Returns G.B.*
[83] S. Williams, *Farming in the Midlands*, 15.
[84] *Agric. Returns G.B.*; Min. of Agric., Fisheries, and Food, *Agric. in the West Midlands* (1974), 54.

LIMING, HARROWING, AND DRILLING WITH HORSE TEAMS AND TRACTORS AT KINGSTONE, 1938

HAND-SINGLING MANGOLDS AT KEELE, 1940

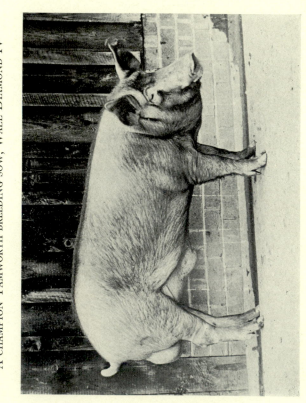

RIDGE AND FURROW AND WATER MEADOWS ON THE TEAN AT STRAMSHALL, 1948

A CHAMPION TAMWORTH BREEDING SOW, WALL DIAMOND IV

A TAMWORTH BOAR

in favour of continuous corn-growing. In the early 1970s, for example, a farmer at Tamhorn pursued a rotation of tick-beans, wheat, barley, barley, oats, and barley.[85] On the other hand rotation grass has generally occupied at least a third and often nearly half of the arable area since the Second World War.[86]

Market-gardening shared in the expansion of arable in the 1940s. The area of market-garden crops, 1,932 a. in 1938,[87] had increased to 4,355 a. in 1948 and fluctuated around 3,000 a. from the 1950s to the early 1970s (see Table III). Over half was normally under brassicas, while parsnips became increasingly popular. Market-gardens were still sited mainly in the south-east and on the fringe of the Black Country, where casual labour was available for the harvest.[88]

GRASSLAND AND STOCK

The conversion of arable to permanent grass continued fairly steadily from 1875 to 1939, except during the brief reversion to arable caused by the First World War. By 1939 permanent grass occupied 78 per cent of the total crops and grass. The grass acreage, however, reached its peak in 1910, and it grew most rapidly before 1890. The proportion of meadow increased from 25 per cent of permanent grass in 1875 to 32 per cent in 1889; thereafter it fluctuated between 26 and 32 per cent until the 1930s.[89] The increase in meadow in the late 19th century meant that more buildings were needed to store hay. Hay barns were a prominent improvement on the Trentham estate in the 1880s.[90] In 1896–7 Lord Hatherton built hay sheds for almost all his tenants.[91] Hay barns were also built between 1868 and 1895 on Lord Ferrers's Chartley estate.[92] Between 1881 and 1906 F. R. Twemlow built five Dutch and two hay barns on his farms in Tyrley, Standon, and Betley.[93] The condition of grassland tended to deteriorate, especially after the First World War; rough grazing, estimated at 4,787 a. in 1893, increased to 9,132 a. in 1911 and 28,215 a. in 1939.[94] During and after the Second World War it became clear that the yield of hay from temporary grass on newly ploughed land was much higher than that from old meadows; the average yields from 1939 to 1948 were 29.9 cwt. an acre from rotation grass and 20.6 cwt. an acre from meadow. By the early 1970s, however, the difference was much less marked, the figures being 37.2 cwt. and 32.9 cwt. respectively. The proportion of rotation grass mown was therefore reduced from 70 per cent in the late 1940s to 57 per cent in 1972.[95]

New methods of grass preservation were developed from the late 19th century. Staffordshire was prominent in the early development of silage-making in the 1880s. In 1884 there were 16 silos of 37,195 cubic feet capacity; in 1889 105 silos with a capacity of 227,182 cubic feet. Such expansion was unusually rapid. In 1885 ten counties had more silos than Staffordshire, but in 1889 only Kent, Lancashire, and the West Riding of Yorkshire.[96] Despite the promising start silage remained relatively unimportant until after the Second World War. One farmer stated in 1917 that he had given up making silage because of the smell.[97] In the late 1940s loading machinery became available, and the quantity of silage made grew from 7,047 tons in 1947 to 64,887 in 1950, though even then the area occupied by crops for silage was less than a

---

[85] *Staffs. Farming Newsletter, Feb. 1976* (published with *Stafford Newsletter*, 6 Feb. 1976).
[86] *Agric. Returns G.B.*
[87] Myers, *Staffs.* 599.
[88] Min. of Agric. *Agric. in W. Midlands*, 58.
[89] *Agric. Returns G.B.*
[90] Perren, 'Agric. Depression', 244, 265–6.
[91] Sturgess, 'Agric. Staffs.' 291.
[92] Ibid. 473.
[93] S.R.O., D.952/3/1.
[94] Myers, *Staffs.* 667.
[95] *Agric. Returns G.B.*
[96] Ibid. 1884–9.
[97] 'Agric. Our Vital Ind.' 8 Sept. 1917.

tenth of that used for hay.[98] Pit silos were then used.[99] but, as elsewhere, tower silos had become common by the 1970s. The first grass-drier in Staffordshire was installed on a farm at Ashley in 1936; green crops, temporary grassland, and permanent grassland were cut in rotation for drying, up to four crops a year being obtainable from each. A second drier was installed at Swythamley in 1940.[1] By the 1970s dried grass was increasingly popular as fodder, but much of it may have been brought in from elsewhere by the Lincolnshire company which controlled its distribution.[2]

TABLE IV: AVERAGE NUMBERS OF CATTLE, SHEEP, AND PIGS IN STAFFORDSHIRE 1866–1973

	Cattle	Sheep	Pigs
1866–70	118,775	317,410	53,205
1871–5	135,463	310,394	55,941
1876–80	131,770	293,084	50,145
1881–5	141,746	237,283	52,639
1886–90	148,784	252,768	52,275
1891–5	158,201	276,748	52,740
1896–1900	158,385	247,564	53,635
1901–5	163,747	214,650	50,048
1906–10	168,910	238,693	49,723
1911–15	174,215	210,439	49,167
1915–20	185,369	180,291	37,323
1921–5	177,337	127,703	43,893
1926–30	183,552	176,782	40,403
1931–5	196,507	199,427	51,929
1936–40	215,035	205,246	58,064
1941–5	226,646	108,948	30,181
1946–50	233,788	81,171	32,971
1951–5	240,173	115,470	90,318
1955–60	236,028	165,935	98,421
1961–5	253,648	207,349	104,485
1966–70	265,992	156,260	99,537
1971–3	283,034	134,334	117,038

Source: *Agric. Returns G.B.*

The number of cattle increased from 138,940 in 1875 to 300,803 in 1973 (see Table IV). The only significant set-back was a fall from 189,276 animals in 1919 to 166,367 in 1920. The increase is largely attributable to the continued expansion of dairying.

[98] *Staffs. County Council Development Plan 1951: Survey Rep. and Analysis*, 129.
[99] Ibid.
[1] Myers, *Staffs.* 588.
[2] *Staffs. Farming Newsletter, May 1976* (published with *Stafford Newsletter*, 21 May 1976).

In the late 19th century the proportion of cattle to land, and that of milking cows to barrens, rose. In 1875 there were 11·32 dairy cows and heifers for every 100 cultivated acres, and 4·35 other cattle over 2 years old. In 1900 the figures were 13·27 and 3·7 respectively.[3] The increased emphasis on milking cows was widespread. In Harborne and Handsworth parishes milking cows increased from 5 a hundred acres in the mid 1870s to 6 in the mid 1890s.[4] In five Moorland parishes, though the number of cattle declined between the late 1870s and the late 1890s, the proportion of milking cows and heifers rose.[5] On T. Carrington Smith's farm at Admaston in Blithfield the tyings for cows increased from 18 in 1856 to 63 in 1908, when there were also from 12 to 20 surplus animals kept in the fields.[6] At Trentham home farm there were in 1874 23 dairy cows and 33 feeders; by 1897 the ratio was almost reversed, there being 28 dairy cows and 23 feeders. On F. R. Twemlow's farm at Tyrley stores and feeders predominated in the 1880s, but cows and heifers in milk or in calf outnumbered them by the 1900s.[7] Farmers kept flying herds instead of breeding their own stock, so that more milkers could be supported.[8] New farm-buildings were generally adapted to dairying. Between 1881 and 1906 Twemlow built new cow-houses for his tenants on four farms, modernized those on two others, and rebuilt a dairy.[9] On Lord Ferrers's estate at Chartley between 1868 and 1895 at least 16 cow-sheds, 9 dairies, and 9 calf-houses were built.[10]

The intensification of dairying was accompanied by a change of emphasis from cheese production to liquid-milk sales. The change was precipitated by large-scale imports of American cheese in 1879, which reduced cheese prices disastrously. In north Staffordshire some farmers gave up dairying altogether. By 1881 cheese-making had been 'nearly done away with' round Lichfield, where labour difficulties aggravated the price fall; farmers were 'nearly all sending their milk away as milk'.[11] By 1890 milk was 'the chief article on which the farmer depends' in the Rocester area,[12] and cheese-making was rare round Burton-upon-Trent by 1888.[13] Most of the milk was sent by rail to London.[14] By 1910 the Great Northern Railway ran a special milk train daily to London from Egginton Junction outside Burton.[15] Other towns also provided a market for liquid milk. About 1880 much milk from the Lichfield area went to Birmingham, as did a prize-winning farmer's milk from Tatenhill in the early 1880s.[16] In 1898 farmers on the Sandwell estate in West Bromwich sold their milk to that town.[17] On the Trentham estate the farmers near the London & North Western Railway line sold their milk to London, the others to the Potteries.[18] In the early 1890s the milk traffic was an important item in the receipts of the North Staffordshire Railway.[19] Access to the railway services and reasonable rates of carriage were essential. In 1894 T. Carrington Smith drew the attention of the Royal Commission on Agriculture to the difficulties caused by a large increase in railway charges the previous year.[20] In 1897 Lord Hatherton complained repeatedly that no trains stopped at Penkridge on Sundays to enable his tenants to send their milk to Stafford and Wolverhampton; his representations to the railway company had failed to persuade it to alter the time-

[3] *Agric. Returns G.B.*
[4] Sturgess, 'Agric. Staffs.' 365.   [5] Ibid. 428.
[6] T. Carrington Smith, *Story of a Staffs. Farm* (Stafford, 1909 edn.), 13–14 (copy in W.S.L.).
[7] S.R.O., D.952/2/3/14; /15, p. 25; /16.
[8] Sturgess, 'Agric. Staffs.' 399.
[9] S.R.O., D.952/3/1.
[10] Sturgess, 'Agric. Staffs.' 473.
[11] *Mins. of Evid. Com. Agric. ii* (1881), pp. 189, 192.
[12] *Agric. Gaz.* N.S. xxxii. 485, 605.
[13] Sturgess, 'Agric. Staffs.' 392.
[14] Ibid. 48; *Mins. of Evid. Com. Agric. ii* (1881), p. 192;

Carrington Smith, *Staffs. Farm*, 37.
[15] C. S. Orwin and E. H. Whetham, *Hist. of Brit. Agric. 1846–1914*, 363.
[16] *Mins. of Evid. Com. Agric. ii* (1881), p. 192; 'The Farm-Prize Competition, 1884', *J.R.A.S.E.* 2nd ser. xx. 587.
[17] Sturgess, 'Agric. Staffs.' 100.
[18] R. Perren, 'The Landlord and Agric. Transformation, 1870–1900', *Ag. H.R.* xviii(1), 48.
[19] *Com. Labour: Agric. Labourer, Vol. I (VI)* [C.6894–vi], p. 91, H.C. (1893), xxv.
[20] *Mins. of Evid. Com. Agric. Depression* (1894), p. 280.

table.[21] It was partly to deal with such problems that farmers combined to found the Staffordshire Dairy Farmers' Association in 1897; many local branches were established. Its other objects were the establishment of a London milk agency to sell direct to the customer and undercut the London dairies, and the prevention of competition from adulterated milk.[22]

Not all dairy farmers turned permanently to liquid-milk selling after 1879. The makers of the best cheese were unaffected by American competition. Milk production too was higher in summer than in winter, so that surplus milk could be made into cheese (sometimes for use on the farm) or butter. Where cheese-making equipment was maintained, farmers could shift from cheese-making to milk-selling and back again in response to short-term variations in cheese or milk prices.[23] An alternative was to sell the milk to local cheese-factories. A farmers' co-operative cheese-factory was established at Lichfield in 1873, but the venture failed through lack of support.[24] In 1880, however, there were factories at Alstonefield and Ellastone; in 1885 one was started at Croxden; others had been opened by 1888 at Hamstall Ridware and King's Bromley, by 1892 at Ilam, Mayfield, and Waterhouses, and by 1893 at Leigh and Rocester. Several were co-operatives.[25] Thereafter the number of factories varied; apparently only three survived in 1912.[26] Staffordshire farmers were also served by factories just outside the county; there was, for example, one at Market Drayton (Salop.) by 1880[27] and another at Marston Montgomery (Derb.) by 1893.[28]

This pattern of production and marketing of dairy goods apparently continued during and after the First World War. Some prominent farmers still made Cheshire or Derbyshire cheese on the farm; others, until recently cheese-makers, were selling milk to local markets, cheese-factories, or urban wholesalers, chiefly in London but also in Manchester, Birmingham, and the Black Country.[29] A farmer at Abbots Bromley had his cows calve in autumn to produce more milk in winter, when there was normally a shortage.[30] Falling dairy prices in the 1920s and early 1930s encouraged direct selling of milk locally.[31] In 1933 two-thirds of licences for retailing milk in the city of Stoke-on-Trent were held by producer-retailers, while on the outskirts of Wolverhampton producer-retailers were 'a very numerous body'.[32] The establishment in 1933 of the Milk Marketing Board, which guaranteed a minimum price, was favourably received in Staffordshire; the first chairman was a retired Staffordshire farmer, Thomas Baxter of Freeford.[33] The board's protection may have caused a reversion to wholesale milk-selling, apparent after the Second World War. By c. 1950 less than a quarter of dairy farmers in the Black Country were retailers.[34]

Falling prices between the World Wars drew attention to the need to increase milk yields by better breeding and feeding. To that end the Staffordshire Milk Recording Society was established in 1921; in 1926 98 members recorded the yields of 1,535 cows in 100 herds, but thereafter membership declined. In 1929 the county Agricultural Committee urged the government to increase its grants to such societies, so that small

[21] *Staffs. Advertiser*, 13 Nov., 25 Dec. 1897.
[22] Ibid. 13 Nov.–25 Dec. 1897; Orwin and Whetham, *Brit. Agric.* 364–5.
[23] Sturgess, 'Agric. Staffs.' 393–4.
[24] *Memo. of Assoc. of Lichfield Co-operative Cheese Factory Co.* (copy in S.R.O., D.661/19/10/22); *Mins. of Evid. Com. Agric.* ii (1881), p. 193. It is not listed in *P.O. Dir. Staffs.* (1876) or *Kelly's Dir. Staffs.* (1880).
[25] 'Agric. Our Vital Ind.' 22 Sept. 1917; *Kelly's Dir. Staffs.* (1880; 1884; 1888; 1892); *Com. Labour: Agric. Labourer*, I (VI), 91.
[26] *Kelly's Dir. Staffs.* (1896 and edns. to 1912).
[27] Ibid. (1880).

[28] *Com. Labour: Agric. Labourer*, I (VI), 91.
[29] 'Agric. Our Vital Ind.' 12 May, 9 and 30 June, 17 and 28 July, 1, 15, 22 Sept. 1917, 10 Aug., 30 Nov. 1918, 17 May, 14 June, 3 July 1919; 'Farming Interviews', 10 Dec. 1927, 14–28 Jan., 19 Apr. 1928; *Wages and Conditions of Emp. in Agric.* 307.
[30] 'Agric. Our Vital Ind.' 9 June 1917.
[31] *N.F.U. Record* (*Staffs. Section*), x (9), 4 (copy in W.S.L.).
[32] Ibid. x (10), 3.
[33] Ibid. x (11), 7; x (12), 3–4; Pepperall, *Baxter*, 145 sqq.
[34] Davies, 'Agric. of W. Midland Conurbation', 229.

producers should not be deterred from recording by high fees; the proposal was apparently ineffectual.[35] The society's records proved the superiority of Friesians in Staffordshire.[36] In the mid 1920s a Friesian herd at Tittensor gave the highest yield in England.[37] Nevertheless Dairy Shorthorns still predominated in 1939, although many farmers kept Friesians or Ayrshires.[38] The chief change in the feeding of dairy cows was a much greater use of concentrates. In the late 19th century expenditure on feed probably remained at about the level reached by the mid 1870s, though falling prices may have allowed more to be bought. On T. Carrington Smith's farm at Admaston, for example, expenditure on feed between 1876 and 1908 averaged 91 per cent of that of 1876, or about 35s. an acre.[39] That may have been a typical level.[40] In 1917 an intensive dairy farmer at Abbots Bromley was spending £4 an acre on feed.[41] By the late 1930s expenditures of £10 an acre on feed were common; some farmers dispensed with arable entirely, with considerable saving in labour costs, and bought all their fodder. Daily yields of up to $3\frac{1}{2}$ gallons a cow, or 2 gallons an acre, were obtained.[42] Purchased foods were much more varied than in the mid 19th century; they included soya, linseed, cotton, ground-nut, and palm-kernel cakes, maize-flakes and maize-meal, sharps, brewers' grains from Birmingham and Burton, tapioca, bran, wheat, oats, beet pulps, and compound cakes and meals; many farmers still mixed their own cattlefood.[43] In the inner areas of the Black Country cows were commonly stalled throughout the year and fed entirely on concentrates; calves were purchased in autumn, so that the farmer benefited from the high price of winter milk.[44]

The adoption of milking-machines was slow in the early 20th century, but towards the end of the First World War labour shortage encouraged a few farmers to buy them.[45] Between October 1917 and September 1918 the Staffordshire War Agricultural Committee received only one application for petrol for milking machinery,[46] but some farmers may have had steam-powered machines. Although the labour difficulties made it risky to rely on hand-milking, the milking-machines available lost up to a quarter of the milk.[47] A farmer at Stone had a machine which he did not use, since the labour of maintenance was as great as that of hand-milking; another at Tixall had one for use at harvest-time only.[48] By 1942, however, there were 1,451 milking-machines in the county, and by 1944 1,625; in both years Staffordshire had more than any county except Lancashire and Cheshire.[49] In 1951 the milking-machine was said to be essential even on small dairy-farms,[50] and by 1954 there were 3,495.[51]

During the Second World War the shortage of imported feed reduced milk output in the county from $64\frac{1}{2}$ million gallons in 1939–40 to $51\frac{3}{4}$ million in 1941–2; in the south Staffordshire towns the cow-keeping system collapsed, since farmers had to grow their own feed. From 1943, however, the decline was reversed. In 1949–50 77 million gallons of milk were obtained; Staffordshire was the fourth largest milk-producing county. Autumn calving had eliminated seasonal variations in milk production.[52] By 1965 it had further increased to over 92 million gallons.[53] Dairy cows increased from

[35] *Staffs. Milk Recording Soc.: Seventh Official Handbook with Ann. Rep., year ending Oct. 1934*, 12–13, 24–5 (copy in W.S.L. Pamphs. *sub* Agric.); S.R.O., County Agric. Cttee. Mins. 1920–33, p. 222.
[36] *Seventh Official Handbook*, 20.
[37] 'Farming Interviews', 12 May 1928.
[38] Myers, *Staffs*. 590.
[39] Carrington Smith, *Staffs. Farm*, 34.
[40] e.g. *Agric. Interests Com.: Digest* (1881), p. 269.
[41] 'Agric. Our Vital Ind.' 9 June 1917.
[42] Myers, *Staffs*. 591, 618, 620.
[43] Ibid. 618–26, 629.
[44] Davies, 'Agric. of W. Midland Conurbation', 108, 241.

[45] 'Agric. Our Vital Ind.' 12 and 26 May, 11 Aug. 1917.
[46] S.R.O., War Agric. Cttee. Mins. 1915–20, Exec. Cttee. 10 Apr. 1918.
[47] 'Agric. Our Vital Ind.' 19 Oct. 1918.
[48] Ibid. 29 June, 28 Sept. 1918.
[49] *Agric. Returns G.B.* 1939–44.
[50] *Staffs. County Council Development Plan 1951: Survey Rep. and Analysis*, 130.
[51] *Agric. Returns G.B.*
[52] *Staffs. County Council Development Plan 1951: Survey Rep. and Analysis*, 130; Davies, 'Agric. of W. Midland Conurbation', 226–7.
[53] S. Williams, *Farming in the Midlands*, 91.

97,865 in 1959 to 121,211 in 1973;[54] production was concentrated in larger units.[55]

Measures to improve the quality of milk began with the certified milk schemes of the 1920s but were more successful after the war. There were 299 Tuberculin Tested herds in October 1949, and 600 in July 1951.[56] Modernization to meet T.T. requirements and higher standards of cleanliness was aided by improvements in water-supply; 1,400 farm water-supply schemes were completed in the 1940s.[57] It also required improvements to buildings. By 1951 a few farmers had adopted the open-yard parlour system, but most retained double-stall cowsheds.[58] Rebuilding of cattle housing continued in the 1950s and 1960s. The most popular new type had timber cubicles for the cows, with straw litter and solid-floored passageways. Cattle were more often housed loose than before, and the number of herring-bone parlours increased.[59]

There were also changes after the war in the breeds of dairy cattle. By 1965 the Friesian had generally replaced the Dairy Shorthorn; there were 80,000 of the former and only 4,600 of the latter.[60] The availability of artificial insemination enabled farmers to improve the quality of herds. By 1965 two-thirds of all dairy herds entirely depended on it.[61] Between April 1974 and March 1975 the Milk Marketing Board carried out 48,376 dairy inseminations in Staffordshire and west Derbyshire; 44,394 were Friesian, 1,459 Jersey, 1,429 Ayrshire, and 1,020 Guernsey.[62]

Stock-rearing decreased in importance down to the Second World War. As has been seen, from the later 19th century fewer dairy farmers reared herd replacements. In the Moorlands at the end of the First World War rearing was said to be still the most usual type of farming, but it was gradually being ousted by dairying.[63] Between the World Wars the proportion of young stock to dairy cattle in the county declined.[64] By 1939 store cattle were not generally reared but were bought in from neighbouring counties, Wales, and Ireland.[65]

While fattening for beef has remained generally far less significant than dairying, it has been important in the southern arable districts since the late 19th century, when falling prices of corn and of imported feed encouraged the development of intensive stall-feeding of bullocks. Though beef prices fell by 25 per cent between the 1870s and 1893, that was offset by the fall in production costs.[66] Between 1867 and 1871 beef sales accounted for 25 per cent of income at Pool farm at Gailey in Penkridge, and 17 per cent at Teddesley home farm, but between 1893 and 1897 the figures were 60 per cent and 32 per cent respectively. Whereas in the late 1860s beef and mutton were about equally important on those farms, by the mid 1890s beef predominated.[67] Fattening bullocks remained the chief livestock enterprise in the southern arable areas down to the Second World War,[68] and occasionally elsewhere, as at Draycott-in-the-Moors in 1918 and Eccleshall in 1928. Farmers conformed to the fashion for selling animals younger, to produce baby beef.[69]

During the Second World War the fattening enterprises were maintained with difficulty owing to the high cost of feed, but higher fatstock prices had brought about a revival by 1951.[70] Nevertheless in 1965 there were 13·2 dairy cows to every beef cow

[54] *Agric. Returns G.B.*
[55] *Staffs. County Structure Plan 1973, Rep.* 148.
[56] *Staffs. County Council Development Plan 1951: Survey Rep. and Analysis,* 130.
[57] Ibid. 133–4.
[58] Ibid. 131.
[59] Min. of Agric., *Agric. in W. Midlands,* 54–5.
[60] Williams, *Farming in Midlands,* 100.
[61] Ibid. 129–30.
[62] Ex inf. Milk Marketing Bd., Cattle Breeding Centre, Tean (1976).
[63] *Wages and Conditions of Emp. in Agric.* 308–9.

[64] *Agric. Returns G.B.*
[65] Myers, *Staffs.* 592.
[66] Sturgess, 'Agric. Staffs.' 356–7; *Mins. of Evid. Com. Agric. Depression* (1894), p. 279.
[67] Sturgess, 'Agric. Staffs.' 300–1.
[68] *Agric. Returns G.B.* 1915, pp. 50–1; *Staffs. County Council Development Plan 1951: Survey Rep. and Analysis,* 126.
[69] 'Agric. Our Vital Ind.' 31 Aug. 1918; 'Farming Interviews', 7 Apr. 1928.
[70] *Staffs. County Council Development Plan 1951: Survey Rep. and Analysis,* 126.

in the county. In the late 1960s and early 1970s beef production was greatly expanded, despite the set-back of the foot-and-mouth epidemic of 1969. Cows and heifers kept for producing beef calves increased from 6,888 in 1965 to 15,478 in 1973, and bullocks between 6 months and 2 years old from 29,108 to 36,280.[71] This reflected the growing popularity of suckler herds, and the interest shown by dairy-farmers in fattening animals on grass for sale at 14 to 18 months.[72]

By the late 1930s Herefords were the chief breed of store cattle, though Hereford-Shorthorn and Shorthorn-Welsh crosses were also kept.[73] In the 1970s the suckler herds included Blue-Greys, Galloway crosses, pedigree Herefords, pedigree Aberdeen Angus, Sussex, and Charolais, but Hereford-Friesian crosses predominated.[74] In 1974–5 artificial inseminations by the Milk Marketing Board from Hereford bulls exceeded those from all other beef breeds combined, though Aberdeen Angus, Charolais, and Simmental inseminations were numerous, and other foreign breeds including Blondes d'Aquitaine, Chianinas, Limousins, and Maine-Anjous were used more often than the other English beef breeds.[75]

Sheep-farming has become less significant in the 20th century than in the 19th (see Table IV). Between the 1870s and the First World War the number of sheep in the county tended to fall. After the war, as F. R. Twemlow put it in 1919, 'sheep have been given up as a bad job. They cannot be used at home, nor can they be sold at market for a fair price, under the present system of control.'[76] There were 212,016 in 1915 but only 108,616 in 1923. Thereafter there was a slow recovery to 225,773 in 1939, encouraged by the protective legislation and marketing regulation of the 1930s. The flock declined again during and after the Second World War; the blizzards of 1947 left only 73,459. There was a further recovery to 216,515 in 1962, followed by renewed decline until 1971.[77]

Not only did numbers fall, but methods of management changed. The traditional predominance of arable farms in sheep-fattening persisted until the First World War; in 1915 stocking rates were highest in the arable areas of south Staffordshire and round Eccleshall.[78] In the late 19th century greater demand for lamb rather than mutton affected the composition of flocks. The proportion of lambs rose from 40 per cent in 1870–4 to 54 per cent in 1893–7, and by 1893 more than half the sheep over 1 year old were breeding ewes rather than wethers. Flying flocks were kept; ewes and lambs were bought in the autumn and fat lambs sold off in the spring.[79] In the late 1930s that was still the predominant system, though the north-east of the county was a rearing area, lambs being sold off as stores. Near towns sheep were less often kept owing to the threat from dogs. Wool was mostly sent directly or indirectly to Bradford.[80]

The breeds of sheep kept also changed, perhaps because of a shift from fattening or folding sheep on arable to keeping them less intensively on grassland.[81] In the late 19th century the Shropshire sheep remained predominant, especially in the southern arable areas, as its early maturity suited it to the fat-lamb trade.[82] Indeed the proportion of Shropshires in the county may have risen, since stocking rates in the Moorlands, where other breeds were kept, declined.[83] From 1881 prizes were offered for no other breed at the Staffordshire Agricultural Society's shows.[84] By 1900, however, other breeds were being tried, less specific to arable farms than the Shropshire. A

[71] Agric. Returns G.B.
[72] Min. of Agric. Agric. in W. Midlands, 55.
[73] Myers, Staffs. 592.
[74] Min. of Agric. Agric. in W. Midlands, 55.
[75] Ex inf. M.M.B.
[76] S.R.O., D.952/2/3/17, bdle. of docs. concerning Com. on Agric. 1919, observations by F. R. Twemlow, 21 Aug.
1919.
[77] Agric. Returns G.B.
[78] Ibid. 1915, pp. 50–1.
[79] Sturgess, 'Agric. Staffs.' 355–6.
[80] Myers, Staffs. 592.   [81] V.C.H. Wilts. iv. 109–10.
[82] Sturgess, 'Agric. Staffs.' 554.
[83] Ibid. 428.   [84] Ibid. 247.

farmer near Stafford kept Cheviot ewes in the early 1880s.[85] At Trentham home farm c. 1900 about half the flock were Shropshires, the rest Cluns or Welsh Mountain sheep.[86] Between 1898 and 1916 F. R. Twemlow kept a mixed flock at Tyrley, with Shropshire, Clun, and Cheviot ewes, crossed usually with Oxford rams but sometimes with Cotswolds, Hampshires, or Suffolks.[87] In 1917–19 flocks were still predominantly Shropshire; Oxford or Hampshire rams were used for crossing. Some farmers, however, kept Kerries or occasionally Cluns, and at Clifford's Wood, Swynnerton, there was a pedigree Hampshire flock.[88] Thereafter the Shropshire declined. Its decline, apparently begun by a foot-and-mouth epidemic in 1922, is reflected in the number of registered breeding flocks in Staffordshire. In 1920 there were 18 with 1,409 sheep, in 1930 8 with 855 sheep, in 1940 5 with 253 sheep, in 1950 2 with 136, and in 1976 1 with 96.[89] In the later 1920s perhaps half the sheep-farmers were still keeping them, but Cluns and Kerries were increasingly favoured, and occasionally Cheviots, Mashams, or Dorset Downs were found. Other Down breeds were still used for crossing, while Gritstones still occurred in the Moorlands.[90] By 1939 few Shropshires were left. In the Maer Hills district half-breds and Cheviots predominated, Suffolks being used for crossing; elsewhere Cluns, Kerries, Gritstones, and crosses between Cheviots and Border Leicesters and between Suffolks and Kerries were found. Oxford rams had been replacing Suffolks for crossing, since they gave a heavier lamb.[91]

In 1960 the breeds used were chiefly Cluns and Kerries, with some Mashams and Scotch Half-breds; Oxford rams were still the preferred cross. In the 1960s Kerries were often replaced by Scotch and Welsh Half-breds, and the Suffolk ram once again replaced the Oxford. Colbred ewes were tried. Most farmers kept their sheep on grass; intensive rotation grazing and winter housing were tried but abandoned. There was, however, some revival of fattening on arable.[92] A farmer at Tamhorn in the 1970s, for example, kept Dorset Horns and fed them off cabbage and broccoli stalks in winter.[93] The proportion of sheep kept in the Moorlands to those in the lowland areas, however, increased in the 1960s, and some Moorland farms were exclusively devoted to sheep.[94]

Pig-keeping continued as an adjunct of dairying and was widespread in the county.[95] The population averaged c. 50,000 until the First World War (see Table IV), falling to 33,037 in 1919. The reduction was not entirely made up until the 1930s, and the Second World War brought a further decline to 24,198 in 1943 and 21,029 in 1947. By 1954, however, the population had reached 110,535. It remained around 100,000 until the 1970s; in 1973 there were 121,627.[96]

In the late 1930s pigs were kept everywhere but were most numerous in the west. There were both small herds of 3 or 4 pigs and large enterprises of up to 500 animals. There were a few large pig-breeders in the east, but other large-scale pig-farmers bought pigs as stores and fattened them for pork or bacon.[97] In the early 1970s breeding and fattening were both practised everywhere except in the north-east. Most herds were small, and most housing was old-fashioned, though some farmers used round-house fattening piggeries. The association of pig-keeping with dairying had become

[85] *J.R.A.S.E.* 2nd ser. xx. 544.
[86] Perren, 'Agric. Depression', 191.
[87] S.R.O., D.952/2/3/15, p. 160; /16, 1 and 29 June 1898, 1 Jan. 1899, 18 Aug., 6 Oct. 1900, 14 Aug. 1901, 1 Jan., 16 Aug. 1902, 8 Sept. 1906, 1 Jan. 1908; /17, 1 Jan. 1916.
[88] 'Agric. Our Vital Ind.' 26 May, 2 and 9 June, 7 and 21 July, 4–18 Aug., 1 Sept.–6 Oct. 1917, 29 June, 10–24 Aug., 28 Sept., 12 and 26 Oct., 9 Nov., 21 Dec. 1918; 25 Jan., 15 and 29 Mar., 26 Apr., 17 May, 14 June, 9 Aug. 1919.
[89] Ex inf. the sec., Shropshire Sheep Breeders' Assoc.

and Flock Book Soc. (1976).
[90] 'Farming Interviews', 10–31 Dec. 1927, 14 Jan.–11 Feb., 17 Mar., 14–28 Apr., 26 May, 16 June 1928.
[91] Myers, *Staffs.* 592.
[92] Min. of Agric. *Agric. in W. Midlands*, 55–6.
[93] *Staffs. Farming Newsletter, Feb. 1976* (published with *Stafford Newsletter*, 6 Feb. 1976).
[94] Min. of Agric. *Agric. in W. Midlands*, 56; Williams, *Farming in Midlands*, 103.
[95] Myers, *Staffs.* 592–3.
[96] *Agric. Returns G.B.*
[97] Myers, *Staffs.* 592–3.

less marked; many new enterprises were on corn farms where bedding was readily available and manure disposal convenient.[98]

In 1918–19 various breeds of pig were kept including Large and Middle Whites, Large Blacks, Berkshires, Gloucester Old Spots, Tamworths, and crosses.[99] By the late 1920s, however, Large Whites were apparently the most popular.[1] In the late 1930s Middle and Large Whites, the Wessex, the Essex, and a cross between the Saddleback and Large White were the commonest breeds.[2] All save the Middle White were popular in the 1960s, and the Swedish Landrace had been introduced. In the early 1970s the Large White and Landrace predominated.[3]

Poultry-keeping greatly increased, especially in the 1920s and early 1930s, though numbers fell during the World Wars: on holdings of over 1 a. there were 260,997 fowls in 1885, 696,680 in 1913, 566,536 in 1921, 1,451,599 in 1934, 777,381 in 1944, and 2,044,850 in 1961. Numbers subsequently declined to 1,253,065 in 1973.[4] Before the Second World War fowls were kept chiefly for their eggs, sold mainly in the Potteries and the Black Country.[5] In 1928 a farmer at Weston Coyney was rearing Rhode Island Reds, White Leghorns, and White Wyandottes on a large scale for egg-laying.[6] Egg-production continued to predominate after the Second World War. In 1962 there were 2,856 farms with 957,632 laying hens. In the 1960s battery-houses and other forms of intensive housing became general; hybrid strains of egg-layers were used. Broiler chickens became more important; they rose from 9·1 per cent of all fowls in 1960 to 22·3 per cent in 1973. They were also more densely housed and more rapidly fattened than before. Broiler enterprises were fewer than egg-laying ones, but on a larger scale: in 1962 there were on average 1,512 broilers in each unit, but only 337 egg-layers. In the early 1970s many Staffordshire broilermen were still independent of hatcheries and processing plants. Turkeys increased from 9,088 in 1885 to 19,357 in 1933 and 79,114 in 1962. By the early 1970s Christmas turkeys were an important product.[7]

AGRARIAN ECONOMY AND SOCIETY

In the late 19th century some of the great estates of Staffordshire were still growing. Lord Harrowby, for example, bought 418 a. in 1890 and a further 116 a. in 1891; the Sandon estate, which had been 4,100 a. in 1856, covered 6,170 a. in the late 1890s. Others had reached their full extent and diminished slightly: Lord Hatherton's at Teddesley from 11,298 a. in 1863 to 10,858 a. in 1904; Lord Ferrers's at Chartley from 7,821 a. in 1883 to 7,551 a. in 1900. The duke of Sutherland's at Trentham had already declined from 10,507 a. in 1857 to 10,434 a. in 1878.[8] Nevertheless the proportion of owner-occupied farm-land in the county decreased from 11·77 per cent in 1890 to 10·27 per cent in 1900.[9] In 1910 11·3 per cent of farms were owned or mainly owned by their farmers. The proportion was higher among smallholdings of under 5 a., but much lower among medium-sized farms of 50 a. to 300 a.[10]

In the early years of the 20th century the great estates began to break up. Lord Ferrers sold the Chartley estate in 1904; nearly half went to one purchaser, much of

[98] Min. of Agric. *Agric. in W. Midlands*, 56.
[99] 'Agric. Our Vital Ind.' 28 Sept., 5 and 12 Oct., 9 Nov., 21 Dec. 1918, 25 Jan., 15 Feb., 5 July, 27 Sept. 1919.
[1] 'Farming Interviews', 10, 24, 31 Dec. 1927, 7 and 21 Jan., 11 Feb., 7 and 14 Apr. 1928.
[2] Myers, *Staffs.* 593.
[3] Williams, *Farming in Midlands*, 115–16; Min. of Agric. *Agric. in W. Midlands*, 56.
[4] *Agric. Returns G.B.*; Myers, *Staffs.* 593.

[5] Myers, *Staffs.* 593; Williams, *Farming in Midlands*, 114.
[6] 'Farming Interviews', 24 Mar. 1928.
[7] Williams, *Farming in Midlands*, 114; Min. of Agric. *Agric. in W. Midlands*, 57; *Agric. Returns G.B.*
[8] F. M. Reid, 'Economic and Social Aspects of Land-ownership in the 19th Cent.' (Oxford Univ. B.Litt. thesis, 1956), 81; Sturgess, 'Agric. Staffs.' 537.
[9] *Agric. Returns G.B.* 1900.
[10] Ibid. 1910.

the rest being fragmented.[11] Lord Macclesfield sold his Croxden estate and other lands in north Staffordshire in 1913, some of it to the tenants,[12] and in 1914 the duke of Sutherland sold most of his property at Tittensor in Stone and Great Wyrley in Cannock.[13] Between 1918 and 1921 much more land was thrown on the market, though sales were perhaps less extensive in Staffordshire than elsewhere.[14] The estates were generally sold in lots and many farms were bought by their tenants. In 1918 2,938 a. of the Giffards' Chillington estate, Lord Anglesey's 5,091-a. Burton estate, 880 a. of Lord Stafford's land round Stafford, much of Lord Shrewsbury's property including 6,475 a. at Alton, the Sneyd-Kinnersleys' estate of 2,394 a. at Loxley Park, and the Staffordshire estates of the earl of Wilton and Baroness Zouche were advertised for sale.[15] In 1919 R. A. Dyott sold over 700 a. at Fulfen and Whittington; Lord Bradford sold outlying parts of the Weston estate; the duke of Sutherland sold the rest of the Trentham estate; Sir Oswald Mosley sold most of his 3,825-a. estate at Rolleston; Sir Charles Wolseley sold 865 a. of the Wolseley Park estate, more than half passing to the tenants; and Lord Hatherton disposed of over 2,300 a. in Penkridge parish.[16] In 1921 the marquess of Crewe sold most of his 4,493-a. Madeley estate, complaining of abnormal super-tax. Most of the property went to the tenants.[17] The prices at the Alton sale apparently averaged about £32 13s. an acre, or only 17 years' purchase, but those at Rolleston averaged almost £43 an acre, those at Loxley almost £42 an acre, and those at Madeley £40, fairly high prices for the period.[18] The proportion of owner-occupied farm-land rose to 14½ per cent (covering 13¾ per cent of farms) in 1920, and to nearly 17 per cent in 1921. Since the prices of agricultural products fell almost immediately, some farmers were probably unable to bear the cost of their land purchases: 7,000 a. had reverted from owner-occupiers to tenants by 1922.[19]

Sales continued in the 1920s and 1930s, especially in the depression years after 1929. In 1927 Sir Smith Hill Child advertised 3,309 a. at Draycott-in-the-Moors and 1,320 a. at Stallington.[20] In 1929 Sir William Bromley-Davenport's 2,524-a. estate at Wootton and Ellastone was up for sale,[21] and Lord Wrottesley sold outlying parts of his property.[22] In 1930 most of the late Sir Francis Villiers Forster's 2,500-a. Lysways estate round Longdon was broken up.[23] In 1932 Lord Anglesey advertised Beaudesert,[24] and in 1933 Lord Bagot sold 6,959 a. at Blithfield, most of his property.[25]

There were further sales after the Second World War. In 1947 Lord Dudley put Himley Hall and 2,712 a. on the market;[26] Lord Hatherton sold 2,562 a. of the Teddesley estate then,[27] and over 1,520 a. in Penkridge and 2,976 a. in Teddesley Hay in 1953.[28] In 1949 Lord Shrewsbury sold his estates in Colwich, Salt, Enson, Hopton, and Coton.[29] In 1951 the Harpur Crewe estate offered 10,753 a. in Alstonefield for sale[30] and the executors of Ralph Sneyd sold what remained of the Keele estate (4,407 a.).[31]

[11] W.S.L., Sale Cat. E/1/1; *Staffs. Advertiser*, 17 Sept. 1904.

[12] W.S.L., Sale Cats. E/1/15, E/2/1; *Staffs. Advertiser*, 19 July 1913.

[13] W.S.L., Sale Cat. E/2/4; *Staffs. Advertiser*, 1 Aug. 1914.

[14] F. M. L. Thompson, *Eng. Landed Society in the 19th Cent.* 329-30.

[15] *Staffs. Advertiser*, 15 and 22 June, 31 Aug., 2 and 9 Nov. 1918; W.S.L., Sale Cats. E/2/8 and 10.

[16] *Staffs. Advertiser*, 31 May, 27 Sept., 11 and 25 Oct., 29 Nov. 1919; W.S.L., Sale Cat. E/3/25; *V.C.H. Staffs.* v. 111, 113-16, 120.

[17] *Staffs. Advertiser*, 17 Dec. 1921; W.S.L., Sale Cat. F/5/5.

[18] *Staffs. Advertiser*, 2 and 9 Nov. 1918, 25 Oct. 1919, 17 Dec. 1921; Thompson, *Eng. Landed Soc.* 332.

[19] *Agric. Returns G.B.*; K. A. H. Murray, *Hist. of Second World War: Agric.* 18.

[20] W.S.L., Sale Cat. D/2/8.

[21] Ibid. E/3/10.

[22] Ibid. E/3/12; *Staffs. Advertiser*, 26 Oct. 1929.

[23] W.S.L., Sale Cat. D/2/9; *Staffs. Advertiser*, 1 Nov. 1930.

[24] W.S.L., Sale Cat. C/2/6.

[25] Ibid. C/2/9; *Staffs. Advertiser*, 23 Sept. 1933.

[26] W.S.L., Sale Cat. E/1/16; *Staffs. Advertiser*, 19 Jan. 1947.

[27] W.S.L., Sale Cat. C/3/31; *Staffs. Advertiser*, 1 Nov. 1947.

[28] *V.C.H. Staffs.* v. 110, 183.

[29] *Staffs. Advertiser*, 11 June 1949; W.S.L., Sale Cat. E/4/14.

[30] W.S.L., Sale Cats. E/3/26-7.

[31] Ibid. E/4/16; *Staffs. Advertiser*, 2 Nov. 1951.

Lord Harrowby offered his 895 a. at Marston for sale in 1960.[32] After the death of the 6th Lord Bagot in 1961 most of the remaining Blithfield estate was also on the market.[33] The rest of the Wrottesley estate, 3,260 a., was sold in 1963.[34]

The decline of the old estates was matched by a further growth of owner-occupation. By the early 1940s 29 per cent of holdings and 25 per cent of farm-land were farmed by their owners.[35] By 1960–1 over 44 per cent of farms, covering 34 per cent of farm-land, were owner-occupied; a further 9 per cent, covering $13\frac{1}{2}$ per cent of farm-land, were predominantly owned by their occupiers. Altogether $47\frac{1}{2}$ per cent of farm-land was owner-occupied, slightly less than the national average. By 1970 $58\frac{1}{2}$ per cent of farms, covering $53\frac{1}{2}$ per cent of farm-land, were wholly or mainly owned by the farmers, and 52 per cent of farm-land was owner-occupied. The extent of owner-occupation remained approximately constant down to 1973.[36]

TABLE V: NUMBER OF AGRICULTURAL HOLDINGS CLASSIFIED BY ACREAGE 1875–1970

	Over 1 a. up to 5 a.	Over 5 a. up to 20 a.	Over 20 a. up to 50 a.	Over 50 a. up to 100 a.	Over 100 a. up to 150 a.	Over 150 a. up to 300 a.	Over 300 a. up to 500 a.	Over 500 a. up to 700 a.	Over 700 a. up to 1,000 a.	Over 1,000 a.	Total
1875	10,870			1,406	1,566		230	37		2	14,111
1880	10,947			1,393	1,551		248	33		3	14,175
1885	3,560	4,141	2,064	1,410	1,577		229	32		4	13,017
1890	3,253	6,297									
1895	3,194	4,224	2,171	1,435	1,596		224	28		4	12,876
1900	No returns collected										
1905	2,740	6,035		3,052			242				12,069
1910	2,658	5,956		3,066			228				11,908
1915	2,596	3,661	2,226	1,478	752	876	212				11,801
1920	2,094	3,392	2,233	1,534	756	861	207				11,077
1925	1,910	3,141	2,206	1,550	751	828	198				10,584
1930	1,650	2,875	2,177	1,601	711	834	182				10,030
1935	1,553	2,694	2,146	1,636	712	803	154	13	4	0	9,715
1940	1,354	2,487	2,155	1,624	692	795	154	11	2	0	9,274
1945	1,555	2,643	2,109	1,603	734	774	159	17	1	0	9,595
1950	1,660	2,574	2,067	1,545	739	766	165	12	4	0	9,532
1955	1,805	2,418	2,028	1,557	721	746	167	15	4	0	9,461
1960	1,607	2,158	1,900	1,539	721	771	183	24	6	1	8,910
1965	1,529	1,986	1,693	1,446	702	756	182	32	14	1	8,341
1970	446	1,272	1,449	1,284	608	682	217	58	22	9	6,047

Sources: *Agric. Returns G.B.*; for 1890, *Return Agric. Holdings* [Cd. 3408], p. 5, H.C. (1907), lxvi. In 1940 and 1942 slight changes were made in the official classifications, but they do not materially affect the figures from 1940 until 1967. In 1967 and 1968, however, many holdings of under 10 a., with little production, were deleted: *Agric. Returns G.B.* 1968–9, page xii note a, and table 63A, notes a and b.

Although there were more landowners, farms became larger, and the number of farms declined faster than the area of farm-land (see Table V). The average farm (including smallholdings of more than 1 a.) increased from *c.* 42 a. in 1875 to *c.* 60 a. in

32 W.S.L., Sale Cat. C/3/29.
33 Ibid. E/4/18.
34 Ibid. C/3/17.

35 Min. of Agric. and Fisheries, *National Farm Survey of Eng. and Wales (1941–1943)* (H.M.S.O., 1946), 93.
36 *Agric. Returns G.B.*

1960. In 1960 the average area of farms over 15 a. was 91 a.; by 1973 it was 112 a.[37] In the late 19th century growth in farm sizes was slow; there was little rise in the proportion of those over 300 a., but some consolidation of smaller ones. On some estates, indeed, the financial difficulties of the larger farmers resulted in the break-up of holdings. On the Keele estate seven farms were divided between 1874 and 1900, and on the Chartley estate two farms, each of which had covered over 300 a. in 1853, had disappeared by 1900.[38] Large farms became less common on the Teddesley estate in the late 19th century, but there were also fewer smallholdings.[39] On the duke of Sutherland's estates in the 1880s it was sometimes necessary to reduce the size of farms in order to let them, though there were also some amalgamations.[40] On the Mainwaring family's estates the average farm at Biddulph was a little smaller in 1881 than in 1868, but a little larger in 1906; at Whitmore and Acton farm sizes fell between 1881 and 1906.[41] Between the World Wars the proportion of farms over 300 a. in the county remained virtually unchanged, but those between 20 and 300 a. became relatively more numerous at the expense of smallholdings. The number of smallholdings rose after the Second World War but declined again from c. 1960. Medium-sized farms also were often consolidated into larger units in the 1960s and early 1970s. In 1973 less than 6 per cent of farms were over 300 a., but they covered over 30 per cent of farm-land; there were 8 farms over 1,000 a., occupying 10,252 a. altogether. Holdings under 100 a. formed over 70 per cent of the total but covered only one-third of the cultivated area.[42]

Despite the general increase, farms still varied in size according to their region and function. In the late 19th century sheep-farms, most of which were in the south, were generally larger than cattle farms. In 1880 holdings under 100 a. supported 44 per cent of the cattle but only 18 per cent of the sheep; holdings over 300 a. supported 39 per cent of the sheep but fewer than 16 per cent of the cattle.[43] On the Dyott estate at Freeford, consisting predominantly of arable-and-sheep farms, most farms c. 1880 were between 170 a. and 300 a.; on the duchy of Lancaster's estate in the Needwood forest dairying area, three-quarters of the farms were under 200 a. and five-eighths under 100 a.[44] In most parishes in the Uttoxeter poor-law union, which included the dairying district from Croxden to Abbots Bromley, the average farm in the 1880s was below 100 a. and often below 50 a.; there were few farms over 300 a.[45] In 1951 the largest farms, of between 200 a. and 400 a., predominated in the southern arable areas, medium-sized farms, of between 70 a. and 150 a., in the central dairying area, and the smallest holdings in the Moorlands and urban areas.[46] On the Harpur Crewe estate, which covered much of the northern Moorlands, two-thirds of all farms over 20 a. were under 100 a.[47] In the Black Country arable farms were generally larger than dairy-farms.[48] In the 1960s over 85 per cent of Moorland farms were still under 100 a.[49]

The combination of bad weather and low prices in the late 1870s and early 1880s resulted, as elsewhere, in a reduction of tenants' working capital, difficulties in paying rents, and increased turn-over of farms. A Staffordshire farmer giving evidence to the Royal Commission on Agriculture in 1881 thought that both large and small farmers had been hit.[50] Another witness considered that while the large farmers were surviving

[37] *Agric. Returns G.B.* In 1967 and 1968 many smallholdings were deleted from the census, so that comparisons between earlier and later figures for all farms are impossible.
[38] Sturgess, 'Agric. Staffs.' 398.
[39] Ibid. 306.
[40] Perren, 'Agric. Depression', 121, 253.
[41] S.R.O. D.(W.) 1743/additional/12, pp. 17–25; /14/1–2.
[42] *Agric. Returns G.B.* [43] Ibid.
[44] *Mins. of Evid. Com. Agric.* ii (1881), p. 643; *Agric.*

Interests Com.: Digest (1881), p. 83.
[45] *Com. on Labour: Agric. Labourer, 1 (VI)*, 91, 99.
[46] *Staffs. County Council Development Plan 1951: Survey Rep. and Analysis*, 131.
[47] W.S.L., Sale Cats. E/3/26–7.
[48] Davies, 'Agric. of W. Midland Conurbation', 195–7.
[49] F. J. Johnson, 'Settlement Pattern of NE. Staffs.' (Univ. of Wales M.A. thesis, 1964), 343–434, 440.
[50] *Mins. of Evid. Com. Agric.* ii (1881), p. 650.

by reducing stocks, farmers with under 50 a. were worse hit and would not be able to afford the expense of cultivation in 1882.[51] On the Keele estate in the 1880s, however, it was the large tenants who could not pay the rent, perhaps because they had proportionately more arable than the smaller farmers, who paid regularly.[52] Although some landlords had unlet farms on their hands c. 1880,[53] that was not general: on the Trentham estate farms did not long remain in hand, and on the Teddesley estate there were no vacancies in the 1880s.[54] Nevertheless farms changed hands more rapidly. In 1894 a farmer at Blithfield stated that almost every farm round his had changed hands twice in recent years.[55] At Teddesley the turn-over of tenants was much greater in the 1870s and 1880s than in the 1850s and 1860s, though it was slightly less in the 1880s than in the 1870s. Less than a quarter of tenants who entered between 1861 and 1880 were still there after 1886.[56] Fourteen out of Lord Harrowby's 25 farms changed hands between 1880 and 1882.[57] At Trentham there were 15 changes of tenancy on the larger farms in the 1880s.[58] On the Chillington estate, on the other hand, farms changed hands no more often in the 1870s than the 1860s, and less frequently in the 1880s. The turn-over was still lower in the 1890s.[59]

The new tenants in many cases were of a lower social standing than the old and had a different attitude to work. In 1879 a labourer blamed the older farmers' difficulties partly on extravagances such as sending daughters to boarding-schools.[60] Larger farms round Blithfield had had perhaps two female domestics in the 1850s. The newcomers, who came from north Staffordshire, Derbyshire, and Cheshire, were accustomed to a lower standard of living and to farm-hands living in. They dispensed with the maids; they and their families did the housework and dairying. Farmers holding as much as 400 a. would do their own farm work.[61] The migration from the north and west continued into the early 20th century. In 1910 a farmer at Weston in Standon claimed that two-thirds of North Staffordshire farmers were, like him, Cheshire men,[62] and in 1928 all the farmers round Edingale were said to be migrants from Cheshire.[63] Farmers also came from Cornwall, Scotland, and west Shropshire.[64]

The reduction of agricultural rents in Staffordshire in the late 19th century was less than in many other parts of England, partly because the county was already predominantly pastoral. Rents fell further in south than in north Staffordshire, and further on arable farms than on grass ones. Serious difficulties for both landlords and tenants generally began in the late 1870s. The rental value of farm-land at Trentham began falling in 1877; it was than 42s. 11d. an acre, but by 1881 was down to 38s. 11d. In 1879 there were rent reductions averaging 13½ per cent on six farms, but three of the reductions were temporary.[65] At Freeford Richard Dyott gave remissions of 10–15 per cent between 1878 and 1881; remissions of 10–20 per cent were general round Lichfield at that period.[66] After the wet summer of 1879 Lord Crewe gave his tenants a 15–25 per cent allowance.[67] Lord Harrowby gave temporary reductions to Sandon tenants of 10–20 per cent between 1878 and 1880.[68] The Revd. F. C. Twemlow returned 5·7 per cent to one farmer at Tyrley in 1878 and his son made allowances of

[51] *Agric. Interests Com.: Digest* (1881), pp. 271–2.
[52] Sturgess, 'Agric. Staffs.' 170, 519.
[53] *Mins. of Evid. Com. Agric. ii* (1881), p. 193.
[54] Sturgess, 'Agric. Staffs.' 298; Perren, 'Agric. Depression', 146.
[55] *Mins. of Evid. Com. Agric. Depression* (1894), p. 231.
[56] Sturgess, 'Agric. Staffs.' 296–7.
[57] Reid, 'Landownership', 87.
[58] Perren, 'Agric. Depression', 264.
[59] Sturgess, 'Agric. Staffs.' 357–8.
[60] *Staffs. Advertiser*, 2 Aug. 1879.

[61] *Mins. of Evid. Com. Agric. Depression* (1894), pp. 233–4; above, p. 116.
[62] *Staffs. Weekly Sentinel*, 24 Dec. 1910.
[63] 'Farming Interviews', 28 Apr. 1928.
[64] Ibid. 31 Dec. 1927, 21 and 28 Jan., 21 Apr., 16 June 1928; 'Agric. Our Vital Ind.' 16 and 23 June, 11 Aug. 1917, 24 Aug., 9 Nov. 1918, 15 Feb., 5 July, 18 Oct. 1919.
[65] Perren, 'Agric. Depression', 256, 301.
[66] *Mins. of Evid. Com. Agric. ii* (1881), p. 651; *Agric. Interests Com.: Digest* (1881), pp. 271–2.
[67] Perren, 'Agric. Depression', 115.
[68] Reid, 'Landownership', 60–1.

11–18 per cent on two farms in 1880–1.[69] In 1880 W. T. C. Giffard permanently reduced some rents at Chillington and gave a temporary 10 per cent allowance on the rest.[70] At Teddesley Lord Hatherton gave a temporary rebate of 10 per cent in 1881.[71]

The landlords at first hoped that rent reductions would remain temporary. Lord Dartmouth's agent thought in 1879 that it would be necessary to offer 'a still more liberal hand' to farmers for a year or two; a reduction of 15 per cent would be needed on light lands, but of up to 25 per cent on cold heavy soils.[72] At Trentham indeed farm rents rose again after 1882 and by 1886 were well above the 1878 level; but thereafter reductions were unavoidable and continued into the 1890s. By 1900 farm rents were over 8 per cent below their 1870 level, and rents per acre had fallen to 31s. 11d.[73] Elsewhere reductions became permanent. The rents on Lord Dartmouth's Sandwell estate were 10 per cent lower in the late 1880s than in the late 1870s.[74] On the Chartley estate they were 13 per cent lower in 1895–1900 than in 1875; at Keele 9 per cent lower in 1894–1900 than in 1879; on the duchy of Lancaster estates 22–24 per cent lower in 1894 than in the 1870s; at Sandon 18 per cent lower in 1899 than in 1878; at Blithfield 10–12 per cent lower in 1894 than in the 1870s.[75] The rental of the Maer Hall estate was 15 per cent lower in 1891 than in 1881, and rents per acre 13⅓ per cent lower.[76] Some estates escaped more lightly. The Bill family's rental on 11 Moorland farms fell by only 2 per cent between 1876 and 1888.[77] The rents of some farms on the Twemlow family's estates at Tyrley, Standon, and Betley were up to 17 per cent more an acre in the late 1890s than in the 1870s, though other rents had been reduced by up to 15 per cent an acre and there were frequent temporary rebates.[78] The greatest reductions were apparently on estates in the south of the county with a high proportion of arable: at Teddesley rents fell by 23 per cent between 1877 and the mid 1890s, and at Chillington by 32 per cent between 1873 and the mid 1890s.[79] It was claimed in 1894 that, apparently since the 1870s, rents in the county had not been reduced on average by more than 10 per cent; on large arable farms they had fallen by 20 per cent, but often they had not fallen at all on medium-sized pasture farms.[80] That may have been an optimistic picture: between 1879–80 and 1894–5 the value of lands assessed for income tax under Schedule A fell by 18·4 per cent. In the same period the rateable value of land fell less than 10 per cent in the Moorlands and in the Stoke and Newcastle poor-law unions, and by between 10 and 20 per cent in most of the rest of the county; in Seisdon, Lichfield, West Bromwich, and Wolverhampton unions, which contained much arable land, the fall was more than 20 per cent.[81]

Farm rents in most areas were generally between 25s. and 33s. an acre in the earlier 20th century and did not keep pace with inflation.[82] There were some minor fluctuations. The rent of larger farms on an estate at Draycott-in-the-Moors remained c. 25s. an acre from 1906 to 1921 but had risen to 28s. by 1927.[83] Rents on the Stone Aston estate rose from c. 25s. an acre in 1914 to c. 30s. in 1942.[84] At Blithfield, on the other

[69] S.R.O., D.952/2/3/23, p. 232; /24, pp. 50–1, 66.
[70] P. J. Doyle, 'The Giffards of Chillington, a Catholic Landed Family, 1642–1861' (Durham Univ. M.A. thesis, 1968), 345.
[71] Sturgess, 'Agric. Staffs.' 278.
[72] S.R.O., D.564/8/1/17, Thynne to Dartmouth, 2 Oct. 1879.
[73] Perren, 'Agric. Depression', 301, 430.
[74] Sturgess, 'Agric. Staffs.' 515.
[75] Ibid. 518–19; Final Rep. Com. Agric. Depression [C.8540], p. 18, H.C. (1897), xv; Mins. of Evid. Com. Agric. Depression (1894), pp. 231–2.
[76] S.R.O., D.1213/5/1.
[77] Sturgess, 'Agric. Staffs.' 520.

[78] S.R.O., D.952/2/3/23–5.
[79] Sturgess, 'Agric. Staffs.' 513–14.
[80] Mins. of Evid. Com. Agric. Depression (1894), p. 232; Final Rep. Com. Agric. Depression, 18.
[81] Com. Agric.: Statements showing decrease or increase in rateable value and gross annual value of lands under Schedule A [C.8300], pp. 7, 10, and map, H.C. (1897), xv.
[82] W.S.L., Sale Cats. C/2/6 and 9; C/3/17, 29, 31; D/2/17 and 20; D/2/131/71; E/1/1 and 15–16; E/2/1, 4, 8, 10, 17; E/3/3 and 25–7; E/4/15–16, 18; F/4/12. Only rents of farms over 20 a. in each catalogue have been analysed here.
[83] Ibid. F/4/12, E/3/3, D/2/131/71 (farms over 20 a.).
[84] Ibid. D/2/17 and 20 (farms over 20 a.).

hand, rents had to be reduced by 3 per cent in 1932.[85] In the Black Country between the two World Wars rents fell because of the increasing acidity of the soil.[86] Where intensive dairying was practised much higher rents could be afforded: thus in 1929 the rent of the Burton House model dairy farm in Castle Church was over £4 16s. an acre.[87] In the 1950s and 1960s rents rose rapidly, averaging £3 14s. an acre in 1962 and £7.32 in 1971; the latter figure was 26 per cent above the national average.[88]

The later 19th century was marked by a shift in responsibility for permanent or long-lasting improvements from tenant to landlord. In 1872 the Staffordshire Chamber of Agriculture proposed an elaborate scheme of compensation for tenants' improvements.[89] The scheme may have affected tenancy agreements, which by 1875 were including clauses giving tenants greater compensation. On the duke of Sutherland's estates partial compensation was given for manures used in the last 3 years of tenancy and for oilcake used in the last two.[90] Lord Harrowby and Richard Dyott of Freeford provided compensation for unexhausted improvements, as did Lord Lichfield on his Eccleshall property.[91] Most Staffordshire landlords, however, contracted out of the 1875 Agricultural Holdings Act, which established a non-compulsory scheme for tenancy agreements. One of Dyott's tenants, however, who himself held under the Act, thought in 1881 that landlords were anxious to meet tenants fairly and that agreements usually gave fair compensation.[92] By 1881 Lord Lichfield's agreements, for example, provided allowances for manure, straw, hay, cake, and artificial fertilizers, and compensation for draining and for seeds for pasture.[93] Some attempts were made to meet the 1875 Act's extension of the period of notice required for yearly tenants from six months to one year. Dyott, for example, had by 1881 altered many tenancies in that sense.[94] On the duke of Sutherland's estates that change awaited the compulsory provisions of the 1883 Agricultural Holdings Act.[95] Another effect of the Act was to consolidate the practice whereby the landlord provided, repaired, and improved farm buildings.[96] On the Sandon estate under the 3rd earl of Harrowby (d. 1900) the rate of landlord's spending on new buildings per acre of farm-land was only 17 per cent of that under the 2nd earl (d. 1882), but repair expenses were $10\frac{1}{2}$ per cent higher. From 1884 the earl took over responsibility for maintaining labourers' cottages from the farmers.[97] Landlords also generally provided seeds and manure when land was laid down to pasture.[98]

In the 20th century the terms of agricultural tenancies depended increasingly on national legislation. That did not, however, greatly affect the period of tenancy, which generally continued to be from year to year as in the mid 19th century, but legislation granted the tenant more immunity from eviction. From the late 1940s such longer leases as survived were generally converted as they expired to yearly tenures in accordance with the Agricultural Holdings Act, 1948. From c. 1970 new agreements sometimes took the form of owner-tenant partnerships based on profit-sharing; that form became commoner but still applied to only a small proportion of tenures in the mid 1970s.[99] Tenures usually began at Lady Day on stock- and dairy-farms, at Michaelmas on arable farms.[1]

[85] S.R.O., D.(W.) 1721/3/280.
[86] Davies, 'Agric. of W. Midlands Conurbation', 53.
[87] W.S.L., Sale Cat. E/4/4.
[88] Min. of Agric. *Agric. in W. Midlands*, 16–17.
[89] See p. 102.
[90] Perren, 'Agric. Depression', 164–5.
[91] W. E. Bear, *Relations of Landlord and Tenant in Eng. and Scot.* (1876), 122–3; Reid, 'Landownership', 59; *Mins. of Evid. Com. Agric. ii* (1881), p. 646.
[92] Perren, 'Agric. Depression', 161; Sturgess, 'Agric. Staffs.' 462; *Mins. of Evid. Com. Agric. ii* (1881), p. 189;

Agric. Interests Com.: Digest (1881), pp. 271–2.
[93] S.R.O., D.615/E(L)/1/2.
[94] *Mins. of Evid. Com. Agric. ii* (1881), p. 645.
[95] Perren, 'Agric. Depression', 171.
[96] *Mins. of Evid. Com. Agric. ii* (1881), p. 651; *Mins. of Evid. Com. Agric. Depression* (1894), p. 234.
[97] Reid, 'Landownership', 71, 94.
[98] *Mins. of Evid. Com. Agric. Depression* (1894), p. 232.
[99] Ex inf. Min. of Agric., Stafford Area Office (1976); Agric. Holdings Act, 1948, 11 & 12 Geo. VI, c. 63.
[1] Min. of Agric. *Agric. in W. Midlands*, 16.

The numbers occupied in agriculture greatly declined. In 1871 there were 31,029, in 1921 24,820, and in 1973 12,131.[2] The proportion of labourers to farmers also declined, especially in the late 19th and early 20th centuries. In 1871 the workforce included 11,038 farmers and their families, 14,127 out-labourers, and 4,997 farm servants;[3] by 1911 there were still 10,264 farmers and their working relatives but only 12,460 farm servants and labourers.[4] The decline in the number of available labourers was exceptionally rapid in the 1870s, and by the early 1880s farmers were complaining of the difficulty of getting skilled dairymaids and farm-hands and of the poor quality of the workers.[5] The ploughing-up campaign of the First World War increased the demand for labour. By 1918 help was provided by the Women's Land Army and by prisoners of war. Farmers again complained that work was poorly done; skilled workers were few, and owing to the call-up only the less vigorous young men were available.[6] Subsequently the number of labourers declined again to 11,481 in 1939. Renewed attempts to raise production increased the number to 14,908 in 1945 through the employment of more women, more casual workers, and from 1944 prisoners of war (see Table VI). After the war there was another sharp reduction in hired labour. By 1973

TABLE VI: WORKERS EMPLOYED ON AGRICULTURAL HOLDINGS, EXCLUDING THE OCCUPIER, HIS WIFE, AND FAMILY 1939–45

	Regular Workers			Casual Workers			Total
	Male	Female	Women's Land Army[a]	Male	P.O.W.[a]	Female	
1939	9,204	671		1,265		341	11,481
1940	8,762	621		1,246		569	11,198
1941	8,697	824		1,637		846	12,004
1942	8,717	1,548		1,990		1,152	13,407
1943	8,588	1,754		2,071		1,172	13,585
1944	8,875	1,315	688	2,039	418	885	14,220
1945	8,995	1,217	635	2,204	1,009	848	14,908

Source: *Agric. Returns G.B.* The figures are for 3 June in each year.

[a] Separate figures are not available before 1944.

there were only 4,438 hired workers, greatly outnumbered by the 7,633 farmers and family workers; hired workers formed less than 30 per cent of the regular full-time workforce. Casual labour was used increasingly in the early 1970s.[7]

In 1879 a labourer estimated that agricultural wages were only some 12s.–15s. a week, though farmers complained that such rates were ruinous.[8] By 1881 15s. or 16s. was a common wage for ordinary labourers, though one witness to the Royal Commission on Agriculture paid 18s. or more; up to 21s. was paid to stockmen and other skilled workers. Those rates often included a rent-free cottage; when rent was charged it was generally £4–£4 10s. a year. Labourers were thought to be better off. They ate more meat, but

[2] *Census*, 1871 (excluding Land Proprietors); ibid. 1921; *Agric. Returns G.B.* 1973.
[3] *Census*, 1871.
[4] Ibid. 1911.
[5] *Mins. of Evid. Com. Agric.* ii (1881), pp. 184, 186, 191–2.
[6] *Wages and Conditions of Emp. in Agric.* 308, 310–11.
[7] *Agric. Returns G.B.*
[8] *Staffs. Advertiser*, 2 Aug. 1879.

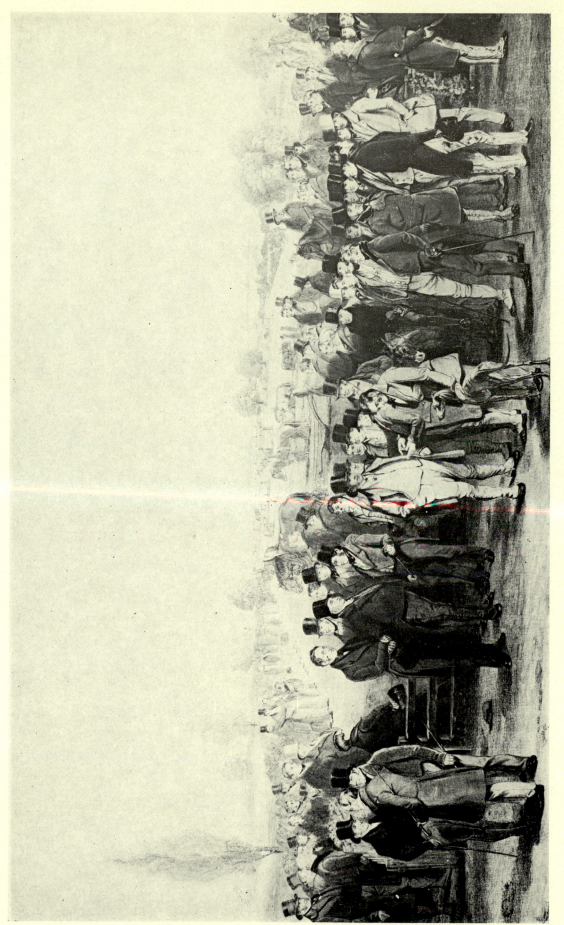

PLOUGHING MATCH AT GROUNDSLOW ON 18 AUGUST 1837

Queen Elizabeth's, Tamworth, in the 1820s

Queen Mary's, Walsall, c. 1854

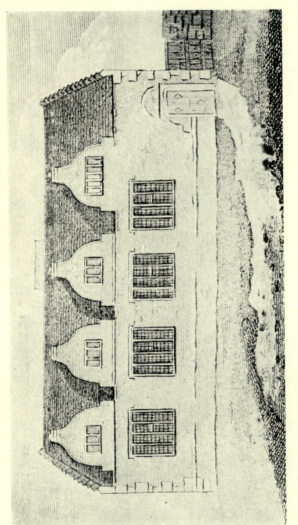

Lichfield in the 1790s

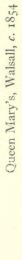

Wolverhampton in 1837

GRAMMAR SCHOOLS

were no better clothed.[9] In the early 1890s Carrington Smith stated that wages had fallen from 17s. in the 1870s to 15s. but that the position of labourers had 'wonderfully improved'; they ate more meat and had potato ground and carriage of coal provided free.[10] Sometimes higher rates of pay obtained: at Trentham farmers in 1892 paid 17s. to 19s. for a 63-hour week.[11] In 1894 demands for wage increases there were met by a reduction in hours for estate labourers.[12] Cash wages in Staffordshire remained c. 15s.–16s. for ordinary labourers down to 1914, and earnings c. 18s.–20s.; skilled stockmen received a further 1s. 6d. to 2s.[13] During the First World War weekly wage rates, which from 1917 were subject to a minimum imposed under the Corn Production Act,[14] rose rapidly. By July 1917 the wage averaged 24s. By May 1918 the wages of ordinary labourers varied from 26s. to 27s., and those of wagoners and stockmen could be up to 30s. In that year the Agricultural Wages Board raised the minimum to 35s.[15] By September 1919 the labourer's rate was 38s. 6d. for 50 hours in summer and 48 in winter.[16]

Craftsmen generally had a free cottage, though there was a shortage of cottages for ordinary labourers and many lacked drains and washing facilities. Cottage rents in 1918 ranged from 2s. to 2s. 6d. a week. Perquisites included free haulage of coals, free potatoes, manure, and milk, and sometimes free pig-litter, free firewood, and cheese at wholesale prices.[17] Hours were long: a 12-hour day was normal, and in July 1918 the county War Agricultural Committee fixed the minimum at 57 hours a week.[18] In the early 20th century yearly or half-yearly hiring of labourers persisted at least in the north-east, especially on smaller farms.[19] There were still autumn hiring fairs at Burton, Tamworth, Fazeley, and Longnor.[20] Workmen's diet continued to improve. In 1905 their fare in eastern Staffordshire was said to include porridge and bacon for breakfast, meat and vegetables for dinner, bread and cheese for tea, and sometimes meat or porridge or both for supper.[21] As late as 1917 home-brewed beer was still given to workers at harvest, especially in the south-west and west of the county.[22] Piece-work payments had largely disappeared by then, though they were commoner in the arable south than in dairying districts. Turnip-hoeing and -singling, hedge-cutting, and potato-getting were sometimes paid by piece.[23]

The weekly wage had risen to 46s. 6d. by 1921, but after decontrol in that year it fell to 30s. in 1924. County wage committees were set up under the Agricultural Wages (Regulation) Act, 1924, and the Staffordshire committee raised the minimum wage to 31s. 6d. in 1925 for a 54-hour week.[24] In 1932 the wage was reduced to 30s.; it rose again to 31s. 6d. in 1934, to 32s. 6d. in 1936, and to 34s. in 1937.[25] From 1940 a national minimum wage, then 48s., was fixed. Wages thereafter rose almost every year. In 1976 the minimum weekly wage ranged from £36.50 for labourers to £45.65 for first-grade workers. Actual wages varied considerably but were normally over the minimum; labourers often received craftsmen's rates, while some foremen and stockmen might

[9] *Agric. Interests Com.: Digest* (1881), pp. 269, 322, 325, 338–9, 343; *Mins. of Evid. Com. Agric. ii* (1881), pp. 184, 643, 647.
[10] *Mins. of Evid. Com. Agric. Depression* (1894), p. 234.
[11] Perren, 'Agric. Depression', 313.   [12] Ibid. 317–18.
[13] *Rep. on Wages and Earnings of Agric. Labourers in U.K.* [Cd. 346], pp. 28, 40, H.C. (1900), lxxxii; *2nd Rep. on Wages, Earnings and Conditions of Employment of Agric. Labourers in U.K.* [Cd. 2376], pp. 28, 37, H.C. (1905), xcvii; *Rep. on Decline in Agric. Pop. of Gt. Brit. 1881–1906* [Cd. 3273], p. 107, H.C. (1906), xcvi; *Wages and Conditions of Emp. in Agric.* 312; F. E. Green, *Hist. of Eng. Agric. Labourer 1870–1920*, 337.
[14] Murray, *Hist. of Second World War: Agric.* 14.
[15] *Wages and Conditions of Emp. in Agric.* 312; *Rep. of Procs. under Agric. Wages (Regulation) Act, 1924, for year*

ending 30 Sept. 1925 (H.M.S.O. 1926), App. vii.
[16] *Staffs. Advertiser*, 13 Sept. 1919; Green, *Eng. Agric. Labourer*, 337.
[17] *Wages and Conditions of Emp. in Agric.* 315, 317.
[18] Ibid. 311–12; S.R.O., War Agric. Cttee. Mins. 1915–20, 25 July 1918.
[19] *Com. on Labour; Agric. Labourer, 1 (VI)*, 92; *Rep. on Wages of Agric. Labourers*, 15.
[20] *Rep. on Wages of Agric. Labourers*, 17.
[21] *2nd Rep. on Wages of Agric. Labourers*, 231.
[22] S.R.O., War Agric. Cttee. Mins. 1915–20, Exec. Cttee. 4 and 11 Aug., 8 Sept. 1917.
[23] *Wages and Conditions of Emp. in Agric.* 313.
[24] *Rep. of Procs. under Agric. Wages (Regulation) Act, 1924, for year ending 30 Sept. 1925*, 37 and App. vii.
[25] Ibid. for 1932–7.

earn over £60 including overtime pay. Rent-free housing was often provided, and workers sometimes received allowances of milk or potatoes, or free use of machinery or farm vehicles. Working hours had been reduced to 40 by 1974, but overtime working was widespread.[26]

Unionization of agricultural workers made slow progress in Staffordshire. In 1881 few labourers belonged to unions, fewer indeed than in 1875.[27] A Freeford farmer stated: 'We have not heard much of Mr. Arch and his friends in our neighbourhood, but . . . that feeling which was put forth by them about the country did very great injury in the minds of the labourers generally'; it had destroyed the patriarchal feeling between employers and employed.[28] In 1899 the Workers' Union did some recruiting but could not hold its membership for long.[29] There were renewed efforts to unionize workers after the First World War, and in 1919 the Agricultural Labourers' Union recruited members round Stafford and negotiated with the farmers, demanding special rates for harvest overtime and a 48-hour week for £3 basic wage. The farmers agreed to pay overtime of 1s. 6d. an hour but refused to negotiate on wages, and a strike was held; it broke after four weeks.[30]

The union (later the National Union of Agricultural Workers) made little further progress in Staffordshire until 1941, when a new organizer was appointed. At least 37 branches were established in the 1940s and 11 more by 1956, when only three of those founded before 1941 survived. Despite that expansion there were still fewer than 200 fully-paid members in 1962, but by the mid 1970s the union (from 1968 the National Union of Agricultural & Allied Workers) estimated that 60–65 per cent of farm workers in the county were members. The number of branches, however, was reduced by lapses and amalgamations to 30 in 1973.[31]

Staffordshire farmers too were late in appreciating the advantages of union organization; the county was one of the last two to federate with the National Farmers' Union. Local branches were founded at Abbots Bromley and Burton-upon-Trent in 1918, and six more were established early in 1919. In May 1919 a county N.F.U. organization committee was set up by the Staffordshire Chamber of Agriculture, which dissolved itself for the union's benefit. Further local branches were founded late in 1919. Despite its late start Staffordshire took a prominent part in the union's affairs between the World Wars, particularly in its work on marketing reform. As a result there were Staffordshire farmers among the original members of the Milk, Potato, and Pig Marketing Boards. By the end of 1919 1,016 farmers had joined the union; there were 3,345 members in 1924, 4,215 in 1939, and 5,478, some 60 per cent of the county's farmers, in 1959. Thereafter the membership included a declining number but a rising proportion of the county's dwindling total of farmers. In 1970 there were 4,056 members, over 66 per cent of all farmers in the county, and in 1976 3,555 members. There were then 17 Staffordshire branches and 4 joint branches with other counties.[32]

A development of the late 19th and early 20th centuries was the statutory provision by parish and county councils of allotments for labourers and of smallholdings to keep

[26] Murray, *Hist. of Second World War: Agric.* 83–5, 124, 189, 211; ex inf. the sec., Staffs. Agric. Wages Cttee. (1961), and Min. of Agric., Stafford (1976); Min. of Labour (later Dept. of Employment), *Time Rates of Wages and Hours of Labour* (1946–59); *Time Rates of Wages and Hours of Work* (1960–76).

[27] *Agric. Interests Com.: Digest* (1881), pp. 388–9.

[28] *Mins. of Evid. Com. Agric. Depression* (1894), p. 191.

[29] C. S. Orwin and E. H. Whetham, *Hist. of Brit. Agric. 1846–1914*, 336.

[30] Green, *Eng. Agric. Labourer*, 308–9; *Staffs. Advertiser*, 13–27 Sept. 1919.

[31] National Union of Agric. Workers, *Rep. and Balance Sheet for 1956*, 155–6; National Union of Agric. & Allied Workers, *Ann. Rep. and Balance Sheet 1973*, 188–9; ex inf. the Staffs. and Ches. district organizer (1977).

[32] Pepperall, *Sir Thos. Baxter*, 63, 66–7; *Staffs. Farmer*, xlv (6), 1, 4–8; *Staffs. Advertiser*, 20 Sept. 1919; ex inf. the assistant sec., Staffs. Branch N.F.U., Stafford (1977).

enterprising young men on the land.[33] In 1906 it was said that there was no difficulty in obtaining allotments in the administrative county. Many were in fact untenanted, while the price of allotment produce had fallen. Smallholdings of 20–60 a., however, were much sought after, although there had been no applications to purchase holdings from the county council; would-be purchasers lacked the capital to put up buildings.[34] Walsall, Smethwick, and Wednesbury borough councils, Handsworth and Perry Barr urban district councils, and Cheslyn Hay and Great Wyrley parish councils bought 91 a. for allotments, divided among 511 tenants. The county council, however, did nothing.[35] In the first two years following the Small Holdings and Allotments Act, 1908, the county council received 258 applications for holdings and approved 148. It bought only 807 a. and did not use its powers of compulsory purchase.[36] By the end of the First World War it was found that the most successful holdings were dairy-farms of 40–50 a.; the arable farms had been unsuccessful, and farm labourers seldom sought allotments.[37] The council continued to buy land for smallholdings; between the World Wars it acquired 5,530 a., which it divided into 233 holdings of various sizes.[38] The holdings were generally in groups since the council's policy was to buy whole estates or farms and to subdivide them.[39] Few cottage holdings were set up since they were found to be mismanaged. The waiting list for holdings remained long in 1939, and during the Second World War 46 applications for holdings under 6 a. and 185 for holdings over 6 a. were received.[40] By 1951 the council owned 311 smallholdings grouped in 36 estates totalling 7,893 a.[41] Between 1949 and 1961 it created only 17 holdings because of the high cost of land and equipment.[42] Some smallholdings were provided by other local authorities. In 1964 Stoke-on-Trent had 195 a., Walsall 4 a., and Wolverhampton 142 a. as smallholding land.[43] From *c.* 1970 the county council began to amalgamate smallholdings. In 1976 it owned 229 holdings covering 8,596 a.[44]

AGRICULTURAL EDUCATION

The 1890s saw great advances in the provision of agricultural education. In 1891 Lord Hatherton established an agricultural technical school at Penkridge for the children of labourers on his estate and organized a series of dairy lectures and demonstrations on his farms.[45] More important for the future was the work of the county council's technical instruction committee, set up in 1890 under the Technical Instruction Act, 1889.[46] In 1891 the committee engaged two peripatetic instructors to give lectures on agriculture at villages throughout the county. In the winter of 1891–2 general lectures on agriculture were given at 23 villages, and short courses on dairy work at ten. Butter- and cheese-making demonstrations were arranged. By 1895 there were separate courses in the making of Cheshire and Staffordshire cheese, and by 1898 there was a travelling dairy school. The committee organized competitions in butter-making at the Staffordshire Agricultural Society's annual show from 1892; successful competitors were given scholarships to the Denbighshire and the Montgomery Dairy Schools. In 1892 Robert Cock was appointed lecturer in horticulture and bee-keeping;

[33] *Departmental Cttee. of Inquiry into Statutory Small-holdings: 1st Rep.* [Cmnd. 2936], pp. 4–32, H.C. (1965–6), vii; Orwin and Whetham, *Hist. of Brit. Agric.* 330–5.
[34] *Rep. on Decline in Agric. Pop. 1881–1906*, 75–6.
[35] *Return relating to Local Authorities (Acquisition of Land)*, H.C. 182, p. 18 (1903), ix.
[36] *Returns . . . Small Holdings*, H.C. 145, p. 3 (1910), lxxiv.
[37] *Wages and Conditions of Emp. in Agric.* 318.
[38] Ex inf. County Estate Agent (1961).
[39] e.g. *V.C.H. Staffs.* v. 127.
[40] S.R.O., County Agric. Cttee. Mins. 1933–49, p. 226.
[41] *Staffs. County Council Development Plan 1951: Survey Rep. and Analysis*, 131.
[42] Ex inf. County Estate Agent (1961).
[43] *Inquiry into Statutory Smallholdings: 1st Rep.* 268.
[44] Ex inf. Deputy County Land Agent (1976).
[45] Sturgess, 'Agric. Staffs.' 288–9.
[46] 52 & 53 Vic. c. 76.

by 1895 he had made over 700 visits to villages, given over 825 lectures and demonstrations, and examined 3,337 beehives. Apparently as a result of his work the number of exhibits of honey at the county show more than doubled from 1892 to 1894. From at least 1895 Cock also lectured in poultry-keeping. By 1899 the committee was sponsoring manurial experiments, and by 1904 courses in hedging and farm hygiene were provided. By 1899 it also granted short-term agricultural scholarships for farmers' sons to attend winter courses of up to 7 weeks at suitable institutions.[47]

In 1898 an agricultural side was opened at Brewood grammar school, providing a three-year course of theoretical and practical instruction in agriculture and related subjects. The technical instruction committee provided a building grant and three (by 1913 five) agricultural scholarships.[48] In the years before the First World War the teaching of agricultural and horticultural subjects at council schools was greatly extended. In 1904 four schools offered gardening courses. By 1913 there were 192, and 8 schools offered poultry-keeping and 7 bee-keeping courses.[49] Staffordshire also benefited from the more advanced instruction provided at Harper Adams College at Edgmond (Salop.), which was established in 1901 under the will of Thomas Harper Adams, an Edgmond farmer (d. 1892). It was originally aided by grants from the county council, which appointed two governors. Courses were provided in agriculture, dairying, and related sciences.[50]

In 1913 there were plans to establish a farm institute near Stafford,[51] but they were postponed until after the First World War. In 1919 the War Agricultural Committee opened its former tractor depot at Dunston in Penkridge as a training depot for men working in agriculture; in the same year the county council bought Rodbaston Hall (also in Penkridge) and the depot was transferred there. A farm institute was finally opened at Rodbaston in 1921.[52] It provided 22-week winter courses for youths of 16–20 who intended to make their living from the land, and 17-week summer courses in dairying, poultry-keeping, and domestic science for women over 16. There was a 300-a. farm attached, which was run as a commercial venture.[53] The institute was requisitioned in 1940; it was later used to train Land Girls on short courses, and a hostel was built. In October 1944 the institute was reopened on pre-war lines with an additional summer course for men.[54] In the 1950s and 1960s the number of students was greatly increased, and the buildings were extended. In 1967 the institute became the Staffordshire College of Agriculture.[55]

From the Second World War until 1975 the agricultural side at Brewood was devoted to teaching G.C.E. Agriculture. From 1973 the farm attached to the school was used as a farm centre to introduce visiting children from urban primary and special schools to farming. It continued that work after the school closed in 1975.[56]

[47] S.R.O., Staffs. County Council Technical Instruction Cttee. Min. Bk. 1890–2, pp. 11, 15, 19, 31, 41; *Staffs. County Council: Technical Instruction Act, 1889; Local Taxation (Customs & Excise) Act 1890: Rep.* . . . p. 6 (copy in min. bk.); *Staffs. County Council Technical Instruction Cttee. Dir.* (1895 and later edns. to 1899); *Com. on Labour: Agric. Labourer, I (VI)*, p. 91; G. Balfour, *Ten Years of Staffs. Educ. 1903–1913* (Staffs. County Council Educ. Dept. 1913), 47–9 (copy in W.S.L.); *Bd. of Agric. and Fisheries: Rep. on Distribution of Grants for Agric. Educ. and Research 1904–5* [Cd. 2808], pp. 177–8, H.C. (1906), xcvi.

[48] *Staffs. County Council Technical Instruction Cttee. Dir.* (1899), 19; Balfour, *Ten Years of Staffs. Educ.* 46.

[49] Balfour, *Ten Years of Staffs. Educ.* 74.

[50] Ibid. 44–5; Salop. R.O. 119/40, statement of facts (1914); R. Kenney, 'Education, Training and Advice', *Century of Progress 1875–1975: Shropshire & West Mid-* lands Agric. Soc. Centenary Brochure [1975], 38–40 (copy in W.S.L. Pamphs. *sub* Agriculture); ex inf. the principal (1977).

[51] Balfour, *Ten Years of Staffs. Educ.* 42.

[52] S.R.O., War Agric. Cttee. Mins. 1915–20, 27 Mar., 8 May, 11 and 25 Sept. 1919; *Staffs. Advertiser*, 20 Sept. 1919; *V.C.H. Staffs.* v. 122.

[53] Staffs. County Council Educ. Cttee. *Prospectus of courses . . . at the County Farm Institute, Rodbaston, Penkridge* (c. 1933; copy in W.S.L. Pamphs. *sub* Agriculture).

[54] Ex inf. Mr. H. E. Wells, principal (1961).

[55] Ex inf. Mr. Wells (1961) and Mr. D. Golland, Schools Liaison Officer (1976); *Express & Star*, 9 June 1969.

[56] Ex inf. Mr. Golland; Staffs. County Council Educ. Cttee. *Farm and Countryside* (guide to Staffs. Coll. of Agric. c. 1976; copy in W.S.L. Pamphs. *sub* Agriculture).

SCHOOLS

THIS section contains histories of the more important or educationally significant public and endowed grammar schools in Staffordshire. Other schools have been treated, or are reserved for treatment, elsewhere in the *History*.

BREWOOD GRAMMAR SCHOOL

THE grammar school at Brewood was founded, probably *c.* 1550, by Dr. Matthew Knightley (d. 1561), rector of Cossington (Leics.) and a native of Brewood, Sir John Giffard (d. 1556) of Chillington in Brewood, and Sir John's son and heir Sir Thomas (d. 1560).[1] The initiative apparently came from Knightley, who is traditionally regarded as the founder: in 1628 it was alleged that the bulk of the school's endowment, land and property in the parishes of Brewood and Bushbury and at Willenhall in St. Peter's, Wolverhampton, had been bought either by Knightley or with money given by him. A 20*s.* rent-charge from land at Hartley Green in Gayton was given by Sir John Giffard.[2] The endowment seems also to have included land in Lapley, although in 1676 it was decided in Chancery that the school was entitled only to rent-charges of £2 10*s.* on the land in question.[3] The income from the endowment was to support a master, and if possible an usher, who would teach, without charge, grammar and other 'convenient and necessary' learning to boys and young men of Brewood parish and elsewhere.[4] It has been suggested that the foundation was intended to replace a defunct chantry school at Brewood, but there is no evidence that such a school existed.[5]

Initially there seems to have been only a master, but an usher had been added by 1613.[6] The first master of whom much is known, John Hilton, was at Brewood in the early 17th century. He was granted a beneficial lease of school property in 1617 to reward his 'rare diligence, pains, and industry', and in the 1680s it was recalled that in his time the school had had a high reputation, attracting many outsiders and persons of quality.[7]

At first the management of the school and its property seems to have been left in the hands of the Giffards. Trustees had been appointed at the time of the foundation, but they appear to have been content to defer to the Giffards as the leading family in Brewood.[8] About 1625 it was alleged in Chancery that Walter Giffard (d. 1632) had appropriated the school estates to his own use, leased them in his own name at inadequate rents, and paid only £18 to the master and £6 13*s.* 4*d.* to the usher out of an income of £37 6*s.* 2*d.* It was also claimed that although able masters were needed to combat popery in Brewood, Giffard, himself a papist, had appointed unsuitable and ignorant men. In view of Hilton's later reputation that claim at least was probably malicious. A decree of 1626 established a new body of trustees, to whom Giffard was to hand over all the school property and all arrears of income. Although Peter Giffard (d. 1663), Walter's son and heir, was named as a trustee, the decree effectively ended Giffard management of the school. A further decree of 1726 reorganized the trust and laid down that in future the rents from the school property, less a rent-collector's pay, were to be divided between the master (two-thirds) and the usher (one-third).[9]

In the later 17th century the school had apparently declined. At least one boy went on to university in the 1660s.[10] In the later 1670s there were usually about 30 pupils. By the later 1680s there were generally only between 10 and 20, and they were merely 'little boys'. The master seems to have been competent, but nevertheless it was claimed that the gentry were losing faith in the school. Only one trustee still sent his sons there; others had taken their boys away and had sent them instead to Lichfield, Shrewsbury, or Wolverhampton.[11]

In the 18th century the school recovered and flourished. It had a good reputation under James Hillman (d. 1731) and an even better one under William Budworth (1731–45). At the time of his appointment Budworth was master of Rugeley grammar school. When he went to Brewood he found the school buildings in disrepair; he returned to Rugeley until 1733, by which time the buildings had been put in order. Richard Hurd, bishop of Lichfield and Coventry 1774–81 and of Worcester 1781–1808, was sent to Brewood shortly before Hillman's death and was Budworth's pupil at Rugeley and Brewood; he later wrote that Budworth had possessed every talent of a schoolmaster 'in a degree . . . rarely found in any of that profession since the days of Quintilian'. In 1736 Samuel Johnson unsuccessfully applied to Budworth for the post of usher.[12] Budworth held the livings of Brewood and Shareshill as well as the mastership and kept a curate who

[1] D. Thompson, *Hist. of Brewood Grammar Sch. 1553–1953* (Cannock, n.d. [1953]), 3–5; *S.H.C.* 1931, 188–93.
[2] *5th Rep. Com. Char.* H.C. 159, pp. 552, 691 (1821), xii; W.S.L. 117/93/49.
[3] *S.H.C.* 1931, 189; *5th Rep. Com. Char.* 553–4.
[4] *S.H.C.* 1931, 189 (probably early 1570s, mentioning only schoolmaster); *5th Rep. Com. Char.* 552 (1628, mentioning schoolmaster and, if possible, usher).
[5] Thompson, *Brewood Grammar Sch.* 3–4.
[6] *S.H.C.* 1931, 189; C 93/10/20.
[7] Thompson, *Brewood Grammar Sch.* 10, quoting lease;

C 91/21/22 m. 5v.
[8] *S.H.C.* 1931, 189–90.
[9] [J. Hay and W. Parke], *Notes and Collections relating to Brewood* (Wolverhampton, priv. print. 1860), 42–4; C 93/10/20; C 93/54/17.
[10] *Admissions to St. John's Coll., Cambridge*, ii (ed. J. E. B. Mayor), 4.
[11] C 91/21/22 mm. 5v.–6.
[12] A. L. Reade, *Johnsonian Gleanings*, vi (priv. print. 1933), 46–8; *Notes and Coll. relating to Brewood*, 105–7; *D.N.B. sub* Budworth.

taught Latin grammar to the younger boys; the usher taught writing and accounts. Boarders at the school included sons of leading Staffordshire families, and other boys were sent to board in the town so that they could attend the school as day-boys. Since the boarders paid only £14 a year and the day-boys nothing, the income from the school was never great; both curate and usher received meagre stipends.[13]

Dr. George Croft (1780–91),[14] who achieved a modest eminence as preacher and divine, gave an account of his curriculum, aims, and methods at Brewood in a pamphlet published in 1784. His approach was more liberal than that of many of his contemporaries at country grammar schools: although the classics and religious instruction retained their usual primacy his pupils were also taught history, geography, and natural history. French, dancing, music, drawing, writing, accounts, and arithmetic were optional subjects, care being taken that 'one branch may not interfere with another'. Croft advocated the use of newspapers as aids to the teaching of geography and as publications which 'make the pupils acquainted with the common occurrences and transactions of life and with the intelligence of the day'. Older boys were encouraged to read the *Annual Register* and the *Monthly Review*.[15]

The Staffordshire gentry apparently found the curriculum attractive. The school may have lost their patronage after Budworth's death, but under Croft a number of them sent their sons to Brewood.[16] More space was needed. The school consisted of a long, single-storey school-house of the 16th or 17th century in School Road in which both master and usher taught, with an adjoining house for the master.[17] Budworth had repaired or rebuilt one or both of them.[18] Croft entered into negotiations for the purchase of two houses opposite the school-house.[19] In 1791 he resigned, and the purchase was completed in 1799 by his successor Hamlet Harrison (1792–1810). The money was provided by two of Budworth's pupils who had become trustees, Bishop Hurd and Sir Edward Littleton, Bt.; they also paid for the conversion of the houses, one of which became the usher's house and the other schoolrooms for his use. School Road was diverted round the back of the two houses, and the stretch of roadway between them and the old buildings was turned into a playground. Because more accommodation was available the usher was permitted to take boarders.[20]

The trustees dismissed Harrison in 1810. They found that he had neglected the school for farming, acquired school land irregularly and rent-free, and punished the boys with undue severity. Although the Charity Commissioners found in 1821 that the school had flourished under his mastership and the county families certainly sent their children to him, the trustees seem to have been justified. The 1st

Lord Hatherton, who spent six years at Brewood under Harrison, recalled that the master was 'completely disqualified' for his post and remarked that 'even with better capacities I could have learned but little'.[21]

It was presumably as a result of Harrison's misconduct that his successor Henry Kempson (1810–41) received detailed instructions from the trustees. He was made responsible for teaching the classics to the older boys while the usher was to give the younger ones a grounding in Latin grammar and to teach them English, geography, writing, and arithmetic. By the 1820s the upper school (Kempson's) and the lower school (the usher's) had virtually become separate establishments; each issued its own bills and had its own scale of fees. The lower school apparently had to rely on day-boys. Although the usher was permitted to take boarders, by 1817 he no longer had accommodation for them in his house. To remedy the deficiency a Robert Kenyon opened a boarding-house in Brewood for grammar-school boys in 1817, employing on his own account a classical master and a writing master. The venture failed, a National school was founded in the parish, and in 1820 there were only 21 boys in the lower school compared with 36 in 1817.[22]

Kempson's mastership saw a controversy over the nature and function of the school. He realized that the school needed to offer a broad curriculum. The endowment income of some £400 was insufficient to provide salaries for a larger staff, and only slight relief was provided by a bequest of £1,000 from Richard Hurd (d. 1827), a nephew of the bishop, and by the sale of a few acres of land in 1830.[23] Nor did fees bring in sufficient profit, although 25 of the 35 boys in the upper school in 1820 were boarders.[24] Kempson and the usher, looking for new sources of income, began to charge the free pupils for heating, text-books, slates, and instruction in writing and arithmetic. That provoked opposition in the town, and in 1831 there were demands that the fees should be dropped and that non-classical subjects should be recognized as integral parts of the curriculum. Kempson and the usher maintained that according to the founder's intentions and the 1810 regulations their duties were limited to instruction in the classics; other subjects were taught, but as an act of favour, and had to be paid for. The leading protesters threatened proceedings in Chancery, but no action was in fact taken. In 1840, in response to renewed and more widespread complaints from the townspeople, the trustees drew up fresh regulations. Latin, Greek, mathematics, writing, English grammar, history, and geography were to be taught without charge; dancing, drawing, and French on payment of a fee. Latin was compulsory and was to be taught solely by the headmaster, who was to have complete control of the school. Masters were no longer required to be in holy orders, the number of

13 *Gent. Mag.* lxii (1), 292–3; (2), 683–6, 785–8, 1001.
14 *D.N.B.*
15 G. Croft, *A Plan of Education Delineated and Vindicated* (Wolverhampton, 1784), 35–9 (copy in W.S.L. Pamphs. *sub* Brewood).
16 *Notes and Coll. Brewood*, 47–8.
17 *V.C.H. Staffs.* v. 23.
18 Reade, *Johnsonian Gleanings*, vi. 47; *Gent. Mag.* lxii (2), 685.
19 *Notes and Coll. Brewood*, 45.
20 Thompson, *Brewood Grammar Sch.* 19–20; *V.C.H.*

Staffs. v. 23–4; S.R.O., D. 260/M/F/5/133, Hurd to Littleton 1792–1801.
21 Thompson, *Brewood Grammar Sch.* 23–6; *5th Rep. Com. Char.* 555–8; C. R. Fay, *Huskisson and his Age*, 310.
22 Thompson, *Brewood Grammar Sch.* 26–9, 32; *5th Rep. Com. Char.* 559–60; Parson and Bradshaw, *Dir. Staffs.* (1818), 296.
23 Thompson, *Brewood Grammar Sch.* 29–32; *5th Rep. Com. Char.* 555; *Notes and Coll. Brewood*, 45.
24 *5th Rep. Com. Char.* 559.

pupils was to be limited, and the right to admit boys was reserved to the trustees, who bound themselves to give preference to applicants from local parishes. A committee was established to arrange an annual examination by a visiting examiner. In 1841 the trustees decided that the maximum number of boys allowed in the upper school should be 40, of whom 20 could be boarders. The usher was allowed 8 boarders only. A separate master was to teach writing and arithmetic; his pupils were to pay £1 a year.[25]

The reforms appear to have satisfied local opinion.[26] In 1842 the trustees obtained an Act empowering them to sell the school's land at Willenhall, which was thought to be suitable for mining.[27] They sold it privately in 1853 and aroused another controversy. They were accused of having sold the land below its market price; the purchaser resold the land at auction; and the Charity Commissioners held an inquiry. The affair was not settled financially until 1862, and meanwhile the school's income was reduced.

In the early 1850s the school had, besides the headmaster and usher, an assistant master, a French master, a drawing-master, and a drill-sergeant. During the 1850s the old school-house was replaced by a hall and classrooms, and a schoolroom and dormitories were added to the usher's house.[28] Boys were sent to university, and there were successes in the Oxford and Cambridge local examinations. The headmaster, the Revd. J. H. Brown (1850–60), and the usher were, however, unbusinesslike; they fell into debt, the school suffered, and when the trustees finally forced Brown to resign there were only 27 pupils, of whom only two were boarders.[29]

Brown's successor, the Revd. Richard Wall (1861–72), had run a successful private school at Birkenhead and brought 50 boarders with him to Brewood. As those boys left, their places were taken by Staffordshire boys, mainly from around Wolverhampton, where the grammar school was temporarily in difficulties. There were 91 boys (65 of them boarders) in 1865 and 98 in 1868. A new house was built for the headmaster in 1862 or 1863. Wall maintained a high standard of teaching. Himself a mathematician, he employed an assistant master to teach the classics, an English master, and a French master, and paid visiting masters to teach chemistry, drawing, music, and drill. He successfully imposed his authority on the usher or second master, the Revd. William Rushton (1842–75), who claimed a virtual independence for the lower school despite the 1840 ruling that control of the entire school was vested in the headmaster. The dispute was submitted for arbitration to Frederick Temple, headmaster of Rugby; in 1866 he condemned Rushton's claims and praised Wall's management of the school.[30]

After Wall another period of decline set in. His successor, J. H. Taylor (1872–4), was a harsh disciplinarian and appears to have been biased against the day-boys, possibly because he hoped that he might be able to eradicate that less profitable element from the school altogether. Within a year of his arrival the number of pupils had fallen to 33 and there were only 7 day-boys. His conduct aroused considerable indignation in Brewood, and that, combined with his apparent failure to maintain Wall's standard of teaching and his attempts to force Rushton, now old and sick, to retire, led the trustees to dismiss him.[31] Under T. E. Rhodes (1875–99), formerly headmaster of Uttoxeter grammar school, teaching improved, but numbers remained low and, in the 1890s, declined still further; there were 45 boys in 1886 but only 18 in 1896. Rhodes attributed the lack of boarders to the establishment of new boarding-schools in the Midlands and that of day-boys to emigration from the Brewood area caused by agricultural depression; in fact the population of Brewood had declined steadily since the 1830s.[32]

The notable features of Rhodes's headmastership were the establishment of links with the county council and his recognition that the school must primarily serve the local farming community. A Scheme of 1877 transferred control to a board of governors including representatives of local authorities, and another of 1897 required the school to provide free education for 12 boys chosen from local elementary schools. The school's character had already begun to change: in 1875 the Endowed Schools Commissioners had accepted the local argument that there was no demand for a 'first-grade' school preparing boys for the universities in an area where most boys were destined for careers in farming or trade, and had classed Brewood as a 'second-grade' or 'commercial' school. By 1896 Rhodes had decided that the best way of making use of Brewood's buildings and endowment would be 'to convert it into an agricultural boarding-school', using its small farm at Brewood, part of the endowment, for educational purposes. The 1897 Scheme sanctioned the establishment of an agricultural side in which theoretical and practical farming would be taught, on condition that the county council made an annual grant. The grant was paid from 1898. The council also established agricultural scholarships and gave a building grant for a new laboratory and new farm buildings. It sent boarders to the school for training in agriculture. An agricultural committee consisting of governors and representatives of the county council was established to superintend the management of the farm.[33]

In the 20th century Brewood developed as a small day- and boarding-school with a strong agricultural side. By a Scheme of 1910 the county council representation on the board of governors was increased; in 1920 the governors sold what remained of the school's property, except the school itself and its farm, and Brewood became a maintained county secondary school. It continued as a grammar school after 1944, when the county council finally took over the management of the boarding-house. A new boarding-house was opened at Wheaton Aston New Hall in Lapley in 1950, and new laboratories and

[25] Thompson, *Brewood Grammar Sch.* 32–43.
[26] For the next 2 paras. see, unless otherwise stated, ibid. 44–57.
[27] 5 & 6 Vic. c. 18 (Private).
[28] Thompson, *Brewood Grammar Sch.* 56; C. Dunkley, *Brewood Grammar Sch.* (Cannock, 1936), 18–19; J. Hicks Smith, *Brewood* (Wolverhampton, 1874), 27.
[29] *Schs. Inquiry Com. vol. xv* [3966–XIV], p. 390, H.C.

(1867–8), xxviii (12).
[30] Thompson, *Brewood Grammar Sch.* 56, 58–63; *Schs. Inq. Com. vol. xv*, 385–93; Dunkley, *Brewood Grammar Sch.* 19.
[31] Thompson, *Brewood Grammar Sch.* 64–72.
[32] Ibid. 73, 75; *V.C.H. Staffs.* i. 320.
[33] Thompson, *Brewood Grammar Sch.* 74–83; above, p. 148.

farm buildings were added at the school in the early 1950s.[34]

In 1970, when the county council was reorganizing its secondary schools into large comprehensives, Brewood had 192 pupils and was regarded as too small to continue a separate existence.[35] From 1972 the number of pupils was allowed to dwindle, and by 1975, when the school was closed, there were only 47 day-boys and 13 boarders.[36] The buildings were used as an annexe to Wolgarston comprehensive school in Penkridge from 1975 until 1977, when Brewood Church of England (Controlled) Middle School was opened in them. From 1975 the school farm was used to show parties of urban schoolchildren the work of a farm.[37]

THE SCHOOL OF ST. MARY AND ST. ANNE, ABBOTS BROMLEY

THE school was established by the amalgamation in 1921 of St. Anne's School and St. Mary's School, both in Abbots Bromley.

ST. ANNE'S. In 1872 the Revd. E. C. Lowe, a close associate of Canon Nathaniel Woodard, the Anglo-Catholic educationalist, became provost of the Midland Division of the Corporation of St. Mary and St. Nicolas (the 'Woodard Schools').[1] He immediately began to realize a scheme for founding girls' schools in the Midlands on the pattern established by Woodard for his boys' schools. Woodard had little enthusiasm for female education, and in 1873 Lowe, acting on his own initiative, bought a house for a middle-class girls' boarding school in High Street, Abbots Bromley, where his brother was vicar. The school opened as St. Anne's School in 1874 with fees of 25 guineas a year. The girls were to be 'prepared for the homely duties of life by making them good accountants and good needlewomen', and they were to be taught to a level which would qualify them to become governesses or school-mistresses. Piano, German, Latin, and private singing lessons might be taken as extras. The school was supervised by a lady resident aided by two governesses. Lowe had appealed successfully for teachers at no salary or very low pay. The curate of Abbots Bromley was appointed chaplain. Besides the main school there were a day-school for village children and an industrial school to train poor girls for domestic service. Some St. Anne's girls were encouraged to stay on as student teachers. There were 28 pupils by the end of 1874 and 50 by the end of 1875. A new wing including a dining-room and a dormitory was therefore begun in 1875 to house 50 girls. A chapel was also begun; it was consecrated in 1881. The lady resident resigned in 1875 and was succeeded by Alice Mary Coleridge, Lowe's sister-in-law and a great-niece of the poet; she was at first known as lady-in-charge or lady sub-warden, and from 1891 as lady warden. From 1875 there was also a headmistress subordinate to her.

Discipline was strict in the school's early years;

silence was compulsory on Fridays, and each week badly behaved girls were compelled to criticize their own conduct before the assembled school. Religious observance too was an important part of the girls' life. They were frequently catechized, and elaborate processions were held on saints' days. By 1878 the curriculum was widening: all pupils learnt the elements, divinity, English history, literature, French, music, and needlework, and some studied Latin, book-keeping, or Euclid. Girls were prepared for the Cambridge local examinations. Physical education began in 1878, and in 1884 a cricket club was established. From the 1890s increased attention was paid to music and drama, and in 1897 an assembly hall was opened to commemorate Queen Victoria's Jubilee.

In 1890[2] St. Anne's was formally included in the Woodard corporation. Miss Coleridge resigned the wardenship in 1898; her successor was not interested in the school, and from her resignation in 1901 the wardenship lapsed. The headmistress thus gained more independence. Under Marcia Alice Rice (1900–21) St. Anne's greatly expanded and the standard of teaching improved. From 1900 the school ceased to advertise itself as a middle-class school but continued to emphasize its Anglican character. Between 1900 and 1907 mathematics and Latin became a normal part of the curriculum and more girls learnt German. A sixth form was established in 1901 and a school museum opened. Property adjoining the school was bought in 1904 and converted in 1905 to include more dormitories and classrooms and a science room, a technical kitchen, and a music studio. There were 120 girls by 1905 and 150 by 1907. From 1906 scholarships were won at Oxford and Cambridge. A trained games mistress was appointed in 1901; she introduced basket-ball and golf and from 1906 lacrosse. Despite the improvements Miss Rice discouraged competition: prizes were abolished in 1915. She also relaxed the school's severe discipline and set up a school council of older girls and staff. Religion remained important; thus in 1904 St. Anne's joined the United Girls School Mission in South London. When Canon Lowe died in 1912 he left a large bequest to the school, enabling extensions to be built. One wing, including sitting-rooms, kitchens, and dormitories, was opened in 1914, but the First World War prevented the completion of the building programme. In 1920, following an inspection by the Board of Education, St. Anne's was recognized as a public secondary school; about that time a junior school was established, run by Froebel-trained teachers and admitting girls from 4 years upwards.

ST. MARY'S. By 1882 it was clear that many prospective parents could not afford the fees at St. Anne's.[3] Accordingly Lowe, encouraged by Miss Coleridge, decided to continue his scheme by founding a second school, St. Mary's, for lower-middle-class girls, particularly daughters of the poorer clergy. It was opened in a rented house at the end of Bagot Street, Abbots Bromley. There were at first 5 girls, under the immediate supervision of a lady-

[34] Thompson, *Brewood Grammar Sch.* 83–7.
[35] *Express & Star*, 19 Feb. and 9 May 1970.
[36] *Stafford Newsletter*, 25 July 1975.
[37] Ibid. 15 Aug. 1975; ex inf. Staffs. County Council Educ. Dept. (1977).
[1] Unless otherwise stated, this section is based on Violet M. Macpherson, *Story of S. Anne's, Abbots Bromley,*

1874–1924 (Shrewsbury, n.d.), and on Marcia A. Rice, *Story of St. Mary's, Abbots Bromley* (Shrewsbury, 1947).
[2] K. E. Kirk, *Story of Woodard Schs.* 148. Rice, *St. Mary's,* 169, implies that it was not incorporated until after 1897.
[3] For this section see Rice, *St. Mary's.*

in-charge and the more remote control of Miss Coleridge. Later in 1882 Agnes Gamlen, an old St. Anne's girl, was appointed mistress. Two more teachers were obtained *c.* 1884. The staff was further augmented by girls of 17 and 18 kept on at school in return for teaching the younger children. The early curriculum was much the same as that at St. Anne's, though apparently taught to a lower level; in 1884, however, the harmonium, piano, French, and Latin were extras. Higher subjects were taught by St. Anne's staff, and some girls moved up to St. Anne's after leaving. St. Mary's also shared St. Anne's chapel. Discipline was kept with rewards and punishments on the lines of those at St. Anne's. By 1886 there were 30 boarders at £21 a year and some 20 day-girls at 30s.; in 1890 the school consisted of 49 boarders only.

The expansion of the school made further accommodation necessary, and several cottages in the village were rented in the 1880s to provide dormitories. In 1886 a site on the main street facing St. Anne's was acquired for a permanent school building, begun in 1889 and opened in 1893. Owing to lack of funds, however, it remained incomplete: only the kitchen, dining-room, and dormitories were built, and there were no purpose-built classrooms. In 1890 the last lady-in-charge retired and Miss Gamlen became headmistress. By the mid 1890s she had built up a waiting list. From 1891 St. Mary's entered for the Cambridge local examinations, though the senior examination was seldom attempted. By 1896 book-keeping and shorthand were taught, but by 1898 both they and Latin had been abandoned, though botany had been introduced. The school's numbers continued to grow in the 1890s. A row of small houses next to St. Mary's had been bought by 1895.

By 1900 St. Mary's had been formally included in the Woodard corporation. From that time it ceased to advertise itself as a school for the lower-middle classes and gained greater independence from St. Anne's. Expansion continued: there were 61 girls in 1901, 99 in 1912, 110 in 1917, and 124 in 1921. In 1906 a school hall was built and two more houses in the village were bought for conversion into a sanatorium. Congestion was partly relieved when in 1910–11 a new wing was built to the design of Sir Aston Webb; it included classrooms, dormitories, and staff accommodation. The early 20th century also saw an improvement in the results obtained in public examinations. Domestic-science classes began in 1905, and the first university-educated teacher was appointed in 1909. In 1915 the entrance age was raised from 7 to 8 and the leaving age from 17 to 18 years. Nevertheless, up to amalgamation with St. Anne's St. Mary's continued to charge low fees and it remained the policy not to prepare girls for university entrance.

The School of St. Mary and St. Anne. By *c.*

1920 the main distinction between St. Mary's and St. Anne's was that of the scale of fees, and Miss Gamlen's retirement in 1921 enabled the Midland Chapter of the Woodard corporation to amalgamate the schools in accordance with a recommendation of the Board of Education's school inspectors.[4] Exhibitions were established to reduce the fees to the old St. Mary's level for those who needed them.[5] The amalgamation was successful, and the school received a laudatory inspection from the Board of Education in 1925.[6] It expanded slowly up to the Second World War and more rapidly during it. There were 300 girls in 1923, 305 in 1931, 372 in 1938, and 448 in 1945.[7] The girls' performance in public examinations continued to improve until at least the late 1930s.[8] In 1922 the assembly hall was enlarged, and in 1924 a temporary block was built to commemorate the jubilee of St. Anne's.[9] In 1934 the former chaplain's house was converted to provide a house for junior girls from 7 to 11 years.[10] In 1936 extensions to St. Anne's main building, including a hall, a dining-room, and house-rooms and dormitories, were opened. Laboratories were also built in the 1930s.

In 1945 the school still consisted entirely of boarders, but in 1950 two day-girls were admitted and by 1955 there were 26. The number of boarders reached 474 in 1965; from then to 1977 there were generally between 450 and 475, including a rising proportion of expatriates' daughters. In the 1970s the demand for day-places grew, because comprehensive education was being imposed in maintained schools and because new houses were being built in Abbots Bromley. More day-girls were admitted every year from 1970, and in 1977 there were 89 out of a school of 564. Nevertheless teaching still revolved round the boarders, and classes were held on Saturdays.[11]

The curriculum remained predominantly academic after the Second World War; economics was introduced, while Latin and Greek continued to be taught. Religion and music remained of great importance in the school's life. The traditional stress on cricket was gradually abandoned and by 1977 only a token game was played each year. Instead more emphasis was placed on activities which the girls could continue after leaving school, including tennis, badminton, judo and yoga.[12] From *c.* 1950 building began anew. A further wing of St. Anne's came into use in 1951, allowing a new school-house to be created. A new library was opened in 1952; in 1956–8 the assembly hall was rebuilt, and in 1957 a swimming-pool was built. In 1961 the science block was extended. A new entrance hall to St. Anne's was built in 1962–3; in 1965 the jubilee wing was demolished and replaced by a block which included a sanatorium. In 1968 and 1969 the St. Mary's building was extended to provide study-bedrooms and a common-room, and flats for house-mistresses. A block with study-bedrooms and common-rooms

[4] Unless otherwise stated, this section is based on *S. Mary and S. Anne: the Second Fifty Years*, ed. Anne Wells and Susan Meads (Derby, 1974).

[5] *Kal. Corp. SS. Mary and Nicolas for year 1923*, 116–17; ibid. *for year 1932*, 92.

[6] Margaret E. Hall and Violet M. Macpherson, *Marcia Alice Rice* (Shrewsbury, 1961), 78.

[7] Ibid. 97; *Kal. Corp. SS. Mary and Nicolas for year 1923*, 117; *for 1938*, 94–8; Rice, *St. Mary's*, 284; ex inf. the school secretary (1977).

[8] *Kal. Corp. SS. Mary and Nicolas for 1926* and later edns. to 1938.

[9] Hall and Macpherson, *Rice*, 71.

[10] *Annual Leaflet of Guild of S. Mary & S. Anne*, xiv. 6 (copy at sch.); ex inf. Miss M. E. Foster of Abbots Bromley (1977).

[11] Ex inf. the headmistress, the school secretary, and Miss Foster.

[12] Ex inf. the headmistress and Miss R. H. Hunter, third mistress.

was built at St. Anne's in 1974 to commemorate that school's centenary.

BURTON-UPON-TRENT GRAMMAR SCHOOL

THERE was a school at Burton by 1453, when the schoolmaster was accused of threatening murder.[1] It may have been a grammar school connected with Burton abbey,[2] though in 1524 there were complaints that the abbey had no instructor in grammar.[3] The origins of a separately endowed school are obscure. The first steps are attributed to William Bene, abbot from 1502 to 1530 or 1531, who is said to have given money to Ralph Sacheverell to buy lands as an endowment for a school.[4] The donation has been identified with a beneficial lease of the manor and tithes of Littleover in Mickleover (Derb.) granted by the abbey to Sacheverell in 1517.[5] In 1529 or 1530 Ralph's son or uncle Sir Richard Sacheverell was licensed to alienate lands in Orton on the Hill (Leics.) and Breaston in Wilne (Derb.) which later formed the endowment of the school.[6] A school was functioning apparently in 1531,[7] and in his will proved 1534 Sir Richard left a wardship to his nephew Ralph on condition that he complete the foundation of the school as soon as possible.[8] Ralph settled the Orton and Breaston lands in trust in 1538. The trustees were to maintain a school for all those, rich and poor, who came to Burton to study grammar, and were to pay the income of the land, then 8 marks, to the master.[9] The abbot had already appointed a master in 1537 at a salary of £5. By 1545 his duties included teaching Latin grammar, Greek grammar, and logic, and his salary had been raised to £20, apparently paid out of the endowments of Burton college. There was also an usher, paid a £10 salary.[10]

The master was pensioned off at the dissolution of the college,[11] but the school survived. A schoolhouse in the churchyard is mentioned in 1549; it was repaired in 1567 and extended in 1568.[12] In 1582–3 or 1591 Dame Elizabeth Paulett, daughter of Walter Blount of Nether Hall, Burton, among other donations gave a £9 rent-charge on the former St. Mary's Priory at Clerkenwell (Mdx.) (later Clerkenwell House) to the school; £3 was to go to the master and £6 to the usher.[13] By 1656 the master had a house next to the school, which he occupied rent-free.[14] Masters and ushers are recorded in the later 17th century; in 1693 the usher was chosen by the feoffees of Lady Paulett's charity with the consent

of Lord Paget, the lord of the manor and a trustee.[15]

In 1708 Paget, as sole surviving trustee, drew up detailed statutes.[16] The school was to be free to sons of parents resident in Burton parish intending to learn Latin, Greek, and Hebrew. When the usher's salary had been made up to £20, it was also to be free for English teaching; if there were fewer than 80 pupils from Burton, free schooling was to extend to the poorest children of Stapenhill (Derb., later Staffs.). Diseased children were excluded. Sons of parents assessed to the poor-rate were to pay admission fees of 1s. 6d. to the master and 1s. to the usher and those not assessed were to pay 6d. to each master. Pupils were to attend from 7 a.m. to 5 p.m. between 1 February and 1 November, and from 8 to 11 a.m. and 1 to 4 p.m. in winter. They were allowed 20 to 26 days' holiday at Christmas and 6 days at Easter and at Whitsun but were not to be absent otherwise for more than 6 days unless sick. They had to attend church twice on Sundays and other days of public worship and were to be examined on the texts and substance of sermons. Boys who could speak Latin were forbidden to speak English; pupils were to be tested monthly with exercises in grammar, history, declamation, and prosody. The master and usher were to be Anglicans, and the master was also to be an Oxford or Cambridge graduate; in appointments of masters former pupils were to be preferred to others equally qualified. The usher was to be capable of teaching the upper school in the master's absence. Provisions were made to control absence or neglect by either teacher, and a body of visitors was constituted. Each year 20s. was to be allowed to poor pupils for cleaning the school and ringing the bell.

The school continued as a classical school during the 18th and early 19th centuries; John Jervis, Earl St. Vincent (1735–1823), learnt Latin and Greek there.[17] The rent-charge on Clerkenwell House was redeemed in 1795.[18] In 1812 there were only 18 pupils, but the number had risen to 60 by 1818.[19] From that time to the late 1870s there were generally some 50 to 70.[20] In the early 19th century the school was losing its classical emphasis: in 1820 the master stated that there had not been more than 20 grammar pupils at any time since 1795.[21] In the early 1820s the master taught 18 to 20 boys Latin, and the usher taught the rest the elements. The educational standard was reduced by the admission of lower-class boys whose parents sought an English education only, and it was difficult to enforce attendance because parents took their boys away for harvest and other work. The income was £9 from Lady

---

[1] G. E. Radford, *Hist. of the Burton upon Trent Grammar Sch.* (Derby, 1973), 9.

[2] Ibid.

[3] *V.C.H. Staffs.* iii. 209.

[4] *11th Rep. Com. Char.* H.C. 433, p. 558 (1824), xiv.

[5] Radford, *Burton Grammar Sch.* 14–15; *S.H.C.* 1937, 182–3.

[6] Radford, *Burton Grammar Sch.* 15.

[7] *L. & P. Hen. VIII*, x, pp. 77–8.

[8] Radford, *Burton Grammar Sch.* 15–16; Prob. 11/25 (P.C.C. 15 Hogen).

[9] C 93/2/21; C 2/Jas. I/B 41/48; Bodl. MS. C.C.C. c. 390/2, f. 176.

[10] E 315/105, f. 12; Radford, *Burton Grammar Sch.* 16; *V.C.H. Staffs.* iii. 297–8; Bodl. MS. C.C.C. c.391/1, f. 19.

[11] *V.C.H. Staffs.* iii. 298.

[12] Radford, *Burton Grammar Sch.* 5–7; S.R.O., D.(W.) 1734/3/4/49, 1st paper, p. [1].

[13] *11th Rep. Com. Char.* 553, 558; Radford, *Burton Grammar Sch.* 17–18; Bodl. MS. C.C.C. c.390/2, f. 176, giving date as 25 Eliz. and source of rent as land in Fenny Bentley (Derb.).

[14] W. Molyneux, *Burton-on-Trent* (Burton, n.d. [1869]), 93.

[15] L.J.R.O., B/A/4/3, f. 30v.; /7, 11 Feb. 1695/6; /13, 15 Dec. 1692; /22, 22 Feb. 1693/4; B/A/11b, 9 Nov. 1693.

[16] Radford, *Burton Grammar Sch.* 173–8.

[17] Ibid. 8, 30; E. P. Brenton, *Life and Correspondence of John, Earl of St. Vincent* (1838), i. 15.

[18] *11th Rep. Com. Char.* 554.

[19] *Digest of Returns to Sel. Cttee. on Educ. of Poor*, H.C. 224, p. 856 (1819), ix(2).

[20] Radford, *Burton Grammar Sch.* 49; *Educ. Enquiry Abstract*, vol. ii, H.C. 62, p. 872 (1835), xlii.

[21] F. G. Gomez, 'Endowed Schs. of Staffs. in the 18th cent.' (Leeds Univ. M.Phil. thesis, 1977), 227–8.

Paulett's endowment and £452 from the school lands, then 120 a. in Orton and 122 a. in Breaston; it had greatly increased following a renewal of the Orton lease in 1812. The master received two-thirds of the net rents and one-third of Paulett's gift, the rest going to the usher. The master had a house adjoining the school, but it was unsuitable and was let to a pauper.[22] The school-house was rebuilt on its existing site in 1834.[23]

By 1839 mathematics and 'the higher branches of literature' were apparently taught, and in 1843 the headmaster had 10 or 12 boarders.[24] J. T. Mac-Michael, headmaster 1843–51, introduced the teaching of mechanics, elementary chemistry, history, and geography.[25] A Chancery Scheme of 1858 allowed the headmaster to be a graduate of any English university but forbade him to hold any other preferment. The school was to be open to all sons aged 8 to 16 of parents resident in the parish, provided that they knew the elements. There were to be fees of £7 for boarders, boys in the upper school, and day-boys in the lower school who were not parishioners, and of £2 for other day-boys in the lower school. Five boys in each school were to be taught free. French and German were to be part of the curriculum.[26]

By 1865 French, drawing, and music were taught; more than half the boys in the upper school then learnt Greek and some learnt physics, though mathematics was apparently neglected. Drill was available in summer as an extra. The standard of work was generally high, though in the lower school it was reduced by the presence of some very young and barely literate boys. Few professional men sent their sons to the school; they were dissuaded partly by snobbery, partly by the state of the building. It was damp and insanitary, and there were only two rooms and no playground.[27]

A Scheme of 1873 amalgamated the school foundation with three other Burton charities, including the charity school of Richard Alsop. A board of governors was established which included representatives of local authorities. The grammar school formed the upper school for boys, and separate lower schools for boys and girls were established. Tuition fees of £6 to £10 were to be charged. The headmaster might be a graduate of any British university. He was to receive a stipend of £150 and a capitation fee of £2 to £4 for each boy.[28] The grammar school was required to move as soon as possible to new buildings with accommodation for 120 boys, and it was transferred to a new building in Bond Street in 1877. There was then a staff of six, including a visiting French master. C. U. Tripp, headmaster c. 1873–c. 1883, encouraged botany and geology as hobbies, founded a natural history society, and introduced cross-country running, cricket matches, and a school cap. During his later

years, however, the number of pupils and the standard of teaching declined.[29] A Scheme of 1884 merged the lower boys' school with the grammar school; the girls' school became a high school.[30] The merger increased the number of pupils at the grammar school, while Tripp's successor, T. W. Beckett (1884–1900), restored its academic quality.[31] By the end of the 19th century the Bond Street buildings were inadequate,[32] and several prefabricated temporary classrooms had been added.[33]

Numbers increased again under R. T. Robinson (1900–30), the first lay headmaster and a noted mathematician. There were 134 boys in 1907, 200 in 1920, and 300 in 1932. The increase took place perhaps partly because the school became the official secondary school for the borough under the 1902 Education Act.[34] A Scheme of 1905 laid down that if there was not room in the school for all applicants, borough children were to be preferred. A Scheme of 1909 required at least eight free places to be given to boys from Burton elementary schools; others were to pay fees of £5 to £12 and the age-range was to be 8 to 18 years.[35] A physics laboratory was built c. 1902 and another extension, including a biology room, in 1911.[36] The land at Breaston was sold in 1903 and that at Orton in 1918, to pay for extensions to the girls' high school.[37] About 1900 Robinson introduced morning school on Saturdays to allow games on Wednesday afternoons, although they were run by a sports club and not by the school and few boys played them.[38] The curriculum was revised c. 1934 to include more subjects and more games. Preparatory forms were abolished in 1947, and Spanish was taught from 1948.[39]

BURTON GRAMMAR SCHOOL.
Or on a cross engrailed azure five mullets argent in the first quarter a mitre azure
[Granted 1955]

The school was granted voluntary controlled status in 1951.[40] Numbers continued to grow in the mid 20th century; in 1952 there were 534 pupils.[41] The buildings became increasingly congested, and in 1957 the school moved to new buildings for 540 boys at Winshill.[42] It continued to expand: in the

[22] *11th Rep. Com. Char.* 559–60.
[23] Radford, *Burton Grammar Sch.* 7; W.S.L., Staffs. Views, ii, p. 190.
[24] Radford, *Burton Grammar Sch.* 33, 36–7.
[25] Ibid. 38–9.
[26] *Schs. Inquiry Com. vol. xv* [3966–XIV], p. 396, H.C. (1867–8), xxviii (12).
[27] Ibid. 394–6, 398.
[28] Radford, *Burton Grammar Sch.* 41, 45, 179–80.
[29] Ibid. 47–8, 57–8.
[30] Ibid. 181.
[31] Ibid. 58–9.

[32] Ibid. 48.
[33] Ibid. 83.
[34] Ibid. 49, 59; D. G. Stuart, *County Borough: the Hist. of Burton upon Trent 1901–1974*, i (Burton, 1975), 146–7.
[35] Bd. of Educ. Schemes, 3 Nov. 1905, 9 Nov. 1909.
[36] Radford, *Burton Grammar Sch.* 48.
[37] Ibid. 31, 193, 200.
[38] Ibid. 79; Stuart, *County Boro.* i. 147.
[39] Radford, *Burton Grammar Sch.* 66–7.
[40] Ibid. 71.
[41] Ibid. 49.
[42] Ibid. 66–8, 71–2.

later 1960s there were generally *c.* 600 pupils.[43] A new sports pavilion, built in 1962, was used as a classroom by 1965; three new classrooms were built in 1967.[44] In 1975 the school merged with the girls' high school and the Ada Chadwick secondary modern school to become the mixed comprehensive Abbot Beyne School. The buildings of all three schools were retained.[45]

COTTON COLLEGE, FORMERLY SEDGLEY PARK SCHOOL

UNTIL the later 18th century such Roman Catholic schools as there were in England catered mainly for the upper classes or provided only elementary education.[1] Richard Challoner, vicar apostolic of the London District 1758–81, entrusted to William Errington, one of his priests, the task of founding a boarding-school where middle-class boys, including those aspiring to the priesthood, would receive a secondary education. In 1762, after two false starts in Buckinghamshire and Wales, Errington opened a school in a house at Betley under the Revd. John Hurst. It has been suggested that the house, which belonged to James Corne, a convert, was the later Tower House. Eighteen boys were admitted during the first year.

The arrangement was intended to be temporary as larger accommodation was needed. Errington soon took a lease of Park Hall in Sedgley with some adjoining land from Lord Ward (later Dudley and Ward); the tenancy, however, was only on a year-to-year basis, and the payment of the rent was guaranteed by the Roman Catholic Thomas Giffard of Chillington in Brewood. In 1763 fifteen boys and two masters moved in two covered waggons from Betley to Sedgley. The Revd. Hugh Kendal became president, holding the office until his death in 1781. Errington continued as owner of the school until his death in 1768; it then passed to the vicars apostolic of the Midland District and their successors, the bishops and archbishops of Birmingham.

By 1767 there were 97 boys and 5 assistant masters.[2] During Kendal's presidency more than half the boys whose homes can be identified came from London and the south of England. Boys sometimes came as young as 7 or 8, and they usually left when between 13 and 15. Those wishing to study for the priesthood then proceeded to colleges abroad; 73 future priests attended the school between 1762 and 1781. The basic annual fee at that period was 12 guineas; in time a few boys attended as parlour boarders. The boys had separate beds, although during a period of overcrowding in the early 19th century a few double beds were used for brothers.

Extensions soon became necessary. The Hall itself was a three-storeyed building with two detached blocks, the eastern one consisting of stables and the male servants' quarters, the western one of domestic offices and the female servants' quarters. Kendal built a three-storeyed wing connecting with the eastern block and consisting of a play-room and a

refectory on the ground-floor, classrooms and a chapel on the first-floor, and dormitories on the second-floor. The Hall then became domestic quarters for the teaching staff, the housekeeper, and visitors. At first a walled plot at the entrance to the Hall was used as the playground, but later about an acre in front was enclosed for the purpose.

Kendal was on friendly terms with Lord Dudley and Ward and with his younger son William Ward, who inherited the Hall in 1774. Lord Dudley and Ward even defended his action in letting his property 'for a popish school' when challenged in the House of Lords. Such a school was, however, technically illegal, and during the Gordon Riots of 1780 William Ward, fearing for his property, reluctantly warned Kendal that the school would have to be closed if there were any disturbances locally. Again, on Kendal's death Ward hesitated before agreeing to allow the school to continue.

Kendal's relative and successor Thomas Southworth (1781–93 and 1797–1816)[3] built another extension before 1785. It was a two-storeyed wing connecting with the western block and consisting of an infirmary, a wash-house, and a dormitory with a dairy in the basement. Previously the boys had washed at a pump in the open; even after the extension one side of the wash-house was left open, apparently to allow the farm horses to drink at the trough where the boys washed. Soon afterwards an extension was built on part of the front of the new wing; it consisted of a basement kitchen, a dormitory for the maidservants, and bedrooms for the president and for a master. A bell and bellcot were erected on the roof *c.* 1805. In 1793 or 1794 a wing was added at right angles to the eastern block; it included another dormitory.[4] About the same time an open-air bath was constructed in a field where there was a spring. In 1800–1 an extension was built on the front of the stable block at the end of the east wing; it had a play-room on the ground-floor and a new chapel, dedicated to St. George, above it. Services for a long time remained simple, without music or singing.

By the beginning of the 19th century there were some 150 boys, and a waiting list was started in 1802. Numbers reached 184 in 1808 and for a short time in 1810–11 rose to 212. The boys were divided into six classes, each under its own master for English; there was also a preparatory class. Most of the boys were intended for a commercial career, and the general education, besides providing religious instruction, covered the elements, grammar, composition, geography, and history; the older boys were also taught book-keeping, land-measuring, geometry, and the use of the globes. There were on average some 30 taking French. The classics were intended mainly for church students; there were some 25 studying Latin and two or three Greek. Dancing (including deportment) and drawing were available as extras. Some of the boys had their own gardens. Oral examinations were held at Christmas and midsummer, with some of the neighbouring priests helping. 'Exhibitions', consisting of reci-

[43] Radford, *Burton Grammar Sch.* 49.
[44] Ibid. 72–4.
[45] Ex inf. the sec., Abbot Beyne Sch. (1976).
[1] This article is based on F. C. Husenbeth, *Hist. of Sedgley Park Sch.*, *Staffs.* (1856), and W. Buscot, *Hist. of Cotton Coll.* (1940). Additional information has been supplied by Mr. F. G. Roberts of Cotton, whose help is gratefully acknowledged. For the first three paras. see also F. Roberts, 'Early Hist. of Sedgley Park', *Staffs. Cath. Hist.* i. 32–6; *V.C.H. Staffs.* iii. 112.
[2] *Staffs. Cath. Hist.* xvii. 31.
[3] J. Gillow, *Bibliog. Dict. Eng. Catholics*, iv. 5, shows that they were first cousins once removed.
[4] For a view *c.* 1797 see plate facing p. 160.

tations of prose and poetry, were held at the same time; musical performances were added from 1817 at the request of John Milner, vicar apostolic of the Midland District. Holidays followed; few went home at Christmas, but more did so in the summer.

A building at right-angles to the western wing was erected by Milner in 1807–8 mainly to provide accommodation for church students and their priest; there were also a new dormitory and a laundry for the school. Milner's purchase of Oscott in 1808 made the new wing unnecessary, but part of it was taken over for 'patriarchs', intending church students who were older than the boys at the school.

Joseph Bowdon (1836–44) carried out a general improvement of the school and paid for much of it himself. It included the building of a gallery in the chapel for the choir and visitors and the provision of an enclosed wash-house for the boys. An old boys' association was started in 1839. Bowdon's successor Henry Smith (1844–8) formed a school library. Under Canon James Moore (1861–73) Latin and French became part of the general curriculum and written examinations were introduced. From the time of the centenary in 1863 the school was divided into seniors and juniors, and games, notably cricket, became more organized. Numbers, which had fluctuated for many years, reached 155 in 1865.

In 1836 Bowdon secured a 21-year lease of the premises instead of the yearly tenancy. The change put an end to a scheme, supported by several of the clergy, for moving the school to Old Oscott in Handsworth where the college buildings were to become vacant on the opening of New Oscott. When the lease expired in 1857 Lord Ward refused to grant more than a yearly tenancy. A further request for a long lease in 1863 was also refused. On both occasions the question of a move was again raised, and in 1864 Bishop Ullathorne of Birmingham appointed a commission to consider the future of the school. It recommended a move to Cotton Hall in Alton, which with the adjoining church of St. Wilfrid and 16 a. of land had passed to the diocese of Birmingham in 1857. More land at Cotton was bought in 1865. Cotton Hall was then occasionally used as a holiday retreat by students from Sedgley Park and Oscott who were not spending the holidays at home. In 1868 it became a preparatory school for Sedgley Park, and finally on Canon Moore's death in 1873 the main school moved there. With 106 boys at its reopening in August the school was full to capacity, even though the two top classes had been sent elsewhere. The village school was taken over as an extra dormitory, and a wooden building was erected as a refectory. The next six months brought 40 applications for admission, but they had to be refused.

A wing including a refectory, a classroom, a playroom, a study hall divisible into classrooms, and a dormitory was opened in 1875; it was named the Souter Wing after J. H. Souter, president 1873–84. The Hawksford Wing (after John Hawksford, president 1884–97) was built in 1886–7 partly at Hawksford's expense and contained two play-rooms, a refectory, private rooms, a science room, and a dormitory. The former refectory became a library and hall for plays and concerts. The results of the matriculation examination in 1893 placed Cotton at the head of the Roman Catholic schools of England.

A school magazine, *The Cottonian*, was founded in 1911. To mark the school's 150th anniversary in 1913 electric lighting and central heating were installed.

Under T. L. Williams (1922–9) the school was modernized. The title of president was changed to that of headmaster. The curriculum was altered to meet the examination requirements of the Oxford and Cambridge Joint Board. A sixth-form reference

COTTON COLLEGE. *Azure a chevron argent between three estoiles or the chevron surmounted by an open book also argent binding and clasps gold edged gules*

[Granted 1929]

library was established on the first-floor of the Hawksford Wing, a new cricket ground was laid out, and rugby football was introduced. An annexe was added to the Souter Wing containing a laboratory and lavatories, showers, and baths. The servants' quarters were enlarged and improved. Williams left to become archbishop of Birmingham.

Bernard Manion (1929–41) built a junior school dedicated to St. Thomas of Canterbury in 1932. Two open-air swimming-baths were constructed in 1935. The chapel (St. Wilfrid's church) was extended by two bays in 1937. Under J. W. Dunne (1941–8) the number of boys rose to over 170, and in 1943 the school was recognized as efficient by the Board of Education. A small community of Sisters of La Retraite was established at Cotton in 1942 to look after the domestic side of the school. W. A. Doran (1948–67) created the Archbishop Williams Memorial Library in 1952 next to the reference library in the Hawksford Wing. In 1960 the Faber Wing was added to the annexe of the Souter Wing; it consisted of two storeys, each containing a master's bedroom and bathroom and study-bedrooms for sixth-formers. Two more storeys were added in 1962, consisting of a master's room, a dormitory, and two classrooms. In September 1961 there was a record total of 226 boys. T. G. Gavin succeeded in 1967, and in 1968 he became a member of the Society of Headmasters of Independent Schools. A biology laboratory was built in 1969, and chemistry and physics laboratories were added to it in 1970. A sports hall was built in 1971. A 400-metre running-track was inaugurated in 1972, with space for a rugby pitch inside the oval. In July 1977 there were 207 boys, including 48 in the junior school.

Notable alumni[5] have included John Milner (1752–1826), divine and historian, who as vicar apostolic of the Midland District 1803–26 was the first of many bishops and archbishops produced by the school; John Philip Kemble (1757–1823), actor, who originally studied for the priesthood; John

---

[5] For this para. see also *D.N.B.*

Kirk (1760–1851; president 1793–7), divine and historian; John Chetwode Eustace (?1762–1815), classical antiquary; the Revd. George Oliver (1781–1861), historian; Lt.-Gen. Sir Alfred Keogh (1857–1936), director-general of the Army Medical Service 1905–10 and 1914–18 and rector of the Imperial College of Science 1910–22; and Cardinal Bernard William Griffin (1899–1956), archbishop of Westminster 1944–56.

DENSTONE COLLEGE

IN the 1860s a body of Midland Anglicans who had observed with interest the establishment by Canon Nathaniel Woodard, the Anglo-Catholic educationalist, of his schools in Sussex, began to work to secure a Woodard school for the Midlands. Sir Percival Heywood, Bt., one of the group's leading members, offered a 50-a. site at Denstone for the proposed school; the support of Bishop Lonsdale of Lichfield (1843–67) and of his successor Bishop Selwyn (1867–78) was obtained; and despite heated opposition from those who saw in the scheme a 'great Jesuit plot to contaminate the backbone of England' Woodard's supporters succeeded in raising funds. In 1868 the foundation-stone of the main school building was laid; it was designed in a Gothic style by William Slater and R. H. Carpenter and was in the form of an **H** with two open quadrangles named after Lonsdale and Selwyn. Selwyn agreed to act as visitor and helped to draw up statutes.[1] A target of 320 pupils was set.[2]

The first section of the building to be completed, including the 'great schoolroom' or assembly hall and some dormitories, was dedicated in July 1873; the school opened in October with 46 or 47 pupils at fees of 34 guineas a year. By Christmas there were over 60 boys. The school was placed under the general supervision of the provost of the Midland Division of the Corporation of St. Mary and St. Nicolas; the first provost was the Revd. E. C. Lowe, formerly headmaster of the Woodard school at Hurstpierpoint (Suss.). The teaching staff initially comprised a second master and three assistants; the headmaster, the Revd. W. B. Stanford, was not appointed until 1875. The academic year was at first divided into two halves and ended in June.[3]

Under Stanford (1875–8) and his successor the Revd. D. Edwardes (1878–1903), formerly second master, the school expanded vigorously. There was steady progress in building. A library was opened in 1881. A chapel, begun in 1879, was dedicated in 1887, and a dining-hall was started in 1888. Its opening in 1891 marked the completion of the main block.[4] Laboratories and a gymnasium were built in 1900, and a sanatorium in 1901. The physical enlargement of the school allowed numbers to grow to 250 by 1890; in the 1890s there were generally between 230 and 250 pupils, but a peak of 303 was reached in 1902.[5] Day-boys had been admitted by 1900, and in 1902 a preparatory department was

opened. The school obtained its first university award in 1876; in the 1890s and early 1900s university scholarships were won regularly. By 1900 the school was divided into classical and modern sides and the curriculum included German, Spanish, Hebrew, chemistry, physics, biology, geology, bookkeeping, surveying, shorthand, and typing, in addition to the usual subjects.[6] Games also flourished: a fives court was opened in 1876, while in 1877 a bathing place was acquired and compulsory cricket was introduced. A cricket ground came into use in 1878. By 1884 rugby was evidently played with success. Other outside activities were encouraged from the start. From 1875 an important feature of the school's life was the annual production of a Shakespeare play; Provost Lowe had insisted that the great schoolroom be adapted for the performance of plays. A museum was opened in 1876, and a school magazine was published from 1877; by 1900 there were several debating societies and other clubs.[7]

Edwardes was succeeded by J. Ll. Dove, under whom the number of boys fell to 214 in 1905 and examination results declined. Dove left in 1905 and was replaced by the Revd. F. A. Hibbert (1905–19); from then until the First World War there were again usually between 230 and 250 boys. From 1906 to 1913 examination results improved. Hibbert also began a new building programme. In 1911 the museum was enlarged; in 1912 classrooms were reconstructed and a drill hall, music-school, and changing rooms were built; in 1913 the laboratories were enlarged and electric light installed.[8] During the First World War, presumably because of the increased demand for places in boarding-schools, the number of boys grew rapidly to reach some 330 in 1920. At the same time, however, academic standards seem to have been falling, and after 1920 the school declined. There were some improvements to buildings: the music-school was enlarged in 1920, and huts for science were built; the laboratories were extended in 1923, and new classrooms were built in 1926. By the 1920s, however, if not before, the fact that the school's intake of pupils was largely restricted to the Midlands made it vulnerable to economic fluctuations. Depression not only cut numbers, but by forcing a reduction of entrance qualifications it lowered academic standards; conversely, improvements in standards were caused as much by renewed prosperity as by the efforts of the school authorities. From 1920 numbers declined to 173 in 1931; the school's academic achievement continued to diminish, qualified staff could not be found to fill vacancies, and by the early 1930s Denstone was losing more and more money each year. Under T. A. Moxon (1931–40) economies were put into effect, numbers increased to 283 in 1936, and the school finances were restored. In 1935 two new classrooms were built and an endowment fund was launched. In 1937 the school leased Smallwood Manor in Hanbury to house the preparatory school. Although numbers fell again in the late 1930s, the

[1] Forty Years of Denstone, ed. F. A. H[ibbert] (priv. print. 1913), 20–35.
[2] D.N.B. sub Woodard.
[3] F. A. Hibbert, Short Hist. & Descrip. of Denstone Coll. (1900 edn.), 16; Forty Years of Denstone, 26, 35–6, 39, 42, 44; K. E. Kirk, Story of Woodard Schs. 125; J. Otter, Nathaniel Woodard, 252.
[4] Hibbert, Denstone Coll. 19, 23; Forty Years of Den-

stone, 36–7; plate facing p. 160 below.
[5] Record diptych at Denstone.
[6] Hibbert, Denstone Coll. 68, 71; Forty Years of Denstone, 37, 186–91.
[7] Record diptych; Hibbert, Denstone Coll. 24–7, 31, 58; Forty Years of Denstone, 36, 62; Lich. Dioc. Mag. (1884), 192.
[8] Record diptych; Forty Years of Denstone, 38.

results in external examinations improved. New fives courts were built in 1938, and other extensions, including new studies, an entrance hall, and a domestic block, were completed in 1939.[9]

The decline in numbers was reversed during the Second World War: they rose from 226 in 1942 to 305 in 1947.[10] The school was able to acquire houses for the staff from 1944 and to buy Smallwood Manor in 1945. A 'flight from classics' began in the war years and continued later: by 1956 only a few sixth-form boys, and by 1965 none, studied Greek.[11]

In the later 1940s and early 1950s fewer parents sought boarding-school places for their sons, and the school stagnated. It maintained its numbers, but only by lowering entrance requirements. By the mid 1950s the academic standard was therefore poor, though some university scholarships were won.[12] In the late 1950s, as a result of economic prosperity and of the high birth-rate after the Second World War, registrations increased and B. M. W. Trapnell, headmaster 1957–68, took advantage of the increase to begin a vigorous programme of improvement. By 1958 he had established a new boarding-house and increased the number of boys from 340 to 376. New studies were completed in 1959; in 1960 land was bought for an extra sports field; new laboratories were completed in 1962; an indoor swimming-pool was completed in 1963, and an athletics track had been laid out by then.[13] Trapnell also sought to attract better staff by providing more married quarters, and that policy continued after his departure. Between 1957 and 1969 new building or conversion provided houses for eleven families, and the school also took over houses in the village. A headmaster's house was built in 1964.[14] The increase in registrations enabled Trapnell to raise entrance requirements, and by the early 1960s examination results had improved. German was reintroduced in 1957 or 1958; Russian and sex education were taught from 1958; economics was introduced in 1967 or 1968. In 1960 a tutorial system was started, and in 1963 fagging was abolished.[15]

From Trapnell's later years numbers at the school declined, mainly owing to external causes; in 1972 there were only 303 boys. Thereafter numbers began to increase again, and in order to encourage further growth the school admitted day-boys and day-girls in 1976 and lowered the age of entrance for day-pupils to 11 in 1977. The number of children accordingly rose from 315 in 1975 to 351 at the end of 1977.[16] In 1969 a new music-school was finished. A building to commemorate the school's centenary, including art, pottery, crafts, and drama workshops, was begun in 1973 and finished in 1977.[17]

LICHFIELD GRAMMAR SCHOOL

STATUTES drawn up for Lichfield cathedral probably in 1191 required the chancellor to maintain a school, and the master or rector of the scholars is mentioned in 1272.[1] No more is known of the cathedral school, but there was a grammar school at Lichfield by 1440, when the master was admitted to the town guild. It may have been connected with St. John's hospital. In 1495, however, the proxy of the hospital alleged that there had not been any regular free teaching of grammar in Lichfield for lack of a master and money.[2] In the same year Bishop William Smith endowed the grammar school as part of his refoundation of the hospital. There were to be a master in priest's orders and an usher, both appointed by the master of the hospital and receiving stipends of £10 and £5 respectively. The master was to swear to refuse fees but might accept spontaneous gifts. Both teachers were to reside in the hospital and to have no contact with women. They could each have a month's annual leave with the permission of the hospital master, but the schoolmaster had to find a suitable *locum tenens*.[3]

The first master after the refoundation was apparently Robert Whittington, a pupil at the old school, author of widely used textbooks, and noted as a teacher of Greek as well as Latin. He was master in 1517[4] but had left by 1519. The master was then non-resident, and the usher complained that he received only 40s. a year.[5] By 1526 the school was receiving £10 from Launde priory (Leics.). The payment may have been connected with an obit for Bishop Smith and may also have been the origin of pensions paid out of the Exchequer to the master and usher until at least the 1830s, when the pension to the master was £6 13s. 4d. and that to the usher £5 10s. 11d.[6] The usher's pay, still 40s. in 1535, had been raised to £5 again by the early 1540s.[7] By the early 1530s[8] the master was Richard Walker, later a wealthy pluralist who in 1567[9] gave lands in Longdon and in Curborough and Elmhurst in St. Chad's, Lichfield, to the bailiffs and citizens of Lichfield to provide £3 6s. 8d. a year for the master, £1 13s. 4d. for the usher, and £1 6s. 8d. each to six

[9] Record diptych; Denstone Coll. records, Sch. Cttee. Min. Bk. 1930–55, pp. 3, 14–15, 19, 27–8, 30–2, 37, 47, 51, 55; ex inf. the headmaster (1977). The provost and governors of Denstone Coll. are thanked for permission to examine the records.
[10] Ex inf. the school secretary (1977).
[11] Sch. Cttee. Min. Bk. 1930–55, p. 62; 1955–63, p. 16; Sch. Council Min. Bk. 1964–8, headmaster's rep. for 1965–6, p. 4.
[12] Ex inf. the school secretary (1977); Sch. Cttee. Min. Bk. 1930–55, pp. 72, 92, 121, 136–7, 152; 1955–63, pp. 4, 16, 52.
[13] Sch. Cttee. Min. Bk. 1955–63, pp. 60, 74, 79, 99, 117, 138, 154; ex inf. the school secretary and the headmaster.
[14] Sch. Cttee. Min. Bk. 1955–63, p. 52; Sch. Council Min. Bk. 1968–71, Bldgs. & Plant Rep. May 1970, p. 5.
[15] Sch. Cttee. Min. Bk. 1955–63, pp. 52, 67, 74, 96, 117, 136, 154; Sch. Council Min. Bk. 1968–71, headmaster's rep. for 1967–8.
[16] Ex inf. the headmaster and the school secretary (1977); Sch. Council Min. Bk. 1964–8, headmaster's rep. for

1966–7.
[17] Sch. Council Min. Bk. 1968–71, headmaster's rep. for yr. ended 31 Aug. 1970; *The Field*, 13 Dec. 1973, 1589; ex inf. the headmaster (1977).
[1] *V.C.H. Staffs.* iii. 142, 149. Unless otherwise stated, the rest of this article is based on P. Laithwaite, *Short Hist. of Lichfield Grammar Sch.* (Lichfield, 1925).
[2] L.J.R.O., B/A/1/13, f. 167.
[3] *V.C.H. Staffs.* iii. 281.
[4] R. *Whittintoni Lichfeldiensis Grammatices Magistri Lucubrationes* (London, 1517).
[5] *S.H.C.* 4th ser. vii. 41.
[6] *Subsidy Collected in Dioc. of Lincoln in 1526* (Oxf. Hist. Soc. lxiii), 123; *Valor Eccl.* (Rec. Com.), iv. 165; *7th Rep. Com. Char.* H.C. 129, p. 394 (1822), ix; *Return of Money paid towards Lichfield Grammar Sch.* H.C. 573, p.1 (1839), xli.
[7] *V.C.H. Staffs.* iii. 282; Leland, *Itin.* ed. Toulmin Smith, ii. 100.
[8] *V.C.H. Staffs.* iii 288.
[9] S.R.O., D.(W.) 617/1.

poor boys to be chosen by the bailiffs. In 1577 a group of inhabitants bought a plot of land on the opposite side of St. John Street from the hospital and conveyed it to the corporation in trust as the site of a new school-house to be built as soon as possible; it had been built by 1587.[10] The two gifts gave the corporation influence over the school, and from 1577 it appointed the masters.[11]

Among the school's pupils in the later 16th and early 17th centuries were the Roman Catholic martyr and saint Edmund Genings (1567–91) and the antiquary Elias Ashmole (1617–92), who learnt Latin there probably in the 1630s. In 1648 the master, Samuel Frankland, was one of only two Staffordshire schoolmasters to sign the Testimony.[12] About 1660 the master, Thomas Bevans, reintroduced Greek and added Hebrew to the curriculum. His pupils included the herald and statistician Gregory King (1648–1712) and the philosopher William Wollaston (1660–1724).[13] In 1670 he resigned after a dispute with the corporation and set up a private school, taking many pupils with him.

The school reached its apogee under Robert Shaw (1680–1704) and John Hunter (1704–41). Paradoxically the improvement was due partly to the smallness of the income, which forced the masters to take boarders. The school received some help from the Lichfield conduit lands trustees, who in 1682 or 1683 built a house adjoining the school for the master.[14] By 1697, and probably by 1680, the trustees were giving £10 a year in addition to £20 supplied by the corporation, which also provided a third master to teach writing by 1696.[15] In that year the bishop decided to allow the masters to take fees, but in 1697 the corporation forbade the charging of fees to local children. Shaw was therefore driven to rely on those from boarders. Both he and Hunter were highly reputed as scholars and attracted pupils from a wide area. By 1695 Shaw had at least twelve sons of Staffordshire gentlemen as boarders. Hunter normally employed two ushers, one of whom, Humphrey Hawkins, was in high repute as a teacher and from 1705 received a £5 gratuity from the conduit lands trustees.[16] Under Hunter the school attracted gentlemen's sons both from Staffordshire and from neighbouring counties. He apparently had nearly 100 boarders at times, and he took over several houses near by to accommodate them.[17] Shaw and Hunter had many distinguished alumni, including the judges William Noel (1695–1762), Sir Thomas Parker (?1695–1784), Sir John Willes (1685–1761), and Sir John Eardley Wilmot (1709–92), the essayist Joseph Addison (1672–1719), the poet Isaac Hawkins Browne the elder (1705–60), the mathematician John Colson (1680–1760), the actor David Garrick (1717–79), the physician Robert James (1705–76), the lexicographer Samuel Johnson (1709–84), the

inventor John Wyatt (1700–66), and Thomas Newton (1704–82), bishop of Bristol 1761–82.[18]

After Hunter's time the school declined. The master's income was further reduced when in 1740 his £10 from the hospital funds was withdrawn on the grounds that the school's connexion with the hospital had long ceased. In 1747, moreover, the conduit lands trustees lowered the master's allowance to £8 and cancelled that to the usher, though the latter payment was partly restored in 1749.[19] By 1794 the schoolroom was said to be dilapidated and unfit for master and boys.[20] There may have been some revival under Thomas Harwood (1791–1813), distinguished as an antiquary; among his pupils were Henry Salt (1780–1827), traveller and collector, and John Obadiah Westwood (1805–93), entomologist and palaeographer.[21] In Harwood's last years, however, there were apparently no pupils.[22]

Under Harwood's successor Cowperthwaite Smith (1813–49) there seems to have been a brief recovery, but in Smith's later years the school almost disappeared. From his appointment the corporation allowed him to take fees of 2 guineas a quarter from each boy in his class and 1 guinea from each in the usher's class, while the conduit lands trustees increased their grant to £35. The stipends, however, remained small; the townsmen resented the fees, and in 1821 the conduit lands trustees suspended their grant. Smith, like his predecessors, concentrated on boarders, claiming in advertisements that there were no free boys 'of an inferior grade' on the foundation. In 1821 there were 18 boarders out of fewer than 40 boys.[23] Smith became increasingly negligent, and the severe thrashings which he gave boys deterred parents. By 1834 the usher did all the Latin teaching of the free pupils, although the corporation had paid him no salary since 1829. In 1834 the headmaster's salary was halved. Between 1834 and 1836 there were still from 24 to 28 day-boys, but the usher's salary was stopped apparently in 1836 and he resigned. In 1837 Smith decided to confine his teaching to the classics and lost all his pupils.[24] He could not be removed, and nothing could be done to improve the school until he left.[25]

By 1846 the school building was ruinous, and in 1848 a public meeting decided to rebuild it on the same site.[26] The conduit lands trustees paid for the rebuilding and promised a grant of £50 a year for the headmaster and £25 for the usher. A committee of governors was established representing the trust, the corporation, the Lichfield parishes, and the master of the hospital. The headmaster's salary was increased to £90, though fees were still charged. When the new building was opened in 1850 there were 28 boys, 8 of them boarders. Under J. C. Bentley (1850–4), J. G. Cumming (1855–8), and J. W. Knight (1859–67) the standard of teaching

[10] S.R.O., D.(W.) 617/2; *7th Rep. Com. Char.* 394; plate facing p. 145 above.
[11] J. R. Lindley, 'Hist. of Educ. in Lichfield' (TS. in L.J.R.O.), 89.
[12] A. G. Matthews, *Cong. Churches of Staffs.* 18.
[13] See also *D.N.B. sub* King and Wollaston.
[14] L.J.R.O., D. 53, scrapbk. f. 7; P. Laithwaite, *Hist. of Lichfield Conduit Lands Trust 1546–1946* (Lichfield, 1947), 53. Laithwaite, *Lichfield Grammar Sch.* 36, following *7th Rep. Com. Char.* 394, states that the house was built in 1692.
[15] Lindley, 'Educ. in Lichfield', 44, 50–1.
[16] Ibid. 52; Laithwaite, *Conduit Lands Trust*, 54.
[17] A. L. Reade, *Johnsonian Gleanings*, iii. 134.
[18] *D.N.B.*
[19] Laithwaite, *Conduit Lands Trust*, 54.
[20] *Gent. Mag.* lxiv (1), 413.
[21] *D.N.B.*
[22] *Return of Money Paid towards Lichfield Grammar Sch.* 2.
[23] Laithwaite, *Conduit Lands Trust*, 55; *7th Rep. Com. Char.* 395.
[24] *Return of Money Paid towards Lichfield Grammar Sch.* 1–2.
[25] Laithwaite, *Conduit Lands Trust*, 55; Lindley, 'Educ. in Lichfield', 79.
[26] Laithwaite, *Conduit Lands Trust*, 55; L.J.R.O., D. 53, scrapbk. f. 20.

DENSTONE COLLEGE IN 1968
from the south

SEDGLEY PARK SCHOOL *c.* 1797

County Buildings

The Borough Hall

The Shire Hall *c.* 1680

STAFFORD

improved. Bentley introduced French and German,[27] Cumming taught science,[28] and under Knight the curriculum included classics, mathematics, French, German, and drawing; by 1865 the headmaster was employing two non-graduate assistants.[29] There was again an influx of boarders; in 1860 the diocesan chancellor bought a tavern adjoining the school for inclusion in the school-house,[30] and in 1865 there were 17 boarders and 26 day-boys.[31]

A Scheme of 1876 amalgamated the foundation with Minors's English School and Terrick's educational charity. A body of governors was established, including representatives of local authorities. It could dismiss the headmaster. The head was to have a salary of £150 and capitation fees of £2 to £4, the boys paying fees of £4 to £8 a year. Science was to form part of the curriculum, while Greek and German became extras.[32] Under the new foundation 30 boys were admitted free. Until the early 20th century the school remained small, with between 40 and 50 boys.[33] Eventually an increased demand for boarding places made the old buildings obsolete, and in 1903 a new school designed by T. Hillyer Pyke of East Ham (Essex) was opened at Borrowcop. It contained a hall, classrooms, a laboratory, and boarding accommodation, and there was a 6-a. playing-field adjoining.[34] A Scheme of 1908 provided for the payment of £195 a year to the school from St. John's hospital, and one of 1909 made the school the boys' secondary school for the city and increased the number of free places.[35] Under a further Scheme of 1920 it became one of the county council's maintained schools.[36] Nevertheless R. W. Clarke, headmaster 1918–37, emphasized Lichfield's public-school character and laid great stress on compulsory games.[37] From the First World War the number of pupils increased: there were 46 in 1914, 130 in 1919, 210 in 1932, 250 in 1936, and 289 in 1942. A preparatory department was established c. 1920. In 1932 a new wing including a chemistry laboratory, assembly hall, and gymnasium was added. Boarding ceased in 1937. By 1942, however, most of the boys came from outside the city.[38]

The school continued to expand after the Second World War: in 1947 there were 358 boys, and in 1970 445. The preparatory department closed in 1948 under the 1944 Education Act, but in 1951 the governors bought Maple Hayes and 25 a. of land and converted the house to provide boarding accommodation once more. Fees were charged on a sliding scale according to parents' income. There were 24 boarders at the opening, and a peak of 72 was reached c. 1955. About 1953 a canteen was built at the main school, and the former dining-rooms there were converted into a classroom and a biology laboratory, so that that subject could be taught

at sixth-form level. A science block was added in the early 1960s. In 1961 the headmaster became housemaster of Maple Hayes, and the former headmaster's house was converted to include sixth-form rooms and offices. German was reintroduced c. 1949, and economics was taught from c. 1967; in the 1960s the school was one of the first to teach a general studies course. By 1971 there were 140 boys in the sixth form; nearly a third of leavers went to university. In that year the school was amalgamated with the adjoining Kings Hill secondary modern school to form the mixed comprehensive King Edward VI school.[39]

NEWCASTLE-UNDER-LYME GRAMMAR SCHOOL

ONE of the chantry priests at Newcastle-under-Lyme may have kept a school there.[1] The first clear evidence, however, of a school in the town is in 1565 when the corporation agreed 'to pay William Sabshed our schoolmaster 26s. 8d. for one whole year, and after as the town likes'. His salary was raised to £10 in 1566, and in 1572 the corporation assigned him £2 'toward the farther maintenance of the school so long as he keepeth a school sufficient in the town'; the sum was stated to be as granted 'in aforetime'. Sabshed became a burgess in 1571, one of the two bailiffs of the town in 1587, and one of the twenty-four capital burgesses created by the borough charter of 1590. By 1587, however, he was no longer the schoolmaster. A later master, Richard Palin, resigned in 1602 after being told by the corporation 'of the dislike we had of him in regard he did not profit our scholars'. The master's salary was reduced from £20 to 20 marks (£13 6s. 8d.) in 1621.

In 1602 Richard Cleyton of London, a native of Newcastle, assigned a rent-charge of £10 a year on property in London to his brother Thomas and the corporation of Newcastle to be paid after Richard's death and that of his wife. The money was to provide a master to teach free 30 poor children born in Newcastle. He was to be a graduate of Oxford or Cambridge and was to be appointed by Thomas while he lived and then by the corporation. The gift seems not to have taken effect until 1625, when the corporation arranged for the choice of 30 poor pupils. Meanwhile in 1609 an agreement was made between the corporation and Sir Rowland Cotton of Bellaport in Norton in Hales and Alkington in Whitchurch (both Salop.), M.P. for Newcastle 1605–11 and 1628–9 and mayor in 1614. His uncle, John Cotton of Alkington, a relation by marriage of Richard Cleyton, had died in 1606, leaving £100 to buy land which would produce £10 a year for the

[27] Lindley, 'Educ. in Lichfield', 87.
[28] *Staffs. Advertiser*, 27 Jan., 5 and 12 May 1855, 7 Aug. 1858.
[29] *Schs. Inquiry Com. vol. xv* [3966–XIV], pp. 427–8, H.C. (1867–8), xxviii (12).
[30] Laithwaite, *Conduit Lands Trust*, 55.
[31] *Schs. Inquiry Com. vol. xv*, 427.
[32] Char. Com. Scheme, 23 Oct. 1876 (copy in L.J.R.O., D. 53).
[33] Lindley, 'Educ. in Lichfield', 96, 104; L.J.R.O., D. 53, scrapbk. f. 50.
[34] Lindley, 'Educ. in Lichfield', 101; *Staffs. Advertiser*, 2 May 1903.
[35] Lindley, 'Educ. in Lichfield', 19, 101–2; Bd. of Educ. Scheme, 17 Nov. 1909 (copy in L.J.R.O., D. 53).

[36] Bd. of Educ. Scheme, 6 July 1920 (copy in Staffs. County Council, Treasurer's Dept., Educ. Accountancy files).
[37] L.J.R.O., D. 53, scrapbk. ff. 42–3, prospectus c. 1930.
[38] Lindley, 'Educ. in Lichfield', 103–4; ex inf. (1977) Mr. W. Richards, headmaster 1947–71.
[39] Ex inf. Mr. Richards.
[1] This account is based on T. Pape, *Educ. Endowments of Newcastle-under-Lyme* (Stafford, 1913); G. Griffith, *Free Schools and Endowments of Staffs.* (1860), 184–90; *13th Rep. Com. Char.* H.C. 349, pp. 281–4 (1825), xi; *Schs. Inquiry Com. vol. xv* [3966–XIV], pp. 432–5 (1867–8), xxviii (12). For the Cotton family see *S.H.C.* 1920 and 1922, 8; T. Pape, *Newcastle-under-Lyme in Tudor and early Stuart times*, 108–9; Burke, *Land. Gent.* (1894), i. 408.

master. In 1609 Sir Rowland paid over the money and it was agreed that he or his heirs should nominate the master on the next vacancy and then on every alternate vacancy. In fact during the 17th century the corporation and the Cotton family consulted each other over nominations. In 1610 the corporation used the £100 to buy property in Knutton in Wolstanton, the income to be paid to the master after the owner's death. That had occurred by 1640, when the corporation decided to lease the property to the master, Richard Orme. In 1648 it was leased to his brother, and it remained in the hands of the Orme family until at least the early 18th century.

John Cowell of Knutton (d. 1659) left £100 to the corporation to be invested in land which would produce £5 a year to augment the master's income. The bequest was made on condition that the children of Knutton and Chesterton in Wolstanton should be taught free at the school, but the inhabitants of those places seem never to have exercised the right. In 1665 the corporation duly bought land in Newcastle. In 1673 it decided to appoint an usher at £5 a year for three years 'in case the schoolmaster be burdened with a greater number of scholars than he is able to teach'. The appointment had become permanent by 1685, and in that year John Lowe of Marston Montgomery (Derb.) settled a rent-charge in trust to provide £2 10s. a year for the usher. In 1690 William Beard of Newcastle, mayor 1687–8, gave a rent-charge endowing a sermon at St. Giles's church, Newcastle, on the feast of St. Mark (25 April); 10s. was to be paid to the master if he attended with his pupils.

In 1692 William Cotton of Bellaport gave the corporation £100 to be invested in land for the benefit of the master; in return the corporation gave the Cotton family the next four nominations and thereafter every second and third turn. It was also agreed that the master was to teach Latin and Greek free to the sons of burgesses as well as to those of poor inhabitants of the borough, but he was allowed to teach the sons of 'foreigners' for a reasonable fee. He was not to be absent for more than three days a year except on holy days and at customary times. He was to be a graduate of Oxford or Cambridge, learned and of good life, and 'of the Protestant religion, and no papist, Roman priest, Jesuit, or schismatic'. He was to be removed if he should 'hear, say, or sing mass, or shall be scandalous, ignorant, illiterate, or cruel, or negligent by the space of three days'. The corporation in fact kept the £100 in its own hands and paid £5 a year to the school. At the end of 1692 it ordered the books from a library adjoining St. Giles's to be transferred to the school.

The school, which until 1692 had been called a free school, thus became a grammar school. It was so described in the will of Edward Orme (d. 1705), son of Richard and himself a former master, who left £40 to the corporation to be invested for the master. It was presumably because of the change in the nature of the school that Orme also left money to endow an English school in Newcastle, the Orme School opened in 1705.

The free school stood south of the tower of St. Giles's, probably from its earliest days. It was pulled down in 1719–20 with the rebuilding of the church, and in August 1720 the corporation ordered a malthouse which it had bought to be converted into a school-house. The building of a new school in Church Street was begun in 1722. Standing below the level of the churchyard it became damp, and by the early 19th century the site was needed for an enlargement of the churchyard. About 1820 a new school was opened on the corner of Hanover Street and School Street; it was built by subscription, the corporation giving the site and 60 guineas. A building of stuccoed brick, it was in a Tudor style with castellated corner turrets and consisted of a single hall with a room for the headmaster at one end.

In the later 18th century there were on average some 10 free boys a year; in 1817 there were only two. In 1824 there were 12 free boys, nearly 40 other day-boys, and 21 boarders. The ordinary day-boys paid 6 guineas a year for the classics and 2 guineas for writing and accounts; if the free boys wished to learn writing and accounts, they too had to pay. It was noted that 'some of the free boys are considerably advanced in classics, and one at least will soon go to one of the universities'. The headmaster then in office had been appointed in 1817 by the corporation, whose turn it had been. The income from endowments in 1824 was £94. Until 1841 the headmaster ran the property himself and took the rents. In that year Chancery appointed a body of trustees, one of whom received the rents and paid them to the headmaster. By 1864 there were 53 day-boys and 12 boarders; the ordinary day-boys paid £8 8s. a year, and the charge to foundationers for English subjects was 4 guineas a year. The curriculum was predominantly classical, and at admission boys had to be able to read and write. The headmaster, who had been appointed by the trustees, was also vicar of St. George's, Newcastle, and was often absent on his clerical duties during the afternoons; there were, however, two full-time assistant masters. The school building was inadequate and academic standards were low; the professional men of the town and its leading businessmen had a poor opinion of the school.

In 1872 a Scheme of the Endowed Schools Commissioners amalgamated Newcastle's educational charities and replaced the grammar school and the Orme School by a boys' high school, a boys' middle school, and a girls' school. The headmaster of the grammar school was given a pension, and the school building was abandoned.[2]

RUGELEY GRAMMAR SCHOOL

THE grammar school at Rugeley may have originated in a chantry school, but there is no clear evidence of a school there before the reign of Elizabeth I. She is traditionally said to have permitted the diversion of rents from cottages and lands in Rugeley, formerly applied to support a mass-priest in the parish church, to pay the salary of a schoolmaster. In 1567, when the Crown granted a lease of the property for £3 10s. 4d., Thomas Reeve, schoolmaster, was among the under-tenants.[1] The land was held by

---

[2] For the history of the three new schools see *V.C.H. Staffs.* viii. 65–7, which wrongly ascribes the 1872 Scheme to the Charity Commissioners.

[1] *S.H.C.* 1915, 220; E. C. Toye, 'Rugeley Grammar Sch.' *Rugeleian*, 7th ser. i. 31 (copy in W.S.L. Sch. Mags.).

trustees of a grammar school in 1585; in 1590 it was claimed that the rents had been employed time out of mind for the use of such a school. It appears that the income was inadequate to support a competent master and that the parishioners had raised money to augment it.[2] By 1638 the rent was £18 1s. 4d.[3] The school may have lapsed in the mid 17th century: in 1657 the rents were said to be misused, and a decree of 1662 ordered the arrears to be paid to new trustees.[4] If there was a lapse, the school had been revived by 1675 when Job Seyton was master.[5]

There was at first no school building, and lessons were apparently held in the church.[6] Walter Landor (d. 1706) left £100 to build a school, and his executor added nearly £100 to provide a house for the master. The school building was begun in 1707; Francis Tomkinson, master 1683–1715, paid for the fittings.[7] In 1710 the school lands were stated to cover 44 a.[8] The school continued as a classical school in the early and mid 18th century. The most distinguished master was William Budworth, who came to Rugeley in 1727 or 1728. After six months he refused to teach English, and in 1731 many inhabitants protested, claiming that English had been taught in the school for 60 years. In the same year Budworth accepted the mastership of Brewood grammar school, but he did not leave Rugeley until 1733. From 1731 to 1733 his pupils included Richard Hurd, who came from Brewood school to study under him and returned thither with him. Budworth's refusal to teach English resulted in the establishment of an English school at Rugeley in 1734.[9] In 1772 Paul Parkyns, head of that school and a layman, was appointed master of the grammar school. Ralph Weston, a trustee, objected to the appointment on the grounds that Parkyns would not be able to teach the classics. Parkyns was therefore obliged to agree to teach both the elements and the classics and to prepare boys for the universities; he was also to take care of the boys' morals and train them in Anglican principles, and to quit the post if required.[10] On his death in 1789 he was succeeded by his son, another Paul; Weston again objected, claiming that many inhabitants of Rugeley who wished their children to qualify for liberal professions had had to send them to distant boarding-schools to learn the classics.[11]

The value of the school property was increased by the inclosure of the Rugeley open fields in 1755 and by an exchange in 1781. The rents, however, remained only £31 12s. until 1809, when they were increased; in the early 1820s the income was £258 7s. excluding the value of land held directly by the master. New rules were drawn up when John Clarke was appointed master in 1810. He was to teach geography as well as the elements and the classics, to preside in school during school hours, to read prayers daily, and not to take more than 20 boarders without the trustees' consent. Boys were not to be admitted under 7 years of age, but those living outside as well as inside the parish were to be eligible. Clarke heightened the house and built a new schoolroom. He often had more than the maximum number of boarders: there were 26 at Midsummer 1820 and 23 at Christmas 1821. About 1821 there were also 20 free and 3 fee-paying day-boys. Only three of the free boys were taught the classics. The fee-paying day-boys, of whom a maximum of 11 was permitted, came from outside the parish; the children of inhabitants were taught free whatever their parents' station in life. His income from endowments and boarding fees enabled him to employ two assistants and a French master.[12]

Clarke's successor Thomas Bonney (1826–53) increased the number of day-boys from some 20 in 1834 to some 45 in 1851; he is even said to have had 83 boys at one time.[13] Among his pupils were his son T. G. Bonney (1833–1923), the geologist, and William Palmer (1824–56), the Rugeley poisoner.[14] Under Bonney the curriculum apparently consisted of the elements, the classics, and geography, but a resolution of the trustees in 1855 required his successor Edward Pitman (1853–76) to teach in addition French, mathematics, and civil engineering.[15] In 1859 numbers were down to 30, of whom 5 were boarders, and the teaching was becoming less classical and more commercial.[16] In 1865 the teaching was being done by an assistant. Mathematics was treated as an extra, and only 3 boys learnt it; of the 26 day-boys, only 8 learnt Greek, though the Latin teaching was adequate. Drill formed part of the curriculum. The fee of £8 a year charged to day-boys from outside the parish kept their numbers low, while the parish boys' free education increased 'their natural indifference to learning'. Boys were admitted who could scarcely write or spell. The headmaster received £225 from the endowment and apparently paid the assistant £70. The schoolroom was enlarged in 1866, and by 1867 there were 32 day-boys and 17 boarders; all learnt Latin, 25 French, 6 German, and 5 Greek.[17] Pitman was also vicar of Pipe Ridware; in his latter years as master he was distracted by clerical duties and illness, and the school declined. In 1872 there were only 18 day-boys.[18]

After much public discussion a Scheme was introduced in 1875 which replaced the trustees by a board of governors including representatives of local authorities. There were to be a 5s. entrance fee and capitation fees of £2 to £4 for each boy; the headmaster's salary was fixed at £150. Sons of parents living in Rugeley were to be eligible for exemption from fees. If funds permitted, leaving exhibitions at higher institutions could be awarded. No boy

[2] W. N. Landor, 'Hist. of Rugeley' (TS. in W.S.L.), ii. 214–15 (new nos.); Req. 2/33/91.
[3] S.R.O., D.(W.) 1792/20, copy rental of Rugeley sch. land.
[4] C 93/24/1 rot. 7; 7th Rep. Com. Char. H.C. 129, p. 276 (1822), x.
[5] Landor, 'Rugeley', ii. 225.
[6] E. C. Toye, 'Rugeley Grammar Sch.' Staffs. Life, v (3), 10; Rugeleian, 7th ser. i. 32.
[7] Rugeleian, 7th ser. i. 33–4; Landor, 'Rugeley', ii. 225.
[8] 7th Rep. Com. Char. 278.
[9] Rugeleian, 7th ser. i. 34; Landor, 'Rugeley', ii. 226; above, p. 149.
[10] Rugeleian, 7th ser. i. 35–6; Schs. Inquiry Com. vol. xv

[3966–XIV], p. 447, H.C. (1867–8), xxviii (12).
[11] Rugeleian, 7th ser. i. 36; S.R.O., D.(W.) 1792/20, esp. R. Weston to (?)R. Hurd, 30 Aug. 1793.
[12] V.C.H. Staffs. v. 159; 7th Rep. Com. Char. 278–80; S.R.O., D.(W.) 1788, P.10, B.6, list of boys at Rugeley sch.
[13] White, Dir. Staffs. (1834), 511; (1851), 474; Rugeleian, 7th ser. i. 36.
[14] D.N.B.; V.C.H. Staffs. v. 152.
[15] White, Dir. Staffs. (1851), 474; Schs. Inquiry Com. vol. xv, 447.
[16] Landor, 'Rugeley', ii. 231.
[17] Schs. Inquiry Com. vol. xv, 446–7.
[18] Rugeleian, 7th ser. i. 36.

was to be admitted under 8 or stay after 15, unless he had the governors' permission to stay until sixteen. Greek ceased to be a prescribed subject, while German, history, and science were added. There was to be an entrance examination. Pitman was to retire on a pension, and future headmasters were not to have cure of souls.[19] Pitman's successor was the former assistant, Richard Boycott (1876–94), who improved the school, made games part of the curriculum, and attracted more pupils. External examinations were held from 1875. A new school hall was built in 1886, and between 1877 and 1890 a playing-field of 1½ a. was acquired. In 1890 there were 78 boys in 7 forms, and their work was said to be generally satisfactory.[20] A lecture room was built in 1905 and a woodwork shop in 1908. The school had a sports ground in Wolseley Road, Rugeley, by 1910. The improvements were not matched by an increase in numbers; in 1907 there were 70 boys, including 5 boarders.[21]

A Scheme of 1909 constituted the school a public secondary school, required the headmaster to be a graduate of a United Kingdom university, raised the leaving age to 18, and permitted the governors to start a preparatory department. That department existed by 1916.[22] By 1920 there were 120 boys, of whom only one was a boarder.[23] A sixth form had been established by 1926 and the school began to win university scholarships. In 1927 the playing-field was enlarged. In 1931, under a Scheme of 1930, the school was taken over by the county council and became a maintained secondary school; the endowment was to be applied to the upkeep of the buildings and providing grants and scholarships.[24] From that time numbers steadily increased to 317 in 1952. In 1932 three wooden classrooms were built, and in 1936 new buildings including a gymnasium, a hall, and laboratories were opened.[25] Girls were admitted in 1953.[26] From the late 1950s the school's intake was restricted apparently to Rugeley urban district. Examination results improved in the 1960s, but sport declined.[27] In 1968 the school was merged into the Fair Oak comprehensive school; a Scheme of 1972 permitted the grammar school's endowment, then almost entirely consisting of stock, to be used for the benefit of that school.[28]

KING EDWARD VI GRAMMAR SCHOOL, STAFFORD

THOMAS Counter (or Countre), rector of Ingestre (d. c. 1500), devised property at Haughton, Stafford, and Dunston in Penkridge worth £4 13s. 4d. a year

to maintain at the collegiate church of St. Mary, Stafford, a chantry priest who would also act as schoolmaster.[1] Leland was told that Counter and 'Sir Randol', a Stafford chantry priest, were the founders of the town's grammar school,[2] and in 1548 the chantry commissioners decided that Counter's foundation was a free grammar school. Counter may in fact simply have endowed an existing school attached to St. Mary's. Schoolmasters occur in Stafford in the late 14th century,[3] and in 1473 the bishop of Coventry and Lichfield was maintaining three boarders at a school in the town.[4]

In 1529 the school was housed in a building next to St. Mary's churchyard.[5] In 1548 the chantry commissioners ordered that it should be allowed to continue; the master was granted £4 5s. a year, the sum which, after the deduction of tithes, he had formerly received from Counter's bequest. He also received 2s. a year from a croft at Rickerscote in Castle Church and some money under the terms of the will, proved in 1547, of Robert Lees, a Stafford ironmonger.[6] The school-house was, however, part of the property seized by the Crown in 1548.

The burgesses petitioned Edward VI for an adequately endowed school, and in 1550 the king established 'the Free Grammar School of King Edward VI'. It was endowed with lands and tithes in and around Stafford worth £20 a year which had belonged to the prebend of Marston in the dissolved college of St. Mary and to the Stafford hospitals of St. John the Baptist and St. Leonard.[7] Control was vested in the burgesses. They were to appoint a master and an usher; they were empowered to make statutes regulating the management of the school whenever necessary, taking the advice of the bishop of Coventry and Lichfield; and they were licensed to acquire further property for the school to the value of £20 a year.[8] Shortly afterwards they converted the disused chapel of St. Bertelin at the west end of St. Mary's into a school-house. Henry, Lord Stafford, then claimed the property which had belonged to St. John's hospital, and after a lawsuit lasting several years gained various concessions from the burgesses, including the right to nominate the master and usher. In 1596 the burgesses bought the right of nomination from his son Edward, Lord Stafford. Later they made two other payments to extinguish the Stafford claims.

When Elizabeth I granted to the burgesses in 1571 what remained in royal hands of the property of the college of St. Mary she made them responsible for paying the master the £4 5s. a year assigned to him in 1548.[9] The first augmentation of the endowment came from Robert Sutton, rector of St. Mary's

[19] Staffs. Advertiser, 16 May, 26 Dec. 1874; Endowed Schs. Com. Scheme, 28 June 1875 (copy in Staffs. County Council Treasurer's Dept., Educ. Accountancy files).
[20] Rugeleian, 7th ser. i. 37–8.
[21] Rugeleian, 7th ser. i. 39; Kelly's Dir. Staffs. (1912).
[22] Bd. of Educ. Scheme, 13 July 1909 (copy in Staffs. C.C. Educ. Accountancy files); Char. Com. Scheme, 3 Oct. 1916 (copy ibid.).
[23] Rugeleian, 7th ser. i. 40; H. H. Hutchinson, 'R.G.S. 1920–52', Rugeleian, 7th ser. i. 42.
[24] Bd. of Educ. Scheme, 26 Nov. 1930 (copy in Staffs. C.C. Educ. Accountancy files).
[25] Rugeleian, 7th ser. i. 42; Staffs. Life, v (3), 12.
[26] A. J. Holt, 'My years at R.G.S.' Rugeleian, 7th ser. i. 43.
[27] T. B. Smart, 'Rugeley Grammar Sch. 1958–68', Rugeleian, 7th ser. i. 46; Staffs. C.C. Educ. Accountancy files.

[28] Express & Star, 23 July 1968; Dept. of Educ. and Science Scheme, 16 Feb. 1972; Staffs. C.C. Educ. Accountancy files.
[1] Unless otherwise stated, this article is based on J. S. Horne, Notes for a Hist. of K. Edw. VI Sch., Stafford (Stafford, 1930), and C. G. Gilmore, Hist. of K. Edw. VI Sch., Stafford.
[2] Leland, Itin. ed. Toulmin Smith, v. 18.   [3] See p. 260.
[4] W.S.L., S.MS. 335 (i), m. 20. The ref. given by Gilmore, K. Edw. VI Sch. plate facing p. 2, is incorrect.
[5] W.S.L., S.MS. 366 (iA), p. 6; W.S.L., H. M. Chetwynd 121, deed of 1609.
[6] S.H.C. 1926, 7.
[7] For those foundations see V.C.H. Staffs. iii.
[8] Bradley, Charters, 79–92, wrongly dating letters patent 1551.
[9] Ibid. 99–107.

(d. 1587), who devised property to provide, among other benefactions, four exhibitions of 26s. 8d. a year at the grammar school for poor boys from Stafford and Foregate Street and also payments to the master and for the repair of the school-house. Nothing was paid until 1599, when a commission of charitable uses decreed that annual payments of 30s. to the master and 46s. 8d. to the usher were to be made in addition to the four exhibitions, and that 30s. a year was to be reserved for repairs to the school-house and St. Mary's church.[10]

No early school statutes have survived. Later evidence reveals that only boys from the town itself were entitled to free schooling: John Dearle, master 1709–49, claimed that such had been the custom under previous masters and successfully maintained it against parents who alleged that boys who lived within three miles of the town shared the privilege. As for the curriculum, statutes of 1750 which laid down that the school was to be 'forever free for the teaching of the Latin, Greek, and Hebrew tongues, or any of them' probably reflected earlier practice and were possibly repeating a previous regulation. Five books delivered to Edward Greene, master in the 1560s, consisted of standard texts — Virgil, Horace's *Odes*, and a collection of Cicero's speeches — and two handbooks for teachers of the classics, Petrus Crinitus's *De honesta disciplina* and Andre Rodrigues's *Liber memorabilium exemplorum*.[11] A classical curriculum did not meet with everyone's approval: in the early 17th century some burgesses claimed, unsuccessfully, that the £4 5s. granted by Elizabeth I to 'a schoolmaster in Stafford' need not necessarily be paid to the master of the grammar school, and suggested that it should instead form the stipend of 'any schoolmaster whom they please, either who shall teach to write or cipher or cast accounts, so it be in Stafford'.[12]

In the 1550s and 1560s boys were going on to university,[13] and by c. 1600 the school was attracting boarders.[14] In the later 17th century it was patronized by some of the Staffordshire gentry, such as the Congreves of Stretton in Penkridge and the Mainwarings of Whitmore.[15] In the early 18th century Dearle was able to charge fees of between £1 and £4 a year for day-boys from around Stafford, and took boarders from other towns in the county and even from London and Doncaster. In 1753 his successor had 'as many boarders as his house will well contain'.[16] It was claimed in the early 18th century that the school's endowments were no longer adequate to support it, and there were disputes between the schoolmaster and the corporation over finance and management. The teachers' salaries, however, do not appear to have been unduly meagre. In 1722 the master was paid £57 2s 2d. and the usher £26 8s. 8d. by the corporation, besides what they received in fees from boarders and day-boys.

The bill of a boarder who was at the school in 1789 shows that by then visiting masters taught French, dancing, writing, and drawing and that there was a drill-sergeant in attendance. By the 1790s the school was also providing elementary and commercial education. In 1794 the usher taught writing, arithmetic, and accounts. A new usher, appointed in 1796, was permitted to teach writing and accounts and to charge a small fee for doing so. That was the type of education which most Stafford parents wanted for their children. In 1818 it was stated that although Lily's Latin Grammar and the Westminster Greek Grammar were still used at the school not a sixth of the boys ever asked to learn the classics, 'being principally destined for commerce and manufactures'. The school devoted itself chiefly to teaching English grammar, writing, and arithmetic, an arrangement made by the masters 'within the last twenty years' in an attempt to render the school useful to the poorer townspeople.[17] In the 1820s the master was teaching about 15 'classical' and about 15 'English' scholars and the usher taught about 70 boys English grammar, reading, writing, and accounts. All tuition was free for Stafford boys, and the only qualification for admission was the ability to read in the New Testament. Stafford retained 'but to an inconsiderable extent the character of a grammar school'.[18]

The man responsible for the changes was Joseph Shaw, master 1780–1825, who went to Stafford from the grammar school at Hawkshead (Lancs.). There he had taught William Wordsworth, who later praised him as an 'excellent master' and a fine teacher. At Stafford he involved himself in municipal politics, twice becoming mayor.[19] By taking note of what the townspeople required of the school he increased the number of pupils. In 1795 there were 59 Stafford boys receiving a free education and 19 fee-paying pupils;[20] in 1818 there were some 120 boys and, as has been seen, in the early 1820s about 100.[21]

In 1801 St. Bertelin's chapel was demolished and the school found temporary accommodation in the chapel of Noell's alms-houses in Mill Street. Later that year it moved to a newly built school-house in Gaol Square, which according to one critic was 'ill adapted both in point of situation and structure to the purposes of a school'.[22] In 1813 the building was taken down and re-erected at the Gaol Square entrance to North Walls.

George Norman, master 1826–60, reacted strongly against Shaw's policy of giving the townspeople what they wanted. Shaw had provided a free 'English' education for 85 boys at a time and was in the habit of asking tradesmen whether they knew of any children who wished to go to the school.[23] Norman and his usher, Joseph Smith (1826–45),[24] maintained that they were there merely to teach the classics. The number of pupils fell. In 1835 a Chancery Scheme, remarking that there were 20

---

[10] C 93/1/16.
[11] W.S.L., S.MS. 366 (iB), loose page headed 'Books delivered to Mr. Greene the schoolmaster of Stafford'.
[12] S.R.O., D.(W.) 1721/1/4, p. 145.
[13] *Admissions to Gonville and Caius Coll., Cambridge, Mar. 1558/9 to Jan. 1678/9*, ed. J. and S. C. Venn, 4, 10.
[14] S.R.O., D.(W.) 1721/1/4, p. 146.
[15] *Admissions to St. John's Coll., Cambridge*, i (ed. J. E. B. Mayor), 135; ii (ed. Mayor), 150.
[16] W.S.L., S.1549(2), *sub* Stafford, unident. newspaper cutting dated 22 Dec. 1753.

[17] N. Carlisle, *Endowed Grammar Schs. in Eng. and Wales*, ii. 493.
[18] *11th Rep. Com. Char.* H.C. 433, p. 584 (1824), xiv.
[19] Bradley, *Charters*, 207.
[20] W.S.L. 7/65/00.
[21] Carlisle, *Endowed Grammar Schs.* ii. 493; *11th Rep. Com. Char.* 584.
[22] Keen, *Letter to Inhabitants of Stafford*, 27 n.
[23] *Staffs. Advertiser*, 11 Mar. 1843.
[24] For the date of Smith's appointment see S.R.O., D. 1323/A/1/4, p. 112.

boys or fewer at the school and that there was little demand for the classics among Stafford parents, sanctioned the appointment of an 'English' master, who was to be chosen by the mayor, the rector of St. Mary's, and the master of the grammar school. He was to teach reading, writing, arithmetic, geography, history, and the elements of mathematics, and was to be paid £100 a year out of the income of the Queen Elizabeth Grant property. In 1836 the school, with other corporation charities, was placed in the hands of trustees appointed by the Lord Chancellor. In 1840 an English master was appointed, and it was agreed that he should share the grammar-school building with Norman and Smith. He was allowed to charge the pupils fees. In 1843 he was unexpectedly ejected by Norman, a move which provoked great resentment in the town. A public meeting was told that Norman and Smith, who between them received some £300 a year, had only 4 pupils. Norman retorted that it was to the townsmen's discredit that so few of them sent their sons to the school for a free classical education.[25] Later in the year the trustees revised the school statutes, but there was little improvement. Although it was agreed that an English master, to be paid £100 a year from the Queen Elizabeth Grant property and from capitation fees, should be added to the staff, the classics remained the backbone of the curriculum. Latin was compulsory for boys aged over ten, Greek for boys aged over fourteen. Boys living in the ancient borough were to be admitted free. The masters were allowed to take boarders. In the appointment of masters preference was to be given to clergymen over laymen if candidates were of equal merit. By a Scheme of 1858 the school was reorganized as an explicitly Anglican establishment; there were to be 17 Anglican trustees and the master and usher were to be Anglicans, though not necessarily clergymen. The curriculum was to include French and commercial subjects. Entrants to the school had to be at least seven years of age, able to read and write English, and free from infectious diseases. All boys had to pay fees of up to £6 a year. The Scheme aroused strong opposition among Stafford nonconformists, and in 1859 there was a public inquiry into the management of the school. The trustees' right to emphasize the school's Anglican character was vindicated, but the inspector who held the inquiry concluded that, were it not for the English school, the grammar school would scarcely exist and that the English school itself was no better than a good National school and much more expensive.

In 1860 Norman was finally forced to retire, and the trustees attempted to revive the school. In 1862 it was moved from its cramped premises in Gaol Square to a building in Newport Road, designed in a 'modified Gothic' style by Henry Ward of Stafford. There were two large schoolrooms, with accommodation for 104 boys; an adjoining house for the headmaster contained some classrooms and several bedrooms or dormitories for boarders.[26] In 1865 the school consisted of classical and commercial departments. Instruction in the classics was still the school's ultimate purpose; although Latin was not generally taught in the commercial department an exception was made for 'promising' boys who were likely to be

transferred to the classical department. The older boys in the classical department were taught Greek. The headmaster taught chemistry and geology as extras, out of school hours. The boys, 37 in the classical department and 35 in the commercial, were 'rather a dull lot, carefully taught'. Few of them were the sons of professional men; the school had, however, recently provided some working-class boys with a good education. In 1867 there were 63 dayboys and 7 boarders.[27]

A Scheme of 1873 vested control in a board of governors, including representatives of local authorities. The bishop of Lichfield's powers as visitor reverted to the Crown. The endowments of various Stafford charities were appropriated to the use of the school. It was reorganized as a two-stream day school. In the Commercial School (ages 8–14) Latin was a voluntary subject, but it remained compulsory in the High School (ages 10–16). All boys took history, geography, and natural science. Greek became an extra. All boys had to pay fees, but some scholarships were available.

Since fees formed an essential part of the school's income it was imperative to keep the number of pupils high. In 1876, however, there were only 35, and although there were 70 in 1881 the number had fallen by 1884 to 38. For lack of money teachers had to be dismissed and improvements to the buildings postponed. Nevertheless scholastic standards were improving. There were further improvements under A. E. Layng, the school's first lay headmaster (1884–1901). He promoted the study of modern languages, science, and mathematics, had extra classrooms built, and persuaded the governors to provide a laboratory. From the 1890s the school was able to use Stafford Technical College for science, art, and handicraft lessons. In his last years as headmaster Layng became a savage disciplinarian, and parents were reluctant to send their boys to the school.

The school recovered under E. O. Powell (1901–24). In 1903 it began to receive government grants, and at about the same time the borough and county councils began to make annual grants in return for free scholarship places for boys from local schools. In 1904 a first floor was built over the main schoolroom and 3 classrooms were added. In 1909 the two-stream division was abolished. The school was beginning to be affected not only by the influx of boys sent on local-authority scholarships but also by the rapid growth of the town; by 1911 there were 124 pupils and the school buildings were already regarded as cramped. The First World War brought a further increase in the number of pupils; in 1918–19 there were 183 boys. It also brought a considerable increase in costs, and in 1918 the governors decided that the school could no longer afford to remain independent. It was handed over to the county council in 1920 and became a maintained grammar school for boys. In 1928 a new wing was opened; it contained 9 classrooms, 3 laboratories, handicraft and art rooms, a dining-room, and an octagonal Speech Hall. By 1939 there were 336 pupils. There were about 500 in the early 1950s and some 600 in 1966.[28]

In 1976 the grammar school was absorbed into a co-educational comprehensive school, King Edward

25 S.R.O., D. 892/1, pp. 12–13, 18–19, 29–30; *Staffs. Advertiser*, 25 Feb., 11 and 25 Mar. 1843; below, pp. 272–3.
26 *Staffs. Advertiser*, 10 May 1862.
27 *Schs. Inquiry Com. vol. xv* [3966–XIV], pp. 451–3, H.C. (1867–8), xxviii (12).
28 Ex inf. Staffs. County Council Educ. Dept. (1966).

VI high school, which was opened in West Way in the buildings formerly occupied by Stafford Girls' High School. The grammar-school buildings in Newport Road became Chetwynd middle school.[29]

ALLEYNE'S GRAMMAR SCHOOL, STONE

THOMAS Alleyne (d. 1558), rector of Stevenage (Herts.), devised property in Hertfordshire, Kent, Leicestershire, London, and Staffordshire to Trinity College, Cambridge, largely to endow free grammar schools at Stone, Uttoxeter, and Stevenage.[1] The master of each school was to be paid £13 6s. 8d. a year. The rules which Alleyne drew up for the conduct of the schools stipulated that each was to educate without charge children who lived 'within two or three miles' and had a firm grounding in grammar. The masters were permitted to receive as fee-paying pupils children who lived further away. School hours were to be from 6 a.m. (7 a.m. from Michaelmas to Lady day) to 11 a.m. and from 1 to 5 p.m. The children were to be allowed one free afternoon a week and there was to be a week's holiday at Whitsun and about ten days at Easter. All pupils were to talk to each other solely in Latin, not only in school but also in the streets and at play.

Alleyne had apparently been supporting a schoolmaster at Stone during his own lifetime, and within a few months of Alleyne's death Trinity College appointed a new master. In 1567 it was claimed that there were 80 pupils at the school, but otherwise little is known of it or its masters in the 16th century. It declined under a Mr. Rose and his successor John Faldoe (1614–29). There was then a year's vacancy. Thomas Berry, appointed in 1630, was allowed the master's salary for 1629–30 to repair the schoolhouse, decayed because of Faldoe's negligence. In 1649 Thomas Chaloner, who had been ejected from the headmastership of Shrewsbury School in 1645, became master.[2] Within a month he had increased the number of pupils at Stone from 37 to 60, and by June 1650, shortly before he left, there were 154. His reputation led parents to send their boys to Stone, and when he left he probably took most of the pupils with him.

During the first two centuries of its existence the school occupied part of the buildings of the dissolved Stone priory. In 1749 the priory church, which had served since the Dissolution as Stone parish church, began to collapse. Plans were made to rebuild the church on a new site and a new home had to be found for the school; in 1758 the trustees appointed to manage the building of a new church decided to put up a new school-house as well. Trinity was apparently not consulted. The new building stood next to the churchyard; each of its two storeys contained one room, the lower being occupied by the school and the upper being used by the parish. At intervals since the late 17th century the parish had contributed towards the repair of the former school-house, and it seems gradually to have assumed full responsibility for repairs to the new building.

From c. 1790 the masters, while continuing to draw the stipend allotted to them under Alleyne's will, began to let the school to teachers who supported themselves by taking fee-paying pupils.[3] By the early 19th century the classics had been abandoned and only the elements were taught. When the senior bursar of Trinity visited Stone in 1824 he discovered that nobody in the town remembered a grammar school there; in 1841 the rector of Stone described the school as nothing more than 'a dame's school, if I may use the term, as it is kept by a man'.

In the early 1840s Trinity set about reviving the school. It had already received counsel's opinion that it was bound by Alleyne's will to provide and maintain a school building as well as to pay the master's salary. Since the ownership of the existing building was divided between the college and the parish, the college owning the lower storey and the parish the upper, it was decided to move the school to a new site. Land was bought in what later became Station Road, and a new building, named Cambridge House, was opened there in 1844.

The first master at Cambridge House was Charles Boreham, who owned a private school in the town. He was appointed in 1843 and apparently took his first grammar-school pupils in temporary premises that year. He advertised in the county newspaper that he would not only be in charge of the new school but would also continue to run his private school. The local clergy protested to Trinity. Boreham thereupon abandoned the idea of running two schools simultaneously and concentrated upon the grammar school. In return the college raised his salary to £100, emphasizing that the augmentation would continue only so long as his management of the school was satisfactory. Boreham was permitted to offer both commercial and classical courses, but it seems that the elements and religious knowledge were the only subjects which he offered and that Latin was not in fact taught. Regulations drawn up in 1843 limited the number of boys to 30, six of whom were to be taught free except for the cost of books. Admission was restricted to boys whose parents or guardians lived in Stone parish. The Anglican character of the school was emphasized in the regulations and was maintained despite protests from Stone nonconformists.

The number of pupils during Boreham's mastership (1843–58) never reached the 30 allowed by the regulations: the highest number on the books at any time was 27 and the average attendance throughout his mastership was 19 boys. During the later years of the mastership there were complaints about Boreham's shortcomings as a teacher and accusations that he neglected the school for farming. In 1858, when there were only 11 pupils, Boreham was persuaded to resign and George Wade was appointed. Under Wade (1858–84) the standard of teaching improved, the curriculum was broadened to include history, geography, French, and Latin, and a master's house was built with accommodation for 10 or 12 boarders. In 1865 Wade had over 30 boys, including a few boarders.[4] Only boarders attempted French or Latin. The day-boys, who generally came to the school at the age of 12 from the local National school and stayed only a year or two, wanted merely

[29] Ex inf. Educ. Dept. (1977).

[1] Unless otherwise stated, this article is based upon N. A. Cope, *Alleyne's Grammar Sch., Stone, Staffs. 1558–1958* (n.d. [1958]). For the Uttoxeter school see below. For the Stevenage school see *V.C.H. Herts.* ii. 69–71.

[2] For Chaloner see also *V.C.H. Salop.* ii. 145, 150, 155.

[3] F. G. Gomez, 'Endowed Schs. of Staffs. in the 18th cent.' (Leeds Univ. M.Phil. thesis, 1977), 230.

[4] For this, and the rest of the para., see *Schs. Inquiry Com. vol. xv* [3966–XIV], pp. 457–61, H.C. (1867–8), xxviii (12).

a commercial education. In 1858 the number of free places had been increased to eight. In 1865 the school was up to the standard of a good National school, 'with an upper class . . . superior to any that would be found in an ordinary National school'.

A Scheme of 1886 ordered Trinity to give £3,000 for the purchase of a new site for the school and the provision of new buildings and to increase its annual payment to £400. A board of governors was established, including nominees of the college and of the Stone school board. The reorganized school was intended primarily as a day-school for the Stone area, but there were also plans for it to take some boarders. A widely based curriculum was laid down, and the governors were instructed to provide a leaving exhibition tenable at a university or other place of advanced education.

Alleyne's entered new premises at Oulton Cross, just outside Stone, in 1889; the buildings, which included a master's house, were designed by W. Hawley Lloyd of Birmingham. The number of pupils remained low; it was not until the mid 1890s that there were more than 50 boys. Under the headmastership of W. J. Harding (1894–1913) a library was built up and greater emphasis was laid on the value of physical training: school sports were instituted and a gymnasium and a tennis-court were built. By 1909 there were over 70 boys, including 13 boarders, and the school had both preparatory and secondary departments. In 1907 Alleyne's began to receive a government grant, and in 1909 the governing body was reconstituted to include representatives of the county council and of Stone urban and rural district councils. The number of pupils declined after 1910 but grants from government and from the county council enabled the school to continue.

Under H. M. Fraser (1916–36) Alleyne's began to grow again; by 1920, when it became a maintained school under the control of the county council, there were 100 boys. By the time Fraser retired it had become a secondary day-school: the preparatory department closed in 1925 and the school ceased to take boarders in 1934.

In 1936 the county council decided to convert Alleyne's into a co-educational grammar school, the first of its type in the administrative county. The building and reconstruction necessary before girls could be admitted had not been completed by the outbreak of the Second World War, and the first girls did not enter the school until 1944. In 1969 the school was merged with Granville secondary modern school, Stone, to form the comprehensive Alleyne's School.[5]

QUEEN ELIZABETH'S GRAMMAR SCHOOL, TAMWORTH

IN 1384 a lane in Tamworth leading from Gungate to the churchyard of the collegiate church of St.

Edith was known as Schoolmaster's Lane,[1] but nothing is known of the school. It may have been connected with St. Edith's. There is, however, no evidence that the church supported a school in the Middle Ages, and it is probable that a permanent grammar school was not established in the town until the 1530s, when one was endowed by John Bailey of Syerscote in Tamworth. Under a royal licence of 1536 Bailey's executors founded a chantry in St. Edith's and endowed it with property in and around Tamworth worth some £5 10s. a year; the chaplaincy was used to augment the stipend of one of the clergy at the church, the St. George, or morrow-mass, priest. In accordance with Bailey's wishes the priest was to keep a free grammar school at Tamworth. In 1526 Bailey and his brother Robert, of London, had endowed a close fellowship at St. John's College, Cambridge, stipulating that preference in elections was to be given to Tamworth men;[2] the grammar school was presumably intended to provide a regular flow of suitable candidates.

The school had been opened by the time Leland visited Tamworth in the earlier 1540s.[3] It survived the dissolution of the college of St. Edith in 1548. The master, Richard Broke, was confirmed in office by the chantry commissioners and was granted a stipend of £10 13s. 2½d., the amount which he had been paid as schoolmaster and St. George priest before the dissolution. When Edmund Downing and Peter Ashton were granted the college property in 1581 the rent-charges which they were obliged to pay included that stipend.[4] The pre-Dissolution school-house was, however, lost. In 1548 the St. George priest had a house in which he lived and taught school; by 1550, when the house was sold by the Crown, it was in the hands of a tenant.[5] In the 1590s the school was held in a house in Lower Gungate which the corporation rented from Sir John Bowes of Elford; in 1594 Sir John granted the house to the town for the school's use.[6]

In 1588 Elizabeth I made Tamworth corporation the governors of the school, which was named 'the Free Grammar School of Elizabeth, Queen of England, in Tamworth'. There was to be one master, appointed by the corporation; for his stipend the corporation was allotted the rent-charge of £10 13s. 2½d. In 1664 Charles II confirmed his predecessor's grant and gave the corporation the further privilege of drawing up, with the consent of the high steward of the borough, statutes for the school. The corporation was at the same time confirmed in its tenure of the school-house in Lower Gungate.[7]

Little is known of the school, apart from the names of various masters,[8] until the mastership of George Antrobus (1659–1708). Antrobus was an able teacher and the school flourished.[9] He found it necessary to employ assistants. In the 1690s he had an usher and an under-usher.[10] The Revd. William Paul, a Jacobite who was executed in 1716 for taking

[5] Express & Star, 11 July 1969, 3 Oct. 1970.
[1] H. Wood, Boro. by Prescription: a Hist. of the Municipality of Tamworth (Tamworth, 1958), 82.
[2] V.C.H. Staffs. iii. 314; T. Baker, Hist. of St. John's Coll., Cambridge, ed. J. E. B. Mayor, i. 370; R. F. Scott, 'Notes from the Coll. Records', The Eagle, no. 119 (1899); archives of St. John's Coll., Cambridge, 58.33 and 58.34.
[3] Leland, Itin. ed. Toulmin Smith, ii. 104.
[4] C. F. R. Palmer, Hist. and Antiquities of Collegiate Church of Tamworth (Tamworth, 1871), 49, 53–6.

[5] Ibid. 31, 53.
[6] C. F. R. Palmer, Hist. of Town and Castle of Tamworth (Tamworth, 1845), 426.
[7] Ibid. 426–7.
[8] For some early masters see ibid. 427. Sam. Shaw (d. 1696), nonconformist divine, was master 1656–7: D.N.B.; L. Fox, A Country Grammar Sch.: a Hist. of Ashby-de-la-Zouch Grammar Sch. 51–7.
[9] Palmer, Town and Castle of Tamworth, 427–31; Wood, Boro. by Prescription, 128.
[10] L.J.R.O., B/V/10, notitia cleri c. 1693.

part in the 1715 rising, had apparently been usher some time between 1701 and 1709.[11] Antrobus's reputation attracted boarders to Tamworth; they included William Whiston, writer and defender of Arianism, who stated in later life that Antrobus had been an excellent teacher.[12] The 15-year-old Viscount Hastings, son of Theophilus, earl of Huntingdon, was a boarder for a short while before going up to Oxford in 1693. A report sent to his father in 1692 gives some idea of the management of the school. Hours were from 7 a.m. to 11 a.m. and from 1 p.m. to 5 p.m., except on Thursdays, when school finished at 3 p.m., and Saturdays, when there was no afternoon school. Whenever holidays were granted they were taken on Tuesdays. A few books only were read at a time: Lord Hastings's form was reading Juvenal and the Greek Testament, and 'they say parts in the Grammar'. There was also a 'small system of rhetoric', and for homework the boys did themes or Latin or English verse.[13]

The school maintained its high reputation under Antrobus's successor, Samuel Shaw, M.D. (1708–30).[14] After having published in 1692 a *Disputatio de utero* Shaw turned his attention from medicine to the classics. He published three text-books: *A Short and Plain Syntax for the Instruction of Children* (1725, with a second edition in 1727), *A Grammatical Dictionary* (1726), and *A New Grammar Composed out of the Classic Writers* (1730).[15] He had a low opinion of Lily's Latin Grammar, still the authorized school text-book, and was probably influenced in that by his acquaintance the grammarian Richard Johnson (d. 1721), headmaster of the free school at Nottingham 1707–18.[16] Although it was William Willymott's *Peculiar Use and Signification of Certain Words in the Latin Tongue* (1704) that Shaw considered 'the most useful school book that ever was published', he also remarked that 'every schoolboy', by which he presumably meant every Tamworth schoolboy in his care, had a copy of Johnson's *Noctes Nottinghamicae: or Cursory Objections against the Syntax of the Common Grammar* (1714). He was one of those who believed that children should learn Latin from text-books which gave the rules in English and was intolerant of lexicographers and grammarians who, instead of collecting their material 'out of the classics', merely parroted the work of their predecessors.[17] Fundamentally he was, however, a traditionalist: he regarded the classics as the backbone of the curriculum and did not question the supremacy customarily accorded to grammar in teaching them.

The success of the school under Antrobus and Shaw is reflected in the number of benefactions which it received and by the fact that it proved

necessary to extend the school-house. Sir Francis Nethersole (d. 1659) of Polesworth (Warws.) bequeathed a £5 rent-charge to the master on condition that up to six children at a time from Polesworth and from Warton in Polesworth should be taught Latin and Greek at the school without charge. William Ashley of 'Spinkefield' (probably Springfield) in Essex, a native of Tamworth, bequeathed to the schoolmaster a rent-charge of £10 a year from property in Essex by will dated 1666. Other bequests included that of the Revd. John Rawlet (d. 1686) of Newcastle-upon-Tyne, also a native of Tamworth, who bequeathed a rent-charge of £2 a year to the master and left his library of 934 books to the school 'for the use of succeeding schoolmasters and such students of the town as shall need them'. The books were placed in Guy's alms-houses in Tamworth.[18] Samuel Frankland (d. 1691), another native of Tamworth, master of the grammar school at Lichfield and later of that at Coventry, established a scholarship worth £10 a year at St. Catharine Hall (later St. Catharine's College), Cambridge, for a boy from Tamworth School.[19] In 1674, at Antrobus's request, the corporation agreed to the addition of a further bay to the school-house, 'the same being now too strait'.[20] In 1677 Antrobus opened a fund for building a new schoolroom. Almost £159 was contributed in sums of 10s. and upwards, many gave less than 10s., and some people living in and around Tamworth helped by working on the building or by lending their teams to haul building material. The new schoolroom, which was of brick with stone dressings and adjoined the master's house, was opened in 1678. Samuel Shaw undertook repairs and improvements.[21]

Little is known of the school's affairs under Thomas Ebdall (1730–3), William Sawrey (1733–41), and John Princep or Prinsep (1741–52).[22] It prospered under Simon Collins (1752–93), who took boarders and taught the classics to a large number of day-boys from Tamworth; his pupils apparently included Sir William Parker (1781–1866), admiral of the fleet.[23] John Oldershaw (1793–1805) seems to have been a satisfactory master, but a rapid decline set in under C. E. Collins (1805–13), Simon Collins's son. The number of pupils dropped, and finally the mastership became a sinecure. After Collins's resignation early in 1813 the school was closed for six months.

When Samuel Downes was appointed later in 1813 an attempt was made to ensure that the master could no longer neglect the school with impunity. Previous masters had been appointed for life. Downes could be dismissed on six months' notice. He was told to teach the elements and English grammar and was

[11] *D.N.B.*
[12] Ibid.; Whiston, *Memoirs* (1749), 17, 19.
[13] Hist. MSS. Com. 78, *Hastings*, ii, p. 225; *Complete Peerage*, vi. 660.
[14] Palmer, *Town and Castle of Tamworth*, 431–2.
[15] The 1st edn. of the *Short and Plain Syntax* was advertised as 'lately published' in the *Daily Courant*, 25 Nov. 1725. Copies of the 2nd edn. and of the other books cited are in B.L.
[16] *D.N.B. sub* Ric. Johnson; Shaw, preface to 2nd edn. of *Short and Plain Syntax*; F. Watson, *Eng. Grammar Schs. to 1660*, 280.
[17] Shaw, *Short and Plain Syntax* (2nd edn.), preface and pp. 3, 10.
[18] *12th Rep. Com. Char.* H.C. 348, pp. 543–4, 554 (1825), x; Palmer, *Town and Castle of Tamworth*, 466–9; Wood,

Boro. by Prescription, 92–3; *Index to P.C.C. Wills*, xi (Index Libr. lxxvii), 229; *Tamworth Chars.* H.C. 299, pp. 205, 207 (1867), liv. For other bequests to the school see *12th Rep. Com. Char.* 544, 547, 552–3. For Sir Fra. Nethersole and the primary school which he founded at Polesworth see *D.N.B.*; *V.C.H. Warws.* ii. 176, 369; iv. 187.
[19] Palmer, *Town and Castle of Tamworth*, 430–1; *V.C.H. Warws.* ii. 327.
[20] Wood, *Boro. by Prescription*, 129.
[21] Palmer, *Town and Castle of Tamworth*, 428–30, 432; *Tamworth Chars.* 193; see plate facing p. 145 above.
[22] For the next 2 paras. see, unless otherwise stated, Palmer, *Town and Castle of Tamworth*, 432–4, 436–8; *12th Rep. Com. Char.* 544.
[23] Stated in 1867 to be an alumnus: *Staffs. Advertiser*, 10 Aug. 1867. For him see *D.N.B.*

empowered to charge pupils 4 guineas a year for that. In 1814 the school buildings were repaired by the corporation, part of the money being raised by public subscription. Downes gathered some 12 pupils, including 3 or 4 boarders. He later ceased to take boarders and apparently lost interest in the school. In 1823 it was at 'a very low ebb'. There were only 4 boys. Downes taught them Latin from 10 a.m. until noon, and they went to other schools in the afternoons. The elements were apparently not taught; in 1820 Sir Robert Peel, father of the statesman, had established a free school for 100 poor boys in the town where such instruction could be had. Without boarders or private pupils the grammar school was moribund. Its income, about £34, was insufficient to maintain it. Again it became deserted; Downes lived on in a dilapidated building with no pupils. In September 1826 the corporation at last expressed its disapproval, and soon afterwards Downes resigned.

After the appointment of T. P. Lammin as master in 1827 the schoolroom and the master's house were repaired by public subscription. Lammin succeeded in reviving the school, and in 1834 the trustees of Rawlet's charity increased their annual payment to the master from £2 to £6. In 1835 there were 43 boys, about half of them boarders and 'half-day scholars'. Thereafter the school declined because of Lammin's ill-health. He died in 1837.[24]

In 1837 Chancery took the school and other municipal charities out of the hands of Tamworth corporation and gave control to trustees who later that year appointed Henry Handley master. Handley had been usher at the grammar school at Chipping Norton (Oxon.) and had kept private schools in Gloucestershire. At Tamworth he inherited 14 day-boys; by 1838 he also had 4 boarders, and in the early 1840s there were 28 day-boys and a few boarders, never more than eight. Handley later claimed that his efforts had been hampered by the bad feeling aroused in the town when the charities were taken out of the corporation's hands and by the struggle between the Peels and the marquesses Townshend for political control of Tamworth: parents, he said, had been persuaded not to send their boys to the school and townspeople had refused to contribute towards the maintenance of its buildings. The school also suffered when Sir Robert Peel's School was improved c. 1850 and 'a higher class of instruction . . . suitable for the middle class' was introduced there. Of Handley's 20 middle-class boys 16 immediately left for Peel's School. Only 8 pupils remained; later there were twelve. In 1862 an inspector from the Charity Commission found little more than a dame school: it contained 'eight small children of the poorer classes' who were taught the elements. Since 1837 the capitation fee had been reduced in stages from 4 guineas a year to 3d. a week. The schoolroom was 'lofty and well suited to its purpose' but very damp; the master's house was ruinous. Handley had entirely lost the confidence of the townspeople. The trustees were reluctant to

dismiss him since he was old and without his salary would be a pauper.[25] In 1863 he was pensioned off,[26] and the school temporarily lapsed.

Later in 1863 the school was handed over to a separate body of governors which included the mayor and the vicar of Tamworth ex officio. They immediately set about re-establishing the school on a new site. Money was to be raised by selling the buildings in Lower Gungate, by assigning money from other Tamworth charities to the school, and by public subscription. The old school buildings were sold in 1864. Rawlet's charity increased its annual grant to the master to £10 and provided £200 towards re-building the school. Port's charity, a Tamworth apprenticing charity, gave £2,000 towards the re-building.[27] In 1865 the school governors chose a site on the Ashby road for the school and appointed a master, J. W. Davis.[28]

In 1866 a Scheme for the school was published. Boys from Tamworth were to pay capitation fees of £8; the headmaster, who was to be in holy orders and a graduate of Oxford or Cambridge, was to be allowed to take boarders, and the curriculum, which included Latin and Greek, was designed to qualify boys for university entrance or for commercial life.[29] The proposals aroused considerable opposition in Tamworth. Opponents claimed that the distance of the site, ½ mile from the town, and the high capitation fees would exclude from the school the poor boys for whom it had been founded. The Marquess Townshend supported the trustees; Sir Robert Peel, 3rd bt., one of the M.P.s for the borough, led a vigorous but unsuccessful attack on them and raised the matter in Parliament.[30]

Meanwhile a house in the town had been rented, and in 1866 Davis began work there.[31] In 1867-8 the new school, designed in a Gothic style by Nicholas Joyce of Stafford, was built on the Ashby road site. It consisted of a single range of building; a master's house with accommodation for 26 boarders stood in the centre, flanked on one side by servants' quarters and domestic offices and on the other by a large schoolroom sufficient for 80 pupils.[32] A Scheme of 1868 set up a new body of governors, two of whom were to be appointed by the town council. The headmaster, who was to be a graduate of an English university or of Trinity College, Dublin, and an Anglican, was empowered to employ assistant masters, and he and the assistants were allowed to take boarders. Capitation fees were retained, £8 for day-boys from Tamworth, £12 for day-boys from elsewhere. Free schooling was to be provided for six foundation scholars and six Port's Scholars, all chosen by competitive examination. The curriculum was to consist of Latin, Greek, French, mathematics, algebra, arithmetic, book-keeping, English grammar, history, geography, and writing; German, natural sciences, drawing, and music were to be offered as extras. Parents or guardians were to have the right to insist that their boys should specialize in one or more subjects.[33]

It appears that in practice the curriculum was

[24] Palmer, *Town and Castle of Tamworth*, 434–5; *Tamworth Chars.* 109, 193.
[25] *Tamworth Chars.* 6, 192–4, 216.
[26] Ibid. 23–9.
[27] Ibid. 18–23, 29–37, 117, 122–35.
[28] Ibid. 38.
[29] Ibid. 47.
[30] Ibid. 52 sqq.; H. C. Mitchell, *Chapter in Hist. of*

Tamworth Grammar Sch. (Tamworth, 1940; copy in Tamworth Public Libr.).
[31] *Tamworth Chars.* 42; *Crockford* (1895), 350.
[32] *Tamworth Chars.* 48; Mitchell, *Chapter*, 18–23, 26; *Staffs. Advertiser*, 10 Aug. 1867; *Tamworth Official Guide* [c. 1962], 26.
[33] *Schs. Inquiry Com. vol. xv* [3966–XIV], p. 463, H.C. (1867–8), xxviii (12).

much narrower than planned. About 1880, towards the end of Davis's headmastership, the principal subjects were Latin, Divinity, and English grammar, with Greek as an extra. There was one assistant master, who taught history and geography. Science was apparently not taught, although Davis's publications included *Simple Chemistry* and *Mechanics of Agriculture* as well as books of Latin and Greek exercises. There was little money, and Davis supplemented a meagre salary by taking boarders, doing some farming, and occasionally taking services in neighbouring churches.[34] In the 1890s the county council began to help the school by making grants towards the cost of teaching chemistry and drawing,[35] but until the appointment of T. J. Barford as headmaster in 1900 the curriculum apparently remained on the whole old-fashioned and the school seems to have stagnated; there were only 21 boys when Barford came.[36]

Barford modernized the curriculum, and in 1903 there were 60 boys. In 1904 a laboratory and a lecture theatre were added to the buildings. By 1906 the school was receiving grants from government and from two county councils but was still in financial difficulties; in 1910 the governors transferred it to Staffordshire county council, and it became a maintained secondary school. The county council added a gymnasium and an art room. In 1912 there were 89 boys.[37]

By 1936 there were over 160 boys, and in 1937 extensions to the school were officially opened on the site of the headmaster's house of 1867–8. The extensions, which included an assembly-room fitted up as a gymnasium, a handicraft room, an art room, and two classrooms, made it possible for the 1910 gymnasium to be converted into a library and for other rooms to become a school dining-room and kitchen. The lecture theatre and laboratories were modernized.[38]

In 1960 the grammar school was merged with Tamworth Girls' High School to form a mixed grammar school in Ashby Road. In 1977 there were 518 pupils.[39]

TETTENHALL COLLEGE

IN 1862 a group of bankers and businessmen, members of Queen Street Congregational chapel in Wolverhampton, decided to establish a Free Church boys' boarding-school in the area.[1] Prominent nonconformists from other counties became involved in the scheme, and a joint-stock company, the Midland Counties Proprietary School Co. Ltd., was established in 1863. The company bought the Hall, Tettenhall, and 6½ a. adjoining, appointed Robert Halley, the principal of an Indian mission college, as headmaster, and opened the school in August 1863 as Tettenhall Proprietary School. The curriculum included 'all the usual branches of an English and classical education', French, elementary drawing and singing, scripture, and 'the elements of natural, moral, and social science'. German, chemistry, instrumental music, and more advanced drawing were optional extras. The directors also promised to promote the health and happiness, moral and religious welfare, and manners and deportment of the pupils, each of whom was to have a separate bed in the dormitory. The academic year was divided into two twenty-week terms beginning on 1 August and 1 February. The fees were 40 guineas a year for boys entering under 14 years of age and 50 guineas for those entering over fourteen. There were reductions for weekly boarders and for second and later pupils from a single family, and a few scholarships for nonconformist ministers' sons were promised.

From the first the school suffered financial difficulties. A share capital of £20,000 was planned, but by 1865 only £12,300 had been subscribed. Moreover the response to the initial advertisement was disappointing; in the first year there were only 17 pupils. The number had risen to 38 by 1865; though insufficient to cover current costs, it obliged the directors to go ahead with new building. By 1864 a gymnasium and play-shed had been built; the main school building, designed in a Gothic style by George Bidlake of Wolverhampton, was completed in 1867; the Hall became the headmaster's house. The expense of building necessitated economies in salaries, while from 1869 day-boys and also day-boarders, who stayed to tea and evening preparation, were admitted in order to increase receipts. Numbers, however, remained few; the blame was attributed to Halley, whose poor discipline impressed parents unfavourably, and he resigned late in 1869. Nevertheless the standard of teaching in his time was high. Although opposed to a purely utilitarian education, he favoured mathematics and science. One of the school's earliest pupils was R. F. Horton (1855–1934), Congregational divine and first nonconformist president of the Oxford Union.[2]

In 1869 the name of the school was changed to Tettenhall College and the number of terms increased to three. Under the new headmaster, A. W. Young (1870–91), the school's academic reputation was high, the number of pupils rose, reaching 108 in 1877, and the financial situation improved. In 1881 Tettenhall was the only school from which more than one boy obtained five distinctions in the Cambridge local examination; one was Arthur (later Sir Arthur) Harden (1865–1940), the chemist.[3] Young expanded the teaching of science, and in 1886 a chemistry laboratory and lecture room was built. Games were encouraged; a swimming-bath and a covered play-room were built in 1876. From 1877, however, trade depression in the West Midlands reduced admissions, while in Young's later years the

[34] Mitchell, *Chapter*, 23, 25; R. Simms, *Bibliotheca Staffordiensis* (Lichfield, 1894), 134–5. Mitchell's recollections were faulty: e.g. Davis was a Cambridge man.
[35] S.R.O., CC/B/16/2, pp. 106, 226; /3, pp. 86, 260, 362; /4, pp. 49, 234.
[36] Tamworth Grammar Sch. appeal booklet, 1903 (copy in Tamworth Public Libr.).
[37] Ibid.; H. C. Mitchell, *Tamworth, Tower and Town* (Tamworth, 1936), 119; *Tamworth Grammar Sch. Yearbk. 1906*, 15 (copy in Tamworth Public Libr.); G. Balfour, *Ten Years of Staffs. Educ. 1903–13* (Staffs. County

Council, 1913), 26.
[38] Mitchell, *Tamworth*, 119; *Staffs. Advertiser*, 6 Feb. 1937.
[39] *Tamworth Official Guide* [c. 1962], 26; ex inf. Staffs. County Council Educ. Dept. (1977).
[1] Unless otherwise stated, this article is based on G. V. Hancock, *Hist. of Tettenhall Coll.* (Tettenhall, priv. print. 1963), and for the period from 1963 on information from Mr. Hancock. For this para. see also *Staffs. Advertiser*, 18 July 1863.
[2] *D.N.B.*
[3] Ibid.

quality of teaching declined. By 1891 there were only 70 pupils. The next headmaster, J. H. Haydon (1891–1905), succeeded in reversing the decline in scholarship and in numbers, which rose to 120 in 1897. The school secretary toured midland and northern towns, contacting local Congregational and Baptist ministers to enlist their support. Haydon, a devoted cricketer, was noted for his encouragement of hobbies and sport. Despite the improvements financial difficulties recurred; the board economized by putting every contract out to tender.

In the early 20th century the school's financial problems worsened. By 1905 the number of boys had fallen to 74, and Haydon resigned. The headmastership of R. L. Ager (1906–13) was characterized by a further decline in numbers and by the board's repeated and mainly unsuccessful approaches to prominent local and national nonconformists for grants and loans. The board made matters worse by excluding day-boys. Several loans by A. B. Bantock of Wolverhampton, one of the directors, helped to preserve the school, but by 1910 closure was planned. In 1911, however, an increase in fees and an appeal to old boys enabled the school to continue.

In 1916 a new trust scheme abolished the holding company, incorporated the school, and enabled any profits to be ploughed back into it. Partly because of the organizing ability of A. H. Angus, headmaster 1913–25, and partly because of the demand for boarding places during the First World War, the number of boys rose from 62 in 1914 to 134 in 1918, and Angus built up a waiting list. The chemistry laboratory was re-equipped in 1913. An inspection in 1920 showed that the boys were well treated and that discipline was good. New playing-fields were bought in 1921 and privileges were granted to sportsmen. Angus's successor P. J. Day opened a junior school. In his time, however, discipline was weak and examination results were poor; the number of boarders declined and Day resigned in 1927. He was followed by Horace Pearson, a former second master. The school was almost immediately affected by the great slump: numbers continued to fall, and in 1928–9 there were again financial losses, salary cuts, and more loans from Bantock. The school had been losing its nonconformist character: c. 1931 over two-thirds of the boys were Anglicans. A decision in 1933 to readmit day-boys and the recovery of the West Midlands from the slump increased the number of pupils to about 120 by the late 1930s. An inspection in 1934 found that though there was little work of distinction in the school the teaching of geography and chemistry was outstanding; in the previous three years five boys had gone to Birmingham University. Games, moreover, were 'not overdone'. Examination results improved in the late 1930s, and in 1937 the school obtained its first university scholarship since 1908.

The Second World War brought threats that the school buildings would be requisitioned, and there was again a financial crisis. By then, however, the school was benefiting from a succession of gifts and legacies. Bantock died in 1938, leaving £5,000 immediately and £20,000 after the death of his wife.

About the same time G. Falkner Armitage of Altrincham (Ches.) left £500, while S. H. Clay gave £2,000 for university scholarships in 1938 and left a larger fund for the same purpose in the 1940s. Also in the 1940s the Industrial Fund granted £12,500 for science teaching. Under F. D. Field-Hyde, who succeeded Pearson in 1941, the school rapidly expanded. Growth was made possible by the purchase in 1943–4 of Tettenhall Towers and 26½ a. adjoining the school, providing space for new playing-fields and buildings. By 1963 the Towers housed seven forms, music rooms, a library, and a gymnasium; it also provided accommodation for nine resident staff. A new sports pavilion was opened in 1953, a building with five classrooms in 1954, and a new science block in 1958; the former chemistry laboratory became the headquarters of the art department. A biology block opened in 1960 connected the new classrooms and the science block and enabled biology to be taught internally for the first time; previously pupils had attended Wolverhampton Technical College. The new building was again extended in 1968 and 1975. In 1970 the former stables of the Towers were converted to serve as a library, and in 1977 squash courts were built.

The physical expansion of the school was accompanied by growth in numbers. During the Second World War more boarders were taken, but later growth was mainly in day-boys. There were 121 boys in 1941 and 191 in 1943. By 1960 there were 384, of whom 103 were boarders, 89 day-boarders, and 192 day-boys. Numbers declined to 294 in 1965 but rose again to 385 in 1977. From 1945 to 1962 Staffordshire county council sent five sponsored boarders and five sponsored day-boarders.[4] The proportion of pupils in the sixth form and that of those going to university increased from the 1940s onwards. The proportion of nonconformists continued to decline: in 1963 there were only 75 out of 350 boys. In 1965 the school joined the Headmasters' Conference; at the same time the former junior school for boys under 11 was replaced by a lower school taking boys from 8 to 13. Day-girls were admitted to the sixth form in 1969, and in 1972 the Drive School in Wrottesley Road, Tettenhall, was bought as a pre-preparatory school for boys and girls from 4 to 8 years old.

ALLEYNE'S GRAMMAR SCHOOL, UTTOXETER

ALLEYNE'S school at Uttoxeter, like its sister foundations at Stone and at Stevenage (Herts.), was founded under the will of Thomas Alleyne (d. 1558).[1] Possibly Alleyne supported a schoolmaster at Uttoxeter during his lifetime,[2] as he had apparently done at Stone and Stevenage. The school's early years seem to have been successful: in 1567 it was claimed that there were some 80 pupils. In 1592, after the death of a master, the rector of Leigh stated that if a suitable successor were appointed he would have as pupils not only the boys whom the rector himself would send to the school but also the sons of gentry. Most of the 16th- and 17th-cen-

---

[4] Ex inf. Staffs. County Council Educ. Dept. (1977).
[1] Unless otherwise stated, this article is based upon W. G. Torrance, *Hist. of Alleyne's Grammar Sch., Uttoxeter, 1558–1958* [Uttoxeter, 1959]. For details of the foundation

and endowment of the 3 schools see the account of Stone grammar school above.
[2] Bodl. MS. C.C.C. c.390/2, f. 180.

tury masters seem in fact to have been satisfactory. Boys were regularly sent to university.[3] Under John Herbert, appointed in 1692, conditions deteriorated; the townspeople complained that whereas the school had previously been filled with boys from Uttoxeter and the sons of persons of quality from near by, they now had to send their sons elsewhere to ensure that they received a good education. Herbert soon resigned.[4] Philip Bouquett, master 1696–1700, was a fellow of Trinity and later became Regius Professor of Hebrew at Cambridge.[5] Although none of the early-18th-century masters stayed long, it seems that the teaching was then adequate: in 1718, for example, it was reported that 40 boys were being taught Latin and Greek and that 'the schoolmaster does his duty'.[6] Boys were going on to university.

The original school-house stood in what came to be known as School Lane, later Bridge Street. It was rebuilt in 1735–6 and was altered and extended in 1765, each time at the expense of the trustees, Trinity College, Cambridge. The college could well afford the payments, since its income from the property left by Alleyne continued to rise. As early as 1726 counsel's opinion had been taken, by whom is unknown, on the possibility of forcing Trinity to increase its payments to the school; matters had apparently gone no further, and the master's salary remained the £13 6s. 8d. specified by Alleyne. Masters could supplement that by taking boarders: in 1766 the master advertised for them, stating that he took a few in his own house and that there were genteel families in the town 'ready to receive young gentlemen'; the school offered 'classical, commercial, and other branches of useful literature' and had visiting masters who taught French, dancing, and drawing.[7] Masters could also hope for a local living: Thomas Phillips, appointed in 1716, was also perpetual curate of Marchington. Nevertheless Trinity found it difficult to attract qualified men to the school. William Holmes, appointed master in 1766, did not graduate until 1771; Zachary Barker, appointed in 1778, apparently never graduated, although he was in orders and so presumably qualified to teach the classics.[8] After Barker's death in 1805 Thomas Osborne, the parish clerk, was appointed master. He taught the elements, probably all that most of the townspeople wanted for their boys. In 1818 it was stated that they regarded a commercial as more important than a classical education, 'which is seldom required for their children'. There were then only 14 boys at the school.[9]

Osborne died in 1846. Trinity improved the position of his successor, John Kinder (1846–55), by renting a house at Dove Bank for his use and adding £100 to his stipend. Kinder was better qualified than Osborne, but his way of running the school was disliked by some townspeople. He restricted the number of pupils to 30, only 8 of whom were taught free. He also insisted that the school was an Anglican institution; in 1852, although he had somewhat re-

laxed his previous rules, daily attendance at services in the parish church was still compulsory and many children were being excluded because their parents were nonconformists. His rigidity was made to appear more marked by the fact that Osborne had, in his later years, been a Methodist.

In 1852 a committee led by several prominent townsmen was set up to press for the reform and reorganization of the school. Trinity was asked to provide more money and to force the master to admit pupils without denominational restrictions. It was unwilling to do so, and the committee opened proceedings against it in Chancery. In 1856 judgement was given in favour of the committee. It was laid down that although the college was bound only to pay the sums stipulated in Alleyne's will it was also responsible for the proper maintenance of the school, having regard to the needs of the modern town; since Alleyne had died a papist there could be no ground for asserting that the school was an Anglican foundation. It was suggested that the college and the committee should combine to make mutually satisfactory arrangements for the reorganization of the school. The advice was duly accepted, and in 1856 the college drew up new regulations. Religious instruction, which was to be that of the Church of England, was not to be compulsory, although every boy had to attend school prayers and Bible-reading classes. Latin, Greek, and mathematics were to be offered for those boys who wished to go on to university; for those who did not there was to be a commercial course consisting of English, geography, history, writing, and arithmetic with book-keeping. There were to be up to 70 day-boys, of whom 10 were to be free scholars and the rest fee-paying local boys, and the schoolmaster was permitted to take up to 20 boarders. It was also agreed that the college should provide new school buildings on a site at Dove Bank adjoining the house which had been rented for Kinder and should raise the schoolmaster's stipend to a reasonable sum. The new school-house at Dove Bank was opened in 1859; it was a brick building designed in the Elizabethan style by H. I. Stevens of Derby and a London architect named Robinson.[10] The college also bought the schoolmaster's house at Dove Bank and some adjoining land.

Under the first schoolmaster at Dove Bank, W. W. Harvey (1855–64), the school grew and improved its academic standing. There were 26 pupils in 1855, 50 in 1857. Boys began to sit the Oxford and Cambridge local examinations, foundation scholarships were awarded by examination, and in 1863 regular inspections of the school were instituted at Harvey's request. T. E. Rhodes (1864–75) continued Harvey's work. He was dissatisfied with the state of the school when he arrived, but an inspector who visited it in 1865 considered that 'it was as good as the average'. In the second half-year of 1864 there were 71 day-boys and 11 boarders. Most of them were in the classical department, taught by Rhodes and an assistant master. A second assistant master taught

[3] See e.g. *Admissions to Trinity Coll., Cambridge*, ed. W. W. Rouse Ball and J. A. Venn, ii, *passim*.
[4] For his Christian name see L.J.R.O., B/V/10.
[5] L.J.R.O., B/A/4/22, 25 Sept. 1696; *D.N.B.*
[6] L.J.R.O., B/V/5, Uttoxeter 1718.
[7] *Aris's Birmingham Gaz.* 7 Apr. 1766.
[8] F. G. Gomez, 'Endowed Schs. of Staffs. in the 18th

cent.' (Leeds Univ. M.Phil. thesis, 1977), 281.
[9] Carlisle, *Endowed Grammar Schs.* ii. 498.
[10] *Staffs. Advertiser*, 23 July 1859, ascribing the design to 'Messrs. Stevens and Robinson of Derby and London'. For H. I. Stevens see e.g. Harrison, Harrod & Co. *Dir. Derbs.* (1860), 63.

the commercial department. There had been 27 boys in the commercial department when Rhodes arrived, but he had dismissed the master in charge and nine boys had left to join a private school which the dismissed master established. The boys at the grammar school were well behaved and the school was highly thought of locally; 7 or 8 boys travelled to it by rail daily from Tutbury, Rocester, and nearby villages. In November 1867 there were, however, only 49 pupils.[11] Numbers continued to fluctuate. In 1871 there were 90 boys, including 23 boarders; 53 were in the classical department. In 1883 there were only 36 boys. All of them learnt Latin and some learnt Greek; there was no longer a commercial department. The schoolmaster, Thomas Allen (1877–87), had a woman assistant and a pupil-teacher to help him. There were no boarders.

In the 1880s complaints again arose in the town. It was claimed that the school needed a larger endowment so that it could provide adequately for local needs. It was also felt that there ought to be some local men on the governing body. In 1886, in response to the complaints, the school was again re-organized. It was given a board of governors containing representatives of Trinity and of the Uttoxeter vestry. The college increased its annual grant to £400; the headmaster received £150 of that and £50 was earmarked for a leaving exhibition. The headmaster also received a rent-free house and capitation fees of £2 to £4. Under the 1886 Scheme, modified in 1898 when the vestry governors were replaced by representatives of the county council and the urban district council, and 1901, when a representative of Derbyshire county council was added to the board, the school revived and flourished. New buildings were added, the curriculum was widened, and the school again took boarders. J. F. Acheson (1887–1901) made science a regular part of the curriculum and built a small laboratory. Under A. T. Daniel (1901–23) a new laboratory was built east of the 1859 school-house and the school bought the first playing-field which it had owned.

In 1921 the governors handed the school over to the county council and it became a maintained secondary school.[12] It was still comparatively small; although the number of boys reached 100 in 1922 it then generally remained in the 80s or 90s until 1926. In that year a new block of buildings was opened; it included four classrooms, a lecture theatre, and an art room. Thereafter numbers gradually rose; in 1937 there were some 140 boys. Until at least the early 1930s there were still a few boarders. In the 1930s the school began to co-operate with Uttoxeter High School for Girls and shared that school's assembly hall and chemistry laboratory. After the Second World War several new buildings were added to the grammar school, including, in 1957, a chemistry laboratory. In the early 1960s there were just over 300 boys. In 1964 the grammar school and the girls' high school were merged to form a mixed grammar school with almost 600 pupils. In 1974 the school became the comprehensive Thomas Alleyne's High School.

QUEEN MARY'S GRAMMAR SCHOOL, WALSALL

THE foundation of a grammar school at Walsall was recommended by the chantry commissioners in 1548. Nothing was done until 1554, when the Crown established a grammar school at the petition of George and Nicholas Hawe and other inhabitants of the town.[1] 'The Free Grammar School of Queen Mary at Walsall' was to have a master and an usher; it was endowed by the Crown with some 300 a. of chantry lands in Walsall, Tipton, and Norton Canes valued at £10 a year, and was placed under the control of a board of governors drawn from the more discreet and honest inhabitants of Walsall parish. Vacancies on the board were to be filled by co-option. No statutes or regulations appear to have survived, but it seems probable from later evidence that the right to a free education was confined to boys from Walsall parish who could read and write.

The first known master, a Mr. Petypher, was appointed in 1555–6, and George Hawe, by will proved 1558, devised a building in St. Matthew's churchyard to serve as a school-house and a master's residence. Among the early schoolmasters was William Sclater (1599–1604), the divine. During the 17th century the school was well served by its masters and evidently had a good reputation in the district, occasionally receiving the sons of local gentlemen. Among the pupils of Richard Lowe (master 1611–46) was Sir Edward Leigh of Rushall (1603–71), the writer. In the mid 17th century some of the schoolmasters were fugitives from political persecution: Francis Storre (1646–50) had been ejected by the royalists from the ushership of Wolverhampton grammar school, while John Toy (1650–60) had been ejected from the mastership of the King's School, Worcester, by the parliamentarians. In 1648 Storre was one of only two Staffordshire schoolmasters to sign the Testimony.[2] Toy was the author of a text-book on Latin verse composition which he dedicated to John, son of John Persehouse of Reynold's Hall, Walsall, apparently one of his pupils. Another pupil was Phineas Fowke (1638–1710), the physician. At the Restoration Toy returned to Worcester; Thomas Barfoot, a puritan who had occupied Toy's post there from 1653,[3] was master at Walsall from at latest 1664 to 1666. His pupils there included Richard Hough (1651–1743), bishop of Oxford (1690–9), Lichfield and Coventry (1699–1717), and Worcester (1717–43), and John Somers, Baron Somers of Evesham (1651–1716), lord chancellor 1697–1700.[4]

In the later 17th and the 18th centuries Walsall, unlike some other grammar schools in the county, was not hamstrung by financial difficulties. Although the governors were accused of corruption in 1685 during the course of a town feud and although

[11] *Schs. Inquiry Com. vol. xv* [3966–XIV], pp. 464–7, H.C. (1867–8), xxviii (12). Torrance, *Alleyne's*, 41, states that there were 79 boys at the school when Rhodes arrived, 42 of them in the classical dept.
[12] This para. is based on Torrance, *Alleyne's*, 63 sqq.; S.R.O., CEG/19/1 and 2; W. G. Torrance, *Following Francis Redfern, pt. ix* (Uttoxeter, n.d. but 1974), 5 (copy in W.S.L. Pamphs. *sub* Uttoxeter); inf. from Staffs.

County Council Educ. Dept. (1977).
[1] Unless otherwise stated, this article is based on D. P. J. Fink, *Queen Mary's Grammar Sch. 1554–1954* (Walsall, priv. print. 1954).
[2] A. G. Matthews, *Cong. Churches of Staffs.* 18.
[3] *V.C.H. Worcs.* iv. 487.
[4] For Leigh, Fowke, Hough, and Somers see also *D.N.B.*

a commission of charitable uses remarked unfavourably in 1726 on the low rents asked for school land, no property was alienated and the school's income rose more than sufficiently to allow the governors to pay salaries which would attract competent masters. By the 1740s the master's salary had been raised to £50 and that of the usher to £20, and there were further increases in the later 18th century. Nevertheless there was a growing surplus after payment of salaries.[5]

By the 1760s various schools offering not only classical but also commercial and elementary education had been established in and around Walsall. The governors of the grammar school were aware of the threat presented by such schools, and when in 1776 William Brownell, formerly proprietor of a private school in the town, was appointed usher they broke with tradition by requiring him to teach a few boys writing and arithmetic at no extra charge. In 1789 they appointed a third master whose sole duty was to teach the elements gratis. Boys receiving an elementary education were, however, expected to move on later to the traditional classical course: in 1793 it was laid down that those incapable of that were to be expelled. From that year the governors ran a separate preparatory school which provided elementary education for 40 boys until they were old enough to enter the grammar school.

As the industrialization of Walsall and the surrounding area advanced, the potential value of the school's property, especially that of an estate over the Coal Measures at Tipton, increased proportionately. In 1797 the governors obtained an Act[6] empowering them to sell mines and to sell or exchange dispersed or uninclosed lands; the sale money was to to paid into Chancery and disbursed thence to the governors as required. In return the governors bound themselves to start new schools in Walsall and to build a chapel of ease, St. Paul's, in the town. The Act required that the governors, the usher, and the masters and mistresses of any schools organized by the governors were to be Anglicans, while the headmaster was to be minister of St. Paul's.

In 1800 the governors sold a lease of the mining rights at Tipton for over £12,000, and for the next 50 years the Tipton mines financed all major additions to the foundation. From 1802 onwards the governors were able to support several elementary schools in and around Walsall, over which the master of the grammar school exercised a general control.[7] In 1815 the grammar school moved to new premises in Park Street, where a three-storeyed house was bought and converted into two schoolrooms and two masters' houses. In 1833 Thomas Rogers, headmaster since 1824, was accused of absenteeism, and in 1835 the governors held an inquiry into the running of the school. It showed that there were 61 boys, 21 taught by the headmaster and 40 by the usher. The standard of classical learning was not high, the boys in the master's top class (who were, however, aged only about 12) reading no more than simple Latin texts; Greek was not taught, but both geography and English and Roman history were included in the curriculum for the older boys, while the younger boys learnt geography,

reading, spelling, and Latin grammar. The usher taught the boys in his care all those subjects except history. Rogers's conduct of the school deteriorated, and in 1837 he was dismissed.

His successor, C. F. Childe (1837–9), was permitted to take four boarders as private pupils, a privilege allowed to one of his predecessors but not known to have been exercised. He proposed a scheme for the reorganization of the school, and it came into force in 1838. The school was divided into two sections: a grammar school of up to 60 boys, which included in its curriculum not only Latin and Greek but also history, geography, English grammar, elocution, mathematics, book-keeping, and general science, and a commercial school of up to 40 boys, which taught all the subjects offered by the grammar school save the classics. Boys were not allowed to move from one school to the other, nor was any boy under 8 to be received into either. Applicants for entry to the grammar school had to be able to read and had to possess a grounding in English grammar and arithmetic; reading only was required for the commercial school.

Childe's successor, W. G. Barker (1839–53), was allowed to take up to twelve boarders as private pupils, but the boarding side of the school appears never to have been of great importance. In 1850 the school, which since 1847 had occupied the grand stand on the race-course, moved to a new brick building in Lichfield Street designed in the Tudor style by Edward Adams, a local architect and a former pupil.[8] In 1854 there were 134 pupils, of whom 50 were in the grammar school. During the 1850s and 1860s the governors came under pressure from two directions. The nonconformists in the town wished to end Anglican control of the school, while the masters, led by A. C. Irvine, headmaster 1858–81, wanted to open it to boys from a wider area, to hold competitive entrance examinations, and to charge fees.

Under a Scheme of 1873 the school became undenominational and the posts of headmaster and minister of St. Paul's were separated. A new board of governors was set up, including representatives of the improvement commissioners and the local school board. The school property was vested in the Charity Commissioners. The school itself, no longer restricted to boys from Walsall parish, was again divided into two parts. The grammar school was succeeded by a high school for boys of 8 to 17 years. Its curriculum according to the Scheme was to include at least one scientific subject, a foreign language, Latin, and singing. The commercial school was replaced by a lower school for boys of 7 to 15, with a curriculum which was to include elementary Latin or French, a science, surveying, and political economy. The Scheme provided that entrance to the high school was to be by examination in the elements and English geography; the entrance examination to the lower school omitted geography. Fees of £5 to £12 a year were to be charged at the high school and of £2 to £4 at the lower school; so ended the school's tradition of free education. Exhibitions granting exemptions from fees were permitted, but not more than twenty per

[5] F. G. Gomez, 'Endowed Schs. of Staffs. in the 18th cent.' (Leeds Univ. M.Phil. thesis, 1977), 284–5.
[6] 37 Geo. III, c. 70 (Priv. Act).
[7] For schools, other than the grammar school, run by the governors see V.C.H. Staffs. xvii. 255.
[8] See plate facing p. 145.

cent of the places were to be free or partially so. At least ten boys were to be wholly exempt from fees. Half of the exhibitions in the lower school were for Walsall elementary-school boys.

In 1893 a further Scheme merged the high school and the lower school (the name of which had proved a check on its development) into a single high school for boys and raised the age of entrance to 10 and the leaving age to 18 years. The 1873 Scheme had recommended the establishment of a girls' school as part of the foundation, and in 1893 Queen Mary's High School for Girls was founded under the new Scheme; it occupied buildings in Upper Forster Street adjoining the boys' buildings in Lichfield Street. Also in 1893 the boys' buildings were extended to include physics and chemistry laboratories and a gymnasium. Numbers, however, declined. In 1891 there had been 112 boys in the high school and 85 in the lower; in 1896 there were only 117 in the combined school. From the later 1890s numbers increased again, and there were 155 boys in 1903. In 1904 the town council's representation on the board of governors was enlarged and representatives of the county council and of Birmingham University were added. As a result of the establishment of the girls' school it was laid down that at least three of the governors were to be women. At the same time the leaving age at the boys' school was raised to 19 and the governors were empowered to set up a pupil-teacher centre there. Also in 1904 a dining-hall and workshops were added.

Numbers at the boys' school had increased to 204 by 1906, and H. E. Marshall (1906–26) succeeded in raising them to 534 by 1923. In 1909 the school's style was changed to Queen Mary's Grammar School, and it became a secondary school for the borough under the 1902 Education Act. In 1913 other classrooms were enlarged and 9½ a. of the Mayfield estate in Sutton Road was bought for a playing-field. By 1917 further accommodation was needed, and in 1918 the governors took a lease of Moss Close in Mellish Road; the junior forms moved into it. The rest of the Mayfield estate was bought in 1921 except for the house, which was bought in 1924 as a preparatory school for the girls' high school. Moss Close was bought in 1926. Plans for new buildings at Mayfield for the boys' school had to be postponed for lack of money; meanwhile numbers declined to 429 in 1930. In the 1930s they rose again, and a new wing was added to the Lichfield Street buildings in 1933. During the Second World War the school became congested: there were 631 boys in 1943.

In 1947 the school became voluntary aided. By 1954 numbers had fallen to around 530, but in the later 1950s and early 1960s they rose again. In 1956 there were some 560 boys, of whom 100 were in the sixth form;[9] in 1963 there were 625 altogether and 186 in the sixth form.[10] In 1956 the teaching of geology and applied mechanics was introduced.[11] In the late 1950s the new buildings at Mayfield were at last begun. Meanwhile in 1960 the headmaster's house was converted to division rooms and a music room.[12] In 1961 the first part of the Mayfield buildings, consisting of a science block and five classrooms, were completed; the senior forms moved into it, and the junior forms moved from Moss Close to Lichfield Street. Moss Close was then closed and was demolished in 1964.[13] In 1963 a coach-house at Farchynys Hall, Bontddu (in Llanaber, Merion.), was bought as an adventure centre for the school.[14] In March 1965 the rest of the school moved to Mayfield, although the buildings were not completed until the autumn. Designed by Robert Matthew, Johnson-Marshall & Partners round two quadrangles, they included, besides the science block, an assembly hall, a dining-hall, a gymnasium, a library, an arts and crafts wing, a covered sports area, and houses for the headmaster and caretaker.[15] The old buildings were handed over to the girls' school.[16]

From 1966 Walsall education committee made a succession of proposals to fit the school into a comprehensive system, and steps were taken to limit the intake. In 1966, although Walsall borough had been enlarged to include Willenhall and Darlaston, the committee, then controlled by the Labour party, decided not to admit children from those areas to the grammar school. That decision was reversed in 1967 when the Independents gained control of the borough council.[17] In 1973 the education committee, then again under Labour control, allowed parents only one choice of secondary school for their children, and there were far fewer applications to the grammar school.[18] Between 1968 and 1977 there were generally some 630 pupils.[19] The sixth form was reorganized in 1971; from then on fewer pupils spent a third year in it and its numbers declined from 193 in that year to 172 in 1974. The number of university places gained was unaffected by the decline.[20] An appeal for £45,000 was launched in 1965 to provide extra facilities; most of it had been raised by 1966,[21] and despite the school's uncertain future the governors continued to put up new buildings in the late 1960s and early 1970s. An indoor swimming-pool was finished in 1970 and squash courts in 1971.[22] In 1973 a sports pavilion was completed at Walsall, and extensions were built at Farchynys so that it could serve as a laboratory for field studies and a centre for reading parties.[23] It was stated in 1975 that biology, German, economics, music, general studies, and computer studies as well as geology had all been introduced or greatly extended in the previous 20 years.[24]

[9] *The Marian*, viii (1), 6–7 (copy in Walsall Central Libr.).
[10] Ibid. xii (1), 7.
[11] Ibid. viii (1), 7.
[12] Ibid. xii (2), 11.
[13] Ibid. ix (8), 3; x (10), 5; *Express & Star*, 24 Feb. 1964; *Official Opening of New Buildings of Queen Mary's Grammar Sch. Walsall* (copy at sch.).
[14] *The Marian*, xii (1), 12; Walsall Central Libr., News-cuttings, vol. i, p. 17.
[15] *Walsall Observer*, 5 Mar. 1965; *The Marian*, xii (5), 8; *Opening of New Buildings*.
[16] *V.C.H. Staffs.* xvii. 255.
[17] *Express & Star*, 9 and 18 Nov. 1966; *Evening Mail*, 5 July 1967.
[18] *Express & Star*, 9 Jan., 23 Feb. 1973.
[19] *The Marian*, xii (9), 5; xii (11), 5; xii (12), 5; xiii (1), 5; xiii (2), 5; xiii (3), 6; ex inf. Mr. J. S. Anderson, deputy headmaster (1977).
[20] *The Marian*, xii (11), 5; xii (12), 4–5; xiii (1), 6; xiii (2), 7; xiii (3), 6; *Queen Mary's Grammar Sch. Speech Day 1975: Prize Giving; 1976: Prize Giving* (copies at sch.).
[21] *Opening of New Buildings*.
[22] *Express & Star*, 16 May 1970; *Queen Mary's Grammar Sch. Walsall: Official Opening of Swimming Bath* (copy at sch.); *The Marian*, xii (12), 3.
[23] *The Marian*, xiii (2), 7–8.
[24] Ibid. xiii (3), 6.

STAFFORD: VIEW FROM THE NORTH-EAST *c.* 1680

The market-place in the later 1850s

View from the south-west, 1883

STAFFORD

WOLVERHAMPTON GRAMMAR SCHOOL

A FREE grammar school was founded at Wolverhampton by Sir Stephen Jenyns (d. 1523), a native of the town who became a London merchant-tailor and was lord mayor in 1508–9.[1] It existed by 1512, when at Jenyns's instigation the Merchant Taylors Company obtained licence to acquire lands to the annual value of £20 to support it. In 1513 Jenyns himself received licence to grant Rushock manor (Worcs.), worth £15 a year, to the company to provide stipends for a master and an usher. The manor was conveyed to the company in 1515. The balance of the property permitted by the licence of 1512 was probably the school-house, with accommodation for master and usher, in John's Lane (later St. John's Street). Jenyns apparently built it on the site of his family home. The Merchant Taylors returned Rushock to Jenyns rent-free for his life and the lives of his wife and son-in-law John Nechells; the family evidently retained the management of the school until Nechells's death in 1531. Nechells gave a £1 annuity for the usher.

From the foundation no restrictions were placed upon the admission of pupils from outside Wolverhampton: the townspeople declared in 1626 that the school had always been for boys both from Wolverhampton parish and from other parts of the kingdom. Statutes were drawn up by the Merchant Taylors in 1573. An admission fee of 4d. was to be paid to the master on behalf of each boy. At admission the boys were to be literate in English and to know the catechism in English and Latin; those later found unapt to learn grammar could be expelled. The statutes provide the earliest known curriculum for the school. The boys were to learn Latin from the *Colloquia* of Vives, the Latin Catechism of Alexander Nowell, and the works of Terence, Ovid, Horace, Virgil, and Cicero; they were to learn Greek from Isocrates, Xenophon, and Homer. The statutes were primarily based upon those of the company's London school, and the textbooks were probably recommended by Richard Mulcaster, master of that school. Revised statutes of 1616 added Maturin Cordier's *Colloquia* to the Latin works and Theognis to the Greek.

From the first the Merchant Taylors appear to have been conscientious trustees and were prepared to increase the stipends sufficiently to attract competent teachers. Until the early 17th century the company appointed the master only; he in turn appointed the usher. Thereafter the company appointed both. In the 17th century the masters and ushers were sometimes former teachers at the company's London school. In 1531, when the company took over the management of the school, the income from Rushock was £18. The company reserved £6 for such items as repairs; the master received £10 and the usher £2, in addition to Nechells's annuity. Stipends were raised several times during the 16th century, and after a further increase in 1605 the master received £20 and the usher £10 a year. Randolph Woolley, a former master of the company (d. 1616), left £100 to augment the stipends by £5 a year. The Merchant Taylors also paid for the building of a new school-house in 1590–1 on the site of the old, which had been burnt down, and in 1605 Henry Offley, a prominent member of the company, gave land for a playground.

Nevertheless the company faced a succession of complaints from Wolverhampton about the running of the school. In 1572 it dismissed the master after complaints from the townspeople. Richard Barnes, master 1605–10, aroused local opposition by reprimanding recusant parents for not sending their children to church; several therefore removed their sons to other schools. The Merchant Taylors defended Barnes, but after the townspeople had brought proceedings in Chancery alleging breach of trust, the company compromised by dismissing him and by building a gallery in the parish church in 1611 for the use of the pupils. The gallery was designed to seat 60 to 70 boys; in 1609 there had been 69 pupils, but the number had fallen in Barnes's last year. He had, however, persuaded the company in 1608 to grant the school's first university exhibition. His dismissal at first restored relations between company and town; the school's statutes were revised in minor details by the townspeople in 1616 with the company's approval, and provision was made for an annual examination of the school by a local clergyman. The examinations did not prevent the school's renewed deterioration; the usher was dismissed for negligence in 1618, and his successor's dismissal was ordered in 1623, temporarily rescinded in 1624, and confirmed in 1627. Such difficulties encouraged some inhabitants to bring further Chancery proceedings in 1626 alleging that the company had retained most of the Rushock profits and that the resulting small stipends were the cause of the masters' inadequacies. In 1627 the company decided that the master should have yearly tenure only. A Chancery decree of 1628 confirmed that Rushock manor belonged to the school, required that the master be approved by the bishop, and ordered the examination of the company's accounts relating to the school. The audit, not completed until 1642, exonerated the company.

In 1640 a visiting committee found the school-house ruinous and recommended that the stipends be augmented, a writing-master appointed, and a house for the usher built. The Civil War at first prevented any action. The usher, Francis Storre, was ejected by the royalists in 1642 and again in 1645, and the war frequently interrupted communication between the Merchant Taylors and the school. In 1648 a new usher was appointed at a salary of £26 13s. 4d., with a further £6 6s. 8d. to teach writing. The master's salary was then raised to £40 and was increased to £45 in 1649. The new usher was discharged for royalism in 1650, and in 1651 Storre returned. In 1658 John Coles (c. 1624–1678), the translator,[2] was appointed master. He complained repeatedly in the 1660s and early 1670s that the salary was inadequate and irregularly paid and that he received no support from the townsfolk. The salary was increased to £50 in 1664 and to £68 6s. 8d. in 1674. Coles's successor, Isaac Backhouse, was a former schoolfellow of Titus Oates at Merchant Taylors' School; he was accused by Oates in 1681 of involvement in the Popish Plot but was acquitted. He attracted pupils from near-by schools

[1] Unless otherwise stated, this article is based on G. P. Mander, *Hist. of Wolverhampton Grammar Sch.* (Wolverhampton, 1913).

[2] *D.N.B.*

and took many gentlemen's sons as boarders. He resigned in 1685 and was succeeded by John Plymley, who neglected his duties. In 1710 it was claimed that there were only six boys in the immediate care of the master, and Plymley was dismissed, though he received a pension out of the school revenues. The school building was also decayed. It was rebuilt to the design of William Smith of Tettenhall; the new building, completed in 1713, had two wings providing houses for master and usher, and a schoolroom in the centre.[3]

Difficulties continued for much of the 18th century. The reduction in the master's salary because of Plymley's pension made it hard to attract or retain suitable masters. Plymley died in 1734, but from 1760 to 1773 another pension absorbed £40 out of the £70 available to the master. Several of the 18th-century ushers held other preferments. Moreover from 1700 or earlier the school faced competition from private schools in the town. There were renewed attacks on the Merchant Taylors' trusteeship in the 1750s. The teaching of William Robertson, master 1768–83, was well regarded, but the number of boys continued to fall. About 1777 there were only 5 boarders and fewer than 30 day-boys.

In 1778 proceedings were again brought against the company, which in 1784 appointed trustees and relinquished control. The school had closed when Robertson died in 1783; before reopening it in 1785 the trustees added an extra schoolroom in the playground. New rules limited the number of boarders to 40 under the headmaster and 12 under the usher. From 1776 the Rushock rents had been gradually increased, and in 1785 the headmaster's salary was raised to £150 and the usher's to £80. An extra under-master was appointed to teach writing and mathematics. In 1785 98 day-boys were elected, but many were soon withdrawn because their parents wanted them to receive a less classical education. In 1788 a drawing-master and French and German masters were appointed.

In the later 1790s the headmaster gave up taking boarders, and the number of boys fell to about 70. His successor, William Tindall (1799–1830), quarrelled with his ushers, and by 1803 there were only 22 day-boys. By 1810 the school's unpopularity was encouraging vandalism to the buildings. Generally, however, there were between 50 and 60 boys, including boarders, during Tindall's mastership, and in 1822 the number reached 84. Despite his shortcomings as a teacher, Tindall bullied the trustees into increasing his salary to £500 in 1814 by threatening to bring a suit in Chancery against them.

The Charity Commissioners' inquiry in 1819 showed that the most important reason for the school's small numbers was the townsfolk's dislike of a classical education. According to Tindall the gentry, who sought a classical education for their sons, sent them to Rugby; respectable tradesmen generally sent their boys to the grammar school as day-boys and took them away at thirteen or fourteen. They were never taught by the headmaster as their parents wanted them to be qualified only for the trades they were to enter. On the other hand Tindall taught all his boarders, however young. All boys in the school studied the classics, writing, and geo-graphy; most learnt drawing, and about 20 French. The drawing classes, which were free, proved increasingly attractive to would-be draughtsmen in the local japanning trade; the consequent entry of working-class children into the school had by 1830 begun to discourage middle-class parents from sending their sons. Agitation therefore arose for a return to a more strictly classical curriculum. In 1831 the drawing-mastership was abolished and it was decided that no French master should be appointed when the incumbent retired. A further fall in attendance resulted; in the 1830s there were rarely more than 50 boys, few of whom studied the classics. In 1841, therefore, the former writing-master was made usher in the hope of converting the usher's school to a commercial department. The number of pupils reached 123 in 1844 but later fell away again; boarders also became fewer since the district round the school was becoming a slum. In the 1840s boys seldom stayed more than two years, and there were seldom more than two in the top class. The curriculum was confused by a practice by which different masters taught the same subject to the same class on the same day.

After further controversy a Chancery Scheme of 1854 ordered that masters be appointed to teach French, German, drawing, and writing. The headmaster and usher should be Anglicans and graduates of Oxford, Cambridge, or Durham. At admission sons of residents in St. Peter's parish were to be given priority; boys must be at least 8 years old and able to read English. The maximum number of day-boys was set at 100, and that of boarders was fixed at 20 for the master and 10 for the usher. Entrance fees and half-yearly capitation fees, both of £2, were to be paid. Provision was made for an annual exhibition. The Scheme did not allow either the alteration of the duties of the masters or an increase in the size of the staff. T. H. Campbell, appointed headmaster in 1855, tightened discipline, acquired the use of a cricket-field, and appointed an assistant master at his own expense. In 1861, however, he dismissed him. The standard of teaching consequently declined, and Campbell resigned in 1863 because of lack of support from the trustees; there were then only 42 boys.

A new Scheme took effect in 1864, despite much local opposition.[4] It divided the school into a commercial department under the usher and a classical, or advanced, department. Capitation fees were raised and salaries lowered. The headmaster or the trustees might appoint such staff as they thought fit. Perhaps because of the Scheme, perhaps because of the ability of Thomas Beach, headmaster from 1865, the school suddenly became attractive to parents. By April 1867 there were 100 boys in the upper school and 77 in the lower, and candidates for admission were being rejected. By 1874 there were 233 boys. New buildings, designed by Giles & Gough of London in a Gothic style, were begun at Merridale in 1874, and the school moved there in 1875. It continued to flourish under Beach's direction, winning many university awards. He also encouraged sport: in the 1870s cricket, football, and athletics were put on an organized basis. He was, however, an extreme conservative; when the

---

[3] For a view in 1837 see plate facing p. 145. By then the façade had been slightly altered.

[4] *Staffs. Advertiser*, 1 May 1858, 20 Apr.–4 May 1861.

Charity Commissioners in 1889 advocated the appointment of a science master he resigned.

Beach's successor, Henry Williams, established a separate modern side in the upper school, appointed a seventh assistant master, fitted up a laboratory, and opened a school library. From 1890 scholarships were granted to elementary-school boys.[5] Williams found, however, that space was lacking for adequate science teaching and that money could not be raised to improve the facilities; at the same time the school's income from Rushock was declining. He therefore resigned in 1895. He was followed by J. H. Hichens, formerly science master at Cheltenham College. A science block was built in 1897; the cost was met by grants from the borough and county councils and by private subscriptions. Hichens also established a preparatory department for boys from 8 upwards. He reorganized the games and introduced drill.[6] The number of boys increased from 131 in 1895[7] to 212 in 1901, but declined again during the year before Hichens's departure in 1905. Under his successor Watson Caldecott (1905–23) the school again expanded. In 1908 it became the secondary school for the borough, and the town council supported at first 13 free pupils and later more.[8] Also in 1908 the buildings were modernized and new ones opened including a larger physics laboratory. A house and 5 a. of land were bought in 1911 for the junior school. By 1913 there were 300 boys. An annual grant was received from the county council by 1914.[9] In 1920 the school sold the Rushock estate.[10] In 1922 there were 560 boys, and there continued to be normally over 500 throughout the 1920s.[11] Extensions, including seven classrooms, a workshop, an art room, a physics laboratory, and a library, were opened in 1931,[12] and two more classrooms and a staffroom were built in 1939;[13] the boarding-house, however, had been closed in 1936.[14] The number of boys rose during the Second World War, reaching 583 in 1944.[15]

The school became voluntary aided in 1945.[16] The preparatory department had therefore to be closed in 1947;[17] as a result the number of pupils fell to 511, but later rose again.[18] In the late 1940s and early 1950s the school attracted staff of high ability; many later became headmasters of other grammar schools. The sixth-form curriculum was enlarged to include English and history and from c. 1957 geography and biology. From c. 1961 biology was also taught at a lower level.[19] The inclusion of the former headmaster's house in the school in 1956 gave more classrooms,[20] and in 1958 an appeal was launched to provide a further endowment and more new buildings.[21] A block containing three classrooms, a biology laboratory, changing-rooms, a dining-hall, and a stage was opened in 1960; other buildings were converted to provide extra chemistry and physics laboratories.[22] In 1964 the number of boys reached 604, of whom 186 were in the sixth form. Russian was then introduced into the curriculum.[23] Another new building was opened in 1969, replacing the former junior-school building; it included a gymnasium, music room, and five classrooms.[24] The school's endowment was increased by a legacy of over £60,000 from Henry Hallmark (d. 1973), chairman of the governors 1954–71.[25] By 1975 there were 647 boys, of whom 190 were in the sixth form.[26] The school had largely lost its classical character, and in 1977 only four boys were learning Greek.[27]

THE ROYAL WOLVERHAMPTON SCHOOL

IN 1850 John Lees, a Wolverhampton lock and key manufacturer, opened an asylum and school in Queen Street, Wolverhampton, for thirteen orphan boys.[1] He had been inspired by pity for those orphaned in the cholera epidemic of 1849, and particularly for children of middle-class parents, for whom he considered the loss the more disastrous. The pupils were to enter between the ages of 7 and 11 and to leave at 13 years. Not more than two children of the same family were to be admitted; diseased or crippled children were excluded. The pupils were to be brought up on Anglican principles and to wear a dress modelled on that of Christ's Hospital in London. Later in 1850 two more boys and four girls were admitted. The first inmates were maintained at Lees's own expense, but he arranged for the appointment of a committee and sought subscriptions from the public. Those subscribing a guinea or more were to become members of the institution and to vote at the election of children; they were to have an extra vote for each extra guinea. Such provision for elections encouraged subscriptions.

At the opening ceremony Lees implied that the orphanage was to serve Wolverhampton and its neighbourhood, but he soon decided to enlarge it and to admit orphans from elsewhere. He bought a site at Goldthorn Hill in 1852 and launched an appeal for a building fund. The new building, known as the Wolverhampton Orphan Asylum, was opened in 1854; designed in an Elizabethan style by Joseph Manning of Corsham (Wilts.), it had a main block and two wings and included schoolrooms, dining-

[5] *Boro. of Wolverhampton: Council Mins. and Reps. from 9 Nov. 1889 to 31 Oct. 1890*, 304–5; *1893–4*, 495.
[6] *Corp. of Wolverhampton: Council Mins. & Reps. 1897–8*, 60; *1898–9*, 249.
[7] Ibid. *1895–6*, 323–4.
[8] *Boro. of Wolverhampton: Ann. Reps. of the several Cttees. 1907*, 14; *1908*, 11; *1909*, 11; *1910*, 13; *1911*, 13; *1912*, 12.
[9] Ibid. *1914*, 12–13.
[10] *Wulfrunian*, xx. 52 (copy in Wolverhampton Central Pub. Libr.).
[11] *County Boro. of Wolverhampton: Council Mins. 1922–23*, 43; *Council Mins. and Reps. 1923–24*, 49; *1925–26*, 36; *1926–27*, 40; *1927–28*, 36; *1928–29*, 37; *1929–30*, 38.
[12] *County Boro. of Wolverhampton: Council Mins. and Reps. 1931–32*, 45.
[13] *Wulfrunian*, xxx. 192, 253.

[14] Ibid. xxxvi. 216.
[15] Ibid. xxxiii. 94, 180.
[16] *Wolverhampton & W. Midlands Mag.* (Dec. 1975), 20–1 (copy in Wolverhampton Central Pub. Libr.).
[17] *Wulfrunian*, xxxiv. 8, 115, 229, 233.
[18] Ibid. 229; ibid. xxxv. 271, 394, 503, 612.
[19] Ex inf. the headmaster (1977).
[20] *Wulfrunian*, xxxviii (5), 22.
[21] Ibid. xxxvi. 380.
[22] Ibid. xxxvii. 69, 152; xxxviii (5), 22.
[23] Ibid. xxxvii. 559–60.
[24] Ibid. xxxviii (6), plate opp. p. 4; xxxix (10), 10.
[25] Ex inf. the headmaster.
[26] *Wulfrunian*, xli (3), 5.
[27] Ex inf. the headmaster.
[1] Unless otherwise stated, this article is based on F. L. Steward, *Hist. of Royal Wolverhampton Sch. 1850–1950* (Wolverhampton, 1950).

rooms, dormitories, sick wards, and accommodation for a master and a matron. A trust was established in 1855. Children who had lost both parents and had no friends able to support them, and fatherless children who were without a stepfather and whose mother could not support them, were to be eligible. Not more than two children of the same parent were to be admitted. The governors could take without election a child whose sponsor had paid 100 guineas, or a deserving child in extreme cases.[2] The boys and girls were separately housed and taught.

In the later 19th century the number of children greatly increased: there were 51 in 1860, 145 in 1870, 244 in 1880, and 325 in 1900. The expansion required repeated enlargement of the buildings. Lees gave a further $2\frac{1}{2}$ a. adjoining the school in 1860. By will proved 1863 he gave £1,000 for the enlargement of the building and £300 for a new entrance lodge; he also left £700 to maintain one child and £2,000 towards the endowment. The lodge and two new wings were completed the same year. An infirmary was built in 1868 and a gymnasium in 1872; in 1875 the girls' wing was greatly enlarged. Extensions in 1881 included a swimming-bath and a covered playground. A chapel, designed by F. T. Beck of Wolverhampton, was completed in 1895.

The curriculum at first consisted of the elements with scripture, history, and the catechism. The children, and especially the girls, spent much time on menial tasks; each girl did $2\frac{1}{2}$ hours' sewing daily. The girls had to mend and darn the clothes of the whole school and also worked in the laundry. Every year the children were given an oral examination in public in English subjects, religious knowledge, and arithmetic. By 1871 the examinations were so popular with the public that the number of spectators had to be limited by tickets, issued only to subscribers and their families. From that time also the curriculum was expanded, at first mainly by including technical subjects. The school adopted the Science and Art Department's drawing scheme in 1871 for the boys and in 1879 for the girls. From 1872 the boys were taught shorthand, and from 1875 the girls were allowed to learn the piano at their friends' expense. French was introduced to the girls' school in 1882. By 1886[3] the boys were attending the Science and Art Department's science classes, which included mathematics, geography, and geology, for a fee of 2s. a term, abolished in 1892. In 1899 the leaving age was raised to fourteen.

As the school grew the rules for admission were altered, generally in a more restrictive sense. In 1858 children of parents who had received poor-relief were excluded; from 1865 not more than one child of the same parents could be admitted, though from 1866 children of living but insane fathers were allowed. From 1876 the parents were to have been in or above the position of clerks or master tradesmen, with incomes sufficient to procure a liberal education for their children. In 1878 the rule was amended: orphans of professional men, self-employed farmers and businessmen, and clerks, and fatherless children respectably descended were

eligible; the orphans of journeymen, tradesmen, artisans, labourers, and servants were specifically excluded. By 1886 the boys and girls could be visited on one afternoon in April and one in October.[4]

From the late 19th century the Freemasons acquired increasing influence over the school. St. Peter's Lodge, Wolverhampton, had become a subscriber by 1863, but by 1875 only four lodges, all local, were as yet subscribing. In the early 1890s, however, Warwickshire and Worcestershire lodges began to subscribe. In 1893 the Provincial Grand Lodge of Staffordshire made a donation, and the lodge was held at the school in 1894 for the laying of the foundation-stone of the chapel. There were 24 lodges subscribing by 1899, and 233 by 1934.[5] In the earlier 20th century most of the governors were Masons and many of the pupils were Masons' children.

In commemoration of a visit to the school by the duke and duchess of York to celebrate its jubilee in 1900, Queen Victoria agreed that the name be changed to the Royal Orphanage of Wolverhampton. A new dormitory was built in 1900. In 1904 the maximum age of entry for boys was raised to 12 and the leaving age to 15; thenceforth one son and one daughter of the same parent could be in the school at the same time. An inspection in 1906, however, revealed that the boys' school was overcrowded and insanitary. The governors therefore decided to limit admissions to the number of leavers and to begin a new building programme. An extra wing, including classrooms and dormitories, was built in 1906. The girls' schoolroom was modernized in 1908, and a new dining-hall and dormitory were built for them in 1909. In 1910–11 a further wing, comprising a classroom, a reading room, a physics and chemistry laboratory, and dormitories, was built on to the boys' school; two wings were added to the girls' school, with a reading room, a classroom, and dormitories. From 1913 two children, of either sex, of the same parent were allowed; by December 1914 there were 345 children.

In 1921 the school applied for recognition by the Board of Education as an efficient secondary school. After an inspection of the school in the same year the board agreed to recognize the boys' department provided that a better-qualified teaching staff could be acquired, the Burnham Scale adopted, and the leaving age raised to 16; those things done, recognition was granted in 1922. By 1924 four new masters with honours degrees had been appointed and several boys were doing advanced work. The girls' department, however, required further improvements; after extensions had been built including classrooms, better baths, and staff bedrooms, it was recognized as efficient in 1927. In 1928 a new wing provided girls' common-rooms and dormitories. By 1934 the boys' curriculum included French, German, Latin, physics, and music, and the girls' included botany. Normal school holidays were by then provided.[6]

When the school became recognized it was thought desirable to establish a separate junior school for the younger children, who were to be admitted at the age of five. In 1930 Graiseley Old

---

[2] *Ann. Rep. 1887: Wolverhampton Orphan Asylum*, 15. Copies of *Ann. Reps.* cited are in Wolverhampton Central Libr.

[3] Ibid. 25.

[4] Ibid. 4.

[5] *Ann. Rep. for 1899: Wolverhampton Orphanage*, 83–4; *Royal Orphanage Wolverhampton: Ann. Rep. for 1934*, 111–123.

[6] *Ann. Rep. for 1934*, 9, 13.

Hall in Claremont Road was bought, and a junior school was built in the grounds. It was opened in 1932; there were then 47 children under 9 years old. It was recognized as an efficient preparatory school in 1934. In 1937 it was reorganized to allow girls to proceed to the senior school at 8 and boys at 11 years. At the same time it was divided into a junior and a preparatory department.

In 1944 the orphanage was renamed the Royal Wolverhampton School. There were then 138 pupils in the boys' school, 82 in the girls' school, and 83 juniors. The admissions policy was relaxed in 1945:

THE ROYAL WOLVERHAMPTON SCHOOL. *Azure on a chevron argent between three bezants a cross pattee gules all within a bordure or charged with three Stafford knots gules*
[Granted 1946]

the governors were permitted to admit motherless children and eligible children without election and to vary the prescribed age at which a child might enter and leave the school.

After the Second World War the school at first continued to flourish. Music teaching was expanded, a new library was built in 1950, and the teaching of chemistry was introduced in the lower forms in 1954. Science had, however, to be dropped from the girls' curriculum in 1954 since a science mistress could not be obtained.[7] In 1960 a new pavilion was opened and a new gymnasium begun.[8] By then, however, the cost of maintaining the children had greatly increased, while owing to improved provision for orphans in state schools the demand for places, especially in the girls' school, was declining. In the early 1960s the school suffered a large and growing financial deficit, and the number of pupils fell from some 360 in the mid 1950s to 286 in 1963.[9] The governors therefore obtained licence to admit fee-paying pupils in 1963. In 1964 they secured a Scheme which closed the girls' senior school while retaining the boys' senior school and the mixed junior school and permitted the admission of fee-paying unbereaved children, as either boarders or day-pupils. The Wolverhampton and Staffordshire education committees and the Lichfield diocesan education committee were given powers to nominate governors.[10] In 1965, to provide for a planned increase in numbers, the buildings were altered to include four new classrooms, a new physics laboratory, study bays, and study bedrooms.[11] A new block built in 1968 provided physics laboratories and dining-rooms. By 1977 there were 320 boys in the senior school, mainly boarders. Besides the normal academic curriculum, woodwork, metalwork, and engineering drawing were taught, and there was a compulsory course in business studies for the senior boys. Tennis-courts and a new swimming-bath had been built.[12]

[7] *Royal Wolverhampton Sch., Wolverhampton: Ann. Rep. for 1946*, 14–15; *1950*, 23; *1954*, 20, 23.
[8] Ibid. *1960*, 15–16.
[9] Ibid. 12; *1962*, 12; *1963*, 13.

[10] Ibid. *1963*, 12; *1964*, 3, 5–7, 16; *1964/5*, 1, 5–6.
[11] Ibid. *1964/5*, 6.
[12] *Public Schs. Yr. Bk.* (1977), 775–7; *Express & Star*, 23 Sept. 1968.

THE UNIVERSITY OF KEELE

THE university college of North Staffordshire, later the university of Keele, was the first of the new universities established in Great Britain after the Second World War.[1] Schemes for a university college for the Potteries had been in the air since 1890. In 1945 E. S. Cartwright, the historian R. H. Tawney, and Gladys Malbon, who had been intermittently involved as tutors or organizers in adult education in the Potteries since 1901, 1908, and 1939 respectively, brought forward new proposals and began negotiations with the University Grants Committee. In 1948 the U.G.C. approved a scheme for a university college in North Stafford-shire with power to grant degrees under conditions of effective external sponsorship. In April 1949 Stoke corporation bought Keele Hall and 154 a. of land for the college. By the end of May Oxford, Manchester, and Birmingham universities had agreed to sponsor the college, and its charter was sealed in August. It was called the university college of North Stafford-shire. Lord Harrowby became the first president and Lord Lindsay of Birker, master of Balliol College, Oxford, the first principal. In addition to the normal governing bodies of a civic university — court, council, and senate — the charter established an academic council on which the sponsors had majority representation. It was to approve senior appointments, appoint external examiners and receive reports from them, and scrutinize the curriculum and organization of studies. The college council included representatives from Staffordshire county council, Stoke city council, and Burton borough council.

THE UNIVERSITY OF KEELE.
Or on a chevron gules an open book argent in base a scythe proper on a chief wavy gules a Stafford knot between a fleur-de-lys and a fret or
[Granted 1950]

A registrar and a librarian were appointed in 1949, and thirteen professors and two readers early in 1950. The curriculum was not settled until October 1950. The scheme which emerged involved a compulsory foundation year with some 300 lectures. They were supplemented by tutorials (later called terminals and sessionals) and included broad courses on the development of western civilization, on man and his environment, and on the industrial revolution and its consequences. The foundation year was to be followed by a three-year combined honours course. Students were required to take at least five subjects, including at least one from each of three groups of related disciplines. The first group of subjects included ancient and modern languages, English, history, and philosophy; the second economics, political institutions, psychology, geography, the history and practice of education, social science, and political and moral philosophy; and the third mathematics, physics, chemistry, biology, and geology. Two or three of the subjects chosen were to be principal subjects studied for three years, and the rest subsidiary subjects studied for one or two years. The class of degree awarded was to depend on the student's performance in all the subjects studied.

A fortnight after the curriculum had finally been agreed the college opened; there were some 90 male and 50 female students. Accommodation was provided not only in the Hall but in army huts built in the park during the Second World War. The former stables of the Hall, known as the Clock House, were converted to a house for the principal, and in 1951 new buildings for physics and chemistry were begun in the grounds.

A target of 600 students had been set, but because of difficulties in providing residential and teaching accommodation it was not reached until 1956. The curriculum was an obstacle to expansion, since one department could not grow without parallel development in the others. Hardly had the target been reached, however, when the college came under pressure from the U.G.C. to take more students. There were 732 in 1960 and 818 in 1962. More space was thus needed; by 1959 over 400 a. of additional land had been bought. J. A. Pickavance was appointed full-time architect in 1952, and Sir Howard Robertson became consultant architect in 1956. A residential block for students was built on the campus in 1952, and another in 1954–5. They formed the core of one hall of residence; each hall came to consist of a group of detached blocks. A second hall was begun at the Hawthorns in Keele village in 1953, and a third on the campus in 1958. Twenty houses for staff were built on the campus in 1951 and more were begun in 1953. Building also continued throughout the 1950s on teaching blocks and laboratories for physics, chemistry, biology, geography, mathematics, and modern languages; they were grouped north-west of Keele Hall. A large lecture hall was built in the same area in 1954–6. In 1959 work began on a permanent library, designed by Sir Howard Robertson; previously the library had been housed in Keele Hall. The new one was finished in 1966. A students' union building designed by Stillman & Eastwick Field was begun near-by in 1961 and

[1] Unless otherwise stated, this article is based on Sir James Mountford, *Keele: an Historical Critique*, and on inf. from Mr. J. M. Kolbert, assistant registrar of Keele (1977).

opened in 1963. A health centre was also begun in 1961.

The curriculum of the college continued on the lines laid down by the founders, with minor alterations and the addition of new subjects. In 1954 weekly seminars (later called discussion groups) were added to the foundation course, and in 1957 the number of lectures was reduced and their sequence rearranged. From 1954 honours students were allowed to take one subject from the arts and social-science groups combined and one from the science group instead of one from each group as before. They were still required to take at least one science and one non-science subject. In 1957 joint honours courses in international relations and in social analysis were set up, and a lecturer in social statistics was appointed. In 1958 Russian was introduced as a subsidiary subject, and funds were raised for a directorship in music. In 1959 a research chair in communication was established. American studies, introduced in 1960, became a principal subject in 1961.

Although the college could award only B.A. degrees, Birmingham and Manchester universities agreed in the early 1950s to award higher degrees for work done at Keele whether by their own or by Keele graduates. Sheffield and Southampton later made like arrangements. Attention was also paid to adult education. Lindsay had hoped to have an extramural department from the outset, but his plans were opposed by the Oxford Delegacy of Extramural Studies, which still ran the university extension courses in the Potteries, and by the Workers' Educational Association. In 1957, however, a University Extramural Committee for North Staffordshire was set up to represent Oxford, the college, and the W.E.A. and to take charge of adult education in the district. In 1962 a department of extramural studies was established at Keele, and Oxford transferred to it the responsibility for its North Staffordshire courses.

In 1951 Lindsay expressed the hope that the college's charter would be altered to enable it to grant higher degrees. Nothing was done until 1959, when the senate set up a charter committee which negotiated with the sponsors and the U.G.C. By 1961 the agreement of the sponsors to the proposed change had been secured, and in 1962 the college received a new charter constituting it the university of Keele. Princess Margaret, countess of Snowdon, who had been president since 1956, became the first chancellor. The charter abolished the academic council and modified the composition of the council and the senate. The representation of the local authorities in the council and the strength of the professors in the senate were reduced. The three authorities, however, were each given power to appoint a deputy pro-chancellor. Sponsorship ceased and the new university had full powers to grant degrees.

The university participated in the national growth of higher education in the 1960s and 1970s, though its numbers increased less rapidly than did those of most other new universities. By 1977 there were 3,187 students, of whom 674 were post-graduates. In 1962 Peter Shepheard succeeded Robertson as consultant architect, and throughout the 1960s work continued both on student and staff residences and on academic buildings. The Chancellor's Building, designed by Shepheard, was begun in 1962 and finished in 1966. It accommodated the departments of history, American studies, economics, politics, psychology, sociology, law, education, and adult education, and two lecture theatres. A sports centre was begun in 1963 and finished in 1967. In 1964 a chapel was built for Anglican, Roman Catholic, and Free Church services. Designed by G. G. Pace, it is a striking building of blue brick with a nave and two semi-circular eastern towers. Also in 1964 work began on a communication building (finished 1966), a science workshop (finished 1965), and extensions to the physics and chemistry departments (finished 1967) and to the geography department (finished 1966). A fourth hall of residence was begun in 1966. In 1968 the geology department and the health centre were extended, and in 1970 a computer centre was built. A ring road was built round the academic buildings in 1971, enabling traffic to be excluded from the central area by 1973.[2] Extensions to the students' union building, providing space for shops, were completed in 1976, and the first part of extensions to the Chancellor's Building was occupied in 1977. The Clock House was being enlarged in 1977 to house the music department.

The university also continued to expand its curriculum. In 1961 the Nuffield foundation gave £20,000 to provide a foundation-year library. The structure of the foundation-year courses was revised in 1963, when fortnightly essays were introduced, and in 1966. A more extensive revision took effect in 1977. The old system of terminals, essays, and discussion groups was abolished; four-week tutorial programmes know as 'topics' were introduced, more closely related to the lecture course than the discussion groups had been, and involving the presentation by the students of an essay or other suitable work. A telescope was acquired in 1962 and astronomy became a subsidiary subject in 1967. A computer was installed in 1963; a department of computer science was established in the early 1970s. Chairs were established in psychology in 1962, in law in 1964, in Russian in 1968, and in sociology in 1969. Also in 1969 the modern languages department was split into departments of French and German, each headed by a separate professor. On the other hand the departments of philosophy and of moral and political philosophy were merged in 1968. In 1971 a research professor in biochemistry was appointed to head a biochemistry research unit, which was later merged with the biology department to form a department of biological sciences.[3] In the early 1970s departments of international relations, music, and social policy and social work, and a centre for postgraduate medical education and research were set up.[4] In addition more combined courses were made available, including one in integrated physical sciences. The most radical change, however, was the introduction in 1973, as alternatives to the standard four-year courses, of some three-year courses exempting undergraduates from the foundation year.[5] In 1977 nearly half the students starting honours work were doing three-year courses.

[2] Univ. of Keele: Rep. of Vice-Chancellor to Council 1970–71, 7; Univ. of Keele Cal. 1973–74, map facing p. 294.

[3] Rep. of Vice-Chancellor 1970–71, 7.
[4] Ibid. 9; ibid. 1973–74, 10; 1974–75, 12.
[5] Univ. of Keele Prospectus 1973–74, 23–6.

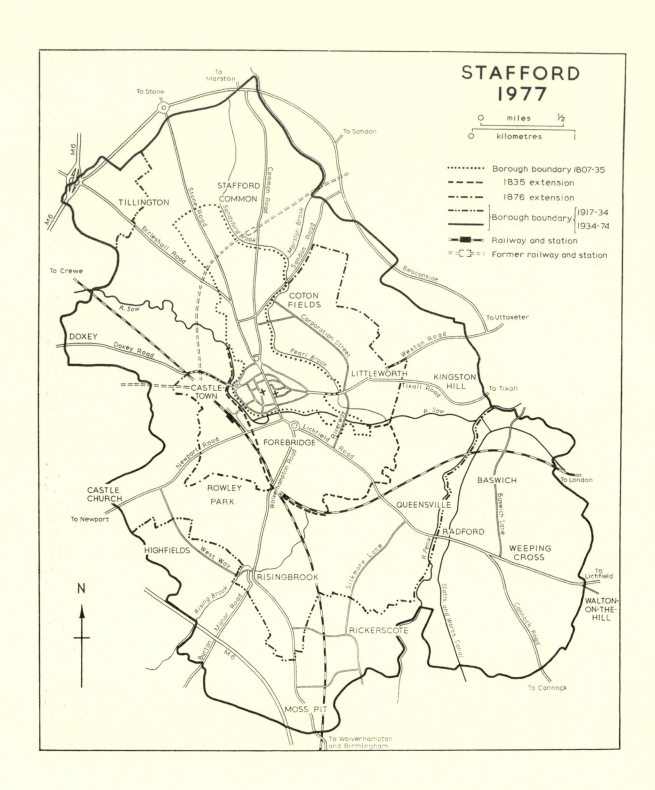

STAFFORD
1977

O miles ½

O kilometres I

·········· Borough boundary 1807-35
– – – – 1835 extension
– · – · – 1876 extension
– ·· – ·· – Borough boundary { 1917-34
———— { 1934-74
—■— Railway and station
= ⊏ ⊐ = Former railway and station

To Marston

To Stone

To Sandon

M6

M6

TILLINGTON

STAFFORD COMMON

To Crewe

R. Sow

DOXEY

Doxey Road

Eccleshall Road

Stone Road

Sandyford Brook

Common Road

Marston Brook

Sandon Road

Beaconside

To Uttoxeter

COTON FIELDS

Corporation Street

Pearl Brook

Weston Road

LITTLEWORTH

KINGSTON HILL

Tixall Road

To Tixall

R. Sow

CASTLE TOWN

FOREBRIDGE

Lichfield Road

Riverway

Newport Road

Wolverhampton Road

BASWICH

To London

CASTLE CHURCH

ROWLEY PARK

To Newport

QUEENSVILLE

RADFORD

Baswich Lane

WEEPING CROSS

HIGHFIELDS

West Way

Rising Brook

RISINGBROOK

Silkmore Lane

R. Penk

Staffs and Worcs Canal

Cannock Road

To Lichfield

WALTON-ON-THE-HILL

N

Burton

M6

Manor Road

RICKERSCOTE

To Cannock

MOSS PIT

To Wolverhampton and Birmingham

THE BOROUGH OF STAFFORD

STAFFORD,[1] the county town and a pre-Conquest borough, lies in the centre of Staffordshire. In 1801 the borough, consisting of the ancient town centre and the liberty of Foregate to the north, covered 364 a.[2] Most of it lay in St. Mary's parish, but part of it formed the parish of St. Chad. The area was increased in 1835 to 610 a. by the addition of the Forebridge portion of Castle Church.[3] In 1876 it was increased to 1,084 a. by additions from Castle Church (part of Newport Road, Castletown, and part of Littleworth) and St. Mary's parish (part of Coton, including the rest of Littleworth).[4] It was further increased to 3,450 a. in 1917 by the addition of more of Newport Road, Rowley Park, Risingbrook, and Silkmore, all from Castle Church, more of Coton, part of Tillington, and the Doxey portion of Seighford.[5] It was increased to 5,089 a. (nearly 8 square miles) in 1934 when Highfields, Burton Manor, Rickerscote, and Moss Pit were added from Castle Church, Baswich, Weeping Cross, and Radford from Baswich parish, and the northern part of Eccleshall Road from Creswell.[6] In 1974 a new borough of 230 square miles was formed consisting of what had been the borough, Stone urban district, and Stafford and Stone rural districts.[7]

The present article is concerned primarily with the history of the area covered by the ancient borough. Some account of the areas added before 1974 is given from the time of their addition. The earlier history of Baswich and Castle Church has been treated in another volume of the Staffordshire History;[8] that of the other new areas is reserved for treatment in a future volume.

The original borough and its liberty lay on a tongue of Keuper Marl and gravel amidst alluvium. The ancient town centre is almost an island, with a loop of the river Sow on the west and south and streams and marshes on the east. The medieval walls followed the limits of the gravel. The town is in a hollow or, as a traveller in 1780 put it, 'seated on a plain, bounded by rising grounds at a very small distance';

the land on the edge of the pre-1974 borough rises to over 300 ft. in many parts.[9] The ground drops to below 250 ft. along the Sow in the town centre and to 239 ft. in the marshy area to the north-east. The centre itself rises to 260 ft. in Earl Street to the north-west of St. Mary's churchyard and again at the east end of Stafford Street.[10] A network of drains running into the Sow was constructed over the low-lying ground outside the town centre in the later 19th century,[11] but the area's liability to flooding was still marked in 1977.[12]

The Sow formed the south-western boundary of the borough.[13] On the north-west the boundary ran up a tributary stream called in 1629 Sparch Pearl ditch. The eastern boundary was Sandyford brook (mentioned in 1432)[14] down to Crooked Bridge. At a perambulation in 1546 it was stated that from there the boundary ran along the Greenway in Coton field, turning south by Crossapenyes croft (Pennycrofts by 1670)[15] to the present Lammascote Road and following that road to the East Gate. By 1807, however, it continued from the Crooked Bridge area down Sandyford brook and then along the bounds of the former royal fish-pool on the north-east of the town; in the latter area it was extended north to Pearl brook (the name of the lower part of Sandyford brook) under an inclosure award of 1807. By that date too the borough included part of the area south of Lammascote Road as far as the Sow; it also included Thieves Ditch meadows between the town ditch and the Sow which had been described as being in the borough in the 1546 perambulation but were stated to be in Forebridge manor in a perambulation of that manor in 1629. In 1807 an area on the east bank of the Sow from the town mill to a point north of Broadeye bridge was transferred from the borough to Forebridge. After the straightening of the Sow east of the town in the early 19th century the boundary continued to follow the line of the old course of the river.[16]

[1] This article was written between 1975 and 1977.
[2] O.S. Book of Ref. to Plan of Par. of St. Mary and St. Chad (1881), 13–14. The adjustment of the boundary in 1807 (see below) made little difference to the acreage.
[3] Census, 1871. V.C.H. Staffs. v. 82, relying on Census, 1831, gives the area of the transferred Forebridge as 317 a., apparently an incorrect figure. V.C.H. Staffs. v. 82–3, is wrong in stating that Castletown and c. 1½ mile of Newport Rd. were added in 1835.
[4] Stafford Corp. Act, 1876, 39 & 40 Vic. c. 196 (Local); O.S. Book of Ref. 21.
[5] Local Govt. Bd.'s Provisional Order Conf. (No. 3) Act 1916, 6 & 7 Geo. V, c. 34 (Local); Census, 1921.
[6] Staffs. Review Order, 1934 (copy, with maps, in S.R.O.); Census, 1951.
[7] Stafford Boro. Official Guide [1976], 21.
[8] V.C.H. Staffs. v.
[9] T. H. Higson, Stafford Survey (Stafford, n.d.), 19–22;

T. Pennant, Journey from Chester to London (1811 edn.), 99.
[10] O.S. Map 1/500, Staffs. XXXVII. 11. 17 (1881 edn.).
[11] V.C.H. Staffs. v. 94.
[12] Higson, Stafford Survey, 58, 60; Stafford Newsletter, 18 Feb. 1977. For what seems to be a reference to flooding of the town centre through the Green Gate in the early 17th century see S.R.O., D. 641/2/C/5/2D, 2nd numbers, f. 2.
[13] For the boundaries to the early 19th century see S.R.O., D.1323/E/1, f. 28v. (1546); D.641/2/E/1/3C, bounds of Stafford manor 1629; W.S.L., copy of lost plan of Stafford; S.R.O., Q/RDc 16, map (1807).
[14] S.R.O. 938/208.
[15] W.S.L., H.M. 26/2, f. 38v. For the widow Crosseapeny who held a pasture in that area in 1535 see S.R.O. 938/224.
[16] S.R.O., D.1323/A/1/8, ntry following 24 Sept. 1861; below, p. 198.

Prehistoric finds in and near Stafford may indicate scattered early settlement, while the Bronze- or Iron-Age hill-fort at Berry Ring is only 2½ miles south-west of the town. There is also evidence of Roman settlement, notably on a site in Clarke Street in the angle between Eastgate Street and South Walls.[17] Stafford has been identified as the island of Betheney or Bethnei where St. Bertelin is said to have had his hermitage before moving to a more remote part; others then occupied the island and called it Stafford,[18] a name meaning a ford by a staith or landing-place.[19] There was presumably some settlement at the river-crossing by 913 when Ethelfleda, the lady of the Mercians, 'built the burh' at Stafford in the course of the struggle against the Danes following the victory of her brother Edward the Elder at Tettenhall in 910.[20] Soon afterwards Stafford became the county town of the new Staffordshire. A mint was established there under Athelstan (924–39), and it continued until the reign of Henry II (1154–89).[21]

Domesday Book apparently records 128 occupied houses in Stafford (with perhaps another 18) and 51 or 52 houses which were waste.[22] Suburbs were evidently developing in Foregate to the north by 1170 and Forebridge to the south by 1288.[23] Although described in 1521 as 'a proper and fair town',[24] Stafford was listed in 1540 among a number of towns where many houses were in a dangerous state of disrepair.[25] It was still in decay in 1575 when Elizabeth I was told during her visit that the causes were the decline of capping and the removal of the assizes.[26] A survey of all the inhabitants, including children, in 1622 listed 384 households and a total population of some 1,550, 'whereof 390 are poor';[27] the hearth-tax returns of 1666 listed 168 households as chargeable and 171 as non-chargeable.[28] To Celia Fiennes in 1698 Stafford was 'an old-built town, timber and plaster pretty much in long peaked roofs of tiling . . . the streets are pretty large and well pitched . . . some of the houses are pretty good.'[29] Defoe in the earlier 1720s found the town 'neat and well built' and 'lately much increased, nay, as some say, grown rich by the clothing trade'.[30]

By 1732 most of the buildings were of brick.[31] The population in 1801 was 3,898.[32]

In the 19th century the north end of the town developed as an industrial suburb based on the footwear industry. By 1831 the population was 6,956.[33] A writer remarked in 1834 that the town had 'generally a very respectable aspect, having both within its limits and in its vicinity many handsome mansions occupied by wealthy families'.[34] Soon after the opening of the Grand Junction Railway in 1837 Stafford developed as a centre of communications, and an industrial suburb grew up near the station. There was an Irish element in the population by 1850.[35] The population was 12,532 in 1861,[36] and by 1868 the town was taking on 'the appearance of the seat of a great manufacture'.[37] In 1871 the increase in population, by then 14,437, was attributed to the flourishing state of trade at Stafford and to the activities of building societies.[38] In 1881 the population was 19,977.[39] There was much industrial development from the early 20th century.[40] The population was 23,383 in 1911, 28,635 in 1921, 40,263 in 1951, 47,806 in 1961, and 55,001 in 1971.[41] There has been a Polish community since c. 1950 when Poles living in camps around Stafford began to settle in the town.[42] There was a small Jamaican community by 1962,[43] and by 1970 there were also Hindus, Sikhs, and Moslems.[44]

Stafford was the birthplace of Izaak Walton (1593–1683), biographer and author of The Compleat Angler;[45] Sir Martin Noell (1614–65), financier;[46] John Prescott Knight (1803–81), portrait painter, whose father, the comedian Edward Knight (1777–1826), worked at the Stafford theatre from 1799 to 1802;[47] Thomas, 1st Earl Brassey (1836–1918), politician and colonial governor, whose father, the engineer Thomas Brassey, was working on the Grand Junction Railway in 1836;[48] and Edward Ilsley (1838–1926), from 1888 Roman Catholic bishop, from 1911 to 1921 archbishop, of Birmingham.[49] Three natives of Stafford have been lord mayor of London: Sir Thomas Offley (?1505–82) in 1556–7,[50] Sir Hugh Homersley (?1565–1636) in 1627–8,[51] and Thomas Sidney (1805–89) in 1853–4.[52]

[17] Alison J. Walker, 'The Archaeology of Stafford to 1600 A.D.' (Bradford Univ. M.A. dissertation, 1976), 6–13, 65–8, 92; P. H. Robinson, 'Pre-Anglo-Saxon Finds from Stafford', T.S.H.C.S. 1968–70, 1–9; below, p. 187.
[18] Church of St. Bertelin at Stafford and its Cross, ed. A. Oswald (Birmingham [1955]), 7, 9; Camden, Brit. (1586 edn.), 330; Plot, Staffs. 409.
[19] E. Ekwall, Concise Oxford Dict. of Eng. Place-names.
[20] V.C.H. Staffs. i. 219; Florence of Worcester, Chronicon ex Chronicis, ed. B. Thorpe, i. 122–3 (giving date as 914).
[21] P. H. Robinson, 'The Stafford Moneyers, 924–1165', T.S.H.C.S. 10–22; Cherry, Stafford, 140–6; S.H.C. 1927, 209–12.
[22] V.C.H. Staffs. iv. 23 and n., 37. The figure of 112 occupied houses given on p. 23 should read 110.
[23] See p. 191; V.C.H. Staffs. v. 83.
[24] L. & P. Hen. VIII, iii(1), p. 509.
[25] Act for re-edifying of towns, 32 Hen. VIII, c. 18.
[26] See pp. 201, 216.
[27] Ruth M. Kidson, 'The Inhabitants of the Borough of Stafford, 1622', T.O.S.S. 1956–59, 16–28. The detailed numbers given for each household add up to 1,554 and the summaries to 1,549; a total of 1,560 is given in the survey itself.
[28] S.H.C. 1921, 44–50. One of the 168 represents an empty house on which Mr. Baddeley of London was charged.
[29] Journeys of Celia Fiennes, ed. C. Morris, 167.
[30] D. Defoe, Tour thro' the Whole Island of Gt. Brit.

(1928 edn.), ii. 478.
[31] Diary of a tour in 1732 . . . made by John Loveday of Caversham, ed. J. E. T. Loveday (Roxburghe Club, 1890), 11.
[32] V.C.H. Staffs. i. 329.
[33] Ibid.
[34] White, Dir. Staffs. (1834), 109.
[35] Staffs. Advertiser, 10 Aug. 1850, p. 4.
[36] Census, 1861.
[37] Staffs. Advertiser, 26 Dec. 1868, p. 4.
[38] Census, 1871.
[39] Ibid. 1881.
[40] See p. 220.
[41] Census, 1911–71.
[42] Stafford Newsletter, 25 Nov. 1977.
[43] Ibid. 11 Aug. 1962.
[44] Staffs. Advertiser, 10 Sept. 1970, p. 8.
[45] D.N.B.; below, pp. 244, 268.
[46] See p. 266.
[47] D.N.B. sub Knight, Edw.; H. Dyson, John Prescott Knight R.A.: a Catalogue (Stafford Hist. and Civic Soc. 1971).
[48] D.N.B.
[49] J. J. Delaney and J. E. Tobin, Dict. Cath. Biog. 585–6; Who Was Who 1916–28.
[50] D.N.B.
[51] St. Mary's, Stafford, Par. Reg. (Staffs. Par. Reg. Soc. 1935–6), 14; A. B. Beaven, Aldermen of City of London, i. 13.
[52] Staffs. Advertiser, 16 Mar. 1889.

William Withering (1741–99), physician, botanist, and mineralogist, was in practice at Stafford from 1767 to 1775 and was sole physician at the Staffordshire General Infirmary opened in 1766.[53] George Baker (?1773–1847), musician, was organist of St. Mary's from 1790 to 1800; he was repeatedly reprimanded by the corporation for neglecting his duties and was prohibited from playing his own favourite composition, 'The Storm'.[54] Notable M.P.s have included John Bradshaw (1602–59), regicide, and R. B. Sheridan (1751–1816), dramatist.[55]

William I defeated the Staffordshire and Cheshire rebels in a battle at Stafford in 1069. He passed through the town again in the campaign of 1070, when a castle was built.[56] The 'Stanford' besieged in 1153 by the future Henry II was formerly identified as Stafford but has since been shown to be Stamford (Lincs.).[57] During the Barons' Wars the town was apparently royalist at first: the devotion of the burgesses was commended in September 1261.[58] It seems later to have changed sides and was captured by royalist forces in 1263.[59] Richard II was taken through Stafford in 1399 as a prisoner on his way to London.[60] In the revolt of January 1400 Henry IV ordered the bailiffs to arm the able-bodied men of the town and bring them to join him at London.[61] He passed through in 1403 after the battle of Shrewsbury.[62] The future Henry VII stopped at Stafford in 1485 to negotiate with the Stanleys before the battle of Bosworth. Elizabeth I visited the town on progress in 1575, and James I was received there in 1617 on his way south from Scotland.[63] In the Civil War Stafford was at first held by the royalists. Charles I stayed at the High House in September 1642; during the visit Prince Rupert is said to have shot holes in the weathercock of St. Mary's from the garden of the house.[64] The town resisted two Parliamentarian assaults in February 1643, but Sir William Brereton captured it by stealth in May.[65] It then became the seat of the parliamentary county committee.[66] William III passed through in 1690 on his way to Ireland.[67] In the campaign of 1745 Stafford was the rendezvous of a division of the duke of Cumberland's army assembled in November; the duke stayed there, according to tradition at Chetwynd House, in December.[68]

GROWTH OF THE TOWN. The street plan as shown by Speed in 1610[69] developed long before

then, and it remained substantially unaltered until the later 20th century. Roman finds of the 3rd or 4th century in Clarke Street in the angle of Eastgate Street and South Walls suggest early reclamation of the marsh, but perhaps for agriculture rather than settlement. The Saxon defences may not have enclosed so large an area as the later walls, which followed the limits of the gravel. On the east side the Saxon rampart may have followed the line of Salter Street and Tipping Street rather than North and South Walls; the theory is strengthened by the fact that Tipping Street has also been called Diglake, a name perhaps suggesting a ditch. In addition the pottery kiln in operation south of the junction of Eastgate and Tipping Streets in the 10th or 11th century is likely to have been outside the walls. The centre of the early settlement may in fact have been around the highest part of the town in the area which became the ecclesiastical centre.[70]

The axis of the town has long been the main street between the North and South Gates, with the market-place mid-way along it and the two parish churches on opposite sides of the street. It was referred to as the high street in the late 13th century, a name which persisted for all or part of it. Gaolgate Street, the stretch north from the market-place, was known both as the Rothermarket and as Cow Street between the 15th and the 17th centuries, presumably from a cattle market held there. The name Gaolgate Street came into use in the 17th century, the North Gate being then used as a gaol. Greengate Street, the southern part of the main street, was known as Southgate Street by the late 15th century; it was also known as Green Street in the later 16th century, and the name Greengate Street was in use by 1681.[71] The market-place, having had the shire hall built in its centre in the late 16th century, became an open square again in the 1790s when the new shire hall was built on its eastern side.[72] In 1834 the main street was described as 'commodious and well paved'; it contained 'many well stocked shops and several excellent inns and spacious mansions, some of which are noble specimens of the antique half-timbered houses of England, in the highest state of perfection, their fantastic fronts having either been renewed, or preserved by many coats of paint'.[73] In 1856 a Russian cannon captured at Sebastopol was placed in Market Square; it was removed to Pitcher Bank in Eastgate Street in 1869 and sent to Chester castle in 1876.[74] The corporation erected a stone

[53] D.N.B.; Staffs. Life, Sept. 1951, 14–15, 18, 21.
[54] D.N.B.; S.R.O., D.1323/A/1/3, pp. 47, 127, 135, 179, 207, 216–17, 220; the marquess of Anglesey, One-Leg, 22.
[55] D.N.B.; below, pp. 237–8.
[56] F. M. Stenton, Anglo-Saxon Eng. (1971 edn.), 595–7; Orderic Vitalis, Eccles. Hist. ed. Marjorie Chibnall, ii. 228, 236.
[57] By Z. N. and C. N. L. Brooke, 'Henry II, Duke of Normandy and Aquitaine', E.H.R. lxi. 86–7, correcting L. Delisle, Recueil des Actes Henri II, i. 61.
[58] Close R. 1259–61, 488.　　[59] V.C.H. Staffs. iii. 242.
[60] Isobel Morcom, 'A thousand years of royal visits to Stafford', T.S.H.C.S. 1974–6, 76.
[61] Cal. Close, 1399–1402, 34; E. F. Jacob, The Fifteenth Cent. 25.
[62] V.C.H. Staffs. i. 239; T.S.H.C.S. 1974–6, 76.
[63] T.S.H.C.S. 1974–6, 76–9; S.R.O., D.(W.) 1721/1/4, f. 114.
[64] T.S.H.C.S. 1974–6, 79–80; Plot, Staffs. 336.
[65] Hist. MSS. Com. 78, Hastings, ii. 90–1; S.H.C. 1941, 138.
[66] S.H.C. 4th ser. i, pp. xiii, 32.
[67] T.S.H.C.S. 1974–6, 81.

[68] D.N.B. sub William Augustus; Staffs. Advertiser, 4 Apr. 1914; Cherry, Stafford, 148.
[69] See p. 188. For the dating of Speed's plan see S. A. H. Burne, 'Early Staffs. Maps', T.N.S.F.C. liv. 62. See also W.S.L., copy of lost plan of Stafford, the date of which is given as c. 1600 by H. L. E. Garbett, 'Note on an Old Plan of Stafford', T.N.S.F.C. lviii. 56; Mr. R. A. Lewis, Advisory Officer (History) in the Staffs. County Council Educ. Dept., suggests that it may have been drawn in connexion with the dispute over the repair of the Green Bridge in 1629 (below, p. 197), since some of the details mentioned in the course of the dispute appear on the plan.
[70] Walker, 'Archaeology of Stafford', 10, 12–13, 19–20, 92; below, p. 216. Clarke St. itself apparently dated from the late 1830s and was at first called Charles St.: W.S.L., D.1798/358; White, Dir. Staffs. (1851), 345. It does not, however, appear in the 1841 Census Returns.
[71] Kettle, 'Street-names', 46.　　[72] See pp. 201–2.
[73] White, Dir. Staffs. (1834), 109.
[74] 'Reminiscences of an old Stafford Resident', T.O.S.S. 1932, 47; S.R.O., D.1323/A/1/8, 3 Feb. 1869; /9, 27 Oct., 1 Dec. 1874, 2 Mar. 1875, 4 Jan. 1876; W.S.L., D.1798/435, John Shallcross's memo. bk. 18 Jan. 1876.

drinking-fountain designed by George Wormal in the square in 1887 to commemorate Queen Victoria's jubilee; it was removed in 1934 to allow more parking space and the widening of the main street.[75]

Eastgate Street occurs as the street leading to the East Gate in the later 13th century and by name *c.* 1300.[76] It is in fact older: one Orm of Eastgate occurs in the 12th century, and the Clarke Street area was occupied then.[77] In 1834 Eastgate Street was considered the principal side street of the town.[78] The open space half-way along it was called the Horsefair in the 17th century but became known as Pitcher Bank from the crockery market held there

the early 19th century they were known respectively as Near Backwalls and Far Backwalls. They were officially named South Backwalls and North Backwalls in 1838 and South Walls and North Walls in 1924.[82] Tipping Street may be the Typpernslane (or Typperuslane) of 1365. It occurs as Dog Lane between 1390 and 1501 and as both Tipping and Chipping Street in the 16th century. Diglake was an alternative name by the end of the century and became the usual name in the 18th century. It was officially named Tipping Street in 1838.[83] Martin Street occurs variously as Martin Lane and St. Martin's Lane from the late 15th century. By the

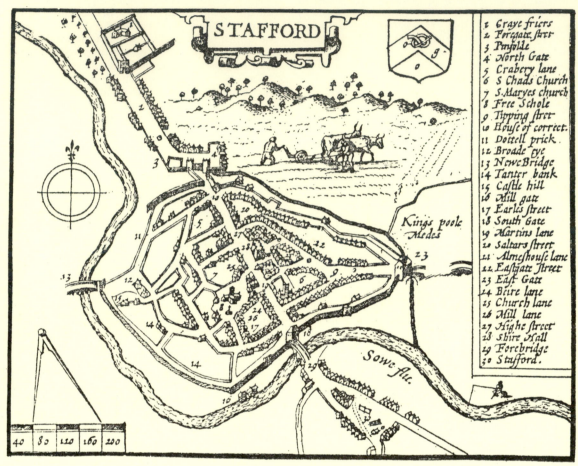

PLAN OF STAFFORD 1610

in the 19th century.[79] In 1804 the residents of Eastgate Street were given permission by the corporation to plant lime trees on each side of the street,[80] and there were still lime trees along it in 1977. Lammascote Road continuing the street eastwards outside the walls may be of Iron-Age origin.[81]

A number of side streets lead from Eastgate Street to the main street. Two led south and north along the inside of the walls from the East Gate: that on the south occurs in 1397 as the way leading from the East Gate to the South Gate and that on the north in 1466 as the way near the King's Pool. By

end of the 17th century it was becoming known as Smoky Lane. It was officially named Martin Street in 1838.[84] The Greengate Street end was closed to traffic in 1958.[85] The name St. Martin's Lane survived in the early 19th century for the road leading from Martin Street to Market Square. It was probably the lane leading to the shire hall mentioned in 1390 and Almshouse Lane of the 17th century. It was renamed Martin's Court in 1838 but had become St. Martin's Place by 1879.[86] The Martin Street area was taken over and extensively rebuilt by the county council from the 1890s.[87] The south-

[75] *Staffs. Advertiser*, 22 Oct. 1887, 14 and 28 Apr. 1934.
[76] Kettle, 'Street-names', 46.
[77] See p. 245; Walker, 'Archaeology of Stafford', 92.
[78] White, *Dir. Staffs.* (1834), 109.   [79] See p. 214.
[80] S.R.O., D.1323/A/1/3, p. 275.   [81] See p. 196.
[82] F. B. Stitt, 'Stafford Borough Court Rolls, 1396–7', *T.S.H.C.S.* 1974–6, 33; Kettle, 'Street-names', 53.

[83] Kettle, 'Street-names', 52.
[84] Ibid. 48; W.S.L., H.M. uncat. 28, deed of 7 Dec. 1696; S.R.O., C/C/D/C/1, 10, 12–14.
[85] Ex. inf. the boro. planning officer (1977).
[86] Kettle, 'Street-names', 42, 48; *Cal. Close*, 1389–92, 281; O.S. Map 1/500, Staffs. XXXVII. 11. 17 (1881 edn.).
[87] See p. 202.

eastern quarter of the town centre, forming St. Chad's parish, had a population of some 500 in 1851 and was then described as destitute.[88] South and North Walls were largely rebuilt with council houses in the earlier 20th century,[89] and the area between Eastgate Street and South Walls was cleared in the 1960s and 1970s, mainly for a new telephone exchange, a new police station, magistrates' court, and probation office, and a new road. Market Street on the north side of the shire hall was formerly known as the Pig Market; it had its present name by 1834.[90] Salter Street, the western extension of Eastgate Street, occurs as Salters Lane from the late 14th century. By the early 19th century it was known as Vine Street, from the Vine inn which stood there by 1782.[91] It was officially named Salter's Street in 1838, but the use of Vine Street continued. From the mid 1870s it was called Salter Street.[92] The Gaolgate Street end was closed to traffic in 1973.[93]

Broadeye by the crossing of the Sow at the western end of the town was probably the site of the castle of 1070.[94] It occurs by name in 1290 and was apparently an inhabited area by then.[95] Butts were maintained there by the corporation in the earlier 17th century.[96] The streets to the east (officially named Broad, Queen, and Mount Streets in 1838) existed by the early 17th century.[97] By the late 1830s the Broadeye area was a working-class district consisting of twenty or thirty streets, courts, and passages.[98] It was approached from Gaolgate Street along Crabbery Street, the 1838 name for Crabbery Lane which occurs from 1411,[99] and also along Stafford Street, the 1838 name for what was called Lewis's Lane in the 17th and 18th centuries and Jerningham's Row and Stafford Row in the earlier 19th century.[1]

The way round the inside of the walls continued on the west side of the main street. The Greengate Street end was known as Mill Bank by the early 19th century.[2] The continuation from the mill to Broadeye was called Tenterbanks by the early 17th century, taking its name from a rack used for drying cloth; there was mention of 'le teynter on the walls' in 1468.[3] That part of the street was also known as Kitling Lane.[4] From Broadeye it continued as Dottell Prick by 1600 (presumably le Dottons Prykys of the late 15th century).[5] After the opening of the gas-works in 1829 that stretch became Gas Lane but was officially named Dottell Street in 1838; it was called Chell Road by 1841. It continued along the line of the walls to the North Gate as

Bull Hill, a name which occurs by the 17th century. With the rebuilding of the area in the 1970s the whole stretch became Chell Road.[6]

An inner road parallel to Tenterbanks along Mill Street and Earl Street to Broad Street occurs as Mill Street from 1287–8 and as Mill Lane from the late 15th century. By the late 16th century the northern part was known as Earl Street; the name was subsequently used for the whole street, but the southern part was officially named Mill Street in 1838.[7] Cherry Street (before 1838 Talbot Lane or Street) ran from the west end of Mill Street to Broadeye.[8] The sequence of streets between Tenterbanks and Mount Street formed by Water Street, Church Lane (Bier Lane before the 18th century), Albion Place, and Chapel Street existed by the 17th century and ran along the western boundary of St. Mary's churchyard. From 1774 the churchyard was extended westward, reaching Earl Street by the early 19th century.[9]

The first major change in the western part of the town centre was the building of Victoria Road from the southern end of Cherry Street to the railway station in 1865–6 to provide a more direct route from the station to the town centre than the existing way along Newport Road. It included the construction of a bridge over the Sow, which was rebuilt in 1933.[10] The area at the junction of Cherry, Earl, and Mill Streets was opened up as Victoria Square when the County Technical School was built on the corner of Earl and Cherry Streets in the mid 1890s.[11] The borough war memorial in the centre of the square was unveiled in 1922; the county war memorial at the station end of Victoria Road was unveiled in 1923.[12] About 1969 the section of Victoria Road north of Tenterbanks was blocked off.[13] In 1908 Victoria Pleasure Grounds (later Victoria Park) were opened on 4 a. on the west bank of the river between Victoria, Station, and Newport Roads; they included a bandstand. Another $1\frac{3}{4}$ a., including a bowling-green, on the east bank was added in 1911, with Coronation Bridge linking the two parts. A further $2\frac{1}{2}$ a. on the east bank north of Victoria Road was added in 1930, with tennis courts and a children's paddling pool.[14] In the early 1960s cottages at Broadeye were demolished, and the street pattern was subsequently modified for road improvements. Cherry Street and parts of other streets were absorbed by extensions to the College of Further Education completed in 1975.[15] From the mid 1960s[16] to the mid 1970s the area

[88] M. W. Greenslade, 'Stafford in the 1851 Religious Census', *T.S.H.C.S.* 1974–6, 70.
[89] See p. 233; Stafford Libr., Stafford Hist. and Civic Soc. photographic coll., vol. on waterworks, etc., photograph of 8 cottages in North Walls erected 1934. A block of 4 cottages in North Walls bears the date 1912.
[90] Kettle, 'Street-names', 47; below, p. 214.
[91] Kettle, 'Street-names', 50; W.S.L., D.1798/581.
[92] S.R.O., D.1323/1/5, p. 327; White, *Dir. Staffs.* (1851), 345; *P.O. Dir. Staffs.* (1860; 1868; 1872; 1876); *Kelly's Dir. Staffs.* (1880); O.S. Map 1/500, Staffs. XXXVII. 11. 17 (1881 edn.).
[93] Ex inf. the boro planning officer.
[94] See p. 200.
[95] *Cal. Inq. p.m.* ii, p. 482; *S.H.C.* 1939, 116.
[96] S.R.O., D.1323/E/1, ff. 151, 261v.
[97] Speed, *Map of Staffs.* (1610); Kettle, 'Street-names', 43, 49.
[98] Kettle, 'Street-names', 38.
[99] Ibid. 45.   [1] Ibid. 52.   [2] Ibid. 48.
[3] Ibid. 52; Speed, *Map of Staffs.* (1610).

[4] Kettle, 'Street-names', 47.
[5] Ibid. 45; S.R.O., D.641/1/2/76, rot. [3]; D.1323/E/1, f. 48v.; Speed, *Map of Staffs.* (1610).
[6] Kettle, 'Street-names', 43–4.
[7] Ibid. 45, 48. For a reference to Earl Lane in 1564–5 see W.S.L., S.MS. 369, p. 125.
[8] Kettle, 'Street-names', 44.
[9] Ibid. 42, 44, 49, 51, 53; Wood, *Plan of Stafford* (1835); below, p. 245. For Church Lane in the 18th and early 19th cents. see S.R.O., D.3130/24; W.S.L. 754/36.
[10] *Staffs. Advertiser*, 9 Sept. 1865, 14 July 1866, 28 Jan. 1933.
[11] O.S. Map 1/2,500, Staffs. XXXVII. 11 (1902 edn.).
[12] *Stafford Newsletter*, 11 Feb. 1966, p. 20; *Staffs. Advertiser*, 2 June 1923.
[13] Stafford Coll. of Further Educ. *Bulletin*, no. 9 (Feb. 1969; copy at the college); *Stafford Newsletter*, 1 May 1970, p. 21.
[14] *Staffs. Advertiser*, 20 June 1908, 26 Aug. 1911, 26 July 1930.
[15] See p. 265.   [16] *Stafford Newsletter*, 27 Mar. 1964.

north from Crabbery Street to Chell Road was developed as two shopping precincts.

Lack of surviving medieval buildings and of adequate documentation makes any assessment of the appearance of the town before the 16th century, except for the walls and churches, a matter of speculation.[17] The surviving late-16th- and early-17th-century buildings and those known from later illustrations reveal a pattern still evident in late-

some other prominent timber features like window oriels were often enriched with carved ornament. The roofs were commonly gabled above large dormers on the main elevations, and while some were probably tiled those on the smaller houses were thatched.

Most of the houses in the main street and around the market-place were of two, or exceptionally three, storeys with attics and had frontages two rooms wide;[20] there was sometimes a short rear wing

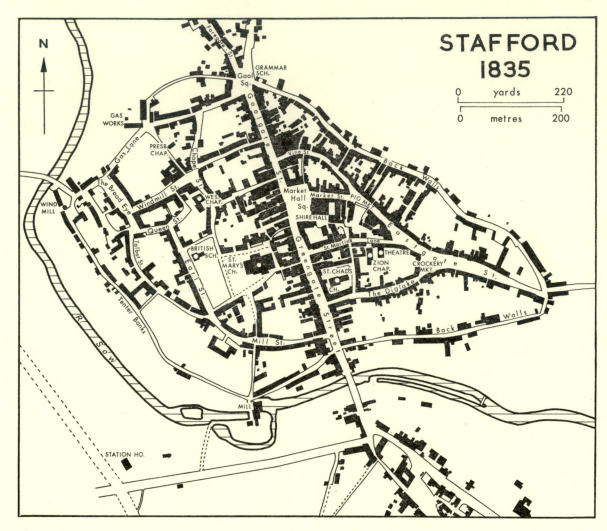

17th-century documents.[18] They show that within the built-up area there was considerable variety in the scale of buildings and hence in the status of their inhabitants. The more prosperous houses were concentrated along Greengate and Gaolgate Streets. Timber-framing with an infill of wattle and daub was the universal walling material, and in the more elaborate buildings such as the High House in Greengate Street[19] the main panels were often sub-divided by curved and cusped braces. Each floor level was marked by a jetty on the principal fronts, and the brackets supporting the jetties as well as

providing space for at least one more room. No. 50 Greengate Street, demolished in 1965, was of that type.[21] So, superficially, were 'Shaw's House'[22] between the High House and the Swan Hotel, and no. 56 Greengate Street (Jenkinson's Restaurant), but they originally lacked attics. Moreover, since each of them has two adjacent ranges at right angles to the street they may preserve elements of under-lying medieval plans. The High House, built apparently in 1595, is of exceptional size and has the plan of an **E**; the short central range houses a staircase.[23]

[17] Thanks are offered to Mr. A. G. Taylor of the Staffs. County Council Planning Dept. for help with the following account of Stafford's buildings.
[18] Marie Rowlands, 'Houses and People in Stafford at end of 17th cent.' *T.S.H.C.S.* 1965–7, 46–56.
[19] See plate facing p. 192.
[20] W.S.L., Staffs. Views, ix. 85, 89–90.

[21] Staffs. County Council Planning Dept., Conservation Section photographs, 517/65–524/65, 538/65–541/65.
[22] F. W. B. Charles, 'Ancient High House, Greengate Street, Stafford', 4 (duplicated booklet, 1975; copy in W.S.L., C.B. Stafford).
[23] Ibid. *passim.*

Although there were thus some large houses, several of the outlying streets had stretches without buildings,[24] and towards the edge of the built-up area, as in Mill and Eastgate Streets, the lesser houses were of only one storey with attics. Some of them had frontages of only a single room, a form which was exemplified in the alms-houses in Eastgate Street[25] and in nos. 57 and 64 Eastgate Street (demolished in 1977). Others, like nos. 76 and 77 Eastgate Street, were two bays wide and more substantially built; others still, for example no. 11 Church Lane (demolished in 1963)[26] and no. 36 Mill Street, were cruck-built. Such one-storey houses may have been the most usual type, although small two-storeyed houses such as no. 30 Eastgate Street were probably also relatively common.[27]

Brick first appears as a walling material in the mid 17th century at the Swan Hotel[28] and was displacing timber-framing in the early 18th century.[29] At Chetwynd House (now the Central Post Office) brick is combined with stone decoration, notably in the capitals of the Corinthian pilasters, to create an elegant and symmetrical façade of c. 1700,[30] and there are many later-18th-century frontages, particularly in Greengate Street and the streets adjacent to the former Horsefair. Some, as at Eastgate House[31] and the William Salt Library,[32] are on older buildings which were remodelled. The design of such façades followed national fashion. Most of the houses were of two or three storeys and consisted of a range parallel with the street and one or more short wings at the rear containing the staircase.

No specific area of 18th-century expansion can be recognized in the town centre, and there may have been little new building for the poorer inhabitants, who presumably continued to live in, and to modify in small ways, 17th-century or earlier buildings. Working-class housing of the 19th century in the centre of the town was concentrated in courtyards and alleys between Eastgate Street, Clarke Street, and South Walls, and in the Broad Street and Princes Street areas.[33]

Until the 19th century Foregate consisted mainly of Foregate field and was part of Marston manor, but it also enjoyed the privileges of the borough by 1206.[34] A suburb was evidently developing outside the North Gate (later the Gaol Gate) by 1170 when a Seman of Foregate (*de extra portam*) occurs.[35]

The Franciscan friary founded at Stafford by 1274 probably stood from the start at the junction of Foregate Street and Browning Street, known to have been its site by the 14th century.[36] Foregate Street was mentioned by name in 1411.[37] Browning Street occurs as Brownings Lane in 1633 and continued as such until renamed in 1838.[38] By the early 17th century Foregate Street was lined with buildings as far as the junction with Browning Street, and the settlement was then referred to as Foregate village;[39] it was also known as Forehead by the 1640s, a usage which continued until the beginning of the 19th century.[40] In 1644 buildings within musket shot of the town walls, including the former friary, were demolished by order of the parliamentary county committee to make an attack on the town more difficult.[41] In 1666 several people were presented at the Marston manor court for building cottages on the waste and commons in Foregate.[42] By 1727 there were several buildings around the point where the main road forks to Eccleshall and to Stone.[43] A Quaker meeting-house was opened in Foregate Street in 1730 and the Staffordshire General Infirmary in 1766.[44] In 1793 a new county gaol was opened on part of Foregate field, and the present County Road running from Foregate Street to the entrance of the gaol existed by 1807.[45] Gaol Square seems to have been created c. 1800 with the demolition of the former county gaol and part of the Gaol Gate.[46] Gaol Road running north from the square was built c. 1803.[47]

With the inclosure of Foregate field in 1807 the area began to be built over, and in the course of the 19th century an industrial suburb developed as the footwear industry became concentrated in that part of the town. Already by 1808 three houses had been built on the Crofts; they were probably the first part of Union Buildings, which led off Gaol Road south of the gaol.[48] By 1820 the Eccleshall road was built up as far as the then borough boundary and beyond; the stretch to the boundary was known as Brook Street by 1838 and until the 1950s.[49] A National school was opened in Gaol Road in 1825 and Christ Church in Foregate Street in 1839.[50] By 1838 New Street, Friar Street, and Cross Street on the north side of Browning Street had been built, with the corresponding part of Fancy Walk;[51] Wright Street to the east of the new streets existed by 1851.[52] That area was cleared in the 1960s and 1970s; the rebuilding of New Street was completed

[24] Speed, *Map of Staffs.* (1610); W.S.L., copy of lost plan of Stafford.
[25] W.S.L., Staffs. Views, ix. 76; below, p. 267.
[26] Planning Dept., Conservation Section photographs, 335/63.
[27] See also W.S.L., Staffs. Views, ix. 76, 78.
[28] F. W. B. Charles, 'Swan Hotel, Greengate Street, Stafford' (TS. 1966; copy in W.S.L., C.B. Stafford).
[29] See p. 186.
[30] See plate facing p. 209. The tradition that the house was built c. 1740 (Cherry, *Stafford*, 148) appears unfounded. The interior has early-18th-century panelling.
[31] The date-stone of 1683 on the façade presumably refers to the original build and was reset at the refronting.
[32] See plate facing p. 193.
[33] O.S. Map 1/2,500, Staffs. XXXVII. 11 (1881 edn.); above, pp. 188–9, and below, p. 232.
[34] S.R.O., Q/RDc 16, map; below, p. 222.
[35] *S.H.C.* i. 61–2.
[36] See p. 207.
[37] *Cal. Fine R.* 1405–13, 223.
[38] S.R.O., D.1323/E/1, f. 201B; D.1323/A/1/5, p. 327.

[39] Speed, *Map of Staffs.* (1610); E 134/9 Jas. I East./15; E 134/10 Jas. I East./33.
[40] *S.H.C.* 4th ser. i. 201; S.R.O., D.1323/E/2, pp. 129–30.
[41] See p. 199.
[42] S.R.O., D.590/437/3.
[43] S.R.O., D.240/E(A)/2/221.   [44] See pp. 234, 253.
[45] See p. 204; S.R.O., Q/RDc 16, map.
[46] W.S.L., M. 606, quarter sessions order 1793; below, pp. 199, 204.
[47] S.R.O., D.1323/A/1/3, p. 245; D.1323/E/2, p. 129.
[48] W.S.L., D.1798/573/3; W.S.L. 756/36; abstract of title of property there 1818 (in private possession in the 1960s).
[49] C. and J. Greenwood, *Map of Staffs.* (1820); S.R.O., D.1323/A/1/5, p. 326; *Stafford Official Guide* (edns. of the 1950s).
[50] See pp. 248, 260.
[51] Wood, *Plan of Stafford* (1835); Dewhirst & Nichols, *Map of Stafford* (1838); *Staffs. Advertiser*, 17 Jan. 1835, p. 1, advert. for sale of newly erected house in a new street off Brownings Lane.
[52] H.O. 107/1999.

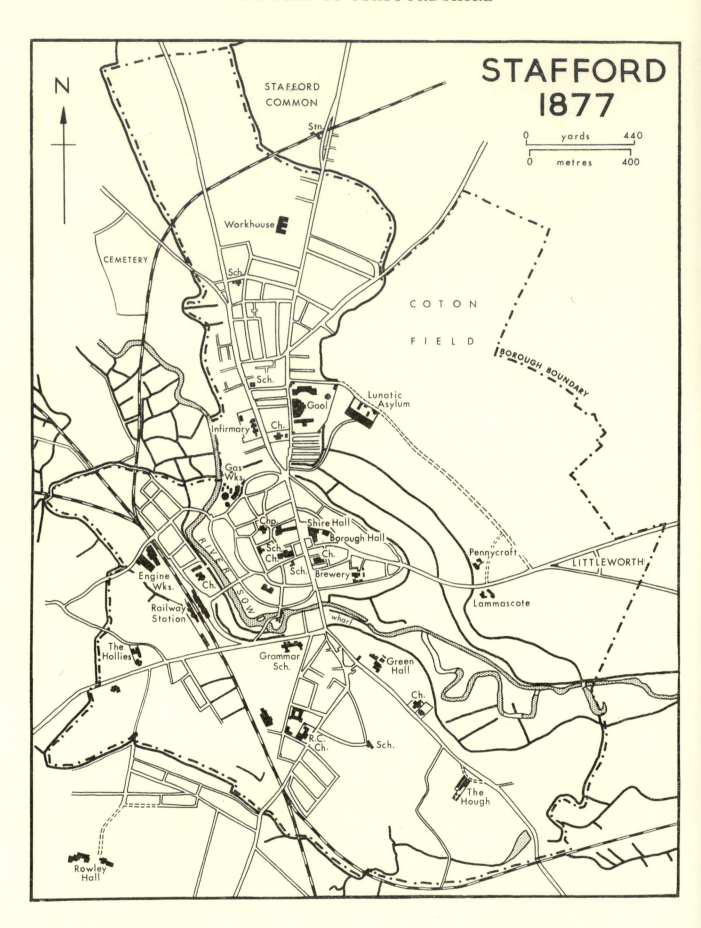

STAFFORD: THE HIGH HOUSE, GREENGATE STREET, *c.* 1835

CARTOON OF 1806
when R. B. Sheridan abandoned his parliamentary seat at Stafford for one at Westminster

Stafford Mill, demolished 1957

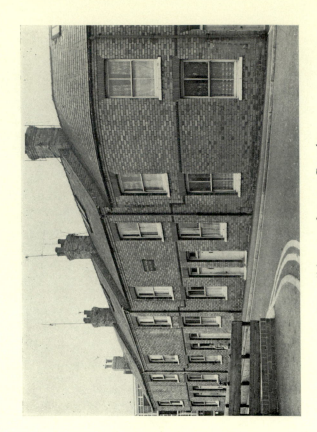

Council houses of 1901 at Broadeye

The Picture House, Bridge Street

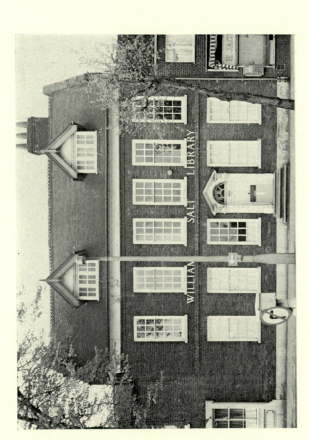

The William Salt Library, Eastgate Street

STAFFORD

in the early 1960s, and other rebuilding was in progress in 1977.[53]

There was a marked rise in the population in the 1860s, and houses and factories were built over pasture land and gardens.[54] Peel and Victoria Terraces running between the Marston and Sandon roads had been begun by 1861.[55] Marsh Street (the northern extension of New Street) and Rowley Street connecting it with the Marston road date from 1865;[56] Rowley Street was described in 1873 as 'the most attractive of the new thoroughfares which . . . owe their existence to the increasing trade of the town'.[57] Victoria and Lloyd Streets off Gaol Road north of the gaol, Wogan Street and Albert Terrace between the Marston and Sandon roads, and Princess Terrace (later Princess Place) to the north all existed by 1871.[58] Tillington Street linking Marsh Street with the Stone road was opened in 1875;[59] it was a continuation of Lovatt Street which ran from the Marston road and had been built shortly before. Streets were being built by 1877 off the Marston road north and south of Common station, opened in 1874 just beyond the borough boundary.[60] Yet in 1876 the mayor stated that there was 'a hundred or two of houses absolutely required to accommodate working men' in the northern part of the town.[61] The population of the district was described in 1884 as consisting 'almost entirely of workers in the shoe trade or engineering'.[62]

Building continued, although fewer new streets were laid out before the 1920s. Izaak Walton and Alliance Streets off the Eccleshall road just beyond the boundary were being laid out c. 1880; there were then several villas in the Eccleshall road itself, and more houses had been built there by 1900.[63] The first of the salt works by Stafford common was opened in 1893.[64] In the early 20th century several houses were built along North Street (later Stone Road) and Sandon Road.[65] Council estates were built on either side of Stone Road north of the railway in the late 1920s and earlier 1930s. The privately built Holmcroft estate west of Stone Road dates from the mid 1930s, and there was also private building in the period between the two

World Wars along Eccleshall Road and Sandon Road.[66] The council built houses at Holmcroft in the late 1940s and at Tillington in the late 1950s.[67] A privately built estate on Stone Road at Tillington was begun in the later 1950s and was extended on both sides of Crab Lane to Eccleshall Road in the earlier 1960s.[68] The private Parkside estate on the borough boundary east of Stone Road was begun in the mid 1960s,[69] and building continued into the 1970s. The M6 motorway access point on Eccleshall Road at Creswell was opened in 1962.[70] The link road to the Stone road was continued east to the Sandon road along the borough boundary in the mid 1970s. Industrial estates were developed in the 1970s in the area to the south between the Marston road (Common Road) and Sandon Road. There was extensive demolition in the 1970s in Gaol Square and in the fork between Foregate Street and Gaol Road to make way for the roundabout at the northern end of a relief road running east of the town centre. It involved the removal of a clock which had itself in 1930 replaced a drinking-fountain erected in 1889 in memory of Thomas Sidney by his widow. The fountain was surmounted by a shaft bearing lamps and a figure of Samson, which was replaced by a clock in 1916. The whole structure was destroyed in 1928 when a motor-van backed into it.[71]

The area east of the town, occupied by the royal fish-pool, Coton field, and hamlet of Littleworth, has been developed largely as a residential district. After the inclosure of much of Coton field in 1880 new streets were eventually laid out. A school was built at Littleworth in the mid 1880s 'in view of the probable erection of house property on Coton field'.[72] Corporation Street running from Weston Road to Sandon Road dates from the mid 1890s.[73] Crooked Bridge Road, the ancient access road from Foregate to Coton field,[74] was extended to join it, and council houses were built there in 1902.[75] The first part of Oxford Gardens (originally Oxford Street) running from the northern end of Corporation Street was built in the early 1900s,[76] and the streets

[53] *Stafford Newsletter*, 9 July 1960, 26 Aug. 1961, 19 Jan. 1963.
[54] *Staffs. Advertiser*, 20 Dec. 1873, p. 4.
[55] R.G. 9/1907; date-stone of 1862 in Peel Terrace; *Staffs. Advertiser*, 6 Feb. 1864, p. 7.
[56] S.R.O., D.1323/J/2, 1 Aug. 1865.
[57] *Staffs. Advertiser*, 20 Dec. 1873, p. 4.
[58] R.G. 10/2816; date-stone of 1871 in Victoria St.
[59] *Staffs. Advertiser*, 3 Apr. 1875.
[60] *Boro. of Stafford* (plan of 1877; copy in W.S.L., M.765); S.R.O., D.1490 Add., nos. 31, 94, 97; below, p. 198.
[61] *Stafford Boro. Extension Bill: Mins. of Evidence, 1876*, 12 (reprinted from the official rep.; copy in W.S.L. Pamphs. *sub* Stafford).
[62] *Souvenir of Golden Jubilee of St. Patrick's* (1945; copy at Blessed William Howard High Sch., Stafford).
[63] O.S. Map 6", Staffs. XXXVII. NW., NE., SE. (1889–90 and 1902 edns.); date-stones of 1878 and 1881 in Sandon Rd., 1882, 1883, 1887, 1888, and 1890 in Peel Terrace, 1887 in Albert Terrace, 1888, 1893, 1894, and 1898 in Stone Rd., and 1890 in Tillington St.
[64] See p. 221.
[65] S.R.O., D.1490 Add., 1909–11, 1913–15; O.S. Map 6", Staffs. XXXVII. NE. (1925 edn.). The Stone road north of the railway was called Stone Rd. by c. 1919; the part south remained North St. until c. 1929 when it too became Stone Rd.: *Halden & Haywood's Dir. Stafford* (1920), pp. 51, 61; O.S. Map 6", Staffs. XXXVII. NE. (1925 edn.); below, p. 262.

[66] Ex inf. the boro. surveyor (1963); W.S.L., Sale Cat. B/2/7; S.R.O., D.1490 Add., 1928–33; Stafford Libr., Stafford Hist. and Civic Soc. photographic coll., unlabelled vol. of photographs of public works; O.S. Map 6", Staffs. XXXVII. NW., NE. (prov. edn. with addns. of 1938).
[67] Ex inf. the boro. surveyor.
[68] *Stafford Official Guide* (edns. of c. 1961 and c. 1964) street plan.
[69] *Stafford Newsletter*, 6 Oct. 1967.   [70] See p. 196.
[71] *Staffs. Advertiser*, 29 June, 6 July 1889, 28 Sept. 1895, 12 May 1928. A lamp pillar erected with the clock in 1930 was removed during road improvements c. 1970. In 1977 the figure of Samson was in Stafford Mus. and Art Gallery. For Sidney see below, p. 270.
[72] *Staffs. Advertiser*, 2 May 1885; below, p. 262.
[73] S.R.O., D.834/8/1/1, plan of 1893; D.1490 Add., nos. 263 and 352 and entries from May 1895; *Halden & Son's Dir. Stafford* (1893), 31; (1904), maps of new streets; O.S. Map 6", Staffs. XXXVII. SE. (1902 edn., revised 1900); below, p. 262.
[74] S.R.O., D.1323/E/1, f. 28v. (reference to Crooked Bridge over Sandyford brook in 1546); S.R.O., D.240/E(A)/2/221. The road was realigned in 1864 to allow for the extension of the county gaol: *Staffs. Advertiser*, 29 Oct. 1864; below, p. 205.
[75] O.S. Map 6", Staffs. XXXVII. SE. (1902 edn.); below, p. 233.
[76] S.R.O., D.1490 Add., from Mar. 1900; *Staffs. Advertiser*, 3 Jan. 1903, p. 6; 14 Feb. 1903, p. 4; O.S. Map 6", Staffs. XXXVII. NE., SE. (1902 and 1925 edns.).

running from the southern end date from the same period.[77] Houses were also built along Weston Road as far east as Littleworth in the early 20th century.[78] The first houses on the council's Coton Field and Lammascote estates were built in 1913–14,[79] and Riverway, continuing Corporation Street over the Sow to Lichfield Road, was opened in 1914.[80] In the 1920s the Coton Field and Lammascote estates were extended and two more council estates were built north of Weston Road and at Littleworth.[81] There was also private building in the period between the two World Wars around the extension of Oxford Gardens to the then borough boundary and along Weston and Tixall Roads. The Gate inn was built c. 1932 on the site of the former Littleworth toll-house at the junction of Weston and Tixall Roads.[82] The Kingston Hill golf course south of Weston Road was opened in the early 1920s, replacing a small course on Stafford common.[83] The engineering works of W. H. Dorman & Co. Ltd. on Tixall Road dates from the late 1920s.[84] Beaconside, running from Weston Road to Sandon Road along the then boundary, was laid out in 1937.[85] Royal Air Force No. 16 Maintenance Unit was opened in 1939 on a site east of Beaconside and partly within the borough.[86] A housing estate for the R.A.F. was built on the opposite side of Beaconside in 1950; blocks of flats were added in 1968.[87] The Coton Farm council estate on Douglas Road, including some Air Ministry houses, was built in the early 1950s. Further development there was completed in 1969 after the corporation had taken over much of the Coton Field allotments in 1964, and more building was in progress in 1977.[88] Council flats, the first in the borough, and old people's bungalows were built at the south end of Corporation Street in 1952; the near-by 16-storey Pennycrofts Court was completed in 1968.[89] The privately built estate north of Weston Road on the then boundary was built in the later 1950s and that on Tixall Road south of the golf course in the later 1960s.[90] Fairway on the Lammascote estate was extended over the Sow to the new St. Leonard's Works of English Electric in 1962.[91] In 1976 work began formally on the inner relief road running east of the town from Gaol Square across the former royal fish-pool and over the Sow south of Lammascote Road to Lichfield Road.[92]

At the time of its transfer to the borough from Castle Church in 1835 the suburb of Forebridge still centred on the Green. It was, however, expanding and was 'in all respects closely connected with the remainder of the town'.[93] The railway from Birmingham, opened in 1837, ran along the southern and western boundaries, and bridges were built over it on the Wolverhampton and Newport roads.[94] The Lichfield road crossed the London line, opened in 1847, by a level-crossing at Queensville until a bridge was built in the late 19th century.[95] The name Queensville was adopted as the new name of the hamlet of Spittal Brook in 1838 to commemorate Queen Victoria's coronation; the brook formed the southern boundary of Forebridge and crossed under the Lichfield road at that point.[96]

St. Paul's church in Lichfield Road was opened in 1844,[97] and 'the little suburb of the Hough' grew up along the road about then;[98] St. Leonard's Avenue dates apparently from c. 1880.[99] West of Wolverhampton Road Friars Road, which had a few buildings at its north end by 1835, had several houses by the middle of the century.[1] Friars Terrace (so called by 1871 and possibly the line of an old road to Rowley Hall) was part of Friars Road by 1861, with Middle Friars and Barracks Road as side roads. Barracks Road (renamed Park Street by 1871) took its name from the militia (later police) barracks at its junction with Friars Terrace. Austin Friars had been built by 1868, with a police station at its west end, and Telegraph Street by 1871.[2] Most of the streets on the east side of Wolverhampton Road date from the 1860s and 1870s,[3] although Cramer Street dates from the 1880s[4] and Alexandra Road from the beginning of the 20th century.[5] New buildings for the grammar school were completed in Newport Road in 1862.[6] In the 1860s a brewery was opened west of the Green in the area of the former Austin friary.[7] Part of the Green was laid out as a garden in 1878 and another part, which was waste land, was inclosed.[8] The Oval was laid out over the grounds of

[77] S.R.O., D.1490 Add., from Sept. 1900; *Halden & Son's Dir. Stafford* (1904), maps of new streets; datestones of 1908 and 1909 in Cambridge St.; below, p. 249.
[78] O.S. Map 6″, Staffs. XXXVII. SE. (1925 edn.).
[79] See p. 233.
[80] Plaque on bridge.
[81] See p. 233.
[82] O.S. Map 6″, Staffs. XXXVII. NE., SE. (prov. edn. with addns. of 1938); Stafford Libr., Stafford Hist. and Civic Soc. photographic coll., vol. labelled 'Street Improvements'.
[83] *Halden & Haywood's Dir. Stafford* (1922), where it appears as Stafford Artizan's Golf Club Course; ex inf. Mr. R. H. Dartford of Stafford (1977).
[84] See p. 219.
[85] Ex inf. the boro. surveyor (1963).
[86] Ex inf. the station commander, R.A.F. Stafford (1963).
[87] Ex inf. the boro. surveyor (1963) and local residents (1976).
[88] Ex inf. the boro. surveyor (1963; 1977); *Stafford Newsletter*, 27 Sept. 1952, 29 Sept., 13 Oct. 1967.
[89] Ex inf. the boro. surveyor (1963; 1977); *Staffs. Advertiser*, 4 Apr. 1952.
[90] Local inf.; *Stafford Newsletter*, 6 Oct. 1967.
[91] The bridge was officially opened in Oct.: ex inf. the boro. surveyor (1963).
[92] *Stafford Newsletter*, 5 Mar. 1976.
[93] *V.C.H. Staffs.* v. 83, 90–1, 98; Wood, *Plan of Stafford*

(1835); *1st Rep. Com. Mun. Corps.* H.C. 116, App. III, p. 2025 (1835), xxv. For the house of Austin friars and the medieval hospitals see *V.C.H. Staffs.* iii. 273–4, 290–4.
[94] S.R.O., D.1323/L/1, 24 Jan. 1834, 16 and 24 Apr. 1835, 5 Aug. 1836; D.1323/A/1/5, pp. 475–6.
[95] 'Reminiscences of an Old Stafford Resident', *T.O.S.S.* 1932, 45; O.S. Map 6″, Staffs. XXXVII. SE. (1889 and 1902 edns.).
[96] *Staffs. Advertiser*, 30 June 1838; Dewhirst & Nichols, *Map of Stafford* (1838); H.O. 107/973; Calvert, *Stafford*, 94.
[97] See p. 248.
[98] H.O. 107/973; H.O. 107/1999; Calvert, *Stafford*, 94.
[99] O.S. Map 6″, Staffs. XXXVII. SE. (1889 edn.); date-stone of 1883.
[1] Wood, *Plan of Stafford* (1835); H.O. 107/1999.
[2] R.G. 9/1907; R.G. 10/2819; *P.O. Dir. Staffs.* (1868; 1872); O.S. Map 6″, Staffs. XXXVII. SE. (1889 and 1902 edns.); below, p. 197.
[3] W.S.L., D.1798/530/1F, deed of 10 Apr. 1877; ibid. 530/7; S.R.O., D.1490 Add., from Apr. 1876; date-stone of 1876 in Shrewsbury Rd.; *Boro. of Stafford* (plan of 1877).
[4] S.R.O., D.1490 Add., from Dec. 1881; O.S. Map 1/500, Staffs. XXXVII. 15.3 (1881 edn.); date-stones of 1882 and 1883.
[5] *Staffs. Advertiser*, 26 Apr. 1902, p. 6; S.R.O., D.1490 Add., from Apr. 1902; date-stone of 1909.
[6] See p. 166.
[7] See p. 221.
[8] *Staffs. Advertiser*, 6 July 1878.

Green Hall in the mid 1890s and was gradually built up with middle-class houses; large houses were also built in the corresponding part of Lichfield Road in the later 1890s.[9] The central library was opened on the site of Green End House at the junction of Lichfield and Newport Roads in 1914, and the road there was widened at the same time.[10] The Odeon cinema on a near-by site was opened in 1936.[11] An important development took place in the early 20th century when Siemens Bros. & Co. Ltd., having bought land between Lichfield Road and the railway in 1900, opened an electrical engineering works there in 1903.[12] In that year it also built an estate for its workers on the Stychfields part of the site.[13] The influx of new workers was probably responsible for the further development of St. Leonard's Avenue and the building of St. George's Road and Christopher Terrace in the early years of the century.[14] Queensville Avenue dates from the years between the two World Wars.[15] Council houses were built at the end of St. George's Road in the late 1950s,[16] and the St. Leonard's Works of Siemens' successor, the English Electric Co. Ltd., was opened to the east in 1962.[17] In the 1970s demolition was carried out in the fork of the Lichfield and Wolverhampton roads to make way for the roundabout at the southern end of the relief road.

Castletown (also known in the later 19th century as Newtown)[18] grew up round the railway station, opened in 1837. Growth was further encouraged by the opening of Henry Venables's sawmills in Doxey Road in 1864 and W. G. Bagnall's engine works in Castle Street in 1876. In 1876, however, it was stated that most of the inhabitants were railway workers, such as engineers, stokers, and engine cleaners. A school was built in 1863 and a church in 1866.[19] The hamlet of Doxey to the west developed as a suburb from the late 19th century.[20] Building plots there were advertised in 1898 as 'a rare opportunity to railway servants, the land being within a few minutes' walk of the engine sheds'.[21] In 1913 Universal Grinding Wheel Co. Ltd. opened

a works on Doxey Road between Castletown and Doxey; in 1935 it built a small estate in Greensome Lane, Doxey, for its employees.[22] A mission church was built in Doxey in 1914.[23] Council estates were built there in the late 1940s and early 1950s,[24] and subsequently there has been private building.

The Newport Road area west of the railway developed as a residential district.[25] In 1876 it contained '62 houses of the villa class' occupied by 'people who are in trade or have business in Stafford'.[26] More were built in the later 19th century, notably in Rowley Avenue.[27] In the early 20th century small houses were built along the south side of Newport Road.[28] On the north side Upmeads, designed by Edgar Wood and dating from 1908, has been described as 'one of the most interesting houses of the date in the whole of England'.[29] The Castle golf course north of the road was opened c. 1911.[30] There was much private building from the 1950s to the 1970s along the north side of the road and in the open country on either side; it included the High Park estate laid out c. 1960 over the grounds of the late-19th-century Highfield Manor.[31]

Rowley Park was laid out over part of the grounds of Rowley Hall by the Staffordshire Land, Building, and Improvement Co. Ltd., formed in 1866 to build 'suburban residences of a superior class'. The scheme failed to attract customers, and the company was wound up in 1871. The building of houses continued over the next century. The Hall itself became a girls' reformatory c. 1930.[32] Playing-fields were opened over another part of the grounds in 1960.[33]

A few villas were built in the Rowley Bank area of the Wolverhampton road in the later 19th century. The terraces in Rowley Grove and those in Park Crescent on the main road date mainly from the early 20th century.[34] At Risingbrook to the south houses were built along the main road in the early 20th century. More were built there and in new

[9] Ibid. 23 Dec. 1893; S.R.O., D.1490 Add., nos. 633, 646, 667; date-stone of 1895 on house on corner of Lichfield Rd. and the Oval; W.S.L., Sale Cat. A/1/6, p. 16; O.S. Map 6", Staffs. XXXVII. SE. (1902 edn.).

[10] *Staffs. Advertiser*, 21 Mar. 1914; Roxburgh, *Stafford*, 104, 107.

[11] *Staffs. Advertiser*, 10 Oct. 1936.   [12] See p. 220.

[13] S.R.O., D.1490 Add., nos. 915, 940; *Staffs. Advertiser*, 26 Dec. 1903, p. 4; *Eng. Electric and its People* (Mar. 1955), 19 (copy in Stafford Libr.); B. E. Collingwood, 'Study of the effects of the foundation of the electrical engineering ind. on the growth and social development of the boro. of Stafford', 13–16, 30–1 (copy in W.S.L., Th. 17). The houses were sold to the Sutton Dwellings Trust after the merger of Eng. Electric with G.E.C. in 1968: ex inf. Mr. H. Abrahams, G.E.C. Power Engineering Co. Ltd. (1977).

[14] See pp. 220, 263; *Staffs. Advertiser*, 2 Jan. 1904, p. 6; S.R.O., D.1490 Add., nos. 879, 883, 887, 944; date-stones of 1909 in St. Leonard's Ave. and 1910 and 1913 in St. George's Rd.; O.S. Map 6", Staffs. XXXVII. SE. (1902 and 1925 edns.).

[15] O.S. Map 6", Staffs. XXXVII. SE. (prov. edn. with addns. of 1938).

[16] Ex inf. the boro. surveyor (1963).

[17] See p. 220.

[18] *Stafford Boro. Extension Bill: Mins. of Evid.* 37, 49, 66; W.S.L., Sale Cat. A/1/6, p. 38.

[19] H.O. 107/973; H.O. 107/1999; R.G. 9/1907; R.G. 10/2819; *Stafford Boro. Extension Bill: Mins. of Evid.* 65, 78, 111; date-stone of 1848 in Doxey Rd.; *Boro. of*

Stafford (plan of 1877); below, pp. 218–19, 249, 261.

[20] Dates on houses 1892–1909.

[21] W.S.L., Sale Cat. A/1/6, pp. 6, 30–1.

[22] See p. 220; *Staffs. Chronicle*, 25 Jan. 1951.

[23] See p. 249.   [24] Ex inf. the boro. surveyor (1963).

[25] *V.C.H. Staffs.* v. 83. Brunswick Terrace, a side road by the railway, dates from the early 1850s: deed of 1938 relating to no. 12 and referring to 'an earlier lease of 1851' (in possession of the owner, 1962); *P.O. Dir. Staffs.* (1854). Castle Ho. is wrongly described in *V.C.H. Staffs.* v. 84, as county council offices instead of as government offices.

[26] *Stafford Boro. Extension Bill: Mins. of Evid.* 12, 27.

[27] O.S. Map 6", Staffs. XXXVII. SW. (1890 and 1901 edns.), SE. (1889 and 1902 edns.).

[28] Ibid. SW., SE. (1925 edn.); S.R.O., D.1490 Add.

[29] Pevsner, *Staffs.* 250. See also *V.C.H. Staffs.* v. 83–4.

[30] *Halden & Haywood's Dir. Stafford* (1912), 26.

[31] For Highfield Manor see O.S. Map 6", Staffs. XXXVII. SW. (1901 edn.); P. Murray and R. Frost, *Victorian and Edwardian Staffs. from old photographs*, nos. 22–4.

[32] *Staffs. Advertiser*, 11 May, 24 Aug. 1867, 18 Feb., 11 Mar. 1871; *Stafford Boro. Extension Bill: Mins. of Evid.* 13, 27, 35–8; W.S.L., D.1798/580; W.S.L., M.694; W.S.L., Sale Cat. A/1/6, pp. 33–4; *V.C.H. Staffs.* v. 84 (wrongly naming the co. as a result of an error in *P.O. Dir. Staffs.* (1868), 648), 90; below, p. 205.

[33] *Stafford Newsletter*, 4 June 1960, p. 15.

[34] *Boro. of Stafford* (plan of 1877); O.S. Map 6", Staffs. XXXVII. SE. (1889, 1902, and 1925 edns.); date-stones of 1884 and 1902 in Rowley Grove; S.R.O., D.1490 Add.

side roads in the period between the two World Wars.[35] In the mid 1920s the British Reinforced Concrete Engineering Co. Ltd. built an estate in Burton Manor Road for its employees; it converted Burton Hall into a social club.[36] Several council estates were built in the Risingbrook area after the Second World War. The first was east of the Wolverhampton road and dates from the late 1940s and early 1950s; flats were added at the south end of Merrivale Road in the mid 1950s, and the estate was extended on either side of that road in the later 1960s and early 1970s. The Manor estate west of the Wolverhampton road was built in the 1950s.[37] To the north-west are the two Highfields estates, no. 1 built in the mid and later 1950s and no. 2 dating from the earlier 1960s; two 16-storey blocks of flats were completed in 1967.[38] West Way was built through Highfields linking the Wolverhampton and Newport roads. In the 1960s and 1970s there was considerable private building along Burton Manor Road and in new side roads off it.[39] At Moss Pit there was some private building along the Wolverhampton road in the earlier 20th century, notably in the 1920s.[40] An estate designed by E. Bower Norris of Stafford was built over the grounds of Burton House west of the road in the later 1940s by the English Electric Co. Ltd. for its employees; after the merger of the company with G.E.C. in 1968 the houses were sold to the borough council, which in turn sold some of them to the occupants.[41] A council estate consisting mainly of prefabricated houses was built east of the main road in 1950; the area was redeveloped with both council and privately built houses in the 1970s.[42] Private estates were built on either side of the main road south to the borough boundary from the later 1950s to the 1970s. The M6 motorway was opened through the south-eastern part of the area in 1962.[43]

At Rickerscote, already a considerable hamlet in the earlier 19th century, there was private building in the 1920s and 1930s. The St. Peter's Gardens council estate dates from the earlier 1950s.[44] There was private building along Silkmore Lane and Silkmore Crescent in the period between the World Wars, and the works of the British Reinforced Concrete Engineering Co. Ltd. was opened on the site of Silkmore farm in 1926. The group of roads to the east running off the Lichfield road date from the same period, and they were linked to Silkmore Lane by the building of Lancaster Road in the earlier 1960s.[45] The council estate around Exeter Street and Sidney Avenue at the southern end of Silkmore Lane was built in the earlier 1950s and extended in the later 1960s. The council houses in Meadow Road to the north date from 1950.[46] The late-18th-century Silkmore Hall was demolished in 1962; Hall Close, an estate of council flats intended for pensioners and their younger relatives, was completed over the site in 1967.[47]

The Weeping Cross area of Baswich was already developing as a residential district in the 1830s. There was considerable private development there and at Radford in the years between the two World Wars, and several private estates were built from the 1950s on both sides of the Lichfield and Cannock roads and of Baswich Lane. Building was still in progress in 1977. From the late 19th century there was some industrial development at the north end of Baswich Lane between the railway and the canal.[48]

COMMUNICATIONS. With its position at a river crossing and its status as the county town Stafford has always had some local importance as a centre of communications. On the other hand the main road from London via Lichfield and Stone to the north-west of the country by-passed Stafford, following the Trent valley east of the town. By the 14th century Stafford was linked to it by the Stone road, and the roads to Sandon and to Uttoxeter via Weston-upon-Trent were probably other early links. The town had a postmaster c. 1680, and from 1785 to 1808 the Holyhead post route lay through Stafford.[49] The main roads out of the town were turnpiked in the later 18th century. The three turnpike trusts were amalgamated in 1867 and abolished in 1880.[50] The first part of the Staffordshire stretch of the M6 motorway was opened in 1962 as a by-pass running west of the town with access points at Creswell and Dunston.[51]

There is evidence to suggest that the causeway carrying what is now Lammascote Road across the marshy area on the east side of the town was constructed in the Iron Age.[52] The road east from the

[35] S.R.O., D.1490 Add.; O.S. Map 6″, Staffs. XXXVII. SE. (1925 edn. and prov. edn. with addns. of 1938).
[36] *Stafford: an Industrial Survey* (Stafford, 1932), 49, 51 (copy in W.S.L. Pamphs. *sub* Stafford); M. Greenslade, *St. Austin's, Stafford* (Stafford, 1962), 29 (copy in W.S.L. Pamphs. *sub* Stafford).
[37] Ex inf. the boro. surveyor (1963; 1977); *Stafford Newsletter*, 27 Sept. 1952, 22 Dec. 1956.
[38] Ex inf. the boro. surveyor (1963; 1977); *Stafford Newsletter*, 22 Oct. 1960, 19 Nov. 1965, 28 Apr., 26 May, 27 Oct. 1967.
[39] *Stafford Newsletter*, 12 Jan. 1963, 6 Oct. 1967, 17 Apr. 1970; local information (1977).
[40] S.R.O., D.1490 Add.; O.S. Map 6″, Staffs. XLIV. NE. (prov. edn. with addns. of 1938).
[41] '*English Electric*' *Housing Estates* (n.d. but apparently 1952; copy in Stafford Libr.); *English Electric and its People* (July 1948), 3–5; local inf. (1977).
[42] Ex inf. the boro. surveyor (1963; 1977); *Stafford Newsletter*, 27 Sept. 1952. [43] See below.
[44] *V.C.H. Staffs.* v. 84; S.R.O., D.1490 Add.; O.S. Map 6″, Staffs. XLIV. NE. (prov. edn. with addns. of 1938); ex inf. the boro. surveyor (1963); *Stafford Newsletter*, 27 Sept. 1952.
[45] S.R.O., D.1490 Add.; O.S. Map 6″, Staffs. XXXVII.

SE., XLIV. NE. (prov. edn. with addns. of 1938); *Stafford Official Guide* [c. 1964], street plan; below, p. 220.
[46] Ex inf. the boro. surveyor (1963; 1977); *Stafford Newsletter*, 16 May 1969.
[47] *V.C.H. Staffs.* v. 94; *Stafford Newsletter*, 28 Apr. 1962, 18 June 1965; ex inf. the boro. surveyor (1977).
[48] *V.C.H. Staffs.* v. 2–4 (where Weeping Cross should be described as south, not north, of the church); S.R.O., D.1490 Add.; O.S. Map 6″, Staffs. XXXVII. SE. (prov. edn. with addns. of 1938); *Stafford Official Guide* (edns. of the 1950s, 1960s, and 1976), street plan; *Stafford Newsletter*, 21 May 1960, 12 Jan., 3 May 1963, 13 Jan., 6 Oct. 1967, 17 Apr. 1970; below, p. 221.
[49] *V.C.H. Staffs.* ii. 275–7; xvii. 11; S. A. H. Burne, 'The Coaching Age in Staffs.' *T.N.S.F.C.* lvi. 52, 59; *S.H.C.* 1934(1) 124–6; below, p. 237. For the Stone road see S.R.O., D.593/A/2/27/5 and 8; E. J. S. Parsons, *The Map of Britain circa 1360 known as the Gough Map*, 36.
[50] Stafford District Turnpike Roads Act, 1866, 29 & 30 Vic. c. 50 (Local and Personal); Annual Turnpike Acts Continuance Act, 1878, 41 & 42 Vic. c. 62.
[51] *V.C.H. Staffs.* ii. 284.
[52] P. H. Robinson, 'Pre-Anglo-Saxon Finds from Stafford', *T.S.H.C.S.* 1968–70, 4–6.

town was mentioned in the 13th century.[53] The 'bridge of the king's fish-pool' which was repaired in 1257 presumably carried the road over the dam of the pool, later the dam of Eastgate mill.[54] The bridge outside the East Gate by the mill was rebuilt in 1399–1400; in the early 17th century it was a single-arch stone bridge.[55] There was another bridge to the east over Pearl brook; in the mid 18th century its repair was the corporation's responsibility.[56] It was on the Eastgate dam that the bailiffs and councillors met Elizabeth I when she came to Stafford from Chartley in 1575.[57] The road was turnpiked as part of the Stafford–Uttoxeter road in 1793.[58] By 1820 there was a toll-gate at the junction with the Tixall road at Littleworth; it was discontinued in 1878, and the demolition of the toll-house was ordered in 1880.[59]

The road to Lichfield and to Cannock which leaves Stafford by the Green Bridge over the Sow occurs c. 1200: Radford bridge by which it crosses the Penk c. 1½ mile south-east of the town centre was mentioned in the reign of John.[60] At Weeping Cross in Baswich the road forks to Lichfield and to Cannock. The road from Stafford to Cannock was turnpiked in 1793,[61] and by 1834 there was a toll-gate at Weeping Cross, which continued in use until the road was disturnpiked.[62] The Lichfield branch was never turnpiked, although it became part of the Holyhead post route in 1785.[63] The Green Bridge was probably the 'great bridge' mentioned c. 1200,[64] and it occurs in 1285 as the bridge of Stafford.[65] For its maintenance the Crown in 1351 made a three-year grant to the bailiffs and townsmen of pontage on goods for sale brought into the town over the bridge.[66] By the later 16th century it was a five-span stone bridge, although two of the middle spans were planked over. In 1583 the two spans were rebuilt by the corporation with stone taken from the town walls between the South and East Gates.[67] The name Green Bridge was coming into use by the 1590s.[68] In 1615 it was established that by long custom the corporation and the lord of Forebridge manor shared responsibility for the bridge, presumably because the boundary between the borough and Forebridge was held to run down the middle of the river.[69] In 1629–30, after some dispute, the corporation agreed to take over the whole responsibility and carried out repairs to the Forebridge half with stone from

Tixall heath.[70] In the late 17th century, however, it was again responsible for only part.[71] The bridge was rebuilt in 1781–2 as a single-span bridge, apparently of brick and stone, to the design of Richard Baker; the corporation paid a third of the cost and the county the rest.[72] It was widened in 1860, and the present parapet of iron railings probably dates from then.[73]

The road to Wolverhampton leaves the Lichfield and Cannock road at the Green in Forebridge. It was turnpiked as part of the Stone–Wolverhampton road in 1761.[74] There was a toll-gate at Risingbrook at the junction with the Coppenhall road by 1831; it continued in use until the disturnpiking of the Wolverhampton road.[75]

The road west to Stafford castle originally left the town at Broadeye and then followed the present Castle Street and the footpath beyond. That was the route which Elizabeth I took in 1575 when she went from the town to dine at the castle. There was then a wooden bridge over the Sow at Broadeye, referred to as the new bridge.[76] By the early 19th century Broadeye bridge was of stone and of four or five arches.[77] In 1810 there was still an ancient wooden extension, carrying the road over the marshy ground to the west.[78] In the mid 19th century the maintenance of the bridge was the responsibility of Lord Stafford.[79] A new bridge was built in 1866 and widened in 1878.[80] The road to Doxey, mentioned in 1419,[81] also leaves the town over Broadeye bridge.

Another route west from the town along the line of the present Newport Road was in use by the 1740s. Half a mile to the west it followed what is now Rowley Avenue to the grounds of Rowley Hall and then the road that runs westwards from the lodge.[82] The present direct line to Castle Church dates from the end of the 18th century, presumably as a result of the turnpiking of the road in 1793.[83] There was a toll-gate west of the junction with Friars Road in the earlier 19th century.[84] In the early 17th century the road to Rowley Hall seems to have followed a more southerly course along the present Friars Terrace.[85] The new line may date from the mid 17th century: it was stated in 1704 that part of the way from Forebridge to the Green common (which straddled Newport Road near Rowley Avenue) was taken out of land called the Friars during the Civil War.[86]

[53] S.H.C. viii (1), 171, 186. [54] Close R. 1256–9, 48, 85.
[55] S.R.O., D.641/1/2/40a; Speed, Map of Staffs. (1610); W.S.L., copy of lost plan of Stafford.
[56] S.R.O., D.(W.) o/8/2, p. 179.
[57] S.R.O., D.1323/E/1, f. 36.
[58] 33 Geo. III, c. 153.
[59] C. and J. Greenwood, Map of Staffs. (1820); 41 & 42 Vic. c. 62; S.R.O., D.1323/L/2, 30 Sept. 1880; D.1323/A/1/10, pp. 422–3.
[60] V.C.H. Staffs. v. 2. [61] 33 Geo. III, c. 153.
[62] Staffs. Advertiser, 18 Jan. 1834; S.R.O., D.1323/L/2, 20 Oct. 1879.
[63] S.H.C. 1934(1), 125–6.
[64] S.R.O., D.(W.) 1721/1/1, f. 28.
[65] S.H.C. 1911, 188–9; S.H.C. vii(1), 121, 185.
[66] Cal. Pat. 1350–4, 167.
[67] W.S.L., S.MS. 369, p. 138; S.R.O. D.641/2/C/5/2d, ff. 10–11; D.641/2/E/1/3/C; D.1323/E/1, f. 38.
[68] S.H.C. 1930, 376; S.R.O., D.1323/E/1, f. 109v.
[69] S.R.O., D.641/2/E/1/2; D.1323/E/1, f. 113.
[70] S.R.O., D.641/2/C/5/2; D.1323/E/1, ff. 171–3.
[71] S.R.O., D.1323/A/1/2, p. 24.
[72] S.R.O., Q/FAa 1, pp. 53–4, 57–8, 61, 70–1; D.1033/1, pp. 275, 293–4; D.(W.) o/8/1, pp. 359, 383, 390; W.S.L.

26/38/22; plate facing p. 209 below.
[73] Date on keystone; Roxburgh, Stafford, 102 (giving the date as 1866).
[74] 1 Geo. III, c. 39; L.J. xxx. 98.
[75] S.R.O., D.1323/L/1, 9 May 1831, 8 June 1832; D.1323/L/2, 20 Oct. 1879.
[76] S.R.O., D.1323/E/1, f. 36; W.S.L., copy of lost plan of Stafford. It is not clear what type of bridge is shown by Speed, Map of Staffs. (1610).
[77] Roxburgh, Stafford, 99.
[78] Stafford Libr., Pamphs. Box B (copy in W.S.L., C.B. Stafford).
[79] S.R.O., D.1323/A/1/7, f. 85v. and p. 94.
[80] Roxburgh, Stafford, 100, 102; S.R.O., D.1323/A/1/10, pp. 185, 187, 190–2, 247, 443; Kelly's Dir. Staffs. (1880).
[81] S.R.O. 938/376.
[82] J. Smith, New Map of Staffs. (1747); B.L. Eg. MS. 2872, ff. 46v., 57v.
[83] Yates, Map of Staffs. (1799 edn.); 33 Geo. III, c. 153.
[84] S.R.O., Q/RDc 15a, map II.
[85] Speed, Map of Staffs. (1610); W.S.L., copy of lost plan of Stafford.
[86] S.R.O., D.3130/45, interrogatories and depositions about the Green Common, 1704.

The road to Eccleshall may be the Tillington Lane which occurs in 1546.[87] It is probably also the Creswell Lane mentioned in 1547 when Robert Lees of Stafford left 2s. a year to repair 'the horse causeway' there.[88] It was turnpiked in 1763[89] and towards the end of the 18th century became part of the Holyhead post route.[90] By 1820 there was a toll-gate a short distance north of the junction with the Stone road; this was presumably the Tillington gate which was in use when the road was disturnpiked.[91]

The Stone road, as seen above, is mentioned from the 14th century. Although the corporation tried to include it in the Act of 1729 turnpiking the main Holyhead road through Lichfield and Stone,[92] it was not turnpiked until 1761, as part of the Stone–Wolverhampton road. For a short time from 1785 it was used by the Holyhead post.[93]

The road to Hopton and Sandon is mentioned from the 13th century[94] and was turnpiked in 1763.[95] It ran from Foregate Street along Browning Street and Sandon Road.[96] By 1546 there was a bridge over Pearl brook at Sandyford; it occurs as a corporation responsibility in the 17th and 18th centuries and was then apparently of wood.[97]

The road to Marston originally ran from a point between Browning Street and the fork of the Eccleshall and Stone roads. After the inclosure of Foregate field in 1807 it became a continuation of Gaol Road.[98] 'The Bier Bridge or Burial Bridge' carrying the road over Sandyford brook is mentioned in the later 1620s; its repair was the corporation's responsibility in the 17th and 18th centuries.[99]

In 1765 the Saracen's Head in Market Square hired out four-wheeled chaises to go anywhere in England.[1] By the later 1790s Stafford was on the route of daily coaches to London, Chester, Birmingham, and Manchester, and there was a coach to Liverpool three times a week. The coaching inns were the Star and the George adjoining each other on the west side of Market Square, and the Swan and the Bear facing each other in Greengate Street. Carriers left weekly for London and for Birmingham.[2] The opening of the railway in 1837 immediately had an adverse effect on existing coach traffic. Coaches, however, were introduced to serve the station and covered a wide area, including Shrewsbury, the Potteries, Derby, and Nottingham. Local omnibuses too were started.[3]

The Staffordshire and Worcestershire Canal, opened in 1772, passes under the road to Lichfield and Cannock c. 1½ mile south-east of the town centre at Radford, which was described in 1782 as a port to Stafford.[4] There was a scheme in 1798 for a branch canal from there to the town,[5] but instead a tramway was opened in 1805 from Radford wharf to a wharf south of Green Bridge. The owner went bankrupt in 1813, and the rails and stock were offered for sale in 1814.[6] Under a lease of 1814 a new link between the canal and the town was built by a group composed mainly of south Staffordshire coalmasters. It consisted of a short branch from the main canal to the Sow below Baswich; the Sow itself, made navigable for barges and straightened; and another short cut from the Sow east of Green Bridge to a coal wharf at the south end of the bridge. The wharf was still in use in the early 1930s, but the cut had been filled in by 1939.[7]

The Grand Junction Railway between Birmingham and Warrington was opened in 1837 with a small station at Stafford on the north side of Newport Road.[8] The station soon proved inadequate, and a new one was built in 1843–4, designed by John Cunningham of Liverpool in an Elizabethan style.[9] Stafford continued to grow in importance as a railway centre, and the station was rebuilt on a larger scale on a site to the north in 1861–2; the new building was designed in an Italian style by the railway company's architect, W. Baker.[10] A direct approach from the town centre was built in 1865–6,[11] and in 1866 the North-Western hotel (later the Station hotel) was opened opposite the station, an Italianate building designed by Robert Griffiths of Stafford;[12] it was demolished in 1972. The station was rebuilt again in 1961–2 to the design of W. R. Headley, the architect of the London Midland region of British Railways.[13]

The line to Lichfield and Rugby and so to London was opened in 1847.[14] The line to Wellington (Salop.) was opened in 1849; the section from Stafford to Newport was closed in 1964.[15] The line to Uttoxeter was opened in 1867, with a station in Marston Road (Common station) from 1874. The line was closed to passenger traffic in 1939, and in

[87] S.R.O., D.1323/E/1, f. 28v.
[88] W.S.L. 77/45, ff. 63–64v.
[89] 3 Geo. III, c. 59; L.J. xxx. 405.
[90] S.H.C. 1934(1), 126.
[91] Greenwood, Map of Staffs. (1820); J. Phillips and W. F. Hutchings, Map of Staffs. (1832), showing it nearer the borough boundary; S.R.O., D.1323/L/2, 18 Feb. 1867, 20 Oct. 1879.
[92] S.R.O., D.1323/A/1/2, p. 342.
[93] S.H.C. 1934(1), 125–6.
[94] S.R.O. 938/250, 258, and 286; W.S.L., H.M. Chetwynd 7, deed of 25 Mar. 1417.
[95] 3 Geo. III, c. 59.
[96] S.R.O., D.240/E(A)/2/221; Yates, Map of Staffs. (1775 edn.); Phillips and Hutchings, Map of Staffs. (1832); S.R.O., Q/RDc 16.
[97] S.R.O., D.1323/E/1, ff. 28v., 202; S.R.O., D.(W.) 0/8/2, p. 21 (1st nos.); S.R.O., D.1033/1, pp. 168, 385.
[98] S.R.O., D.240/E(A)/2/221; Yates, Map of Staffs. (1775 and 1799 edns.); S.R.O., Q/RDc 16.
[99] S.R.O., D.641/2/C/5/2A, f. 6; D.590/437/4; D.1033/1, p. 385.
[1] Aris's Birmingham Gaz. 18 Feb. 1765.
[2] Univ. Brit. Dir. iv. 437–8; Wood, Plan of Stafford (1835).
[3] Staffs. Advertiser, 1 and 8 July 1837; Osborne's Guide

to Grand Junction Railway (1st edn. 1838), 65.
[4] V.C.H. Staffs. ii. 288; v. 2; T. Pennant, Journey from Chester to London (1782 edn.), 106.
[5] Staffs. Advertiser, 10 Feb. 1798.
[6] K. Brown, 'Stafford's First Railway', Railway Mag. lxxxv. 333–5; Staffs. Advertiser, 2 Nov. 1805; W.S.L., H.M. uncat. 27; J. Farey, General View of Agric. of Derb. iii (1817), 415.
[7] S.R.O., D.660/8/16, lease of 1 Apr. 1814; B.L., O.S.D. 211; 'Reminiscences of an Old Stafford Resident', T.O.S.S. 1932, 45, 47; Halden & Haywood's Dir. Stafford (1933); Railway Mag. lxxxv. 335.
[8] V.C.H. Staffs. ii. 306–7; Staffs. Advertiser, 8 July 1837; Wood, Plan of Stafford (1835).
[9] Staffs. Advertiser, 2 Mar. 1844; plate facing p. 209 below.
[10] Staffs. Advertiser, 18 May 1861, 1 and 22 Feb., 1 Mar. 1862; V.C.H. Staffs. ii. 327; The Builder, 9 June 1860, p. 371.   [11] See p. 189.
[12] Staffs. Advertiser, 14 July 1866.
[13] Ibid. 29 Dec. 1962, 5 Jan. 1963; Pevsner, Staffs. 244; ex inf. British Railways, London Midland Region (1975); plate facing p. 209 below.
[14] V.C.H. Staffs. ii. 308–9; C. R. Clinker, Railways of the West Midlands, a Chronology 1808–1954, 18.
[15] V.C.H. Staffs. ii. 309; ex inf. Brit. Railways.

1951 the freight service was withdrawn except over the stretch between Stafford and Common stations. That stretch too was closed to general freight in 1968, although it was kept open for traffic to a private siding. The Common station buildings were demolished in 1973.[16]

WALLS AND GATES. The fortifications erected by Ethelfleda in 913 probably consisted of earth and timber defences round the settlement; they may well have enclosed a smaller area than the later defences.[17] Stafford was a walled town in 1086[18] and remained such until the 17th century, with four gates on the roads into the town from north, south, east, and west. In the late 11th century the castle was part of the defences on the north-west, while in the mid 13th century the king's fish-pool was recognized as part of those on the north-east.[19] The river gave protection on the west and south, and the Thieves Ditch ran below the walls on the north-east and south-east.[20] A military observer described Stafford in January 1660 as 'so naturally defended with ditches and water that if the frost were gone it could be made very tenable'.[21]

In 1224 the king ordered the sheriff to spend up to 20 marks 'on walling our town of Stafford' (ad villam nostram Staff' claudendam).[22] A few weeks later the burgesses received a two-year remission of their aid to help them to wall their town (ad villam suam claudendam) and in 1227 a year's remission to fortify it (firmandam).[23] In 1233 the king gave them sixty oaks from Cannock forest to repair three gaps in the walls.[24] They also received many grants of murage between 1233 and 1341.[25] About 1600 the walls were mainly of stone, but the stretch between the town mill and a point beyond Broadeye bridge consisted of wooden palisades, and there was another wooden section on the north-east. To the west of the South Gate there was a tower with a gate beyond leading to the mill; to the east there were two gates giving access to the public tip by the river.[26] Buttresses east of the North Gate were mentioned in 1599.[27] In 1583 the corporation used the stretch of wall between the South and East Gates as a quarry for work on the Green Bridge,[28] but it was still repairing the walls in 1620.[29] A borough ordinance of 1473–4 forbade any digging

or planting within 6 ft. of the walls.[30] There are, however, several references to gardens below the walls,[31] and in 1644 it was stated that the fortifications had been seriously damaged by the 'rooting and trampling' of swine and cattle.[32] The fortifications were strengthened in 1643 and 1644.[33] The Parliamentarians, who captured the town in 1643, demolished buildings in Foregate and on the Green in 1644 to make an attack on the town more difficult, and the King's Pool, the Green common, and other land were flooded 'for the security of this town'.[34] By the early 1670s the walls were in ruins.[35]

There is mention of what was probably the North Gate in 1170,[36] and it occurs by that name in 1445.[37] By the later 15th century it was the largest of the gates, and with two flanking towers it projected from the line of the walls.[38] There was mention of a bridge there in 1619[39] and of a draw-bridge in 1643 and 1644.[40] On the occasion of James I's visit in 1617 the mayor ordered 'the way and passage of the gate' to be widened, the causeway being less than 3 yd. wide and dangerous for both coaches and horses.[41] The North Gate became known as the Gaol Gate in the earlier 17th century as a result of its use as a gaol.[42] It was ruinous by 1678, and in the late 17th century a house of correction for the borough was built on the site, with an arch on the east side through which the road passed; a passage ran over the arch to the county gaol flanking it on the other side. The whole structure was demolished in stages between 1796 and 1820.[43]

The South Gate was known as such by the late 14th century.[44] It was also known as the Green Gate by 1612,[45] and both names were still in use in 1674.[46] A passage for pedestrians was made on the west side of the arch by an order of the borough council of 1723.[47] The gate was demolished in 1777.[48] Richard Whitworth of Batchacre in Adbaston claimed that the demolition was carried out on his initiative 'to make a noble opening at the entrance of the town'. Between 1804 and 1807 he converted adjacent premises to the south-east into Castle Whitworth, with a martello tower and swivel guns.[49]

The East Gate was mentioned in the later 12th century.[50] It was taken down c. 1800, but part of the north side was left standing.[51] That was moved

[16] V.C.H. Staffs. ii. 315; Clinker, Railways of W. Midlands, 61, 63; ex inf. Brit. Railways.
[17] See pp. 186–7.
[18] V.C.H. Staffs. iv. 37.   [19] See pp. 200, 210.
[20] O.S. Map 1/2,500, Staffs. XXXVII. 11 (1881 edn.); V.C.H. Staffs. v. 94; S.R.O., D.1323/E/1, f. 28v.
[21] Cal. S.P. Dom. 1659–60, 299.
[22] Rot. Litt. Claus. (Rec. Com.), i. 613.
[23] Pat. R. 1216–25, 459; 1225–32, 37.
[24] Close R. 1231–4, 335.
[25] e.g. Cal. Pat. 1232–47, 26; 1247–58, 103; 1338–40, 213.
[26] W.S.L., copy of lost plan of Stafford; Erdeswick, Staffs. 144–5.
[27] S.H.C. 1934(2), 9.   [28] See p. 197.
[29] S.R.O., D.1323/E/1, f. 109v.
[30] W.S.L., S.MS. 369, p. 97.
[31] S.H.C. 1926, 6; S.R.O., D.1323/E/1, ff. 46v.–47v.; W.S.L. 7/1/00, transcript of lease of 14 Nov. 1607; W.S.L., H.M. uncat. 26, deed of 30 June 1635.
[32] S.H.C. 4th ser. i. 71.
[33] S.R.O., D.1323/E/1, ff. 266v., 268v.; S.H.C. 4th ser. i. 64–5, 71.
[34] S.H.C. 4th ser. i. 35, 64, 67–8, 72, 76, 82, 88, 90–1, 98, 105, 107, 119, 220, 228, 251, 297, 303; S.R.O., D.641/2/G/1/1, Stafford Castle rents 1643–5, pp. 1, 4–5; above,

p. 187. The date of demolition is wrongly given as 1642 in V.C.H. Staffs. v. 83.
[35] R. Blome, Britannia (1673), 204; S.R.O., D.649/3, p. 105.
[36] See p. 191.   [37] Cal. Pat. 1441–6, 393–4.
[38] B.L. Add. Ch. 40765, mentioning the barbican of the great north gate (1471); W.S.L., copy of lost plan of Stafford.
[39] S.R.O., D.1323/E/1, f. 97.
[40] S.H.C. 4th ser. i. 12, 220.
[41] S.R.O., D.(W.) 1721/1/4, f. 121v.
[42] E 134/9 Jas. I East./15; S.R.O., D.1323/E/1, ff. 97, 98v. (1619), 109v. (1620). In S.R.O., D.(W). 1721/1/4, f. 121v. (1618), it is called the North Gate.
[43] See p. 204.   [44] S.R.O., D.641/1/4A/14, rot. 5.
[45] Kettle, 'Street-Names', 51.
[46] W.S.L., H.M. uncat. 23, deed of 11 Dec. 1674.
[47] S.R.O., D.1323/A/1/2, p. 242; W.S.L. 26/38/22.
[48] S.R.O., D.(W.) 0/8/1, pp. 326, 336.
[49] 'Whitworth MSS. in Salt Libr.' T.O.S.S. 1931, 30; W.S.L. 26/38/22.
[50] See p. 245. It can be seen on the view of Stafford facing p. 176.
[51] Pitt, Staffs. 289; White, Dir. Staffs. (1834), 116; W.S.L. 7/1/00, drawing of 1883.

for road widening in 1939 and set against the end wall of a cottage further along North Walls. When the cottage was demolished in 1964 it was left free-standing.[52]

John Speed stated that there was a fourth gate on the west, and his plan of 1610 shows one at Broadeye bridge.[53] Celia Fiennes too stated in 1698 that there had formerly been a gate there.[54] By the later 1620s it seems that only the other three gates existed.[55]

CASTLE. There was a tradition in Elizabethan times that the mound then known as Castle Hill and standing south-east of Broadeye bridge was the site of a tower built in 913 by Edward the Elder, brother of Ethelfleda.[56] The tradition is improbable.

A castle was built in the town by William the Conqueror in 1070, after the rebellion of 1069. The site belonged to the manor of Chebsey, of which Henry de Ferrers was lord in 1086, and it has been suggested that Henry had some duty in connexion with the castle. It had been destroyed (*destructum*) by 1086, presumably with the coming of more peaceful times.[57]

Orderic Vitalis declared that Henry I entrusted *custodiam Stephordi castri* to William Pantulf in 1102.[58] If the phrase does indeed refer to a castle in Stafford town as has often been supposed, and not to the Stafford family's castle at Castle Church west of the town,[59] the Conqueror's castle must have been rebuilt. If it was rebuilt, it cannot have lasted long, or, at any rate, have long remained in royal hands; apart from one possible instance, and that a trifling one,[60] the county farm was not burdened with its maintenance up to the death of John. Nor was the Crown interested in it in other ways.[61] It seems most reasonable to suppose that Pantulf's castle was at Castle Church.[62]

In many counties the sheriff occupied a castle and exercised his authority from it. In Staffordshire he did not need to do so, for until 1344 he was also sheriff of Shropshire, and Shropshire possessed two castles which were at his disposal — one of them, Bridgnorth castle, only just over the Staffordshire border. It is possible that, on the

rare occasions when 'Stafford castle' is mentioned in the earlier 14th century,[63] Bridgnorth is intended. Nevertheless it is also possible that what remained of the castle in the town, though 'destroyed' for military purposes, continued in use as a county gaol until the later 13th century.[64]

The castle probably stood at Broadeye. There is a reference c. 1200 to the old castle by the river.[65] Castle Hill or Old Castle Hill at Broadeye can be traced from 1397,[66] and it was stated c. 1600 to have been 'in memory fortified with real walls'.[67] It has been alternatively suggested that the castle stood at Bull Hill to the north-east[68] and that the name, which occurs by 1631, may derive from the bailey. It is more probable that the land took its name from a messuage called the Bull which stood in the area in the 16th century.[69]

THE COUNTY TOWN. Stafford gave its name to the shire which was created round it in the 10th century,[70] but early references to its function as a county town are few. It appears in Domesday Book as the chief town of Staffordshire, and all the principal landowners of the county had property there.[71] The county court is recorded there in 1176,[72] and by 1185 the sheriff had a gaol in the town.[73] Lichfield, however, was the normal stopping-place of the eyre.[74] The justices of the peace met at Wolverhampton and Penkridge as well as Stafford in the earlier 1360s, but in the early 15th century Stafford was their usual meeting-place.[75]

By the early 16th century Staffordshire gaol deliveries were held at Stafford, and in 1528 they were ordered to be held there.[76] By 1544, however, they had been transferred to Wolverhampton.[77] It was stated in 1559 that by ancient custom Stafford was the place for county inquisitions, gaol deliveries, and assizes, the town lying centrally in the county. All such sessions had lately been moved elsewhere, and an Act was passed that year ordering them to be held at Stafford except when there was contagious sickness there.[78] In 1570 the bishop described Stafford as 'the shire town, where both the assizes and sessions with many other meetings of all estates and persons are commonly kept because it is in the middle of the shire'.[79] In 1564, 1566, and 1571 gaol

[52] *Stafford Newsletter*, 20 Mar. 1964; *Staffs. Weekly Sentinel*, 22 July 1939.
[53] J. Speed, *Theatre of Empire of Great Britaine* (1611 edn.), 69; above, p. 188.
[54] *Journeys of Celia Fiennes*, ed. C. Morris, 167.
[55] S.R.O., D.641/2/C/5/2D, ff. 18, 20–1; W.S.L., copy of lost plan of Stafford.
[56] Camden, *Brit.* (1695), 531, 538; W.S.L., copy of lost plan of Stafford.
[57] Orderic Vitalis, *Eccl. Hist.* ed. Marjorie Chibnall, ii. 228, 236; *V.C.H. Staffs.* i. 221–2; iv. 25–6, 48; F. M. Stenton, *Anglo-Saxon England* (1971 edn.), 595–7; above, p. 187.
[58] Orderic Vitalis *Eccl. Hist.* ed. Chibnall, vi. 24–5.
[59] *V.C.H. Staffs.* v. 84.
[60] *S.H.C.* ii (1), 91 (1199–1200): 'in reparacione gaiole et ferramento castelli de Stafford 20s.' Eyton (ibid. 97) took this to mean that the gaol was in the castle and that *ferramentum* referred to prison gear; it need, however, mean no more than iron work.
[61] *Rot. Litt. Claus.* (Rec. Com.), i. 69, appears to relate not to Stafford but to Seaford (Suss.).
[62] The latest study of the problem is by D. M. Palliser, 'The Castles at Stafford', *T.S.H.C.S.* 1971–3, 1–17. He disagrees with Ella Armitage, *Early Norman Castles*, 213.
[63] e.g. *Cal. Fine R.* 1319–27, 373; *Cal. Close*, 1307–13, 402.
[64] And see p. 203.
[65] *T.S.H.C.S.* 1971–3, 3, 14.
[66] See p. 231; J. B. Frith, 'Account of the bailiffs of borough of Stafford for 1411–12', *T.O.S.S.* 1939, 21; W.S.L., H.M. Chetwynd 7, deeds of 1429 and 1439.
[67] W.S.L., copy of lost plan of Stafford.
[68] P. T. Dale, 'Some notes on the ancient buildings and streets of Stafford', *T.O.S.S.* 1934, 23; F. J. Cope, 'The Walls of Stafford', *T.O.S.S.* 1938, 39–40.
[69] S.R.O., D.1323/E/1, f. 188; Kettle, 'Street-names', 43.
[70] F. W. Maitland, *Domesday Book and Beyond* (1907 edn.), 187; F. M. Stenton, *Anglo-Saxon Eng.* (1971 edn.), 337. Much of the research for this section was carried out by Miss Ann J. Kettle.
[71] *V.C.H. Staffs.* iv. 23, 37; Maitland, *Domesday Book and Beyond*, 174.
[72] R. W. Eyton, *Antiquities of Shropshire*, ii. 264 n.
[73] See p. 203.
[74] *S.H.C.* iii (1), 34, 79.
[75] *Procs. before J.P.s in 14th and 15th Cents.* ed. Bertha H. Putnam, 289, 333–4.
[76] B.L. Add. MS. 35205; J. S. Cockburn, *Hist. of Eng. Assizes 1558–1714*, 20, 35.
[77] *L. & P. Hen. VIII*, xx (1), p, 320.
[78] S.R.O., D.1323/E/1, ff. 20–21v.; *Statutes of the Realm*, iv (1), 350.
[79] S.P. 46/14 f. 162.

deliveries were held there.[80] By 1572, however, the assizes were no longer held at Stafford: in that year there was a Bill to revive the statute of 1559, but the Lords vetoed it.[81] In the mid 1570s the assizes were held at Wolverhampton.[82] When Elizabeth I visited Stafford in 1575 she was told that one reason for its decay was that the assizes had been transferred elsewhere. She promised to have them brought back, and in 1579 she duly sent instructions to the circuit judges through Lord Stafford to hold their sessions at Stafford.[83] In 1587 or 1588, however, the summer assizes were at Wolverhampton.[84] The reason given by the judges for the removal from Stafford was the lack of an adequate hall there, and the rebuilding of the shire hall was undertaken in the later 1580s to remedy that want.[85] Assizes are recorded at Stafford in 1590 and 1601,[86] and although assizes and gaol deliveries were occasionally held at Wolverhampton in the earlier 17th century[87] Stafford was by then established as the assize town.[88] It was at Stafford that the parliamentary county committee was set up in 1643.[89]

In 1660 a general muster was ordered at Stafford because of its central situation and 'because it is the county town and it may seem a wrong to it not to have the county business done in it'; various Staffordshire gentlemen, however, preferred Lichfield, and the order was withdrawn.[90] Speed in the early 17th century considered Lichfield 'more large and of far greater fame' than Stafford as well as 'much her ancient'.[91] Defoe in the earlier 1720s found little in Stafford to justify his detour to visit it; Lichfield on the other hand was the best town in the county for 'good conversation and good company' and the principal town in the north-west after Chester.[92] In 1747 Stafford was described as 'very much increased and improved of late in politeness and gentility'.[93] A traveller in 1787 thought it 'a dull, idle place', while another in 1792 found it 'very mean, though the county town', with inns that were 'merely ale-houses and fit for the market folks only'.[94] The October race-meeting established in 1763, however, attracted people to the town. In 1795 a county newspaper, the *Staffordshire Advertiser*, was launched at Stafford.[95] James Amphlett, editor of the *Advertiser* from 1804 to 1810, later remembered that period as one when Stafford society had 'an elevated distinction in the county'; William Horton of Chetwynd House, a leading footwear-manufacturer, was 'the Amphi-

tryon of the borough', regularly entertaining Sheridan and 'all the wits and bright spirits of the age' who accompanied him.[96] Yet in 1819 the future Lord Campbell, then a barrister on the Oxford circuit, described Stafford as 'the dullest and vilest town in England', an opinion echoed by an assize judge in the earlier 20th century.[97] Dickens, after a night at the Swan in 1852, pronounced Stafford 'as dull and dead a town as any one could desire not to see'.[98] A new arrival in 1856 thought that he 'had never been in such an uncouth, outlandish place to be called a county town'. By 1866, however, he considered that the foundation of the Staffordshire County Club in Salter Street in 1863 had made the town more attractive to the gentry, while the villas planned on the Rowley Hall estate would make it comparable with other county towns.[99] Stafford's position as the administrative centre of the county was confirmed with the formation in 1889 of the county council, which met in the town. Stafford became the seat of a Crown court in 1972.[1]

A hall in Stafford where the county court met existed by the 1280s.[2] As already seen, the shire hall in use in the later 16th century had by then proved too small. It was replaced by a new hall, and by 1606 the old building was being leased out by the corporation. It was occupied as a house by Matthew Dorrington in 1616, and the corporation still received rent from it in the early 1660s. It adjoined or was part of the booth hall on the corner of the present Market Square and Greengate Street.[3]

Work had begun on the new hall in Market Square by 1587 with Laurence Shipway as master mason. It continued in phases and was not finished until 1607, although the hall was probably in use before then. The cost was met by subscriptions collected throughout the county and by gifts in kind, and it was probably the difficulty of raising enough money that delayed the work. The final stage included a 'chequor' modelled on that at Warwick.[4] The building consisted of a hall supported on colonnades; the open space below was paved. It was described in 1634 as 'the chief fabric and the grace of the whole town, if it were handsomely and cleanly kept', and Plot c. 1680 considered it the most beautiful of the 'civil public buildings' in the county.[5] Repairs had become necessary by 1626, and a dispute arose between the county justices and the corporation, which also used the

[80] *Cal. Pat.* 1563–6, 37, 104; 1569–72, 215; Cockburn, *Eng. Assizes*, 146.
[81] Cockburn, *Eng. Assizes*, 35 n.
[82] S.R.O., Tp. 804, ff. 191, 191v., 199v., 202v.
[83] S.R.O., D.1323/E/1, f. 36; Folger Shakespeare Libr., Washington, L. a. 244 (ref. supplied by Prof. A. G. Petti of Calgary Univ.).
[84] S.R.O., Tp. 804, f. 237v.   [85] S.R.O., D.(W.) 1744/33.
[86] Hist. MSS. Com. 3, *4th Rep. I*, p. 332; W. D. Cooper, 'Expenses of Judges of Assize', *Camd. Misc.* iv (Camd. Soc. [1st ser.], lxxiii), 53–4, 57.
[87] S.R.O., D.1323/E/1, ff. 175v., 199v.; Cockburn, *Eng. Assizes*, 35.
[88] S.R.O., D.1323/E/1, bailiffs' and mayor's accts. *passim*, and f. 231v.; S.R.O., D.(W.) 1721/1/4, unnumbered folios *sub* 1600; Cockburn, *Eng. Assizes*, 34.
[89] *S.H.C.* 4th ser. i.   [90] S.R.O., D.260/M/F/1/6, f. 66.
[91] J. Speed, *Theatre of Empire of Great Britaine* (1611 edn.), 69.
[92] D. Defoe, *Tour thro' the Whole Island of Gt. Brit.* (1928 edn.), ii. 478–80.
[93] J. Smith, *New Map of Staffs.* (1747).

[94] H. Skrine, *Three Successive Tours in the North of Eng., and great part of Scotland* (1795), 2; *Torrington Diaries*, ed. C. Bruyn Andrews, iii. 135–6.
[95] See pp. 256, 258.
[96] *S.H.C.* 4th ser. vi. 188, 195–6.
[97] F. D. MacKinnon, *On Circuit 1924–1927*, 71, 172, 188, 227, 258.
[98] In 'A Plated Article', *Household Words*, 24 Apr. 1852, re-issued in *Reprinted Pieces*.
[99] W.S.L. 7/15/00, cutting of July 1866; *P.O. Dir. Staffs.* (1868).
[1] *Staffs. Quarter Sessions 1362–1971* (Staffs. County Council, 1972), 15; *Stafford Newsletter*, 21 Jan. 1972, p. 10.
[2] W. A. Morris, *Early Eng. County Court* (Univ. of California Publications in History, vol. xiv, no. 2), p. 151.
[3] S.R.O., D.1323/E/1, ff. 47, 304; S.R.O., D.(W.) 1721/1/4, f. 108v.; below, p. 213.
[4] S.R.O., D.(W.) 1721/1/4, accts. on unnumbered folios at end; *Staffs. Advertiser*, 24 Sept. 1836.
[5] *Relation of a Short Survey of 26 Counties*, ed. L. G. Wickham Legg, 55; Plot, *Staffs.* 371–2; plate facing p. 161 above.

hall. It was settled in 1639 when the corporation agreed to pay £20 then and one-tenth of the cost of future repairs and to convey the site to the justices.[6] Extensive work was carried out in the 1720s, and in 1769 the space under the hall was paved with Hartshill quarries.[7]

By 1790 the hall was in bad repair, and in 1793 the county quarter sessions ordered an advertisement for designs for a new hall; the corporation agreed to pay a tenth of the cost of building it. Work began in 1795 under an Act of 1794 and was completed by 1798. A caretaker's house was added in Market Street in 1798-9. The shire hall is in a classical style and was designed by John Harvey, a pupil of Samuel Wyatt who seems also to have contributed to the design. It was built over the site of several houses east of the former hall.[8] There was a market-place behind the hall until 1854 when extensions were built over it.[9]

In the 17th century it seems to have been the practice for the assize judges to stay in a private house at the expense of the corporation, which also presented wine to them and made provision for their retinue and horses.[10] In the late 17th century the Exchequer was allowing the corporation £20 a year through the sheriff towards expenditure on the judges.[11] In 1799 the corporation resolved to stop presenting wine and ale to them in view of the increase in their salaries.[12] In the 1790s the sheriff was lodging them at a cabinet-maker's at the south end of the High House, and c. 1800 Miss Ferny-hough of Bull Mount gave them hospitality.[13] Although one of John Harvey's plans of 1794 for the shire hall included a house on the south side for the judges,[14] it was not until 1799 that the county quarter sessions decided to build such a house. Designed apparently by Joseph Potter of Lichfield, the county surveyor, it was finished in 1802.[15] Until 1808 it was also used as an hotel.[16] It had been extended along St. Martin's Place by 1879.[17]

The county council at first met either in the borough hall or in the shire hall. In 1891 it bought the properties on the north side of Martin Street as the site for a council chamber and offices, and the County Buildings were opened in 1895. They were designed by H. T. Hare of London in a baroque style and are of red brick and Hollington stone.[18] They were extended to the corner of Martin Street

and St. Martin's Place in 1899 under Hare's direction.[19] In 1915 a block of offices was opened on the opposite side of Martin Street east of St. Chad's Passage. Another block was built further east on the site of the Lyceum theatre in the late 1920s, and another on the west side of St. Chad's Passage in the early 1930s. All three blocks are in a style designed to harmonize with County Buildings. Another block was built in Eastgate Street c. 1936 and was later extended.[20] In 1964 a seven-storey block was opened on a site between Tipping and Martin Streets, which included the site of the Diglake, a house in Tipping Street bought by the county council shortly after the Second World War and used as offices.[21] Three more ranges were built between Tipping Street, St. Chad's Passage, and Martin Street in the 1970s, the last being completed in 1976 and incorporating the site of the Martin Street Congregational church.

A chief constable was appointed for the county in 1842; from the first his office was probably on the Green in Forebridge, where it was in 1851.[22] A new office was completed, apparently in 1858, on the site of the Blue Posts inn next to the judges' house in St. Martin's Place.[23] The site was absorbed into the new County Buildings and the chief constable moved into Eastgate House on the corner of Eastgate and Martin Streets, which had been bought by the county council in 1891 with the other Martin Street property. In 1893 a superintendent's house was built on the site of the Goat inn in Eastgate Street adjoining Eastgate House.[24] In 1952 Baswich House at Weeping Cross was acquired as the site of a new county police headquarters and training-centre. The first buildings were opened in 1957, and the chief constable moved there in 1961. Eastgate House was then taken over by staff from the Diglake.[25] In 1976 the adjoining super-intendent's house was used as county council offices.

On the establishment of the county education committee in 1903 its offices were housed in the technical school on the corner of Victoria Square and Earl Street. New offices were opened on an adjoining site in Earl Street in 1905.[26] The education department moved into the new ranges in Tipping Street and St. Chad's Place in 1974 and 1976, although retaining the old buildings.[27]

[6] S.R.O., Q/SO 3, f. 8v.; Q/SO 4, ff. 81v.-82, 269 and v.

[7] S.R.O., Q/SO 12, ff. 53v., 69, 90; S.R.O., D.(W.) 0/8/1, p. 256.

[8] S.R.O., Q/AS 1; S.R.O., D.1323/A/1/3, p. 109; W.S.L., M.606; Act for building a new shire hall for the county of Stafford, 34 Geo. III, c. 97; Univ. Brit. Dir. iv. 437; Staffs. Advertiser, 4 July, 1 Aug. 1795; W.S.L., Staffs. Views, ix. 99-101, 103; S.R.O., C/A/5/1; H. M. Colvin, Biog. Dict. Eng. Architects, 271. For a design by John Nash see Country Life, 6 Jan. 1950.

[9] Staffs. Advertiser, 15 July 1854; S.R.O., Q/AE 1, no. 1; S.R.O., C/A/5/2-4.

[10] S.R.O., D.1323/A/1/1, pp. 277, 333; D.1323/A/1/2, p. 64; D.1323/E/1, bailiffs' accts. passim.

[11] S.R.O., D.1323/A/1/2, p. 1.

[12] S.R.O., D.1323/A/1/3, pp. 205, 208.

[13] R. Whitworth, Narrative of Facts relating to what is called the Judges' House or Lodgings (Stafford, 1811), 7, 9-11 (copy in W.S.L., S.1773).

[14] City of London R.O., Surveyor's Justice Plan no. 157.

[15] W.S.L., M.606; Colvin, Biog. Dict. Eng. Architects, 469, 748.

[16] W.S.L., M.606; Whitworth, Narrative of Facts, 12; Sir John Wrottesley, Letter addressed to Inhabitants of

County of Stafford (Wolverhampton, 1811), 4-5 (copy in W.S.L., S.1773); S.R.O., C/A/5/1.

[17] O.S. Map 1/500, Staffs. XXXVII. 11.17 (1881 edn.).

[18] Staffs. County Council Record (1895), pp. i-iii; plate facing p. 161 above.

[19] Staffs. County Council Record (1899), 2; (1900), 92.

[20] Ibid. (1915), pp. vii-viii; Year Book of County Council of Staffs. (1929-30), 124; (1932-3), 118; (1936-7), 125; (1937-8), 125; Stafford Libr., Stafford Hist. and Civic Soc., vol. labelled 'Street Improvements'.

[21] Stafford Newsletter, 27 Jan. 1962, 7 Feb. 1964; ex inf. the county treasurer's dept. (1976).

[22] S.R.O., Q/SO 34, adjourned sess. Mich. 1842; Williams's Com. Dir. Stafford and the Potteries (1846); White, Dir. Staffs. (1851), 329.

[23] S.R.O., Q/APc 1/4, p. 39 (first cttee. meeting at the constabulary office); Harrison, Harrod & Co. Dir. Staffs. (1861); W.S.L. 7/15/00.

[24] Staffs. County Council Record (1895), pp. iii-iv; date on supt.'s house.

[25] V.C.H.. Staffs v. 4; Stafford Newsletter, 28 Dec. 1957, 27 Jan. 1962.

[26] G. Balfour, Ten Years of Staffs. Educ. 1903-1913 (Staffs. County Council Educ. Dept. 1913), 94-5.

[27] Ex inf. the county treasurer's dept. (1976).

In 1916 the county council accepted a grant from the Carnegie United Kingdom Trust to establish rural libraries through village schools.[28] Staffordshire was the first English county to establish a rural library service, and some urban areas without access to libraries were included. A sub-committee of the education committee was formed, and the books were housed in the unfinished electrical engineering school in Cherry Street behind the education offices. In 1920 the repository was moved to the Co-operative Hall in Browning Street and in 1921 to premises in Cherry Street. The county council became a library authority in 1922 (for rural areas only until 1931) with continued support from the Carnegie Trust. Additional premises were acquired in Earl Street in 1943. They were closed when the first part of the new headquarters was opened in 1958 on the site of the former militia (later police) barracks on the corner of Friars Terrace and Park Street. All headquarters departments were moved there from Cherry Street in 1961.

In the mid 1630s a treasury was built under the shire hall for the rolls and records of the clerk of the peace.[29] It was 'repaired, glazed, fitted, and made more useful' in the earlier 1660s, largely at the clerk's expense.[30] By the later 18th century the records were kept in a private office, but with the building of the new shire hall they were moved to a room there near the clerk's office.[31] Quarter sessions decided in 1815 that the office was unfit for the custody of the records and ordered the building of a room over the existing office.[32] About 1907 the records were transferred to an attic in County Buildings, which in 1947 became a temporary county record office in the charge of a county archivist who was also the William Salt librarian. A record office on a site behind the William Salt Library in Eastgate Street was opened in 1961. It was enlarged in 1972.[33]

A gaol in Stafford is first mentioned in 1185,[34] and enough was then spent upon it to make it likely that that was the year of its construction. Between 1194 and 1214 expenditure on the fabric continued,[35] a fact which suggests completion or enlargement rather than repair. Deliveries are traceable from 1230 and were not infrequently ordered up to 1241. For many years after that, however, the prison is seldom mentioned, and evidence of delivery is absent. Bail writs show that in the mid 13th century

Staffordshire prisoners were kept in Shropshire gaols. The fact that in 1272 Stafford gaol was threatening to fall and its repair was then ordered suggests that for some time the building had been insecure. In 1285-6 delivery was resumed. Meanwhile, in 1281, the prison in Bridgnorth castle had collapsed. The prisoners were moved to less secure custody in the castle, and the lack of security may explain why after 1284-5 that castle was seldom delivered and after 1302-3 not at all.[36] Stafford deliveries are rare until 1293,[37] after which delivery commissions are common for the rest of Edward I's reign.[38] There is the strong presumption that thenceforth the gaol for Staffordshire was fixed at Stafford, although in 1337 many Staffordshire prisoners were tried at Shrewsbury,[39] perhaps because repairs ordered in 1332 had not yet been completed.[40]

In 1390 county prisoners were being kept in the borough gates.[41] Since extensive prison works were being carried out between 1391 and 1394, it is likely that a new prison was then built.[42] At all events in 1442-3 references to the 'old' prison begin to occur, and that building had evidently been discarded as a place of confinement, for stone from it was then applied to other uses.[43] The new prison consisted of a gaol chamber with a 'dungeon' below it.[44] Later evidence shows that the prison was at the end of or 'near' Crabbery Lane and 'towards' Broadeye.[45]

From 1347 the county gaol is sometimes called Stafford castle,[46] and the usage is common in the 15th and 16th centuries.[47] There is no necessity to suppose that the usage implies a fortification; in other towns in which there were both a county and a borough gaol the word castle was applied to the former for distinction's sake, even though a true castle is known not to have existed or to have been used for prisoners.[48]

Staffordshire was one of the many counties in which, under the Gaols Act, 1531,[49] the justices of the peace were ordered to investigate the adequacy of the gaols and, if they were insufficient, to have new ones built. The Act and similar ensuing legislation were widely ignored.[50] There is no clear evidence of what was done in Staffordshire. Stafford 'castle' was apparently a gaol in 1519,[51] but in 1559 it was being said that there was no county gaol at Stafford and that the borough was allowing the sheriff to use its own gaol.[52] The gaol of Staffordshire, how-

[28] For this para. see M. K. Gibson, 'Staffs. County Libr. 1915-1974' (diploma thesis 1974-5, College of Librarianship, Aberystwyth; copy at County Libr. H.Q., Stafford). For the library established for the county c. 1646 see below, p. 258.

[29] *S.H.C.* 4th ser. vi. 67-8.

[30] S.R.O., Q/SO 7, f. 68v.

[31] S.R.O., Q/SBl, E.1800, E.1803. The record room shown in *S.H.C.* 4th ser. vi, plate facing p. 69, was probably for the borough.

[32] S.R.O., Q/SO 26, f. 61.

[33] *S.H.C.* 1927, 120; *Archives*, iv. 205-8; *Stafford Newsletter*, 25 Mar. 1961; ex inf. the county archivist (1976).

[34] R. B. Pugh, *Imprisonment in Medieval Eng.* 73.

[35] *S.H.C.* i and ii (1). On two occasions (1206, 1214) allowances were made simply for 'the gaols' of the county, Newcastle-under-Lyme being the other: *V.C.H. Staffs.* viii. 14. Two of the 4 gaols for which the sheriff of Shropshire received allowance in 1207 were probably Staffs. gaols.

[36] Pugh, *Imprisonment*, 73-4. Some of the later commissions may be for the delivery of Bridgnorth town prison.

[37] Ibid. 74.

[38] Evidence of Pat. R.

[39] J.I. 3/131 rot. 1.

[40] *Cal. Close*, 1330-3, 503.

[41] Ibid. 1389-92, 215.

[42] Pugh, *Imprisonment*, 74.

[43] S.R.O., D.641/1/2/54.

[44] E 101/587/8 and 9.

[45] W.S.L. 7/2/oo (refs. to deeds of 1464, 1469, and 1715); S.R.O., D.1323/E/1, f. 46v.; note by J. S. Horne of deed of 1665 in scrapbk. on Stafford gaol in Mr. Horne's possession (1976). When the Wesleyan chapel at the end of Crabbery St. was extended in 1842 and 1870 two walls of large red stones were removed (W.S.L. 7/2/oo); some of the stones were still visible in a wall N. of the chapel in 1976.

[46] J.I. 3/131 rott. 14d., 15.

[47] Evidence of *Cal. Pat*; *S.H.C.* n.s. vi (1), 107; and see below.

[48] Pugh, *Imprisonment*, 67 n., 78.

[49] 23 Hen. VIII, c. 3.

[50] Pugh, *Imprisonment*, 343-6.

[51] C 66/633 m. 20d.

[52] S.R.O., D.1323/E/1, f. 20v. (copy of Priv. Act 25 Jan. 1 Eliz. I).

ever, was again delivered in 1564,[53] and there is a reference to the gaol of Stafford castle in 1569[54] and to a keeper of the county gaol in 1602.[55] In the early 17th century the lower part of the North Gate was used as the county gaol.[56]

A new gaol by the town wall east of the North Gate[57] probably came into use in 1621.[58] Work continued for some years thereafter.[59] When finished, the building was of stone and possessed two dungeons,[60] and there was a wooden house for the gaoler.[61] In 1647 the gaol was said to be decayed, and repairs, possibly amounting to extensions, were carried out soon after.[62] In 1686 it was again reported to be inadequate,[63] and in consequence the county sought from the borough the land on which the North Gate then stood, undertaking to leave a passage between that site and 'the present stone gaol'. Its petition was granted in 1687,[64] and the gaol was then enlarged.[65]

Howard found the prison too small. He especially condemned the cramped felons' day-room and courtyard and the lack of air in the male dungeon, which was imperfectly ventilated by two funnels. A lofty room above the female dungeon was full of lumber. On the other hand the debtors' court and the debtors' hall, called the free ward or county chamber, were spacious. There was a chapel, and a stream flowed near by but not, to Howard's regret, within the walls.[66]

A house of correction for the county, standing on the town wall south-east of the North Gate,[67] had been completed by 1599.[68] It was out of use by 1630,[69] but in 1649 its re-establishment was ordered.[70] It is not known whether the order was then complied with, but a county house of correction was again in use at Stafford in 1660.[71] By 1662, however, it seems to have been institutionally fused with the county gaol.[72] Gaol and bridewell had earlier often shared a keeper or governor.[73] At the end of the 17th century it seems that a new county house of correction was built on the site of the North Gate. The gate was ruinous in 1678,[74] and the borough agreed to lease the site to the county

in 1687 in compliance with the petition mentioned above. The rebuilt bridewell stood to the west of the gaol and was connected with it by a passage forming an archway over the main road.[75] Howard found separate day- and work-rooms for men and women; there was a court but it was not used because it was insecure.[76] When, as explained below, a new gaol was built, a house of correction was incorporated with it. The old house of correction was demolished in stages between 1796 and 1820.[77]

In 1786 a county meeting recommended the justices to build a new gaol at a 'proper' distance from the centre of the town and to incorporate, if possible, improvements suggested by Howard.[78] Accordingly under an Act of 1787[79] a new building began to rise upon the Crofts in Foregate field and was opened in 1793.[80] It was designed by William Blackburn.[81] The old building was demolished, and in 1801 part of the site was used for the new grammar school.[82]

The new three-storey brick prison, enclosed within a boundary wall, was approached through a stone gate-house on the west, which was separated from the gaoler's house by a garden. A passage led eastwards through the house into a large inner courtyard. In 1805 the felons' prison contained 7 day-rooms and 118 cells. The house of correction had a day-room and 13 cells. There was a chapel.[83] Subsequently the prison was enlarged several times and radically redesigned. The first enlargement occurred c. 1819, increasing the capacity to 224.[84] In 1832–3 a new house of correction was built at the north end of the site in the form of a crescent to the design of Joseph Potter, the county surveyor.[85] Two round angle-towers (or keeper's lodges) were described in 1843 as lately built, and two more at the remaining angles were then recommended for the security of the prison; they had been built by 1856.[86] In order to make it possible to operate the 'separate' system a new block was erected at the south end of the site in the mid 1840s to the design of Joseph Potter's son Joseph.[87] Between 1852 and 1854 the female prison was pulled down and a

[53] Cal. Pat. 1563–6, pp. 37, 104. [54] Ibid. 1566–9, p. 428.
[55] Sta. Cha. 5/S 40/20. [56] See pp. 227–8.
[57] W.S.L., H.M. uncat. 35 (Norbury), Ferreday v. Parton, 1695; Cherry, Stafford, 18; W.S.L. 7/3/00, sketch plan of Gaol Sq. area.
[58] See p. 228; Sta. Cha. 8/45/13 f. 25.
[59] S.R.O., Q/SO 2, f. 126; Q/SO 4, f. 180v.; Q/SR, T.1638, no. 11.
[60] S.R.O., Q/SR, M.1638, no. 1.
[61] Sta. Cha. 8/45/13 f. 32; S.R.O., Q/SO 6, ff. 88v., 99.
[62] S.R.O., Q/SR, T.1647, no. 25; Q/SO 5, ff. 312, 378.
[63] S.R.O., Q/SR, M.1686, no. 7.
[64] S.R.O., D.1323/A/1/1, p. 335.
[65] S.R.O., Q/SR, T.1687, no. 5B; Q/SO 10, 28 July 1687.
[66] J. Howard, State of the Prisons (1777 edn.), 327; (1780 edn.), 310–11; Howard, Acct. of . . . Lazarettos (1789 edn.), 158 n., 173.
[67] Speed, Map of Staffs. (1610).
[68] S.H.C. 1935, 229–30; S.R.O., D.1323/E/1, f. 42v.
[69] S.R.O., D.1323/E/1, f. 176v.; S.R.O., Q/SO 4, f. 175v.
[70] S.R.O., Q/SO 5, ff. 251, 308.
[71] S.R.O., Q/SR, A. 1659/60, no. 2.
[72] In the early 1650s 3s. rent was paid 'for gaol and seat' (S.R.O., D.1323/E/1, f. 295v.); the same rent was paid to the borough for the county house of correction in 1619 (ibid. f. 96), for the house of correction and the 'seat at door' in 1622, 1630, and 1631: ibid. ff. 122v., 169v., 187v. In 1662 the rent was 'for the new gaol, lately a house of correction' and 'for a stone step and seat': ibid. f. 300v. For another example of such a fusion see V.C.H. Wilts. vi. 182.
[73] Sta. Cha. 8/45/13, f. 7; S.R.O., D.1323/E/1, ff. 122v.,
187v.; S.R.O., Q/SO 5, pp. 211, 308. A reference to Jas. Almond as keeper of the houses of correction in 1635–6 (S.R.O., D.1323/E/1, f. 221B) may suggest that county and borough houses shared a keeper.
[74] S.R.O., D.1323/A/1/1, p. 272.
[75] Ibid. /3, p. 221; Cherry, Stafford, 18; B.L. Eg. MS. 2872, f. 57v.
[76] Howard, State of the Prisons (1780 edn.), 312.
[77] S.R.O., D.1323/A/1/3, pp. 152, 205, 221; /4, p. 20; Staffs. Advertiser, 10 Aug. 1799; below, p. 217.
[78] S.R.O., Q/SB, M.1786, no. 169.
[79] 27 Geo. III, c. 60.
[80] From the evidence of the salaries of the gaoler and 2 turnkeys from 13 May: S.R.O., Q/SO 20, f. 236v. (ref. supplied by Mr. A. Standley, training principal officer at Stafford prison (1977), who also provided some of the material used in the following paragraph).
[81] W.S.L., M.917 and 1004.
[82] S.R.O., Q/SMe 4, 18 July 1793; ibid. 5, 10 Oct. 1793 adj. to 11 Nov.; Staffs. Advertiser, 13 June 1795; W.S.L. 7/15/00, notice of auction of part of site 1799; S.R.O., D.1323/A/1/3, p. 230.
[83] Gent. Mag. lxxvi (2), 1188–9 (J. Neild's rep.); White, Dir. Staffs. (1834), 122.
[84] Acct. respecting Gaols, H.C. 135, pp. 42–3 (1819), xvii; Returns of Gaols, H.C. 400, p. 50 (1821), xxi.
[85] White, Dir. Staffs. (1851), 330–1.
[86] Staffs. Advertiser, 7 Jan. 1843; S.R.O., Q/AE 1.
[87] The Builder (1846), 346; Staffs. Advertiser, 8 Jan. 1842, 12 Apr. 1845, 13 Mar. 1847; S.R.O., Q/FAa 1/14, 1 Aug. 1846.

mixed block of two divisions was built partly on the old site and partly on a newly purchased plot to the east. A chapel was also built on the new site, cruciform and 'devoid of prison aspect'. The prison thus became the 'largest and most important' in the inspector's district in which it lay.[88] The crescent building, long criticized for its poor ventilation,[89] was altered and enlarged to the design of Robert Griffiths, the county surveyor, between 1864 and 1866 to provide extra cells, and the means to enforce the 'separate' system was complete.[90] In 1868 the prison could hold 732.[91] A circular kitchen was built c. 1866–7 on a new site on the south-east extending to Pearl brook. By the early 20th century it had been replaced by a kitchen north of the 1840s block.[92] A male hospital was completed on the south-eastern site in 1886, replacing a hospital on the north-west opened in 1821.[93] A tread-wheel was installed in 1822,[94] and by 1834 there were eight.[95] By 1893 there were two, for grinding corn and pumping water; by 1895 the one which pumped water was used only occasionally.[96] The tread-wheel was abandoned in 1901–2.[97] From 1916 to 1921 the prison was used as a military detention barracks and then remained unoccupied until 1939 when it was reopened as a civilian prison.[98] The last of the corner towers, that on the north-west, was demolished for road-widening in the early 1950s.[99] The chapel was pulled down in 1952–3 after being damaged by subsidence and was replaced by a hut. In 1976 Roman Catholic services were transferred there from the Roman Catholic chapel of the later 19th century.[1] A new gate-house was built in 1953.[2]

The County Refuge (later the County Industrial Home) was opened in Sandon Road in 1878. It was built by subscription to provide work for friendless women and had three main departments, for cooking, sewing, and laundry. It was thought to be the first of its kind in the country. By 1928 it had become a Home Office reformatory for girls, which c. 1930 moved to Rowley Hall.[3]

THE COLLEGE ESTATE. In 1086 the thirteen prebendary canons of St. Mary's, Stafford, held 3 hides in free alms. The estate, which included fourteen houses in the town, was worth 20s. in 1066 and 60s. in 1086.[4] By the mid 13th century there were tenants not only in Stafford but also in Orberton, Worston, and Whitgreave in St. Mary's parish and in Butterton in Trentham. In 1251 Henry III issued a charter to the dean and chapter of St. Mary's to replace another granted by him which had been stolen. It gave them a court which was exempt from the jurisdiction of royal officers, and their tenants were to be free of suit to any other court. The dean and chapter had their own gallows and the right to infangthief and outfangthief. Their tenants were quit of customs and tallages except those tallages paid by other exempt churches.[5] By the Dissolution the dean and chapter owned property in various parts of the county.[6] Their estate, worth just under £100 a year,[7] then passed to the Crown.

The Crown soon started to alienate parts of the estate.[8] The first big alienation was the grant of the deanery to Henry, Lord Stafford, in 1550; it included lands and tithes in Hopton, Whitgreave, Tillington, Castle Church, Creswell, Ingestre, and Tixall and was worth £44 8s. 2d. a year.[9] In 1553 Lord Stafford sold it to John Maynard of London,[10] and on Maynard's death in 1557 it was divided between his three daughters, Frances, Elizabeth, and Susan. The largest share went to Frances, and in 1564 she and her husband Walter Robertes sold it to William Crompton of London and later of Stone. In the same year Crompton bought Susan's share also. In 1609 his grandson Thomas Crompton bought Elizabeth's share from her son William Sparry.[11] By the time of his death in 1603, however, Thomas's father, another William Crompton, had sold some of the property to Thomas Blackborne, the town clerk (d. 1604), and Thomas Crompton sold more of it.[12]

Another part of the collegiate property, tithes belonging to the prebend of Marston from the town, Foregate, Foregate field, and Lammascote, was granted to the grammar school in 1550.[13] The property in Whitgreave belonging to the prebends of Coton and Marston was sold in 1553 and 1554.[14] In 1571 Elizabeth I granted the residue of the collegiate property, consisting of lands and tithes in Stafford, Coton, Marston, Salt, and Rugeley, to the burgesses of Stafford to provide stipends for the rector, assistant curate, and schoolmaster of Stafford and the curate of Marston; the rest of the income

[88] 17th Rep. Prison Inspectors, S. and W. Dist.[1495], pp. 66, 68, H.C. (1852), xxiv; 19th Rep. [1853], pp. 99–100, 106, 109, H.C. (1854), xxxiv; R. G. Alford, Notes of Eng. Prison Buildings (Parkhurst, priv. print. 1910), vi. 40–1; Staffs. Advertiser, 3 Apr. 1852.

[89] From 1856: 21st Rep. Prison Inspectors, S. and W. Dist. [2133] p. 69, H.C. (1856), xxxiii.

[90] 29th Rep. Prison Inspectors, N. Dist. [3326,] p. 52, H.C. (1864), xxvi; 30th Rep. [3520] p. 91, H.C. (1865), xxiii; 31st Rep. [3715], p. 99, H.C. (1866), xxxvii. The building bears the date 1864.

[91] 32nd Rep. [4029], p. 94, H.C. (1867–8), xxxiv.

[92] Staffs. Advertiser, 2 July, 22 Oct. 1864, 7 Jan. 1865; 31st Rep. 99; 32nd Rep. 96; Alford, Eng. Prison Buildings, vi. 42–3.

[93] Staffs. Advertiser, 10 Apr. 1886. For the earlier hospital see ibid. 28 July 1821; S.R.O., Q/AE 1.

[94] Dyott's Diary 1781–1845, ed. R. W. Jeffery, i. 346.

[95] White, Dir. Staffs. (1834), 123.

[96] 16th Rep. Prison Commrs. Pt. 2 [C. 7197–I], p. 79, H.C. (1893–4), xlvii; 17th Rep. Pt. 2 [C. 7509–I], p. 77, H.C. (1894), xliv.

[97] Rep. Prison Commrs. for 1901–2 [Cd. 1278], p. 509, H.C. (1902), xlvi.

[98] Roxburgh, Stafford, 132.

[99] Staffs. Advertiser, 1 June 1951.

[1] Ex inf. Mr. A. Standley; Alford, Eng. Prison Buildings, vi. 43.

[2] Stafford Newsletter, 27 June 1953.

[3] Staffs. Advertiser, 21 Sept. 1878; Kelly's Dir. Staffs. (1928; 1932); W.S.L., Sale Cats. A/2/12 and C/3/4; O.S. Map 6″, Staffs. XXXVII. SE. (1889 and 1902 edns.).

[4] V.C.H. Staffs. iv. 37, 44.

[5] Ibid. iii. 303, 305.

[6] S.C. 12/14/76.

[7] S.H.C. 1915, 240.

[8] V.C.H. Staffs. iii. 308.

[9] Cal. Pat. 1550–3, 18.

[10] S.H.C. xii (1), 212–13. V.C.H. Staffs. v. 95, citing Cal. Pat. 1550–3, 66–7, gives the date as 1551, which was in fact the date of the licence for alienation.

[11] Cal. Pat. 1560–3, 399–400, 601; 1563–6, 4; W.S.L., S.MS. 402, ff. 15v.–16; S.H.C. xiii. 230, 232; S.H.C. N.S. iii. 33–4; C 142/145 no. 24; C 142/312 no. 155.

[12] C 142/283 no. 107; C 142/299 no. 159; W.S.L., S.MS. 369, p. 144; S.MS. 402, f. 16. V.C.H. Staffs. v. 95, gives the date of the death of Wm. Crompton the younger as 1604 and that of Blackborne as 1607; those dates are in fact the dates of the inquisitions post mortem.

[13] Bradley, Charters, 81.

[14] V.C.H. Staffs. iii. 308.

was to be used for the repair of St. Mary's and for charitable works in the town. Payments were still made in respect of the Queen Elizabeth Grant in 1977.[15]

The collegiate buildings included a house for the dean and apparently two separate houses for the canons and the vicars choral.[16] The dean's chamber in or adjoining the churchyard was mentioned in 1295.[17] By the beginning of the 15th century his house included a hall, principal chamber, chapel, pantry, and buttery.[18] The Crown sold it with the rest of the deanery estate to Lord Stafford in 1550; it was owned by Thomas Blackborne at his death in 1604. A building described in 1546 as 'the house wherein divers ministers did lie' and in 1549 as the capital messuage of the priests of the former collegiate church was by then in the tenure of the newly established vicar of St. Mary's on a 60-year lease. The Crown sold it in 1549 to three speculators.[19] A building on the south side of the churchyard known as the College House occurs from the early 17th century as part of the corporation's property. By 1615 it was occupied by the master of the grammar school, and part of it was normally let to the masters until 1725 when John Dearle left it after a dispute with the corporation over the rent; William Hammersley, usher at the school and curate at St. Mary's from 1666 until his death in 1716, lived in the other part. It continued to be let as two separate tenements for a short time. It was, however, in a poor condition and was demolished in 1736. The profits from the sale of the timber were assigned to the workhouse which was established in the outbuildings in 1738.[20] St. Mary's National school was built on the site of the workhouse in 1856.[21]

There was a barn 'commonly called the tithe barn' at Broadeye in 1694.[22] It was probably the tithe barn in Gaolgate ward mentioned in the earlier 18th century.[23] A tithe barn in Coton field is mentioned in 1861, and it still stood at the junction of Tithe Barn Road and St. John's Walk in the early 1920s.[24]

OTHER ESTATES. In 1086 there were 18 burgesses in Stafford belonging to the abbey of St. Evroul's manor of Marston.[25] Two burgages in Stafford which Thomas de Erdington apparently held for life from the priory of St. Thomas near Stafford c. 1199 were described as of the fee of St.

Evroul.[26] It is not clear whether they were within or without the walls. No more is known of any St. Evroul property within the walls, but the lords of Marston held the lordship of Foregate even after it was attracted to the borough in or before the 13th century.[27] Those rights had passed to St. Evroul's daughter-house of Ware (Herts.) by 1306, and after the suppression of Ware in 1414 they were granted in 1415 to the priory of Sheen (Surr.).[28] In 1535 Sheen held lands and tenements in Foregate worth 26s. 8d. a year.[29] In 1540 the property, then including two-thirds of the tithes of Foregate field, was granted by the Crown to Sir John Giffard of Chillington in tail male.[30] It then descended in the Giffard family[31] until it was split up into allotments under the Stafford inclosure of 1807.[32]

In 1086 Burton abbey held five houses in the borough. No more is known of them, and the abbey held no property in Stafford at the Dissolution.[33]

By 1170 Kenilworth priory (Warws.) or its daughter-house of Stone held land allegedly in Stafford which had belonged to Walter, described variously as son of Gutha, Jutha, or Inett. The property, however, was associated with land in Castle Church which had been given by Robert de Stafford to Stone priory between 1138 and 1147; it may thus have been outside the borough. In 1292 Kenilworth released its rights in both properties to Stone.[34] At the Dissolution Stone priory held a burgage and 2s. rent in Stafford.[35]

About 1174 Gerard son of Brian gave his new foundation of St. Thomas near Stafford property in Stafford, probably a burgage, reserving a rent of 8d., of which 6d. was later released to the priory by Adam, priest of Stowe.[36] The canons were also given houses in Stafford by Ralph, the archdeacon of Stafford; Christine of Wolverhampton gave the land on which the houses stood.[37] In the late 12th and the 13th centuries the priory acquired many other small properties and rents in the town by gift or purchase, and c. 1250 Robert de Stafford gave it a rent-charge of 3 marks out of Stafford mill.[38] In 1352 Ralph, earl of Stafford, gave a meadow next to the town, which the canons alienated before 1432,[39] and in 1365 Henry le Schyrreve gave them a house in Tipping Street.[40] The priory was licensed in 1383–4 to buy further property in the town[41] and in 1414 to buy a house and 5 a. in Stafford and Coton and two tofts in Stafford.[42] In 1415 or 1416 it acquired a house and 20 a. in Stafford and Marston from Richard Colman of

[15] Bradley, *Charters*, 99–107; below, pp. 239–40.
[16] For a discussion of the buildings, much of it conjectural, see L. Lambert's two booklets (copies in W.S.L.), *St. Mary's and the Coll. Quarter of Stafford* (Birmingham, 1925); *The Queen Elizabeth Grant and the Coll. Estate in the Town of Stafford* (Stafford, 1939).
[17] *Cal. Pat.* 1292–1301, 158.
[18] *Cal. Inq. Misc.* vii, pp. 184–5.
[19] *S.H.C.* 1915, 240–1; *Cal. Pat.* 1549–51, 126.
[20] S.R.O., D.1323/E/1, ff. 64v., 99v. sqq.; S.R.O., D.(W.) 1721/1/4, f. 113v.; S.R.O., D.1323/A/1/1, pp. 7, 17, 194, 256; /2, pp. 182–3, 248–9, 265, 412–13, 449; D.1323/F/1, reverse pages, pp. 20–1, 67, 70; W.S.L. 49/112(B)/44, relator's proofs, ff. [5–6]; J. S. Horne, *Notes for Hist. of K. Edw. VI Sch.*, Stafford (Stafford, 1930), 25–6, 30, 70.
[21] See p. 261.
[22] W.S.L., H.M. uncat. 27, deed of 4 July 1694.
[23] S.R.O., D.(W.) 0/8/18 (1735); W.S.L., H.M. uncat. 23, land-tax assessment for Stafford boro. 1742.
[24] S.R.O., D.1323/A/1/8, 6 Feb. 1861; O.S. Map 6″,

Staffs. XXXVII. SE. (1889, 1902, and 1925 edns.).
[26] *S.H.C.* viii (1), 184.   [25] *V.C.H. Staffs.* iv. 46.
[27] See p. 222.
[28] *V.C.H. Herts.* iv. 455–7; E 326/8056; *S.H.C.* 1911, 151; 1914, 103–4; S.R.O. 938/417.
[29] *Valor Eccl.* (Rec. Com.), ii. 51.
[30] *L. & P. Hen. VIII*, xv, p. 470; *S.H.C.* 1914, 104.
[31] *S.H.C.* n.s. v. 117–99; S.R.O., D.590/369c.
[32] S.R.O., Q/RDc 16.
[33] *V.C.H. Staffs.* iii. 201, 204; iv. 43.
[34] *S.H.C.* ii (1), 210–11; vi (1), 13; Dugdale, *Mon.* vi. 223, 232; *Cal. Pat.* 1334–8, 308–9.
[35] *Valor Eccl.* iii. 113; Dugdale, *Mon.* vi. 233, listing the burgage only.
[36] *V.C.H. Staffs.* iii. 260, wrongly giving the rent as 8s.; *S.H.C.* viii (1) 132, 185.
[37] *S.H.C.* viii (1), 133; *V.C.H. Staffs.* iii. 260.
[38] *S.H.C.* viii (1), 135–6, 184–6; below, p. 211.
[39] S.R.O. 938/196 and 208.
[40] Ibid./198.   [41] *S.H.C.* viii (1), 185.
[42] *Cal. Pat.* 1413–16, 290–1.

Lichfield.[43] Humphrey, earl of Stafford, released other lands in Stafford to the canons in 1425.[44] At its dissolution St. Thomas's held at least 32 houses and tenements, at least 20 cottages, a shop, and several chief rents, gardens, barns, and other property in Stafford and Forebridge, besides the rent-charge on the mill. The total was valued at £14 in 1535, with outgoings totalling 20s. 10d., but at £35 11s. 8d. in 1543.[45]

In 1185 the Templars held a 2s. rent in Stafford of the fee of Geoffrey Marmion and Thomas son of Noah; Geoffrey had given it to them.[46] No more is known of it.

Lilleshall abbey (Salop.) held a moiety of a house in Stafford by 1189 and acquired the other half in that year. Apparently in the 13th century it held 5 burgages in Stafford given by John the fuller of Stafford and 3 given by William de Gresley, one of the latter being at the East Gate.[47] The canons had apparently alienated their Stafford property by the Dissolution.[48]

In the later 12th century the Hospitallers held property in St. Chad's parish: 6d. was owed to them from property there granted by Gerard son of Brian to his daughters at that time.[49] In 1535 the prior of St. John of Jerusalem was paid 8d. rent by the prior of St. Thomas near Stafford for two houses in Eastgate Street, perhaps the property granted by Gerard.[50]

Apparently in the mid 13th century Gilbert, son of Hugh of Coton, gave Dieulacres abbey a house in Foregate, reserving a rent of 8d. The abbey still held a croft in Foregate at the Dissolution.[51]

In 1273 Ralph Wymer held ¾ carucate at 'le Lombercote' east of the borough of the prior of Ware's manor of Marston for 2s. a year.[52] In the early 15th century it was held by Nicholas Bradshaw (d. 1415), and later by his brother Roger; it had passed to Humphrey, earl of Stafford, by 1434.[53] It then descended with the Stafford barony.[54] By 1788 it formed part of Lammascote farm.[55] Under the Stafford inclosure of 1807 parts of it were allotted to Lord Talbot, to John Collins and William Keen, and to the corporation. Sir William Jerningham, heir to the Stafford barony, exchanged a further part with Lord Talbot for land adjoining Coton field.[56] In 1896 Lord Stafford sold Lammascote farm to the corporation. A sewage works was opened on the part between the Sow and the Penk in 1897.[57] Houses were built on another part from 1913-14.[58] There was a farm-house by 1778, north of Lammascote Road, and farm buildings south of the road.[59] Riverway school was opened on the site of the farm buildings in 1939, and Pennycrofts Court was built on that of the house in 1968.[60] The form 'Lammascote' has not been found before 1775;[61] early forms suggest that the name means 'lambcot'.[62]

The Franciscans had settled in Stafford by 1274.[63] By the mid 14th century, and probably from the start, their friary was in Foregate on the east side of the main road north of the junction with Browning Street.[64] In 1306 Henry Grocock granted them a plot in Foregate to make a curtilage.[65] Philip Chetwynd gave them 1½ a. in Foregate field near the friary in 1430,[66] and in 1435 they received 1 a. there from William Bradshawe and 1½ a. from the priory of St. Thomas.[67] By 1538 the friars held 6 'lands', presumably in Foregate field. In that year the friary was sold to James Leveson of Wolverhampton.[68] His grandson Walter Leveson of Lilleshall (Salop.) sold it in 1581 to Matthew Dorrington of Stafford, who gave it to his son John, a London grocer, in 1582.[69] In 1611 and 1612 it was held by Richard Dorrington.[70] It had passed by 1644 to Sir Richard Dyott.[71] The buildings were then demolished to facilitate the defence of the town.[72]

In 1337 Richard of Billington sought licence to grant two houses and two curtilages in Stafford to Ranton priory.[73] At the Dissolution the priory held a burgage let at will for 2s. 4d., another on lease to the prior of St. Thomas for 2s., and a curtilage and barn worth 3s. 4d.[74]

Ralph, earl of Stafford, received licence in 1352 to grant rents in Stafford worth £5 a year to the master and brethren of St. John's hospital, Forebridge. The endowment was in support of a chaplain saying mass daily in the hospital chapel. Ralph's son-in-law John, Lord Ferrers of Chartley, seems to have granted two houses in Stafford to the hospital.[75] In 1535 the hospital was owed 4s. 4d. in rent-charges from lands in Stafford belonging to

[43] S.R.O. 938/417; S.H.C. viii (1), 176, wrongly giving Sheen priory as the donor.
[44] S.R.O. 938/206.
[45] S.R.O. 938/29; Valor Eccl. iii. 111.
[46] Recs. of Templars in Eng. in 12th cent. ed. Beatrice A. Lees, 31.
[47] B.L. Add. MS. 50121, ff. 43, 48.
[48] None is listed in Dugdale, Mon. vi. 265, or S.C. 6/Hen. VIII/3009 rott. 14-30.
[49] S.H.C. viii (1), 131.
[50] Valor Eccl. iii. 111.
[51] S.H.C. n.s. ix. 327-8; V.C.H. Staffs. iii. 231, 233; S.C. 6/Hen. VIII/3353 rot. 39d.
[52] S.H.C. 1911, 151; S.R.O. 938/266, gift by John and Denise del Orme to Adam Gilbert, n.d. but later 13th cent.
[53] S.R.O., D.641/1/2/53, rot. 2; /54, rot. 2; C 139/10 no. 20.
[54] S.R.O., D.641/1/2/95, rot. 4d.; D.641/2/G/1/1, rentals Mich. 1624 and Lady Day 1626; D.(W.) 1721/1/1, f. 140; W.S.L., H.M. uncat. 24, case concerning right of common in Lambercoate, 1749; H.M. Chetwynd 121; Act for inclosing lands in or adjoining the parish of St. Mary, Stafford, 39 & 40 Geo. III, c. 70 (Local and Personal).
[55] B.L. Eg. MS. 2862, ff. 52v.-53.
[56] S.R.O., Q/RDc 16.
[57] Staffs. Advertiser, 18 Sept. 1897; O.S. Map 6",
[58] See p. 233.
[59] B.L. Eg. MS. 2862, f. 53.
[60] See pp. 194, 263.
[61] Yates, Map of Staffs. (1775).
[62] e.g. 'Lambercote' in 1433-4 (S.R.O., D.641/1/2/53, rot. 2); 'Lambcotts' in 1537 (S.R.O., D.(W.) 1721/1/1, f. 140); 'Lambercoats' in 1550 (Bradley, Charters, 81); 'Lamberscot' in 1788 (B.L. Eg. MS. 2862, ff. 52v.-53); 'Lamberscott' in 1846 (L.J.R.O., B/A/15/Coton, nos. 29, 35-6).
[63] V.C.H. Staffs. iii. 270.
[64] E 326/4704.
[65] Ibid. /8506; S.H.C. 1911, 283-4.
[66] E 326/4802.
[67] Ibid. /4706; E 329/373.
[68] V.C.H. Staffs. iii. 270-1.
[69] Ibid. v. 80; S.R.O., D.593/A/2/27/17; D.661/2/317, 320, 325, 723.
[70] E 134/9 Jas. I East. /15; E 134/10 Jas. I East. /33.
[71] S.H.C. 4th ser. i. 72, 105-6.
[72] E 326/4706 and 4802; E 329/373; V.C.H. Staffs. iii. 271.
[73] S.H.C. 1913, 60-1.
[74] Valor Eccl. iii. 111, 115 (giving 2 burgages for 2s. 4d. and omitting the barn); S.C. 6/Hen. VIII/3352 rot. 11.
[75] V.C.H. Staffs. iii. 291.

Staffs. XXXVII. SE. (1902 edn.).

St. Thomas's priory.[76] By 1548, when it was suppressed, the hospital had three houses and other property allegedly in Stafford but probably in Forebridge. In 1550 Edward VI granted them, with the other possessions of the hospital, to Stafford grammar school. The tenants, however, resisted the grant, and the hospital, restored in or before 1556, seems to have retained the property until its final dissolution in 1560. The burgesses then granted the estate to Lord Stafford in fee farm.[77] Following litigation by the headmaster and usher a Chancery decree of 1612 subjected the former hospital's property to rent-charges payable to the school.[78]

The other property granted to the grammar school by Edward VI in 1550 included the tithes of Foregate field, Foregate, and Lammascote, and those of the high street, all formerly belonging to the prebend of Marston in St. Mary's, and rent-charges on two houses in Eastgate Street, one in Foregate Street, and a cottage in the borough, which had formed the endowments of various obits.[79] The school also held two rent-charges on two houses in Foregate Street left by Robert Lees in 1547.[80] Part of the tithes were assigned by the burgesses to Lord Stafford under the grant of 1560. They apparently passed to Robert Sutton, rector of Stafford (d. 1587), and then to his successor John Palmer, from whom they were recovered in 1612 for the use of the school.[81] Part of the tithes of Foregate field may have been granted to William Fowler in 1705; they had been lost to the school by the early 19th century. Those of Lammascote were exchanged in the Stafford inclosure of 1807 for lands in Castle Church.[82] One of Lees's rent-charges was lost between 1736 and 1823.[83] In 1823 the school still received small payments for tithes in the town and 13s. from houses there.[84] It still held various small properties in Stafford when it was suppressed in 1976. In 1977 a scheme was being prepared to divert the income to a group of schools in Stafford including the King Edward VI, Graham Balfour, Walton, and Rising Brook high schools, and a proposed school near Tixall Road.[85]

By 1535 Croxden abbey drew rent from a curtilage and garden in Stafford let to a tenant at will.[86]

ECONOMIC HISTORY. AGRICULTURE. By the mid 15th century the inhabitants of Stafford were claiming pasture rights in the three common fields of Coton manor, but the prior and canons of St. Thomas near Stafford as lords of Coton claimed the right to keep the fields in severalty. In 1455, under an award made by the duke of Buckingham as arbitrator, one of the fields, Pool (later Coton) field north-east of the town, was leased by the canons to the bailiffs, burgesses, and commonalty of Stafford for 99 years at a rent of 9 marks (£6); the corporation gave up its claims in the other two fields for that period.[87] By 1543 the rent was £4.[88] In 1554 a further dispute was settled by Lord Hereford as arbitrator, and Brian Fowler, then lord of Coton, granted another 99-year lease in return for a fine of £10, a rent of £4, and the provision of 'an able billman on foot to serve the king in his wars' as directed by Fowler. On the expiry of that lease Walter Fowler challenged the corporation's rights, but in 1669 a Chancery decree recognized the burgesses' right of common pasture in all three fields in Coton; in fact an agreement was made allowing the burgesses to continue to occupy Coton field during Walter's lifetime at a rent of £40. In 1699 Walter's son William granted them a 99-year lease of the field, then 180 a., at a rent of £20; in addition the mayor was to pay £20 a year to the poor in Noell's alms-houses, and the Fowlers were to nominate two inhabitants of the borough to the alms-houses and also to be quit of toll on stock sold by them at the borough fairs and markets.[89] In 1705 Fowler granted a new 99-year lease reducing his family's share of the rent to £12 but raising the payment to the alms-houses to £28. He also agreed to convey the inheritance of the field to the corporation, which in 1708 secured the necessary royal licence for the alienation, but no conveyance was made.[90] The corporation continued in occupation after the lease had expired in 1804, and in 1830 Earl Talbot as lord of Coton tried unsuccessfully to oust it.[91] It applied to him in 1838, and to his son in 1854, for the conveyance of the equitable fee,[92] and in 1874 the court of Chancery recognized that the field had become the corporation's property under an earlier decree.[93]

After the making of the 1455 lease the bailiffs and burgesses agreed to share out the field; the bailiffs (and later the mayor) had their own acres, the 'masters' (presumably the capital burgesses) had three acres each, and the rest of the burgesses 'and other commoners' received one or two acres. After the cutting of hay and corn the land was available as common pasture. Acres were apparently allocated by the bailiffs and by the church-wardens of St. Mary's in the later 16th century. In 1611 there were 99 tenants; 'clay' acres were let at 4d. each and 'sand' acres at 6d.[94] There was mention of a 'meadow'

---

[76] *Valor Eccl.* iii. 111.

[77] *V.C.H. Staffs.* iii. 292; Bradley, *Charters*, 82–4. Some of the property listed in the grant to the school was clearly in Castle Church, while lists of 1612 of the former hospital property show houses in Forebridge but none in the borough: C. G. Gilmore, *Hist. of K. Edw. VI Sch., Stafford*, 131–2; W.S.L., M. 941.

[78] *11th Rep. Com. Char.* H.C. 433, p. 582 (1824), xiv; W.S.L., M. 941.

[79] *11th Rep. Com. Char.* 579; above, p. 205.

[80] *11th Rep. Com. Char.* 583.

[81] Gilmore, *K. Edw. VI Sch.* 125; W.S.L., M. 941.

[82] *11th Rep. Com. Char.* 581.

[83] Ibid. 583.

[84] Ibid. 581.

[85] Gilmore, *K. Edw. VI Sch.* 128; Staffs. County Council, Treasurer's Dept., Educ. Accountancy files; ex inf. Treasurer's Dept. (1977).

[86] *Valor Eccl.* iii. 125; S.C. 6/Hen. VIII/3353 rot. 46d.

[87] B.L. Add. MS. 36542, ff. 188–189v.

[88] S.R.O. 938/29.

[89] S.R.O., D.(W.) 1790/D/7, 1669 Chancery decree and 1701 agreement; W.S.L., C.B. Stafford, copy of 1699 agreement; W.S.L., S.MS. 369, p. 119; S.R.O., D.1323/A/1/1, pp. 90 sqq. For the bounds of Coton field in 1670 see W.S.L., H.M. 26/2, ff. 38–9; it is also shown on the Coton tithe map (L.J.R.O., B/A/15, Coton).

[90] W.S.L., D.1798/537/2/1; W.S.L., S.MS. 402, f. 70.

[91] *Staffs. Advertiser*, 4 and 18 Dec. 1830; White, *Dir. Staffs.* (1834), 121.

[92] W.S.L., D.1798/537/2/9; *Staffs. Advertiser*, 28 Oct. 1854, p. 8. A draft conveyance was prepared in 1847: D.1798/537/2/2.

[93] *Staffs. Advertiser*, 18 July 1874, p. 5.

[94] S.R.O., D.(W.) 1790/D/7, 1669 Chancery decree; *Cal. Pat. 1549–51*, 362–3; Ann J. Kettle, 'Black Book of Stafford', *T.S.H.C.S.* 1965–7, 6, 28; S.R.O., D.1323/E/1, ff. 54v.–55, 68–9, 74–5.

The Royal Brine Baths, Greengate Street, demolished 1976

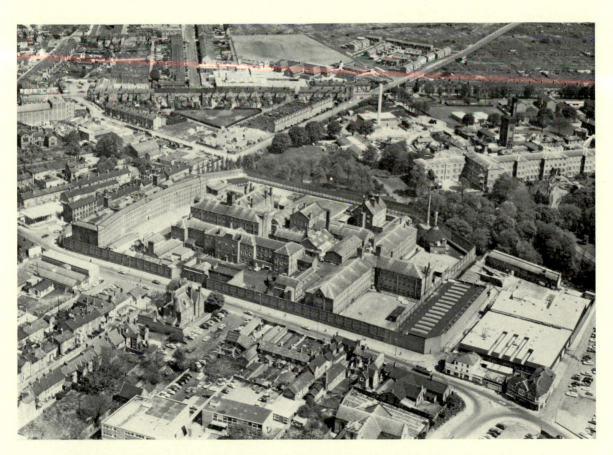

The gaol from the south-west, 1972, with St. George's Hospital in the right background

STAFFORD

The Green Bridge in 1841

Chetwynd House, Greengate Street, in 1841

The railway station in 1844

The railway station in 1967

STAFFORD

acre in 1652,[95] but by 1700 the distinction was between 'corn' and 'grass' acres.[96] Rents were collected by the churchwardens at least between the mid 16th and the later 17th centuries,[97] but the responsibility had passed to the chamberlains by the early 18th century.[98]

In 1670, to meet the legal costs of the dispute with the Fowlers, a new system of distribution was introduced. The mayor and councillors were given the first choice of acres and were allowed two each; an entry fine of 40s. was imposed unless the councillor had advanced that amount towards the cost of the lawsuit. The remaining acres, 'so far as they will extend', were to be divided among the burgesses at the rate of one each, with 10s. added to the rent for the first year and 5s. for the second; burgesses who had advanced money towards the suit during the previous six years were to have that allowed against the additional charges, and they were also to have preference in the choice of acres. A widow was to retain her husband's land during her widowhood. The mayor assisted by some of the councillors was to handle the distribution.[99] In 1674 the corporation, having ordered a reduction of the rents by half, decided to view the field in order to fix 'an equality of the rates'.[1] In 1696 it ordered that no burgess should dispose of his acre without the consent of the mayor and council,[2] and in 1697 it restricted acres to those burgesses who were householders in the borough.[3] In 1699 the mayor was given sole responsibility for the distribution. It was also ordered that any holder of an acre who became a charge on the town through poverty should have his acre seized by the mayor to be used towards his maintenance. Another order provided that everyone taking possession of an acre should in future pay the equivalent of a year's rent to 'the poor's box'.[4] In 1700 the profits from the crop of grass acres in the year following a vacancy and all the profits from Coton field over £40 a year were for the future assigned to the poor in the alms-houses.[5] In 1701 it was made a general rule that entry fines of 10s. on a grass acre and of twice the annual rent on a corn acre were to be paid to the alms-house poor.[6] By that time most of the rents were 4s., 4s. 6d., or 5s.[7] In 1745 there were 171 or 172 tenants, holding mostly at those rents; entry fines were then 5s. on tillage acres and 10s. on grass acres. Pasture rights after the cutting of corn and hay were enjoyed by all the burgesses.[8] From 1763 races were held in October on part of the field.[9]

New regulations were made in 1769 after disputes had arisen over the distribution of acres. The mayor retained responsibility for allocation. No councillor was to receive his two acres during the year of his election without the mayor's consent.[10] In the early 19th century the councillors' entitlement was reduced to one acre, but dissatisfaction with the system continued. Distribution, still in the hands of the mayor, was a matter of patronage and acres were not given to the poorer burgesses. Rents were 4s., 5s., or 6s. according to the quality of the land.[11] Regulations drawn up in 1836 restricted acres in future to needy burgesses, to be chosen in order of seniority as burgesses. No one was to hold more than one acre, and councillors were no longer eligible. Pauperism, however, was still a disqualification. By 1851 rents had become fixed at 5s., with entry fines of 5s. and 10s. as before.[12] Needy burgesses were defined in 1867 as those worth less than £200 and having an income (other than earnings) of less than £10 a year.[13] By the earlier 1850s ½-a. plots were being granted,[14] and by 1880 the average holding was ¾ a.[15] By 1854 the average age of tenants was about 60, and many, being too old to cultivate the land properly, were selling or leasing their plots.[16] Nearly 30 a. was derelict by 1876.[17]

In 1879 it was ruled in Chancery that the corporation could not levy a rate until the Coton field acres were let at competitive rents. The corporation gave the tenants notice to quit, but a group of burgesses prepared to challenge the ruling. To avoid litigation a settlement was agreed. It was embodied in the Stafford Corporation Act, 1880, whereby the 180 a. of Coton field, including 20 freehold acres which the corporation was authorized to buy, were vested in the corporation and all common rights were extinguished. Seventy acres was reserved as freemen's allotments, up to 20 a. was to be laid out as a public pleasure ground, and the rest could be sold.[18] By the earlier 1960s the freemen's allotments were partly derelict, and under the Stafford Corporation Act, 1964, the corporation took two-thirds of the land for development.[19]

Foregate field, occupying most of Foregate, was a common field belonging to the manor of Marston. Inhabitants of Stafford held land there, and the borough authorities as well as the Marston court took part in the organization of the field. At the end of the 18th century it was cultivated on a three-course rotation. All householders in the borough enjoyed pasture rights there, the burgesses enjoying more extensive rights than other householders; the corporation paid a grass-fee to the lord of Marston.[20]

[95] S.R.O., D.1323/A/1/1, p. 49.
[96] Ibid. /2, pp. 86, 94; W.S.L., H.M. 26/2, f. 34.
[97] W.S.L., S.MS. 366 (iA), p. 22; T.S.H.C.S. 1965–7, 6; S.R.O., D.1323/E/1, churchwardens' accts.; S.H.C. 4th ser. i. 276.
[98] S.R.O., D.(W.) 0/8/2, pp. 26–7; W.S.L., H.M. 32.
[99] S.R.O., D.1323/A/1/1, pp. 217–18.
[1] Ibid. pp. 236, 241.
[2] Ibid. /2, p. 48.
[3] Ibid. p. 53.
[4] W.S.L., H.M. 32.
[5] S.R.O., D.1323/A/1/2, pp. 86, 90, 92.
[6] Ibid. p. 94.
[7] S.R.O., D.1323/A/2/1, 12 June 1699.
[8] S.R.O., D.(W.) 0/8/2, pp. 171–5 and reverse pages, 1740 decree, p. 27; 1st Rep. Com. Mun. Corp. H.C. 116, App. III, p. 2028 (1835), xxv.
[9] See p. 256.
[10] S.R.O., D.(W.) 0/8/1, pp. 254–5, 284.

[11] 1st Rep. Com. Mun. Corp. App. III, 2028, 2030; White, Dir. Staffs. (1834), 121.
[12] S.R.O., D.1323/A/1/5, pp. 185–9, 243; White, Dir. Staffs. (1851), 329.
[13] S.R.O., D.1323/A/1/8, 8 Nov. 1867.
[14] Ibid. /7, pp. 135–6, 219–20.
[15] Stafford Corp. Act, 1880, 43 & 44 Vic. c. 73 (Local). For a detailed plan of the field in 1880 see O.S. Map 1/2,500, Staffs. XXXVII. 7 and 11 (1881 edn.).
[16] Staffs. Advertiser, 28 Oct. 1854, p. 8.
[17] S.R.O., D.1323/A/1/10, p. 6.
[18] Ibid. pp. 441–2; 43 & 44 Vic. c. 73 (Local), giving the date of the ruling as 1878.
[19] 1964, c. 12 (Local); Stafford Newsletter, 19 Jan. 1964.
[20] Act for inclosing lands in or adjoining the parish of St. Mary, Stafford, 39 & 40 Geo. III, c. 70 (Local and Personal); S.R.O. 938/188; S.R.O., D.641/1/4A/11, rot. 2d.; T.S.H.C.S. 1965–7, 21, 28; E 134/9 Jas. I East./15; E 134/10 Jas. I East./33; S.R.O., D.1033/1, p. 561.

Householders also had pasture rights in Marston and Port fields and Blakefield meadow, all in Marston on either side of the present Common Road; again the burgesses enjoyed more extensive rights. Householders enjoyed pasture rights in the ancient part of Lammascote farm, from the cutting of the crops until Candlemas in the cultivated part and from Michaelmas until Candlemas in the rest; the burgesses enjoyed more extensive rights. Householders had rights throughout the year on the 2½-a. Eastgate common on the south side of Lammascote Road, partly within Forebridge manor.[21]

All those rights were extinguished under an inclosure Act of 1800, and the award of 1807 allotted the householders instead 117 a. of Foregate and Marston fields and 8 a. called Stone Flat in Port field. Management of what came to be called Stafford common was vested in an annual meeting of householders worth £5, and rules were adopted at a meeting in 1803.[22] By 1834 cattle were grazed from May until Christmas on the main part and for the rest of the year on Stone Flat. Each householder could graze two cows or one horse and each burgess three cows or one cow and one horse. A maintenance fund was raised by charging 4s. or 5s. a year for each cow and 9s. or 10s. for each horse and by a levy for carriages and stalls on strangers coming to the races which were held on the common from 1820.[23] By 1851 over 200 cows and 80 horses were grazed.[24] In 1876 it was stated that, out of 2,300 ratepayers entitled to exercise common rights, only 130 did so.[25] In 1864 the first of several military reviews was held on the common, and by the 1870s it was frequently used for fêtes, cricket matches, and other entertainments. There was a small golf course in the early 20th century.[26] In 1976 the common was 200 a. in area, with farmers paying for grazing horses between May and October.[27]

The general management of the pastures was in the hands of the borough council and the borough court leet, but by the later 16th century the details were the responsibility of the Six Men, who were still appointed by the leet in 1747.[28] Two swineherds were paid by the bailiffs in the early 15th century.[29] A herdsman and a shepherd supervised the grazing of the fields by the later 16th century, with the council laying down the wages to be paid to them by the owners of cattle and sheep; both officials still existed in 1704.[30] A hayward was appointed by the leet in 1842.[31] A pinner was appointed by the leet in the 18th century and by the

corporation in the 19th and early 20th centuries.[32] Under the inclosure Act of 1800 a pinner was appointed for Stafford common at the annual meeting of commoners, and in 1976 there was still an overseer who supervised the common during the grazing season.[33]

In 1851 the remains of the Green field between the Lichfield and Wolverhampton roads and the Green common on either side of Newport Road (both in Forebridge) were inclosed under an Act of 1800. Five acres on the Lichfield road were allotted to the parishioners of Castle Church. Known as the Green common, the land was used for grazing until the First World War. It was used for allotments from 1917 until its sale to the English Electric Co. Ltd. in 1957.[34]

FISHERIES. The king had a fish-pool beyond the walls on the north-east side of the town by 1157,[35] and it was regularly repaired by the sheriff in the later 12th century.[36] In 1197–8 the custody was granted to William son of Wymer and his heirs at a rent of ½ mark,[37] but the Crown continued to be responsible for repairs.[38] In the mid 13th century the pool provided the king with bream, pike, and tench, and the sheriff or the keeper was responsible for fishing it.[39] In 1250 the king ordered four pike and four bream to be given to the dean of Stafford.[40] In 1253 the sheriff was ordered to sell the fish in the pool except for 'the little fish called frit' and without destroying the bream there.[41] By 1257 the king had had the dam taken down, but in that year he allowed the townsmen to rebuild it at their own expense in view of the part played by the pool in the defences of the town.[42] Early in 1281 John the queen's sauce-maker, William the king's fisherman, and a boy fished the pool and John despatched the fish to the king in Wales.[43] In 1282 the queen was given permission for her men to take fish from the pool for her use.[44]

A William Wymer was succeeded in the custody of the pool by his son Ralph in 1268.[45] At his death in 1273 Ralph was stated to have been entitled to all the fish except pike and bream when the king had the pool fished; when the king had it dragged Ralph was also entitled to eels in the outlet of the pool. He was succeeded by his brother Henry.[46] At the *Quo Warranto* proceedings in 1293 Henry claimed in addition all fish escaping through the outlet and also the reeds growing in the fishery; in return he paid ½ mark and was responsible for the

[21] 39 & 40 Geo. III, c. 70 (Local and Personal); S.R.O., Q/RDc 16; W.S.L., copy of lost plan of Stafford; B.L. Eg. MS. 2872, ff. 52v.–53.
[22] 39 & 40 Geo. III, c. 70 (Local and Personal); S.R.O., Q/RDc 16 (including copy of Act); *Stafford Boro. Extension Bill: Mins. of Evidence, 1876* (reprinted from the official rep.), 6–7 (copy in W.S.L. Pamphs. *sub* Stafford); White, *Dir. Staffs.* (1834), 121.
[23] White, *Dir. Staffs.* (1834), 121; below, p. 256.
[24] White, *Dir. Staffs.* (1851), 329.
[25] *Stafford Boro. Extension Bill: Mins. of Evid.* 30.
[26] Ibid. 8, 20; above, p. 194, and below, p. 256.
[27] *Stafford Newsletter*, 19 Mar. 1976.
[28] *T.S.H.C.S.* 1965–7, 12–13, 26; W.S.L., H.M. uncat. 28.
[29] J. B. Frith, 'Account of the bailiffs of borough of Stafford for 1411–12', *T.O.S.S.* 1939, 23.
[30] *T.S.H.C.S.* 1965–7, 11–12, 14, 25–6, 28; S.R.O., D.1323/A/1/2, p. 107.
[31] *Staffs. Advertiser*, 26 Feb. 1842.
[32] See p. 229.

[33] 39 & 40 Geo. III, c. 70 (Local and Personal); White, *Dir. Staffs.* (1834), 121; (1851), 329; *Stafford Newsletter*, 19 Mar. 1976.
[34] *V.C.H. Staffs.* v. 94–5; S.R.O., Q/RDc 15a; D.804/9–10; D.3130/45, interrogatories and depositions about Green common, 1704; W.S.L., H.M. uncat. 64.
[35] *S.H.C.* i. 23.
[36] Ibid. 37, 72, 98; ii (1), 54.
[37] Ibid. ii (1), 75.
[38] *Rot. Litt. Claus.* (Rec. Com.), i. 529; ii. 39; *Cal. Lib.* 1226–40, 183; 1251–60, 8, 175, 391, 453; *Close R.* 1256–9, 85; 1268–72, 205.
[39] *Close R.* 1237–42, 104; 1247–51, 149, 493; *Cal. Lib.* 1245–51, 223, 371–2.
[40] *Close R.* 1247–51, 254.
[41] Ibid. 1251–3, 336.
[42] Ibid. 1256–9, 48, 85.
[43] Cherry, *Stafford*, 31.
[44] *Cal. Pat.* 1281–92, 52.
[45] *S.H.C.* 1911, 141.
[46] Ibid. 151.

maintenance of the dam. The fishery, however, was held to be forfeit to the Crown.[47] It was still in the king's hands in 1327.[48]

By 1345 the pool was held by Simon de Rugeley on a ten-year lease at a rent of 2 marks. He then petitioned for a grant in perpetuity with permission to raise the head of the pool and build a mill there.[49] At the subsequent inquiry the jurors stated that it would improve the defences of the town if the pool were repaired and raised. Simon's request was duly granted, and to the rent was added the service of holding the king's stirrup when he first mounted his palfrey on visits to Stafford.[50] Soon afterwards Simon granted the pool and the mill which he built there to St. Thomas's priory near Stafford without the king's permission. The alienation was revealed in 1349 after Simon's death, and in 1350 the pool and the mill were given by the king at the same rent and service to Ralph, Lord Stafford.[51] They then remained in the Stafford family. By the early 1430s there was pasture called the King's Pool north of the mill-pool, but the pool was still in use as a fishery. The dam was still maintained c. 1560: in 1606 a man of 66 recalled how Henry, Lord Stafford (d. 1563), 'did come down in a summer time to the said King's Pools and was then in a green coat and was amongst certain masons and other workmen which were then repairing the dam of the said King's Pools'. By 1606 the pool had disappeared, although the area became flooded in bad weather. There was then an underground sewer draining the southern part into the Sow.[52] The parliamentary committee flooded the area in the mid 1640s to strengthen the town's defences.[53] It remained a tract of rough land until the mid 1970s when the relief road was built across it and car-parks were laid out.

The grant of Stafford mill to William son of Wymer by Hervey Bagot and his wife in the late 12th century included fishing rights in the vicinity,[54] and in 1250 William Wymer claimed the right to fish the mill-pool.[55] The Staffords held a fishery in 'the pond of le Brodhe' (Broadeye) in the later 13th century,[56] perhaps the 'vivarium de Sowe' in the Foregate area mentioned in 1453.[57] By the 15th century they had fishing rights in the Sow from the mill to Tillington[58] and in 1444 leased them to the corporation for 20 years.[59] In the mid 1640s the parliamentary committee exercised the fishing rights in the river and mill-pool sequestrated from Lord Stafford. In 1644 it banned unauthorized fishing from boats on the river and in 1645 ordered 'the waters about Stafford that belong to the state' to

be fished twice a week for the committee's own use.[60]

In 1828 an angler complained that the burgesses were dragging the Sow with fine-mesh nets and destroying the fish. He also described how, when the pike came up the ditches along the river in the spawning season, a 'host of unwashed artificers' destroyed them with snares, spears, and nets on the strength of King John's charter.[61] In 1863 the corporation adopted a report from its fishery committee asserting the immemorial right of the burgesses and inhabitants to a free fishery in the Sow from a place called the Withies above Broadeye bridge down to the confluence with the Penk below Baswich; it banned all netting, poisoning, and spearing of fish between those points.[62] By 1875, however, the corporation had apparently limited its claim to the stretch of the river within the borough,[63] and its jurisdiction there was recognized by the Stafford Corporation Act, 1876.[64] In 1877 it duly passed by-laws banning trimmers and night-lines with live bait and fixing close seasons for angling.[65] It was employing a river bailiff in 1879.[66]

MILLS. In 1086 the canons of Stafford had a mill, but it is not clear that it was in the town.[67] From 1164–5 the burgesses held of the king a mill on the Sow south-west of the town centre.[68] The rent ceased to be mentioned after 1173,[69] and it was probably then that the mill passed to Robert de Stafford. It remained the property of the Staffords and their successors until 1879 and was normally leased out.[70]

Robert de Stafford leased the mill to William son of Wymer and his heirs.[71] The lease was renewed by Robert's sister Millicent and her husband Hervey Bagot, who succeeded to the Stafford barony in 1193–4. They granted William and his heirs the suit of their tenants in the liberty of Bradley, who in addition were to maintain the pool; the grant also included the right to timber from a wood at Bradley for repairs to the building.[72] The mill remained in the tenure of the Wymer family until at least 1273.[73] About 1250 Robert de Stafford, grandson of Hervey and Millicent, gave the prior and canons of St. Thomas near Stafford a rent-charge of 3 marks out of the 10 marks rent;[74] after the Dissolution the gift was stated to have been in return for an undertaking by the canons not to take corn out of the town for grinding at the priory mill.[75] At least between the earlier 15th and the earlier 16th centuries the mill was known as the port mills,[76] presumably to distinguish it from Eastgate mill.

By the earlier 17th century damage was being

[47] *Plac. de Quo Warr.* (Rec. Com.), 717–18.
[48] *Cal. Mem. R.* 1326–7, p. 268.
[49] *S.H.C.* 1913, 112.
[50] *Cal. Pat.* 1345–8, 40.
[51] Ibid. 1348–50, 503; *S.H.C.* 1913, 134–5; W.S.L., copy of lost plan of Stafford.
[52] S.R.O., D.641/1/2/40a; /1/2/53, rot. [2 and d.]; S.R.O. 938/208; E 134/4 Jas. I East./15; W.S.L., copy of lost plan of Stafford.
[53] See p. 199.
[54] S.R.O., D.(W.) 1721/1/1, f. 28.
[55] *S.H.C.* iv (1), 116, 118; *S.H.C.* 1911, 151.
[56] *Cal. Inq. p.m.* ii, p. 482. For other references to a fish-pond at Broadeye at that time see S.R.O. 938/257 and 278.
[57] S.R.O., D.593/A/2/27/12.
[58] S.R.O., D.641/1/2/53, rot. [2]; /71, rot. [3].
[59] W.S.L., H.M. uncat. 26, deed of 8 Mar. 1443/4.
[60] *S.H.C.* 4th ser. i. 99, 140, 255–6; S.R.O., D.641/2/G/1/1, Stafford Castle rents 1643–5, p. 3.

[61] *Weekly Register*, 24 May 1828.
[62] S.R.O., D.1323/A/1/8, 23 Sept. and 22 Dec. 1862, 7 May 1863.
[63] Ibid. /9, 6 July 1875.
[64] 39 & 40 Vic. c. 196 (Local).
[65] S.R.O., D.1323/A/1/10, p. 79.
[66] Ibid. p. 266.
[67] *V.C.H. Staffs.* iv. 44.
[68] *S.H.C.* i. 39.
[69] Ibid. 36–69 *passim*.
[70] See e.g. *S.H.C.* ii (1), 32, 37–8; S.R.O., D.641/1/2/53, rot. [2]; D.641/2/G/1/1 and 3.
[71] *S.H.C.* ii (1), 28, 32.
[72] S.R.O., D.(W.) 1721/1/1, f. 28. For Bradley liberty see *V.C.H. Staffs.* iv. 76–7.
[73] *S.H.C.* iv (1), 80, 115–16, 118; *S.H.C.* 1911, 151; *Cal. Inq. p.m.* ii, p. 12.
[74] *S.H.C.* viii (1), 148.   [75] S.R.O. 938/29.
[76] S.R.O., D.641/1/2/53, rot. [2]; /108, rott. [2d., 4].

caused by the raising of the 'head sills' at the mill. In the 19th century there were constant complaints about the mill: the damming of the river there caused it to stagnate in the town and to flood the area to the north.[77] The Stafford Corporation Act, 1876, authorized the corporation to buy Stafford mill and St. Thomas mill and to demolish them both in order to improve the flow of the Sow.[78] The corporation bought Stafford mill in 1879 but, instead of demolishing it, built a weir there and provided additional flood-gates.[79] By 1937 motor-power as well as water-power was used at the mill, which was then concentrating on the production of feed for cattle and poultry.[80] In 1957 it ceased work and was demolished. The corporation laid out the site as an extension to Victoria Park, with the two undershot water-wheels left in position.[81]

The building which was demolished had been erected in 1834 by George Brewster; in 1837 he also built a malt-house near by in Water Street which survived in 1977.[82] Moat House south of the mill site was formerly the mill-house; it was occupied by the girls' high school from 1903 to 1907, and from 1946 it was the headquarters of the Staffordshire branch of the National Farmers' Union.[83]

The grant of the custody of the king's fish-pool to William son of Wymer and his heirs in 1197–8 included permission to build a mill there if they wished.[84] The mill which Simon de Rugeley built outside the East Gate in the later 1340s[85] still existed in 1546,[86] but c. 1570 it was in ruins. It was used as a barn until the timber was removed by Lord Stafford c. 1600.[87] In 1456 there was a house in Eastgate Street known as the Mill-house, but it formed part of the Ingestre estate.[88]

In 1617 a group of councillors, including the mayor Thomas Cradock, recommended that the corporation should build a malt mill. The income was to be used first to meet the expense of the royal visit that year and then to provide a regular income for the town. The inhabitants were to be 'gently entreated' to grind their malt at the mill, but it was to be run in competition with existing malt mills.[89] There were then three: Matthew Cradock's in Salter Street, owned in 1561 by his grandfather Matthew Cradock as a horse-driven wheat and malt mill;[90] Richard Drakeford's, mentioned in

1610;[91] and Francis Dorrington's. Dorrington opposed the scheme, having 'well nigh enchanted all the burgesses to come to his mill'. The council, however, agreed to the proposal, but being unable to erect a new mill at once, it took over Cradock's mill for two years as it was the best of the three. Drakeford and Dorrington closed theirs.[92] By 1622 there was a separate town malt mill, and the other three were all in use about then.[93] At least between 1632 and 1640 the corporation was renting the Dorrington mill.[94] By 1653 it had its own mill in Salter Street, which was usually farmed out.[95] In 1617 the council appointed three overseers to account for the income,[96] but by 1620 and until 1729 there were two mill masters or reeves each year.[97] From 1729 until at least 1738 the council appointed a salaried reeve.[98]

Despite the original plan to run the mill competitively, the Cradock family was soon accusing the authorities of having in 1622 imprisoned an alehouse-keeper who insisted on grinding at the Cradock mill and of releasing him only when he promised to use the town mill.[99] In 1690 the council ordered all inhabitants to grind their malt at the town mill in future on pain of a fine; alehouse-keepers who refused were to lose their licences.[1] In 1691 it ordered that no alehouse-keeper should in future receive a licence unless he entered into a bond to grind at the malt mill,[2] and in 1725 it threatened victuallers and innkeepers with the forfeiture of their bonds.[3] By the 1720s, however, 'steel or hand mills' for grinding malt were in use in the town. As a result the corporation's income from the mill, by then assigned for the support of the poor, fell sharply and it became necessary to levy a poor-rate.[4] In 1743 the churchwardens and overseers of the poor took a 51-year lease of the mill from the corporation and applied the profits to the running of the workhouse.[5] They were still working the mill in 1775,[6] and it was described as 'lately used' as a malt mill in 1780 when the corporation leased it to George Boulton for 99 years.[7] By the time that the lease expired, the mill had been demolished.[8]

In 1795 the corporation leased land at Broadeye to John Wright, a banker, and Francis Brookes for the building of a windmill, which was completed in 1796.[9] Materials from the old shire hall were

[77] Trinity Coll., Cambridge, mun. box 32; W.S.L., H.M. uncat. 23; S.R.O., D.1323/J/1/2, 4 Oct. 1864, 5 Sept. 1865; below, p. 232.
[78] 39 & 40 Vic. c. 196 (Local).
[79] S.R.O., D.1323/A/1/10, pp. 246–7, 284; Roxburgh, Stafford, 17–18.
[80] Stafford Newsletter, 8 May 1937.
[81] Ibid. 19 Oct. 1957; R. Sherlock, Ind. Arch. Staffs. 188.
[82] Sherlock, Ind. Arch. Staffs. 188; White, Dir. Staffs. (1834), 149; (1851), 355; plate facing p. 193 above.
[83] Stafford Revisited, 1841–1907, by a descendant of Rector Dickenson (Stafford, n.d.), 13 (copy in poss. of Mr. J. S. Horne, Stafford, 1976); ex inf. the assistant sec., Staffs. branch of N.F.U. (1977).
[84] S.H.C. ii (1), 75.
[85] See p. 211; W.S.L., copy of lost plan of Stafford.
[86] S.R.O., D.1323/E/1, f. 28v.
[87] E 134/4 Jas. I East./15; W.S.L., copy of lost plan of Stafford.
[88] S.H.C. xii (1), 324.
[89] S.R.O., D.(W.) 1721/1/4, f. 119.
[90] Ann J. Kettle, 'Three 17th-cent. Surveys of Property in Stafford', T.S.H.C.S. 1968–70, 33–6.
[91] S.H.C. n.s. iii. 51.
[92] S.R.O., D.(W.) 1721/1/4, ff. 119–20.
[93] S.R.O., D.1287/10/2, incomplete draft petition of Joan

and Matt. Cradock.
[94] S.R.O., D.1323/E/1, ff. 196v.–197, 242.
[95] S.R.O., D.1323/A/1/1, pp. 130, 206; /2, pp. 2, 32, 77, 91, 106, 124, 169, 224; D.1323/F/1, reverse pages, pp. 36, 83; S.R.O., D.(W.) 0/8/2 (1694, 1700, 1702); W.S.L., H.M. 32, chamberlains' accts. 1708.
[96] S.R.O., D.(W.) 1721/1/4, f. 120.
[97] S.R.O., D.1323/E/1, ff. 103v. sqq.; D.1323/A/1/1, pp. 22, 365, 378; /2, pp. 124, 224, 247, 339.
[98] S.R.O., D.1323/A/1/2, pp. 343, 363, 368, 435, 456.
[99] S.R.O., D.1287/10/2, petition of Joan and Matt. Cradock.
[1] S.R.O., D.1323/A/1/1, pp. 369, 373, 377.
[2] Ibid. p. 379. [3] Ibid. /2, p. 268.
[4] W.S.L. 77/45, f. 19; W.S.L. 49/112(B)/44, relator's proofs, f. 3.
[5] S.R.O., D.(W.) 0/8/1, p. 41; D.(W.) 0/8/18.
[6] S.R.O., D.1323/K/1, 6 Aug. 1775.
[7] S.R.O., D.(W.) 0/8/1, p. 362.
[8] Cherry, Stafford, 82–3.
[9] S.R.O., D.1323/A/1/3, pp. 138–9; cast-iron plate on exterior inscribed 'IW 1796'; R. Wailes, TS. Rep. on Castle Hill Windmill, Broadeye, Stafford (1950; copy in possession of Mr. J. S. Horne of Stafford), noting a beam on the fourth floor bearing the date 1795. The lease was from Mar. 1796.

used, and a carving of the royal arms from the hall was placed over the doorway of the mill.[10] The Wright family was still working it *c.* 1818.[11] Steam-power had been introduced by 1847,[12] and the mill remained in use until the early 1880s.[13] The building was subsequently used as a grain-store and from 1925 as a shop, but it was derelict by the later 1930s.[14] The tower still stood in 1977.

There was a windmill in Foregate in the later 16th century: land in Foregate field was described in 1585 as 'shooting upon the windmill'. Mill flat in the field was mentioned in 1615.[15]

MARKETS AND FAIRS. There was a market-place in Stafford in the later 12th century.[16] The market was held on Saturday by 1382, the earliest date at which the day is indicated.[17] A Tuesday market was added in 1912 for the sale of farm produce, and it soon developed into a general market.[18] A market on Friday afternoons was begun in 1955 and became a market for the whole of Friday in 1961.[19] Markets continued to be held on Tuesdays, Fridays, and Saturdays in 1977.

The area still known as Market Square remained the market-place until the 19th century. It is presumably the 'high' market-place mentioned in 1310,[20] which may have replaced an earlier market site since there was a reference in the later 13th century to the old market-place.[21] By the 15th century there was a booth hall on the corner of the square and Greengate Street with a shambles and storage-space for stalls beneath it; a house there was still called the Shambles in 1815.[22] A market cross stood in the centre of the market-place by the earlier 15th century.[23] It was repaired 'and set in fresh colours' for Elizabeth I's visit to Stafford in 1575.[24] It was removed when the new shire hall was built in the square in the late 16th century,[25] but there was still a market cross in the mid 17th century.[26] A market bell was cast or recast at Walsall in 1641–2 and was still hanging in the 'guildhall' (presumably the shire hall) in 1735.[27] When the shire hall was rebuilt in the 1790s, a space with an arcade on three sides was provided at the rear for a market dealing in eggs, cheese, poultry, and vegetables; the rest of the market continued in Market Square.[28] When the guildhall was built on the west side of the square in 1853–4 a market hall was built behind it, designed, like the guildhall, by Charles Trubshaw, the county surveyor, and the market held behind the shire hall was transferred there. The approach was by a tunnel entrance from Market Square.[29] The new market hall and the guildhall were separated by a militia store and a space where by 1865 stalls were set up.[30] In 1867 the market hall was extended over that intervening area to the design of Robert Griffiths of Stafford, with a second entrance in Crabbery Street. The whole hall was then named St. John's Market.[31] In 1880 a butchers' market, designed by N. Joyce of Stafford, was added at the west end, with entrances in Crabbery Street and Albion Place, and Market Square was cleared of butchers' stalls. The Noah's Ark inn in Crabbery Street was bought by the corporation and part of it converted into a market office and refreshment room; the rest remained a public house until 1967 when it became the markets office.[32] An extension at the Albion Place end of the butchers' market seems to have been added in 1882, and by 1889 it was used for the sale of fish, cheese, wool, and crockery.[33] In 1927 the remaining stalls were removed from Market Square to allow additional parking space for cars and buses, and another extension was opened in 1928 on the north-east of the market hall.[34] During the Second World War the hall was requisitioned as a food depot and R.A.F. store, and a small market was again held in Market Square. It continued until St. John's Market was released in 1946. The former butchers' and fish markets became available in 1948 and were converted into an extension of the general market.[35]

Between the 15th and 17th centuries Gaolgate Street was known variously as the Rothermarket and Cow Street[36] and was presumably the site of a cattle market. A few cattle were brought to the Saturday market in the early 1830s, but space was limited and there were no pens.[37] In 1838 cattle markets every other Monday were started in Eastgate Street, and by 1839 they were held in Market Square; they seem, however, to have been short-lived.[38] In 1852 the corporation was considering the establishment of a monthly cattle market[39] and in the 1860s the provision of a smithfield.[40] Private smithfields were opened next to the Junction inn

[10] Calvert, *Stafford*, 19. Wailes, Rep. on Castle Hill Windmill, notes that most of the main timbers were apparently re-used.
[11] Parson and Bradshaw, *Dir. Staffs.* (1818), 221.
[12] Sherlock, *Ind. Arch. Staffs.* 188.
[13] It is listed in *Kelly's Dir. Staffs.* (1880; 1884) but not in *Halden's Stafford Dir.* (1883).
[14] Ex inf. Mr. Horne; Roxburgh, *Stafford*, 3.
[15] S.R.O., D.661/2/190 and 315.
[16] *S.H.C.* viii (1), 131, grant by Gerard son of Brian. He founded St. Thomas's priory near Stafford between 1173 and 1175 and was still living in the later 1180s: *V.C.H. Staffs.* iii. 262.
[17] *Cal. Pat.* 1381–5, 145.
[18] *Stafford Corporation Markets: Official Guide* [1936], 17 (copy in W.S.L. Pamphs. *sub* Stafford).
[19] Ex inf. the markets inspector (1962).
[20] S.R.O. 938/190.   [21] Ibid. /184.
[22] *S.H.C.* N.S. x (1), 79; S.R.O., D.1323/A/1/3, p. 422; W.S.L. 788/36, deed of 26 Apr. 1815.
[23] S.R.O. 938/209.   [24] S.R.O., D.1323/E/1, f. 36.
[25] Ibid.; S.R.O., D.(W.) 1721/1/4, shire hall accts. at end, 4 July 1590.
[26] W.S.L., S.MS. 369 *sub* 1684.
[27] S.R.O., D.1323/E/1, f. 260; Keen, *Letter to Inhabitants of Stafford*, 57.

[28] Act for building a new shire hall for the county of Stafford, 34 Geo. III, c. 97; Stafford Shire Hall Act, 1853, 16 & 17 Vic. c. 72 (Local and Personal); White, *Dir. Staffs.* (1834), 124; *S.H.C.* 4th ser. vi, plate facing p. 69.
[29] *Staffs. Advertiser*, 4 and 11 Mar. 1854; *Stafford Corp. Markets*, 15.
[30] *Staffs. Advertiser*, 4 Mar. 1854; S.R.O., D.1323/A/1/8, 2 Aug. 1865.
[31] *Staffs. Advertiser*, 10 Aug. 1867 (describing the demolished building as the old police barracks); *Stafford Corp. Markets*, 15.
[32] *Staffs. Advertiser*, 24 July, 18 Dec. 1880; S.R.O., D.1323/A/1/10, p. 315; *Stafford Corp. Markets*, 21; O.S. Map 1/2,500, Staffs. XXXVII. 11 (1881 and 1901 edns.); ex inf. the market supervisor (1976).
[33] *Stafford Corp. Markets*, 15, 18; *Rep. Com. Market Rights and Tolls*, vol. viii [C. 6268-II], p. 97, H.C. (1890–1), xxxviii.
[34] *Stafford Corp. Markets*, 17.
[35] *Stafford Official Guide* [c. 1964], 31–2.
[36] See p. 187.
[37] White, *Dir. Staffs.* (1834), 124.
[38] *Staffs. Advertiser*, 20 Jan., 17 Mar. 1838, 12 Oct. 1839. None is mentioned in White, *Dir. Staffs.* (1851), 332.
[39] S.R.O., D.1323/A/1/7, f. 38v.
[40] Ibid. /8, 21 Dec. 1863, 3 Feb. 1869.

in Newport Road in 1861,[41] the Talbot in Victoria Road in the mid 1870s,[42] and the Sun in Lichfield Road a few years later.[43] In the later 1880s fortnightly cattle markets were held in the streets, but they were suffering from the competition of the smithfields; the corporation was still hoping to establish its own smithfield when it could afford to do so.[44] After the First World War trade at the two remaining private smithfields declined, with an adverse effect on trade generally in the town. The shopkeepers urged the council's markets committee to open a public smithfield, and in 1930 the corporation took over the Talbot smithfield. Sales were held every other Tuesday with special sales about once a month on Saturdays; sales of farm produce and poultry were held every Friday. With the introduction of restrictions on the sale of fat cattle during the Second World War the smithfield was used mainly for small-stock sales and as a grading centre. It was closed in 1953, and in 1977 the site, intended originally for a new civic centre, was being used as a car-park.[45] Sales were then held every Friday at the privately run Sun smithfield.

A pig market was held in the east ward by the early 1660s,[46] probably in Market Street where it was held in the later 18th century.[47] By the earlier 1830s, and possibly by 1813, it had moved a short distance to Eastgate Street where 'some miserable pales for swine' were erected.[48] In 1874, when the borough hall was about to be built there, the council ordered the removal of the market to the more spacious Pitcher Bank but in 1875 changed the proposed site to Gaol Square.[49] A sheep market was held by 1813, apparently in conjunction with the pig market.[50] It was held in Eastgate Street by 1849.[51] Both markets still existed in 1877.[52] Sheep were included in the monthly Saturday sales at the Talbot smithfield in the 1930s.[53]

A crockery market was held by 1835 in the large space at the junction of Eastgate and Tipping Streets which had been known in the 17th century as the Horsefair and which as a result of the new market became known as Pitcher Bank.[54] In 1865 the council ordered that crockery was not to be sold in the streets and that stalls were to be provided in Market Square.[55] The crockery market had been moved into the market hall by 1889,[56] but in the early 20th century a small pitcher market was held in Market Square; it was removed in 1927.[57]

Borough ordinances of 1566 included regulations on the conduct of the market.[58] The bailiffs were to

ensure every market day that there was no engrossing or forestalling, and the sale of corn, meat, and other foodstuffs on market days was restricted to the market. The bailiffs, accompanied by the wardens of the butchers, were to check the quality of the meat offered for sale there. The bailiffs were also to see that no one apart from freemen and burgesses set up stalls; the regulation did not, however, apply to 'foreign' butchers and victuallers, who were to have free access to the market. In 1689 two clerks of the market were appointed by the council.[59] In 1692 the council ordered the mayor to put a stop to the secret buying of corn in the market, with consequent evasion of toll, by ensuring that no corn was sold there before the ringing of the 11 a.m. bell.[60] An inspector of the market was appointed by the council in 1856.[61]

A corn exchange was established c. 1820. It was held in the shire hall from at least 1910 and may have moved there from the street in 1848. By the 1920s business was declining, and in 1928 it was decided to close the exchange.[62]

In 1261 the king granted the burgesses the right to a fair on the eve of St. Matthew, the feast, and the six days following (20–27 September).[63] By 1315 there was also a fair on the feast of St. Peter and St. Paul (29 June).[64] A third fair, on the feast of the Finding of the Cross (3 May), was granted in 1412.[65] That year a special patrol and watch was provided for each of the fairs, and the bailiffs walked the fairs.[66] A fourth fair, on the Tuesday before Shrove Sunday and the three days following was granted in 1614.[67] By then the September fair was dealing in horses,[68] and the area at the junction of Eastgate and Tipping Streets was known as the Horsefair.[69] In 1665 there was mention of 'white beef' sold at the May fair,[70] and in 1679 there was an attempt to establish a hop fair as part of the September fair.[71] In 1683 the corporation changed the date of the June fair,[72] presumably to Midsummer Day (24 June), the date authorized in the charter of 1685. The charter also granted a fifth fair, on 4 December, which like the June fair was to deal specially in cattle and horses.[73] The June fair later reverted to 29 June, but with the change in the calendar in 1752 it was held on 10 July (29 June Old Style). In 1781, however, it was moved to the Saturday before 29 June; it was then primarily a wool fair.[74] In that year too the September fair, which had become primarily a colt fair by the 1740s, was made a three-day event, on 16, 17,

[41] Staffs. Advertiser, 16 Nov. 1861.
[42] Ibid. 27 May 1876.
[43] Ex inf. Geo. Horne & Sons, Stafford (1962).
[44] Rep. Com. Market Rights and Tolls, vol. viii, 96.
[45] Staffs. Advertiser, 12 Apr. 1930; Stafford Corp. Markets, 21–3; Stafford Official Guide [c. 1964], 65.
[46] S.R.O., D.1323/E/1, f. 303.
[47] Kettle, 'Street-names', 47; B.L. Eg. MS. 2872, f. 57v.; W.S.L., M. 41.
[48] S.R.O., D.660/8/16, lease of 27 July 1833; D.1323/A/1/3, p. 400; White, Dir. Staffs. (1834), 124; Wood, Plan of Stafford (1835).
[49] S.R.O., D.1323/A/1/9, 27 Oct., 1 Dec. 1874, 2 Mar., 6 Apr. 1875.
[50] Ibid. /3, p. 400.   [51] Ibid. /6, p. 474.
[52] Staffs. Advertiser, 28 Apr. 1877.
[53] Stafford Corp. Markets, 23.
[54] Wood, Plan of Stafford (1835); see below.
[55] S.R.O., D.1323/A/1/8, 4 May 1865.
[56] Rep. Com. Market Rights and Tolls, vol. viii, 97.
[57] Stafford Corp. Markets, 17.

[58] Ann J. Kettle, 'Black Book of Stafford', T.S.H.C.S. 1965–7, 5–6, 9–10, 15–16.
[59] S.R.O., D.1323/A/1/1, p. 364.
[60] Ibid. /2, p. 14.
[61] Ibid. /7, p. 378.
[62] Staffs. Advertiser, 22 Dec. 1928, pp. 3, 7.
[63] Cal. Chart. R. 1257–1300, 36.
[64] S.H.C. x (1), 52.
[65] Cal. Chart. R. 1341–1417, 446.
[66] J. B. Frith, 'Account of the bailiffs of borough of Stafford for 1411–12', T.O.S.S. 1939, 21.
[67] Bradley, Charters, 170.
[68] S.R.O., D.(W.) 1721/1/4, f. 12v.
[69] S.R.O., D.1323/E/1, ff. 227, 303v.; D.1323/F/1, reverse pages, p. 60; W.S.L., H.M. uncat. 29, corp. rent book 1705, p. 14.
[70] S.R.O., D.641/2/G/1/1, disbursements 1665–6.
[71] Cherry, Stafford, 95.
[72] Cal. S.P. Dom. 1683 (July–Sept.), 144.
[73] Ibid. 1685, 192; Lond. Gaz. 26–30 Nov. 1685, no. 2090.
[74] S.R.O., D.(W.) o/8/1, pp. 328, 368.

and 18 September.[75] There were by then four other fairs, customarily held on the Tuesday before Shrovetide, 14 May, 2 October, and 4 December.[76]

In the early 19th century the Shrovetide, May, and September fairs dealt in horses and cattle, the June fair in wool, the October fair in colts, and the December fair in cattle and pigs.[77] By 1834 there was a fair for cattle and horses at the beginning of April; it was still held in 1851.[78] The wool fair in June was held in Eastgate Street in 1839, apparently as a revival.[79] The May fair had lapsed by 1845 but was revived in that year.[80] The September fair had lapsed by 1851.[81] A cheese fair in the market-place was instituted in November 1838, and it was held in February and October in 1839;[82] it was presumably the forerunner of the cheese and bacon fair held on 21 February in the 1850s.[83] The October fair was apparently a sheep fair in the 1860s and 1870s.[84] In 1875 the mayor still proclaimed the May fair in state.[85] By the early 20th century the surviving fairs were cattle fairs in May, October, and December and monthly cheese fairs.[86]

During the 19th century the fairs attracted farmers and dealers from all over the country and also dealers in Irish cattle.[87] In the later 19th century there were complaints about the danger to property and to individuals and about 'the disgusting filth and indecent scenes' resulting from the holding of cattle fairs in the streets.[88] In 1909, despite some resistance, the council removed the fairs to land on Lammascote farm.[89] A decline followed, apparently because the site was too far from the railway station and was inadequately equipped. The fairs were later held at the smithfields but by the 1930s had ceased.[90]

TRADE AND INDUSTRY. A summary of Stafford's economic life made in the early 17th century was probably broadly true of the entire period before the rise of the town's modern industries: most of the inhabitants, it was stated, were 'men of trade or mechanics, as maltsters, innkeepers, vintners, butchers, tailors, clothworkers, glaziers, plumbers, tanners, mercers, shoemakers, glovers, and the like'.[91] In the 17th and early 18th centuries the richest and most influential townsmen were generally retailers, and the largest occupational groups consisted of retailers such as mercers and butchers.[92] Stafford's position as an administrative centre enabled the townspeople to obtain a wide market for their goods and services. It may well have been outsiders who

bought the wares of the two prosperous goldsmiths who were established in the town in the mid 13th century.[93] One of the reasons for Stafford's decay which the townspeople gave Elizabeth I in 1575 was the removal of the assizes from Stafford.[94] Sessions and assize business not only attracted professional men, such as the attorneys who by the 17th century had settled in the town,[95] but also helped to keep other businesses alive. Stafford was a small town and was not on one of the country's main roads: it was presumably people on official business and market folk who helped maintain the 82 keepers of unlicensed tippling-houses who were fined in 1614 or the 62 licensed alehouse-keepers who occur in 1753.[96] In 1811 it was stated that at sessions time the inns were 'thronged with the solicitors, the parties, and the witnesses in causes'.[97]

The 1206 charter granted the burgesses freedom from toll throughout the king's lands save at London.[98] In the 1280s they successfully made use of the privilege when defending their right to sell cloth and wool retail in Newcastle-under-Lyme,[99] and there is evidence that some of them had even wider commercial interests. In 1277 Stafford men were employed by the king to take supplies to the army in Wales.[1] In 1282 William de Pickstock of Stafford was sending wool to Flanders, and during the earlier 14th century other Stafford merchants were active in the wool-trade;[2] in 1337 the townsmen in fact claimed that Stafford's life was dependent on commercial activity outside the town.[3] In 1464 a petition concerning traffic on the Severn mentioned Stafford as one of the Midland towns harmed by interference with the free passage of goods up the river from Bristol to Shrewsbury.[4]

In the 18th and early 19th centuries the town was the headquarters of the most important of the small groups which carried on the profitable business of 'undertaking' church briefs. There was a group of undertakers in Stafford c. 1710, perhaps the trio who undertook a brief in 1714, William Green, Edward Ward, and Henry Walker.[5] Robert Hodgson of Stafford was the country's leading undertaker in the mid 18th century. He was in business with a partner by 1732 and on his own from 1735; in 1754 he stated that he had been undertaking briefs 'for near thirty years past'. His father had been responsible for a reduction in charges which had driven another Stafford man out of the business. In 1754 three more Stafford men, John Byrd, John Hall, and John Stevenson, entered the field and

[75] Ibid. p. 368; J. Smith, *New Map of Staffs.* (1747).
[76] S.R.O., D.(W.) o/8/1, p. 368.
[77] Roxburgh, *Stafford*, 114, 116.
[78] White, *Dir. Staffs.* (1834), 125 (giving 3 Apr.); (1851), 332 (giving 1st Tues. of Apr.).
[79] S.R.O., D.1323/A/1/5, pp. 324, 340; *Staffs. Advertiser*, 23 Feb., 15 June 1839.
[80] *Staffs. Advertiser*, 10 May 1845.
[81] It is not listed in White, *Dir. Staffs.* (1851), 332.
[82] *Staffs. Advertiser*, 27 Oct., 10 Nov. 1838, 23 Feb., 12 Oct. 1839. It was still held in Feb. 1840: ibid. 22 Feb. 1840.
[83] *P.O. Dir. Staffs.* (1850; 1854; 1860).
[84] *Staffs. Advertiser*, 6 Aug. 1864; S.R.O., D.218/1, p. 39.
[85] W.S.L., D.1798/435, John Shallcross's memo. bk. 14 May 1875.
[86] S.R.O., D.1323/C/18/2, p. 9; *Stafford Corp. Markets*, 15; *Kelly's Dir. Staffs.* (1912).
[87] *Stafford Corp. Markets*, 21.
[88] *Staffs. Advertiser*, 5 Oct. 1861, p. 3; 21 May 1864, p. 4; 28 May 1864, p. 4; *Stafford Boro. Extension Bill: Mins. of Evidence, 1876*, 11 (reprinted from official rep.; copy in

W.S.L. Pamphs. *sub* Stafford).
[89] *Stafford Newsletter*, 2 May 1959 (reprinting from ibid. 1 May 1909); *Staffs. Advertiser*, 24 Sept. 1910, p. 1.
[90] *Stafford Corp. Markets*, 15, 21.
[91] S.R.O., D.(W.) 1721/1/4, f. 52.
[92] K. R. Adey, '17th-cent. Stafford', *Midland Hist.* ii. 164.
[93] *S.H.C.* xi. 310.   [94] See p. 201.
[95] *Midland Hist.* ii. 153.
[96] S.R.O., D.1287/10/2, Matt. Cradock's Bk., pp. 119–22; S.R.O., D.1323/G/1, 1 Oct. 1753.
[97] [T. Lister], *Letter to Sir John Wrottesley, Bart. . . . by a Magistrate of the County of Stafford* (Lichfield, 1811), 10 (copy in W.S.L., S.1773).
[98] See p. 222.   [99] *V.C.H. Staffs.* viii. 44.
[1] *Cal. Pat.* 1272–81, 226–7.
[2] *Sel. Bills in Eyre* (Selden Soc. xxx), 77–8; *Cal. Close, 1307–13*, 558; 1327–30, 237; 1337–9, 148, 269, 430; 1339–41, 170, 302, 308; 1341–3, 212, 443; 1343–6, 152, 154, 400; 1349–54, 65; *S.H.C.* 1917–18, 19, 53, 74.
[3] *Cal. Pat.* 1334–8, 428.   [4] *Rot. Parl.* v. 569–70.
[5] W. A. Bewes, *Church Briefs*, 35, 56.

eventually replaced Hodgson, who seems to have gone out of business c. 1765. Until the virtual abolition of the system of briefs in 1828 a near monopoly of brief-undertaking remained in the hands of members of the bank which Stevenson established in Stafford.[6] The system had long been under attack; one of the complaints against it had been that too many of the briefs introduced had been from Staffordshire and the adjoining counties and that too much attention had been devoted to them by the undertakers.[7]

The town's trades and crafts were, with few exceptions, those common in all small or medium-sized towns. Of the specialist crafts the earliest known is potting: an Anglo-Saxon kiln discovered south of the junction of Eastgate and Tipping Streets in 1977 has been dated to the 10th or the 11th century, and the ware excavated with it is of a type which has been found elsewhere in the West Midlands.[8] A William the potter occurs in the town in 1275.[9] By then, however, the principal commodities dealt with in the town appear to have been leather and wool.

A Richard the cordwainer who occurs in 1170 may well have been a burgess of Stafford.[10] By the 1270s and 1280s there were tanners, shoemakers, and glovers at work in the town.[11] In 1476 a guild of shoemakers consisting of sixteen masters made an agreement with the town authorities regulating apprenticeship and trading by non-burgesses. The influence of the guild is seen in 1614 when its wardens seized shoes at a fair, claiming that they were sub-standard, and were upheld by a committee appointed by the mayor to examine the shoes.[12] Shoemakers, glovers, and tanners were all active in the town in the 17th century.

In 1286 the burgesses successfully claimed as an immemorial custom the monopoly of the sale of wool by the fleece (that is to say, the retail sale of wool) in the town, and it was stated in 1341 that most of the townsmen, including the 'better sort', derived their livelihood from 'husbandry of wool and lambs'.[13] In the 13th and 14th centuries, as already mentioned, some men engaged in the wool-trade, and in the later 16th and early 17th centuries the wealth of one of the town's leading families, the Cradocks, seems to have been founded on wool.[14] Mercers and tailors occur from the 1270s, among the first known Stafford tradesmen.[15] Capping was a Stafford trade by 1498[16] and in the 16th century was important in the town: the 1571 Act for the Making of Caps named Stafford as one of the places which had suffered because people no longer wore knitted

woollen caps.[17] The Act's attempt to compel people to wear them was unsuccessful. When Elizabeth I visited Stafford in 1575 the decay of capping was put forward as a reason for the town's decline, and she promised to renew the Act.[18] Nothing was done and capping did not revive.

There does not appear to have been a guild merchant in the borough. In theory, however, the burgesses were well protected from competition. Their successful claim in 1286 to a monopoly of retail wool sales has been mentioned, while by the 1560s, and doubtless long before, burgesses and freemen alone were allowed to sell in the market; 'foreign' butchers and victuallers were exempt from the rule.[19] The 1614 charter relaxed the rule slightly by allowing outsiders to sell goods in the borough wholesale and in the market; they were not, however, to keep shops or to follow 'any mystery, occupation, or manual art' without the permission of the mayor and aldermen.[20] Several craft and trade guilds existed. As already mentioned the shoemakers' guild of 1476 was still active in 1614. A butchers' company occurs in 1566,[21] a company of 'innkeepers, bakers, etc.' in 1590,[22] with a separate 'company and society of bakers' by 1693,[23] a company of drapers and clothiers in 1609,[24] a company of glovers in 1614–15,[25] a company of saddlers in 1672,[26] a company of cloth-workers, dyers, tailors, and bodice-makers in 1682,[27] and a company of chandlers in 1701.[28] The borough authorities exercised some control over the guilds. The 1605 charter confirmed the bailiffs' customary right to swear 'the custodians and guardians of each art, society, and mystery', and the 1614 charter vested the right in the mayor.[29] Regulations drawn up by the shoemakers in 1476 and by the bakers in 1699 were agreed with the town authorities.[30]

In practice the economic life of the town was not so exclusive as it was in theory. By the later 14th century Stafford's development as a commercial centre had led to the presence of a class of *tensarii*, persons who, having settled in the town and not being burgesses or freemen of a craft, were allowed to trade and practise crafts in return for certain payments.[31] The shoemakers' guild ordinances of 1476 recognized the presence of such men.[32] The 1614 charter allowed outsiders to trade or work at a craft if they secured the licence of the mayor and aldermen.[33] By the mid 17th century many outsiders were trading and working without licences, and in 1650 the council ordered them to desist on pain of a fine of 3s. 4d. a week. In 1689 the fine was fixed at 10s. a month; the offence then was not

[6] W.S.L., M.762A/II; Bewes, *Church Briefs*, 50–5; R. S. Sayers, *Lloyds Bank in the Hist. of Eng. Banking*, 1–2.
[7] Bewes, *Church Briefs*, 39.
[8] *Stafford Newsletter*, 20 May 1977.
[9] S.R.O., D.641/1/4A/1.
[10] *V.C.H. Staffs.* ii. 230.
[11] S.R.O., D.641/1/4A/1 and 3.
[12] *V.C.H. Staffs.* ii. 230–1.
[13] *S.H.C.* vi (1), 166; *Inq. Non.* (Rec. Com.), 131.
[14] *S.H.C.* 1917–18, 345; 1920 and 1922, 22–3; 1926, 34; 1933 (2), 62–3; *St. Mary's, Stafford, Par. Reg.* (Staffs. Par. Reg. Soc. 1935–6), 24, 54; Erdeswick, *Staffs.* p. lviii; E 134/9 Jas. I East./15 m. [3].
[15] S.R.O., D.641/1/4A/1 and 2.
[16] S.R.O., D.641/1/2/85, rot. 1.
[17] 13 Eliz. I, c. 19.
[18] S.R.O., D.1323/E/1, f. 36; N. B. Harte, 'State Control of Dress and Social Change in Pre-Industrial Eng.' *Trade, Government and Economy in Pre-Industrial Eng.* ed. D. C.

Coleman and A. H. John, 138, 153–4.
[19] See p. 214.
[20] Bradley, *Charters*, 168.
[21] Ann J. Kettle, 'Black Book of Stafford', *T.S.H.C.S.* 1965–7, 6.
[22] W.S.L. 77/45, f. 54v.
[23] S.R.O., D.1323/F/1, reverse pages.
[24] W.S.L. 77/45, f. 54v.
[25] S.R.O., D.1287/10/2, Matt. Cradock's Bk., p. 284.
[26] W.S.L. 77/45, f. 54v.
[27] S.R.O., D.1323/F/1, reverse pages, pp. 15–19.
[28] Ibid. /A/1/2, p. 97.
[29] Bradley, *Charters*, 123, 163.
[30] H. L. E. Garbett, 'The Agreement with the Stafford Shoemakers', *T.O.S.S.* 1936, 18; W.S.L., H.M. uncat. 23.
[31] S.R.O., D.641/1/4A/13, rot. 4.
[32] *T.O.S.S.* 1936, 18–19.
[33] Bradley, *Charters*, 168.

simply unauthorized activity but also the refusal to regularize the position by becoming a burgess.[34] In 1699 the fine for unlicensed trading or pursuit of a craft was raised to 20s. a week; freemen of London were then stated to be exempt from the rule.[35] The council was in fact willing enough to admit suitable 'foreigners' as burgesses on payment of a fee, normally £10;[36] in 1696 it was agreed that one-third of such fees should be paid to the company of the trade concerned.[37] The 1827 charter repeated the ban on unauthorized economic activity by outsiders,[38] but in 1834 it was noted that 'this *restrictive clause* has never been enforced; indeed, the spirit of freedom and toleration which now exists would not submit to it, and it is a matter of surprise that it should have been suffered to form a part of a charter of the 19th century'.[39] The old system had evidently long since broken down. Licences were still being applied for and granted in the early 18th century,[40] but some of the guilds and companies were probably already moribund: although there was a chandlers' company in 1701, in 1707 George Keen was licensed as a chandler because there was 'an occasion and necessity for a chandler here'.[41]

In the 1720s Defoe found Stafford 'lately much increased; nay, as some say, grown rich by the clothing trade, which they have fallen into but within the reach of the present age, and which has not enriched this town only, but Tamworth also, and all the country round'.[42] It is not clear whether he meant that the town's wealth came from making cloth or from marketing it. There was certainly some trade in the raw material: by the 1780s the June fair was primarily a wool fair.[43] Until the 19th century there was also some textile working, but it seems always to have been on a small scale. Four men, each described as a 'dyer and clothworker', headed the list of recipients when the corporation granted a charter to the town's clothworkers, dyers, tailors, and bodice-makers in 1682.[44] Other dyers occur in 1698 and in 1716, when Stephen Townsend, a dyer, bought Mostylee mill in Stone and converted it into a fulling-mill.[45] The master weaver who worked in Forebridge in the 1690s,[46] the jersey-weaver who was sworn a burgess in 1702, the websters who were admitted as burgesses in 1724 and 1727,[47] and the weaver who occurs in 1757[48] were probably all stocking-knitters. A few men described as stocking-weavers or -knitters occur in the mid 18th century.[49] There was a jersey-comber,

who prepared wool for spinning, in Forebridge in 1697.[50] Several thread-makers worked in the town between at least 1750 and 1818,[51] and there was a ribbon-weaver in the later 18th century.[52] Part of the old house of correction had been converted into a cotton manufactory by 1803 and was being used as such in 1805.[53] There was a silk-mill in the town by 1835, and it apparently still existed in 1861.[54]

There was a hat manufacturer at Stafford in the later 1790s, and in 1818 hat-making was said to be a 'considerable' industry in the town; there were then two firms of hat manufacturers and six straw-hat makers. There were 9 makers of straw hats in 1834 and 8 in 1851.[55]

From the later 18th century the town's footwear industry developed rapidly.[56] William Horton (1750–1832), whose works in Mill Street was apparently the first boot and shoe factory in Stafford, supplied London, Manchester, and Bristol with his products and before the Napoleonic Wars had a flourishing export trade to America and the Baltic countries. At an election dinner in the town his friend Sheridan proposed the toast: 'May the manufactures of Stafford be trodden under foot by all the world.'[57] Despite a general depression in the industry in the early 19th century the number of employers in the town increased. There had been 5 principal manufacturers in 1787; by 1818 there were 20. Peace brought further expansion. By 1834 there were 26 manufacturers and by 1851 29. Much of the making and finishing was done by out-workers in near-by villages until the mid 19th century, but in 1855 the mechanization of the industry in Stafford began. Thereafter all stages of manufacture were gradually concentrated in factories. By 1861 the trade employed almost 2,000 people in the town. In the later 19th century there was a boom and some large factories were built, mainly in the north end of the town. By the early 1880s there were 39 manufacturers.[58] There followed a long decline as tariff barriers shut off oversea markets and ever larger sums of money were needed to build, equip, and maintain factories. Firms went out of business or were amalgamated with former competitors. The fact that Stafford specialized in the production of women's shoes made its manufacturers especially vulnerable when rapid changes in fashion became common, and in the later 1930s such changes were regarded as having contributed to the decline of the industry in the town. By then there were only nine factories left;

[34] S.R.O., D.1323/A/1/1, pp. 29, 362.
[35] Ibid. /A/1/2, p. 75.
[36] See e.g. ibid. pp. 53, 57.
[37] Ibid. p. 50.
[38] Bradley, *Charters*, 198.
[39] White, *Dir. Staffs.* (1834), 119 n.
[40] S.R.O., D.1323/A/1/2, *passim*.
[41] Ibid. p. 123.
[42] D. Defoe, *Tour thro' the Whole Island of Gt. Brit.* (1928 edn.), ii. 478.
[43] See p. 214.
[44] S.R.O., D.1323/F/1, reverse pages, p. 15.
[45] Ibid. /A/1/2, p. 57; L. E. Helsby and others, 'Water Mills of the Moddershall Valley' (TS. in W.S.L.), chap. 4, para. 2.
[46] S.R.O., D.1323/A/1/2, reverse pages, pp. 1–2.
[47] S.R.O., D.1323/A/1/2, pp. 101, 250, 302.
[48] S.R.O., D.1323/G/1, 3 Oct. 1757.
[49] Ibid. 14 July 1746, 11 Jan. 1747/8, 9 Jan. 1758, 14 July 1760.
[50] S.R.O., D.1323/A/1/2, reverse pages, p. 2.

[51] W.S.L., D.620B(30)/10 deeds of 25 May 1750 and 30 June 1777; S.R.O., D.1323/G/2, reverse pages, 13 July 1778; *Univ. Brit. Dir.* iv. 439; Parson and Bradshaw, *Dir. Staffs.* (1818).
[52] S.R.O., D.1323/G/2, reverse pages, 7 Oct. 1782; *Univ. Brit. Dir.* iv. 439.
[53] *Staffs. Advertiser*, 12 Mar. 1803; S.R.O., D.1323/F/2, p. 56.
[54] *V.C.H. Staffs.* ii. 216.
[55] *Univ. Brit. Dir.* iv. 440; Parson and Bradshaw, *Dir. Staffs.* (1818), pp. lxiv, 224, 226; White, *Dir. Staffs.* (1834), 151–2; (1851), 356.
[56] For the following para. see, unless otherwise stated, *V.C.H. Staffs.* ii. 231–5.
[57] Pitt, *Staffs.* 294. There are other slightly different versions of the toast: see e.g. Calvert, *Stafford*, 23; D. Wilks, *Fragments of Stafford's Past* (Stafford, 1932), 18.
[58] *Stafford Boro. Extension Bill: Mins. of Evidence, 1876* (reprinted from the official rep.), 12 (copy in W.S.L. Pamphs. *sub* Stafford); *Halden's Stafford Dir.* (1880), 81; (1881), 4, 57; (1883), 45.

they still employed some 3,000 people, but over half of those were employees of one firm, Lotus Ltd. By *c.* 1950 the number of factories had fallen to five.[59] By 1958 Lotus alone was left, and in 1977 its works in Sandon Road was still the only shoe factory in the town.

The firm, for long the largest in the trade in Stafford, had been founded by Thomas Bostock, who was making boots and shoes in Gaolgate Street in 1822.[60] By 1833 he had taken his son Edwin (d. 1883) into parnership; it was probably about then that the firm moved to Greengate Street.[61] By 1850 Edwin had taken over and had moved to a works in Foregate Street. It was there that in 1855 the closing-machine was introduced, representing the first stage in the mechanization of the local industry.[62] In 1871 Edwin also got control, on his brother Thomas's death, of a shoe factory which Thomas had established at Stone. Edwin Bostock's firm became a limited liability company as Edwin Bostock & Co. Ltd. in 1898. In 1901 the large Stafford works, stretching from Foregate Street to the Sow, was burnt down.[63] Production was transferred to temporary premises until 1903, when the factory in Sandon Road was completed. Its layout reflected new trends in factory design. The British footwear industry was beginning to face serious competition from highly mechanized American manufacturers, and the firm's technical adviser for the design of the factory was the manager of a Massachusetts shoe-machinery company, J. J. Heys, a native of Walsall who had lived in Stafford before emigrating to America.[64] The factory was extended in 1910, 1912, the early 1920s, 1946, and 1947. In 1919 Edwin Bostock & Co. Ltd. and Frederick Bostock Ltd. of Northampton, a footwear manufacturing firm established by another of Edwin's brothers, amalgamated and took the name Lotus Ltd.[65] The Bostock family retained control of Lotus until 1971, when it was acquired by Argo Caribbean. In 1973 it was taken over by Debenhams. In May 1977 Lotus employed some 1,000 people in Stafford.[66]

The growth of the town's footwear industry in the 19th century led to the establishment of a few firms of boot and shoe wholesalers. The largest has been R. T. Jennings & Son (from 1959 Jen Shoes Ltd.). In the early 1890s the firm, which was then making footwear in St. Chad's Place, entered the general wholesale trade.[67] That side of its business grew, and *c.* 1914 it gave up manufacturing.[68] In 1933 it moved to Marsh Street, and by *c.* 1950 it

was handling over 1¼ million pairs of footwear a year.[69] In 1962 it moved to premises in Newport Road.[70]

The footwear industry provided a market for allied trades in the town. There were, for example, 4 tanners and 9 curriers in Stafford in 1818 and a tanner and 10 curriers and leather-cutters in 1851.[71] When he died in 1860, T. B. Elley, a prominent footwear manufacturer, owned a tanyard in North Walls, a fellmonger's yard which could deal with 1,000 skins a week, and curriers' shops in North Walls capable of employing 40 men.[72] The production of wooden heels also became important. Lasts and heels had been made in the town from at least the later 18th century. There were 2 last- and heel-cutters in the mid 1780s, 2 heel-makers in the later 1790s, 2 last-makers in 1818, and 5 in 1851.[73] By the late 19th century, however, most of the heels needed were apparently imported from the Continent. Heel-making was revived *c.* 1906 by Markham & Roberts Ltd. in Glover Street, from 1911 Vik Heels Ltd. The outbreak of the First World War and the consequent interruption of supplies from abroad stimulated production.[74] In the early 1920s there were three firms in the town.[75] Heels Ltd., later Heels (Stafford) Ltd., which began production in 1920, was to be the most successful. By the early 1930s it was the largest maker of wooden heels in the British Empire, and in the late 1940s it could produce some 400,000 dozen pairs a year.[76] The introduction of plastic heels reduced the demand for its products, and its large works, in Friars Terrace, closed in 1967.[77] The presence of the heel firms in turn generated other business in the town. The Stafford Timber Co., with a sawmill in Rickerscote Road (occupied in 1977 by Cox Long Ltd.), was established in 1928 by the proprietor of Heels Ltd. specifically to cut and supply beech wood for the heel manufacturers.[78] Another firm of timber merchants, Henry Venables Ltd., though having much wider interests, also provided wood for heels. The founder of the firm, Henry Venables, established a sawmill in Foregate Street in 1860 before moving to the Castletown sawmills in Doxey Road in 1864.[79]

In the 1850s, and presumably earlier, small firms of carpenters and joiners produced the pine-wood boxes lined with paper in which shoes for export were packed.[80] By the early 20th century large footwear manufacturers made their own packing cases and the cardboard boxes for individual pairs of footwear,[81] but other firms still had to rely on outside suppliers such as C. J. Nevitt, who

[59] *Stafford Official Guide* [*c.* 1938], 22–3; [*c.* 1950], 43.
[60] Pigot, *New Com. Dir.* (1822–3), 482.
[61] *V.C.H. Staffs.* ii. 234; White, *Dir. Staffs.* (1834), 148.
[62] Slater, *Nat. Com. Dir.* (1850), Staffs. p. 86; *V.C.H. Staffs.* ii. 232.
[63] TS. hist. of Lotus Ltd. (copy in W.S.L.), 53, 58, 72–7.
[64] Ibid. 78–80, 82–3; *Staffs. Advertiser*, 20 June, 26 Dec. 1903.
[65] *V.C.H. Staffs.* ii. 234–5.
[66] Ex inf. the firm (1977).
[67] *Halden & Son's Dir. Stafford* (1892), 42; (1894), 67.
[68] It last appears as a footwear manufacturer in *Halden & Haywood's Dir. Stafford* (1914), 91.
[69] Ibid. (1934), 122; *Stafford Official Guide* [*c.* 1950], 45, 47.
[70] Ex inf. the firm (1977).
[71] Parson and Bradshaw, *Dir. Staffs.* (1818); White, *Dir. Staffs.* (1851), 352.
[72] *Staffs. Advertiser*, 9 and 16 June, 18 Aug. 1860.
[73] *Bailey's Brit. Dir.* (1784), 442; *Univ. Brit. Dir.* iv.

439–40; Parson and Bradshaw, *Dir. Staffs.* (1818); White, *Dir. Staffs.* (1851), 354.
[74] *Halden & Son's Dir. Stafford* (1907), 91; *Halden & Haywood's Dir. Stafford* (1912), 94; *Staffs. Advertiser*, 2 Jan. 1915.
[75] *Halden & Haywood's Dir. Stafford* (1922), 81.
[76] *Stafford: an Industrial Survey* (Stafford, 1932), 75 (copy in W.S.L. Pamphs. *sub* Stafford); *Stafford Official Guide* [*c.* 1950], 47.
[77] It occurs in *Stoke-on-Trent Area P.O. Telephone Dir.* (Jan. 1967) but not in an edn. published later the same year.
[78] *Stafford: an Industrial Survey*, 75–7; ex inf. Mr. C. J. Venables of Stafford (1977).
[79] *Stafford: an Industrial Survey*, 79–80; *Stafford Official Guide* [*c.* 1950], 47; ex inf. Mr. Venables.
[80] J. Venables, 'A short account of the Venables family and the business founded by Henry Venables in 1855', 3–4 (copy in W.S.L. Pamphs. *sub* Biog.).
[81] See e.g. mention of facilities at the new Bostock factory in 1903: *Staffs. Advertiser*, 26 Dec. 1903.

was making cardboard boxes in Bailey Street by 1880 and remained in business there until 1914 or 1915.[82] Among other firms of cardboard-box and packing-case manufacturers has been Shoe Findings Co. of Marston Road, since 1946 Stafford Box Co. It was established c. 1919 and developed as a supplier for the footwear industry; by c. 1950 it had diversified into other specialized packing fields.[83]

The shoe trade also attracted metal-working and engineering concerns. The 'cutlery' that was being made in the town in 1818[84] was probably shoe-makers' knives. John and William Keats, inventors and manufacturers of footwear machinery, settled in Stafford c. 1886 and, as Keats Bros. & Co., established a works in Gaol Road. From c. 1890 they were at the Albion Works, Marston Road. In 1904 the firm became Keats & Bexon Ltd. and in 1916 it moved to Corporation Street, where it continued to make shoe-repairing machinery until 1966.[85] Raworth Bros., later Raworth & Son, made press knives and other cutlery at the Walton Works in Izaak Walton Street from the 1920s until about the time of the Second World War.[86]

Some firms which had been established initially to cater for the footwear trade later moved into other fields. In 1870 W. H. Dorman opened a works in Foregate Street to make press knives and other tools and machinery for the footwear industry. By the 1890s the firm (from 1897 W. H. Dorman & Co. Ltd.) was making machinery for other industries, and in 1903 it began to make petrol engines, which became its speciality. From the late 1920s it concentrated on diesel engines. In 1921 it had bought a site of some 20 a. in Tixall Road. A new works was opened there in 1928–9, and by 1932 it included iron and aluminium foundries and the firm's heavy machinery department. In 1939 the Foregate Street works was closed and all the firm's activities were concentrated in Tixall Road. Dormans became a subsidiary of English Electric Co. Ltd. in 1961, and in 1977 it was trading as G.E.C. Diesels Ltd.[87]

John Evans was making knives, iron lasts, presses, and other machinery for the shoe trade in Fancy Walk by 1881.[88] The business had, by the early 1890s, been taken over by Richard Lloyd, and it later became Lloyd & Yates and Lloyd, Yates & Knight. In 1894 it moved to the Globe Works in Stone Road. In 1905, by then Yates & Knight, it began to make screw-cutting tools. Other products, such as cutting wheels and combination centre drills, were added, and by 1917 the firm was well established as a maker of machine tools. In 1917 it was taken over by J. J. H. Lines. It continued to concentrate

on tool making, from 1938 as J. H. Lines Ltd. Traces of its origins remained; after the Second World War it was still making press knives.

Spic and Span Shoe Polishes Ltd., later Spic and Span Chemical Products Ltd. and subsequently Evode Ltd., was established in 1932 in Glover Street where it made floor and shoe polishes, the latter mainly for Lotus Ltd.[89] From 1938 it began to diversify into the general manufacture of chemically based waterproofing products. Its principal market became the building industry; in the mid 1970s most of its products, such as concrete additives, adhesives, and specialized paints, were for builders. It still maintained its connexion with the footwear industry, into which in 1948 it had successfully introduced adhesives made from synthetic rubbers and resins, but it ceased making polishes in 1962. In 1956 it took over Vik Supplies Ltd., the former Vik Heels Ltd. In 1953 it bought a 20-a. site in Common Road where Stafford Brick Works had operated from 1915 to c. 1938,[90] and in 1954 it opened a new factory there. The works was later enlarged several times; in the early 1960s the Glover Street premises were closed and all work was transferred to Common Road. In May 1977 the Evode Group employed some 800 people in Stafford.

Other firms with little or no interest in Stafford's old staple trade were attracted to the town from the later 19th century because of its good railway connexions and the availability of cheap land. Among the more notable arrivals were several engineering firms.

In 1875 W. G. Bagnall, who had gained his engineering experience at an uncle's iron-foundry at Wolverhampton, acquired a millwright's business in Castletown. In 1876 he built his first locomotive there, and the works, in Castle Street, later became known as the Castle Engine Works. During the next 85 years his firm, later W. G. Bagnall Ltd., produced 1,869 steam and diesel locomotives and a few electric and petrol locomotives. The works was expanded and modernized several times. In the late 1940s the firm became a subsidiary of Heenan & Froude Ltd., a Worcester-based engineering firm which in 1959 sold it to Dormans. When Dormans was taken over by English Electric in 1961 locomotive construction at the Castle Works ceased.[91] In 1977 the works housed the Stafford Engineering Product Division of G.E.C.

In 1893 W. O. Rooper, owner of a Greenwich firm which made emery wheels and artificial-sandstone grindstones, transferred part of his operations to Stafford, where he was already a partner

[82] Kelly's Dir. Staffs. (1880); Halden & Haywood's Dir. Stafford (1915), 65.
[83] Halden & Haywood's Dir. Stafford (1920 and later edns. sub 'Box Makers'); Stafford Official Guide [c. 1950], 47.
[84] Parson and Bradshaw, Dir. Staffs. (1818), p. lxiv.
[85] V.C.H. Staffs. ii. 170–1; Halden's Stafford Dir. (1887 and later edns.); ex inf. Mr. T. W. West of Stafford (1977).
[86] The firm first appears, as Raworth Bros., engineers, in Kelly's Dir. Staffs. (1924). It first appears in Halden & Haywood's Dir. Stafford in the issue for 1928, where it advertises (p. 126) as a maker of press knives. It advertises in the directory as Raworth & Son 1933–7 but remains Raworth Bros. in the trades directory section 1928–46.
[87] V.C.H. Staffs. ii. 153; Stafford: an Industrial Survey, 61–7.
[88] This para. is based on Halden's Stafford Dir., later Halden & Son's Dir. Stafford, and subsequently Halden &

Haywood's Dir. Stafford (to 1916 sub 'Machinists and General Mechanics' and thereafter sub 'Engineers'); Stafford Official Guide [c. 1959], 47–8.
[89] This para. is based, unless otherwise stated, on Stafford Newsletter, 31 Dec. 1960, 6 Jan. 1962, 11 Feb. 1977, supplement; Architects' Jnl. 29 Aug. 1962; Stafford Official Guide (1976), 47; Evode: a Short Review of Group Activities (n.d. but c. 1976; copy in W.S.L. Pamphs. sub Industry); information from Evode Ltd. (1962 and 1977).
[90] Halden & Haywood's Dir. Stafford (1916), 67; (1938), 105. The Stafford Brick Yard in Common Rd. from the 1860s to c. 1880 was a separate works a short distance N. of the later works: P.O. Dir. Staffs. (1868); Kelly's Dir. Staffs. (1880); O.S. Map 1/2,500, Staffs. XXXVII. 7 (1881 edn.); O.S. Map 6", Staffs. XXXVII. NE. (1925 edn.).
[91] V.C.H. Staffs. ii. 159, 163–4; A. C. Baker and T. D. A. Civil, Bagnalls of Stafford, 11–24.

in Rooper & Harris Ltd., an electrical business. Rooper & Harris established a works in Eastgate Street, later moving to Castle Street. In 1905 the firm was bought by a rival concern, Moser, West & Bateman Ltd. of Greenwich, which in turn transferred its manufacturing activities to Stafford. In 1913 Universal Grinding Wheel Co. Ltd., a recently established Sheffield company which had also been acquired by Moser, West & Bateman, opened a factory at Doxey to make vitrified grinding-wheels, a new type of abrasive wheel which had been developed abroad; in 1914 Moser, West & Bateman was voluntarily wound up and its assets were transferred to Universal Grinding Wheel. The Doxey factory was extended during the First World War, and in 1921 Universal Grinding Wheel concentrated its manufacture of all types of grinding-wheel there and closed the Castle Street works.[92] Later the company expanded, extended the range of its products, and added to the Doxey factory. From 1942 it also produced there white aluminous abrasive, until then not made in Great Britain.[93] In the later 1950s the factory, on its 44-a. site, was the largest of its kind in Europe, and in the mid 1970s the company was Europe's largest manufacturer of grinding-wheels. In May 1977 it employed some 1,600 people at Stafford.[94]

In 1900 Siemens Bros. & Co. Ltd. of Woolwich, a cable-laying firm of German origin which was anxious to establish itself as a manufacturer of heavy electrical equipment, bought land in Forebridge for a new works.[95] It began building in 1901, and in 1903 it opened the large Dynamo Works, adjoining the railway and on the west side of the Lichfield road. In 1906 Siemens Bros. Dynamo Works Ltd. was formed to run the works and to carry on the heavy electrical engineering side of the parent company's business. Products of the Stafford works ranged from generators, electric motors, and electric locomotives to domestic appliances. It was always run at a loss, and after the First World War Siemens decided to sell it. In 1919 the works and the heavy electrical engineering side of Siemens's business were purchased by the newly formed English Electric Co. Ltd. From 1930 English Electric flourished under the direction of G. H. Nelson, later 1st Lord Nelson of Stafford (d. 1962). The main works, which covered some 56 a. in 1932, was extended in the later 1940s, and in 1960 a new transformer works was opened there. In 1962 a new factory, to produce meters, relays, and other precision devices, was completed off St. Leonard's Avenue. The former Dorman works in Foregate Street was taken over in 1942; Dormans itself and its subsidiary, Bagnalls, were acquired in 1961. In 1968 English Electric merged with General Electric Co. Ltd. to form the General Electric and English Electric Companies; G.E.C. was the dominant partner and in 1970 gave its name to the whole

group.[96] The merger was followed by some reorganization and rationalization of the work of the Stafford factories to link them more closely with the activities of the group's other factories elsewhere in the country. In the mid 1970s the site in Lichfield Road housed the Generator Division of G.E.C. Turbine Generators Ltd., making generators for gas- and steam-turbine drives; the High Voltage Unit of G.E.C. Switchgear Ltd., making gas and air blast circuit-breakers and current and instrument transformers; the Power Transmission Division of G.E.C. Switchgear Ltd., working on the engineering of power systems and engaged in the development of converter valves; G.E.C. Transformers Ltd., with its headquarters at Stafford, producing large transformers; and G.E.C. Rectifiers Ltd., making rectifiers for a wide range of applications. On the site there was also a laboratory and a foundry producing castings in non-ferrous metals. The Castle Works still made components for equipment produced at Lichfield Road, while G.E.C. Diesels Ltd. at the Dorman works in Tixall Road and G.E.C. Measurements Ltd. at the St. Leonard's Works continued to make the same items that they had produced before. In May 1977 G.E.C. had some 8,200 employees at its various works in Stafford.[97]

The British Reinforced Concrete Engineering Co. Ltd., designers of reinforced concrete structures and manufacturers of welded steel wire mesh and rods for use as concrete reinforcement, moved to Stafford from Manchester in 1926.[98] The new site consisted of some 20 a. south of the town bounded by the railway line, the Lichfield road, and Silkmore Lane. By 1932 the works had almost doubled in size and covered about 5 a.; in the later 1950s it covered over 9 a. In May 1977 B.R.C. employed some 750 people at Stafford.

The establishment of these engineering firms effectively destroyed the supremacy which the footwear industry had once had in the economic life of the town. The change was becoming noticeable by the later 1880s,[99] but it was only in the early 1900s, with the arrival of Siemens, that the pattern of employment began to change rapidly. Siemens brought some 800 employees from Woolwich to Stafford[1] and immediately became one of the town's most substantial employers. By 1921 there were 2,034 metal-workers living in the borough and only 1,867 footwear workers,[2] and although in the later 1930s there were about 3,000 workers in the town's nine shoe factories, by then E.E.C. alone employed some 4,000 people in Stafford.[3] Engineering has since become the town's staple industry, with G.E.C. dwarfing all the other firms.

Other industries in the town in the 19th and 20th centuries have included brewing, the manufacture of soft drinks, and salt-making. In the mid 18th century Stafford ale had a good reputation,[4] but the

[92] *Staffs. Chron.* 25 Jan. 1951; *Halden & Son's Dir. Stafford,* later *Halden & Haywood's Dir. Stafford* (1894–1904 sub 'Machine Makers'; 1905–16 sub 'Grindstone and Emery Wheel Maker'); *Stafford: an Industrial Survey,* 77–9.
[93] *Staffs. Chron.* 25 Jan. 1951.
[94] *Stafford Official Guide* [c. 1959], 49; (1976), 47; ex inf. the firm (1977).
[95] For this para. see *V.C.H. Staffs.* ii. 157–9.
[96] See e.g. R. Jones and O. Marriott, *Anatomy of a Merger,* 289–313.

[97] Ex inf. the firm (1977).
[98] This para. is based on *Halden & Haywood's Dir. Stafford* (1927), 95; *Stafford: an Industrial Survey,* 47–51; *Stafford Official Guide* [c. 1959], 42–3; (1976), 47; information from the firm (1977).
[99] *Halden's Stafford Dir.* (1887), 3.
[1] *Early Hists. of some Companies of the English Electric Group* (Stafford, n.d.), 5 (copy in W.S.L. Pamphs. sub Industry).
[2] *Census,* 1921. [3] *Stafford Official Guide* [c. 1938], 22–3.
[4] *Eng. Illustrated* (1764), ii. 242.

town's proximity to Burton and its lack of an adequate water-supply ensured that its brewing never became of more than local significance. No wholesale brewers are known until 1834, and most of the firms which occurred thereafter were short-lived. Only two, or possibly three, breweries survived for more than a few years. One in Foregate Street, apparently established in the 1840s by Henry Trubshaw, became known as Stafford Brewery and seems to have continued under various owners until

Stafford from the later 19th century until about the end of the Second World War.[11] Several firms were involved; probably the longest-lived was that of W. D. Batkin (from 1912 W. D. Batkin Ltd.) of the Eclipse Works in Gaol Road. Batkin bought his premises there in 1902 from another firm of mineral water manufacturers, Hardman & Openshaw (established in 1886), which had moved to Gaol Road in 1895 and had built a new works there in 1898. Batkins manufactured its own soft drinks on the

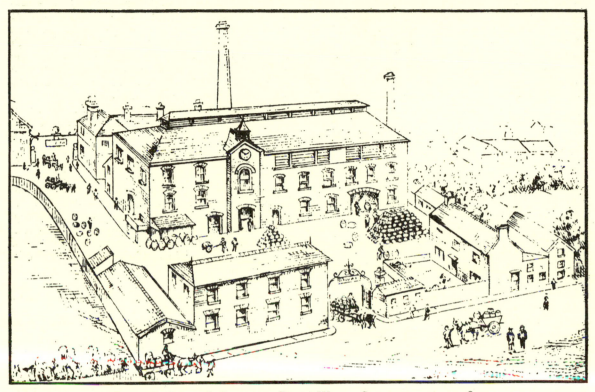

HUMBY & BAILLIE'S BREWERY, SOUTH WALLS, STAFFORD, IN THE 1890s

the mid 1860s.[5] Two other breweries were set up in the mid 1860s. One, the Green Brewery, was established on the west side of the Green, Forebridge, by John Bishop, an ale and porter merchant.[6] Control passed to Charles Eley c. 1879;[7] the firm became Eley & Tatham in 1888, Eley, Tatham & Nesbitt in 1894, and Eley's (Stafford) Brewery Ltd. in 1899.[8] In 1928 it was taken over by W. Butler & Co. Ltd. of Wolverhampton, which later that year closed the brewery and sold the premises.[9] The other brewery established in the mid 1860s had been set up in South Walls by George Hartridge. It passed through various hands until 1899, when Eley's took over the then owners, Humby & Baillie, and closed it.[10]

Mineral water and other soft drinks were made in

premises until c. 1945 and traded from there until 1966.

Brine deposits were discovered beneath Stafford common in 1877 during the search for a water supply for the town, and in 1893 the Stafford Salt and Alkali Co. began to make salt at a works near Common railway station. In 1894 the company added a works on the canal at Baswich; a pipeline running through the town from the common supplied it with brine. By 1900 two other firms had saltworks by the common, and new works were later built there and at Baswich. In the later 1960s, after various mergers and closures, three plants were still working, an open-pan works by the common and two vacuum plants at Baswich.[12] By then, however, there were complaints that the brine-

[5] Hen. Trubshaw: *P.O. Dir. Staffs.* (1850); White, *Dir. Staffs.* (1851), 350. T. A. Woollett: *P.O. Dir. Staffs.* (1854). T. M. Heathorn: ibid. (1860); Harrison, Harrod & Co. *Dir. Staffs.* (1861). B. Farmer: *P.O. Dir. Staffs.* (1864).
[6] *P.O. Dir. Staffs.* (1868). For Bishop see ibid. (1864). For the site see O.S. Map 1/500, Staffs. XXXVII. 11. 23 (1881 edn.).
[7] *Halden's Stafford Dir.* (1880), 69.
[8] Ibid. (1884 and later edns. to 1891); *Halden & Son's Dir. Stafford* (1892 and later edns. to 1900).
[9] *Staffs. Advertiser*, 31 Mar., 21 Apr., 22 Dec. 1928.
[10] *P.O. Dir. Staffs.* (1868; 1872; 1876); *Halden's Stafford*

Dir. (1880 and later edns. to 1891); *Halden & Son's Dir. Stafford* (1892 and later edns. to 1900). For the site see O.S. Map 1/500, Staffs. XXXVII. 11. 22 (1881 edn.).
[11] This para. is based on C. Ecclestone, 'Digging into your local history', *Old Bottles and Treasure Hunting* (Feb. 1976; copy in Stafford Libr.); Margaret M. Owens, 'The New Premises of Parkes of Stafford—a Brief History' (copy in W.S.L., C.B. Stafford); 'Borough' Guide to Stafford (Cheltenham, n.d. but c. 1908), 46 (copy in W.S.L. Pamphs. sub Stafford); information from Mr. N. Plant of Stafford, a former manager of Batkins (1977).
[12] *V.C.H. Staffs.* ii. 250–1.

pumping was causing subsidence and damaging buildings in the northern part of the town; in 1970 a court order banned further pumping, and salt-making in the town ceased.[13]

LOCAL GOVERNMENT. THE BOROUGH. Stafford appears in Domesday Book as a borough which in Edward the Confessor's reign had paid £6 to the Crown and £3 to the earl of Mercia in place of all customary dues. After the Conquest the earl's share escheated to the king, and by 1086 the total payment had dropped to £7, half of which William I gave to Robert de Stafford.[14] Stafford is the only borough recorded as paying less after the Conquest than before; that was probably the result of its sufferings following the rebellion of 1069, which are attested by the large number of waste messuages in 1086.[15] There were then eighteen burgesses on the king's demesne in the town and eighteen attached to the manor of Marston belonging to Roger, earl of Shrewsbury. All the tenants-in-chief in the borough paid geld annually to the king, and all had sac and soc.[16]

In 1153 Henry, duke of Normandy, granted Stafford with much of the county to Ranulf, earl of Chester, but the grant had no permanent effect.[17] In 1206 King John issued a charter to the town conferring on it the status of a free borough, but it seems to have been largely a confirmation of existing rights rather than a new grant.[18] The burgesses were to enjoy sac and soc, toll and team, infangthief, and all their other ancient liberties and those held by all free boroughs in England except London. They were to be exempt from tolls throughout the king's lands except in London. No suits concerning tenements in the borough or pleas concerning debts contracted there and pledges made there were to be heard outside the borough. The burgesses were also exempted from pleas under the writ of *mort d'ancestor* in favour of the custom of the borough. The charter may have been recognizing the custom of Borough English, which was probably the usage in Stafford by 1390 and certainly so by the 16th century. It was apparently still observed in the 1830s.[19] Although it was stated in 1851 to have been abandoned,[20] a share in a house in Eastgate Street was described that year as held by the custom of Borough English.[21]

The charter provided that the borough was to be held at the ancient fee-farm rent. No amount was mentioned, but by 1242 the burgesses were paying a farm of 5 marks (£3 6s. 8d.).[22] That had been the amount paid by the borough as an aid in 1129–30 and 1155–6 and probably in 1154–5.[23] The sums paid by the borough as a *donum* or an *assisa* in the later 12th century were often much higher, but in 1161–2 the sheriff accounted for 5 marks from Stafford borough and in 1173–4 for the same as an *assisa*.[24] The charter of 1206 gave the burgesses the right of accounting for the fee-farm rent direct to the Exchequer, a right which they were also exercising in the case of tallages by 1242.[25] The 5-mark fee-farm continued to be paid to the Crown[26] until 1672 when it was redeemed by the corporation.[27] At least between the early 15th century and 1802 the borough also paid a fee-farm rent of £1 13s. 8d. to the Stafford family and its successors,[28] perhaps a survival of the share of the borough rent granted to Robert de Stafford by William I.

The borough claimed in 1293 that the suburb of Foregate, though part of Marston manor, had enjoyed the borough's privileges by 1206, and a jury upheld the claim.[29] In other respects, however, Foregate remained within Marston manor until the beginning of the 19th century. Holders of property there owed suit to the manor court. The borough bailiffs were summoned to the court, and in 1678 the chamberlains were fined for failing to repair a bridge on the boundary between Foregate and Marston township. It was recalled in 1612 that the prior of Sheen as lord of Marston had held his court in Foregate village.[30]

The charter was confirmed by the Crown in 1228.[31] It was confirmed again in 1315 when new privileges were granted. The burgesses, so long as they dwelt in the borough or its suburb, were not to be placed with outsiders on any assizes, juries, or inquisitions, and only men of the borough were normally to sit on assizes, juries, and inquisitions concerning the borough or its suburb. The burgesses were granted freedom from murage throughout the kingdom. They were to have a coroner, elected by themselves, and their own gaol.[32] Further confirmations of the charters were granted in 1341, 1379, 1390, 1400, 1414, 1440, 1478, 1511, 1548, 1554, and 1560. Henry VII confirmed Edward IV's confirmation 'upon a resumption by parliament', and in 1550 and 1605 the Crown confirmed the incorporation of the town.[33]

The chief officers of the borough were originally styled reeves. Walter *prepositus* occurs from 1164 and possibly from 1155.[34] In the 13th century there

[13] *Stafford Newsletter*, 28 Nov., 4 Dec. 1969, 5 Feb., 19 June, 7 Aug 1970; *Express & Star*, 30 and 31 July 1970.
[14] *V.C.H. Staffs.* iv. 24, 37.
[15] J. Tait, *Medieval Eng. Borough*, 153; *V.C.H. Staffs.* i. 221; iv. 23.
[16] *V.C.H. Staffs.* iv. 37, 46.
[17] *S.H.C.* ii (1), 221, 224; *Reg. Regum Anglo-Norm.* iii, no. 180; F. M. Stenton, *First Cent. of Eng. Feudalism* (1961 edn.), 240–1.
[18] For the charter see Bradley, *Charters*, 1–17.
[19] *Cal. Close*, 1389–92, 282 (ref. in 1390 to the custom of the town); C 1/191 no. 43; C 1/237 no. 80; *S.H.C.* viii (2), 147; *S.H.C.* n.s. ix. 162–4; W.S.L., H.M. uncat. 29, envelope labelled 'Borough Parliamentary Election 1690'; T. Pennant, *Journey from Chester to London* (1811 edn.), 99; *Univ. Brit. Dir.* iv. 437; White, *Dir. Staffs.* (1834), 117. Pitt, *Staffs.* (1817), 294, however, states that he had found no evidence of its being observed.
[20] White, *Dir. Staffs.* (1851), 326.
[21] S.R.O., D.1329/1.
[22] *Pipe R.* 1242 (ed. H. L. Cannon) 10.

[23] *S.H.C.* i. 3–4, 20, 22.
[24] Ibid. 35, 71.
[25] *Pipe R.* 1242, 8; *Cal. Lib.* 1245–51, 295.
[26] See e.g. J. B. Frith, 'Account of the bailiffs of borough of Stafford for 1411–12', *T.O.S.S.* 1939, 21; *Cal. Close*, 1435–41, 156, 216; *Rot. Parl.* vi. 598; S.R.O., D.1323/E/1, f. 102.
[27] See p. 268.
[28] See e.g. *T.O.S.S.* 1939, 21; S.R.O., D.1323/E/1 and 2.
[29] *S.H.C.* vi (1), 287.
[30] E 134/9 Jas. I East./15; E 134/10 Jas. I East./33; S.R.O., D.590/530; above, p. 209.
[31] Bradley, *Charters*, 19.
[32] Ibid. 35–7.
[33] Ibid. 45, 50–1, 54–5, 62–3, 65–70, 75, 79–92, 94–5, 97–8, 108 sqq.; some of the dates are wrongly translated by the editor. For the 1390 confirmation see *Cal. Close*, 1389–92, 209, and for Henry VII's S.R.O., D.(W.) 1721/1/1, f. 139v.
[34] L. Margaret Midgley, 'Some notes on "Old Stafford" and "Old Staffordians"', *T.S.H.C.S.* 1974–6, 10–11.

were two reeves at a time.[35] By 1275 they were called bailiffs, and there were also sub-bailiffs then.[36] At least by the early 14th century the bailiffs held office for one year.[37] At the beginning of his reign Henry VII laid down the procedure for the appointment of the bailiffs. The town council was to choose four candidates from among its members, with none of the ordinary burgesses present; two of the four were then to be chosen bailiffs by the rest of the council and all burgesses who were householders resident within the liberty of the borough. The ordinance was confirmed by Henry VIII in 1510.[38] The procedure may represent an oligarchic tendency. It was stated early in the 17th century that while the dukes of Buckingham were recorders from about the mid 15th century, the office of bailiff was held by 'cappers, smiths, barbers, tanners, tailors, and other handicraft men'; the last duke (1485–1521), however, and his son Henry, Lord Stafford (recorder from 1542), used their authority as recorders to bring in 'a more civil government'.[39] Borough ordinances of 1566 reduced the amount of entertainment required from the bailiffs.[40] The charter of 1605 confirmed the existing method of electing the bailiffs, naming the Monday after the feast of St. Luke (18 October) as election day. If a bailiff vacated his office or was removed from it, responsibility for appointing a successor lay with the other bailiff and the council. A bailiff could appoint a deputy from among the councillors. The charter confirmed the bailiffs' customary right to swear the wardens of the guilds and to appoint the lesser officials of the borough.[41]

The charter of 1206 implies the existence of a borough court, and a view of frankpledge for the town was mentioned in 1219.[42] Records of a few sessions of the court between 1275 and 1307 show that it then met on Mondays at three-weekly or fortnightly intervals and even weekly on occasion.[43] By the 1380s and 1390s it was meeting every other Monday.[44] It was held before the bailiffs.[45] In 1395 a court leet was held in August and in 1397 in July,[46] and a court leet held after Easter is mentioned in the bailiffs' accounts for 1411–12.[47] In 1482 it was stated by a defendant that there had always been a king's court held before the bailiffs every Monday in the guildhall to deal with matters relating to tenements in the town.[48] In 1561 the bailiffs were holding a monthly court on Mondays.[49] Borough ordinances of 1566 described it as a court of record and ordered the bailiffs to keep the records in the treasury.[50] The ordinances also laid down that the bailiffs were to take two petty inquests a year, every

member of which was to have 4d. from the treasury.[51] The charter of 1605 included three-weekly courts of record in the general list of privileges confirmed.[52]

The bailiffs and *communitas* of the town were mentioned in 1305 when they appeared as prosecutors in the court, but there is no record before the 15th century of any governing body other than the court. A decision establishing that two men possessed the freedom of the town was made in the court in 1305 by *seniores*.[53] In 1394 and 1395 the court dealt with several matters concerning burgess rights, and at the 1395 leet the bailiffs with the assent of the burgesses laid down the penalties to be imposed on any burgess or *tensarius* who prosecuted a fellow townsman by royal writ outside the liberty of the town.[54] An ordinance of 1399 restraining the bailiffs from taking revenues from waifs, strays, and forfeitures was made by certain burgesses sworn in the great court and acting with the community of the town.[55] A town council existed by 1476 when the bailiffs 'and their brethren the Twenty-five' approved a set of regulations drawn up by the shoemakers' guild.[56] As already seen, the Twenty-five were given the chief authority in the election of the bailiffs in 1500–1. An ordinance of 1546 concerned with craftsmen in the borough was made by the bailiffs, the Twenty-five, and the burgesses,[57] and during the reign of Edward VI a town clerk was appointed by the bailiffs, the Twenty-five, 'and burgesses and commons'.[58] About the late 1540s the burgesses claimed that they were being excluded by the Twenty-five from privileges to which they had a right, and an agreement was made between the two sides providing that the burgesses should be represented on the inquisition of the leet and that one of the two chamberlains should be a burgess.[59] In 1566, however, ordinances relating to all sides of the town's life were passed by the bailiffs and Twenty-five only and confirmed by them in 1590.[60] The charter of 1605 reduced the number of councillors or capital burgesses to twenty-one. It nominated the first twenty-one, who were to hold office for life but could be removed for misconduct by the bailiffs and the other capital burgesses; vacancies were to be filled by the bailiffs and capital burgesses from among the most upright and discreet inhabitants and residents of the borough. The charter recognized the bailiffs and twenty-one capital burgesses assembled together as the supreme authority in the borough.[61]

The charter of 1548 granted the borough a commission of the peace.[62] In 1561 borough sessions of

[35] S.R.O. 938/178, /182, /184–5, /253. Reeves occur in the Memoranda Rolls from 1220: E 159/4 m. 1.
[36] E 159/49 m. 37; S.R.O., D.641/1/4A/1–2. Three are listed in Jan. 1293: *S.H.C.* vi (1), 256. For a similar change of title at Shrewsbury see Una Rees, 'Provosts of Shrewsbury, 1200–1300', *Trans. Shropshire Arch. Soc.* lix. 43–4.
[37] Bradley, *Charters*, 203. The reference to the mayor, bailiffs, men, and whole community of Stafford in 1301 in connexion with a subsidy (*Cal. Close*, 1296–1302, 461) is presumably a confusion with other towns.
[38] S.R.O., D.(W.) 1721/1/1, f. 143.
[39] S.R.O., D.(W.) 1721/1/4, f. 28 (2nd numbering); W.S.L., S.MS. 369, pp. 93, 110.
[40] Ann J. Kettle, 'Black Book of Stafford', *T.S.H.C.S.* 1965–7, 24.
[41] Bradley, *Charters*, 117–23.
[42] *Rot. Litt. Claus.* (Rec. Com.), i. 396.
[43] S.R.O., D.641/1/4A/1–5.
[44] Ibid. /11–14.
[45] Ibid. /3; ibid. /13, rot. 1.

[46] Ibid. /13, rot. 4; F. B. Stitt, 'Stafford Borough Court Rolls, 1396–7', *T.S.H.C.S.* 1974–6, 32.
[47] *T.O.S.S.* 1939, 17–18, 23.
[48] *S.H.C.* n.s. vi (1), 146. See also *S.H.C.* n.s. iv. 107.
[49] W.S.L., S.MS. 366 (ii).
[50] *T.S.H.C.S.* 1965–7, 6.
[51] Ibid. 9.
[52] Bradley, *Charters*, 127.
[53] S.R.O., D.641/1/4A/4.
[54] Ibid. /13, rott. 1, 1d., 2d., 4.
[55] *1st Rep. Com. Mun. Corp.* H.C. 116, App. III, p. 2025 (1835), xxv.
[56] H. L. E. Garbett, 'The Agreement with the Shoemakers of Stafford', *T.O.S.S.* 1936, 18.
[57] B.L., Hargrave MS. 288, f. 41.
[58] S.R.O., D.(W.) 1721/1/4, f. 173v.
[59] *1st Rep. Com. Mun. Corp.* App. III, 2025.
[60] *T.S.H.C.S.* 1965–7, 3.
[61] Bradley, *Charters*, 112–17, 120–1.
[62] Ibid. 75–7.

the peace with gaol delivery were held in March and October before the bailiffs as justices and the recorder.[63] The charter of 1605 nominated the bailiffs as justices and excepted cases of felony from their jurisdiction.[64]

A clerk of the court existed by 1395.[65] A clerk was paid a fee of ½ mark by the bailiffs in 1411–12.[66] Henry, Lord Stafford, after being made recorder in 1542, appointed a town clerk, 'who took a corporal oath for the due executing of the place'.[67] In 1548–9 the borough appointed a 'steward or town clerk' to hold office for life, and the bailiffs assigned him an annual rent of 4 marks in addition to customary fees and profits. He promised that he or a lawful deputy would keep the records of the court and other town muniments, advise the bailiffs, and carry out all other duties customarily connected with the office; he also agreed to live in the town.[68] There was a borough treasurer by 1411–12,[69] and by the early 1530s the town's finances were handled by two chamberlains.[70] As mentioned above, the charter of 1315 gave the burgesses the right to elect a coroner, but the first known coroner was Thomas Worswick, who was coroner for both the county and the borough in 1602.[71] There was a recorder by 1459[72] and a steward by 1613 with the town clerk as his deputy.[73]

By 1613 a group of which Matthew Cradock was a prominent member was pressing for a new charter replacing the bailiffs by a mayor and reconstituting the council as ten aldermen and ten capital burgesses; the aim was openly stated to be the limitation of the influence of the 'vulgar burgesses'.[74] There was strong opposition within the town. There were also opponents outside it; the bishop of Coventry and Lichfield, for example, was alarmed by the proposal to revive the exempt jurisdiction of St. Mary's and jealous for the commercial interests of Lichfield and Eccleshall. Most of the county authorities, however, supported the proposed charter, which was granted in 1614.[75] The town was reincorporated in the name of the mayor and burgesses of the borough of Stafford. Cradock was nominated first mayor, and from 1615 the mayor was to be elected by the retiring mayor and the councillors on the Monday after St. Luke's day from among the aldermen. He could appoint a deputy from among previous mayors and, failing them, from the more experienced aldermen. The ten aldermen and the ten capital burgesses were also named in the charter. Vacancies among the aldermen were to be filled by the mayor and councillors from the burgesses at large and vacancies among the capital burgesses from residents of the borough; councillors could be expelled for misconduct. The earl of Northampton was nominated high steward for life; subsequent high stewards were to be elected

by the mayor and councillors. Robert Aston was nominated recorder during the pleasure of the mayor and councillors, who were to elect future recorders. There were to be two or more serjeants-at-mace, one appointed by the mayor and the rest by the resident burgesses. The justices were to be the mayor, the recorder, and two aldermen; the charter nominated the first two aldermanic justices, but from 1615 they were to be chosen by the mayor and councillors on the Monday after St. Luke's day. Capital offences were excepted from the jurisdiction of the borough justices. The mayor and councillors were empowered to appoint a deputy recorder, a clerk, a chamberlain, and the customary constables and lesser officers, and the mayor and his deputy were given the bailiffs' right of swearing the wardens of guilds. The borough was granted a three-weekly court of record to be held on Mondays in the guildhall before the mayor, recorder, and aldermen or any two of them (including the recorder). No stranger was to trade regularly in the borough without the permission of the mayor and aldermen, and the town was granted a Shrove-tide fair. The borough's right to a coroner and a prison was confirmed along with all other privileges granted by previous charters. The charter ended with a clause safeguarding the rights of the bishop.

To enhance the office of mayor the council later in 1614 assigned him during his term of office fines and perquisites of court and also the revenues from waifs, strays, and forfeitures which, as mentioned above, the bailiffs had been denied in 1399; he was not required to account for the money.[76] By 1699 the mayor received tolls, the surplus from the Coton field rents, and profits from weights and measures as well as the revenues assigned in 1614; the money was 'for his extraordinary expenses and support of the grandeur of his office'.[77] In November 1622 the new mayor gave a dinner and a supper on three occasions; for the first he received a large number of presents in kind. The retiring mayor also gave a dinner and a supper.[78] In 1797 the mayor was still giving a treat at his election. He then received 50 guineas a year towards his expenses, and after increases in 1808 and 1812 the sum was raised in 1813 to 100 guineas.[79] In 1833, however, he had no emoluments or allowance from the corporation.[80]

The corporation's privileges were confirmed in 1664–5.[81] It appointed the duke of Monmouth high steward in 1677, but in 1682 the Tory mayor Sampson Birch collaborated in the duke's arrest at Stafford. At the same time Birch urged the council to surrender the charter to the king. The council demurred on the ground of the expense of obtaining a new charter.[82] In reporting the proceedings to the king, Birch stated that he was 'so grievously sensible of the unsoundness of the major part of the

[63] W.S.L., S.MS. 366 (ii).
[64] Bradley, *Charters*, 123–5.
[65] S.R.O., D.641/1/4A/13, rot. 1d.
[66] *T.O.S.S.* 1939, 20.
[67] W.S.L., S.MS. 369, p. 110.
[68] S.R.O., D.(W.) 1721/1/4, ff. 173v.–174.
[69] *T.O.S.S.* 1939, 20.
[70] W.S.L., S.MS. 366 (iA), f. 5v.
[71] W.S.L., S.MS. 369, p. 143.
[72] Ibid. p. 93.
[73] S.R.O., D.(W.) 1721/1/4, f. 52v. (2nd numbering). The steward mentioned in the 1566 ordinances (*T.S.H.C.S.* 1965–7, 24) could be the town clerk (see above).
[74] For an account of the struggle for the charter see

S.R.O., D.(W.) 1721/1/4, ff. 13 sqq. (2nd numbering). For the Cradock family see J. S. Horne, 'Portrait of Mathew Cradock 1520–1592', *T.O.S.S.* 1937.
[75] Bradley, *Charters*, 133–75, where the date is wrongly given as 1615.
[76] S.R.O., D.(W.) 1721/1/4, ff. 90v.–91.
[77] W.S.L., H.M. 32. The Coton field rents are deleted from the same list in S.R.O., D.1323/A/1/2, p. 74.
[78] S.R.O., D.(W.) 1721/1/4, ff. 158v.–161v.
[79] S.R.O., D.1323/A/1/3, pp. 174, 176, 342, 377, 398.
[80] *1st Rep. Com. Mun. Corp.* App. III, 2026.
[81] C 66/3079 mm. 21–3.
[82] 'Arrest of Duke of Monmouth in Stafford, 1682', *T.O.S.S.* 1932.

Marston Road, showing former shoe factories

The Closing Room at Lotus Ltd. *c.* 1930

STAFFORD: THE FOOTWEAR INDUSTRY

The union workhouse in 1843

Noell's Alms-houses in 1837

STAFFORD POOR RELIEF

common council that I may too truly say they stink for want of amputation'; but he also reported that he had secured the admission of '50 or more loyal gentlemen of worthy quality of our county and parts adjacent . . . to prevail against the numerous dependent lesser-rate men here'. The king replied that he hoped to reduce the cost of any new charter.[83] In 1683 the council transferred the high stewardship from Monmouth to Lord Ferrers.[84] In 1684 it petitioned the king that on the surrender of the charter he would grant a new one containing additional privileges.[85] A new charter was granted by James II in 1685, nominating the mayor, aldermen, and capital burgesses, and the steward, recorder, and town clerk; the burgesses' right to elect one of the serjeants-at-mace was vested in the mayor and council. The king reserved the right to remove officers and members of the corporation.[86] In 1687 James took advantage of the death of an alderman to appoint a Roman Catholic, Dr. Benjamin Thornburgh, to the vacancy, and he was duly sworn both alderman and justice. Later the same year he was elected mayor, and the king dispensed him from taking the oaths of allegiance and supremacy.[87] In May 1688 James dismissed the high steward, the recorder, the two aldermanic justices, three other aldermen including Sampson Birch, three capital burgesses, and the town clerk and nominated replacements. Some of the nominees were admitted, but the council declined to admit the others because they were not resident in the borough. In addition some refused to act. By royal order in October those who had been dismissed were reinstated and the old charter was restored.[88]

The charter of 1685 provided for quarter sessions. In the mid 17th century sessions were still held twice a year,[89] but by 1744 they were quarterly.[90] By the earlier 1830s they dealt only with civil matters and the occasional appeal, criminal cases being committed to the county, and that appears already to have been the practice in the mid 18th century.[91] In the earlier 1830s petty sessions were held weekly.[92] A twice-yearly court leet was held before the borough justices in the early 1620s, but by the mid 18th century it was held in October only, before the deputy steward.[93] The three-weekly court of record ceased to be held in 1781.[94] There was no borough coroner in the earlier 1830s, although the right to one had been confirmed in successive charters; the county coroner acted instead.[95]

The 17th century was a time of increasing financial difficulty. The main sources of borough revenue by the 15th century were tolls, rents, perquisites of court, and fines.[96] In 1617 a borough malt mill was brought into use to provide a regular income.[97] In 1650 a council meeting was held to consider ways of raising money, and it was decided to borrow £200 at 6 per cent, the whole council giving security.[98] In 1651 the council assigned the income from the lease of the market tolls towards paying off debts. It also decided to allow creditors 5 per cent interest and forbade the two chamberlains and other collectors to dispose of the town rents without its consent.[99] The dispute with the Fowlers over Coton field in the later 17th century led to new expense and debt, and rents paid by tenants there were raised in 1670 to help towards meeting the cost.[1] By 1691 the malt mill had been mortgaged, and an action of ejectment was then brought against the corporation for failure to pay the annual £20 due on the mortgage.[2] Stricter control of the chamberlains was introduced by the council in 1699.[3] From 1710 a single salaried chamberlain was appointed, although in that year at least an assistant was also appointed.[4] In the 1790s the cost of the new organ in St. Mary's and the £1,000 required as the corporation's contribution towards the new shire hall led to new debts.[5] In 1797 it was decided to stop providing wine at the proclamation of the fairs and in 1799 to stop presenting wine and ale to the assize judges.[6] Rents on corporation property were raised in 1798, and in 1802 the council decided to let property by auction only.[7]

The charter was renewed in 1767.[8] By the mid 1820s the practice had grown up of electing by a majority of the council instead of by a majority of the aldermen and of the capital burgesses separately. *Quo Warranto* proceedings were then instituted and it was held that such elections were void. The corporation was thus dissolved. A new charter similar to that of 1614 was granted in 1827 reconstituting the corporation and nominating the members, the high steward, and the recorder.[9]

A body of improvement commissioners was established by an Act of 1830 to pave, light, watch, clean, and maintain the streets of the borough.[10] The commissioners were the mayor, aldermen, capital burgesses, and everyone owning or occupying property in the borough worth at least £25 a year. The main street from the Green Bridge to the junction of the Stone and Sandon roads in Foregate Street remained the responsibility of the corporation along with most of the streets leading off it in the town centre.

The municipal corporations commissioners in the earlier 1830s found that the closed system of government was causing much discontent.[11] Favouritism was rife and family connexion was influential

[83] *Cal. S.P. Dom.* 1682, 456, 473.
[84] S.R.O., D.1323/A/1/1, pp. 302–3.
[85] *Cal. S.P. Dom.* 1684–5, 229.
[86] Ibid. 1685, 192.
[87] Bradley, *Charters*, 224; W.S.L., S.MS. 369, *sub* 1686, 1687; Hist. MSS. Com. 75, *Downshire*, i, 269; *Cal. S.P. Dom.* 1687–9, 107.
[88] S.R.O., D.1323/A/1/1, pp. 349–50, 354 with printed copies of the order inserted; *Cal. S.P. Dom.* 1687–9, 261, 266, 312.
[89] S.R.O., D.1323/A/1/1, pp. 23, 43.
[90] S.R.O., D.1323/G/1.
[91] *1st Rep. Com. Mun. Corp.* App. III, 2027; D. Hay, 'Crime, Authority and the Criminal Law: Staffordshire 1750–1802' (Warwick Univ. Ph.D. thesis, 1975), 601.
[92] *1st Rep. Com. Mun. Corp.* App. III, 2027.
[93] S.R.O., D.(W.) 1721/1/4, ff. 164, 169; W.S.L. 7/96/00; S.R.O., D.1323/G/1 and 2.
[94] S.R.O., D.1323/G/2; *1st Rep. Com. Mun. Corp.* App. III, 2027.
[95] *1st Rep. Com. Mun. Corp.* App. III, 2027.
[96] *T.O.S.S.* 1939, 17–20.
[97] See p. 212.
[98] S.R.O., D.1323/A/1/1, p. 29.
[99] Ibid. p. 40.   [1] Ibid. p. 193; above, p. 209.
[2] S.R.O., D.1323/A/1/2, p. 5.
[3] Ibid. p. 74.   [4] Ibid. pp. 136 sqq.
[5] Ibid. /3, pp. 69, 151, 159, 169.
[6] Ibid. p. 176; above, p. 202.
[7] S.R.O., D.1323/A/1/3, pp. 189–90, 240.
[8] Bradley, *Charters*, 179.
[9] Ibid. 180–201, where the date is wrongly given as 1828; *1st Rep. Com. Mun. Corp.* App. III, 2026; White, *Dir. Staffs.* (1834), 138.
[10] 11 Geo. IV, c. 44 (Local and Personal).
[11] *1st Rep. Com. Mun. Corp.* App. III, 2027–8, 2030.

in a body many of whose members were related by blood or marriage. The corporation was still in financial difficulties. It had had to pay the costs of the *Quo Warranto* proceedings, and those, with the expense of the new charter, had left it heavily in debt. To meet part of the debt the corporation had raised a mortgage and imposed entry fines on new tenants of corporation property. The interest on the mortgage accounted for nearly half of the expenditure in 1832–3, while the entry fines meant that only low rents could be charged. Even so, much of the debt remained, and the corporation raised a further mortgage in 1835, the last year of its existence in its old form.[12]

In 1835, under the Municipal Corporations Act of that year, a new corporation was created consisting of a mayor, six aldermen, and eighteen councillors elected by the burgesses at large. The bounds of the municipal borough were extended to become those of the parliamentary borough and thus included Forebridge. The new borough was divided into two wards, East and West, each with nine councillors.[13] The corporation did not petition for a court of quarter sessions as was necessary under the 1835 Act, and the court met for the last time in January 1836.[14] The offices of recorder and coroner lapsed with it. A court leet was still held before the deputy steward in 1842.[15] A county court for Stafford and the neighbouring district was established in 1847.[16] The borough council became a board of health in 1872, and in 1874 it petitioned for the abolition of the improvement commissioners.[17] In 1875 the commissioners' powers were transferred to the council, which acted as an urban sanitary authority until it became an urban district council under the Local Government Act, 1894.[18]

The new corporation, having inherited the debt of its predecessor, began selling parts of its property in 1839.[19] New mortgages were raised in 1843 and 1844.[20] About 1850 the mace and insignia were seized for debt.[21] A memorial from the corporation to the Treasury in 1851 proposing a further sale of property provoked a counter-memorial from 850 burgesses demanding that an inquiry should first be held into the borough's finances. It was held in 1852, and in 1853 the Treasury gave permission for a new mortgage.[22] From that year a general borough rate was levied.[23] Financial problems, however, remained. When the improvement commissioners' powers were transferred to the corporation in 1875, so was their debt.[24]

With the extension of the borough in 1876 the number of councillors was raised to twenty-four

and the number of aldermen to eight.[25] In 1924, after the extension of 1917, two new wards were created, North and South, but there was no increase in the number of councillors, each of the four wards having six.[26] A fifth ward, Baswich, was created with the extension of 1934 and the size of the council was increased by three councillors and one alderman. In 1960 the five wards were reorganized into nine, each with three councillors.[27] Under the Representation of the People Act, 1948, the date of the borough elections and mayor-making was changed to May in 1949.[28] In 1974, under the Local Government Act of 1972, a new Stafford district came into being; it comprised what had been the borough, the urban district of Stone, and the rural districts of Stafford and Stone. It was granted the title of Stafford borough by royal charter.[29]

The offices of town clerk and borough treasurer became full-time in 1906.[30] The separate offices of mayor's serjeant and burgesses' serjeant were united in 1919.[31] A meeting on St. Thomas's day (21 December) for the election of chamberlains, schoolwardens, and a churchwarden of St. Mary's was customary by the later 17th century; eventually the only business was the appointment of the churchwarden, and in 1962 the meeting was discontinued.[32]

Working-class burgesses played an influential part in the elections to the new council in 1835, being determined to elect only councillors who would support their candidate for the office of town clerk. A 'working men's committee' ran candidates at the 1854 election with some success, and a group of working-class burgesses accompanied the mayor and councillors to the mayoral service at St. Mary's. At the 1864 election a Local Affairs Association, opposing the adoption of the 1858 Local Government Act, sponsored candidates who won all six seats and ousted the retiring mayor from one of them.[33] Party politics were introduced into council elections in 1919 when six Independent and three Labour candidates were elected. There was a Labour mayor for the first time in 1925–6. Except, however, for a year of Labour control in 1935–6 the Independents remained the dominant party until 1946 when Labour gained control of the council. From 1947 the Independents and Conservatives together balanced Labour, and from 1949 until 1954 the Independents again had a majority. Labour was then in control until 1959 when there was once more a balance. The Independents had a majority from 1960 until 1963 when Labour took control. The Independents were in control from 1965 until 1972 when Labour became the dominant party for the

[12] S.R.O., D.1323/A/1/5, pp. 142–3.
[13] 5 & 6 Wm. IV, c. 76; *Lond. Gaz.* 8 Dec. 1835, pp. 2398–9; S.R.O., D.1323/A/1/5, p. 157.
[14] S.R.O., D.1323/G/3.
[15] S.R.O., D.1323/A/1/5, p. 298; *Staffs. Advertiser,* 26 Feb. 1842.
[16] *Lond. Gaz.* 10 Mar. 1847, p. 1012.
[17] Ibid. 26 Apr. 1872, p. 2064; S.R.O., D.1323/A/1/9, 9 Mar. 1874.
[18] Local Govt. Bd.'s Provisional Orders Conf. (Abingdon, Barnsley, etc.) Act, 1875, 38 & 39 Vic. c. 211 (Local); S.R.O., D.1323/A/1/9, 9 Nov. 1875; *Kelly's Dir. Staffs.* (1896).
[19] S.R.O., D.1323/A/1/5, pp. 302–8, 355, 357–60, 372, 406, 414; /6, p. 148.
[20] Ibid. /6, pp. 86–8, 118, 148–52, 172.
[21] W.S.L., D.1798/435, Steele to Shallcross, 28 May 1851; *Stafford Boro. Extension Bill: Mins. of Evidence,*

1876 (reprinted from the official rep.), 47 (copy in W.S.L. Pamphs. *sub* Stafford).
[22] S.R.O., D.1323/A/1/7, ff. 71, 76v.–80, 91–2, 94–95v.
[23] Ibid. pp. 105–13.
[24] *Stafford Boro. Extension Bill: Mins. of Evid.* 46–7.
[25] *Kelly's Dir. Staffs.* (1880).
[26] *Corp. of Stafford: Yr. Bk.* (1924–25).
[27] Ibid. (1960–1).
[28] 11 & 12 Geo. VI, c. 65; *Stafford Newsletter,* 13 Nov. 1948.
[29] *Stafford Boro. Official Guide* (1976), 21, 23; charter of 15 May 23 Eliz. II (on show in the Guildhall, 1976).
[30] *Corp. Yr. Bk.* (1906–7), 42.
[31] Ibid. (1921–22).
[32] S.R.O., D.1323/A/1/1; *Stafford Newsletter,* 15 Dec. 1962, p. 11; below, p. 230.
[33] *Staffs. Advertiser,* 26 Dec. 1835, 2 Jan. 1836, 4 and 18 Nov. 1854, 29 Oct., 5 Nov. 1864.

rest of the old borough's existence. The new borough of 1974 had a large majority of Independents and Conservatives.[34]

By the 17th century and presumably earlier there were three ways of achieving burgess status: by birth (being born in the borough the son of a burgess); by servitude (serving an apprenticeship in the borough and paying a fee); and by purchase (mentioned in 1566). Admission was by the council.[35] Burgess-silver of 1 mark (13s. 4d.) was paid in 1411–12, but no further details are given.[36] The widow of a burgess, Sir Thomas Littleton, was admitted a burgess in 1501.[37] By the late 17th century any burgess who moved away from the town lost his privileges.[38] Any who received poor-relief were disfranchised: during the 1826 parliamentary election it was noted that 'upwards of 100 bare-breeched burgesses appeared in rags to poll, who had been notoriously abstaining from parish relief to exercise their independent franchise'. It was a time of much unemployment among shoemakers, and the bribes offered at the election were high.[39] The Municipal Corporations Act, 1835, banned the purchase of burgess status.[40] It eventually became the practice for the mayor to admit new burgesses at a meeting of the borough court.[41] In 1974 admission was still by birth or apprenticeship, with the mayor holding a special court when one was required; the term of apprenticeship necessary was reduced in 1964 from seven to five years.[42]

It was usual by the later 17th century to create honorary burgesses. On occasion the practice was used by the mayor for political ends, as in 1682 and apparently at the parliamentary election of 1690.[43] It was presumably to prevent such manœuvres that in 1699 the council passed an ordinance insisting on the ancient custom whereby no new burgess was sworn by the mayor unless first elected by the council.[44] The practice of creating honorary burgesses was challenged in the mid 1820s and held to be invalid by the Court of King's Bench. The corporation, although insisting on its right, ceased to use it for a time.[45] It was later revived, and honorary freemen were still created in the 1970s.[46]

A moot hall was mentioned in 1468 as town property in the tenure of Humphrey Whitgreave,[47] while in 1482 a guildhall was described as the customary meeting-place of the borough courts.[48]

Both a hall and a council house were leased by the corporation with the borough gaol to John Malpas in 1537–8.[49] A new council chamber was fitted up in 1605 in the chancel of the former St. Bertelin's chapel.[50] An office for the mayor was built under the shire hall in 1617. Its immediate purpose was as a place where the king during his forthcoming visit to Stafford could refresh himself and see the town records; the mayor was thus saved the expense of entertaining the king in his house. The structure had the further advantage of strengthening the hall and making 'the walks under the hall more delightful and warmer'.[51] In 1736 the town clerk was given permission to use the office for the transaction of corporation business.[52] By 1744 the various borough courts were evidently held in the shire hall, and rooms were provided for the borough in the new shire hall of the later 1790s in return for its contribution towards the cost.[53] The improvement commissioners too met there.[54]

By 1853 the borough's rooms were required by the county, and in 1853–4 a guildhall designed by Charles Trubshaw was built at the county's expense on the site of the Star inn on the west side of Market Square.[55] A new council chamber was built in 1899–1900.[56] A new guildhall, with an arcade of shops beneath it giving access to the market hall, was built on the same site in 1934–5 to the design of William Plant, the borough surveyor.[57]

The borough hall in Eastgate Street was built in 1875–7, part of the cost being met by H. D. Pochin, M.P. for the borough from 1868 until unseated on petition in 1869. Designed by Henry Ward, the borough surveyor, in a Decorated style it is of brick and stone and has an assembly hall on the first floor.[58] It was extended in 1914.[59] It housed the offices of the town clerk and the borough treasurer from 1906 when the two appointments became full-time.[60]

The charter of 1315 authorized the borough to build and maintain a prison of its own.[61] The prison was built, and it was delivered at intervals between 1328 and 1359.[62] Nothing more is known until in 1537–8 a prison, called 'Peacock's hall', in the North Gate was leased to John Malpas, perhaps the gaoler.[63] It may be that the borough gaol was in the North Gate as early as 1390 when county prisoners were being housed in the gates.[64] In the later 16th century the borough was still using the gates for prisoners,[65] and it was the North Gate which the town put at the disposal of the

[34] Ibid. 8 Nov. 1919, 3 May 1930, 9 Nov. 1935; *Stafford Newsletter*, 9 Nov. 1946, 8 Nov. 1947, 14 May 1949, 29 May 1954, 9 May 1959, 14 May 1960, 10 May 1963, 14 May 1965, 5 May 1972, 8 June 1973.
[35] W.S.L., H.M. uncat. 29, envelope labelled 'Borough Parliamentary Election of 1690'; *T.S.H.C.S.* 1965–7, 25; S.R.O., D.1323/A/1/1, *passim*; /2, p. 207; D.1323/E/1, ff. 52, 63v.
[36] *T.O.S.S.* 1939, 20.
[37] S.R.O., D.(W.) 1721/1/1, f. 139v.
[38] W.S.L., H.M. uncat. 29, 'Boro. Election 1690'.
[39] *S.H.C.* 1933 (1), 61.
[40] 5 & 6 Wm. IV, c. 76, s. 3.
[41] S.R.O., D.1323/A/1/5, pp. 263–4, 314–15, 365–6; *Staffs. Advertiser*, 7 July 1900.
[42] H. Ward, *Freemen in Eng.* 1975, 77–8.
[43] See pp. 224–5, 238. [44] S.R.O., D.1323/A/1/2, p. 229.
[45] *1st Rep. Com. Mun. Corp.* App. III, 2026; *S.H.C.* 1933 (1), 59–60; White, *Dir. Staffs.* (1834), 138.
[46] Ex. inf. the chief executive (1976).
[47] B.L., Hargrave MS. 288, f. 44.
[48] See p. 223.   [49] W.S.L. 7/2/00, p. 7.
[50] See p. 243.
[51] S.R.O., D.(W.) 1721/1/4, ff. 114–118v., 128v.–130v., 132; S.R.O., D.1323/E/1, f. 89.
[52] S.R.O., D.1323/A/1/2, p. 405.
[53] S.R.O., D.1323/G/1 (calling it the guildhall); Act for building a new shire hall for the county of Stafford, 34 Geo. III, c. 97.
[54] S.R.O., D.1323/J/1.
[55] Stafford Shire Hall Act, 1853, 16 & 17 Vic. c. 72 (Local and Personal); *Staffs. Advertiser*, 3 Sept. 1853, 4 and 11 Mar. 1854.
[56] *Corp. of Stafford Yr. Bk.* (1907–8), 44.
[57] *Staffs. Advertiser*, 5 May 1934, 27 July 1935.
[58] Ibid. 5 June 1875, 16 June 1877; plate facing p. 161 above.
[59] *Corp. Yr. Bk.* (1914–15).
[60] *Kelly's Dir. Staffs.* (1908); *Corp. Yr. Bk.* (1906–7), 2.
[61] Bradley, *Charters*, 37–8, 126.
[62] J.I. 1/1457; J.I. 3/122; J.I. 3/127; J.I. 3/131; J.I. 3/214/3.
[63] W.S.L. 7/2/00, p. 7.
[64] See p. 203.   [65] *T.S.H.C.S.* 1965–7, 19, 29.

county for the purposes of a prison in the early 17th century.[66] The prison, which in 1610 possessed a gaol hall,[67] was of two storeys.[68] Some part of the lower one was referred to between 1566 and 1644 as the 'bear hole'[69] and was remembered under that name in 1695,[70] after it had disappeared. It was in a lower room too, called Penkridge in 1620, that the county prisoners were confined before the rebuilding of the county gaol.[71] Between 1631 and 1644 the whole building was often called the town castle.[72] After the Rebellion the gaol seems to have been abandoned. From 1620 until at least 1641 the prisoners benefited from Margaret Temple's bequest to them and the poor in general.[73]

When it acquired its own quarter sessions in 1614 the borough became entitled to a house of correction. In 1621 it took over for that purpose the part of the North Gate that the county had occupied as a gaol.[74] The house of correction, like the borough gaol, probably fell into disuse after the Rebellion. In 1654 it was said to be much 'defaced' and the government allotted money for its repair to set the numerous poor of Stafford to work.[75] In fact nothing appears to have been done.[76] The council ordered a lock-up for 'drunken, idle, and disorderly persons' to be built on to the shire hall in 1682,[77] and it may have partly served the purpose of a borough house of correction. In 1687 the corporation decided to lease to the county 'the land that the old Gaol Gate now stands upon where the late old house of correction was'.[78]

There are instances during the Middle Ages of sanctuary sought by criminals in St. Mary's and in St. Chad's.[79] In 1542 Stafford was made a sanctuary town in place of Manchester, and the borough authorities assigned certain places of sanctuary, including buildings in Tipping Street on the south side of St. Chad's churchyard.[80] A royal mandate to the sheriff followed in the same year stating that ambiguity had arisen so that it was being claimed that the gaol was within the sanctuary; the mandate stressed that it had never been intended to include the gaol and also that prisoners being taken to and from the gaol through any part of the town were not to enjoy sanctuary rights.[81]

By 1546 there was a gibbet on the borough boundary at Sandyford bridge on the Sandon road.[82] The last execution there was in 1793, after which hangings took place at the county gaol.[83] The field-names Gallows Flat and Gallows Leasow north of the Lichfield road at Queensville in the earlier 19th century suggest the site of a gallows, presumably belonging to Forebridge manor.[84]

In 1498 there were stocks in the main street of the town and in a lane by St. Chad's churchyard.[85] There were stocks in the market-place in 1566,[86] and c. 1680 they stood in front of the shire hall.[87] In 1854 the council ordered the stocks to be placed on a movable frame so that they could be shifted into and out of the market-place.[88] In 1835 there were also stocks at the fork of the Lichfield and Wolverhampton roads by the Green in Forebridge.[89] In 1933 a pair of stocks was found in the basement of the borough hall and transferred to the borough museum,[90] where it was on view in 1976.

There was apparently a pillory in the market-place by 1575.[91] In 1612 the corporation paid for the repair of a pillory and a cage as well as of the stocks.[92] In the earlier 19th century a pillory was erected as needed on the north side of Market Square; it was described as 'a kind of box or case, only showing the face of the criminal, and twice the height of the street lamp-posts'.[93] In 1610 the authorities spent money on setting up a whipping-post,[94] which c. 1680 stood behind the stocks in front of the shire hall.[95] In the early 19th century men were whipped at the cart's tail and also at the palisades in front of the hall.[96] A cucking-stool is mentioned in the earlier 17th century.[97] In 1838 a scold's bridle bearing the words 'garrula lingua nocet' was placed on a woman by order of the mayor; it had been found among lumber in the parish workhouse. Later the same year it was repaired and put in a conspicuous place in the mayor's office. It was eventually placed in the borough museum, where it remained in 1976.[98]

A borough pinfold is mentioned in 1498.[99] About 1600 it stood outside the North Gate[1] and was described as of stone in 1662.[2] By the earlier 1830s it had been moved to the junction of Gaol Road and Crooked Bridge Road,[3] where it remained until c.

[66] S.R.O., D.(W.) 1721/1/4, f. 28v.; D.1323/E/1, f. 111v.
[67] S.R.O., D.1323/E/1, f. 52v. [68] Ibid. f. 102.
[69] T.S.H.C.S. 1965–7, 16; S.R.O., D.1323/E/1, f. 273.
[70] W.S.L., H.M. uncat. 35 (Norbury), Ferreday v. Parton, 1695.
[71] Sta. Cha. 8/45/13; S.R.O., D.1323/E/1, f. 102.
[72] S.R.O., D.1323/E/1, ff. 188v., 274.
[73] See p. 271.
[74] S.R.O., D.1323/E/1, ff. 111, 140v.; S.R.O., D.(W.) 1721/1/4, f. 153v.
[75] Cal. S.P. Dom. 1653–4, 407.
[76] The only known ref. at a later date which could indicate that a borough house of correction was in use is an isolated one of 1672 to 'the town castle or house of correction' (W.S.L. 7/2/00, sheet headed 'The Prisons, Stafford'), but it is inconclusive.
[77] S.R.O., D.1323/A/1/1, p. 295. A similar order was made in 1788: D.1323/A/1/3, p. 13. For the Forebridge lock-up see V.C.H. Staffs. v. 83; S.R.O., D.1323/A/1/10, pp. 12, 20.
[78] S.R.O., D.1323/A/1/1, p. 335.
[79] S.H.C. iv (1), 73; xvii. 27; Cherry, Stafford, 1.
[80] L. & P. Hen. VIII, xvii, pp. 207–8; R. W. Heinze, Proclamations of the Tudor Kings, 8; Bradley, Charters, 71; W.S.L., S.MS. 369, p. 114; B.L., Hargrave MS. 288, ff. 50v.–51. The transference was initially to Chester, which successfully resisted.
[81] Bradley, Charters, 71–4, where the date of the mandate is wrongly translated.
[82] S.R,O., D.1323/E/1, f. 28v.

[83] Cherry, Stafford, 80.
[84] W.S.L., S.MS. 471, Castle Church, nos. 1063, 1077, 1079–80. For the gallows of the dean and chapter of St. Mary's see above, p. 205.
[85] S.R.O., D.641/1/2/85, rot. 1.
[86] T.O.S.S. 1965–7, 26.
[87] See plate facing p. 161 above.
[88] S.R.O., D.1323/A/1/7, p. 218.
[89] Wood, Plan of Stafford (1835).
[90] Staffs. Advertiser, 29 July 1933; Stafford Public Libr.: Quarterly Bulletin (Autumn, 1933). For stocks at the police barracks in Austin Friars in 1925 see W.S.L., Stafford Photographs, Misc., pp. 173–4.
[91] Acts of P.C. 1571–5, 373.
[92] S.R.O., D.1323/E/1, f. 70v.
[93] Cherry, Stafford, 17, 79; W.S.L. 7/2/00, p. 15A; Staffs. Advertiser, 7 Aug. 1802.
[94] S.R.O., D.1323/E/1, f. 52v.
[95] See plate facing p. 161 above.
[96] Cherry, Stafford, 17.
[97] e.g. S.R.O., D.1323/E/1, ff. 109v., 172v.
[98] Cherry, Stafford, 79; Staffs. Advertiser, 1 Dec. 1838, 12 Oct. 1878; S.R.O., D.1323/A/1/8, 6 Jan. 1864.
[99] S.R.O., D.641/1/2/85, rot. 1.
[1] W.S.L., copy of lost plan of Stafford; Speed, Map of Staffs. (1610).
[2] S.R.O., D.1323/E/1, f. 300v.
[3] S.R.O., D.1323/A/1/5, p. 72; Wood, Plan of Stafford (1835).

1880.[4] In 1737 the leet appointed an official described as the field-tender and pinner.[5] By 1837 the council appointed a pinner for Coton field,[6] and it continued to appoint a borough pinner until the mid 1920s.[7]

In the later 16th century the town porters were responsible for impounding stray pigs, apparently using a tower on the southern part of the walls as a pound.[8] It had ceased to be so used by 1607,[9] but a pig pound was mentioned in 1635.[10] In 1695 the corporation ordered the erection of a pinfold for swine on a site adjoining St. Mary's churchyard,[11] but in 1766 John Byrd was given permission to take it down.[12]

By 1540 there was a pinfold on the Green in Forebridge.[13] There was still a Forebridge pinfold in 1876.[14]

The common seal in use in the 13th century was circular, 2 in. in diameter, and depicted a three-towered castle with two lions on either side and a fish below. Legend, Lombardic: SIGILLUM COMMUNITATIS VILLE STAFFORDIE. It was still used in 1462.[15] The seal recorded at the heraldic visitations of 1583 and 1614 was similar, but there was a fifth lion instead of the fish and there were differences in the architectural and ornamental detail.[16] Legend, Roman: SIGILLUM COMMUNE VILLE DE STAFFORD. It may date from the time of the charter of 1550, which granted the burgesses a common seal.[17] The earlier seal was in use again by 1764,[18] but in 1826 it was replaced by a new seal based on it and of the same size but differing in the details of the device.[19] Legend, Roman: SIGILLUM COMMUNITATIS VILLAE STAFFORDIAE 1826. A wafer version, 1½ in. in diameter, was in use in 1976.[20]

The impression of another common seal survives, apparently made for Elias Ashmole in the 17th century. It was circular, 1⅛ in. in diameter, with cinquefoil decoration.[21] Legend, Roman: SIGILLUM BURGI STAFFORDIE.

The bailiffs had their own seal by 1464. It was circular, 1⅛ in. in diameter, and depicted a lion.[22] Legend, Lombardic: SIGILLUM OFFICII BALLIVORUM STAFFORDIE. The mayor used it in 1615,[23] but by 1692 he apparently had his own seal: among the items which the outgoing mayor handed to his successor in that year was 'a silver seal of office with a brass seal'.[24] A mayor's seal, which still existed in 1976 but was no longer used, was 1½ in. in diameter and depicted the borough arms.[25] Legend, Sans Serif: BOROUGH OF STAFFORD MAYOR'S SEAL.

When Elizabeth I visited Stafford in 1575 the bailiffs delivered their maces to her and received them back.[26] Those may well have been the two small maces carried by the serjeants which existed in 1623 and 1692[27] and the two small silver maces owned by the corporation in 1976. Each bears a silver disc, the inscriptions on which include respectively the initials CR (probably those of Charles II) and the initials of William and Mary, but the maces themselves are older.[28] A great mace was bought in 1614, and part of the present great mace is of that date. The bowl apparently dates from one of the mayoralties of Thomas Backhouse, 1644–5 and 1654–5, and further remodelling was carried out at the Restoration.[29]

The mayor's chain and badge were bought by subscription in 1870 in recognition of the efforts of Ephraim Austin, mayor 1869–70, to secure a meeting of the Royal Agricultural Society at Stafford. It was enlarged by public subscription in 1883.[30] The mayoress's chain and badge were presented in 1901 by the mayor, W. C. T. Mynors, and his wife.[31]

The items handed over by the retiring mayor in 1623 included a silver badge worn by the beadle.[32] It was described in 1692 as 'the town arms in silver which the bellman wears'.[33]

Plate bought by subscription because the borough had none was presented in 1930.[34]

The borough arms in use in 1583 were those of the

THE BOROUGH OF STAFFORD.
Gules a square castle with four domed towers in perspective argent, a gold pennon on each tower, in chief two Stafford knots and in base a lion of England all or

Stafford family (or, a chevron gules) differenced by charging the chevron with a Stafford Knot, the primary badge of the family. Although those arms

[4] S.R.O., D.1323/A/1/9, 6 Apr. 1875. It had gone by 1880: O.S. Map 1/500, Staffs. XXXVII. 11.7 (1881 edn.).
[5] W.S.L. 7/96/00.   [6] S.R.O., D.1323/A/1/5, p. 262.
[7] *Corp. Yr. Bk.* (1925–26), 7.
[8] *T.O.S.S.* 1965–7, 13, 31; W.S.L. 7/1/00.
[9] W.S.L. 7/1/00.   [10] S.R.O., D.1323/E/1, f. 221A.
[11] S.R.O., D.1323/A/1/2, p. 44.
[12] S.R.O., D.(W.) 0/8/1, p. 231.
[13] *V.C.H. Staffs.* v. 83, where, however, the date is inadequately given.
[14] S.R.O., D.1323/A/10, pp. 12, 20.
[15] W. de G. Birch, *Cat. of Seals in Brit. Museum*, ii. 193; S.R.O., D.593/A/2/27/11; *S.H.C.* 1913, 301 and plate facing p. 300; Cherry, *Stafford*, plate facing p. 57.
[16] W.S.L., S.MS. 16, f. 34v.; S.MS. 371(i), p. 11; Cherry, *Stafford*, 149 and plate facing p. 57.
[17] Bradley, *Charters*, 89. The charter of 1605 also granted a common seal: ibid. 112.
[18] S.R.O., D.590/34.
[19] Birch, *Cat. of Seals in Brit. Museum*, ii. 193; Cherry, *Stafford*, plate facing p. 57, wrongly giving 'villae' as

[20] Ex inf. the chief executive (1976).
[21] Bodl. MS. Ashmole 1138, f. 116.
[22] S.R.O., D.1287/6/2, deed of 20 Aug. 1464. There is an impression without an accompanying document in W.S.L., H.M. uncat. 23.
[23] S.R.O., D.1287/10/2, Matt. Cradock's Bk., p. 204.
[24] W.S.L., H.M. uncat. 45, deed of 14 Nov. 1692.
[25] Ex inf. the chief executive.
[26] S.R.O., D.1323/E/1, f. 36.
[27] S.R.O., D.(W.) 1721/1/4, f. 152; W.S.L., H.M. uncat. 45, deed of 14 Nov. 1692.
[28] P. H. Robinson, *The Stafford Maces* (Stafford, 1973), I, 13–15 (copy in W.S.L. Pamphs. *sub* Stafford).
[29] Ibid. 1–12.
[30] S.R.O., D.1323/A/1/9, 5 May, 1 Oct. 1870; inscription on the reverse of the badge.
[31] Inscription on the reverse of the badge.
[32] S.R.O., D.(W.) 1721/1/4, f. 152.
[33] W.S.L., H.M. uncat. 45, deed of 14 Nov. 1692.
[34] *Staffs. Advertiser*, 8 Nov. 1930.

'villiae'.

appeared on the mace of 1614, the arms recorded at the heraldic visitation of that year were those that remained in use until 1974. The shield on the mayor's badge, however, is derived from the seal of 1826.[35]

A badge was granted in 1962 depicting a domed tower argent ensigned with a staff flying a pennon or with a circlet of Stafford Knots conjoined gold. It remained in use until 1974.[36]

A partial list of reeves and bailiffs and a list of mayors to 1896 is printed by J. W. Bradley in *The Royal Charters and Letters Patent granted to the Burgesses of Stafford A.D. 1206–1828* (Stafford, 1897), pages 202–8. There is a list of mayors from 1836 to 1974 in the corporation's *Year Book* for 1973–4. Some additional names of reeves and bailiffs are supplied by Miss L. Margaret Midgley in the *Transactions of the Stafford Historical and Civic Society*, 1974–6, pages 11–12.

THE PARISHES. From at least 1728 there was a joint vestry for the parishes of St. Mary and of St. Chad, meeting normally at St. Mary's but sometimes in the shire hall.[37] A vestry clerk is mentioned in 1738.[38] A select vestry existed by 1828; it was not appointed after 1837, its duties having passed to the Stafford poor-law union formed in 1836.[39]

There was mention in 1340 of the keepers of the fabric of St. Mary's church[40] and in 1466 of the wardens or holy-water clerks (*gardiani vel aquebaiuli*) there.[41] The two churchwardens of St. Mary's were presenting their accounts to the bailiffs and council by the 1520s,[42] and by the 17th century they were appointed by the corporation.[43] In the 1690s the rector secured the appointment of one of the wardens,[44] and the system of dual appointment remained in force in 1976. The churchwardens were still accounting to the corporation in the 18th century.[45] In 1825 the council discontinued a payment to the chamberlain for keeping the accounts of the wardens, who in future were to keep the accounts themselves.[46]

There was a 'clerk of the church' by 1566.[47] When a new clerk was appointed by the corporation in 1705, the rector appointed a second clerk with the corporation's approval.[48] A sexton was mentioned in 1701 and was apparently identical with the clerk;[49] he was still appointed by the corporation in the early 19th century.[50] In 1670 the corporation appointed four sidesmen;[51] the office existed by 1628–9 when

the mayor paid for dinners for sidesmen as well as churchwardens.[52]

The two churchwardens of St. Chad's are mentioned from 1553.[53]

RELIEF OF THE POOR. The administration of poor-relief was in the hands of the borough until the later 1720s. A borough ordinance of 1566 gave the bailiffs the responsibility of collecting and distributing the compulsory charity payments to the poor ordered by the Act of 1563.[54] By the later 17th century the council was appointing the overseers of the poor, usually four in number.[55] In 1677 the retiring overseers were ordered to account in future to the mayor and churchwardens,[56] but in 1684 the council instructed the churchwardens and overseers to see to the details of relief so that the mayor should no longer be troubled with them.[57] A salaried overseer was appointed in 1700,[58] and the chamberlain acted as overseer at least from 1712.[59]

Responsibility for poor-relief passed to the joint vestry of St. Mary's and St. Chad's parishes in 1727 or 1728.[60] There were four overseers, but at least between 1735 and 1740 there were two at a time serving six months.[61] In 1767 the vestry appointed a salaried standing overseer, who was succeeded by his son in 1772; in 1780 a new standing overseer was appointed for twelve months.[62] The vestry clerk acted as assistant overseer by 1829.[63] In 1836 the borough became part of the Stafford poor-law union.[64]

The cost of relief was met out of borough funds until *c.* 1730. Some of the fines imposed by borough ordinances in 1566 were assigned to 'the poor-man's box'.[65] In 1643 half the fines paid for defaults in the watch were assigned to the poor,[66] while in 1683 and 1718 the fines to be paid by councillors for not wearing gowns were similarly assigned.[67] Around the turn of the century various orders were made assigning part of the income from Coton field to the poor.[68] The salaried overseer of 1700 was paid out of borough funds.[69] By the early 18th century the profits from the malt mill were assigned to the poor. With the spread of 'steel or hand mills', however, profits dropped and a poor-rate became necessary. In addition the poor were becoming more numerous. A rate was imposed when the vestry took charge of relief.[70]

The vestry adopted a stringent attitude to relief.

[35] F. J. Cope, 'The Arms of the Borough of Stafford', *T.O.S.S.* 1934, 47–8; W.S.L., S.MS. 16, f. 34v.
[36] Grant in possession of the chief executive; ex inf. the chief executive.
[37] W.S.L., H.M. 29/9; S.R.O., D.(W.) o/8/18.
[38] S.R.O., D.(W.) o/8/18, reverse pages, p. 22.
[39] *Staffs. Advertiser*, 1 Nov. 1828, 1 Apr. 1837.
[40] S.R.O. 938/343.
[41] W.S.L., H.M. uncat. 26, feoffees to Ralph Lawnder 12 Jan. 1466.
[42] W.S.L., S.MS. 366 (iA).
[43] B.L., Hargrave MS. 288, f. 18; L.J.R.O., B/V/1/55, p. 45; S.R.O., D.1323/A/1/1.
[44] S.R.O., D.1323/A/1/2, pp. 40, 44, 51.
[45] Ibid. pp. 251, 367; W.S.L., S.MS. 365.
[46] S.R.O., D.1323/A/1/4, p. 111.
[47] *T.O.S.S.* 1965–7, 21.
[48] S.R.O., D.1323/A/1/2, p. 113.
[49] Ibid. pp. 48, 95; W.S.L., S.MS. 402, f. 34.
[50] S.R.O., D.(W.) o/8/1, p. 324; S.R.O., D.1323/A/1/3, pp. 379–80.
[51] S.R.O., D.1323/A/1/1, p. 214.
[52] Ibid. /E/1, f. 164–164v.   [53] *S.H.C.* 1915, 239.
[54] *T.O.S.S.* 1965–7, p. 14; Act for the Relief of the Poor, 5 Eliz. I, c. 3.

[55] S.R.O., D.1323/A/1/1, pp. 214, 287, 296, 377.
[56] Ibid. p. 270.
[57] Ibid. p. 308.
[58] Ibid. /2, pp. 82–3.
[59] Ibid. pp. 174, 271.
[60] The last chamberlain described as overseer held office until Dec. 1727: ibid. pp. 300, 316. The vestry was in charge by May 1728: W.S.L., H.M. 29/9.
[61] W.S.L., H.M. 29/9; S.R.O., D.(W.) o/8/18, reverse pages; S.R.O., D.143/A/PO/1.
[62] S.R.O., D.1323/K/1, 4 Jan. 1767, 7 June 1772, 6 Feb. 1780.
[63] *Staffs. Advertiser*, 1 Nov. 1828, 3 Apr. 1830, 4 Apr. 1835.
[64] *3rd Ann. Rep. Poor Law Com.* H.C. 546, p. 164 (1837), xxxi.
[65] *T.O.S.S.* 1965–7, pp. 12, 26.
[66] *S.H.C.* 4th ser. i. 4. For money assigned for the relief of Stafford's poor out of the sale of material from Lichfield cathedral in 1651 see *V.C.H. Staffs.* iii. 174.
[67] S.R.O., D.1323/A/1/1, p. 297; /2, p. 190.
[68] See p. 209.
[69] S.R.O., D.1323/A/1/2, pp. 82–3.
[70] W.S.L. 77/45, ff. 7v., 19; W.S.L., H.M. 29/9; above, p. 212.

In 1728 it bought red cloth in order to badge those receiving relief.[71] In 1738, with the opening of a workhouse, a tighter control was placed on weekly pay, and in 1742 it was decided to stop it altogether outside the workhouse.[72] The rule was later relaxed, but in 1774 the vestry ordered the discontinuance of payments to poor living outside the town and the constant wearing of badges by those receiving pay.[73]

In 1735 a proposal was made at a vestry meeting for the use of a house in St. Mary's churchyard as a borough workhouse, and an assessment of the inhabitants of the borough was duly drawn up.[74] Nothing further was done until 1738 when it was agreed to use £100 given to the town by John, Viscount Chetwynd, in adapting the out-buildings of the former college house on the south side of the churchyard. The corporation granted the churchwardens and overseers a 99-year lease of the premises for the benefit of the poor at a nominal rent. It also gave them money from the sale of timber from the house, with a further £2 10s. to buy materials for employing the poor for a year. The workhouse was opened the same year. John Hill was appointed master at a salary of £15 for himself and his wife, but Samuel Whitley of Wolverhampton was also appointed to set the house in order and instruct Hill in its management for six months.[75] The workhouse consisted of six chambers, hall-place or work-room, kitchen, brew-house, pantry, cellar, store-room, wash-house, and garden.[76] A system of management was drawn up in 1742. A committee of three, one of them representing the corporation, was to be appointed monthly to inspect the house and present the accounts to the vestry. Admission to the house was to be by order of the vestry or one of the committee, and the master was to keep a record of admissions and departures; rules were laid down for the discipline of the house. The master was allowed 12 tons of coal from the pits at Hednesford in Cannock. Inmates who worked about the house or nursed the sick were allowed small remunerations, and those employed outside were allowed to keep half their wages. There was to be a school in the house for children over three; between the ages of five and nine they were to spin, knit, or do other work of use to the parish under the instruction of the master or mistress who was also to teach them reading for half an hour twice a day.[77] In 1743 the churchwardens and overseers took a lease of the malt mill and applied the profits to the workhouse.[78] The vestry farmed the poor in the workhouse to the mistress in 1774 at 2s. a week each.[79] An observer in 1806, who praised conditions at the gaol, found the workhouse ruinous, dirty, and 'really deplorable'. The seventeen poor there were farmed at 3s. 3d. a week each. There was no sick room, and when fever had broken out a few years before 22 out of 48 people died.[80]

In 1829 the vestry bought a site for a new workhouse on 'the road leading to the common field'.[81] The old house, however, was still in use in 1836 when it was taken over by the guardians of the Stafford union as tenants of the corporation.[82] A union workhouse was built in Marston Road in 1837–8 to the design of Thomas Trubshaw of Stafford,[83] and in 1839 the council sold the old building to Thomas Salt.[84]

The building used as the workhouse for Castle Church parish from about the end of the 18th century stood in Forebridge on the corner of Lichfield Road and White Lion Street. It seems to have continued in use until the building of the union workhouse. It was sold in 1839, and Gothic Cottage was built on the site between 1840 and 1842.[85]

In 1948 the former union-workhouse buildings became Fernleigh, consisting of an old people's home and a hospital for the chronic sick, maternity cases, and patients suffering from skin diseases. A new home, the Foxwalls, was opened on an adjoining site in 1971 and the Fernleigh home was demolished. The hospital was replaced by the new Kingsmead Hospital in Corporation Street in 1974, and the building was taken over as offices by the area health authority.[86]

PUBLIC SERVICES. In the 1390s the borough court took measures against the indiscriminate dumping of filth, and in 1397 it ordered the establishment of a public tip at Castle Hill.[87] In 1468 mention was made of a former tip outside the East Gate.[88] In the 16th century there was a tip on the river bank east of the South Gate, approached through gates in the walls, and there were others at the North and East Gates.[89] The cleaning of the market-place occurs as a public charge in 1412. It was the responsibility of the bellman in the later 16th century, but in 1704 the corporation ordered the serjeants to sweep the market-place and the area under the shire hall every Monday.[90] At least from the later 16th century it was an offence to allow pigs to wander in the streets, churchyard, and market-place, and in addition the corporation then banned the erection of pigsties near the streets and the churchyard.[91] A scavenger was appointed in 1753 to remove the muck from the streets.[92]

References to channels in Eastgate Street and

[71] W.S.L., H.M. 29/9, 18 May 1728; S.R.O., D.(W.) 0/8/18, reverse pages, p. 2.
[72] S.R.O., D.(W.) 0/8/18, 3 Sept. 1738, 31 Oct. 1742.
[73] S.R.O., D.1323/K/1, 6 Feb., 3 Apr. 1774, 5 Feb. 1775.
[74] S.R.O., D.(W.) 0/8/18, 7 Dec. 1735 and loose assessment 17 Dec. 1735.
[75] Ibid. 9 Mar., 6 Aug., 3 Sept., 3 Dec. 1738; S.R.O., D.834/11/1–2; S.R.O., D.1323/A/1/2, p. 451; above, p. 206.
[76] W.S.L., H.M. uncat. 28, schedule of 1748; Cherry, Stafford, 82.
[77] S.R.O., D.(W.) 0/8/18, 31 Oct. 1742, much of which is printed in Cherry, Stafford, 81–2.
[78] See p. 212.   [79] S.R.O., D.1323/K/1, 7 Aug. 1774.
[80] Cherry, Stafford, 83.
[81] Staffs. Advertiser, 1 Nov., 27 Dec. 1828, 21 Feb. 1829.
[82] S.R.O., D.1323/A/1/5, pp. 278, 295, 305–7; below, p. 239.
[83] R. J. Sherlock, 'Ind. Arch. in Administrative Staffs'. N.S.J.F.S. ii. 106–7; plate facing p. 225 above.

[84] S.R.O., D.1323/A/1/5, pp. 357, 359–60; S.R.O., D.834/11/3.
[85] W.S.L., D.1798/524.
[86] Ex inf. Staffs. County Council Social Services Dept. and Staffs. Area Health Authority (1976); Stafford Newsletter, 6 Oct. 1962.
[87] S.R.O., D.641/1/1/4A/13, rott. 1–2d.; F. B. Stitt, 'Stafford Borough Court Rolls, 1396–7', T.S.H.C.S. 1974–6, 33–4.
[88] B.L., Hargrave MS. 288, f. 45v.
[89] S.R.O., D.1323/E/1, f. 28v.; Ann J. Kettle, 'Black Book of Stafford', T.S.H.C.S. 1965–7, 11–12, 25; above, p. 199.
[90] J. B. Frith, 'Account of the bailiffs of borough of Stafford for 1411–12', T.O.S.S. 1939, 22; T.S.H.C.S. 1965–7, 16, 32; S.R.O., D.1323/A/1/2, p. 108.
[91] T.S.H.C.S. 1965–7, 7, 12–13, 29–31; S.R.O., D.1323/A/1/1, pp. 226, 268, 283, 290; above, p. 229.
[92] S.R.O., D.1323/G/1, 1 Oct. 1753.

Foregate in 1498[93] probably indicate a system of street drainage. By the later 16th century there was a channel running north along Gaolgate Street from the well in the market-place; another ran south from the well along Greengate Street and discharged into the Sow. Side channels ran into them. Householders were responsible for cleaning the section of channel in front of their houses as well as the corresponding part of the street. Those holding gardens along the town ditch had to scour their side of the ditch annually, while the town porters were responsible for the other side.[94] In 1711 the corporation appointed a man to see that the channels were cleaned.[95]

The maintenance of the streets was another concern of the borough authorities. They received grants of pavage in the later 13th and the 14th centuries;[96] otherwise paving was a charge on the town revenues.[97] By the later 16th century the chamberlains were responsible for it, with the bell-man organizing the work.[98] A paviour was employed by the early 18th century.[99] In 1498 the court imposed fines for leaving carts in various public places, and measures against such obstruction occur regularly thereafter.[1] In 1815 the council resolved that innkeepers in the main street should be requested to remove their signs and fix them to their walls.[2]

A report on sanitary conditions in Stafford in 1839 presents a picture of dirt and disease.[3] The situation of the town in a loop of the Sow with a ditch on the remaining side offered possibilities for good drainage but in fact meant that the town was surrounded by stagnant water, the result partly of the damming of the river at the mill. The state of the Sow was held to be one cause of disease in the built-up areas along the river in Tenterbanks, Broadeye, and Foregate. Conditions in working-class districts such as Broadeye and Backwalls were particularly bad. The houses were cheaply built, had only two small rooms, and were without drainage. Refuse was thrown in front of them and left there, including that from the houses in the main streets which backed on to them. Disease was further encouraged by the sedentary nature of work in the footwear industry and by the workers' habit of violently overworking for half the week after spending the rest in public houses. When stricken with fever the poor were reluctant to go into the infirmary.

The council appointed committees in the 1840s in an attempt to improve conditions.[4] The main road from the Green Bridge to the northern end of the

borough was macadamized in the mid 1840s.[5] In 1849 the borough was divided into seven districts, each under a group of visitors; the seven groups together formed a sanitary committee.[6] A Stafford branch of the Health of Towns Association was established in 1847; it received support from local doctors and other informed people, but there was opposition from those who were afraid of an increase in the rates and from the improvement commissioners.[7]

Lack of a proper drainage system remained a major problem. Lord Lichfield commented on it in 1864, observing that 'the smells in the streets were perfectly frightful'.[8] In that year the commissioners investigated the nuisance caused by the cess-pool for sewage from the gaol and the county asylum which had been formed by damming Sandyford brook. The contents were used to irrigate the meadows belonging to the asylum, to the discomfort of the inhabitants of Red Lion Street, Chapel Terrace, North and South Walls, and Eastgate Street.[9] In 1870 an assize judge declared Stafford 'the most stinking town I was ever in in my life', noting especially the sewage flowing down the open channels in the principal streets.[10] The state of the streets was made worse by their use for cattle markets and fairs.[11]

In 1874 the corporation, having become a board of health in 1872, appointed a medical officer of health.[12] He immediately set about improvements, in particular the replacement of 'the foul middens and reeking cess-pools' with the Rochdale tub system of privies. He was so successful that by 1875 the arrangements for emptying them were overstrained.[13] In 1876 the inhabitants of Sandon Road and the neighbouring area complained of the use of that road by the carts taking night-soil to be deposited in Coton field.[14] A sanitary depot was eventually built in Lammascote Road in 1879–80. A main drainage scheme was put into operation in 1880–1.[15] In 1897 a sewage works was opened on part of Lammascote farm. By then all the streets and about a third of the private property in the town had been sewered, and water-closets began to replace pail-closets.[16] The works was enlarged in the late 1920s and replaced in 1957 by a new works beside the Sow at Brancote Gorse in Tixall. A refuse destructor was installed at the depot when the Lammascote works was opened, and the steam from the burning refuse was used to drive the machinery which pumped the sewage from the depot to the works. The use of the destructor was later discontinued in

[93] S.R.O., D.641/1/2/85, rot. 1.
[94] W.S.L., copy of lost plan of Stafford; S.R.O., D.641/2/C/5/2D, f. [6] (2nd numbering); Roxburgh, *Stafford*, 48; *T.S.H.C.S.* 1965–7, 16, 31, 34.
[95] S.R.O., D.1323/A/1/2, p. 138.
[96] *Cal. Pat.* 1292–1301, 144; 1313–17, 283; 1354–8, 531.
[97] See e.g. *T.O.S.S.* 1939, 22.
[98] B.L., Hargrave MS. 288, f. 19; *T.S.H.C.S.* 27–8, 32.
[99] S.R.O., D.1323/A/1/2, pp. 94, 196, 340, 349, 380; S.R.O., D.(W.) 0/8/1, p. 34.
[1] S.R.O., D.641/1/2/85, rot. 1; *T.S.H.C.S.* 13, 30; S.R.O., D.1323/A/1/1, pp. 226, 251; S.R.O., D.(W.) 0/8/1, p. 442.
[2] S.R.O., D.1323/A/1/3, p. 431; 'Whitworth MSS. in Salt Libr.' *T.O.S.S.* 1931, 30.
[3] For this para. see E. Knight, *Rep. on Sanitary State of Stafford* (copy in W.S.L. Pamphs. *sub* Stafford), from *Reps. Sanitary Condition of Labouring Population of Eng. H.L. pp.* 225–6 (1842), xxvii; W. Fergus, *Vindication of Stafford*

Health of Towns Assoc. (Stafford, 1848), 10–14 (copy in W.S.L. Pamphs. *sub* Stafford).
[4] S.R.O., D.1323/A/1/5, pp. 414, 417; /6, pp. 268, 374.
[5] Ibid. /5, p. 457; /6, pp. 165, 185, 313.
[6] Ibid. /6, pp. 503–5.
[7] Fergus, *Vindication of Stafford Health of Towns Assoc.*; Anon. *Answer to and Observations upon the alleged Vindication . . .* (Stafford, 1848; copy in W.S.L. Pamphs. *sub* Stafford).
[8] *Staffs. Advertiser*, 2 July 1864.
[9] Ibid. 9 Apr., 9 July, 6 Aug. 1864.
[10] Ibid. 23 July 1870.
[11] See pp. 214–15.
[12] S.R.O., D.1323/1/9, 2 July, 5 Aug. 1874.
[13] Ibid. 25 Nov., 1 and 15 Dec. 1874, 22 Jan., 2 Feb., 2 Mar., 7 Sept., 9 Nov. 1875.
[14] Ibid. /10, pp. 2–4.
[15] *Corp. of Stafford: Yr. Bk.* (1906–7), 42–3.
[16] Stafford Corp. Act, 1896, 59 & 60 Vic. c. 63 (Local); *Staffs. Advertiser*, 18 Sept. 1897; above, p. 207.

favour of the tipping of refuse to raise the level of low-lying ground.[17]

Stafford's housing by the early 1920s compared favourably with that of other Staffordshire towns as a result of both private and corporation enterprise.[18] A council committee was appointed in 1899 to prepare plans for working-class dwellings. Nine such houses, consisting of a living-room, a scullery, and two bedrooms, were completed at Broadeye in 1901; six were let at 4s. 3d. a week and three at 4s. 6d. More council houses were completed in Crooked Bridge Road in 1902.[19] In 1913–14 sixty more were built in South Walls, in Harrowby Street on the Lammascote estate, and in Blakiston Street on the Coton Field estate.[20] Large-scale council building began with the extension of the Coton Field and Lammascote estates in the early 1920s, Lammascote being planned as a 'garden city'. Two more estates followed, Littleworth (Cull Avenue) in 1925 and Tithe Barn (north of Weston Road) in 1926–7. The four estates then consisted of 562 houses, and an estate had also been started on Stone Road.[21] Three of the larger firms built estates for their workers in the earlier 20th century.[22] By 1939 the corporation had built over 1,200 dwellings. Between the end of the Second World War and 1959 over 3,000 were added, including bungalows and flats, and private enterprise produced some 2,000 houses. The first council flats were opened in Corporation Street in 1952. The corporation began a slum-clearance programme in the later 1950s, notably in the area north of Browning Street. By the later 1960s it owned over 5,000 dwellings; three 16-storey blocks of flats, two at Highfields and the other at the junction of Lammascote Road and Corporation Street, were completed in 1967 and 1968.[23]

In 1397 several wells in the town, including one in Foregate, were found to be defective, and the borough court ordered them to be cleared.[24] In Elizabethan and Jacobean times the public wells were maintained by two elected well-wardens for each ward under the general supervision of the corporation.[25] There was a well in the market-place by 1597 when a man drowned in it,[26] and a well in the South Ward was mentioned in 1618 and the early 1660s.[27] In 1641 the corporation paid for 'a piece of stonework called a gage' to bring water to the Gaol Gate end of Foregate.[28] A well by the East Gate was mentioned in the early 1660s,[29] and

there were two others by the Green Gate and in Earl Street in 1737.[30] The corporation paid for planking for a reservoir in Mill Street in 1798, and there was a pump on the corner of Mill Street and Church Lane in 1841.[31] There was a public pump near the Lamb inn at Broadeye by 1834 and another near the White Lion in Lichfield Road by 1837.[32] In 1845 the council ordered pumps to be fixed to the public wells in Greengate, Gaolgate, Eastgate, and Foregate Streets.[33] There was a public pump in Tipping Street by 1869.[34] In 1874 the council ordered the well in Tenterbanks to be cleaned and fitted with a pump.[35]

It was claimed in 1851 that Stafford was adequately supplied with water.[36] In 1854, however, the improvement commissioners were informed that the gas-works was tainting the water-supply.[37] In 1864 they were told that the supply 'was saturated with noxious matter . . . When drunk by visitors to the town it invariably produced diarrhoea.'[38] In 1875 the inspector of nuisances stated: 'The subsoil of the borough is saturated with sewage. In many cases the midden, privy cesspool, and pump are contiguous. I recently witnessed house sewage emptied into a yard drain and immediately afterwards pumped from the well.'[39] An analysis of twelve samples of the borough's water in 1882 showed ten unfit for drinking.[40]

There were various private schemes in the earlier 1870s for providing the town with a piped water-supply. In 1874 the council decided to build its own water-works. Parliamentary sanction was secured in 1876.[41] Difficulties were encountered at the various sites chosen for boring because of the presence of salt or because of unfavourable strata, and it was not until 1890 that a works was opened, at Milford in Baswich.[42] It was extended in 1912 and a new reservoir opened in 1928. The works was rebuilt as an electrically operated station in 1953–5. A pumping station was opened at Shugborough in Colwich in 1940, and in 1959 a new source of supply from Gnosall came into use.[43]

Borough ordinances of the later 16th century stipulated that no one was to 'wash clothes, fish, or any other thing, water horses, wash their hands, or wash parsnips' at the common wells.[44] The corporation was providing washing-places by the 17th century. In 1631 and 1639 it repaired the washing-boards and washing-stocks, and in 1639 it paved the

[17] *Corp. Yr. Bk.* (1929–30), 49; *Boro. of Stafford: Opening of New Sewage Disposal Works, Brancote Gorse, Aug. 1957* (copy in W.S.L. Pamphs. *sub* Stafford); T. H. Higson, *Stafford Survey* (Stafford, n.d.; preface dated Dec. 1948), 71.
[18] A. Sayle, *Houses of the Workers*, ed. J. A. Rosevear (1924), 42–3, 138.
[19] S.R.O., D.1323/C/14/1; *Corp. Yr. Bk.* (1907–8), 44; dates on houses; plate facing p. 193 above.
[20] S.R.O., D.1323/C/18/2.
[21] Ibid.; *Staffs. Advertiser*, 11 Oct. 1919; Sayle, *Houses of the Workers*, 136–8; *Invitation to Stafford* (1928), 22, 37 (copy in W.S.L. Pamphs. *sub* Stafford); *Stafford: an Industrial Survey* (1932), 29, 31 (copy in W.S.L. Pamphs. *sub* Stafford); ex inf. the boro. surveyor (1963).
[22] See pp. 195–6.
[23] *Stafford Official Guide* [c. 1959], 27; [1968], 31; *Stafford Newsletter*, 29 Oct. 1960; above, pp. 194, 196.
[24] *T.S.H.C.S.* 1974–6, 33.
[25] Ibid. 1965–7, 11, 30, 32–3; S.R.O., D.(W.) 1721/1/4, ff. 137v., 141. For the wards see below.
[26] *St. Mary's, Stafford, Par. Reg.* (Staffs. Par. Reg. Soc. 1935–6), 121.
[27] S.R.O., D.(W.) 1721/1/4, f. 141; S.R.O., D.1323/E/1,

f. 302.
[28] S.R.O., D.1323/E/1, f. 257, where it is also called 'the cadge'.
[29] Ibid. f. 303.
[30] W.S.L. 7/96/00.
[31] S.R.O., D.1323/E/2, p. 39; W.S.L., Staffs. Views, ix. 77–8.
[32] S.R.O., D.1323/J/1, p. 51; W.S.L., Staffs. Views, ix. 87.
[33] S.R.O., D.1323/A/1/6, p. 200.
[34] Ibid. /8, 8 Nov. 1869.
[35] Ibid. /9, 9 Mar. 1874.
[36] White, *Dir. Staffs.* (1851), 331.
[37] *Staffs. Advertiser*, 9 Sept. 1854.
[38] Ibid. 8 Oct. 1864.
[39] S.R.O., D.1323/A/1/9, 9 Nov. 1875.
[40] Boro. Hall, Stafford, Corp. Order Bk. 1881–7, p. 127.
[41] S.R.O., D.1323/L/2, 3 Oct., 18 Nov. 1872; Calvert, *Stafford*, 88–9.
[42] Calvert, *Stafford*, 89–91; *Staffs. Advertiser*, 22 Mar. 1890.
[43] *Corp. Yr. Bk.* (1930–1), 49, 53; *Stafford Official Guide* [c. 1959], 31–2.
[44] *T.S.H.C.S.* 1965–7, 11, 30.

washing-place by the town walls. In 1642 it provided a washing-stool at the East Gate.[45] By 1702 there were washing-stocks by the mill and at Broadeye as well as at the East Gate.[46] In 1720 the council ordered the inspection and repair of all the washing-stocks.[47] There were still stocks at the mill in 1731 and by Broadeye bridge in 1784.[48]

Edward Whalley's Friary Baths on the Green in Forebridge were opened apparently in 1871. They were probably at the north end of Friars Walk and

to the east in 1974,[51] and it was demolished in 1976 to make way for a civic centre and a supermarket.

Master William the leech occurs in the Stafford court rolls in 1276, and in 1288 John the physician of Stafford was involved in a dispute with Thomas the apothecary.[52] During the outbreak of plague in 1610 the corporation built a pest-house and provided nurses and medical attendance there. It also appointed warders to keep people from Stone, which was also infected, out of the town.[53] In 1630–1

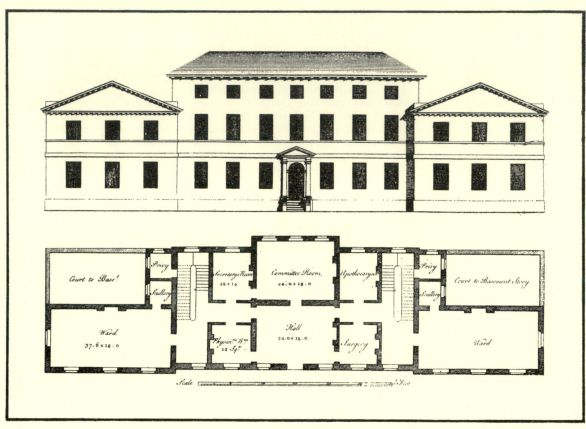

STAFFORDSHIRE GENERAL INFIRMARY: ELEVATION AND PLAN c. 1769

were perhaps the bath-house bought by the corporation from Lord Stafford in 1879.[49] In 1892 the corporation opened public baths by the Green Bridge. The plan was by the borough surveyor, W. Blackshaw, and the architect was George Wormal. A notable feature was the brine bath, to which brine was piped from a spring on Stafford common. The building was extended in 1893. After the visit of the duchess of Teck in 1895 the baths were known as the Royal Brine Baths.[50] The building was closed when the Riverside sports centre was opened

William Walthow and his wife were forbidden to come to Stafford after they had been in an infected house in London.[54] Warders were again appointed in 1665 to keep travellers out of the town.[55] During the cholera epidemic of 1832 a board of health was set up for Stafford, but only one case was recorded in the town.[56]

The Staffordshire General Infirmary was opened by subscribers in 1766 in two houses in Foregate Street.[57] A hospital of 80 beds was built in Foregate Street between 1769 and 1772 to the design of

[45] S.R.O., D.1323/E/1, ff. 188, 234 and v., 262.
[46] S.R.O., D.(W.) 0/8/2, pp. 16, 18.
[47] S.R.O., D.1323/A/1/2, p. 213.
[48] Ibid. p. 363; S.R.O., D.(W.) 0/8/1, p. 405.
[49] Staffs. Advertiser, 22 July 1871; O.S. Map 1/500, Staffs. XXXVII. 11.22 (1881 edn.); S.R.O., D.1323/A/1/10, p. 284.
[50] Staffs. Advertiser, 23 Apr. 1892; Kelly's Dir. Staffs. (1892; 1896); V.C.H. Staffs. ii. 250; Pevsner, Staffs. 244; plate facing p. 208 above.
[51] Plaque in foyer of Riverside Centre.
[52] S.R.O., D.641/1/4A/2 and 3; S.R.O., D.(W.) 1721/1/1, f. 227.
[53] S.R.O., D.1323/E/1, ff. 52v.–54. For other outbreaks see W.S.L., S.MS. 369, p. 105; K. R. Adey, '17th-cent.

Stafford', Midland Hist. ii. 161–3.
[54] S.R.O., D.1323/E/1, f. 184.
[55] S.R.O., D.1323/A/1/1, p. 183.
[56] Stafford Boro. Mus., Stafford Bd. of Health printed notice, 30 Aug. 1832; W. E. Clendinnen and J. B. McCallum, Sanitary Defects of Old Towns (paper read to Sanitary Inst. of Gt. Brit. Oct. 1878), 4 (copy in W.S.L. Pamphs. sub Stafford).
[57] For this para. see R. A. McKinley, 'Foundation of Staffs. General Infirmary', T.O.S.S. 1963–5; Cherry, Stafford, 27–8; S.R.O., D.(W.) 0/8/1, p. 249; S.R.O., D.1323/K/1, 7 Jan. 1770; H. M. Colvin, Biog. Dict. Eng. Architects, 719; White, Dir. Staffs. (1834), 135; Pevsner, Staffs. 247; Kelly's Dir. Staffs. (1900); Roxburgh, Stafford, 64–5; below, pp. 252–3.

Benjamin Wyatt of Weeford. Two wings were added later, and in 1829 a fever ward was built. The building was restored and enlarged between 1892 and 1897 to the design of Sir Aston Webb. A portico of 1829, built with money left by Thomas Mottershaw of Silkmore in Castle Church, was removed to the Congregational church in Martin Street and replaced by a hooded porch. Subsequent additions included a nurses' home opened in 1927 and an L-shaped wing completed in 1938.

About the end of the 18th century money was left to build a ward for the insane at the infirmary. Instead the county justices and the trustees of the infirmary, with the help of subscribers, opened the Staffordshire General Lunatic Asylum north-east of the town centre in 1818 for patients of all social classes. It was designed by Joseph Potter, the county surveyor, and stood in grounds of 40 a. It was enlarged in 1849–50 and several times thereafter. It was renamed St. George's Hospital in the late 1940s.[58] It became an asylum entirely for paupers when Coton Hill asylum for middle- and upper-class patients was opened on Weston Road in 1854. Standing in grounds of 30 a., the new asylum was designed by Fulljames & Waller of Gloucester in a Gothic style and was of pale brick with Bath stone dressings. By 1880 it had been extended. It was closed in 1975 and demolished in 1976 to make way for a new general hospital.[59]

During the smallpox threat of 1872 the corporation converted a barn at Kingston Hill east of the town into a hospital at the expense of the owner, Lord Shrewsbury.[60] From c. 1895 there was an infectious diseases hospital at Kingston Hill run by the Stafford rural district council; it had accommodation for about 10 patients and remained in use until c. 1911.[61] The corporation opened an isolation hospital east of Marston Road north of the railway c. 1900; it had accommodation for about 25.[62] It was replaced in 1907 by a hospital for about 16 at the north end of Tithe Barn Road, which was still in use in 1956 but had become a nurses' training school by 1964.[63] In 1976 the building was used as borough offices.

Burton House maternity home at Moss Pit was opened by the corporation in a converted house in 1944.[64]

In 1948 the hospital at the former workhouse became Fernleigh Hospital. It was replaced in 1974 by Kingsmead Hospital for old people in Corporation Street.[65]

A burial board was set up in 1854, and in 1856 it opened a cemetery of 4 a. in Eccleshall Road in Tillington. Its powers passed to the corporation under the Stafford Corporation Act, 1876. The cemetery was extended several times and reached 22 a. in 1940.[66] A crematorium and cemetery in Tixall Road beyond the borough boundary were opened in 1964.[67]

Two constables were appointed for Stafford in 1285 under the Statute of Winchester, but when one of them died he was not replaced. By 1307 the other was ill, and a single constable was then appointed instead.[68] Two serjeants of the town were mentioned in 1307,[69] and in at least the 17th century the serjeants-at-mace had police functions.[70] It was stated in 1307 that no watch was kept at the gates and that the gates were not shut, and the town was duly fined.[71] In 1390, after 'evil-doers of Wales and Cheshire' had entered the town at night as a result of the lack of ward and had removed prisoners held at the gates, the bailiffs were ordered to repair the gates and keep them shut at night.[72] Extensive repairs were made to the gates in 1411–12, and janitors were being paid that year.[73] In the 16th and 17th centuries there was a watch for each of the three wards (North, South, and East) into which the town was by then divided, and in the later 17th century the tenant of a house at each of the three gates had the duty of 'warning the watch' for the ward.[74] By then too there were three constables, one for each ward.[75] The borough ordinances of the later 16th century ordered a curfew at 8 p.m. on working days and 7 p.m. on Sundays and holidays, with a day bell at 4 a.m. They also limited drinking in ale-houses by labourers and apprentices and ordered the bailiffs to inspect ale-houses for the playing of unlawful games, to deal with the idle and with 'light suspect women', and to keep musicians, minstrels, and waits from going about the town.[76] About 1730 the appointment of the three constables passed from the council to the court leet, which from 1779 appointed four constables.[77]

In 1783 there was formed the 'Forebridge Association for detecting felonies, petty robberies etc. committed on the members thereof'. There were 34 members, and the initial subscription was 10s. 6d. with provision for subsequent payments as required.[78] A Stafford Association for the Prosecution of Felons was formed apparently in 1825. In 1838 the subscription was 12s. a year, including an annual dinner, and it was then said that 'this useful association is much on the increase'. It still existed in 1851.[79]

In the earlier 1830s the borough police force consisted of four constables appointed by the court

[58] Roxburgh, *Stafford*, 71–4; White, *Dir. Staffs.* (1851), 340–1; S.R.O., D.550/1; *Stafford Official Guide* [1950], 38.
[59] *Staffs. Advertiser*, 4 Mar. 1854; *Kelly's Dir. Staffs.* (1880); ex inf. Staffs. Area Health Authority (1976).
[60] S.R.O., D.1323/A/1/9, 14 May, 17 July, 17 Oct. 1872.
[61] *Halden & Son's Dir. Stafford* (1896), 18; (1911), 19; O.S. Map 6", Staffs. XXXVII. SE. (1902 edn.); *Corp. Yr. Bk.* (1907–8), 44.
[62] *Halden & Son's Dir. Stafford* (1902), 19; O.S. Map 6", Staffs. XXXVII. NE. (1902 edn.).
[63] *Corp. Yr. Bk.* (1907–8), 44; *Halden & Son's Dir. Stafford* (1909), 19; (1910), 19; *Stafford Dir.* (1956–57), 130; (1964–65), 147.
[64] Higson, *Stafford Survey*, 67.
[65] See p. 231.
[66] S.R.O., D.1323/C/9/1; 39 & 40 Vic. c. 196 (Local); Lich. Dioc. Regy., B/A/2(i)/P, ff. 398–404; /R, pp. 98–101;
/T, pp. 90–3; *Corp. Yr. Bk.* (1906–7), 44; Higson, *Stafford Survey*, 75.
[67] *Stafford Newsletter*, 24 Apr. 1964.
[68] *S.H.C.* vii (1), 179–80.
[69] S.R.O., D.641/1/4A/5.
[70] B.L., Hargrave MS. 288, ff. 19v.–20.
[71] *S.H.C.* vii (1), 179. [72] *Cal. Close, 1389–92*, 215.
[73] *T.O.S.S.* 1939, 19–20, 22–3.
[74] E 179/177/90; S.R.O., D.1323/E/1, ff. 275, 302, 303v.; D.1323/A/1/1, p. 234; W.S.L., H.M. uncat. 35 (Norbury), Fereday v. Parton, 1695.
[75] S.R.O., D.1323/A/1/1, p. 251.
[76] *T.S.H.C.S.* 1965–7, 18, 20–1, 26–7.
[77] S.R.O., D.1323/A/1/2, p. 223; D.1323/G/1 and 2; D.1033/1, p. 252; W.S.L. 7/96/00.
[78] W.S.L. 7/137/00.
[79] W.S.L., C.B. Stafford; *Staffs. Advertiser*, 26 Jan. 1833, 15 Sept. 1838; White, *Dir. Staffs.* (1851), 329.

leet and two deputies appointed by the magistrates. There was no night watch, although one was said to be much needed.[80] Under the Municipal Corporations Act, 1835, control of the police passed to the borough watch committee.[81] In 1840 the corporation strongly opposed a Bill amalgamating its force with the county's[82] and appointed a chief police officer for the borough. In 1841 a night watch was being maintained.[83] In 1845 the council agreed to amalgamation, but the agreement was ended in 1850.[84] The borough force was finally amalgamated with the county's in 1858.[85] The borough police station was in the new guildhall from 1854.[86] A station was built on the corner of Bath Street and Albion Place in 1931 and extended in 1961.[87]

In the interest of fire prevention the council in 1680 banned the taking of tobacco in the streets and in barns, stables, or other dangerous places; bakers and others with ovens were not to keep more than twenty kids of wood if they lived in closely built streets.[88] The twenty-seven leather buckets in the council house in 1726[89] were presumably fire-fighting equipment. The borough possessed a fire-engine in 1729.[90] A new engine was bought by public subscription in 1743 for use within the borough, with the vestry responsible for its maintenance.[91] A second engine was bought in 1776.[92]

The improvement commissioners took over the engines in 1837, buying the equipment from the vestry and appointing Robert Crewe to maintain the engines and provide twenty men to work them.[93] The engines were kept in Tipping Street by 1851 and were moved to the covered market in 1856.[94] In 1857 they were placed under a superintendent with four firemen paid a regular wage and others paid on an hourly basis. They could be used outside the borough at a charge of one guinea for each engine; payments to the men and for the horses were also required.[95] Another brigade, the Stafford Fire Brigade, was formed in 1865; while apparently of independent origin, it was subject to some control by the commissioners and in 1867 was transferred to them with its engine.[96] A fire bell was installed at the guildhall in 1872; it had been presented to the town in 1855 by the 80th Regiment of Foot (Staffordshire Volunteers), which had taken it at Rangoon

in 1852.[97] The corporation took over the fire brigade from the commissioners in 1876,[98] and in 1877 a volunteer brigade was established.[99] By 1880 it had three engines, kept at the market hall. A station was built in 1884–5 at the junction of Greengate Street and South Walls.[1] A steam engine was bought by public subscription in 1887, apparently in connexion with Queen Victoria's jubilee, and a motor engine in 1927.[2] Control of the brigade passed to the National Fire Service in 1941, and in 1942 a temporary station was opened on the corner of Mill Bank and Water Street. The county council took control in 1948.[3] A new fire station was opened in Lammascote Road in 1969, with the 1942 premises retained as workshops and stores. The Lammascote Road complex included the headquarters of the county's western division and a control room for all emergency calls from within the county. The official opening was delayed until 1971 when all communications became centred there.[4]

The Birmingham District Fire Office had an engine in Crabbery Street from 1841.[5] Between at least 1860 and 1876 the Norwich Union Fire and Life insurance company had an engine at Stafford,[6] while in 1864 a new engine was built for the Stafford branch of the Western Fire and Life.[7] Siemens had its own fire brigade in 1913.[8]

A gas-works in Chell Road (formerly Gas Lane) was opened by William Edwards & Co. in 1829.[9] Street lighting was provided by the improvement commissioners from the winter of 1830–1.[10] The works was sold to the Stafford New Gas Co. in 1846 and extended soon afterwards.[11] The company was reincorporated as the Stafford Gas Co. in 1854.[12] The works was bought by the corporation in 1878 under the Stafford Corporation Act, 1876, and was again extended in 1919 and 1920.[13] It was taken over by the West Midlands Gas Board in 1949. Production ceased in 1964, and most of the works was demolished between 1966 and 1970. In 1976 a single gas-holder remained, containing North Sea gas.[14]

An electricity works was opened by the corporation in 1895 in Foregate Street.[15] It was extended several times and in 1930 was taken over by the North-west Midlands Joint Electricity Authority,

[80] *1st Rep. Com. Mun. Corp.* H.C. 116, App. III, p. 2027 (1835), xxv.

[81] 5 & 6 Wm. IV, c. 76, s. 76.

[82] S.R.O., D.1323/A/1/5, pp. 408, 410–12; W.S.L. 7/138/00.

[83] S.R.O., D.1323/A/1/5, pp. 439, 447–8, 452; W.S.L. 7/139/00.

[84] S.R.O., D.1323/A/1/6, pp. 64–6, 230–1, 537, 548–54.

[85] Ibid. /7, p. 276 and 21 Dec. 1857, 25 Jan. 1858; /8, 15 Oct. 1858, 14 Dec. 1860.

[86] *Staffs. Advertiser*, 4 Mar. 1854.

[87] Ex inf. the chief constable (1962).

[88] S.R.O., D.1323/A/1/1, pp. 284–5.

[89] W.S.L. 77/45, f. 55v.

[90] S.R.O., D.(W.) o/8/2, p. 37 (1st numbering).

[91] W.S.L., H.M. uncat. 26; S.R.O., D.(W.) o/8/18; S.R.O., D.1323/K/1.

[92] S.R.O., D.1323/K/1, 7 July 1776.

[93] Ibid. /J/1, pp. 75, 86.

[94] White, *Dir. Staffs.* (1851), 337; S.R.O., D.1323/J/2, pp. 23, 51.

[95] S.R.O., D.1323/J/2, pp. 50–2.

[96] Ibid. 7 Mar., 3 Oct. 1865, 7 May, 2 July 1867; *Staffs. Advertiser*, 12 Nov. 1864, p. 4.

[97] Calvert, *Stafford*, 76–7; S.R.O., D.1323/A/1/7, pp. 285–7; /9, 2 May 1872; D.1323/J/2, 4 July 1871, 6 Feb. 1872.

[98] S.R.O., D.1323/A/1/10, p. 21.

[99] *Staffs. Advertiser*, 13 July 1878; Calvert, *Stafford*, 74–5.

[1] *Kelly's Dir. Staffs.* (1880); *Corp. Yr. Bk.* (1906–7), 43.

[2] Boro. Hall, Stafford, Corp. Order Bk. 1887–93, p. 12; *Corp. Yr. Bk.* (1927–8), 49.

[3] Ex inf. the chief fire officer of Staffs. (1962); Higson, *Stafford Survey*, 73.

[4] *Stafford Newsletter*, 5 Dec. 1969, 27 Aug. 1971; brochure for official opening 25 Aug. 1971 (copy in W.S.L. Pamphs. *sub* Stafford).

[5] *Staffs. Advertiser*, 1 May 1841; White, *Dir. Staffs.* (1851), 337.

[6] *P.O. Dir. Staffs.* (1860; 1876).

[7] *Staffs. Advertiser*, 31 Dec. 1864.

[8] *Stafford Newsletter*, 10 Feb. 1962, photograph.

[9] White, *Dir. Staffs.* (1834), 124; Wood, *Plan of Stafford* (1835).

[10] S.R.O., D.1323/J/1, pp. 6–7, 20.

[11] White, *Dir. Staffs.* (1851), 331; Stafford Gas Act, 1846, 9 & 10 Vic. c. 114 (Local and Personal).

[12] Stafford Gas Act, 1854, 17 & 18 Vic. c. 22 (Local and Personal).

[13] 39 & 40 Vic. c. 196 (Local); S.R.O., D.1323/A/1/10, pp. 181, 215; *Corp. Yr. Bk.* (1906–7), 42; (1924–5), 51–2.

[14] Ex inf. West Midlands Gas (1976); *Stafford Newsletter*, 27 Mar. 1964, 5 Sept. 1968.

[15] *Staffs. Advertiser*, 19 Oct. 1895.

with the corporation then buying its supply.[16] The undertaking passed to the Midlands Electricity Board in 1948. Generating ceased in 1959. In 1976 the board still used part of the building as a sub-station and the rest was occupied by G.E.C. The board opened a district office in Brunswick Terrace in 1960.

Stafford had a postmaster c. 1680.[17] By the 1790s the post office was run by Arthur Morgan, printer and stationer, and was on the west side of Market Square next to the Star inn where the London-Chester mail coach called and where the excise office was.[18] In 1838 it moved to Tipping Street next to the Crispin, c. 1845 to the corner of Greengate Street and South Walls, and c. 1855 to Eastgate Street next to the Rose and Crown.[19] Three pillar boxes were erected in 1857, near the White Lion in Fore-bridge, at Broadeye, and in Gaol Road; letters could be posted up to 9.30 p.m. for delivery the following morning.[20] The post office was moved to premises on the corner of Market Square and Bank Passage in 1867.[21] In 1914 Chetwynd House in Greengate Street became the head post office of Stafford.[22]

The National Telephone Co. Ltd. opened an exchange in Newport Road in 1887.[23] The telephone exchange in Eastgate Street is dated 1959.

With the opening of the railway in 1837 an omnibus was started between the Swan and the station by John Meeson of the Swan; the driver and a boy acting as a guard wore a scarlet uniform.[24] By 1851 an omnibus and two flys from the Swan and the Vine met every train.[25] Omnibuses plied from Market Square by the later 1880s charging 6d. for any distance up to a mile; on Saturdays they ran between the north and south ends of the town for fares of 2d. and 1d.[26] Motor buses to various parts of the county were introduced c. 1920.[27]

The park and public libraries are treated elsewhere.[28]

PARLIAMENTARY REPRESENTATION. Stafford borough was reprseented by two burgesses in the parliament of 1295, and there is a fairly continuous record of representation by two members thereafter.[29] It was made a one-member constituency by the Instrument of Government in 1653 but regained its second member in 1659.[30] It continued to return two members until 1885 when it again

became a one-member constituency.[31] In 1690 it was stated that by ancient custom the electorate consisted of the resident burgesses only, a fact which was confirmed at the hearing of a petition in 1722.[32] The electorate numbered 190 in 1624,[33] 400 in 1722,[34] 600 in 1816,[35] and 1,176 in 1831.[36] The boundaries of the parliamentary borough were extended to include the Forebridge area of Castle Church parish in 1832,[37] the part of Castle Church immediately west of the borough in 1868,[38] and the Littleworth and Coton area of the municipal borough in 1885.[39] Under the Representation of the People Act, 1918, the borough was merged in the Stafford Parliamentary Division, covering a large area round the town.[40] It became part of the constituency of Stafford and Stone under the Representation of the People Act, 1948.[41]

During the 14th century the members seem normally to have been chosen from among the burgesses.[42] There appears to have been royal interference in 1384 when John de Orwell, serjeant-at-arms to the king, secured one of the seats.[43] The influence of the Stafford family was paramount in the 15th century, one, and often both, of the members being nominated by it. Some royal officials secured a seat, and later in the century a few of the local gentry who were apparently not within the Staffords' sphere of influence sat for the borough.[44] The influence of the Staffords was again marked from the 1540s until the end of the 16th century, and several members of the family represented the borough.[45] Francis Cradock, recorder of Stafford and a member of an important burgess family, held one of the seats from 1584 until his death in 1594.[46] He was re-elected in 1593 against the wishes of the earl of Essex who had his own candidate. Another of Essex's nominees sat for Stafford from 1588 to 1598.[47] It was at Stafford at some time between 1530 and 1532 that the first known by-election took place when Sampson Erdeswick of Sandon was elected.[48]

Stafford sent royalists to both the Parliaments of 1640.[49] In 1654 John Bradshaw the regicide was elected, although as an opponent of the government he did not take his seat.[50] Control of one of the seats by the Chetwynds of Ingestre began in 1661, continuing with few breaks until 1770; on occasion their nominee secured the other seat also.[51] It was stated in 1682 that one seat was by custom in the gift of the high steward. In 1679 and 1681 the duke

[16] The rest of this para. is based on information supplied in 1976 by Mr. C. H. Pettifer, Stafford District Manager of the M.E.B. Part of the building is dated 1939.
[17] W.S.L. 11/20.
[18] Univ. Brit. Dir. iv. 437; Wood, Plan of Stafford (1835).
[19] Staffs. Advertiser, 7 Apr. 1838, 20 Mar. 1841, 28 Mar. 1914; S.R.O., D.1323/A/1/7, pp. 142–3, 205.
[20] Staffs. Advertiser, 15 Aug. 1857.
[21] Ibid. 30 Mar. 1867.   [22] Ibid. 4 Apr. 1914.
[23] Boro. Hall, Stafford, Corp. Order Bk. 1881–7, pp. 483, 505; 1887–93, p. 33; Staffs. Advertiser, 31 Dec. 1887, p. 6; Kelly's Dir. Staffs. (1892).
[24] Staffs. Advertiser, 8 July 1837.
[25] White, Dir. Staffs. (1851), 357.
[26] Halden's Stafford Dir. (1887; 1888).
[27] Kelly's Dir. Staffs. (1921; 1924); Halden & Haywood's Dir. Stafford (1922), 61.
[28] See pp. 189, 203, 258.
[29] S.H.C. 1917–18, 12 sqq.
[30] Ibid. 1920 and 1922, 95, 104.
[31] Redistribution of Seats Act, 1885, 48 & 49 Vic. c. 23.
[32] W.S.L., H.M. uncat. 29, envelope labelled 'Borough

Parliamentary Election of 1690'; T. H. B. Oldfield, Representative Hist. of Gt. Brit. and Ireland, iv. 504.
[33] D. Hirst, The Representative of the People?, 225.
[34] S.H.C. 1933 (i), 35.
[35] Oldfield, Representative Hist. iv. 506.
[36] S.H.C. 1920 and 1922, 212.
[37] 2 & 3 Wm. IV, c. 64. V.C.H. Staffs. v. 82, wrongly states that this was the Reform Act and also wrongly includes Castletown in this extension instead of in that of 1868.
[38] 31 & 32 Vic. c. 46.   [39] 48 & 49 Vic. c. 23.
[40] 7 & 8 Geo. V, c. 64.
[41] 11 & 12 Geo. VI, c. 65.
[42] S.H.C. 1917–18, pp. xxxviii–xxxix.
[43] Ibid. pp. xxxix, 138–9.
[44] Ibid. pp. xlv–xlvii.
[45] Ibid. 311, 315–18, 350, 365, 378, 403–4.
[46] Ibid. 379; C 142/239 no. 97.
[47] S.H.C. 1917–18, 391, 395.
[48] Ibid. 297–9, 303.
[49] S.H.C. 1920 and 1922, 61–3.
[50] Ibid. 98–9.   [51] Ibid. p. xix.

of Monmouth, the high steward, had no difficulty in securing a seat for Sir Thomas Armstrong, most of the burgesses being enthusiastic supporters of the duke. When Armstrong was executed without trial in 1684 on suspicion of complicity in the Rye House Plot, the government sent one of his quarters to Stafford with orders for it to be fixed on a pole and set up in a public place.[52] For much of the period from 1689 to 1737 the Foley family controlled the second seat.[53]

After the 1690 election the defeated Philip Foley alleged that there had been bribery, intimidation, and the manipulation of the electoral roll by the creation of new burgesses after the issue of the writ and the admission of honorary burgesses to the poll.[54] Walter Chetwynd was unseated in 1711 after a petition alleging bribery, treats, and threats at the election of 1710; he was, however, elected at a by-election in 1712. In 1725 Francis Eld was expelled in favour of Viscount Chetwynd, whom he had defeated at a by-election in 1724; his offence was an attempt 'to compromise the election . . . before the same was heard before the Committee of Privileges'.[55] Of the 1780 election Josiah Wedgwood wrote that in contrast to 'our farce' at Newcastle-under-Lyme 'matters are not conducted quite so snugly in our county town. They have four candidates and the highest bidder must carry it, for no Cornish borough is more venal'.[56] Richard Brinsley Sheridan secured one of the seats at that election and held it until 1806 when he moved elsewhere. His maiden speech in the Commons was an indignant reply to a petition against the 1780 election. Yet he had paid 5 guineas each for 248 votes, and in the earlier 1780s his annual expenses in the town came to £144, including £40 on ale-tickets, £10 in fees for 'swearing young burgesses', 5 guineas' subscription to the new infirmary, and 2 guineas' subscription to 'clergymen's widows'. In 1811 he recalled two of his Stafford elections as 'most tough and expensive'. In 1812 he again stood at Stafford but was defeated, apparently because he was unable to pay enough for support: he attributed his failure to the refusal of Samuel Whitbread to advance £2,000 from the sum due to him for his share of the Drury Lane theatre.[57] John Gladstone, the father of the statesman, considered standing for Stafford in 1818 and was told that the price of a vote had risen from 5 to 7½ guineas.[58] At the election of that year one candidate spent £1,458 in 44 public houses.[59] The by-election of December 1826, held during a time of unemployment, was notably corrupt, with the price of a vote rising to £15; there was also much drunkenness and violence. One candidate spent between £6,000 and £7,000, another between

£13,000 and £14,000. When an inquiry was instituted, one of the agents was paid a sum equal to half the expenses of the election to suppress the evidence.[60]

In 1832 Stafford sent two Whigs to the first reformed parliament, but the defeated candidate and the burgesses themselves petitioned against the election. A committee of inquiry in 1833 found that 825 out of 1,049 voters had been bribed, and it recommended the disfranchisement of Stafford. A Bill passed the Commons, but before the Lords could deal with it Parliament was dissolved.[61] Bribery was alleged at the 1835 election, and when one of the members retired later the same year the writ for a by-election was suspended until 1837 and was then carried by only one vote.[62] In 1869 both members elected in 1868 were unseated, the Liberal for intimidation and the Conservative for corruption. During the hearing evidence of corruption at the 1865 election also was brought forward.[63]

From 1835 one seat was normally held by a Conservative and the other by a Liberal.[64] In 1874 Alexander Macdonald, a miners' leader standing as a Liberal, secured one of the seats and thus became one of the first two working-class M.P.s; he continued to represent Stafford until his death in 1881.[65] Of the four members who held the single seat from 1885 until 1918 one was a Conservative (1886–92) and the rest were Liberals.

CHURCHES. Until the 19th century Stafford borough was served by two parish churches. The Saxon church of St. Bertelin and its successor St. Mary's served a parish which included most of the town and an extensive area outside it. The church of St. Chad served a small parish east of Greengate Street. At least between the 15th and 18th centuries St. Mary's was known as the great or high church in contrast to St. Chad's, the low church.[66] In the 19th and 20th centuries several new parishes were formed out of St. Mary's and also out of Castle Church parish, much of which was taken into the borough.

There was a church at Stafford by the 10th century. It was associated with the cult of St. Bertelin, who is traditionally said to have had a hermitage at Stafford.[67] The church served a large area outside the town: in the earlier 15th century the parishes of Creswell, Ingestre, and Tixall, as well as the townships of Marston, Salt, Coton, and Whitgreave within St. Mary's parish, by old custom buried their dead in the church and graveyard of St. Bertelin.[68] The deanery of St. Mary's was described as the deanery of St. Mary and St.

[52] *Cal. S.P. Dom.* 1682, 426, 428, 456; ibid. 1684–5, 78, 80; *S.H.C.* 1920 and 1922, 136, 139–40.
[53] *S.H.C.* 1920 and 1922, pp. xix, 226.
[54] W.S.L., H.M. uncat. 29, envelope labelled 'Borough Parliamentary Election of 1690'.
[55] Oldfield, *Representative Hist.* iv. 503–5; *S.H.C.* 1920 and 1922, 205, 223–4.
[56] *S.H.C.* 1920 and 1922, 301.
[57] Cherry, *Stafford*, 84, 86–7; *S.H.C.* 1920 and 1922, 303, 305; *S.H.C.* 1933 (1), 2 n.; plate facing p. 192 above. For an alternative view of his failure in 1812 see W.S.L. 132/30.
[58] S. G. Checkland, *The Gladstones: a Family Biography, 1764–1851*, 103.
[59] W.S.L. 7/12/00.
[60] *S.H.C.* 1933 (1), 60–1.
[61] Ibid. 78, 80–1, 86–7.

[62] Ibid. 87, 91, 98.   [63] *Staffs. Advertiser*, 15 May 1869.
[64] For this para. see *Dod's Parl. Companion, passim*; D. H. Fletcher, 'Beginnings of Labour Representation: Parliamentary Elections in Stafford 1869–81' (Univ. of Keele M.A. dissertation, 1970); S. R. Broadbridge, 'Alexander MacDonald and Stafford', *Bull. N. Staffs. Labour Studies Group*, i (2).
[65] The other was Thos. Burt, elected for Morpeth (Northumb.).
[66] S.R.O., D.641/1/2/53, m. 2; Bradley, *Charters*, 99; S.R.O., D.1323/A/1/2, p. 99; S.R.O., D.(W.) 0/8/2, reverse pages, 30 Oct. 1708; *The Torrington Diaries*, ed. C. Bruyn Andrews, iii. 136; Kettle, 'Street-names', 49.
[67] *Church of St. Bertelin at Stafford and its Cross*, ed. A. Oswald (Birmingham [1955]).
[68] *Feud. Aids*, v. 19–20.

Bartholomew in 1524, while in 1543 there is a reference to St. Bartholomew's parish, Stafford; Bartholomew was evidently a variant of Bertelin.[69] As a parish church St. Bertelin's was superseded by St. Mary's, which was built on a site immediately to the east probably in the 12th century and is first mentioned by name in 1203.[70] St. Bertelin's was retained as part of the building and by the 15th century was probably used as a guild chapel.[71]

By 1086 the church of Stafford was collegiate, with thirteen canons who occur in Domesday Book both as the priests of the borough and as the king's prebendary canons.[72] In 1136 Jordan, clerk of Roger of Fécamp, held the church of the Crown, probably by grant of Henry I.[73] In that year King Stephen granted it to the bishop and the cathedral churches of Coventry and Lichfield in perpetuity for the soul of Henry I, but Jordan was to continue to hold it for his lifetime. The church was resumed by Henry II. The advowson of the deanery then remained with the Crown until 1446 when Henry VI granted it to Humphrey, duke of Buckingham, in exchange for the patronage of the priory of Wootton Wawen (Warws.).[74] After the forfeiture of Edward, duke of Buckingham, in 1521 the Crown retained the advowson until the dissolution of the college in 1548. The dean exercised a peculiar jurisdiction over the parish of St. Mary, the prebendal estates outside the parish, the parishes of Creswell, Tixall, Ingestre, and Castle Church, the chapel of St. Nicholas in Stafford castle, and the hospitals of St. John and of St. Leonard in Forebridge;[75] it lapsed at the dissolution.

In 1548 the chantry commissioners appointed one of the prebendaries as vicar of St. Mary's.[76] In 1571 Elizabeth I designated the benefice a rectory in the gift of the Crown and appointed the existing vicar as rector.[77] It had become usual by the 18th century, and probably earlier, for the corporation to recommend a candidate for presentation.[78] In 1873 the Crown transferred the patronage to the bishop of Lichfield, who still holds it.[79]

The vicar's stipend was fixed in 1548 at £16 charged on the royal revenues in Staffordshire.[80] By 1570 it had ceased to be paid, and the borough bailiffs, supported by the bishop, petitioned the Crown for an adequate endowment. When in 1571 Elizabeth I granted the burgesses all the collegiate property that had not been sold, the stipend was made a first charge on it.[81] It soon became customary for the corporation to lease all or most of the property to the rector to augment his stipend, a practice which continued until 1704.[82] In 1646, however, the committee for plundered ministers ordered that his salary and the curate's should be increased, apparently by £100.[83] In 1653 the corporation raised the stipend to £80, apparently instead of granting a lease.[84] It is not clear, however, that either of the augmentations was paid, and in 1658 the corporation asked the lord protector to secure an augmentation for St. Mary's of £40, which was granted in 1659.[85] It presumably did not survive the Restoration, and by 1662 the rector was 'in great necessity for money'.[86] On the appointment of a rector in 1704 the stipend was raised to £70.[87] It was later increased several times, and by Chancery order of 1835 it was raised from £180 to £340.[88] An annuity of £25 was granted in 1844 in lieu of certain fees lost as a result of parochial reorganization.[89] In 1977 £340 was still paid to the rector in respect of the 1571 Queen Elizabeth Grant.[90] By will proved in 1912 Elizabeth Wogan of Stafford left £10,000 for the augmentation of the benefice besides £3,000 for the repair of the church.[91]

In 1549 the vicar was tenant of the house which had previously been occupied by the priests of the college and which was then sold by the Crown.[92] The rector later occupied a house in the churchyard as tenant of the corporation, which in 1698 granted his request for a year's remission of rent.[93] In 1708 the corporation bought a house in Greengate Street for the rector; part of the cost seems to have been met by the sale of a house in the same street, which was part of the endowment of Robert Sutton's charity.[94] By 1729 the rector paid only an acknowledgement instead of a full rent.[95] In 1835 the corporation waived its right to the house in favour of the rector in return for recognition of its right to the workhouse adjoining the churchyard.[96] William Coldwell, rector from 1822, lived in a house next door, no. 21 Greengate Street, since his predecessor's widow was allowed by the corporation to

[69] L. & P. Hen. VIII, iv (1), p. 169; xviii (1), p. 200; Church of St. Bertelin, 9 n.
[70] S.H.C. iii (1), 170–1. [71] See p. 241.
[72] V.C.H. Staffs. iv. 37, 44.
[73] For the rest of this para. see, unless otherwise stated, V.C.H. Staffs. iii. 298, 303–9, where the history of the college is related.
[74] Rot. Parl. v. 309.
[75] Feud. Aids, v. 19–20; Valor Eccl. (Rec. Com.), iii. 117–19; S.H.C. 1915, 78, 235, 237.
[76] S.H.C. 1915, 239–40, 243, 245–6.
[77] Bradley, Charters, 101–2.
[78] S.R.O., D.1323/A/1/2, pp. 110, 372; /3, pp. 118–19; /4, p. 24; S.R.O., D.(W.) o/8/1, pp. 61–2. Gregory King stated c. 1680 that the corporation presented (S.H.C. 1919, 212), while even in 1572 the first rector was instituted on the presentation of the burgesses under their common seal (L.J.R.O., B/A/1/15, f. 65v.).
[79] Lond. Gaz. 6 May 1873, pp. 2264–5; Lich. Dioc. Dir. (1975).
[80] L. Lambert, Short Hist. of Coll. of Stafford (Guildford, 1923), 38 (copy in W.S.L.); Bradley, Charters, 99–100.
[81] Bradley, Charters, 99–107; S.P. 46/14 f. 162.
[82] W.S.L., S.MS. 402, ff. 19–21; S.R.O., D.1323/A/1/1, pp. 71, 80, 155–6, 175, 197, 199, 227, 258, 301, 348; /2, pp. 99, 107; D.1323/F/1, reverse pages, pp. 24, 62.
[83] Bodl. MS. Bodl. 323, f. 267v.
[84] S.R.O., D.1323/A/1/1, p. 58. Leases of St. Mary's tithes were granted to other persons in 1649 (for 1 year) and 1650 (for 7 years): ibid. pp. 22, 31.
[85] S.R.O., D.1323/A/1/1, p. 58; Cal. S.P. Dom. 1657–8, 285; S.H.C. 1915, 247.
[86] S.R.O., D.1323/A/1/1, pp. 155–6, 227.
[87] Ibid. /2, p. 110.
[88] Ibid. /2, p. 374; /3, pp. 119, 143, 236, 413, 415, 441; /5, p. 9; W.S.L., S.MS. 365; W.S.L., S.MS. 402, ff. 19, 33v.–34v.; Keen, Letter to Inhabitants of Stafford, 24; 11th Rep. Com. Char. H.C. 433, p. 591 (1824), xiv; Rep. Com. Eccl. Revenues [67], p. 499, H.C. (1835), xxii; S.R.O., D.892/1, pp. 10, 16–17; D.892/3/1.
[89] Lond. Gaz. 10 Sept. 1844, pp. 3119–22, 3229, 3326.
[90] Ex inf. the rector (1977).
[91] Char. Com. files. [92] See p. 206.
[93] L.J.R.O., A/V/1/3, p. 73; S.R.O., D.1323/A/1/2, p. 57.
[94] S.R.O., D.1323/A/1/2, pp. 122, 126, 128, 374; D.3130/44; D.(W.) o/8/1, p. 80; L.J.R.O., B/V/5, Stafford, St. Mary, 1751; Keen, Letter to Inhabitants of Stafford, 36; 11th Rep. Com. Char. 595.
[95] S.R.O., D.(W.) o/8/2, p. 34; D.1033/1, p. 2; D.1323/A/1/3, pp. 119, 143; 11th Rep. Com. Char. 596. In 1719, however, the corporation had decided to charge a rent of £10 a year for 7 years: D.1323/A/1/2, p. 198.
[96] S.R.O., D.1323/A/1/5, pp. 147–9.

continue to live in the rectory. When she died her executor sold the house in ignorance and the money was lost. W. G. Cowie, who succeeded Coldwell in 1867, also lived at no. 21, but it was sold when he became bishop of Auckland (New Zealand) in 1869 and the proceeds were paid to Queen Anne's Bounty.[97] A rectory designed by Robert Griffiths of Stafford was built in Mount Street in 1879–80.[98] A house on the corner of Newport Road and Rowley Avenue became the rectory in 1945 and was replaced in 1974 by a new house in Rowley Avenue built in the grounds of the old.[99]

In 1548 the commissioners appointed one of the vicars choral of the college as assistant curate.[1] He was styled reader between at least 1645 and 1794. By 1666 and until 1753 the curacy was combined with the office of usher at the grammar school, the corporation appointing.[2] The corporation still appointed the curate in 1754 and 1759, but by the earlier 19th century the rector appointed.[3] The curate's stipend was fixed at £8 in 1548. Like the vicar's it had lapsed by 1570, and in 1571 it too was made a charge on the collegiate property granted to the corporation.[4] As seen above, the curate shared in the augmentation ordered in 1646 and apparently in that granted in 1659. The curate was receiving £8 in 1667, and the stipend was raised to £16 in or shortly before 1676.[5] Having granted the curate a year's remission of rent due from his house in 1698, the corporation in 1701 made it a permanent grant so long as the existing curate continued in office and lived in the borough.[6] In 1718 the corporation voted the curate an extra £4 10s. a year, apparently raised by subscription, for reading prayers every morning. It was increased to £5 in 1754. By 1774 the curate received a salary of £26, which the corporation then agreed to continue while excusing him from reading prayers on Wednesdays, Fridays, and holidays 'without a subscription for that purpose'.[7] By the Chancery order of 1835 the curate's salary was raised from £120 to £170,[8] and in 1977 that sum was still paid in respect of the Queen Elizabeth Grant to the sub-rector, the senior of the assistant curates.[9]

There were nine altars besides the high altar by 1526: Jesus, St. Clement's, Trinity, St. Thomas's, St. Catherine's, St. Margaret's, St. Stephen's (apparently in a side aisle), St. Mary Magdalen's, and St. Bertelin's (presumably in St. Bertelin's chapel). There may also have been an altar of St. Nicholas. A Lady chapel was mentioned in the late 1520s, and there was a chapel of St. Thomas the Martyr by 1548.[10]

In 1446 the duke of Buckingham received licence from the Crown to endow a chantry in St. Mary's.[11] The only known chantry, however, is that of St. Thomas the Martyr. It was founded, probably in the late 15th century, by Thomas Counter, rector of Ingestre, for a priest to say mass daily in St. Mary's and keep a school. It was presumably attached to the altar and chapel of St. Thomas. In 1535 its endowments, worth £4 7s. a year, were an estate in Haughton called Bold Hall, another in Dunston called the Hall, and lands in Stafford; in 1549 a croft in Rickerscote in Castle Church was also mentioned.[12] In 1548 the commissioners ordered that the chantry priest should continue as schoolmaster at the same salary.[13] The Crown sold the Haughton and Dunston property in 1549 and the Rickerscote croft in 1550.[14]

A Jesus mass was being celebrated by 1466. It was endowed with lands in Coppenhall and at Silkmore in Castle Church by Humphrey Foxe, who also endowed an obit in the Franciscans' church with lands in Stafford. The Crown made a grant of both sets of property as concealed lands in 1564.[15]

Nine obits were recorded in the chantry certificates in 1548 and 1549, most of them datable to the later 15th and earlier 16th centuries.[16] Four more were established by Robert Lees by will proved in 1547.[17] Some of the income was assigned to the grammar school in 1550.[18] A house in Forebridge on which one of the obits was charged was bought by John Linacres of Forebridge; he died in 1577 leaving to the rector and his successors 3s. rent charged on the house in respect of the obit. It was still paid to the rector in 1714.[19]

In 1411-12 the corporation paid 1d. to the keepers of the light of the high cross,[20] probably a light before the rood in St. Mary's. A rent of 1s. for a light before the crucifix in St. Mary's was noted in 1548,[21] and in 1550 the Crown sold lands in Coton field and in the Crofts in Foregate field given for lights before the crucifix.[22] In 1466 Margery Burgham

[97] S.R.O., D.892/11/1, copy of letter from D. R. Norman to R. L. Lambert; *11th Rep. Com. Char.* 591, 595–6; White, *Dir. Staffs.* (1851), 346; P. T. Dale, 'Notes on ancient buildings and streets of Stafford', *T.O.S.S.* 1934, 18; deed of 1869 in poss. of Staffs. Building Soc., Wolverhampton (1977).
[98] *Staffs. Advertiser*, 3 and 10 Apr. 1875; W.S.L., M.530/4, copy of printed appeal 21 Apr. 1875; S.R.O., D.240/U/349, Smith & Gore to H. G. Bolam, 8 July 1878; *Lond. Gaz.* 11 July 1879, p. 4407; *Lich. Dioc. Ch. Cal.* (1880), 77; *Kelly's Dir. Staffs.* (1884).
[99] Ex inf. the rector (1962 and 1976).
[1] *S.H.C.* 1915, 243, 246.
[2] *S.H.C.* 4th ser. i. 271; W.S.L., S.MS. 402, f. 34v.; S.R.O., D.1323/A/1/1, p. 194; /2, pp. 92, 182, 198, 219; /3, p. 117; S.R.O., D.(W.) o/8/1, pp. 131, 137; W.S.L., H.M. Chetwynd 124; W.S.L., S.1549(2), *sub* Stafford, unident. newspaper cutting 22 Dec. 1753; B.R.L., Lee Crowder 64.
[3] L.J.R.O., B/A/1/21, pp. 42, 81; *Rep. Com. Eccl. Revenues*, 498; White, *Dir. Staffs.* (1851), 334.
[4] See refs. in notes 80 and 81 above.
[5] S.R.O., D.1323/A/1/1, pp. 199, 258; W.S.L., S.MS. 402, ff. 18v.–21, 34v.
[6] S.R.O., D.1323/A/1/2, pp. 57, 92.
[7] Ibid. p. 193; S.R.O., D.(W.) o/8/1, pp. 137, 300; W.S.L., S.MS. 365.

[8] L.J.R.O., B/V/6, St. Mary's, Stafford, 1841.
[9] Ex inf. the rector (1977).
[10] *St. Mary's, Stafford, Par. Reg.* (Staffs. Par. Reg. Soc. 1935–6), p. xxxii; *S.H.C.* 1926, 8, 12; W.S.L., S.MS. 366(iA), p. 7.
[11] For this para. see, unless otherwise stated, *V.C.H. Staffs.* iii. 307–8.
[12] *Valor Eccl.* (Rec. Com.), iii. 120; Lambert, *Coll. of Stafford*, 36–7.
[13] *S.H.C.* 1915, 243.
[14] *Cal. Pat.* 1548–9, 420; 1549–51, 363.
[15] H. L. E. Garbett, 'The Agreement with the Shoemakers of Stafford', *T.O.S.S.* 1936, 18–19; *Cal. Pat.* 1563–4, 62–3.
[16] Lambert, *Coll. of Stafford*, 36–7, 40–1. For dating see W.S.L., S.MS. 369, p. 98; C 1/253 no. 51; *St. Mary's Par. Reg.* p. xxxii; Req. 2/11/57; Req. 2/13/27; B.L. Add. Ch. 44264.
[17] *S.H.C.* 1926, 7.
[18] *Cal. Pat.* 1550–3, 21.
[19] *S.H.C.* 1926, 23; *St. Mary's Par. Reg.* 54; W.S.L., S.MS. 402, f. 34.
[20] J. B. Frith, 'Account of the bailiffs of borough of Stafford for 1411–12', *T.O.S.S.* 1939, 23; *T.O.S.S.* 1936, 19.
[21] Lambert, *Coll. of Stafford*, 40–1.
[22] *Cal. Pat.* 1549–51, 362.

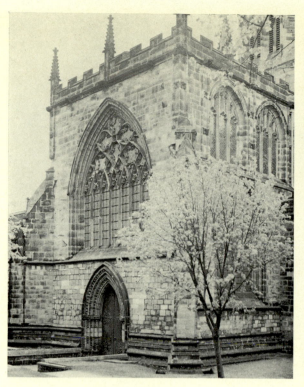

The north transept

The font

View from the south-west in 1794, with St. Bertelin's Chapel on the left

STAFFORD: ST. MARY'S CHURCH

Wesley Methodist Church, Chapel Street, with the former
house for the minister on the left

St. Chad's Church from the north-east, 1837

St. Chad's Church: the junction of the north nave arcade
and the chancel arch

STAFFORD

of Stafford arranged for the maintenance after her death of a lamp in the chancel of St. Mary's 'in honour of the most precious Body and Blood of Our Lord'.[23] The shoemakers' guild was maintaining a light in St. Mary's in 1476.[24] It was stated in 1548 that a rent of 1s. 8d. had been given by Ralph Launder for a lamp in St. Mary's.[25]

The keepers of the light of the high cross were probably the forerunners of the wardens of the rood guild in St. Mary's which existed by 1476.[26] It occurs as the guild of the Holy Cross in the church of Stafford during the reign of Henry VII when it was given a rent of 2s. 8d. from property in Eastgate Street by Richard Clarke of Shredicote in Bradley. There were then two wardens.[27] In the earlier 16th century the two wardens of what was called the brotherhood of the rood were presenting their accounts to the corporation.[28] There was a guild of St. Bertelin by 1425 when Elizabeth, widow of John Baxter of Stafford, left it 6s. 8d.; by 1529 it had two wardens, who accounted to the corporation.[29]

It was claimed in 1571 that the lapsing of the vicar's stipend had meant that for a long time the people of Stafford had received little instruction.[30] By will proved in 1588 Robert Sutton, rector 1572–87, left 6s. 8d. a year for a sermon on the anniversary of his death, apparently 30 November; it was still preached on that date in 1835.[31] By will proved in 1593 Richard Cradock of London gave £100 for the maintenance of a preacher or preachers to read a lecture or sermon at St. Mary's every Sunday morning, but the charity had been lost by the 1730s.[32] John Palmer, rector 1587–1639, was described early in the 17th century as learned and a preacher but was also a non-resident pluralist; in 1635 it was stated that there was seldom any catechizing.[33] Stafford was one of the twelve places in the county which benefited from a double lecture founded by John Machin of Seabridge in Stoke-upon-Trent and given on a monthly rotation from 1653 to 1660.[34] In addition a lecturer, John Greensmith, who was also vicar of Colwich, was appointed in 1655 at a salary of £50. He held the lectureship until the Restoration, and Noah Bryan, the rector appointed in 1657, was ejected c. 1661 in favour of the rector who had been sequestered in 1648.[35] In 1751 there were morning and afternoon services on Sunday, morning prayers on other days, and afternoon prayers on holidays; there was communion on the first Sunday of the month, with about 80 communicants; the rector catechized every Sunday in Lent.[36] When organizing the appointment of a new rector in the mid 1790s the corporation insisted on his agreeing to preach in the morning and the evening on Sundays.[37] In 1830 there were three services on Sunday, prayers on Wednesday and Friday, and an evening lecture on Wednesday; the sacrament was celebrated monthly and at the festivals, and the communicants numbered between 150 and 200.[38] It was noted, however, as part of the general dilapidation of St. Mary's in the late 1830s that, although there were two services on Sundays, 'one would suppose that neither clerk, organist, nor singers ever received anything for their services, they perform them so miserably'.[39] In 1851 there were three services on Sunday and one on Wednesday evening; those on Sunday morning and evening were always full.[40] In 1854 matins was said every day.[41]

By then the first of several new churches had been founded, Christ Church in Foregate Street, opened in 1839.[42] By 1878 there was a mission at Broadeye school, and in that year St. Augustine's school-chapel was opened as an extension to the school building.[43] It was replaced in 1900 by St. Bertholin's on the opposite side of Broadeye. The new church was of brick and wood and designed by George Wormal of Stafford; it was sold in 1940 and demolished in 1964.[44] St. John's, Littleworth, was opened in 1886.[45] St. Bertelin's, on a site at the junction of Holmcroft and Eccleshall Roads given by F. W. Carder, formerly of the near-by Tillington Hall, was built in 1956 as both a church and a hall. A brick building with large windows and a small tower, it was designed by B. A. Miller. A sanctuary and meeting-rooms were added in 1971. There was a curate-in-charge living at no. 27 Holmcroft Road by 1958 and at the specially built St. Bertelin's House, also in Holmcroft Road, by 1966.[46]

The site of the church of *ST. BERTELIN* adjoins the south end of the west front of the later St. Mary's.[47] The first Christian building there was a small wooden chapel which was replaced c. 1000 by one of stone with a chancel and nave. It appears to have been largely rebuilt in the 13th century, and in the 14th century a clerestory and south aisle were added to the nave. There was access by a door from St. Mary's. There were burials in and near St. Bertelin's from its earliest period, and it was still

[23] W.S.L., H.M. uncat. 26. Neither this nor the obit which she also arranged was mentioned in the chantry certificates.
[24] T.O.S.S. 1936, 18.
[25] Lambert, Coll. of Stafford, 40–1.
[26] T.O.S.S. 1936, 18.
[27] W.S.L., M.390.
[28] W.S.L., S.MS. 366(iA), pp. 8–18.
[29] Church of St. Bertelin, ed. Oswald, 10; W.S.L., S.MS. 366(iA), pp. 9–19.
[30] Bradley, Charters, 100.
[31] S.H.C. 1915, 243, 246; 11th Rep. Com. Char. 594–6; Keen, Letter to Inhabitants of Stafford, 35–7; S.R.O., D.1323/E/2, p. 594; St. Mary's Par. Reg. 91.
[32] Prob. 11/82 (P.C.C. 62 Neville); W.S.L. 49/112/44, copy of inf., Attorney-General v. Corp. of Stafford, p. 5.
[33] S.H.C. 1915, 243, 246; L.J.R.O., B/V/1/55.
[34] A. G. Matthews, Cong. Churches of Staffs. 30–1.
[35] S.H.C. 1915, 77, 243, 247; Cal. S.P. Dom. 1655–6, 52; 1657–8, 285.
[36] S.R.O., B/V/5, Stafford St. Mary, 1751.
[37] S.R.O., D.1323/A/1/3, p. 119.

[38] L.J.R.O., A/V/1/3, p. 73.
[39] Osborne's Guide to Grand Junction Railway (1st edn. 1838), 207.
[40] M. W. Greenslade, 'Stafford in the 1851 Religious Census', T.S.H.C.S. 1974–6, 69.
[41] V.C.H. Staffs. iii. 76 n.
[42] See p. 248.
[43] Staffs. Advertiser, 14 Sept. 1878.
[44] Lich. Dioc. Ch. Cal. (1900; 1901); Lich. Dioc. Mag. (1900), 154; Staffs. Advertiser, 7 June 1902, p. 4; Char. Com. files; Staffs. Advertiser and Chron. 27 Feb. 1964; S.R.O., D.834/15/4/4.
[45] See p. 249.
[46] Stafford Newsletter, 14 Apr., 15 Sept., 20 Oct. 1956, 12 Apr. 1963, 19 Mar. 1971; Lich. Dioc. Dir. (1959; 1967); Halden & Haywood's Dir. Stafford (1947), 49.
[47] This para. is based on Church of St. Bertelin at Stafford and its Cross, ed. A. Oswald (Birmingham [1955]); Alison J. Walker, 'The Archaeology of Stafford to 1600 A.D.' (Bradford Univ. M.A. dissertation, 1976), 14–19; information supplied by Dr. P. H. Robinson, formerly of Stafford Boro. Mus. and Art Gallery.

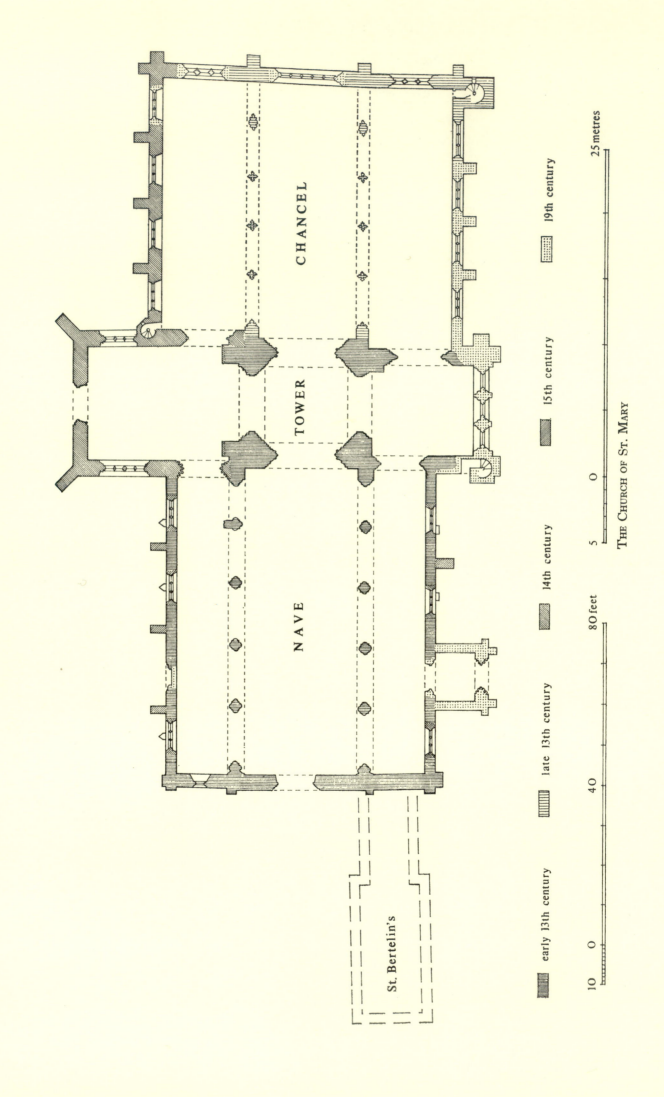

CHANCEL

TOWER

NAVE

St. Bertelin's

THE CHURCH OF ST. MARY

early 13th century

late 13th century

14th century

15th century

19th century

10   0   40   80 feet

5   0   25 metres

a burial place in the earlier 16th century. In the early 17th century it was stated that there had been three aisles in 1550 and that one of them was demolished when the grammar school moved into the building soon afterwards. There is no archaeological evidence of a north aisle; it seems that the three 'aisles' were the chancel, nave, and south aisle and that it was the south aisle which was demolished. The chancel was converted into a council chamber in 1605. St. Bertelin's was demolished in 1801 to provide additional burial space in St. Mary's churchyard. The site was excavated in 1954. The remains were found of a wooden object which was identified as a cross buried beneath the first church; another theory identifies it as a charcoal burial of the 11th or 12th century. After the excavation the plan of the church as rebuilt c. 1000 was outlined with original stone, and a conjectural replica of a cross was placed above the spot where the find was made.

The church of *ST. MARY*, set in a spacious churchyard, is a notable landmark which, in the opinion of Charles Lynam in the late 19th century, gave Stafford 'an air of importance which otherwise it would not possess'.[48] It is built of sandstone and has an aisled chancel, a central tower with octagonal lantern, transepts of which only that on the north now has a clerestory, and an aisled and clerestoried nave with a south porch. Much of its present appearance is the result of restoration and rebuilding in the 19th century; the spacious east end, which is wider than the nave and its aisles, is a relic of the requirements of the medieval college.

Some masonry in the nave and aisle walls is said to be of Norman origin, but the cruciform plan of the present church, with its aisled nave and chancel, is 13th-century and presumably represents the total rebuilding of an earlier church. Work may have been started in the reign of King John who in the mid 16th century was traditionally regarded as the founder of the collegiate church. The nave arcades of five bays are of the early 13th century. The transepts may have been of similar date: a lancet window survives in the south transept. The tower is mid-13th-century; in 1244 the dean was given eight oaks from the wood at Rugeley in Cannock forest 'for making the belfry of the church at Stafford'.[49] The aisled chancel of five bays is of the later 13th century, but the north aisle was rebuilt in, or not completed until, the early years of the 14th century shortly before the north transept was rebuilt.[50] Later in the century three new windows were inserted in the south aisle. Although there was no later enlargement of the plan there was much refenestration and reroofing in the 15th century.

New windows were put into the east wall of the chancel, the south chancel aisle, the south transept, and the north nave aisle. Both nave aisles were heightened and given new buttresses at the same time. The chancel, transepts, and nave were also provided with clerestories below new roofs of lower pitch and the tower was given an octagonal top stage and a spire. In 1594 the spire was blown down and the church seriously damaged; extensive rebuilding was at once carried out, apparently under the direction of Thomas Cleys, a carpenter, but the spire was not replaced.[51] The rector paid for the repair of the chancel on that occasion,[52] but in 1639 the Lord Keeper ruled that under the Queen Elizabeth Grant of 1571 the corporation was responsible for the repair of both nave and chancel.[53] A vestry may have been built at the west end c. 1699, but in 1785 the vestry was in the chancel.[54] A classical south porch had been erected by the late 18th century, and there was then a sun-dial on the outside of the staircase adjoining the south transept.[55] About the beginning of 1758 the church was whitewashed throughout.[56]

By 1777 St. Mary's was in such bad repair that it had to be closed. The upper part of the tower was rebuilt that year by Richard Baker and James Trubshaw, and in 1779–80 Baker carried out work on the roof, the parapets, and the windows.[57] By 1837 the church and its precincts were again so dilapidated that at the visitation of that year the archdeacon, instead of giving the churchwardens detailed directions, instructed them to have the fabric examined by a good architect and to submit his report.[58]

In 1840 George Gilbert (later Sir Gilbert) Scott inspected the church and recommended a restoration.[59] J. W. Russell of Ilam Hall offered £5,000 if another £3,000 could be raised, and in fact much more was forthcoming. Even so there was not enough money for as extensive a restoration as Scott wished. Pugin, however, pronounced it 'the best restoration . . . in modern times'. Work began apparently in 1842[60] and was completed in 1844. Scott rebuilt the south aisle of the chancel and most of the east wall where he inserted a Decorated window in place of the Perpendicular window; he also removed the chancel clerestory. In the south transept he replaced the Perpendicular window, door, and clerestory with three lancets and a steep-pitched roof. A Gothic south porch was substituted for the classical one. The four piers of the tower were in a dangerous state and were largely rebuilt. The octagon was restored: four pinnacles at its base which had disappeared by the end of the 18th century were replaced, and its parapet was rebuilt. The former parapet and other pieces of masonry

[48] Cherry, *Stafford*, 117. For other accounts of the architectural history of St. Mary's see ibid. 116–20; S. A. Cutlack, 'St. Mary's Church, Stafford' (MS. in W.S.L. 242/30, much of it printed in *T.O.S.S.* 1945–6 & 1946–7), 1–12; Pevsner, *Staffs.* 241–2.

[49] *Close R.* 1242–7, 160. *V.C.H. Staffs.* ii. 342, wrongly gives the number of oaks as 80.

[50] See plate facing p. 240.

[51] *St. Mary's Par. Reg.* 111; W.S.L., S.MS. 369, p. 139(b); *Cal. of Shrewsbury Papers in Lambeth Palace Libr.* (Derb. Arch. Soc. Rec. Ser. i), 74.

[52] *St. Mary's Par. Reg.* 111.

[53] Ibid. p. xxxvi. For the Queen Elizabeth Grant see above, pp. 205–6.

[54] S.R.O., D.1323/A/1/2, 63, 112; S.R.O., D.(W.) o/8/1,

[55] See plate facing p. 240.

[56] S.R.O., D.(W.) o/8/1, p. 164; W.S.L., S.MS. 365, Jan. 1758.

[57] S.R.O., D.(W.) o/8/1, pp. 325–7, 338, 344–5, 348, 359; B.L. Ch. Br. B. xvii. 7; tablet in the belfry.

[58] L.J.R.O., A/V/1/3, p. 73.

[59] For this para. see, unless otherwise stated, J. Masfen, *Views of the Church of St. Mary at Stafford* (1852), including Scott's account of the restoration; *Staffs. Advertiser*, 21 Dec. 1844; Cutlack, 'St. Mary's', 14–30; Cherry, *Stafford*, 116, 129; *S.H.C.* 4th ser. vi. 27–8.

[60] S.R.O., D.834/4/1/2, drawings of 1842; W.S.L., Staffs. Views, ix. 43; Lich. Dioc. Regy., B/A/1/30, p. 214.

p. 428.

from the church were used as garden features at Forebridge Villa (later St. Joseph's Convent) in Lichfield Road; other fragments were preserved elsewhere in the neighbourhood of the town.[61] Inside the church Scott found evidence that the level of the east end had formerly risen by stages, and he therefore installed a series of steps. The chancel was laid with Minton tiles. The coating of whitewash and a plaster ceiling were removed. Gas lighting was installed. The builder employed was William Evans of Ellastone, uncle of George Eliot and said to be the original of her Adam Bede. There were further restorations in the late 1870s and between 1947 and 1952. A nave altar was erected in the crossing in 1963.[62]

When Scott inspected the church in 1840, he found that pillars and arches had previously been cut to make room for deep galleries on three sides of the church.[63] The schoolmaster's gallery, used presumably by the grammar school generally, was mentioned in 1692.[64] In 1696 the corporation gave the churchwardens permission to erect two new 'lofts' next to the south and north-west doors in the same style 'as the other new lofts', and in 1706, to meet the demand for seats in the church, it ordered the erection of a gallery on the north side.[65] During Scott's restoration the galleries and box-pews were removed and low pews installed.[66] It was probably then that the mayor's pew, dated 1618, was moved to the parish church of Grendon (Warws.).[67]

The font dates from c. 1200 and is of unusual design. It is of quatrefoil globular shape and is carved with human and animal figures. It bears two inscriptions: 'Tu de Jerusalem ro . . . lem Me faciens talem tam pulchrum tam specialem', and 'Discretus non es si non fugis ecce leones'.[68]

A pulpit is mentioned in 1577.[69] Money was spent in 1612 on 'boards, wainscot, and work about the pulpit' and in 1613 on a canopy and desk.[70] A new pulpit and desk were apparently installed in the later 1750s.[71] By 1840 the pulpit stood immediately in front of the west gallery, so that most of the seats in the nave faced west.[72] The pulpit now at the north-east corner of the nave dates from Scott's restoration.[73]

The alabaster tomb of Sir Edward Aston (d. 1568) and his wife in the north transept, a table tomb with effigies, was formerly in the chancel but had been moved by 1840. It is damaged, apparently as a result of the careless erection of a jury box in the 1790s when the assizes were held in the chancel of St. Mary's owing to the dilapidated state of the

shire hall.[74] The bust of Izaak Walton by R. C. Belt was erected in the recess of the former door in the north aisle in 1878. Since 1930 it has been customary for a laurel wreath to be placed there at a civic service on 9 August, Walton's birthday.[75]

An organ built by John Geib of London was installed in the west gallery by the corporation in 1790; the borough M.P.s, Edward Monckton and R. B. Sheridan, contributed towards the cost.[76] A salaried organist was appointed in 1789, and at least by the early 1820s the salary was paid from the Queen Elizabeth Grant. During Scott's restoration the organ was moved from the west gallery to the north aisle of the chancel. It was enlarged in 1844 and replaced in 1909. The mahogany case from Geib's instrument was retained for one end of the new instrument and was used for a second organ installed at the west end in 1974.

The great bell and the little bell of St. Mary's were mentioned in the late 1520s,[77] and by 1553 there were four bells and a sanctus bell.[78] The treble bell was recast in 1620 at Walsall, and the little bell, now used as a call bell, was recast by Thomas Hancox of Walsall in 1622. The great bell was recast in 1640 and the third bell in 1642, both at Walsall.[79] There is now a peal of ten: (i and ii) 1887, Gillett & Co., Croydon (Surr.), installed for Queen Victoria's jubilee; (iii, iv, and vii) 1709, probably Abel Rudhall the elder of Gloucester; (v, vi, and viii) 1692, Henry Bagley of Chacombe (Northants.); (ix) 1751, recast by Abel Rudhall the younger of Gloucester; (x) 1742, Henry Bagley. The bells were restored and retuned at the Whitechapel Foundry in 1921.[80]

A clock and chimes were mentioned in the late 1520s.[81] In 1698 the corporation confirmed a contract for a new clock and chimes.[82] A set of Westminster quarter chimes was installed in 1887. The present clock, which uses five of the bells, was installed in memory of Ann and Elizabeth Wogan (d. 1909 and 1911) in 1913 after its predecessor had been struck by lightning. A carillon was installed in 1887 but was destroyed at the same time as the clock.[83]

The plate c. 1530 consisted of a silver-gilt cross, 4 parcel-gilt candlesticks, a silver-gilt cup, 2 parcel-gilt silver cruets, 2 parcel-gilt silver censers, a parcel-gilt silver ship, a small silver-gilt pyx, an enamelled parcel-gilt silver pax, a large silver chalice, a gilt chalice, 2 parcel-gilt silver chalices in daily use, a parcel-gilt silver chalice 'which Sir John Torner doth occupy', a broken parcel-gilt chalice, and a

[61] V.C.H. Staffs. v. 98.
[62] Kelly's Dir. Staffs. (1896); Collegiate Church of St. Mary, Stafford (Gloucester, edn. of c. 1970), 21, 27, 30 (copy in W.S.L. Pamphs. sub Stafford).
[63] Masfen, Church of St. Mary, 15. And see L.J.R.O., A/V/1/3, p. 73; W.S.L., Staffs. Views, ix. 68.
[64] W.S.L., H.M. Stafford 28, sale of pews 1692.
[65] S.R.O., D.1323/A/1/2, pp. 51, 118.
[66] Staffs. Advertiser, 21 Dec. 1844.
[67] V.C.H. Warws. iv. 79–80; W.S.L., S.MS. 402, f. 223v.
[68] S. A. Jeavons, 'The Fonts of Staffs.' T.B.A.S. lxviii. 15; plate facing p. 240 above.
[69] S.H.C. 1926, 33.
[70] S.R.O., D.1323/E/1, ff. 69, 75v.
[71] W.S.L., S.MS. 365 sub 1756, 1758.
[72] Masfen, Church of St. Mary, 15.
[73] W.S.L., Staffs. Views, ix. 63, 69.
[74] S. A. Jeavons, 'The Monumental Effigies of Staffs.' T.B.A.S. lxx. 25–6; W.S.L., Staffs. Views, ix. 74–5; Collegiate Church of St. Mary (edn. of c. 1970), 23; S.R.O.,

D.1323/A/1/3, p. 102; Univ. Brit. Dir. iv. 437. For Sir Edw.'s date of death see C 142/152 no. 149.
[75] Staffs. Advertiser, 10 Aug. 1878, 9 Aug. 1930, 15 Aug. 1931; Stafford Newsletter, 13 Aug. 1976.
[76] This para. is based on S.R.O., D.1323/A/1/3, pp. 23, 25, 27–9, 43, 45, 51, 63, 66, 69; /4, p. 44; plates on the 1790 organ case; Collegiate Church of St. Mary (edn. of c. 1970), 25, 31; Masfen, Church of St. Mary, 34; inf. from the rector (1976).
[77] W.S.L., S.MS. 366(iA), p. 6.
[78] S.H.C. 1915, 240.
[79] S.R.O., D.1323/E/1, ff. 103v., 107v., 134v., 251v., 264v.–265; T. S. Jennings, Bells of Church of Saint Mary, Stafford (1959; copy in W.S.L. Pamphs. sub Stafford).
[80] Jennings, Bells of Church of Saint Mary.
[81] W.S.L., S.MS. 366(iA), pp. 6–7.
[82] S.R.O., D.1323/A/1/2, p. 62.
[83] Kelly's Dir. Staffs. (1888); Stafford Newsletter, 1 Mar. 1947.

silver cruet belonging to the rood guild.[84] In 1553 the commissioners noted only two parcel-gilt silver chalices.[85] New communion plate was being paid for in 1623.[86] A list probably of the mid 1720s gives the plate as a silver communion cup, two silver patens, and two flagons; one of the patens and one of the flagons were given by a Mrs. Green.[87] Two silver salvers were added after the corporation ordered their purchase in 1789.[88] The plate still consisted of all those items in 1841,[89] but by the mid 20th century the only item earlier than the 19th century was a silver paten cover of 1622.[90]

The registers date from 1559; entries for the years 1644–67 vary in thoroughness.[91]

The churchyard was mentioned in 1178.[92] A cross, presumably a preaching-cross, still stood in the south-west corner in the early 17th century.[93] By the later 16th century the entrance to the churchyard was through lich-gates, probably under a gatehouse at the south-east corner, which was the main entrance by the late 18th century. In 1566 the three keepers were ordered by the corporation to see that the gates were opened on Sundays and holidays but otherwise kept locked.[94] In 1613 money was spent on the lich-gates and also on other church gates including a 'turning gate';[95] one may have been on the north side of the church, where new gates were paid for in 1756.[96] The court leet ordered the mayor in 1623 to see that the churchwardens enclosed the churchyard so that horses and carts could enter only by the lich-gates, which were to be kept shut except on holidays and for burials; a private key was to be given to each person living in the churchyard and to the parish clerk.[97] In 1636 the bishop forbade access by carts, carriages, and cattle.[98] In 1729 the corporation ordered a shop under the chancel to be converted into a charnel house.[99] It ordered a wall to be built on the north and west sides of the churchyard in 1778, assigning the stone from the demolished Green Gate.[1] In 1774 it bought some gardens on the west side as an extension. It demolished St. Bertelin's in 1801 to provide further space, and another small extension was consecrated in 1820.[2] By 1830 the churchyard was enclosed by a brick wall and by houses but was an open thoroughfare.[3] An ancient footpath dividing the western extension from the old part was closed in 1845 and palisades were erected round the churchyard.[4] In 1856 the churchyard was closed for burials except those in

vaults and walled graves.[5] After the excavation of St. Bertelin's in 1954 the churchyard was laid out as a garden of remembrance which was dedicated in 1956.[6]

The church of *ST. CHAD*, dating from at least the 12th century, formerly served a small parish east of the main street in the town centre. The parish originally included the area round the church, Tipping Street, the south side of Eastgate Street at Pitcher Bank, the corresponding stretch of South Walls, and the area immediately north-east of the Green Bridge. In 1903 the boundary was extended to cover the whole of Eastgate Street and South Walls and the area up to and including North Walls.[7] In the mid 1950s clearance of cottages and migration from the town centre reduced the population so that the church came to serve a congregation rather than a parish.[8] The parish and benefice were united with St. Mary's in 1973.[9]

The parish of St. Chad was mentioned in a deed probably of the later 12th century.[10] Architectural evidence suggests that the church was built in the mid 12th century. An inscription on the north-east pier of the crossing reads 'Orm vocatur qui me condidit'. Orm has not been identified,[11] but he may be the Hormus who witnessed the foundation charter of St. Thomas's priory *c.* 1174 and the Orm of Eastgate whose daughter gave land to the new priory.[12] It has been suggested that the church was founded by the bishop for the tenants of his estate in the borough, 14 messuages in 1086.[13] By the early 15th century, however, it had been appropriated to the prebend of Prees in Lichfield cathedral.[14] The right of appointing a curate remained with the prebendary until the death of Canon Henry Ryder in 1877, when under the Cathedrals Act of 1840 the patronage passed to the bishop.[15] The curacy became a perpetual curacy as a result of an augmentation from Queen Anne's Bounty in 1742; it was styled a vicarage from 1868.[16] Until 1858 the prebendary exercised a peculiar jurisdiction within the parish.[17]

The church was valued at 5 marks a year in 1428.[18] By the early 17th century the property held by the prebendary of Prees as rector of St. Chad's included cottages in the parish, 1½ a. of arable 'in the common field of Stafford', meadow, and certain tithes in and near Stafford. In 1650 the rents from the property amounted to £6 7s. 2d., although their true value

[84] W.S.L., S.MS. 366(iA), pp. 6–8, 16; S.MS. 366(iB).
[85] *S.H.C.* 1915, 240–1.
[86] S.R.O., D.1323/E/1, f. 139v.
[87] W.S.L., S.MS. 365.
[88] S.R.O., D.1323/A/1/3, p. 39.
[89] L.J.R.O., B/V/6, St. Mary's, Stafford, 1841.
[90] S. A. Jeavons, 'Church Plate in the Archdeaconry of Stafford', *T.B.A.S.* lxxiii. 1, 4, 10.
[91] The registers have been printed to 1671 by the Staffs. Par. Reg. Soc. (1935–6).
[92] *S.H.C.* i. 89.   [93] Speed, *Map of Staffs.* (1610).
[94] Ann J. Kettle, 'Black Book of Stafford', *T.S.H.C.S.* 1965–7, 18, 25; S.R.O., D.1323/E/1, f. 75; D.1323/A/1/3, p. 130; plate facing p. 240 above.
[95] S.R.O., D.1323/E/1, f. 75v.
[96] W.S.L., S.MS. 365 *sub* 1756.
[97] S.R.O., D.(W.) 1721/1/4, ff. 167v.–168.
[98] S.R.O., D.1323/E/1, f. 221C.
[99] S.R.O., D.1323/A/1/2, p. 350.
[1] S.R.O., D.(W.) o/8/1, p. 336.
[2] Ibid. pp. 300, 318; S.R.O., D.1323/A/1/3, pp. 55, 322; /4, p. 26; Lich. Dioc. Regy., B/A/2(i)/F, pp. 183–91; *11th Rep. Com. Char.* H.C. 433, p. 584 (1824), xiv.
[3] L.J.R.O., A/V/1/3, p. 73.

[4] *Staffs. Advertiser*, 6 Feb. 1864.
[5] *Lond. Gaz.* 27 June 1856, p. 2246.
[6] *Stafford Newsletter*, 21 Apr. 1956.
[7] Roxburgh, *Stafford*, 21; Wood, *Plan of Stafford* (1835); *Staffs. Advertiser*, 2 Jan. 1904.
[8] *Stafford Newsletter*, 11 Aug. 1956.
[9] *Lich. Dioc. Dir.* (1975), 146.
[10] *S.H.C.* viii (1), 131.
[11] J. Hewitt, 'Inscription recording the building of St. Chad's Church, Stafford', *Arch. Jnl.* xxxi. 216.
[12] *S.H.C.* viii (1), 132, 186.
[13] Calvert, *Stafford*, 44; *St. Chad's, Stafford, Par. Reg.* (Staffs. Par. Reg. Soc. 1935–6), pp. iii–iv; *V.C.H. Staffs.* iv. 37.
[14] *Feud. Aids*, v. 20.
[15] *Rep. Com. Eccl. Revenues* [67], p. 498, H.C. (1835), xxii; *St. Chad's Par. Reg.* p. vi; Cherry, *Stafford*, 132; *V.C.H. Staffs.* iii. 190.
[16] Poor Clergy Maintenance Act, 1 Geo. I, c. 10; below, p. 246; *Lich. Dioc. Ch. Cal.* (1869).
[17] *S.H.C.* 1915, 238; L.J.R.O., BB 17 and 21, LL 9; A. J. Camp, *Wills and their Whereabouts* (1974 edn.), 125; *V.C.H. Staffs.* iii. 74.
[18] *Feud. Aids*, v. 20.

was estimated at £24 5s. 5d.; the tithes yielded £8 16s. 8d. but were valued at £18 6s. 8d.[19] Most of the 35 houses in the parish in 1834 belonged to the prebendal estate.[20] By 1818 and until 1878 the estate was leased to the earls Talbot (from 1856 earls of Shrewsbury), who had to pay a stipend to the incumbent and maintain the chancel.[21]

By the early 17th century the prebendary was allowing the curate the rents paid by the tenants of the Stafford property and the tithes. In 1630, at the request of the bishop, Thomas Morton, the Puritan Feoffees for the Purchase of Impropriations, the lessees of the prebendal estate, assigned a further £10 9s. 3d. a year from the rents.[22] In 1643 the parliamentary committee for the county ordered that the curate should receive a grant from the sequestrated estates of the area and in 1644 assigned him rent from a close in Tillington or an equivalent.[23] In 1646 his income was stated to be £25 and the committee for plundered ministers ordered an augmentation of £50.[24] The parliamentary survey of 1650, however, declared that the curate's only income was that assigned by the prebendary and the 1630 augmentation.[25] A petition from the mayor and other inhabitants of Stafford to the lord protector in 1658 gave the income as £16 and requested an augmentation of £30 a year; one of £40 a year was granted.[26] By 1693 the lessee of the prebendal property was paying the curate £7 a year,[27] and in 1742 the value of the church was given as £7 10s., the amount of the stipend paid by the 19th-century lessees.[28] Four augmentations of £200 each were made from Queen Anne's Bounty in 1742, 1773, 1788, and 1808,[29] and the average annual value of the benefice in 1828–31 was £85 gross and net.[30] The vicar's income in 1875 was £91 10s., consisting of a stipend of £7 10s. from Lord Shrewsbury as lessee of the prebendal estate, £44 from 22 small gardens, £8 from investments, £28 from land at Tillington, and £4 from land in Coton field.[31] A grant of £100 a year was made from the Common Fund in 1878.[32]

No vicarage house was provided until the late 19th century.[33] Lord Shrewsbury as lessee of the rectorial estate promised to assign a house when William Beresford, vicar 1875–82, accepted the living; in fact it was never granted, being one of the houses in Greengate Street demolished in the mid 1870s to clear the western approach to the church. In 1880 the bishop asked the Ecclesiastical Commissioners to grant a house for the vicar, but they had already spent all that was available for St.

Chad's. In 1882 a pair of houses in Tipping Stree, part of the prebendal estate, was assigned in lieu of £40 of the £100 granted in 1878, but it was not until the beginning of the 20th century that the vicar moved to Tipping Street.

By the 17th century and until the mid 19th century St. Chad's was frequently held in plurality with Seighford, St. Mary's, Stafford, or Castle Church. From 1846 to 1854 the curates of St. Chad's were also the ushers at the grammar school, and from 1866 to 1873 the headmasters held the living.[34] In the later 18th and early 19th centuries services were infrequent. By 1782 it had long been customary to hold only one service a month; it consisted of prayers and a sermon and was held in the afternoon of the second Sunday of the month. From 1782 there was a service in the morning every third Sunday. From 1825 there was a service every Sunday, either morning or afternoon, and on Census Sunday 1851 there was a congregation of 123. An evening service was started in 1856.[35] William Beresford established a Sunday school, a clothing club, and a young people's guild and generally improved the life of the church; he also enlarged the building.[36]

The church is built of sandstone and consists of a chancel, a central tower with transepts, and an aisled and clerestoried nave. It appears to date from the mid 12th century and originally to have had an apsidal sanctuary, a chancel, and an aisled and clerestoried nave of four bays; the idea that it had a central tower and transepts at that time is not supported by the archaeological evidence. The surviving parts are richly decorated, the interior of the sanctuary with blind arcading of intersecting arches, the chancel arch and its respond with two orders of beak-headed ornament and chevrons, and the two eastern bays of the nave arcade with chevrons.[37] The east end of the sanctuary was extended and squared off in the 14th century, and about the same time a tower was built over the chancel. It was largely rebuilt and probably heightened c. 1500 by Thomas Counter, rector of Ingestre, and 'Sir Randol', a chantry priest of Stafford.[38] By the early 17th century the church was no longer aisled,[39] and in 1650 it was decribed as 'very small, ruinous, and inconsiderable'.[40] Peter Hales (d. 1643) left a 10s. rent-charge for the repair of St. Chad's; by 1840 it was paid into the churchwardens' general account.[41]

About 1740 the west end fell down.[42] Rebuilding and remodelling were begun in 1743 under the

[19] L.J.R.O., D.30, vol. LV, ff. 66–70, most of which is printed in *T.S.H.C.S.* 1968–70, 40–5.
[20] White, *Dir. Staffs.* (1834), 128.
[21] S.R.O., D.240/U/69; /U/353.
[22] L.J.R.O., D.30, vol. LV, ff. 66, 69–70; *V.C.H. Staffs.* iii. 56–8.
[23] *S.H.C.* 4th ser. i. 195.
[24] Bodl. MS. Bodl. 323, f. 267v.
[25] L.J.R.O., D.30, vol. LV, f. 70.
[26] *Cal. S.P. Dom.* 1657–8, 285; *S.H.C.* 1915, 239.
[27] *V.C.H. Staffs.* iii. 179.
[28] J. Ecton, *Thesaurus Rerum Ecclesiasticarum* (1742 edn.), 115; S.R.O., D.240/U/349; /U/353.
[29] C. Hodgson, *Account of Augmentation of Small Livings by Governors of Bounty of Queen Anne* (1845), p. ccxcvi.
[30] *Rep. Com. Eccl. Revenues*, 499.
[31] *Staffs. Sentinel*, 30 Oct. 1875 (copy of relevant extract in W.S.L. Pamphs. *sub* Stafford).
[32] *Lond. Gaz.* 5 July 1878, p. 3974.
[33] For this para. see W.S.L., C.B. Stafford, notes on St.

Chad's, letter from W. Beresford to Mrs. Cookson, 18 Feb. 1916; W.S.L., St. Chad's Scrapbook; *Lond. Gaz.* 16 June 1882, p. 2798; *Halden & Son's Dir. Stafford* (1902).
[34] *S.H.C.* 1915, 227, 239, 243 (with MS. notes by the editor in W.S.L. copy); *St. Chad's Par. Reg.* p. v; Bodl. MS. Gough 17560, f. 36; J. S. Horne, *Story of Castle Church, Stafford* (Gloucester [1963 edn.]), 12 (copy in W.S.L. Pamphs. *sub* Castle Church); J. S. Horne, *Notes for Hist. of K. Edw. VI Sch., Stafford* (Stafford, 1930), 70–1.
[35] Cherry, *Stafford*, 132; *T.S.H.C.S.* 1974–6, 69; W.S.L., St. Chad's Scrapbook, printed appeal 1860.
[36] *Lich. Dioc. Mag.* 1883, 30.
[37] See plate facing p. 241.
[38] Leland, *Itin.* ed. Toulmin Smith, v. 18 (where the entry is headed Lichfield, evidently in error).
[39] Speed, *Map of Staffs.* (1610).
[40] L.J.R.O., D.30, vol. LV, f. 70.
[41] See p. 268; L.J.R.O., B/V/6/Stafford, St. Chad's, 1840.
[42] Bodl. MS. Gough 17560, ff. 36, 38.

direction of Richard Trubshaw.[43] By the beginning of 1752 the money had run out; the west end had been rebuilt, but the work on the interior was unfinished and the tower and chancel were ruinous. In 1757 the parishioners decided to sell the bells in order to complete the work. As a result of the 18th century remodelling most of the medieval features were covered over. Externally the nave was encased in brick and a classical porch was apparently built at the west end. The tower was given a plain parapet with an urn at each corner. Classical windows were inserted in the nave. The chancel windows were blocked, and three lancets were intruded at the east end. The interior of the church was plastered and whitewashed; new decoration in 1744 included

and 1875 under the direction of Sir Gilbert Scott as a memorial to Thomas Salt. The nave piers, arches, and clerestory were restored. The west end was rebuilt, with a romanesque doorway surmounted by an arcade of five arches, three of them containing windows; above them is a niche containing a statue of St. Chad, given by Scott. A south aisle was built, also in a romanesque style.[46] A north aisle, designed by Robert Griffiths of Stafford following in the main a plan by Scott, was added in 1880.[47] The tower was restored in 1884 by Griffiths, again working to a plan by Scott; the 'pagan parapet' was replaced by an embattled parapet and also by eight pinnacles which were removed in 1910.[48] A north transept, designed by Griffiths in a romanesque

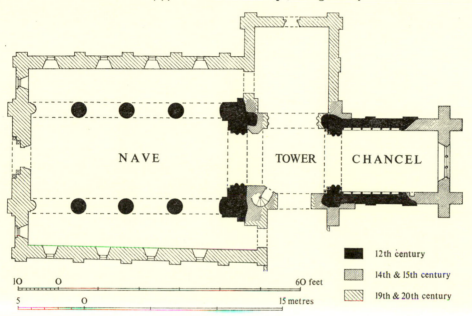

NAVE   TOWER   CHANCEL

10   O   60 feet

5   O   15 metres

■ 12th century

▨ 14th & 15th century

▧ 19th & 20th century

THE CHURCH OF ST. CHAD

'cherubs and circles'. Box pews, a three-decker pulpit, and a new font were installed.

In 1819 and 1832 the church was declared to be in a bad state of repair, but money for improvements was lacking.[44] Repairs were begun in 1854, but the discovery of the medieval work beneath the 18th century plaster led to the restoration of the chancel, the tower, the nave arch, and a small part of the nave. The three-light Decorated east window apparently dates from that time. The ceiling was stripped of plaster. The box pews were replaced by free seats, and a font 'consistent with the architecture of the original building' and a stone pulpit were installed. The work, completed in 1856, was organized by Thomas Salt of Weeping Cross in Baswich and a few others, and the architect was Henry Ward of Stafford.[45] Further work was carried out in 1874

style, was built in 1886; it was made into a chapel and vestry in or after 1937 as a memorial to Henry Henson Jevons, vicar 1915–35.[49] A wooden pulpit and a rood were installed in 1922 as a memorial to Robert McCleverty, vicar 1893–1915.[50] The font cover and the inner porch were designed by Sir Charles Nicholson.[51] A restoration was carried out between 1953 and 1960; the transeptal south-east choir vestry, built in place of an older structure, and the adjoining organ chamber were completed in 1955.[52]

The graveyard of St. Chad was mentioned in 1498.[53] Izaak Walton gave £22 to build a stone wall round it, and in 1672 he assigned rent which could be used by the churchwardens to maintain the church wall.[54] The approach to the church was improved c. 1744, and one of the objects of the sale

[43] For the rest of this para. see W.S.L. 319/40; Bodl. MS. Gough 17560, f. 36; W.S.L., H.M. uncat. 28; W.S.L., Staffs. Views, ix. 111–12 (including a view of 1837 reproduced facing p. 241 below); W.S.L., St. Chad's Scrapbook, photographs of exterior of nave showing pier behind brick casing.
[44] B.L. Ch. Br. C. i. 1; Staffs. Advertiser, 6 Oct. 1832.
[45] Staffs. Advertiser, 20 Apr. 1854, 2 Aug. 1856, 1 Apr. 1875.
[46] Ibid. 21 Mar. 1874, 1 Apr. 1875.
[47] Ibid. 6 Nov. 1880.
[48] Lich. Dioc. Mag. 1884, 62, 188; W.S.L., St. Chad's Scrapbook, cutting; Short Guide and Hist. of St. Chad's

Church, Stafford (copy in St. Chad's Scrapbook); Stafford Newsletter, 16 July 1960, p. 14.
[49] Staffs. Advertiser, 20 Nov. 1886; printed proposal for memorial Mar. 1937 (copy in W.S.L., St. Chad's Scrapbook); plaque in the chapel.
[50] Order of dedication (copy in W.S.L., St. Chad's Scrapbook).
[51] Hist. of St. Chad's (copy in Scrapbook).
[52] Stafford Newsletter, 2 Feb. 1952, 24 Oct. 1953, 7 Aug. 1954, 19 Mar. 1955, 23 Jan., 23 July 1960; ex inf. Mr. R. H. Dartford, churchwarden (1962).
[53] S.R.O., D.641/1/2/85, m. 1.
[54] W.S.L., H.M. uncat. 28; below, p. 268.

of the bells c. 1757 was the raising of money to fence and level the churchyard.[55] It was closed for burials in 1856 except those in vaults and walled graves.[56] In 1863 the churchwardens were letting the grazing for sheep.[57] In 1860 the main approach to the church was through a passage under a building in Greengate Street.[58] During the restoration of the mid 1870s the two buildings in Greengate Street immediately west of the church were demolished; they formed part of the rectorial estate leased to Lord Shrewsbury, who waived his interest in them as a contribution to the restoration fund.[59] The churchyard was then levelled and planted and a wall and gates were built in Greengate Street.[60] Stones which may have been the base of a preaching-cross were discovered at that time;[61] they have been set in the ground beside the main approach. A cross was erected near the west door in 1924 as a war memorial; it was accidentally destroyed during the rebuilding of the shops to the north in 1960, but a replica was erected in 1963.[62]

The church possessed a silver-gilt chalice and paten in 1553.[63] In 1975 none of the plate was ancient.

In 1553 the church had four bells and a sanctus bell and 'one other great bell, which is accustomed to call the parishioners together in all things pertaining to the town of Stafford'.[64] In the later 16th century the great bell was used to call the Twenty-five to council meetings and on the three fair days to summon the Twenty-five, the churchwardens, the schoolwardens, and the chamberlains to attend the bailiffs.[65] It was still used as the town bell in the early 17th century.[66] By 1757 five of the bells were cracked and it was decided to sell them and buy one new bell. There is now a single bell of 1632 by Thomas Hancox of Walsall, with a call bell which is probably the sanctus bell mentioned in 1553.[67]

The registers date from 1636; there are few entries for 1642–4, none for 1645 and 1646, and one for 1647.[68]

CHRIST CHURCH in Foregate Street was begun in 1837 and consecrated in 1839 as a chapel of ease to St. Mary's.[69] In 1844 it was assigned a parish covering the northern part of the town. The living, a perpetual curacy, was styled a vicarage from 1868 and has remained in the gift of the rector of St. Mary's.[70] A grant of £200 was made from Queen Anne's Bounty in 1845 to meet a benefaction, and in 1851 the annual income of the benefice was £126, mainly from pew-rents.[71] The vicarage house in Marston Road had been built by 1849.[72] On Census Sunday 1851 there were congregations of 450 in the morning and 450 in the evening.[73]

A mission room was opened at the Rowley Street school in December 1873; it seems to have continued until c. 1945.[74] St. Aidan's mission church, an iron structure on a site adjoining the vicarage, was opened as a mission and parish room in 1902; it was licensed for divine service in 1908.[75]

Christ Church, a building of white brick with stone dressings, originally consisted of a chancel, transepts, a nave with a west gallery, and a west tower with a bell. It was designed in a mixed Norman and Early English style by George E. Hamilton.[76] In 1863 an apse and aisles were added and the transepts were extended; the architect was T. W. Goodward.[77] A bell cast by Vickers & Sons was installed in 1875.[78] The graveyard was closed for burials in 1873 except those in existing vaults and walled graves.[79]

The church of ST. PAUL on a site in Lichfield Road given by C. H. Webb of Forebridge was begun by 1842 and consecrated in 1844.[80] A parish covering Forebridge, Castletown, and Rickerscote was formed in 1844 out of Castle Church parish.[81] The living, a perpetual curacy, was later (presumably from 1868) styled a vicarage; it has remained in the gift of the incumbent of Castle Church.[82] A grant of £200 was made from Queen Anne's Bounty in 1850 to meet a benefaction, and in 1851 the annual income of the benefice was £121, including £57 from an endowment made by the Ecclesiastical Commissioners.[83] The vicarage house south of the churchyard dates from the early 1850s.[84] On Census Sunday 1851 there were congregations of 86 in the morning and 82 in the evening.[85]

The daughter church of St. Thomas was opened in Castletown in 1866, and a mission church at Rickerscote in 1877.[86] There was a mission in Bailey Street off the Green from c. 1882 to c. 1886.[87]

[55] W.S.L. 319/4/40; W.S.L., H.M. uncat. 28.
[56] Lond. Gaz. 27 June 1856, p. 2246.
[57] S.R.O., D.1398/2/2, accts. 1863.
[58] W.S.L., St. Chad's Scrapbook, printed appeal 1860 and view of Greengate St. entrance.
[59] Staffs. Advertiser, 1 Apr. 1875.
[60] Ibid.; S.R.O., D.1398/2/2, W. Beresford's notes.
[61] Cherry, Stafford, 131; Calvert, Stafford, 46.
[62] Stafford Newsletter, 2 July 1960, 10 May 1963.
[63] S.H.C. 1915, 238.
[64] Annals of Dioc. of Lichfield, iv. 6 (copy in W.S.L. Pamphs.).
[65] Ann J. Kettle, 'Black Book of Stafford', T.S.H.C.S. 1965–7, 17, 31.
[66] S.R.O., D.(W.) 1721/1/4, f. 35v.
[67] W.S.L. 319/4/40; W.S.L., H.M. uncat. 28; Univ. Brit. Dir. iv. 437; A. E. Garbett, 'Church Bells of Staffs.' T.O.S.S. 1953–4, 7–8; C. Lynam, Church Bells of County of Stafford (1889), 27 and plates 77–8; T. S. Jennings, Hist. of Staffs. Bells (priv. print., preface dated 1968), 23, 30 (copy in W.S.L.); Staffs. Sentinel, 30 Oct. 1875 (copy of relevant extract in W.S.L. Pamphs. sub Stafford).
[68] The registers have been printed to 1812 by the Staffs. Par. Reg. Soc. (1935–6).
[69] Staffs. Advertiser, 26 Sept. 1835, 15 July, 28 Oct. 1837, 12 Jan. 1839.
[70] Lond. Gaz. 13 Dec. 1844, pp. 5159–61; White, Dir. Staffs. (1851), 334–5; Lich. Dioc. Ch. Cal. (1869); Lich. Dioc. Dir. (1975).
[71] C. Hodgson, Account of Augmentation of Small Livings by Governors of Bounty of Queen Anne: Supplement (1864), p. lxvii; T.S.H.C.S. 1974–6, 69.
[72] L.J.R.O., B/V/6, Stafford, Christ Church, 1849.
[73] T.S.H.C.S. 1974–6, 69.
[74] Lich. Dioc. Regy., B/A/1/33, pp. 280–1; Staffs. Advertiser, 20 Dec. 1873; Lich. Dioc. Dir. (1946).
[75] Lich. Dioc. Mag. 1902, 200; Lich. Dioc. Regy., B/A/1/37, pp. 82–3.
[76] W.S.L., Staffs. Views, ix. 119–20; Lich. Dioc. Regy., B/A/2(i)/L, pp. 420–1; plaque in the church.
[77] P.O. Dir. Staffs. (1868); Staffs. Advertiser, 17 Oct. 1863, p. 1; Pevsner, Staffs. 246.
[78] Staffs. Advertiser, 8 May 1875; Jennings, Staffs. Bells, 105.
[79] Lond. Gaz. 27 June 1856, p. 2246; 2 Sept. 1873, p. 4039.
[80] Staffs. Advertiser, 27 July 1841, 27 Jan. 1844.
[81] Lond. Gaz. 23 July 1844, pp. 2549–51.
[82] White, Dir. Staffs. (1851), 335; Lich. Dioc. Dir. (1975). The living is first given as a vicarage in Lich. Dioc. Ch. Cal. in the 1885 edn.
[83] Hodgson, Queen Anne's Bounty: Supplement (1864), p. lxviii; T.S.H.C.S. 1974–6, 72.
[84] White, Dir. Staffs. (1851), 335; P.O. Dir. Staffs. (1854).
[85] T.S.H.C.S. 1974–6, 72.
[86] See p. 249.
[87] Lich. Dioc. Ch. Cal. (1883; 1887).

St. Paul's is a stone building designed in a Decorated style by Henry Ward, apparently of Stoke-upon-Trent. It consists of a chancel, transepts, and a nave with a west gallery. There was formerly a bell turret, but in 1887 a tower and spire designed by Robert Griffiths of Stafford were built over the crossing to commemorate Queen Victoria's jubilee.[88] The bell of 1843, by Thomas Mears, was removed for recasting in 1969.[89]

The church of *ST. THOMAS AND ST. ANDREW* at Doxey originated in the church of St. Thomas at Castletown. A site for a church, house, and school in Castletown was bought in 1863, but at first there was enough money to build only the school. The church was built in 1866 by James Tyrer of Tixall Hall, a large shareholder in the London & North Western Railway. The church was intended mainly for the railway workers living in the area, with all the sittings free; it was endowed with shares in various railway companies, and the stone for it was carried free where it passed over the L.N.W.R. line. Tyrer also provided a house for the incumbent in Rowley Avenue, set in an acre of ground.[90] A parish was formed out of St. Paul's parish in 1867.[91] The living, a perpetual curacy, was styled a vicarage from 1868 and was originally in the gift of Tyrer; after his death in 1875 it passed to trustees.[92] The Evangelical preaching of William Kendall, the first incumbent, at once attracted crowds from elsewhere in the town who, it was commented, 'occupy space in a building which was never designed for them . . . Fine silks and satins with extensive crinolines are a bar to the working classes in more ways than one.'[93] The church was designed in a mixed Early English and Decorated style by W. Culshaw of Liverpool. It was of stone and consisted of a chancel and a nave with a west bellcot containing a bell of 1792 by John Rudhall of Gloucester. Culshaw also designed the vicarage house.[94]

In 1936 the Doxey portion of the parish of Seighford with Derrington and Creswell was transferred to St. Thomas's parish.[95] It included St. Andrew's mission church in Doxey Road, built in 1914;[96] a bell in a bellcot over the porch was presented by S. T. Price of Doxey, who was manager of W. G. Bagnall Ltd.'s Castle Engine Works and had the bell cast there.[97]

By 1972 St. Thomas's had become redundant and was then closed and demolished. St. Andrew's was used as the parish church until 1975 when the church of St. Thomas and St. Andrew was opened in Doxey Road. It is a multi-purpose building designed in a modern style by Horsley, Currall & Associates of Stafford.[98] The vicar had moved to a new vicarage house in Doxey in 1965; the vicarage in Rowley Avenue was sold and demolished, and houses were built over the grounds.[99]

The church of *ST. PETER* in Rickerscote Road, Rickerscote, originated in a mission church in School Lane, Rickerscote, opened from St. Paul's in 1877 and also used as a school. A conventional district was established in 1954.[1] St. Peter's church was begun in 1956 and consecrated in 1957.[2] A parish was formed in 1962. The vicarage is in the gift of the bishop of Lichfield and the vicar of St. Paul's.[3] The vicarage house in Rickerscote Road was completed in 1962.[4]

St. Peter's, which is not orientated, was designed, like the house, by C. C. Gray of Walsall[5] and is of brick with stone-mullioned windows. It has a clerestoried nave divided from narrow aisles by square brick piers; the chancel is structurally part of the nave. There are a baptistery and a tower at the 'west' end. The font, altar, lectern, pulpit, and altar rails are of brick.

The church of *ST. JOHN THE BAPTIST* at Littleworth originated in a mission centre dedicated to St. John which was opened from St. Mary's in the new school in Weston Road, Littleworth, in 1886.[6] A mission church was built in Tithe Barn Road in 1902 to the design of George Wormal of Stafford;[7] it is a building of brick with stone dressings and has a bell on the west wall. The Littleworth area was constituted a mission district c. 1920 and a conventional district in 1921. A parish was formed out of St. Mary's in 1928 under a perpetual curate (from 1969 styled a vicar) nominated by the bishop.[8] St. John's church, on a site between Weston Road, Westhead Avenue, and Bedford Avenue given by the earl of Shrewsbury in 1921, was begun in 1927 and opened in 1928. Designed by Sir Charles Nicholson in a Gothic style and incorporating materials from Tixall Hall, demolished shortly before, the permanent part consisted of a chancel of brick and stone, with a Lady chapel on the north and an organ chamber and vestries on the south.[9]

[88] Pevsner, *Staffs.* 248; Pigot, *Nat. Com. Dir.* [1841], Staffs. p. 51; White, *Dir. Staffs.* (1851), 335; *Lich. Dioc. Mag.* 1887, 95, 230.
[89] Jennings, *Staffs. Bells*, 99; *Stafford Newsletter*, 21 Feb. 1969.
[90] Joan Exton, *St. Thomas' Church, Castletown, Stafford* (Gloucester [1972]; copy in W.S.L. Pamphs. *sub* Stafford); *Staffs. Advertiser*, 22 Aug. 1863, 12 May 1866; Lich. Dioc. Regy., B/A/2(i)/R, pp. 58–9. *V.C.H. Staffs.* v. 97, wrongly states that the mission was founded after Castletown was added to the borough.
[91] *Lond. Gaz.* 28 June 1867, pp. 3627–8.
[92] Lich. Dioc. Regy., B/A/2(i)/R, pp. 57–8; *Lich. Dioc. Ch. Cal.* (1869); Crockford (1895, the first edn. to show the patrons as the Hyndman Trustees instead of simply as trustees); *Lich. Dioc. Dir.* (1975); Exton, *St. Thomas' Church*, 9–10.
[93] W.S.L., St. Chad's Scrapbook, unident. newspaper cutting.
[94] *Staffs. Advertiser*, 12 May 1866; Exton, *St. Thomas' Church*, 2, 4, 8–9. The details of the bell were supplied by Mr. J. Burke of Weston (1975); Jennings, *Staffs. Bells*, 87, gives the date as 1799.

[95] *Lond. Gaz.* 14 July 1936, pp. 4507–8.
[96] St. Thomas's par. records, box II; *Lich. Dioc. Ch. Cal.* (1915).
[97] Ex inf. Mr. J. Burke (1976).
[98] Ex inf. Mrs. Joan Exton (1975); *Stafford Newsletter*, 14 Mar., 28 Nov. 1975.
[99] Ex inf. the vicar (1975); St. Thomas's par. records, file for 1960–7.
[1] *V.C.H. Staffs.* v. 97, 99.
[2] *Stafford Newsletter*, 19 May 1956, 21 Sept. 1957.
[3] *Lich. Dioc. Dir.* (1963; 1964; 1975).
[4] Ex inf. the vicar (1963).
[5] *Stafford Newsletter*, 21 Sept. 1957; ex inf. the vicar.
[6] See p. 262; *Lich. Dioc. Ch. Cal.* (1888).
[7] *Staffs. Advertiser*, 3 Jan. 1903; Lich. Dioc. Regy., B/A/1/36, p. 100; S.R.O., D.834/8/1/1.
[8] *Lich. Dioc. Ch. Cal.* (1921–2; 1923; 1929); *Lich. Dioc. Dir.* (1969; 1975); *Lond. Gaz.* 15 June 1928, pp. 4094–6.
[9] *Order of Service for laying of foundation-stone* (1927) and *Order of Service for consecration* (1928) (copies in W.S.L. Pamphs. *sub* Stafford); *Kelly's Dir. Staffs.* (1928); *Dioc. of Lichfield: Year Book of Dioc. Council* (1930), 216; *S.H.C.* 1927, 77.

The nave was a temporary structure of wood and concrete. In 1971 work began on a permanent nave, a rebuilt Lady chapel, and a church hall, which were completed in 1972; the new parts, which are of brick, were designed by C. W. Tomkinson of Forshaw, Greaves & Partners of Newcastle-under-Lyme. A vicarage house was built beside the church in 1970.[10] The former church in Tithe Barn Road, which had been used as the parish hall, was sold in 1972 and converted into a Sikh temple.[11]

St. Alban's mission church in Marston Road within Marston parish (later Marston with Whitgreave) was opened in 1896.[12]

In 1964 a temporary church was opened in West Way on the Highfields estate in Castle Church parish, replacing the school halls which had been used for services, a Sunday school, and meetings. In its place a hall in Lovelace Close used both for services and as a social centre was dedicated in 1967.[13]

ROMAN CATHOLICISM. Until the 18th century the Roman Catholic centres in the Stafford area were at some distance from the borough: at St. Thomas near Baswich, owned by the Fowlers from the 1540s, at Tixall Hall, where the Astons were Roman Catholics from the 1620s or 1630s, and probably at Stafford Castle, the seat of the Staffords until its demolition during the Civil War.[14] There were also priests in the town itself at various times during the reigns of Elizabeth I and James I. The Tulley family of Forebridge sheltered priests under Elizabeth I,[15] and they probably gave a home to their relative Thomas Chedulton, a canon of St. Mary's who became the first vicar there in 1548, resigned c. 1560, but remained in the area until his death in 1589. Robert Sutton, a seminary priest, is said to have spent many years in Stafford before his arrest and execution there in 1587. About 1612 a priest who was living in the town escaped from the pursuivants allegedly through the connivance of Thomas Worswick, the town clerk of Stafford. A priest named Fisher, possibly Thomas Fisher, is said to have been working in Stafford in 1620. In 1641 36 recusants were returned in St. Mary's parish and 4 in St. Chad's; 23 were returned in Baswich and 9 in Castle Church.[16]

After the accession of James II in 1685 a Roman Catholic chapel and school were opened in the town, possibly by Daniel Fitter, the Fowlers' chaplain at St. Thomas. John Leyburn, the vicar apostolic, confirmed 417 people in 1687 at the chapel, which on that occasion seems to have been used as a centre for a wide district; he also confirmed five at St. Thomas. A Roman Catholic, Dr. Benjamin Thornburgh, was elected mayor in 1687 on James II's

instructions.[17] With the flight of James in 1688 the chapel was destroyed by a mob. In 1705 15 papists were returned in the borough, most of them 'of inferior condition'; one, however, was described as a gentlewoman and occurs as the wife of an alderman in 1706. In Baswich 25 were returned and in Castle Church four.[18]

St. Thomas ceased to be a Catholic centre in the 1730s, and the only priest left in the Stafford area was the chaplain at Tixall. In the 1740s Richard Palin, a priest and the heir of the Roman Catholic Palins of Dearnsdale in Bradley to the west of the town, went to live at Dearnsdale; he was, however, in his 70s. He died in 1750, and in 1754 one of his heiresses settled an annuity to support a priest who would say mass at Dearnsdale and in the neighbourhood. Thomas Wilson came to Stafford from Tixall in 1754 and worked in the town until his death in 1766. In 1751 there were stated to be 12 papist families in St. Mary's parish.[19] In 1767 84 papists were returned in the parishes of St. Mary and St. Chad; there were 41 in Baswich and 27 in Castle Church.[20] A few years later Thomas Barnaby came to Stafford from Norfolk, and there has been a regular succession of priests ever since. There is a local tradition that Barnaby used to say mass in the garret of a house on the Green in Forebridge.

His successor, John Corne, who came from Cobridge in Burslem in 1784, lived for a time in Tipping Street, using a building in his garden as a chapel. In 1788 a lease was taken of land on the Wolverhampton road in Forebridge, once part of the Austin friars' estate and by then the property of the Roman Catholic Berington family, formerly of Rowley Hall in Castle Church. A chapel was opened there in 1791, with a house for the priest. A new church incorporating the chapel was built c. 1816, the cost being met by the Jerningham family, the heirs of the Staffords. The present St. Austin's was built on an adjoining site in 1861–2 to the design of E. W. Pugin; the old church then became part of the school.

A mass-centre dedicated to St. Patrick and served from St. Austin's was opened in St. Patrick's school in Foregate Street in 1884.[21] St. Patrick's became an independent mission in 1893,[22] with responsibility for 700 of the 1,200 Roman Catholics served by St. Austin's. An iron church was built in St. Patrick's Street behind the school in 1895. In 1921 a site was acquired in Sandon Road where a presbytery was built in 1926 and a school was opened in 1930. A hall attached to the school was then used as the church until the completion of the present St. Patrick's, built in 1951–3. Designed in a Romanesque style by E. B. Norris of Stafford, it is of straw-coloured brick and consists of chancel, nave, narrow aisles with end chapels, and a narthex.

St. Austin's opened a mass-centre at the Lea-

[10] *Stafford Newsletter*, 17 Nov. 1972; ex inf. the vicar (1975).
[11] See p. 255.
[12] *Stafford Newsletter*, 13 Mar. 1970; *Lich. Dioc. Mag.* 1896, 112; *Lich. Dioc. Dir.* (1975).
[13] *Stafford Newsletter*, 27 Mar., 16 Oct. 1964, 17 Mar. 1967.
[14] This account is based, unless otherwise stated, on M. Greenslade, *St. Austin's, Stafford* (Stafford, 1962; copy in W.S.L. Pamphs. *sub* Stafford). An account of Roman Catholicism in Forebridge, including the successive churches of St. Austin, is given in *V.C.H. Staffs.* v. 97–8; some of the details, particularly in connexion with St.

Joseph's convent, are corrected in *St. Austin's*.
[15] See also *S.H.C.* 1930, 255–6.
[16] *Staffs. Cath. Hist.* v. 8–9, 29, 37.
[17] See p. 225. Thornburgh had been appointed an alderman and J.P. on James's instructions earlier the same year, not in 1686 as stated in Greenslade, *St. Austin's*, 8.
[18] *Staffs. Cath. Hist.* xiii. 8, 14, 40–1.
[19] L.J.R.O., B/V/5, Stafford, St. Mary, 1751.
[20] *Staffs. Cath. Hist.* vi. 9–10, 23; vii. 11–13.
[21] Ed. 7/109/295; G.R.O., Worship Reg. 28588.
[22] *Staffs. Advertiser*, 23 Dec. 1893. This corrects Greenslade, *St. Austin's*, 26.

sowes school on the Weeping Cross estate *c.* 1963. A parish with a resident priest was formed in 1964, and St. Anne's hall, used as a church and a hall and designed by Sandy, Norris & Partners of Stafford, was opened in Lynton Avenue in 1966.[23]

There was a mass-centre served from St. Austin's at Bower Norris Roman Catholic school in Somerset Road, Highfields, from 1966 to 1971.[24]

The Sisters of St. Joseph of Cluny opened a convent in 1903 at Forton House, a former shoe factory in Lichfield Road. In 1905 the community moved to Forebridge Villa, also in Lichfield Road, and opened a private school for girls there. The school was closed in 1971, and the nuns' main work in 1976 was running a guest house for elderly ladies. In addition one of the sisters was headmistress of St. Austin's Roman Catholic primary school, which moved to the convent in 1971.[25]

PROTESTANT NONCONFORMITY.[26] APOS-TOLIC CHURCH.

The Apostolic Church began meeting at the Sheridan Hall in Sandon Road *c.* 1950. In 1968 the members moved to a wooden church at the junction of South Walls and Clarke Street which they had constructed themselves, but it ceased to be used in 1971.[27]

BAPTISTS. About 1650 Stafford had the strongest General Baptist church in the county, with Henry Haggar as its minister. There were two Stafford signatories to a letter of advice and exhortation sent to Cromwell by thirteen Baptist churches in the Midlands in 1651.[28] Colonel Henry Danvers, the governor of Stafford in the early 1650s, became a Baptist while living there.[29] In 1656 the child of an Anabaptist was buried at St. Mary's.[30] It was at a Baptist meeting about that time that the Quaker Humphrey Woolrich first preached in Stafford.[31] John Wade, whose house was returned in 1669 as a conventicle with 300 or 400 adherents, is said to have been a Baptist.[32]

Nothing further is known of Baptists in the town until 1857 when a group with Baptist views withdrew from the Congregational church and began to meet in a room in Eastgate Street. A Sunday school was started in February 1858, and a church was formed in May.[33] In November the Lyceum theatre began to be used for services, and they were still being held there at the end of 1859. From 1859

there was a resident minister.[34] The congregation next met in a room over a music shop.[35] They subsequently had a chapel in Water Street, but by 1864 it was too small. In that year it was taken down and a white-brick chapel erected on the same site; it was registered for Particular Baptists. During the rebuilding services were held in the former grammar school in North Walls, which was lent by the Y.M.C.A.[36] A gallery was inserted in the chapel in 1880.[37] In 1895 a new chapel with a Sunday school adjoining was begun on the Green in Forebridge; it was opened in 1896. Designed in a Tudor-Gothic style by Ewen Harper of Birmingham it is of red brick with stone dressings and consists of an apse and an aisled nave with a gallery over the entrance; there is a north-east tower with a stone spire in open tracery.[38] The Water Street building was let to various organizations, including a group of Brethren, until 1920 when it was sold; it was converted into a grain store and in 1970 was demolished.[39]

A Baptist Sunday school served from the Stafford chapel was started at Rising Brook school in 1948. A church hall used for services was opened in John Amery Drive in 1955, and in 1960 Risingbrook became a separate church. An extension primarily for Sunday-school and youth-club purposes was built in 1977.[40]

A Free Baptist church and Sunday school were opened in 1948 in two huts in Sandon Road. They were replaced by a permanent church in 1970.[41]

BRETHREN. In 1838 Alexander Stewart, the Presbyterian minister at Stafford, was dismissed for 'Plymouth heresies'. He tried to continue to use the Presbyterian church for meetings but then moved to a room in a tavern. The present meeting-room on the corner of Church Lane and St. Mary's Place was opened in 1839. There was originally a small graveyard in front of the room; it was closed for burials in 1856 except those in vaults and walled graves but survives as a forecourt. The group received visits from two pioneers of the Brethren movement, W. H. Dorman, earlier the Congregational minister at Stafford, and J. N. Darby.[42] A split seems soon to have occurred.[43] In 1851 a group of Plymouth Brethren was meeting in a house in Eastgate Street, and on Census Sunday there were attendances of 40 in the morning and 40 in the evening; nothing further is known of the group. Those who continued to use the meeting-room were Exclusive Brethren,

[23] *Cath. Dir. of Archdioc. of Birmingham* (1964), 125; (1967), 125; (1969), 223.
[24] Ex inf. the parish priest of St. Austin's (1975).
[25] For the schools see pp. 260, 264.
[26] Much of the research for this section was carried out by Miss Ann J. Kettle.
[27] *Stafford Newsletter*, 18 Nov. 1950 and 5 Feb. 1971 (first and last announcement of meetings), 29 Nov. 1968.
[28] A. G. Matthews, *Cong. Churches of Staffs.* 34–6.
[29] Ibid. 34; *Cal. S.P. Dom.* 1650, 159, 211, 506, 580; 1652–3, 412.
[30] *St. Mary's, Stafford, Par. Reg.* (Staffs. Par. Reg. Soc. 1935–6), 303.
[31] S.R.O., D.3159/1/1, notes at end of volume.
[32] Matthews, *Cong. Churches of Staffs.* 66, 89.
[33] *Records of an Old Association*, ed. J. M. Gwynne Owen (Birmingham, 1905), 187–8; *Staffs. Advertiser*, 28 Nov. 1857.
[34] *Staffs. Advertiser*, 4 Dec. 1858; R. M. Charley, *Stafford Baptist Church* (1938 edn.), 7 (copy in W.S.L. Pamphs. *sub* Stafford).

[35] *Staffs. Advertiser*, 4 June 1887.
[36] Ibid. 2 Apr., 9 July 1864; G.R.O., Worship Reg. no. 16360.
[37] *Staffs. Advertiser*, 4 June 1887.
[38] Ibid. 13 July 1895, 13 June 1896.
[39] Charley, *Stafford Bapt. Church* (1938 edn.), 12.
[40] Charley, *Stafford Bapt. Church* (1958 edn.), 6–7 (copy in W.S.L. Pamphs. *sub* Stafford); *Stafford Newsletter*, 19 Mar. 1960, 30 Dec. 1977.
[41] *Stafford Newsletter*, 8 Nov. 1963, 3 July 1970; Worship Reg. no. 62388.
[42] S. D. Scammell, *Jubilee and Bicentenary Memorial of the Old Stafford Meeting House* (Stafford, 1887), 25, 35–6 (copy in W.S.L. 7/198/00); F. R. Coad, *Hist. of Brethren Movement*, 76–7; W.S.L., C.B. Stafford, Church Lane Meeting Room; *Lond. Gaz.* 27 June 1856, p. 2246.
[43] The rest of this para. is based on inf. from Mr. G. J. Venables of Stafford (1962); M. W. Greenslade, 'Stafford in the 1851 Religious Census', *T.S.H.C.S.* 1974–6, 70; *Halden & Son's Dir. Stafford*, later *Halden & Haywood's Dir. Stafford* (1897 and later edns. to 1920); W.S.L., C.B. Stafford, Church Lane Meeting Room.

and on Census Sunday there were attendances of 45 in the morning and 45 in the evening at what was then known as the Room. The Sunday school, which was at first held in the Room, moved to the former grammar-school building in North Walls in 1861 and to Crabbery Hall in Crabbery Street in 1896. Two schoolrooms were built behind the Room in 1906; they were extended to the south in 1927. The Church Lane Brethren became an Open Meeting in 1885.

A group of Open Brethren registered the Working Men's Gospel Mission in Brook Street in 1889; it had no connexion with Church Lane. The hall was taken over by the Primitive Methodists in 1902.[44]

An Exclusive Meeting was started in 1895 by two evangelists who used a tent on the grammar-school field in Newport Road and later the Odd Fellows Hall. The meeting was held at the Stafford Institute in Earl Street from c. 1897, and c. 1905 it moved to the former Baptist chapel in Water Street. In 1920 it amalgamated with Church Lane.[45]

In 1930 a group of Exclusive Brethren who had been meeting at Gnosall registered part of no. 11 Crabbery Street. They moved to the Co-operative Hall, Wolverhampton Road, apparently by 1936. It seems to have been this group which registered a meeting-room at the rear of no. 132 Lichfield Road in 1950 and moved to premises behind no. 35 Mill Street in 1951. In 1958 it moved to a meeting-room which it had built in Tipping Street; the room was closed in 1963.[46]

An Open Meeting of Christian Brethren was started at Highfields primary school in 1960. Highfields chapel in Milton Grove was opened in 1961.[47]

CHRISTADELPHIANS. A Christadelphian Bible Class was started c. 1896 in the premises of the former Working Men's Club in Salter Street.[48] From c. 1904 meetings were held at the Stafford Institute in Earl Street, c. 1930 in the Co-operative Guild Room in Salter Street, and from c. 1931 in Currys Buildings, Greengate Street.[49] In 1936 the society moved to the Welton Memorial Institute in Eastgate Street, but by 1946 it was once more meeting in Greengate Street.[50] By 1954 meetings were being held in Crabbery Hall in Crabbery Street,[51] and in 1958 the Christadelphians took over the premises behind no. 35 Mill Street vacated by the Plymouth Brethren.[52] They moved to the Lewis Heath Memorial Institute in Victoria Road in 1969.[53]

CHRISTIAN SCIENTISTS. A group of Christian Scientists began to hold services in a house in Oxford Gardens in 1912. In 1919 a room was hired at no. 16 Tipping Street. The group was recognized by the Christian Science Board of Directors in 1926. In 1963 the society moved to no. 64 Lichfield Road, a house which it had bought and converted into a church, Sunday school, and reading-room.[54]

CONGREGATIONALISTS (INDEPENDENTS), LATER UNITED REFORMED CHURCH. In 1786 James Boden, minister of the Congregational Tabernacle at Hanley, started to preach in the streets of Stafford, despite the hostility of the crowd. An exciseman then opened his house in Martin Street for meetings. The congregation later moved to a house in North Walls behind the Vine inn, and in 1788 a converted building in Salter Street opposite the Vine was registered for worship. Jonathan Scott sent John Wilson as the first resident minister in 1789 and maintained him at his own expense. In 1792 the meeting-house was bought by Wilson and Thomas Goodwin and conveyed by them to trustees; it was stipulated that the ministers were to be of the Independent persuasion. A church with fourteen members was constituted in 1798. In 1800 the County Association reported a marked increase in attendance at the chapel during the previous three months, although Stafford was perhaps 'more deeply sunk in licentiousness' than any other place. A secession to the Wesleyan Methodists in 1803 reduced the membership to seven, and there was again no resident minister until 1810.[55]

In 1811 a site was bought in Martin Street, and Zion chapel was opened there in 1812, a red-brick building with a garden and graveyard in front.[56] The expense caused the congregation and John Chalmers, minister 1815–29, much embarrassment, and for a time Chalmers waived his salary, supporting himself by training missionaries and later by running a school. In 1822 a loan from a Mr. Birch of Armitage, probably Thomas Birch of Armitage Lodge, saved the chapel from conversion into houses. Church membership was then 18, and although there were congregations of 100 in the morning and 200 in the evening, the chapel was too big and a third of it had been partitioned off as a school.[57] A schoolroom and classrooms were built behind it in the later 1830s, and were replaced by new schools and a lecture room in 1863.[58] On Census Sunday 1851 the morning congregation numbered 130 and that in the evening 192.[59] A secession in 1857 led to the foundation of a Baptist meeting.[60] Improvements were begun in 1896, and the chapel was reopened in 1897. The building was extended towards Martin Street and a baroque façade was added including a four-columned portico from Staffordshire General

[44] Worship Reg. no 31656; ex inf. Mr. Venables; below, p. 254.
[45] Ex inf. Mr. Venables.
[46] Ex inf. Mr. Venables; Stafford Newsletter, 5 Apr. 1958; Worship Reg. nos. 52649, 62557, 62962, 66669.
[47] Stafford Newsletter, 1 Oct. 1960; ex inf. Mr. Venables.
[48] Halden & Son's Dir. Stafford (1897); Worship Reg. no. 35824.
[49] Halden & Son's Dir. Stafford (1905); Halden & Haywood's Dir. Stafford (1931; 1932).
[50] Halden & Haywood's Dir. Stafford (1937; 1947).
[51] TS. list of 1954 in copy of Halden & Haywood's Dir. Stafford (1947) at Stafford Libr.
[52] Stafford Newsletter, 26 Apr. 1958. [53] Ibid. 21 Feb. 1969.
[54] Ex inf. the clerk of the Christian Science Soc., Stafford (1962); Stafford Newsletter, 22 Nov. 1963; Worship Reg. no. 69349.

[55] Staffs. Advertiser, 20 Jan. 1934; Yr. Bk. of Cong. Church, Stafford, 1878, 5 (copy in W.S.L. 7/19/oo); Matthews, Cong. Churches of Staffs. 166, 202–3, 261; S.H.C. 4th ser. iii. 128; deeds of Sir Thos. Salt in the possession of Messrs. Trail, Castleman-Smith & Wilson of Blandford, Dors.; W.S.L., M.41.
[56] Yr. Bk. of Cong. Church, Stafford, 1878, 6; S.H.C. 4th ser. iii. 141–2; S.R.O., C/C/D/C/1/12–14; Staffs. Advertiser, 20 Jan. 1934.
[57] Matthews, Cong. Churches of Staffs. 192–3, 265; Roxburgh, Stafford, 123–4. For Thos. Birch see White, Dir. Staffs. (1834), 304.
[58] Staffs. Advertiser, 19 Dec. 1863, 20 Jan. 1934.
[59] H.O. 129/367/1/9. T.S.H.C.S. 1974–6, 70, wrongly gives the morning attendance as 250, which was the total average attendance.
[60] See p. 251.

Infirmary. The interior was extensively altered.[61] In 1965 the building, having been bought by the county council, was demolished, and in 1966 a new church was opened in Eastgate Street.[62]

EVANGELICAL PENTECOSTAL ASSEMBLY. The Covenant Hall in St. Patrick's Street was built in 1933 by the Evangelical Pentecostal Assembly.[63]

FREE EVANGELIST MISSION. Crabbery Hall in Crabbery Street was registered for the Free Evangelist Mission in 1938. The registration was cancelled in 1949.[64]

FRIENDS. The Quaker Miles Bateman came to Stafford 'out of the north' during the mayoralty of Walter Adney (1653–4) and preached in the streets; Adney had him whipped and put in the town gaol. He was followed by Humphrey Woolrich of Newcastle-under-Lyme, who was imprisoned several times 'for declaring truth in the streets and steeple-house at Stafford'.[65] Another Quaker, Thomas Taylor, was under restraint in Stafford from 1662 to 1672, sometimes in prison, sometimes in his house; he managed to write, to teach children, and to preach through the prison window. In 1679 he was fined for preaching at Keele, but the borough officers could find no goods on which to distrain. He was in prison again at Stafford the same year and died in the town in 1682.[66] Several Quakers were imprisoned by the mayor in 1672 for refusing to promise not to meet in Stafford for worship, and there was further persecution in 1674 and from 1683 to 1685; during much of the winter of 1684–5 the Quakers were locked out of their meeting-house.[67]

In 1668 the Quakers bought land in Foregate Street as a burial ground from Matthew Babb of Foregate, who had befriended the first Quakers in the town and had been converted by Woolrich. In 1674 they bought the house where they met and enlarged it, and they extended the burial ground in 1680 and 1725.[68] The present meeting-house on the east side of Foregate Street was built in 1730; much of the cost was met by the sale of the old meeting-house and by a legacy from John Alsop of Ingestre (d. 1728). It is a small red-brick building and still contains the original galleries, overseers' bench, staircase, and panelling.[69] In 1751 there were stated to be only two Quaker families in St. Mary's parish.[70] On the morning of Census Sunday 1851 there was a congregation of eight.[71] A room was added at the rear of the meeting-house in 1892. A hall was erected in front of the building in 1905 and

was used for mission services and adult and Sunday schools. It was later used as a special school and was demolished in 1957.[72]

FULL GOSPEL ASSEMBLY. The Stafford Prayer Group began to meet in a room at the public library in 1961 and moved in 1962 to the meeting-room at the public baths. It afterwards became the Full Gospel Assembly and Prayer Group, and as the Stafford Full Gospel Assembly it moved in 1973 to the community centre in Holmcroft Road.[73]

INDEPENDENTS, see CONGREGATIONALISTS.

JEHOVAH'S WITNESSES. Stafford was visited by Jehovah's Witnesses from the Potteries in the 1920s, and meetings were started in Rowley Street c. 1936. A Kingdom Hall was registered at no. 4 the Green in 1939 and was replaced by another at no. 115B Wolverhampton Road in 1941. Meetings were held in St. Thomas Street from 1946, in Mount Street from 1948, and in Rowley Street from 1950. In 1952 a Kingdom Hall was established in a room behind no. 19 Greengate Street. It was replaced in the earlier 1970s by a hall in converted premises in Fancy Walk, which was dedicated in 1975.[74]

LATTER-DAY SAINTS. Mormons began to meet at the community centre in Holmcroft Road in 1961, and in December a branch of the church was officially organized. It moved in 1962 to the Odd Fellows Hall and later the same year to the Popular Café in Salter Street. It subsequently moved to the Sheridan Hall in Sandon Road, and in 1974 it registered the newly built Wildwood branch chapel in Cannock Road.[75]

METHODISTS. *Wesleyan*. Although John Wesley visited Stafford in 1738 and 1746 he did not then preach there.[76] The Methodist Dr. Thomas Coke preached in the market-place in 1779.[77] A society of sixteen members was formed in 1783 and served by preachers from Burslem. Meetings were held first in a house in Cherry Street and then in a disused stable near by, described by Wesley in 1784 as 'a deplorable hole'. A chapel was built in Cherry Street in 1785. Wesley preached at Stafford every year from 1783 to 1786 and again in 1788, noting in 1785 that 'there are few towns less infected with religion than Stafford'. By 1796 the society no longer existed, and the chapel was sold in 1802. In 1800, however, two lay preachers from the Potteries preached in the town, and from 1803 services were held in a room in

[61] *Staffs. Advertiser*, 13 Mar. 1897; Roxburgh, *Stafford*, 123–4.
[62] *Stafford Newsletter*, 9 July 1965; plaque in Eastgate St. church.
[63] Char. Com. files; *Stafford Newsletter*, 6 Sept. 1958.
[64] Worship Reg. no. 58119; *Kelly's Dir. Staffs.* (1940).
[65] S.R.O., D.3159/1/1, notes at end of volume. For Woolrich see also *V.C.H. Staffs.* iii. 118; *Some Notes on Soc. of Friends in Stafford . . . 1730–1930* (Stafford, 1930), 3 (copy in W.S.L. Pamphs. *sub* Stafford); *D.N.B.*
[66] *D.N.B.*; W. C. Braithwaite, *Second Period of Quakerism*, 85, 223–4; S.R.O., Q/SR, E.1679, no. 4.
[67] S.R.O., D.3159/2/17; J. Besse, *Coll. of Sufferings of People called Quakers* (1753), i. 652.
[68] D. G. Stuart, 'Burial Grounds of Soc. of Friends in Staffs.' *Trans. S. Staffs. Arch. & Hist. Soc.* xii. 44; S.R.O., D.3159/1/1, nos. 28–9, 32–5, 38–9, 41–7, and abstracts of trust deeds.
[69] S.R.O., D.3159/1/1, no. 861; D.3159/2/1, ff. 87, 174v.;

D.1122; Pevsner, *Staffs.* 246; date on meeting-house. For Alsop see Friends' House, London, Official Regs. (ref. supplied by Mr. D. G. Stuart of the Dept. of Adult Education, Keele University).
[70] L.J.R.O., B/V/5, Stafford, St. Mary, 1751.
[71] *T.S.H.C.S.* 1974–6, 71.
[72] *Soc. of Friends in Stafford*, 14–15; *Staffs. Advertiser*, 23 Sept. 1905; *Trans. S. Staffs. Arch. & Hist. Soc.* xii. 44; *Stafford Newsletter*, 20 July 1957.
[73] *Stafford Newsletter*, 16 Dec. 1961, 6 Jan. 1962, 21 Sept., 12 Oct. 1973.
[74] Ex inf. the Stafford presiding minister (1963); Worship Reg. nos. 58839, 59866, 63572; *Stafford and Dist. Guide* (1970); *Stafford Newsletter*, 18 Apr. 1975.
[75] Ex inf. the Stafford branch president (1963); Stafford Libr., list of local churches (1974); Worship Reg. no. 73745.
[76] *Jnl. of John Wesley*, ed. N. Curnock, i. 444–5; iii. 233.
[77] J. Vickers, *Thomas Coke: Apostle of Methodism*, 49–50.

St. Chad's Passage that was part of a currying business. It was served for a short time from Wolverhampton and then from Burslem. There was a secession in 1803 to the Wesleyans from the Congregationalists. From 1805 the Wesleyans held their services in the Presbyterian meeting-house. Stafford was recognized as a preaching-station in Newcastle-under-Lyme circuit in 1807, and in 1808 it became the head of a new circuit.[78] A Sunday school, which was supported by Anglicans also, was started in the room in St. Chad's Passage in 1805; the numbers were so large that later the same year it moved to the assembly-room in the shire hall.[79]

A chapel was built in the present Chapel Street in 1811. It was of brick with stone dressings and was designed in a classical style by W. Jenkins; there was a gallery on three sides. A vestry was added in 1828.[80] The Sunday school was held in the chapel from 1812 until 1842 when a schoolroom was built behind the chapel.[81] A house for the minister was built on the south side of the chapel in 1831, and in 1856 a cottage on the north side was bought for the chapel-keeper.[82] On Census Sunday 1851 there were congregations of 165 in the morning and 200 in the evening.[83]

The chapel was pulled down in 1863, and the present chapel was opened on the same site in 1864. Of red brick with stone and brick dressings, it was designed by Hayley & Sons of Manchester in the form of a basilican church in a Romanesque style with a tower on the left side of the main entrance.[84] The Sunday school moved to the British school in 1863. The present two-storeyed school on the corner of Earl and Queen Streets was built in 1872 to the design of Thomas Roberts of Trentham.[85]

In 1886 a Sunday school used also as a chapel was opened in Rowley Street on a site given by Mary Smith. It was set back from the road to leave room for the chapel which was opened in 1909. The school, of red brick, was designed in a Queen Anne style by G. Wormal of Stafford; the chapel, designed in a Gothic style by C. W. D. Joynson of Wednesbury and Darlaston, is of red brick with terracotta dressings.[86]

New Connexion. Johnson Brothers, who occurs as a Methodist New Connexion preacher in various places from 1807 to 1815, registered three houses in St. Mary's parish for dissenting worship in 1816.[87] A New Connexion chapel in County Road was registered in 1817.[88] The trustees had a site for a new chapel by 1839, but it was not until 1847 that the foundation-stone of a chapel in Gaol Square was laid. It was opened in 1848. Of red brick with stone dressings, it was apparently designed by William Ridgway, although the Doric façade may have been designed by C. Cooper, one of the trustees. There was a gallery on three sides, and beneath the chapel were a vestry and schoolrooms.[89] On Census Sunday 1851 there were congregations of 177 in the morning and 224 in the evening.[90] William Booth visited Stafford in 1857 as an itinerant New Connexion evangelist.[91] The chapel was closed in 1952 and was reopened as a Masonic temple in 1953.[92]

Primitive. In 1836, after earlier attempts had failed, a Primitive Methodist church was formed in Stafford by the Revd. Thomas Russell of the Longton circuit. The ten members met in a room in the north end of the town.[93] A chapel was built in New Street in 1839.[94] It was replaced in 1849 by a larger chapel in Snow Hill at the southern end of Gaol Road, a plain red-brick building with stone dressings.[95] On Census Sunday 1851 there were congregations of 60 in the morning and 110 in the evening; there was also a Sunday school by then.[96] In the mid 1880s the chapel was enlarged and rooms for the Sunday school were added at the rear.[97] The chapel was closed in 1958 and was turned into a garage; it was demolished in 1968.[98]

In 1902 the Primitive Methodists took over the mission hall in Brook Street that had been used by the Brethren. It continued in use until 1962.[99]

A hall serving as a Methodist church, Sunday school, and community centre was opened at Risingbrook in 1956 in succession to a church and Sunday school which had been accommodated for some years at Flash Ley school. An extension primarily for Sunday-school and youth-club purposes was opened in 1963.[1]

In 1956 a site for a Methodist church was acquired at the foot of the Rise, Walton-on-the-Hill. A church was opened in 1961, services having meanwhile been held in Walton village hall, the Leasowes school on the Weeping Cross estate, and private houses.[2]

NEW TESTAMENT CHURCH OF GOD. The New Testament Church of God was meeting at the Co-operative Education Centre in Tipping Street in 1970.[3]

[78] *Wesley Methodist Church, Stafford: Centenary Celebrations* [1964], 4–6 (copy in W.S.L. Pamphs. *sub* Stafford); Scammell, *Stafford Meeting House*, 23–8; *S.H.C.* 4th ser. iii. 5; *Jnl. of John Wesley*, vi. 442–3, 488; vii. 63, 151, 368; W.S.L. 7/18/00, notes from Burslem Circuit Books; *Staffs. Advertiser*, 2 Jan. 1802, notice of auction of chapel in Broadeye; W.S.L., H.M. uncat. 26.
[79] W. Baker, *Centenary Hist. of Wesleyan Sunday Sch., Stafford, 1805–1905* (Stafford, 1905), 5–7 (copy in W.S.L.).
[80] S.R.O., D.1174/3/2/1; *Wesley Methodist Church, Stafford*, 7–9; Baker, *Wesleyan Sunday Sch., Stafford*, 11.
[81] Baker, *Wesleyan Sunday Sch., Stafford*, 9, 12–15.
[82] *Wesleyan Methodist Church, Stafford*, 8.
[83] *T.S.H.C.S.* 1974–6, 70.
[84] *Wesleyan Methodist Church, Stafford*, 10–13; Pevsner, *Staffs.* 243; plate facing p. 241 above.
[85] Baker, *Wesleyan Sunday Sch., Stafford*, 22–8; *Staffs. Advertiser*, 29 June 1872.
[86] Baker, *Wesleyan Sunday Sch., Stafford*, 33 and plate facing p. 36; *Staffs. Advertiser*, 23 Jan. 1886, 1 May 1909; *Stafford Newsletter*, 1 Oct. 1965; *Halden & Son's Dir. Stafford* (1910), 15.

[87] *S.H.C.* 4th ser. iii. 39–40, 42; W. Salt, *Memorial of Wesleyan Methodist New Connexion* (Nottingham, 1822), 163.
[88] *S.H.C.* 4th ser. iii. 42.
[89] S.R.O., D.1174/4/1; *Staffs. Advertiser*, 21 Aug. 1847, 4 and 11 Nov. 1848.
[90] *T.S.H.C.S.* 1974–6, 71.
[91] Catherine Bramwell-Booth, *Catherine Booth*, 165.
[92] *Stafford Newsletter*, 5 July 1952; ex inf. Mr. G. G. Frape of Great Bridgeford (1976).
[93] S.R.O., D.1352/4.
[94] *Stafford Newsletter*, 29 Mar. 1958.
[95] *Staffs. Advertiser*, 2 June 1849; date on former Snow Hill chapel.
[96] *T.S.H.C.S.* 1974–6, 71.
[97] S.R.O., D.1352/4; tablet formerly *in situ*.
[98] *Stafford Newsletter*, 5 Apr. 1958, 29 Mar. 1968.
[99] Ibid. 31 Mar. 1962; S.R.O., D.1303/1/5, schedule of chapels 1902; Worship Reg. no. 46167.
[1] *Stafford Newsletter*, 14 and 21 Apr. 1956, 25 Aug. 1962, 16 Feb. 1963.
[2] Ibid. 7 Oct. 1961.
[3] Worship Reg. no. 72258.

OPEN FELLOWSHIP. The Open Fellowship, offering 'not a creed but a living Christ, not a doctrine but deliverance', began to meet at the Odd Fellows Hall in 1959. It held its last meeting in 1962, 'moving out in faith to evangelize'.[4]

QUAKERS, *see* FRIENDS.

PRESBYTERIANS, LATER UNITED REFORMED CHURCH. The first evidence of Presbyterian sympathies at Stafford dates from 1648 when Richard Bell of Stafford signed the county's Testimony.[5] Noah Bryan, rector of St. Mary's from 1657, was ejected *c.* 1661.[6] John Mott, the ejected curate of King's Bromley, lived at his mother-in-law's house in Stafford in the later 1660s; after being imprisoned for refusing to renounce the Covenant, he was expelled from the town.[7] In 1672 William Turton, the ejected curate of Rowley Regis, was licensed as a Presbyterian teacher at Joseph Wade's house in Stafford, and the houses of Frances Sound and Eleanor 'Moot', probably John Mott's wife, were licensed for Presbyterian meetings.[8]

A meeting-house was opened in Balk Passage in 1689, a building of brick and stone with galleries on two sides; there was a burial ground attached. John Dancer, an ironmonger who was mayor in 1702–3 and 1709–10, subscribed towards the cost and was one of the first two trustees.[9] During the Staffordshire riots against dissenters in 1715 the meeting-house was extensively damaged, doors, galleries, and pews being burnt in the market-place.[10] In 1729 there were 350 hearers, described as Scotch Presbyterians,[11] and in 1751 there were stated to be 20 Presbyterian families in St. Mary's parish.[12] By the end of the 18th century the membership was predominantly Scottish, and with the departure or death of such members the church declined. The meeting-house was shared with the Wesleyans from 1805 until the building of a Wesleyan chapel in 1811.[13] Although William Tooth, the clerk, continued to hold services and there were occasional visiting preachers, there was no resident minister until 1830 when Alexander Macdonald was appointed. A revival then took place.[14] Alexander Stewart, who succeeded Macdonald in 1834, enlarged the meeting-house in 1835–6. Designed by Boulton & Palmer of Stafford in a Decorated style, the extensions consisted of a aisle, vestry, and schoolroom; the fittings were renewed and a sloping floor was inserted.[15] In 1838 Stewart, after being dismissed for heresy, tried unsuccessfully to take over the building for meetings of Brethren.[16] The dispute reduced the membership to three, but by 1842 it had risen to 48; on Census Sunday 1851 there were congregations of 70 in the morning and 150 in the evening, numbers which were stated to be lower than average 'owing to the severity of the day'.[17] A schoolroom for the girls' Sunday school was built in 1868.[18] In 1901 the church was extended southwards over the graveyard, where the last burial had taken place in 1863; a tower was also built.[19] The building remained in use in 1977 as a United Reformed church.

SALVATION ARMY. The Salvation Army was meeting at the Lyceum theatre in Martin Street by January 1888.[20] It registered a barracks in Wright Street in 1890 but had moved to Mount Street by 1892.[21] A barracks in the former grammar-school building in North Walls was registered in 1901 in place of the Mount Street premises and was itself replaced by a hall in Crabbery Street, registered in 1907; the registration was cancelled in 1914.[22] The army had a meeting-room in Brunswick Street *c.* 1920.[23] Part of the Co-operative Hall in Browning Street was registered as a Salvation Army hall in 1922,[24] and it was still in use in 1975. A young people's hall at no. 1 Marston Road was registered in 1930 but was no longer in use in 1954.[25]

SPIRITUALISTS. Spiritualists were meeting at the Assembly Rooms in Tipping Street by 1930. By 1947 they were meeting at the Co-operative Hall in Salter Street, and in 1959 a Spiritualist church was opened in Mount Street. By 1962 the Spiritualists were again meeting at the Assembly Rooms, which they were still using in 1971.[26] The building was no longer in use in 1977.

UNITED CHRISTIAN ARMY. The United Christian Army registered the skating rink in Newport Road for worship in 1882. The group had ceased to meet there by 1896.[27]

UNITED REFORMED CHURCH, *see* CONGREGATIONALISTS; PRESBYTERIANS.

OTHER GROUPS. A meeting-room at no. 34 Ingestre Road was registered for Christians in 1966.[28] Another, adjoining no. 54 Garden Street, was registered, also for Christians, in 1969.[29]

SIKHS. The former parish hall in Tithe Barn Road belonging to St. John's church was sold to the Sikh community in 1972. It was reopened as Sri Guru Nanaksar Gurdwara.[30]

[4] *Stafford Newsletter*, 2 and 16 May 1959, 28 Apr. 1962.
[5] Matthews, *Cong. Churches of Staffs.* 18.
[6] See p. 241.   [7] A. G. Matthews, *Calamy Revised*, 358.
[8] Matthews, *Cong. Churches of Staffs.* 92–3; Matthews, *Calamy Revised*, 498; *St. Mary's, Stafford, Par. Reg.* (Staffs. Par. Reg. Soc. 1935–6), 285, 287, 310.
[9] Scammell, *Stafford Meeting House*, 13–16; W.S.L., S.MS. 369; Bradley, *Charters*, 206–7.
[10] Scammell, *Stafford Meeting House*, 19–22; Assizes 4/18, pp. 242–4; Matthews, *Cong. Churches of Staffs.* 128.
[11] Matthews, *Cong. Churches of Staffs.* 129; Scammell, *Stafford Meeting House*, 19; Roxburgh, *Stafford*, 45.
[12] L.J.R.O., B/V/5, Stafford, St. Mary, 1751.
[13] Scammell, *Stafford Meeting House*, 25–8.
[14] Ibid. 29–33.
[15] Ibid. 33–5; *Staffs. Advertiser*, 27 Feb., 5 Mar. 1836. For Boulton & Palmer see *Staffs. Advertiser*, 25 Apr. 1835, p. 1.

[16] See p. 251.
[17] Scammell, *Stafford Meeting House*, 37–8; *T.S.H.C.S.* 1974–6, 71.
[18] Scammell, *Stafford Meeting House*, 42.
[19] Roxburgh, *Stafford*, 45; Scammell, *Stafford Meeting House*, 43.
[20] Worship Reg. no. 30591.   [21] Ibid. nos. 32007, 33517.
[22] Ibid. nos. 38277, 42242; *Stafford*, ed. C. Hibberd (1906; copy in W.S.L. Pamphs. *sub* Stafford).
[23] *Kelly's Dir. Staffs.* (1924).
[24] Worship Reg. no. 48623.   [25] Ibid. no. 52266.
[26] *Halden & Haywood's Dir. Stafford* (1930; 1947); *Stafford Newsletter*, 9 May 1959, 23 Apr. 1971; ex inf. Stafford and Stone Co-operative Soc. (1962).
[27] Worship Reg. no. 26397 (cancelled 1896 on revision).
[28] Ibid. no. 70478.   [29] Ibid. no. 71980.
[30] Ex inf. the vicar of St. John's (1975); board outside the temple (1975).

SOCIAL AND CULTURAL ACTIVITIES. An annual festival known as the Green Wakes was held on the Green in Forebridge in Castle Church on the two days following the second Sunday in August. It was presumably held in connexion with the feast of the Assumption of the Virgin (15 August), the parish church of Castle Church being dedicated to St. Mary.[31] In the mid 1870s householders living near the Green complained about the nuisance caused by the wakes, and in 1877, following a petition from Forebridge ratepayers, the town council limited the wakes to one day. In 1878 the inclosure of the Green and the removal of three trees round which the sideshows had clustered restricted the wakes further, and they lapsed.[32] They were revived in 1887 on the near-by Green common by a committee of Forebridge residents, the profits being distributed among the poor of Forebridge, and in 1888, 1889, and 1890 they were again two-day events. In 1891, however, the promoters were made to transfer them to a field in Wolverhampton Road, and they were not held again.[33] In the 19th century Forehead wakes were held in October at the north end of town. They too had lapsed by the end of the century.[34]

A pleasure-fair was held in conjunction with the May Fair (14 May) by the 1820s, and it remained the town's principal, and latterly its only, regular pleasure-fair until its abolition in 1919. The various sideshows and entertainments were centred in Market Square.[35] In the mid 19th century a pleasure-fair was also held in conjunction with the fair on 3 April.[36] In the later 19th century other travelling fun-fairs and circuses visiting the town used a field between South Walls and the Sow. Since at least the 1870s Stafford common has also been used for those entertainments.[37]

The traditional sport of 'heaving' in Easter Week survived at least until the early 16th century; money collected was paid to the churchwardens of St. Mary's.[38] A new maypole was erected in 1612 after the old one had been sawn up to make ladders.[39] A hobby-horse dance was performed annually at New Year's Eve to raise funds for St. Mary's until shortly before the Civil War.[40]

There was a bowling-place by the decayed Eastgate mill c. 1600; it was probably the bowling-alley which the corporation owned and maintained in the 1620s and 1630s.[41] There were four greens in the town c. 1800, but by 1835 the sole survivor was that at the Talbot in Talbot (later Cherry) Street. It was converted into a smithfield in the mid 1870s, and bowlers had to go to neighbouring towns until a new green was opened at the Junction hotel in

Newport Road in 1876.[42] By 1976 there were about a dozen private and municipally owned greens in the borough.

There was a cockpit in Foregate in 1662, and probably another at Broadeye.[43] Cock-fighting was among the attractions at Stafford races in 1781 and 1821.[44] Bulls were baited, apparently in Market Square, until 1791, when the corporation forbade the practice within the liberties. It probably continued on the outskirts of the town: after a by-election in 1826 supporters of the successful candidate baited a bull on two successive days, first in a field in Castle Church and then in Coton field.[45]

In 1733 there was three days' horse-racing at Stafford in September.[46] Races were revived in October 1763, when there was a three-day meeting on a new course in Coton field, and October races continued to be held there, patronized by the county gentry. The prince of Wales attended in 1790, and in 1795 a grandstand was built. The meeting lapsed after 1798 but was revived in 1806 on the initiative of Joshua Drewry, the proprietor of the *Staffordshire Advertiser*. In 1820 the races were transferred from Coton field to Stafford common, where they were held until 1847. Autumn meetings were held on the common in 1874 and 1875, and Whitsun meetings in 1902 and 1903 and from 1923 to 1930.[47]

A Stafford Angling Society, later the Izaak Walton (Stafford) Angling Association, existed by the 1880s and by 1900 had a number of affiliated clubs. In the late 1950s the association controlled 15 miles of water, including canals, and had 1,500 members. Since c. 1970 boat traffic on the canals and pollution of the Sow and Penk have tended to drive anglers further afield.[48]

From at least the 1830s the earls Talbot (later earls of Shrewsbury) allowed the corporation an annual coursing day on their estates east of the town.[49] In 1864 a Mayor's Cup and a Corporation Cup were competed for. The day's sport was followed by dinner in one of the Stafford inns; in 1837 it was stated that the Coursing Dinner had assumed the character of the former annual civic feast, which the recently reformed town council had abolished. The Corporation Coursing Meeting was held regularly until 1869. Lord Shrewsbury, who complained of disorderly behaviour at that year's meeting, was apparently incensed in 1870 by a newspaper report suggesting that the corporation considered that it had a right to a day's coursing on his land, and he withdrew the privilege. His son,

[31] 'Reminiscences of an Old Stafford Resident', *T.O.S.S.* 1932, 45; P. T. Dale, 'Some notes on the ancient buildings and streets of Stafford', *T.O.S.S.* 1934, 19; *Stafford Revisited, 1841–1907, by a descendant of Rector Dickenson* (Stafford, n.d.), 12 (copy in possession of Mr. J. S. Horne, Stafford, 1976); *V.C.H. Staffs.* v. 95.
[32] *Staffs. Advertiser*, 18 Aug. 1877, 6 July, 17 Aug. 1878; *Stafford Revisited*, 9, 12; S.R.O., D.1323/A/1/10, pp. 118–19, 125.
[33] *Staffs. Advertiser*, 20 Aug. 1887, 18 Aug. 1888, 17 Aug. 1889, 16 Aug. 1890, 15 Aug. 1891.
[34] *T.O.S.S.* 1934, 19.
[35] *Weekly Register*, 17 May 1828; *Staffs. Advertiser*, 15 May 1875; *Staffs. Chron.* 18 May 1889, 17 Aug. 1901; *Corp. Yr. Bk.* (1919–20).
[36] *P.O. Dir. Staffs.* (1850; 1854; 1860).
[37] *T.O.S.S.* 1932, 46; *Stafford Newsletter*, 22 Oct. 1955; *Staffs. Advertiser*, 10 July 1875.
[38] W.S.L., S.MS. 366(iA), p. 5.
[39] S.R.O., D.1323/E/1, f. 64v.
[40] D. A. Johnson, 'The Stafford Hobby-horse', *T.S.H.C.S.* 1974–6, 59–64.
[41] W.S.L., copy of lost plan of Stafford; S.R.O., D.1323/E/1, ff. 109v., 125, 140, 151v., 173, 234.
[42] *Staffs. Advertiser*, 15 Aug. 1801, 27 May 1826, 27 May 1876; Wood, *Plan of Stafford* (1835); *P.O. Dir. Staffs.* (1850); above, p. 214.
[43] S.R.O., D.1323/E/1, ff. 300–1, 302v.; W.S.L. 790/36.
[44] *Stafford Newsletter*, 25 Apr. 1956; S.R.O., D.149/Z/1.
[45] P. T. Dale, 'Some notes on the ancient buildings and streets of Stafford', *T.O.S.S.* 1933, 35; S.R.O., D.1323/A/3, p. 65; *Staffs. Advertiser*, 30 Dec. 1826.
[46] J. Cheny, *Hist. List of Horse-matches*, 1733, 94–5.
[47] *V.C.H. Staffs.* ii. 364–7 and sources cited ibid. 367 n. 56.
[48] P. Butters, 'Diary of a Staffordian' (TS. in possession of Mr. Butters, 1976), pp. 365–72. And see above, p. 211.
[49] *Staffs. Advertiser*, 9 Dec. 1837, 26 Nov. 1864, 11 Dec. 1869, 24 Dec. 1870, 17 Mar. 1888.

the 20th earl, allowed the corporation to revive the meeting in 1888. It was held at intervals thereafter into the early 20th century.[50]

The first known sports club in the town, Stafford Victoria Cricket Club, was formed in 1844 and still existed in 1864.[51] It is uncertain whether it was related to Stafford Cricket Club, which may have existed by 1847 and was probably put on a permanent basis in 1864. Stafford C.C. played on the Lammascotes until 1889; it then moved to the Hough, which remained its ground in 1976. County cricket matches were played there between the World Wars and again until 1955.[52] The other sports clubs which existed in 1976 included only one professional club, Stafford Rangers Association Football Club, founded in 1876. It originally played on the Lammascotes and then moved to a ground off Stone Road and later to another at Castletown before settling c. 1896 at a ground in Marston Road, which remained its home in 1976. The club, a member since 1969 of the Northern Premier League, won the F.A. Challenge Trophy in 1972.[53]

By the early 17th century Stafford was a recognized stopping-place for touring bands of players. In 1609–10 six companies played in the town: the King's, the Queen's, Lord Stafford's, Lord Dudley's, Lord Derby's, and Lord Mounteagle's.[54] The King's Men are recorded at Stafford fourteen or fifteen times between 1609–10 and 1635.[55] Other companies which visited the town before the Civil War included those of the prince of Wales,[56] the Lady Elizabeth (the daughter of James I),[57] Philip, earl of Montgomery, Lord Chamberlain 1626–41,[58] and Henry, Lord Berkeley.[59] The Stafford authorities also gave gratuities to 'players of our town' and to 'the players of Eccleshall'.[60]

Such performances took place on temporary stages: in 1615–16 the mayor paid 'for setting up stoops for players'.[61] During the later 18th century, and probably earlier, plays and entertainments were given in the shire hall.[62] The 'Theatre' which advertised in 1778 and 1782[63] was probably also the shire hall. By 1786 there was a New Theatre, possibly in Broad Street. Part of the building collapsed in 1787, and although the theatre reopened it cannot have survived for long.[64]

Samuel Stanton, the manager of a theatrical company which was touring the Midlands by the 1770s, used the shire hall when his company visited Stafford, and when the building's demolition and replacement was proposed in 1790 he decided to build a theatre of his own in the town. It was opened in Martin Street in 1792, a small brick building 'scarcely higher than a single-storeyed house' known as the New Theatre or simply as the Theatre.[65] Stanton's company and, later, other companies and individual performers played short seasons there, but except in race week or on special occasions support appears to have been poor.[66] It was at a race-week performance given by Stanton's company in 1794 that Sheridan first saw the actress Harriot Mellon, who became famous under his management at Drury Lane before marrying first Thomas Coutts the banker and then the duke of St. Albans.[67] In the late 1830s a visitor found the theatre dilapidated and remarked that 'it still bears the one original coat of paint of its youthful days'; in the early 1840s the corporation complained about the state of the building.[68] It was extensively repaired and altered in 1847 and was renamed the Lyceum.[69] In 1852 Dickens still found it a 'mouldy little theatre'.[70] It was called the Theatre Royal in 1857,[71] but probably for one season only; it then reverted to being the Lyceum. In 1877 it was enlarged and improved.[72] Further alterations were made in 1912, when it was renamed the Playhouse. In 1915 it was badly damaged by fire, and it was used as a warehouse until 1921, when it was sold to the county council. Council offices were built on the site in the late 1920s.[73]

In the 1860s and 1870s Snape's Travelling Theatre, 'a long wooden building with a stage at one end' made Stafford its winter quarters. The company originally specialized in melodramas but later offered more varied entertainment.[74]

The Albert Hall cinema in Crabbery Street became a concert-party hall in 1919, and the Albert Hall Repertory Company, founded in the 1920s, operated there until 1932.[75] The Sandonia in Sandon Road was opened in 1920 as a theatre specializing in variety shows and musical comedies. A season of opera in English was held there in 1921. It became a cinema in 1923.[76] Between c. 1934 and c. 1940 repertory and variety were presented at the Co-operative Hall in Salter Street.[77]

The town's first cinema was the Electric Picture

[50] See e.g. ibid. 11 Mar. 1893, 19 Jan. 1895, 1 Mar. 1902.
[51] Ibid. 6 and 20 Apr., 11 May, 22 June 1844, 18 June 1864.
[52] Butters, 'Diary of a Staffordian', pp. 342–8.
[53] P. Butters, Cinderella Story: Hist. of Stafford Rangers Football Club (Stafford, 1972); ex inf. Mr. Butters (1976).
[54] S.R.O., D.1323/E/1, ff. 52–3.
[55] Ibid. ff. 52, 72, 104, 105v., 117, 117v., 158av., 159, 163, 163v., 191v., 199v., 207, 215v.
[56] Ibid. ff. 100, 104, 112, 117, 134v., 135.
[57] Ibid. ff. 117, 134v., 176; S.R.O., D.(W.) 1721/1/4, f. 102.
[58] S.R.O., D.1323/E/1, f. 158B.   [59] Ibid. f. 58.
[60] S.R.O., D.(W.) 1721/1/4, f. 107v.; D.1323/E/1, f. 254v.
[61] S.R.O., D.(W.) 1721/1/4, f. 107v.
[62] Aris's Birmingham Gaz. 30 Jan. 1769; W.S.L. Broadsheets 31/1/1–4.
[63] W.S.L. Broadsheets 31/2/1–2.
[64] Ibid. 31/2/3 and 6; Bell's Weekly Reporter, 20 Jan. 1912 (copy in W.S.L.).
[65] S.R.O., D.685/7/1, p. 12A; Memoirs of the late Thomas Holcroft, written by himself (World's Classics edn.), 91–9; Margaret Baron-Wilson, Memoirs of Harriot, Duchess of St. Albans (1840 edn.), i. 88, 96–8, 121–2, 126; W.S.L. Broadsheets 31/2/10–11.

[66] Baron-Wilson, Harriot, Duchess of St. Albans, i. 130.
[67] Ibid. 131; M. Kelly, Reminiscences, ed. R. Fiske, 218.
[68] Baron-Wilson, Harriot, Duchess of St. Albans, i. 121–2; S.R.O., D.1323/A/1/6, pp. 44, 50, 66, 115.
[69] S.R.O., D.1323/A/1/6, pp. 244, 260, 262, 266, 278; Staffs. Advertiser, 13 Nov., 11 Dec. 1847.
[70] 'A Plated Article', Household Words, 24 Apr. 1852, re-issued in Reprinted Pieces.
[71] W.S.L. Broadsheets 31/4/2–3, mentioning 'Mr. Blakemore's next the theatre'. Blakemore lived next to the Lyceum: S.R.O., County Council deed bdle. C 491/11. W.S.L. Broadsheets 31/4/1, advertising 'Theatre Royal, Shire Hall, Stafford', is an election squib.
[72] Calvert, Stafford, 77; Staffs. Advertiser, 29 Sept. 1877, 2 Feb. 1878.
[73] Staffs. Advertiser, 28 Dec. 1912, 5 and 12 June 1915; Stafford Newsletter, 2 July 1955; S.R.O., County Council deed bdle. C 491/11; above, p. 202. For photographs of the theatre after the renaming see S.R.O., D.619.
[74] Staffs. Chron. 26 Jan. 1955.
[75] Stafford Newsletter, 9 July 1955, 26 May 1962; Butters, 'Diary of a Staffordian', pp. 126–8.
[76] Stafford Newsletter, 16 July 1955.
[77] Halden & Haywood's Dir. Stafford (1934 and later edns. to 1940).

Palace in Glover Street, opened in 1910 and closed in 1923.[78] The Albert Hall was a cinema from its opening in 1912 until 1915, and again from 1932 until 1952. The Sandonia was used as a cinema from 1923 until 1963, when it became a bingo hall. Two cinemas were still operating in 1977, the Picture House in Bridge Street, opened in 1914,[79] and the Odeon, at the junction of Newport and Lichfield Roads, opened in 1936.

About 1646 a library was founded in the town 'for the benefit of the county of Stafford by some gentlemen of our country'. It still existed in 1674.[80] It may have been set up for the use of the county justices. Booksellers can be traced from 1658 when John Felton was in business in the town.[81] A circulating library was established in Market Square in 1795 by Joshua Drewry, the founder of the *Staffordshire Advertiser*; he closed it in 1804.[82] The Stafford Book Society, a private club, was founded in 1798 with its headquarters at Arthur Morgan's bookshop in Market Square. The members, mainly professional men, concentrated on works of literature, history, politics, and travel; they took a selection of London reviews but barred technical books and pamphlets. The annual subscription was a guinea, and by 1802 there were 39 members.[83] By 1808 the club had become the Stafford Permanent Book Society and appears to have had premises of its own; from at least 1811 until 1818 they were in either Malt Mill Lane or Salter Street, and from 1819 in Martin Street.[84] There was a librarian by 1814. The club still flourished in 1827, but the library was broken up in 1828.[85] By then John Rogers, a bookseller in Greengate Street, had established a circulating library.[86] In 1834 his was the largest library in the town, with several thousand volumes. A Miss Drewry ran a smaller circulating library, and there was a book society with some 21 members, a newsroom at the Swan with 30 subscribers, and a society which took periodicals.[87]

In 1878 Clement L. Wragge of Oakamoor in Cheadle offered the corporation his collection of ethnographic, zoological, and geological specimens, most of them collected abroad, to form the nucleus of a borough museum. In 1879 Stafford adopted the Free Libraries and Museums Act, and in the same year the collection, housed in the borough hall, was officially opened as the Wragge Museum.[88] An extension to the borough hall was built to house the museum, a library, and the town's school of art. It was opened in 1881 and the Wragge collection was transferred to it. The library section contained only

a reading room, but a lending and reference library was established in 1882, housed in what had formerly been the dining-room of the borough hall.[89] In 1914 a public library, designed by Briggs, Wolstenholme & Thornely of Liverpool and built with the aid of a donation from Andrew Carnegie, was opened at the junction of Lichfield and Newport Roads.[90] The Wragge collection was rehoused there.[91] Open access was introduced in the library in 1929.[92] An art gallery was opened in the building in 1934, and extensions to the building in 1962 included two galleries.[93] In 1976 the Wragge collection was no longer on exhibition; there were instead displays of material relating to the history and archaeology of the Stafford area.

The North Branch Library in Rowley Street was opened in 1936. From 1950 to 1957 there was a library centre at Rickerscote mission church; it was replaced by the South Branch Library in Merrey Road. Branches were opened in Holmcroft Road in the north of the borough and in Lynton Avenue, Baswich, in 1970.[94]

The William Salt Library originated in the extensive collection of books, maps, manuscripts, and pictures formed by William Salt (d. 1863), a London banker who came of a family with long-established Stafford connexions. The collection related principally to the history of Staffordshire, and in 1868 it was offered to the county by his widow. The library was established in 1872 in Old Bank House in Market Square under the management of a body of trustees. In 1918 it was moved to a house in Eastgate Street; an adjoining cottage, bought at the same time, was added when the tenant left in 1934. The collection has been enlarged by numerous gifts and deposits.[95]

Stafford's first newspaper, the weekly *Staffordshire Advertiser*, was founded in 1795 by Joshua Drewry, the son of a Lincoln printer.[96] He went bankrupt in 1819 and control passed to Charles Chester, a Newcastle-under-Lyme printer and stationer who had married one of Drewry's cousins. In 1828 Chester made over the paper to John Drewry Mort and Charles Chester Mort, sons of another of Drewry's cousins. The *Advertiser* belonged to the firm of J. & C. Mort (from 1903 J. & C. Mort Ltd.) until 1955; Morts then sold it with the *Staffordshire Chronicle* to Powysland Newspapers Ltd., which merged the papers to form the *Staffordshire Advertiser and Chronicle*. Thereafter the paper was printed outside the town.[97] In December 1972 Powysland Newspapers sold the title to R. W.

[78] For this para. see Butters, 'Diary of a Staffordian', pp. 120 sqq.; *Stafford Newsletter*, 9 and 16 July 1955, 28 June, 6 and 27 Sept., 22 Nov. 1963; *Staffs. Advertiser*, 20 July, 6 Aug. 1910, 21 and 28 Feb. 1914, 10 Oct. 1936.

[79] See plate facing p. 193.

[80] Bodl. MS. C.C.C. c. 390/2, f. 178.

[81] H. R. Plomer, *Dict. of Booksellers and Printers in Eng., Scot. and Irel. 1641–67*, 73; *1668–1725*, 277, 300–1.

[82] *S.H.C.* 4th ser. vi. 196, 203.

[83] *Rules of Book Soc., Stafford, established 4 June 1798* (copy in W.S.L., Salt Pamphs. (bound ser.), vii, no. 12).

[84] *Staffs. Advertiser*, 4 June 1808, 1 June 1811, 5 June 1819, 3 June 1820, 9 June 1821; Parson and Bradshaw, *Dir. Staffs.* (1818), 218.

[85] *Staffs. Advertiser*, 4 June 1814, 9 June 1827; *Week Register*, 6 and 13 Sept. 1828.

[86] *Weekly Register*, 13 Sept. 1828.

[87] *Staffs. Advertiser*, 18 Oct. 1834. For other 19th-cent. libraries see below, pp. 264–5.

[88] *Staffs. Advertiser*, 13 July 1878, 1 Nov. and 27 Dec.

1879. For Wragge see *Weatherwise* (jnl. of American Meteorological Soc.), xxiii. 222–3, 255 (copy in Stafford Libr.).

[89] *Staffs. Advertiser*, 5 Nov. 1881, 29 July 1882.

[90] Ibid. 21 Mar. 1914; *Staffs. Chron.* 21 Mar. 1914.

[91] *Kelly's Dir. Staffs.* (1916 and later edns. to 1940).

[92] Ex inf. the principal area librarian, Stafford (1976).

[93] Ex inf. the principal area librarian; *Stafford Newsletter*, 17 Feb. 1962.

[94] *Boro. of Stafford Public Libraries, Art Gallery and Museum Ann. Rep.* 1954–5, 1956–7, 1970–1 (copies in Stafford Libr.).

[95] S. A. H. Burne, *Growth of the William Salt Library* (Stafford, priv. print. n.d.; copy in W.S.L.).

[96] For this para. see, unless otherwise stated, *S.H.C.* 4th ser. vi. 186–208; *Staffs. Advertiser*, 5 Jan. 1895, 28 Jan. 1955; *Staffs. Advertiser and Chron.* 4 Jan. 1973. There is a set of the paper in W.S.L.

[97] Ex inf. Mr. P. J. Berrisford, formerly editor of the *Staffs. Advertiser and Chron.*

Hourd & Son, publisher of the *Stafford Newsletter*, and in January 1973 Hourds closed the *Advertiser and Chronicle*. At the peak of its fortunes the *Advertiser* was the county's leading newspaper. By 1823 its circulation was nearly 2,000 copies a week, and by 1837 it had the seventh largest circulation of any provincial newspaper. In 1850 its weekly circulation was *c.* 6,400 copies; by 1859 it had risen to nearly 10,000 copies, and no more than three or four weekly provincial papers outsold it.[98] Drewry had established it as a politically independent ournal, and his successors continued that policy. Its sympathies varied. Under Drewry it had a Whig flavour. In 1841 Sir Robert Peel, who thought it 'by far the most respectable Staffordshire paper', considered that although it was not a party paper it had 'very conservative leanings'. In the early 20th century its politics were regarded as Conservative.[99]

Drewry founded several other papers at Stafford, all short-lived. From February to May 1820 he produced thirteen numbers of *The Bookworm*, 'a literary journal for Staffordshire'. From January to July 1827 he edited and published a weekly newspaper, *Drewry's Staffordshire Gazette*, and from November 1827 to December 1828 he produced *The Weekly Register*, which was in fact a newspaper but which masqueraded as a 'miscellany' in an attempt to evade the payment of stamp duty.[1] In July 1831 he established another weekly newspaper, the *Staffordshire Gazette*, which advocated parliamentary reform. It lasted until September 1832.[2]

From January 1814 until June 1815 James Amphlett, editor of the *Staffordshire Advertiser* 1804–10 and later a peripatetic journalist, published and printed in Stafford a weekly paper, the *Staffordshire Mercury*. From July 1815 he published and printed it at Lichfield as the *Lichfield Mercury and Midland Chronicle*.[3] The *Staffordshire Gazette*, a Conservative weekly, was established at Rugeley in January 1839 by J. T. Walters, but from June 1839 it was printed and published in Foregate Street, Stafford, by John Vickers and Joseph Stringer; it ceased publication in March 1842.[4] In January 1863 the first number of a weekly *Stafford Mercury* appeared, printed and published in Martin Street by Frederic Marshall. It was the first paper to be aimed at a Stafford rather than a county readership. It survived for only 17 issues.[5]

A weekly *Stafford Chronicle* was established in 1877 by W. B. Allison; in 1884 it became the *Staffordshire Chronicle*. Allison was succeeded as proprietor by C. S. Allison, and in 1910 the *Chronicle* passed to Allison & Bowen Ltd. By 1955 a controlling interest in the company had passed to J. & C. Mort Ltd., the owner of the *Staffordshire Advertiser*,

and in that year both newspapers were sold and the *Chronicle* was merged with the *Advertiser*.[6]

In 1906 the *Stafford Newsletter* was launched by R. W. Hourd as a free weekly news-sheet with a circulation of 5,000. It contained a summary of local news and was supported entirely by advertising revenue. The printing was originally done by W. D. Bell of Mount Street, but after eighteen months Hourd set up his own press in Mill Street. On his death in 1932 he was succeeded as proprietor by his son A. E. Hourd (d. 1962). In 1938 the *Newsletter* was formed into a private limited company. When at the end of 1941 the publication of free news-sheets was officially banned, the *Newsletter* became a commercial newspaper. From 1973 it was printed outside the town.[7] In 1974 it also began to distribute a free *Midweek Advertiser* each week, which at first contained only advertisements but from the beginning of 1975 included some local news.[8]

The early success of the *Newsletter* led to the appearance of two or three similar productions. There was a *Stafford Observer* in 1908, published by C. Hibberd of Victoria Road.[9] In 1910 W. D. Bell, the original printer of the *Newsletter*, established *Bell's Weekly Reporter*, which by 1912 incorporated a *Stafford Free Press* and had ceased publication by 1916.[10] A free *Stafford News Shopper*, containing a little local news as well as advertising, was published in 1970; 34 issues appeared, at first fortnightly and then weekly.[11]

Of the town's social and dining clubs the Stafford Liberal Club, wound up in 1893, was claimed to be the oldest; in the 1860s it was believed to have originated in the early 17th century.[12] Two clubs, meeting weekly, were formed in the mid 18th century. One, an all-male affair at which liquor and cards were available, was established in 1749 and probably met at an inn; it may have been the men's club which held an oyster feast in 1760. The other, founded in 1752, consisted of 30 men and women who met at a private house for tea, coffee, and cards.[13] The Stafford Oyster Club, which existed by 1855, met at fortnightly intervals during the oyster season, mostly at the Swan; its regular meetings ended in 1918.[14]

Two friendly societies, the Senior and the Junior, were founded in 1764, and a Female Friendly Society was established in 1771. In 1809 a Union Friendly Society and a Samaritan Friendly Society were formed. By 1856 there were at least ten societies in the town, including several lodges of Odd Fellows; the total membership was over 1,300.[15] An Odd Fellows' Hall, a two-storeyed building of Ruabon brick with Bath stone dressings, designed by George Wormal of Stafford, was opened on the corner of Greengate and Tipping Streets in 1893.[16]

[98] *Staffs. Advertiser*, 4 Jan. 1823, 7 Jan. 1837, 3 Jan. 1852, 7 Jan. 1860.
[99] *S.H.C.* 4th ser. vi. 198–201; A. Aspinall, *Politics and the Press c. 1780–1850*, 466; C. V. Wedgwood, *The Last of the Radicals*, 77.
[1] *S.H.C.* 4th ser. vi. 204–7; sets in W.S.L.
[2] Set in B.L. Newspaper Libr., Colindale.
[3] *S.H.C.* 4th ser. vi. 197. There is an incomplete set in W.S.L.
[4] Set in W.S.L.; S.R.O., D.1287/18/27, bdle. marked 'Knockin correspondence', P. Potter to Lord Bradford, 2 July 1842.
[5] Set in W.S.L. 7/236/00.
[6] Set in B.L. Newspaper Libr., Colindale. There is a set 1891–1955 in Stafford Libr.

[7] Set in Stafford Libr., especially issues of 9 Dec. 1961, 25 Aug. 1962, 28 Sept. 1973.
[8] Set in Stafford Libr.
[9] *Staffs. Chron.* 14 Feb. 1952, describing copy of *Stafford Observer*, no. 10 (May, 1908).
[10] *Kelly's Dir. Staffs.* (1912; 1916); *Bell's Weekly Reporter*, 20 Jan. 1912 (copy in W.S.L.).
[11] Set in W.S.L.
[12] *Staffs. Advertiser*, 10 Sept. 1864, 7 Sept. 1867, 21 Oct. 1893.
[13] W.S.L., H.M. uncat. 23; W.S.L., M. 22, Stafford dining club; S. A. H. Burne, *Occasional Papers* (Stafford, priv. print. 1961), 8–9 (copy in W.S.L.).
[14] S.R.O., D.3086. [15] *Staffs. Advertiser*, 15 Nov. 1856.
[16] Ibid. 23 Sept. 1893.

From 1958 to 1970 the assembly-hall on the first floor was used as an arts centre.[17] In 1976 a room on the ground floor was used as a lodge room by eight lodges of Odd Fellows.[18]

EDUCATION. Schooling was available in Stafford by the later 14th century.[19] Thomas (alias Roger) the schoolmaster of Stafford was one of a group pardoned in 1380 for aiding and abetting a murder.[20] Later the same year Catherine the schoolmistress brought an action in the borough court.[21] In 1396 Thomas Bron, a chaplain, sued Richard Heire for failing to pay the fee to which he had agreed in return for a term's tuition of his son.[22] A similar action was brought in 1397 by John Pepard against Richard Bower for 12d. due for teaching Bower's son.[23] In 1473 the bishop of Coventry and Lichfield was maintaining three poor boys at a school in Stafford, probably the one attached to St. Mary's church which was endowed as a grammar school c. 1500. Its history is treated above.[24]

A school was established in 1685 or earlier for poor Roman Catholics, but it did not survive the destruction of the Roman Catholic chapel in 1688.[25] Private schools are recorded from the 1760s.[26] In 1803 the corporation gave Messrs. Newbould permission to use the room over the new grammar school in Gaol Square on Sunday evenings so that their apprentices could be taught reading and writing.[27] The first religious Sunday school in the borough was started in 1805 by a Wesleyan Methodist and attracted Anglicans as well.[28] Twenty Sunday schools took part in the celebrations for Queen Victoria's jubilee in 1897.[29] Several churches and chapels also organized evening classes in non-religious subjects for children and adults.[30] The first public day school to be opened in the 19th century was that built at St. Austin's Roman Catholic church in 1818; a National school was opened in Gaol Road in 1825.

A school board was established in 1871.[31] At the first election the Church of England secured five of the nine seats,[32] and the nonconformists quickly complained of Anglican dominance of education in the borough.[33] At the time of the elections the churchmen pointed out that the Anglican schools had 1,492 children on their books while the nonconformists had only 400 in their day schools.[34]

At a meeting in 1870 it had been claimed that if a new school were opened in Christ Church district at the north end of the town, Stafford would have all the school accommodation required by the new Education Act.[35] A National school was duly opened in Rowley Street in 1874, and the board built no school until 1895 and only one after that.[36] It started evening classes in 1892 at St. Mary's school and classes for pupil teachers in 1898 at the Corporation Street school.[37]

In 1903 the county council took control of education in the borough.[38] Reorganization along the lines of the Hadow Report of 1926 took place in the late 1930s.[39] The first comprehensive school for the borough was opened in 1967,[40] and in 1976 the schools began to be reorganized into primary, middle (ages 9–13), and high schools.

St. Austin's Roman Catholic Junior Mixed and Infants' (Aided) School. A Roman Catholic school was opened in 1818 on part of the St. Austin's site in Wolverhampton Road. The cost of the building was met by Sir George Jerningham and a Mrs. Frith. A second building was erected in 1847 and used for the girls' department; it was extended in the early 1860s. With the opening of the new St. Austin's church in 1862 the old church was converted into the boys' schoolroom.[41] The boys were transferred to St. Patrick's school in Foregate Street probably soon after its opening in 1868 and certainly by 1884; St. Austin's then became the girls' school for the mission, and both schools were taking infants by 1884. St. Patrick's became a separate mission in 1893, and by 1896 each school was for boys, girls, and infants.[42] By 1910 St. Austin's school was overcrowded. In 1954 part of it moved into the new parish hall, but although the buildings of 1818 and 1847 were then able to be used solely as the school canteen, they soon had to be used for teaching again.[43] The school moved into St. Joseph's convent in 1971.[44]

Stafford National School, later Christ Church National School. A National school attached to St. Mary's was opened in Gaol Road in 1825.[45] In 1854 its two rooms were occupied by a mixed department under a master and an infants' department under his wife; there was also a teacher's house. Attendance averaged 60. Evening classes were then held in the building once a week by voluntary teachers under the direction of the clergy; they were

[17] *Staffs. Advertiser and Chron.* 9 Oct. 1958, 5 Feb. 1970.
[18] Ex inf. the Provincial Secretary, Mid Staffs. District, Independent Order of Odd Fellows Manchester Unity Friendly Soc.
[19] Much of the research for this section was carried out by Miss Ann J. Kettle.
[20] *S.H.C.* xiv (1), 150; *Cal. Pat.* 1377–81, 547.
[21] S.R.O., D.641/1/4A/11, rot. 1.
[22] Ibid. /14, rot. 1 and d.
[23] Ibid. rot. 3 and d.
[24] See pp. 164–7.
[25] A. C. F. Beales, *Educ. under Penalty*, 255, 265; *Cath. Mag.* v. 427 (reprinted in *Staffs. Cath. Hist.* xiv).
[26] See p. 264.
[27] J. S. Horne, *Notes for Hist. of K. Edw. VI Sch., Stafford* (Stafford, 1930), 45.
[28] See p. 254.
[29] *Official Programme of Stafford Celebrations of Diamond Jubilee* (copy in W.S.L. Pamphs. *sub* Stafford).
[30] W. Baker, *Centenary Hist. of Wesleyan Sunday Sch., Stafford, 1805–1905* (Stafford, 1905), 11 (copy in W.S.L.); *Staffs. Advertiser,* 17 June 1848; below, pp. 260–1.
[31] *Lond. Gaz.* 24 Feb. 1871, p. 686.
[32] *Staffs. Advertiser,* 25 Mar. 1871.

[33] Ibid. 8 July 1871.
[34] W.S.L. 7/206/00.
[35] W.S.L. 7/96/00.
[36] See p. 262.
[37] *Stafford (U.D.) Sch. Bd.: Triennial Rep.* (1895), 8, 11 (copy at Stafford Coll. of Further Educ.); (1898), 11.
[38] G. Balfour, *Ten Years of Staffs. Educ. 1903–1913* (Staffs. County Council Educ. Dept. 1913), 13 (copy in W.S.L.).
[39] *Staffs. Advertiser,* 8 Nov. 1930, p. 3; *Stafford Official Guide* (edn. of c. 1938), 24.
[40] See p. 264.
[41] M. Greenslade, *St. Austin's, Stafford* (Stafford, 1962), 28–9 (copy in W.S.L. Pamphs. *sub* Stafford); *Cath. Mag.* v. 429 (reprinted in *Staffs. Cath. Hist.* xiv), giving 1818 as the date of the school; Ed. 7/109/290, giving both 1820 and 1826.
[42] Greenslade, *St. Austin's,* 28; *P.O. Dir. Staffs.* (1872), showing a master for St. Patrick's and a mistress for St. Austin's; *Kelly's Dir. Staffs.* (1896), which, however, gives St. Austin's both as mixed and as for girls and infants.
[43] Greenslade, *St. Austin's,* 29.
[44] Ex inf. the headmistress (1976).
[45] *Staffs. Advertiser,* 25 June 1825.

still held in 1867.[46] In 1857, after the opening of St. Mary's school in 1856, the Gaol Road school was assigned to Christ Church district and became Christ Church National school. The infants' department had been closed by 1858.[47] A new room was added in 1862.[48] The master who took over the school in 1865 found it 'in sad state'; of some 95 boys and 55 girls attending the school 70 did not know their letters.[49] A separate infants' department was established in 1872.[50] In 1874 the boys were transferred to the new Rowley Street school, and Gaol Road became a girls' and infants' school.[51] The inspector's report for 1874 criticized it for 'general inefficiency' and part of the government grant was withheld. The report stated that the infants should at once become a separate department, and in 1875 the recommendation was duly carried out.[52] A classroom was added in 1885.[53] In 1909 the school was closed, and the pupils, averaging 250 girls and 96 infants, were transferred with the staff to Corporation Street school.[54] In 1977 the building was occupied by the R.A.F. Association.

British School. A British school was opened in 1834 in temporary premises in St. Chad's Lane,[55] and in 1836 it moved to a new building on a site in Earl Street given by Lord Stafford and Mr. Jerningham. There were separate rooms for boys and girls, and the school was run by a master and his wife.[56] In January 1838 there was an average attendance of 160 boys and 120 girls.[57] By 1847 the building needed repair,[58] and the school was closed in 1853.[59] After improvements it was re-opened in 1862 by a committee representing various denominations. The average attendance was 64 boys and 37 girls, which had risen to some 145 by 1864.[60] A classroom was added in 1887.[61] In 1893 the managers offered the school to the school board, but the Education Department would not approve the buildings. The school was taken over by the board in 1894 as a temporary measure, and in 1895 the pupils were transferred to the new Corporation Street school.[62] In 1896 the building passed to the Stafford Institute, which moved in 1964 to the new Lewis Heath Memorial Institute in Victoria Road;[63] the Earl Street building was demolished.

Infant Training School. An Infant Training School was started in 1838 in the new schoolroom adjoining the Presbyterian chapel.[64] In June 1839 the trustees invited the public to attend an exam-ination of the children, and 110, most of them 3 or 4 years old, went through the examination 'in such a manner as to excite the astonishment of all present'.[65] The school was closed in 1844, revived in 1846 and finally closed in 1860.[66]

Ragged School. A ragged school was established in 1848,[67] and by 1850 it had an average attendance of 90.[68] It was carried on under the auspices of the Y.M.C.A. by 1868[69] and was described as a night school in 1869.[70] It still existed in 1897, when it was apparently held in St. Augustine's school-chapel at Broadeye.[71]

St. Mary's Church of England School. A National school was built on the site of the parish workhouse to the south of St. Mary's churchyard in 1856. It was designed by G. G. Scott in a style harmonizing with that of the church; the buildings are of brick cased with stone from Weston-upon-Trent and have Bath stone dressings. The west and south ranges were built in 1856. They consisted of separate boys' and girls' schools, each with a classroom attached, and a teacher's house.[72] The third range, on the east, was added as the infants' school in or soon after 1857.[73] In 1874 a wing was added to the boys' schoolroom.[74] Evening classes for young men and women were started at the school in 1856.[75] The girls were transferred to Tenterbanks school in 1911.[76] The infants' department was closed in 1926, and the school then became a boys' school, which was known until c. 1930 as the Collegiate School.[77] It was closed in 1939.[78] The buildings still stood in 1976, being used as a refectory by the college of further education and as a parish hall.

St. Thomas's School. A schoolroom was built in 1863 on a site in Castletown acquired for a church and school.[79] In 1867 there was an attendance of upwards of 100. Both mixed and infants' departments were housed in the one room until a classroom was added in 1868.[80] By 1877 the porch of the extension had been enlarged as a classroom and an infants' school had been added to the main range.[81] With the opening of Tenterbanks school in 1911 the infants' department was closed, but the mixed department continued until 1926.[82] The building was then used by various organizations for meetings, and in 1958 it was converted into a parish centre.[83] In 1976 it was used by a firm of electrical wholesalers, the church having been rebuilt on a new site at Doxey.

[46] Ed. 7/109/292; S.R.O., CEL/38/1, p. 71.
[47] Ed. 7/109/286 and 292.
[48] *Staffs. Advertiser*, 14 June 1862.
[49] S.R.O., CEL/38/1, p. 1; Ed. 7/109/286.
[50] S.R.O., CEL/38/1, p. 125; CEL/37/1, p. 1.
[51] Ibid., CEL/37/1, p. 13.
[52] Ibid. pp. 22–3, 25.
[53] *Kelly's Dir. Staffs.* (1888).
[54] S.R.O., CEL/37/1, p. 484.
[55] *92nd Rep. Brit. and Foreign Sch. Soc.* (1897), 378; *Staffs. Advertiser*, 15 Nov. 1834.
[56] *Staffs. Advertiser*, 23 Jan., 9 Apr. 1836; Ed. 7/109/287.
[57] *Staffs. Advertiser*, 6 Jan. 1838.
[58] Ed. 7/109/287.
[59] *Staffs. Advertiser*, 24 May 1862.
[60] Ed. 7/109/287; *Staffs. Advertiser*, 25 June 1864.
[61] S.R.O., D.693/1, 28 Jan., 3 June, 25 July 1887.
[62] *Stafford (U.D.) Sch. Bd.: Triennial Rep.* (1895), 14–16; *Halden & Son's Dir. Stafford* (1895).
[63] *Stafford Newsletter*, 28 Aug. 1964.
[64] *Staffs. Advertiser*, 24 Feb., 3 Mar. 1838; Roxburgh, *Stafford*, 42, 45.
[65] *Staffs. Advertiser*, 15 and 22 June 1839.
[66] W.S.L. 7/18/00, newspaper cutting.

[67] *Staffs. Advertiser*, 9 Dec. 1848, 6 Jan. 1849; White, *Dir. Staffs.* (1851), 336.
[68] *Staffs. Advertiser*, 9 Nov. 1850.
[69] Ibid. 11 Jan. 1868.
[70] S.R.O., CEL/38/1, p. 70.
[71] *Staffs. Advertiser*, 13 Apr. 1889; *Official Programme of Stafford Celebrations of Diamond Jubilee*, list of schools in procession.
[72] *Staffs. Advertiser*, 17 December 1853, 29 Mar., 11 and 18 Oct. 1856.
[73] S.R.O., D.812, box 5; *Staffs. Advertiser*, 2 Mar. 1861, reprinting an article from *The Builder* (1861), 117–18.
[74] *Lich. Dioc. Ch. Cal.* (1875), 77.
[75] *Staffs. Advertiser*, 11 Oct. 1856.   [76] See p. 264.
[77] *Lich. Dioc. Year Book* (1926), 120; *Halden & Haywood's Dir. Stafford* (1930).
[78] Ex inf. Mr. A. E. Mottershead of Stafford (1978).
[79] *Staffs. Advertiser*, 22 Aug. 1863.
[80] Ibid. 4 May 1867; *Lich. Dioc. Ch. Cal.* (1869), 76; S.R.O., D.812, box 5.
[81] S.R.O., D.812, box 5; W.S.L., M. 765.
[82] *Halden & Son's Dir. Stafford* (1911); *Staffs. Advertiser*, 3 Apr. 1926.
[3] *Stafford Newsletter*, 14 June 1958.

St. John's Church of England Junior Mixed and Infants' (Controlled) School, formerly Eastgate Infants' School. Eastgate infants' school was opened in 1863 as a branch of St. Mary's National school in a temporary schoolroom at the east end of South Walls. The site was given by the earl of Shrewsbury. The average attendance in 1865 was some 54.[84] After repeated complaints by the inspectors about the unsuitability of the building the government grant was suspended in 1883.[85] In 1886 the school moved to a new building, used also a mission church, on a site at Littleworth given by the earl of Shrewsbury.[86] It was then reorganized, with mixed and infants' departments in separate rooms.[87] In 1887 it was renamed St. Mary's Littleworth National school[88] and *c.* 1923 St. John's Church of England school.[89] It acquired controlled status in 1951.[90] The original building in South Walls was used as a garage by the 1970s and was demolished in 1976.

St. Patrick's Roman Catholic Schools. The first St. Patrick's Roman Catholic school was opened in 1868 for boys, girls, and infants. The two-storeyed building on the corner of the present Foregate Street and St. Patrick's Street consisted of a school-room and a classroom. It subsequently became a boys' school only, the girls going to St. Austin's school, but in 1884 an infants' department was started. St. Patrick's became an independent mission in 1893, and by 1896 the school was again for boys, girls, and infants.[91]

In 1930 the children aged under 11 were transferred to a new St. Patrick's junior school on part of the St. Patrick's site between Sandon and Marston Roads (in 1976 St. Patrick's junior mixed and infants' (aided) school). The Foregate Street building became St. Patrick's senior school, which became a secondary modern school under the 1944 Education Act. In 1963 the pupils were transferred to Blessed William Howard school, and the building was converted into a shop.[92]

St. Mary's Broadeye School. A school attached to St. Mary's church was opened at Broadeye in 1868 with an attendance of 80 boys and girls.[93] A new schoolroom and classroom were opened in 1871 and the school became St. Mary's Broadeye National school.[94] A mission chapel added to the building in 1878 was also used as the girls' department.[95] By 1892 the school was for girls and infants only.[96] The buildings were extended in 1898.[97] In 1911 the school was closed and the pupils were transferred to Tenterbanks school.[98] The buildings, at the junction of Broadeye and Duke Street, were later used as a Sunday school[99] and were demolished in the 1960s.

Rowley Street National School. Rowley Street National school at the junction of Rowley and Marsh Streets was opened in January 1874 as an additional school for Christ Church district. The schoolroom was also used as a mission church. It was a mixed school, but girls over 7 years old were not admitted. The boys at the Goal Road school were transferred to it, and the initial attendance was 231.[1] A separate infants' department was established in 1882[2] and a junior girls' department in 1888;[3] on each occasion a new room was added.[4] In 1909 the infants were transferred to North Street and the girls to Corporation Street, and Rowley Street became a boys' school.[5] It became Rowley Street council school *c.* 1926.[6] It was closed *c.* 1939,[7] and in 1976 the buildings were occupied by a firm of furniture removers.

John Wheeldon Junior Mixed and Infants' School, formerly Corporation Street School. Corporation Street school, the first built by the school board, was opened in 1895 for boys, girls, and infants. The numbers presenting themselves on the first morning were more than could be accommodated, but 242 boys and 176 girls were admitted.[8] Two classrooms and a separate infants' block were added in 1900.[9] In 1909 a separate boys' department was built and the infants' building was enlarged.[10] In 1957 the school was renamed after John Wheeldon, the first headmaster and from 1909 to 1922 the head of the boys' department; he had been the last headmaster of the British School, and he was mayor in 1923–4.[11]

Northfields (formerly North Street) Infants' School. North Street infants' school was opened by the school board in 1900.[12] It was enlarged in 1909.[13] About 1929 it was renamed Stone Road council school[14] and in 1958 Northfields infants' school.[15]

Other 19th-century Schools. A day school was opened in 1850 in the schoolroom at the Methodist New Connexion chapel. It was for children of all social classes and offered 'a good English education on terms so moderate as to place it within the reach of all'. Some 65 pupils were admitted at the opening.[16] There was an infants' school at Broadeye in 1850[17] and another in Friar Street at the north end of the town in 1851.[18] St. Paul's Church of England junior mixed and infants' (controlled) school in Garden Street, which originated in an 18th-century charity school, is treated elsewhere, as is the National school at Rickerscote.[19]

[84] Ed. 7/109/294.
[85] S.R.O., D.218/1, pp. 45, 63, 100, 108–9, 118–19, 142–3, 151.
[86] *Staffs. Advertiser,* 2 May 1885, 16 Jan. 1886.
[87] S.R.O., D.218/1, p. 169.
[88] Ibid. p. 178.
[89] *Halden & Haywood's Dir. Stafford* (1924).
[90] Ex inf. the headmaster (1976).
[91] Ed. 7/109/295; above, p. 250.
[92] *Cath. Dir. of Archdioc. of Birmingham* (1931), 151; St. Patrick's Sch. log-book, 1896–1939 (at Blessed William Howard High Sch.), pp. 259, 261; ex inf. the headmaster, Blessed William Howard High Sch. (1976).
[93] *Lich. Dioc. Ch. Cal.* (1869), 76.
[94] Ed. 7/113/Stafford.
[95] *Staffs. Advertiser,* 14 Sept. 1878.
[96] *Kelly's Dir. Staffs.* (1892).
[97] Ibid. (1900).
[98] Ed. 7/108/296A.
[99] O.S. Map 1/2,500, Staffs. XXXVII. 11 (1923 edn.).

[1] Ed. 7/113/Stafford; S.R.O., CEL/38/1, p. 140; above' p. 248.
[2] S.R.O., CEL/38/3, p. 1.
[3] S.R.O., CEL/38/4, p. 1.
[4] *Lich. Dioc. Ch. Cal.* (1884), 74; (1889), 159.
[5] S.R.O., CEL/38/2, pp. 281, 284.
[6] *Halden & Haywood's Dir. Stafford* (1927).
[7] It occurs ibid. (1939) but not in the next edn. (1946).
[8] S.R.O., D.693/2, p. 1; Ed. 7/109/287.
[9] *Staffs. Advertiser,* 20 Oct. 1900.
[10] Ibid. 3 July 1909; *Halden & Son's Dir. Stafford* (1910).
[11] *Stafford Newsletter,* 16 Feb. 1957.
[12] *Halden & Son's Dir. Stafford* (1901).
[13] *Staffs. Advertiser,* 3 July 1909.
[14] *Halden & Haywood's Dir. Stafford* (1930).
[15] *Stafford Newsletter,* 11 Oct. 1958.
[16] *Staffs. Advertiser,* 12 Jan. 1850.
[17] *P.O. Dir. Staffs.* (1850).
[18] White, *Dir. Staffs.* (1851), 336.
[19] *V.C.H. Staffs.* v. 98–9.

SCHOOLS OPENED BY THE COUNTY COUNCIL SINCE 1903.

Barnfields junior mixed and infants' school in Lansdowne Way on the Wildwood estate was opened in 1974.[20]

Blessed William Howard Roman Catholic high school was opened as a mixed secondary school in 1963 on a site between Rowley Avenue and Brunswick Terrace bought in 1939.[21] It became a comprehensive high school in 1971. Extensions to the building were completed in 1972 and 1976.[22]

Bower Norris Roman Catholic junior mixed and infants' aided school in Somerset Road, Highfields, was opened in 1966.[23]

Burton Manor junior mixed and infants' school in Uplands Road was opened in 1955.[24]

Castlechurch junior mixed and infants' school in Tennyson Road, Highfields, was opened in 1962.[25]

Chetwynd middle school was opened in 1976 in the buildings of the former King Edward VI grammar school in Newport Road.[26]

Dartmouth Street senior school, see Kingston secondary modern school.

Doxey junior mixed and infants' school in Doxey Road replaced Tenterbanks school. It opened in 1960 with the infants in the building intended for the junior mixed department. The infants' building was opened in 1961, and the juniors were then transferred from Tenterbanks.[27]

Flash Ley infants' school in Hawksmoor Road was opened in 1951. The adjoining junior mixed school was opened in 1953.[28]

Girls' High School, see Stafford Girls' High School.

Graham Balfour grammar school for boys and girls in Stone Road was opened in 1962. At first it was housed in Trinity Fields secondary school, but in 1963 it moved into a new building on an adjoining site.[29] In 1968 it became the upper school of Graham Balfour Trinity Fields comprehensive school,[30] which in 1973 was renamed Graham Balfour high school.[31]

Green Hall nursery school in Lichfield Road for physically handicapped children was opened by the county council in 1975 in the day care centre which had been run by the Mid-Staffordshire Spastics Association from 1971.[32]

Highfields infants' school and Highfields junior mixed school on adjoining sites in Highfield Grove were opened in 1954, replacing Rising Brook primary school.[33]

Holmcroft infants' school in Young Avenue was opened in 1939. The adjoining junior mixed school was opened in 1969.[34]

King Edward VI high school was opened in 1976 in the buildings of the former girls' high school in West Way.[35]

Kingston middle school in Dartmouth Street was opened in 1939 as Dartmouth Street senior boys' school. It became a secondary modern school for boys under the 1944 Education Act. It was renamed Kingston in 1956 and became Kingston middle school in 1976.[36]

The Leasowes junior mixed and infants' school in Porlock Avenue on the Weeping Cross estate was opened as Stockton Lane junior mixed and infants' school in 1958. The name was changed in 1959. A separate junior school was opened on an adjoining site in 1963.[37]

Marshlands school in Lansdowne Way, Wildwood, originated in a voluntarily run occupation centre for mentally handicapped children which was opened in the Quaker hall in Foregate Street in 1934; earlier there had been a part-time centre at the Wesleyan schoolroom. The Foregate Street centre later passed to the county council's health department. In 1957 the hall was closed and a newly built junior training centre was opened in North Walls. In 1971 it passed to the education department as Stafford day special school. It was renamed Marshlands day special school in 1973. It moved to Wildwood in 1976 as Marshlands school.[38]

Oakridge junior mixed and infants' school in Silvester Way on the Hillcroft Park estate was opened in 1964.[39]

Parkside junior mixed and infants' school in Bradshaw Way was opened in 1974.[40]

Rising Brook high school was opened in 1946 as a primary school.[41] In 1954 the children were transferred to the Highfields schools and the buildings were enlarged to accommodate the new Rising Brook secondary modern school; a further block was added in 1956.[42] In 1976 it became a middle school and the name was changed.[43]

Riverway middle school was opened in 1939 as Riverway senior girls' school and became a secondary modern school for girls under the 1944 Education Act.[44] It was enlarged in 1958.[45] In 1976 it became Riverway middle school, a Church of England (controlled) school.[46]

St. Anne's Roman Catholic junior mixed and infants' (aided) school in Lynton Avenue, Weeping Cross, was opened in 1966.[47]

St. Leonard's junior mixed and infants' school in St. Leonard's Avenue was planned by the school board[48] and was the first school to be opened in the borough by the county education committee. It was begun in the Baptist schoolroom on the Green in 1904 as a temporary measure to meet the pressure caused by the influx of Siemens' workers. The

[20] Ex inf. Staffs. County Council Educ. Dept. (1976).
[21] Greenslade, St. Austin's, 30.
[22] Ex inf. the headmaster (1976).
[23] Ex inf. Educ. Dept.
[24] Stafford Newsletter, 20 Aug. 1955.
[25] Ibid. 8 Sept. 1962.
[26] Ex inf. Educ. Dept.
[27] Stafford Newsletter, 26 Aug. 1961.
[28] Ex inf. Educ. Dept.
[29] Stafford Newsletter, 8 Sept. 1962, 26 Jan. 1963.
[30] Staffs. Advertiser, 5 Sept. 1968.
[31] Ex inf. Educ. Dept.
[32] Ex inf. the head teacher (1977).
[33] Ex inf. Educ. Dept.
[34] Ex inf. Educ. Dept.
[35] Ex inf. Educ. Dept.
[36] Ex inf. Educ. Dept. and the school secretary (1976).
[37] Stafford Newsletter, 7 Nov. 1959; Staffs. Advertiser, 5 Sept. 1963; ex inf. Educ. Dept.
[38] Ex inf. the head teacher (1976); ex inf. Mrs. A. P. Cresswell, Cherry Trees Sch., Wombourn (1976); Stafford Newsletter, 20 July 1957.
[39] Ex inf. Educ. Dept.
[40] Ex inf. Educ. Dept.
[41] Stafford Official Guide [c. 1950], 36.
[42] Stafford Newsletter, 7 Aug. 1954, 26 May, 30 June 1956.
[43] Ex inf. Educ. Dept.
[44] Ex inf. Educ. Dept.
[45] Stafford Newsletter, 23 Aug. 1958.
[46] Ex inf. Educ. Dept.
[47] Cath. Dir. of Archdioc. of Birmingham (1969), 223.
[48] Balfour, Ten Years of Staffs. Educ. 126.

building in St. Leonard's Avenue was opened in 1906.[49]

Sandyford nursery school originated in a day nursery opened *c.* 1943 in the area called the Motty in the triangle formed by Corporation Street, Crooked Bridge Road, and Sandyford Street. In 1946 it became a nursery school. In 1964, since the building had been damaged by subsidence, the school moved into Northfields infants' school. It remained there until 1967 when a new building was opened in Prospect Road.[50]

Silkmore junior mixed and infants' school in Exeter Street was opened in 1948.[51]

Stafford day special school, *see* Marshlands school.

Stafford Girls' High School started in 1903 as a private school in Moat House, Newport Road. In 1907 it moved into buildings in the Oval off Lichfield Road erected by the county council and became the first maintained girls' high school in the administrative county. In 1918 the preparatory department moved into Green Hall, Lichfield Road; it was closed under the 1944 Education Act. A new wing was added at the Oval in 1930.[52] The school moved to West Way, Highfields, in 1963.[53] The buildings there were taken over by King Edward VI high school in 1976.

Stafford North secondary school, *see* Trinity Fields secondary modern school.

Stockton Lane junior mixed and infants' school, *see* the Leasowes junior mixed and infants' school.

Tenterbanks council school was opened in 1911 to take the girls from St. Mary's school, the girls and infants from Broadeye school, and the infants from St. Thomas's school.[54] It was reorganized as a junior mixed and infants' school in 1945. In 1960 the infants were transferred to Doxey school, and the rest of the children followed in 1961.[55] The building was used for a time by the college of art[56] and was demolished in 1967 to make way for an extension to the college of further education.[57]

Tillington Manor junior mixed and infants' school in Paddock Close off Trinity Rise was opened in 1971.[58]

Trinity Fields secondary modern school in Stone Road was opened as Stafford North secondary school for boys and girls in 1960. It was renamed in 1961. In 1968 it became the junior school of Graham Balfour Trinity Fields comprehensive school (from 1973 Graham Balfour high school).[59]

Walton high school in the Rise, Walton-on-the-Hill, was opened as Walton comprehensive school in 1967. It was renamed in 1976.[60]

PRIVATE SCHOOLS. There was a boarding-school for young ladies in Market Square in the earlier 1760s.[61] In 1785 the room over the council chamber in the former St. Bertelin's chapel was converted into a writing-school. By 1797 it was the Commercial School run by Robert Foster, who also provided board at his house. When he died that year his father, R. Foster, took it over as Stafford Academy. On the demolition of St. Bertelin's in 1801 the school moved to a house in Martin Street. By then it took both boys and girls. After Foster's death the same year the academy was taken over by T. Fairbanks, who advertised its reopening at the beginning of 1802.[62] Other schools advertising in the mid 1790s included Miss Foster's academy in Eastgate Street.[63]

One of the more successful of the many 19th-century private schools was a classical and commercial academy opened as a boys' boarding-school *c.* 1820 by John Chalmers, minister at Zion Congregational chapel. It moved to Eastgate Street in 1821. It was still carried on there by his son, the Revd. T. S. Chalmers, in 1863.[64] Eighteen private schools were listed in 1851,[65] but the number had fallen to ten by the end of the century.[66]

In 1903 a girls' private school was opened at Moat House, Newport Road, the forerunner of the Stafford Girls' High School.[67] The Sisters of St. Joseph of Cluny opened a private school for girls at the convent in Lichfield Road in 1905. It was closed in 1971.[68] The only private school in the town in 1976 was Brooklands preparatory school for boys and girls. It was started as a result of the closure of the preparatory department of the girls' high school: in 1945 a group of parents formed a limited company and in 1946 opened a house in Eccleshall Road as a preparatory school. Numbers grew rapidly, and an adjoining house was added. An assembly hall linking the two buildings was opened in 1962. In 1967 a science laboratory and new kitchens were built.[69]

FURTHER AND HIGHER EDUCATION. The Stafford Experimental Society was formed in 1811 to promote the study of the different branches of science. It had a library and met for lectures at the Star inn in Market Square.[70] It was later renamed the Stafford Philosophical Society. By 1828 it was 'either dead or bordering on dissolution', and the idea of reviving it as a mechanics' institute was being canvassed.[71]

A mechanics' institute was formed in 1837 with a reading room and a library.[72] Its lectures were at first held at the Vine and in the mayor's office,[73]

[49] Ed. 7/109/291.
[50] Ex inf. Mrs. M. Adams, head teacher (1976); *Stafford Newsletter*, 21 Apr. 1967. For 2 pieces of land in Foregate field, each called a motty, see B.R.L., Keen 371, deed of 25 Jan. 1766.
[51] Ex inf. Educ. Dept.
[52] *Stafford Girls' High Sch. Mag.* (1928), 2 (copy in W.S.L. Pamphs. *sub* Stafford); *Kelly's Dir. Staffs.* (1908); *Stafford Newsletter*, 28 Sept. 1957.
[53] *Staffs. Advertiser*, 17 Jan. 1963.
[54] Ed. 7/108/296A.
[55] *Stafford Newsletter*, 26 Aug. 1961.
[56] Ibid.; ex inf. Educ. Dept.
[57] *Stafford Newsletter*, 1 Sept. 1967.
[58] Ex inf. Educ. Dept.
[59] *Stafford Newsletter*, 27 Aug. 1960, 16 Dec. 1961, 5 Sept. 1968.
[60] Ex inf. Educ. Dept.
[61] *Aris's Birmingham Gaz.* 21 June 1765.
[62] *Church of St. Bertelin at Stafford*, ed. A. Oswald

(Birmingham [1955]), 10; S.R.O., D.1323/A/1/3, p. 10; *Univ. Brit. Dir.* iv. 439; *Staffs. Advertiser*, 1 July, 30 Dec. 1797, 23 Dec. 1798, 20 June, 21 Nov. 1801, 2 Jan. 1802.
[63] *Staffs. Advertiser*, 30 Jan. 1796.
[64] A. G. Matthews, *Cong. Churches of Staffs.* 193; *Staffs. Advertiser*, 6 Jan. 1821, 4 July 1863; *Nat. Com. Dir.* (1835), 444.
[65] White, *Dir. Staffs.* (1851), 348–9.
[66] *Halden & Son's Dir. Stafford* (1900).   [67] See above.
[68] Greenslade, *St. Austin's*, 30–2; ex inf. the headmistress, St. Austin's R.C. sch. (1976).
[69] *Stafford Newsletter*, 15 Dec. 1962; ex inf. the headmaster and Mr. P. Butters of Stafford (1976).
[70] Cherry, *Stafford*, 92; *Staffs. Advertiser*, 2 Nov., 7 Dec. 1811.
[71] *Weekly Register*, 20 Sept., 4 Oct. 1828.
[72] *Staffs. Advertiser*, 30 Sept., 14 and 28 Oct., 4 Nov. 1837.
[73] Ibid. 9 Dec. 1837, 3, 10, 17 Feb., 15 Sept., 15 Dec. 1838.

but in 1839 it moved to a lecture room in Crabbery Street.[74] It still met there in February 1841,[75] but its annual general meeting in March was held at the Vine. It was then 'by no means in a flourishing state', although classes were held in reading, writing, arithmetic, and drawing and the library consisted of some 200 volumes.[76] Soon afterwards it ceased to exist and the library was sold to pay its debts.[77] The institute was refounded in 1845.[78] By 1850 it had premises in Bath Street and a membership of 220; there was a newsroom and a library of 300 volumes.[79] By 1854 its address was Martin Street,[80] and in 1856 it moved to the Lyceum theatre in that street;[81] by 1879 its premises were a building behind the theatre.[82] In the early 1880s there was a library of some 3,500 volumes.[83] Decline set in as a result of the establishment of the free library in 1882 and of various reading rooms in the town. The institute was dissolved at the end of 1893 and the library sold in 1894.[84]

An art school was started in 1873 by a local committee in association with the Department of Science and Art at South Kensington; its first classes were held in the evenings in the Wesleyan schoolroms in Earl Street.[85] In 1877 it moved to the new borough hall[86] and in 1881 into the extension to the hall.[87] It was taken over by the corporation in 1887 and placed under the free library and museum committee.[88] In 1889 the corporation formed a technical instruction committee,[89] and a technical school was started in 1890, with classes at first in the borough hall and Wogan Street and from 1891 at Crabbery Hall in Crabbery Street.[90] The art school too was taken over by the committee in 1891.[91] As the school of science, art, and technical instruction all the classes were transferred in 1896 to the new County Technical School built by the county council on the corner of Victoria Square and Earl Street; the building is in a classical style and was designed by Bailey & McConnal of Walsall.[92] In 1927 the institution became the County Technical College and Art School, with a board of governors representing both the county and the borough; there were separate directors for college and school.[93]

A new building for the technical college was begun in Tenterbanks in 1937. The shell was requisitioned during the Second World War, and although

occupied by the college from 1948 the building was not completed until 1956. In 1959 a separate college of technology was established and the technical school was renamed Stafford College of Further Education.[94] The first of a series of extensions was completed in 1967, and when the last was finished in 1975 the college occupied a site bounded by Earl Street, Victoria Road, Tenterbanks, and Broad Street; Cherry Street and parts of Queen and Duke Streets had been absorbed into the site.[95]

Staffordshire College of Technology at first occupied part of the Tenterbanks building. It moved in 1962 to a new building at the junction of the Weston road and Beaconside beyond the borough boundary. In 1970 the college became part of the North Staffordshire Polytechnic, formed by merging the Stafford college, Stoke-on-Trent College of Art, and the North Staffordshire College of Technology at Stoke.[96]

Stafford College of Art remained in the Victoria Square building until 1963 when it moved into the premises in the Oval vacated by the girls' high school.[97] It was amalgamated with the college of further education in 1971.[98]

CHARITIES FOR THE POOR. *St. Martin's Lane Alms-houses.* In 1564 the burgesses leased out land in a street leading from the market-place to St. Martin's Lane (later Martin Street) upon which an alms-house had been lately built.[99] The building, or what remained of it, had by 1606 been converted into a 'stable called the Alms-house'.[1]

Palmer's Alms-houses. By will proved 1639 John Palmer, rector of St. Mary's, devised a house in Martin Lane (later Martin Street) divided into two cottages and already occupied by two widows; they were to be used as alms-houses but repaired by the occupants. By *c.* 1800 the cottages had been exchanged for two in Broad Street.[2] A Charity Commission inspector described them in 1859 as 'altogether poor places'. Each contained one small room on the ground-floor and another upstairs.[3] By the early 1920s the alms-houses were receiving a 6s. 8d. rent-charge from the trustees of the Methodist New Connexion chapel in Gaol Road, which was later redeemed for £13 6s. 8d. stock.[4] In 1934 the alms-

[74] *Staffs. Advertiser*, 15 June 1839.
[75] *Staffs. Gaz.* 4 Feb. 1841.
[76] *Staffs. Advertiser*, 6 Mar. 1841.
[77] Ibid. 8 Nov. 1845.
[78] Ibid. 18 Oct., 27 Dec. 1845.
[79] Ibid. 23 Nov. 1850; *P.O. Dir. Staffs.* (1850).
[80] *P.O. Dir. Staffs.* (1854).
[81] *Staffs. Advertiser*, 12 Apr. 1856.
[82] O.S. Map 1/500, Staffs. XXXVII. 11. 17 (1881 edn.).
[83] *Kelly's Dir. Staffs.* (1884).
[84] S.R.O., C.491/11, abstract of title of Stafford corp. to Lyceum theatre and no. 10 Martin St., 1920, p. 5; *Staffs. Advertiser*, 10 Feb. 1894.
[85] *Staffs. Advertiser*, 23 Nov., 14 Dec. 1872; *Cat. of Fine Art Exhibition, Borough Hall, Stafford, 1878* (copy in W.S.L. Pamphs. *sub* Stafford).
[86] S.R.O., D.1323/A/1/10, pp. 115, 129; *Cat. of Fine Art Exhibition, 1878.*
[87] Calvert, *Stafford*, 69; S.R.O., D.1323/A/1/10, pp. 416, 505.
[88] *Staffs. Advertiser*, 1 Jan. 1887; S.R.O., D.1323/C/10/1, pp. 39–40.
[89] S.R.O., D.1323/C/18/1, p. 155.
[90] Ibid. pp. 173–4, 205; *Halden's Stafford Dir.* (1891), 17; *Halden & Son's Dir. Stafford* (1892), 17.
[91] S.R.O., D.1323/C/18/1, p. 212; *Halden & Son's Dir.*

Stafford (1892), 17.
[92] S.R.O., D.1323/C/11/1, p. 3; *Halden & Son's Dir. Stafford* (1897), 16–18, 21; Balfour, *Ten Years of Staffs. Educ.* 39.
[93] *Halden & Haywood's Dir. Stafford* (1928), 21.
[94] 'Hist. of Stafford Coll. of Further Educ.' (1963; TS. at the Coll. of Further Educ.); Staffs. Educ. Cttee. *County Technical Coll., Stafford, 1955* (copy at Coll. of Further Educ.).
[95] The dates have been supplied by the librarian, Stafford Coll. of Further Educ. (1976).
[96] Ex inf. the director, N. Staffs. Polytechnic (1976); *Stafford Newsletter*, 1 Sept. 1962, 27 Mar. 1964.
[97] *Stafford Newsletter*, 30 Aug. 1963.
[98] Ex inf. the librarian, Stafford Coll. of Further Educ.
[99] W.S.L., H.M. uncat. 23, lease of 13 Feb. 1563/4.
[1] S.R.O., D.1323/E/1, f. 47v.
[2] *11th Rep. Com. Char.* H.C. 433, p. 604 (1824), xiv; P. T. Dale, 'Notes on ancient buildings and streets of Stafford', *T.O.S.S.* 1934, 22–3; Keen, *Letter to Inhabitants of Stafford*, 37–8, wrongly giving Palmer's Christian name as Robert. A copy of Palmer's will is in W.S.L., H.M. uncat. 26.
[3] Char. Com. files.
[4] Copies of Char. Com. schemes in poss. of the sec., Stafford United Chars. (1963).

houses were dilapidated, and by 1948 only one was inhabited. In 1959 the funds of the charity were transferred to Stafford United Charities,[5] and in 1962 the alms-houses were demolished.

Noell's Alms-houses. Sir Martin Noell, a London merchant and financier born in Stafford in 1614 and M.P. for the borough 1656–9, had by 1662 built a group of alms-houses in Mill Lane (later Mill Street). The alms-folk, 6 men and 6 women, were to be aged over 50 and either natives of the town or resident there for at least fifteen years.[6] He had not fulfilled his intention to endow the houses when he died of plague in 1665,[7] and the alms-houses remained in the hands of his family until 1691. They were then conveyed to the mayor and four burgesses as trustees and later passed to the corporation, but no alms-folk were appointed until 1701.[8] The corporation used sums given in 1700 to endow the alms-houses, £100 from John Chetwynd of Ingestre, £50 each from Philip Foley and his nephew Thomas Foley, and £12 from Katherine Abnett of Stafford, wife of Humphrey Perye, to pay off debts incurred in buying the tithes of Marston. It charged the tithes with payments to the alms-houses of £10 12s. a year, raised to £12 in 1732.[9] William Fowler assigned to the alms-houses £20 rent from Coton field from 1699 and a further £8 from 1705 in return for the right to nominate two alms-folk. At least in the earlier 18th century the corporation devoted the income from Coton field, after payment of the rent, to the alms-houses and the poor.[10] By 1701 part of the money which it received under Izaak Walton's will was assigned to the alms-houses, and in 1714 it decided to put Richard Bynns's bequest of £50 to the same use.[11]

In 1701 the income of the poor in the alms-houses was stated to be £41 16s. 6d.[12] From 1768 £40 6s. was paid to the alms-folk at the rate of 15s. 6d. a week. In 1808 the income was £46, made up of £12 from Marston tithes, £28 from Coton field, and £6 in coals.[13] By the early 1820s the only regular income was from Coton field; £40 6s. was paid to the alms-folk, and £3 10s. was spent on repairs. Since 1809 the corporation had also made payments to the alms-houses out of the charity of William Farmer and Rebecca Crompton.[14] In 1859 it was still allotting the alms-folk £40 6s. a year, and a further £6 10s. was obtained by leasing out part of the alms-house garden. Each house was provided with a ton of coal at Christmas, and several alms-folk received help from other charities. Most of them were nevertheless

upon the parish.[15] In 1861 each inmate received between 7½d. and 1s. weekly out of the endowments.[16] In 1862 the trustees were permitted to devote the income from various charities to the alms-folk: Startin's, Farmer's, Sutton's 40s., and Walton's and Fowler's as far as applicable. In 1908, however, the alms-houses were still 'miserably endowed'. The alms-folk, 12 married couples, each received 7¾d. a week and consequently had to apply for poor-relief and could not obtain old-age pensions.[17]

In the 20th century the alms-houses received various gifts and bequests. John Shallcross of Stafford (d. 1904), twice mayor of the borough, left £600 to the alms-house trust, the income to be distributed annually; William Marson (d. 1918), a Stafford chemist, left £100 to the repair fund; and Mrs. E. M. Stranaghan gave £100 in 1918, the income to be distributed annually.[18] In 1922 the alms-houses became part of Stafford United Charities, but they continued to receive specific endowments. Henry Woodhouse of Llandudno (Caern.) (d. 1924) left £200 for the general purposes of the alms-houses and to provide annuities of 2s. 6d. to each inmate.[19] In 1924 the corporation redeemed two rent-charges payable towards the maintenance of the alms-houses, that of £28 on Coton field and one of £12 6s. on other corporation property.[20] Olive Jenkinson, by will proved 1948, left £198 15s. 6d. stock to the trustees of Stafford United Charities, the income to be used for the benefit of the alms-folk.[21] Under a Scheme of 1962 the alms-folk pay a small rent.[22]

The age-limit laid down for alms-folk by Noell was not strictly observed until the mid 19th century. John Chetwynd apparently required that his gift be used 'towards the maintenance of poor persons and children' in the alms-houses, and during the 18th century children were occasionally housed there. In 1859 it was said of a seventy-year-old widow that the alms-houses had been her home since she was three.[23]

The alms-houses, a two-storey stone structure forming three sides of a quadrangle and consisting of 12 houses and a chapel, were completed at Noell's expense and gardens were laid out.[24] In 1787 the corporation ordered that the chapel should be converted into two tenements to provide further accommodation for the poor, and in 1801 repairs were sanctioned so that it could be used as a temporary schoolroom for the grammar school.[25] In 1859 the alms-houses were in bad repair, cold, draughty, and wet in bad weather; the chapel was again being

[5] *T.O.S.S.* 1934, 22; Roxburgh, *Stafford,* 46–7; ex inf. the rector of St. Mary's (1962).
[6] G. E. Aylmer, *The State's Servants,* 250–1; *St. Mary's, Stafford, Par. Reg.* (Staffs. Par. Reg. Soc. 1935–6), 168; *S.H.C.* 1920 and 1922, 101–3; S.R.O., D.1323/E/1, f. 302; Keen, *Letter to Inhabitants of Stafford,* 63–4.
[7] *11th Rep. Com. Char.* 596; W.S.L., H.M. uncat. 30/1, indenture of 21 May 1691; Aylmer, *State's Servants,* 251.
[8] W.S.L., H.M. uncat. 30/1, indentures of 9 Oct. 1669, 10 May 1676, 21 May 1691; S.R.O., D.1323/A/1/2, pp. 24, 93.
[9] S.R.O., D.(W.) 0/8/2, p. 8; *11th Rep. Com. Char.* 596–7; W.S.L., H.M. 26/2, ff. 33v.–34; *S.H.C.* 1920 and 1922, 168–9; G. T. Lawley, *Hist. of Bilston* (Bilston, 1893 edn.), 152; W.S.L., H.M. 26/1, unnumbered folio written by Humph. Perye giving family details; W.S.L., H.M. 26/3, f. 34; S.R.O., D.1323/A/1/2, p. 374.
[10] See pp. 208–9; W.S.L. 77/45, f. 24 and v.
[11] See pp. 268–9.
[12] S.R.O., D.1323/A/1/2, p. 95.
[13] S.R.O., D.1033/1, pp. 51 sqq.; D.1323/E/2, pp. 19

sqq.; Keen, *Letter to Inhabitants of Stafford,* 15–16, 65–6.
[14] *11th Rep. Com. Char.* 598–9; below, p. 269.
[15] Char. Com. files.
[16] *Staffs. Advertiser,* 2 Mar. 1861.
[17] Char. Com. files.
[18] Ibid.; *Corp. of Stafford Yr. Bk.* (1907–8), stating that only £542 12s. 9d. was received from Shallcross's legacy.
[19] Char. Com. files.
[20] *Corp. Yr. Bk.* (1924–25).
[21] Char. Com. list of chars. for poor of Stafford in poss. of the rector of St. Mary's (1962).
[22] Char. Com. Scheme, 20 July 1962; ex inf. the sec., Stafford United Chars. (1977).
[23] Keen, *Letter to Inhabitants of Stafford,* 64; S.R.O., D.(W.) 0/8/2, chamberlains' accts. 1730–1, 1731–2; D.(W.) 0/8/18, vestry order 7 Dec. 1740; Char. Com. files.
[24] Keen, *Letter to Inhabitants of Stafford,* 63; W.S.L., H.M. uncat. 30/1, indenture of 21 May 1691; plate facing p. 225 above.
[25] S.R.O., D.1323/A/1/3, pp. 3, 232; J. S. Horne, *Notes for Hist. of K. Edw. VI Sch.,* Stafford (Stafford, 1930), 45.

used as an extra dwelling-house. The whole building was completely restored in, or shortly before, 1866.[26] Between 1960 and 1962 central heating was installed and the buildings were extended at the rear; accommodation was provided for about 30 old people in 22 separate apartments with a resident warden.[27]

Eastgate Street Poor-houses. In 1702 the corporation bought a block of four small cottages on the north side of Eastgate Street, placed poor in them rent-free, and made itself responsible for repairs. In 1808 the cottages, though occupied, were described as scarcely habitable and were still so in 1859.[28] It was stated in 1889 that the corporation had not exercised any rights of ownership since 1804; it had ceased to nominate tenants and had left occupants to do their own repairs. The buildings were demolished *c.* 1880, and in 1977 the site was occupied by nos. 33–5 Eastgate Street.[29]

Lees's Charity. Robert Lees (d. 1547), a Stafford ironmonger, devised a 6s. 8d. rent-charge on his property in Stafford and Forebridge to be distributed yearly among the poor of Stafford. The charity existed by 1555 and was being applied in 1641, but it had lapsed by 1736.[30]

Welles's Charity. Before 1548 Robert Welles (or Willes) gave a rent-charge of 3s. 8d. for the poor.[31] Nothing further is known of it.

Sutton's Charity. By will proved 1588 Robert Sutton, rector of St. Mary's, devised a 40s. rent-charge to be distributed among the poor of Stafford and Foregate Street on his obit day. No payment was made until 1599. The corporation took over the executors' obligations in 1616 and was applying the charity by 1618.[32] Payment lapsed in 1708, but the charity was re-established under a Chancery decree of 1740; the corporation redeemed the rent-charge in 1912–13.[33] In 1836 the charity passed into the control of the Stafford Charity Trustees, and in 1922 it became part of the United Charities.

George Cradock's Charity. By will proved 1611 George Cradock of Stafford, M.P. for the borough 1604–11, left £50 to the corporation to apprentice boys or girls. At first the gift was not applied as no burgess would accept the terms for the premiums; the money was not paid to the corporation until 1632 or 1633. In 1635 or 1636 it was given to the governor of the house of correction to provide work for the poor.[34]

Smith's Charity. Stafford was one of the many places which benefited from the charity established by Henry Smith, a London merchant, by a succession of instruments culminating in a declaration of trust dated 1627. In 1641 his trustees bought the manor of Fradswell in Colwich and assigned £14 a year out of the income to Stafford for general charitable purposes in the town.[35] In the late 1730s the charity was distributed in cloth, shoes, and cash. After 1740 the distribution appears to have been entirely in cash; in the 1770s the payments included occasional grants to boys being apprenticed. By the early 1820s all the money was used to apprentice two or three poor boys a year, but in 1834 it was stated not to have been applied for 15 years.[36] By the late 1850s four boys were apprenticed to shoemakers every year. By 1905 the income was spent on blankets for the poor of St. Mary's and St. Chad's. It was still so spent in 1976.[37] By will proved 1959 Mrs. M. M. P. Cookson left a sum, apparently £500, the income from which was to supply extra blankets. The income in 1976 was between £10 and £25.[38]

Backhouse's Charity. By deed of 1628 Thomas Backhouse alias Chamberlain settled in trust a £2 6s. 8d. rent-charge from land in Castle Church to be distributed yearly among the poor of St. Mary's parish.[39] By 1808 the charity was usually distributed with those of Roger Hinton and Henry Smith.[40] By 1859 it had apparently become merged, like Hinton's, with general church funds,[41] and it was lost by the 1890s.[42]

Dorrington's Charity. In 1630 or 1631 the mayor paid out £1 10s., the rent from a house in Foregate 'given by one Dorrington, which payeth for bread'. In 1643–4, although the house had been pulled down, the mayor paid the beadle for bread £1 12s. 6d. which should have been charged on it.[43] Nothing further is known of the charity.

Charity of Barbara, John, and Prudence Crompton. Barbara Crompton of Creswell (d. 1641),[44] widow of Sir Thomas Crompton, a judge of the Admiralty Court, instructed John, her son and executor, to assure within six years of her death 40s. a year to be distributed among four poor widows of St. Mary's parish. In 1679 Prudence, John's widow and executrix, assigned £41 4s. to assure 40s. a year for the charity, and in 1693 she gave a further £50, part of which was to secure the charity.[45] The corporation administered the charity by 1690.[46] The income was charged on houses in Stafford belonging to the cor-

[26] Char. Com. files.
[27] *Staffs. Advertiser*, 5 July 1962; *Stafford Newsletter*, 7 July 1962.
[28] *11th Rep. Com. Char.* 604–5; Keen, *Letter to Inhabitants of Stafford*, 52–3; B.R.L., Homer 22g; Char. Com. files.
[29] Borough Hall, Stafford, Corp. Order Bk. 1881–7, p. 54; *Staffs. Advertiser*, 16 Mar. 1889, p. 6; W.S.L. 7/237/00, drawing of cottages, apparently copied from one of 1844 by J. Buckler in W.S.L., Staffs. Views, ix. 76.
[30] *S.H.C.* 1926, 7; W.S.L., S.MS. 366(iA), p. 91; W.S.L. 77/45, f. 26v.; S.R.O., D.1323/E/1, ff. 99v., 259.
[31] L. Lambert, *Short Hist. of Coll. of Stafford* (Guildford, 1923), 40–1 (copy in W.S.L.).
[32] C 93/1/16; *11th Rep. Com. Char.* 594–6; Keen, *Letter to Inhabitants of Stafford*, 29–30, 34–7; S.R.O., D.1323/E/1, f. 99v.; above, p. 241.
[33] W.S.L., H.M. uncat. 25, decree of 1726; W.S.L. 77/45, ff. 20 and v., 31v.; Keen, *Letter to Inhabitants of Stafford*, 35–7; *Boro. of Stafford: Abstract of Accts. of Stafford Corp. for year ended 31st Mar. 1913*, 6.
[34] *S.H.C.* 1920 and 1922, 6; S.R.O., D.1323/E/1, f. 221B.
[35] *8th Rep. Com. Char.* H.C. 13, pp. 660–4 (1822), xviii; *11th Rep. Com. Char.* 605; Keen, *Letter to Inhabitants of Stafford*, 67–77; *V.C.H. Staffs.* viii. 72. For Smith and his char. see W. K. Jordan, *Chars. of London 1480–1660*, 117–22.
[36] W.S.L., M. 924; W.S.L., S.MS. 365; W.S.L., H.M. uncat. 27, churchwardens' accts. 1771, 1773, 1775; *11th Rep. Com. Char.* 605; *Staffs. Advertiser*, 1 Nov. 1834.
[37] Char. Com. files; ex inf. the borough secretary (1977).
[38] Ex inf. the borough secretary.
[39] *11th Rep. Com. Char.* 607–8; *Abstract of Returns of Char. Donations, 1786–8*, H.C. 511, pp. 1142–3 (1816), xvi (2), giving income as £2; *V.C.H. Staffs.* v. 99, wrongly giving date of deed as 1629.
[40] Keen, *Letter to Inhabitants of Stafford*, 59.
[41] Char. Com. files; below, p. 269.
[42] *Corp. Yr. Bk.* (1895–6).
[43] S.R.O., D.1323/E/1, ff. 185v., 274v.
[44] Monumental inscription to Barbara in south chancel aisle of St. Mary's, Stafford.
[45] W.S.L., H.M. uncat. 26, deed poll 10 July 1679 and copy of deed of 22 May 1693 between corp. and Prudence Crompton; *11th Rep. Com. Char.* 600–1; S.R.O., D.(W.) 0/8/2.
[46] S.R.O., D.1323/A/1/1, p. 368.

poration, which redeemed the rent-charge in 1912–13.[47] The charity passed into the control of the Stafford Charity Trustees in 1836, and in 1922 it became part of the United Charities.

Hales's Charity. Peter Hales of Stafford (d. 1643) left a rent-charge of 20s. a year on property in Stafford of which half was to maintain St. Chad's church and half was to be distributed to the poor of that parish. By 1786 10s. was distributed in bread, which by the early 19th century was given twice yearly to 30 poor.[48] From 1946 the rent-charge was not received and the charity lapsed.[49]

Fowler's Charity. Simon Fowler (d. 1663), a Stafford alderman, by his will settled £12 a year from land at Reule in Bradley (later in Haughton) in trust for the poor of Stafford: £9 was to be distributed twice yearly in cash; £1 was for a sermon at each distribution, and £2 was to be spent on gowns for six poor of the town, each receiving a gown every third year.[50] In 1847 the charity was still applied as directed, but by 1905 the rector apparently distributed the entire £12 to the poor throughout St. Mary's ancient parish.[51] The rent-charge was redeemed in the early 1970s; the income in 1976 was £11 from stock. By then £2 a year was normally given to the two oldest residents of Noell's alms-houses and the rest distributed in doles of £0.12½ to poor in Christ Church and St. Mary's parishes.[52]

Startin's Charity. By will dated 1667 Richard Startin, a Stafford baker, left £60 to provide the poor of Stafford with at least 1s. in bread weekly.[53] In 1672 the corporation used the bequest to redeem the borough's fee-farm rent of £3 6s. 8d. due to the Crown and decided to pay Startin's dole with the money saved. Izaak Walton was prominent in the transaction[54] and persuaded the corporation to spend not only £2 12s. on bread but the balance, 14s. 8d., on coal for the poor. He gave the corporation a garden, stipulating that if coal was not distributed the rent was to go to St. Chad's for the repair of its wall or for coal for its poor.[55] By 1701 8s. rent from the garden was given to 8 widows,[56] but the payment lapsed c. 1778[57] and in 1808, as in 1859, the corporation was restricting its payments to 1s. a week for bread.[58] By 1895 the £2 12s. was paid to the

grammar school, in whose funds the endowment was lost or sunk, the corporation having redeemed the charge in 1912–13.[59]

Lovett's Charity. By deed of 1676 Robert Crompton of Elstow (Beds.) settled in trust a £1 10s. rent-charge from half of Creswell manor for distribution twice yearly among the poor of Stafford. The gift was in fulfilment of the intention of his grandfather Robert Lovett, a London merchant from Callowhill in Kingstone who died at Elstow in 1657, and of Crompton's uncles, Richard and John Crompton.[60] In 1693 the corporation directed that the charity be used to clothe and equip poor apprentices. By 1736, however, it was usually distributed to six poor widows.[61] It lapsed for some years in the early 19th century owing to a confusion with Rebecca Crompton's charity, but was again distributed by 1846.[62] It passed into the control of the Stafford Charity Trustees in 1836, and in 1922 it became part of the United Charities.

Walton's Charity. By will proved 1684 Izaak Walton left Halfhead farm at Shallowford in Chebsey, then let at £21 10s. a year, to his son Izaak. If the younger Izaak did not marry before the age of 41, the farm was to revert to Stafford corporation, which was to apply £10 of the rent each year to the apprenticing of two poor boys and £5 as a dowry for a maidservant aged over 21 who had 'dwelt long in one service' or for 'some honest poor man's daughter' aged over 21. The administrators were to receive £1 a year between them. The remainder of the rent was to be distributed in coals to the poor of the town.[63] The charity took effect in the mid 1690s when the younger Izaak transferred the farm to the corporation.[64] By 1701 £4 10s. of the coal-money and the £1 a year allowed to the administrators had been assigned to Noell's alms-houses.[65] By 1808 there were complaints that the maids' charity was normally paid to a servant of the mayor, sometimes regardless of length of service. That abuse had been checked by the early 1820s.[66] Part of the farm was sold in the mid 1830s, and the proceeds were invested in £271 11s. 9d. stock; by 1859 it produced £8 2s. 11d. a year, while the rest of the farm was let at £47.[67] In 1873 the stock was transferred to the

---

[47] W.S.L., H.M. uncat. 26, copy of deed of 22 May 1693; *Boro. of Stafford: Abstract of Accts. of Stafford Corp. for year ended 31st Mar. 1913*, 6.

[48] *11th Rep. Com. Char.* 607; *Char. Dons. 1786–8*, 1142–3; Keen, *Letter to Inhabitants of Stafford*, 61; D. A. Johnson, 'The Stafford Hobby-Horse', *T.S.H.C.S.* 1974–6, 61, 63.

[49] Ex inf. the vicar of St. Chad's (1963).

[50] *11th Rep. Com. Char.* 605; Keen, *Letter to Inhabitants of Stafford*, 45–7; *St. Mary's Par. Reg.* 307; W.S.L., H.M. 27/1. *V.C.H. Staffs.* v. 100, treating of Fowler's char. for Forebridge, wrongly gives Reule as once in Gnosall and alter in Bradley.

[51] *Staffs. Advertiser*, 25 June 1859; Char. Com. files.

[52] Ex inf. the rector of St. Mary's (1977).

[53] S.R.O., D.1323/E/1, f. 22; Keen, *Letter to Inhabitants of Stafford*, 43.

[54] S.R.O., D.1323/A/1/1, p. 229; *11th Rep. Com. Char.* 602.

[55] Keen, *Letter to Inhabitants of Stafford*, 43–4.

[56] S.R.O., D.1323/A/1/2, p. 95.

[57] It last appears in the chamberlains' accts. in 1777: S.R.O., D.1033/1, p. 233.

[58] Keen, *Letter to Inhabitants of Stafford*, 45; Char. Com. files.

[59] J. Averill, *Abstract of Stafford Chars. Jan. 31 1895* (copy in poss. of the sec., Stafford United Chars.); *Boro. of Stafford: Abstract of Accts. of Stafford Corp. for year ended 31st Mar. 1913*, 6. The char. is not listed in Char. Com. Scheme, 19 Dec. 1922, setting up the Stafford United

[60] *11th Rep. Com. Char.* 601; W.S.L., H.M. uncat. 28, transcript of deed of 1676. For Lovett see *Staffs. Pedigrees 1664–1700* (Harl. Soc. lxiii), 66, 107; *V.C.H. Beds.* ii. 291; iii. 283; A. H. Johnson, *Hist. of Worshipful Company of Drapers*, iv. 159; monumental inscription to Barbara Crompton in south chancel aisle of St. Mary's, Stafford.

[61] S.R.O., D.1323/A/1/2, p. 28; W.S.L. 77/45, ff. 25v.-26.

[62] *11th Rep. Com. Char.* 601; Keen, *Letter to Inhabitants of Stafford*, 39; *Staffs. Advertiser*, 25 June 1859; Char. Com. files.

[63] Walton, *Complete Angler*, ed. Sir Harris Nicolas (1860), i, pp. ciii–cviii; E. Marston, *Thos. Ken and Izaak Walton*, 114–17. The phrasing of the section of the will dealing with the £5 maids' gift is ambiguous (Keen, *Letter to Inhabitants of Stafford*, 42–3), but apparently Walton intended that the poor man's daughter, like the servant, should receive the money on her wedding day.

[64] W.S.L., H.M. 26/2, ff. 13–15; deeds at Boro. Hall, Stafford, relating to Walton's Char., Izaak Walton the younger to mayor, 19 May 1694; W.S.L., H.M. 32, corp. ordinance 1696.

[65] S.R.O., D.1323/A/1/2, p. 95 (not stating that the £1 mentioned is the sum allotted for the expenses of rent-collecting); Keen, *Letter to Inhabitants of Stafford*, 65.

[66] Keen, *Letter to Inhabitants of Stafford*, 42–3; *11th Rep. Com. Char.* 602–3.

[67] Char. Com. files.

grammar school,[68] apparently in lieu of the apprenticeship premiums.[69] The charity passed into the control of Stafford Charity Trustees in 1836, and in 1922 it became part of the United Charities. The maids' charity was abolished in 1973, and the money was thenceforward applied with the other United Charities' funds.[70]

Hinton's Charity. By will dated 1685 Roger Hinton charged his estate at Rickerscote and Burton in Castle Church with annuities for the poor of various Staffordshire places, including one of £5 for Stafford borough. The charity was not established until 1692, after Chancery proceedings.[71] Although it was then directed that the surplus rents from the estate were to be divided among the places concerned, in fact it was not until the early 19th century that the full economic rent was paid to the charity. By 1808 the income had increased as a result of improvements following the Forebridge Inclosure Act, 1800, and between 1805 and 1820 Stafford received £237 1s. 4d. in six instalments. By 1859 two-thirds of the Stafford money went to St. Mary's and one-third to Christ Church; it was spent on religious books and tracts for the poor and on occasional gifts of food and other comforts. By 1903 the St. Mary's share was spent on coals.[72] A Scheme of 1909 appointed trustees and widened the application.[73] It was replaced by a new Scheme in 1955. The income of the Stafford charity in 1975–6 was £37.52 from stock and £65.29 from the estate trustees; £74 was distributed in gift vouchers.[74]

Charity of William Farmer and Rebecca Crompton. By will dated 1697 William Farmer of Penkridge left £40 to be invested to provide coals for the poor of Stafford. Rebecca Crompton of Creswell (d. 1683 or 1684), daughter of Robert Lovett and sister-in-law of John and Prudence Crompton, had, by will, left land and money to provide 30s. to be distributed yearly among 6 poor widows of Stafford; her daughter, Rebecca Drakeford, left £30 by will dated 1704 to give effect to her mother's wishes. In 1724 the £30 was transferred to the corporation, which, having also acquired Farmer's £40, invested the £70 in 1725 in land at Fulford in Stone, let at £3 10s. a year.[75] Both charities were being paid in 1786, but by 1808, although the income had risen in 1806 to £13 10s., only the 30s. was paid.[76] From 1809 to 1812 that lapsed, but from 1809 £6 10s. was spent on coals for Noell's alms-houses and after 1814 a

further £6 10s. a year was paid into the alms-houses' account.[77] In 1856–7 payments included 30s. to six widows, £12 spent on coal, and £4 2s. 4d. spent on repairs to the alms-houses and expenses.[78] The charity passed into the control of Stafford Charity Trustees in 1836, and in 1922 it became part of the United Charities.

Bynns's Charity. By will dated 1711 Dr. Richard Bynns, rector of St. Mary's, left £50 to the corporation, which in accordance with his wishes decided in 1714 to apply the income to the alms-houses.[79] In 1786 £2 10s. was paid, but payment lapsed soon afterwards,[80] though the charity was one of those placed under the control of the Stafford Charity Trustees in 1836.

Perye's Charity. Humphrey Perye (d. 1716), five times mayor of Stafford, settled in trust a £26 rent-charge from land at Bilston; £6 was for the apprenticing of a boy or girl aged over 14, to be chosen in alternate years from Stafford and Bilston. Stafford children were to be sent to masters living at least 8 miles from the town.[81] In the early 19th century few children applied for the premiums, and at least from 1846 to 1859 the charity was in abeyance, the owner of the land repudiating the rent-charge.[82] A Scheme of 1882, revising one of 1862, required that annual payments of up to £2 a head should be made to three children attending public elementary schools in Stafford borough.[83] The payments were reduced c. 1906 to £1 10s. a head.[84] In the early 1970s the rector of St. Mary's received an annual payment of £6 15s., which was used to provide educational help to poor children.[85]

Lycett's Charity. By deed of 1728 Ann Lycett settled in trust a 20s. rent-charge from land in Seighford, to be paid in two instalments each year to poor members of the Presbyterian chapel in Stafford. It was stated c. 1830 that since 1812 all the money had been spent on repairs to the chapel.[86] The trust was renewed in 1835, but priority was given to the repairs; the land was sold in 1922, and the charity apparently lapsed then, if not earlier.[87]

Toombes's Charity. By will proved 1722 John Toombes, M.D., left a £5 rent-charge on land at Bridgeford in Seighford to be distributed annually to five poor widows of Stafford. In 1976 the rent-charge was being redeemed; the rector of St. Mary's distributed the £5 to five widows, most of them inmates of Noell's alms-houses.[88]

[68] Horne, *K. Edw. VI Sch., Stafford*, 32.
[69] Char. Com. files.
[70] *Stafford Newsletter*, 8 June 1973; ex inf. the sec., Stafford United Chars. (1977).
[71] *7th Rep. Com. Char.* H.C. 129, p. 418 (1822), x; *V.C.H. Staffs.* v. 99; xvii. 273.
[72] *Char. Dons. 1786–8*, 1142–3; Keen, *Letter to Inhabitants of Stafford*, 48–50; *7th Rep. Com. Char.* 420, 422; Char. Com. files.
[73] For details see *V.C.H. Staffs.* v. 100.
[74] Char. Com. files; ex inf. the borough secretary (1977).
[75] Keen, *Letter to Inhabitants of Stafford*, 51–2; L. Lambert, *Chron. Table of . . . church of Blessed Mary . . . Stafford* (Stafford, 1936), 25 (copy in W.S.L.); W.S.L., H.M. uncat. 24, inventory of goods of Rebecca Crompton; *Staffs. Pedigrees 1664–1700* (Harl. Soc. lxiii), 66; above, pp. 267–8.
[76] *Char. Dons. 1786–8*, 1142–3; Keen, *Letter to Inhabitants of Stafford*, 52; *11th Rep. Com. Char.* 600; S.R.O., D.1323/E/2, p. 196.
[77] *11th Rep. Com. Char.* 600–1; S.R.O., D.1323/E/2, pp. 214, 252, 264 sqq.
[78] *1st Rep. Com. Mun. Corp.* H.C. 116, App. III, p. 2029 (1835), xxv; *Staffs. Advertiser*, 25 June 1859; Char.

Com. files.
[79] *11th Rep. Com. Char.* 597; S.R.O., D.1323/A/1/2, pp. 162, 181, 184.
[80] *Char. Dons. 1786–8*, 1142–3; Keen, *Letter to Inhabitants of Stafford*, 66.
[81] *5th Rep. Com. Char.* H.C. 159, p. 594 (1821), xii; *11th Rep. Com. Char.* 606; Keen, *Letter to Inhabitants of Stafford*, 53–4; Lawley, *Bilston*, 152, 237–8; Bradley, *Charters*, 206–7.
[82] *5th Rep. Com. Char.* 596; *11th Rep. Com. Char.* 606; *Staffs. Advertiser*, 2 July 1859.
[83] Copy of Scheme in poss. of rector of St. Mary's (1962); Lawley, *Bilston*, 241.
[84] *Corp. Yr. Bk.* (1895–6 and later edns. to 1944–45).
[85] Ex inf. the rector (1977).
[86] W.S.L., H.M. uncat. 26, bdle. of deeds incl. Old Bull's Head etc. 1668–post 1812, petition relating to meeting-house (watermarked 1828), pp. 5–13.
[87] Deeds relating to Presbyterian chapel, Stafford, in possession of Mr. W. D. Paterson of Stafford (1977), lease and release of 9 and 10 Feb. 1835 and letter of 4 Apr. 1922, GreatRex, Warner & Beswick to Coates.
[88] *11th Rep. Com. Char.* 606–7; *Char. Dons. 1786–8*, 1142–3; ex inf. the rector (1977).

Webb's Charity. By will dated 1760 John Webb of
Stafford left a 40s. rent-charge on two houses there
to be distributed twice yearly to 20 poor widows of
the town in shillings. The charity lapsed *c.* 1843
when a new owner of the houses successfully claimed
that the gift was void under the Mortmain Act.[89]

Kenderdine's Charity. By will dated 1829 John
Kenderdine of Stafford left £250 stock, the interest
to be distributed annually in half-crowns to 50 poor
widows living in Stafford; if 50 widows could not
be found, the number was to be made up with poor
men. In the early 1970s the money was divided between 25 widows from St. Mary's parish and 25 from
Christ Church parish.[90]

Sidney's Charity. By deed of 1857 Thomas Sidney,
a native of Stafford, M.P. for the town in 1847–52
and 1860–5, and lord mayor of London in 1853–4,
settled £700 stock on the mayor, the rector of St.
Mary's, and the incumbent of Christ Church to
provide an annual distribution in money, coals, or
both, to 20 poor widows or widowers aged over 60.
In 1858 Sidney stated that the recipients should
receive the charity for life, if the trustees approved
of their character. In 1976 the income, *c.* £60, was
distributed within the borough as directed.[91]

Rogers's Charity. By deed of 1858 John Rogers of
Leamington Spa (Warws.), mayor of Stafford in
1833–4 and 1841–2, gave £500, the interest to be used
to apprentice three fatherless children, native inhabitants of Stafford, every year. Schemes of 1889 and
1922 provided that the money might be spent on
outfits for children starting work. At least from 1894
to 1944 the income was £15 6s., but by 1974 it had
fallen to £14.90. In 1976 £50 was paid to the Royal
Wolverhampton School.[92]

Hodges's Charity. By deed of 1892 William Hodges
of Southend-on-Sea (Essex), a retired Stafford
footwear manufacturer, vested £2,061 17s. 1d. stock
in the corporation, directing that from 1894 the interest was to be distributed yearly in cash to poor of
the borough over 30 years of age. In 1962 it was
distributed in food vouchers.[93] Application ceased
c. 1966, but in 1977 a new Scheme was being prepared which would permit the trustees to apply the
charity more generally to relieve need among
qualified persons.[94]

The Town Bonds, later the Poor Burgesses Charity.
From the mid 16th century or earlier to 1714 the
borough authorities administered various charities
designed or adapted to provide short-term loans for

needy but deserving tradesmen or for ex-apprentices
setting up in business. The funds, known collectively
in the 17th century as the Town Bonds, were lent in
small sums either interest-free or at low rates of
interest. The interest received was distributed to the
poor.

By deed of 1553 Margaret Kirton, a native of
Stafford and the widow of Stephen Kirton, a London
alderman and merchant-tailor, gave £100 to be lent
interest-free for two-year periods to 10 young freemen, natives, or ex-apprentices of Stafford. She also
gave a 12s. rent-charge on property in Stafford, of
which 2s. was to be distributed yearly to 12 poor
householders.[95] It was still distributed in 1653.[96] A
12s. rent-charge called Savage's gift, distributed to
the poor in 1701, was probably Kirton's rent-
charge,[97] which in 1736 the corporation could not
trace.[98] In 1786 the rent-charge was stated to be
vested in the corporation.[99] Nothing further is known
of it. Of the loan capital £39 12s. was lost between
1683 and 1701; the rest remained in 1720.[1]

By will proved 1575 Richard Blunt (or Blount)
of London, a native of Stafford, gave £20 to help
the poorest people of the town. It was used to provide £5 loans for 4 resident burgesses at 5 per cent
interest for two-year periods. The interest was to be
paid yearly to the poor.[2] The dole was still being
distributed in 1641, but no more is known of it. Of
the capital £10 was lost by loans made in 1675 and
1679; the rest remained in 1720.[3]

By will proved 1582 Sir Thomas Offley, lord mayor
of London 1556–7, a native of Stafford, and brother
of Margaret Kirton, left £100 to provide loans on
the same terms as hers. In pursuance of his wishes
his executors also bought a 12s. rent-charge on
houses in Stafford, of which 2s. was to go to the
poor, and two 12s. 6d. rent-charges on other property in Stafford to provide 24s. yearly for 24 poor of
the town.[4] The doles were still being paid in 1641–2,[5]
and in 1701 one of the 12s. 6d. rent-charges was
being paid to the poor as 'Blore's Gift' of 12s.[6] No
doles were being paid in 1736.[7] In 1786 there were
said to be two 12s. rent-charges, one given by Sir
Thomas and the other by his executors.[8] No more
is known of them. Of the loan capital £35 was
lost between 1667 and 1711; the rest remained in
1720.[9]

William Sale (d. 1588), a canon residentiary of
Lichfield cathedral, bequeathed £20 to provide £5
loans for 'four poor artificers' of Stafford for four-

[89] *Char. Dons. 1786–8,* 1142–3 (giving 1760 as date of will); Keen, *Letter to Inhabitants of Stafford,* 60 (giving 1766); *11th Rep. Com. Char.* 607; Char. Com. files.
[90] Char. Com. files, giving date of will as 1829; G. Griffith, *Free Schools and Endowments of Staffs.* 56–7, 79, giving date as 1828; ex inf. the rector (1977).
[91] Griffith, *Free Schools,* 84–5; S.R.O., D.1323/A/1/7, 30 Nov. 1857, 5 May 1858; *Corp. Yr. Bk.* (1894–5); Char. Com. files; A. B. Beaven, *Aldermen of City of London,* i. 32, 312–13; ii. 146; *Staffs. Advertiser,* 16 Mar. 1889, p. 3; plaque on Sidney's birthplace on corner of Gaolgate St. and North Walls; ex inf. the borough secretary (1977).
[92] Griffith, *Free Schools,* 86; Char. Com. files; *Corp. Yr. Bk.* (1894–5 and later edns. to 1943–44); Bradley, *Charters,* 208; ex inf. the sec., Stafford United Chars. (1977).
[93] Char. Com. files; ex inf. the deputy town clerk (1963).
[94] Ex inf. the rector of St. Mary's and the borough secretary (1977).
[95] W.S.L. 7/64/00, list of loan benefactions; W.S.L. 77/45, f. 18; C. M. Clode, *Early Hist. of Merchant Taylors Company,* ii. 172; Beaven, *Aldermen of London,* i. 101; ii. 32, 171. The gift was presumably by deed, for Marg.

Kirton's will was not proved till 1573: *Wills proved in P.C.C. 1558–1583,* iii (Index Libr. xviii), 183.
[96] S.R.O., D.1323/A/1/1, p. 55.
[97] S.R.O., D.1323/A/1/2, p. 95. The 12s. rent-charge had been said in the earlier 17th cent. to come from a house formerly 'Savage's land': D.1323/E/1, ff. 99, 103, 259.
[98] S.R.O., D.1323/A/1/2, p. 95. [99] *Char. Dons. 1786–8,* 1142–3.
[1] S.R.O., D.1323/A/1/2, p. 208.
[2] Prob. 11/57 (P.C.C. 47 Pyckering); W.S.L. 7/64/00; S.R.O., D.1323/F/1, town-bond loans, 1599.
[3] S.R.O., D.1323/E/1, f. 259; D.1323/A/1/2, pp. 208–9.
[4] Prob. 11/64 (P.C.C. 39 Tirwhite); W.S.L. 7/64/00, list of loan benefactions and transcript of indenture be-tween burgesses, Merchant Taylors, and Offley's exrs.; W.S.L. 77/45, f. 53; *D.N.B.*
[5] S.R.O., D.1323/E/1, f. 258v.
[6] S.R.O., D.1323/A/1/2, p. 95. For identification see W.S.L. 77/45, f. 54; S.R.O., D.1323/E/1, ff. 99, 103, 180, 258v.
[7] W.S.L. 77/45, ff. 18v.–19.
[8] *Char. Dons. 1786–8,* 1142–3.
[9] S.R.O., D.1323/A/1/2, pp. 208–9.

year periods, interest-free; £15 remained in 1720.[10]

By will proved 1591 Mary Leveson, widow of Sir Richard Leveson of Lilleshall (Salop.), gave £10 to the poor of Stafford. In 1599 it had still not been distributed. By 1601 it was employed as a fund providing £5 loans for 2 burgesses for two-year periods at 5 per cent interest, distributed yearly to the poor until at least 1631.[11] In 1673 £5 of the capital was lost; the rest remained in 1720.[12]

By will proved 1593 Richard Cradock of London left £100 to be lent to 10 young men of Stafford borough for two-year periods.[13] The gift is not known to have been applied.

In or before 1599 Joan Phillips bequeathed the town £20 to provide £5 loans for 4 young freemen or ex-apprentices for two-year periods at 5 per cent interest, to be distributed yearly to the poor of Stafford and Forebridge.[14] In 1629–30 £5 was lost, reducing the dole to 15s., which was still distributed in 1641.[15] A further £5 was lost in 1657, and £2 was lost apparently in 1718. In 1720 £8 remained.[16]

In or before 1599 a Mr. Skrymsher gave £5 which was lent to burgesses as a single lot. Until at least the early 1630s 6s. 8d. interest was paid, but by 1641 it had fallen to 5s.[17] Nothing further is known of it.

By will proved 1610 Sir Stephen Slaney, lord mayor of London 1595–6 and a native of Mitton in Penkridge, bequeathed £10 to the poor of Stafford. It was used to provide £5 loans to 2 men of the borough for two-year periods at 5 per cent interest, distributed annually among the poor.[18] By 1618 £5 of the capital had been lost, and the dole had thus been reduced to 5s.; nothing is known of it after 1641. The lost £5 seems to have been recovered later but was lost again in 1674; £5 remained in 1720.[19]

John Webb (d. 1613 while bailiff of Stafford) bequeathed £20 which from 1635–6 was lent to burgesses in £5 lots for two-year periods at 5 per cent. The income was spent yearly on bread for the poor until at least 1641, but no more is known of it. Of the capital £12 was lost between 1667 and 1689; the rest remained in 1720.[20]

Sir Hugh Homersley (or Hammersley), a native of Stafford and lord mayor of London 1627–8, gave the town £50 in 1613 to provide £10 loans for 5 burgesses for two-year periods at half interest, to buy bread for the poor.[21] Hugh Homersley, a London merchant who was son of Hugh Homersley of Stafford and an employee and apparently a relative of Sir Hugh, bequeathed, before 1636, £50 to the poor of Stafford. After payment of his debts only £35 remained for the poor, which Sir Hugh's widow Mary paid to the corporation in 1640, adding a further £15 to make the sum up to £50. The money was lent in £10 lots for two-year periods to 5 freemen. From the 40s. interest 9d. was distributed weekly in bread to 9 poor. The remaining 1s. a year was also distributed among the poor.[22] The doles were still paid in the early 1640s,[23] but no more is known of them. Most of the £100 capital was lost between 1657 and 1694; £42 10s. remained in 1720.[24]

Before 1615 Hugh Atwell gave £2 which was lent to burgesses as a single lot. Interest of 3s. a year was still being distributed to the poor in 1631, but the charity had apparently been lost by 1698.[25]

By will dated 1617 Margaret Temple, a native of Stafford and widow of Sir Alexander Temple of St. Clement Danes (Mdx.), left £15 to the poor of the borough and £15 to poor prisoners in the borough gaol. The fund was divided into three £10 lots lent from 1620 at 8 per cent, and the doles began the same year.[26] In 1635 the rate of interest was reduced to 6 per cent, and by 1698 borrowers were charged half interest.[27] In 1720 the capital was stated to be £35, of which £10 had been lost allegedly in 1626; c. 1735, however, it was said to be £20, divided into four lots.[28] The dole to the prisoners was still paid in 1641 but, like that to the free poor, had lapsed by 1736.[29]

Before 1620 Edward Dorrington[30] gave a sum of money, apparently £5, the interest to be used for a bread-dole. By 1698 the bread-dole had ceased and the £5 was being used to provide one interest-free loan.[31] It remained intact in 1720.[32]

In or before 1620 a bishop of London, possibly John King (1611–21), gave a loan fund from which 6s. 8d. interest was paid to the poor in the early 1620s. In 1736 it was claimed that a bishop of London had given or bequeathed £5 to be lent for two-year

[10] *Wolverhampton Antiquary*, i. 65; *S.H.C.* 1915, 345; S.R.O., D.1323/A/1/2, pp. 208–9; S.R.O., D.(W.) 1721/1/4, f. 162v.; W.S.L. 77/45, f. 5v.

[11] Prob. 11/78 (P.C.C. 59 Sainberbe); C 93/1/16; W.S.L. 7/64/00, list of loan benefactions; S.R.O., D.1323/E/1, ff. 99, 180v., 183v.; /F/1, town-bond loans, 1601.

[12] S.R.O., D.1323/A/1/2, pp. 208–9.

[13] Prob. 11/82 (P.C.C. 62 Neville).

[14] S.R.O., D.1323/F/1, town-bond loans, 1599; /E/1, ff. 99, 100; W.S.L. 7/64/00, list of loan benefactions.

[15] S.R.O., D.1323/E/1, ff. 174 and v., 259; /F/1, town-bond loans, 24 Aug. 1629, 21 Dec. 1629 (?), 25 Aug. 1631. D.1323/A/1/2, p. 209, implies that the £5 was lost by a loan of 1621.

[16] S.R.O., D.1323/A/1/2, pp. 208–9.

[17] S.R.O., D.1323/F/1, town-bond loans, 1599; /E/1, ff. 99 and v., 174 and v., 259; W.S.L. 77/45, f. 6.

[18] J. F. Wadmore, *Some Account of the Skinners Company*, 168–9; Beaven, *Aldermen of London*, i. 74, 110, 182; ii. 42; S.R.O., D.1323/E/1, f. 53; W.S.L. 7/64/00, list of loan benefactions; W.S.L. 77/45, f. 25v.

[19] S.R.O., D.1323/E/1, ff. 99v., 103, 111, 259; D.1323/A/1/2, pp. 208–9; W.S.L., H.M. 26/2, p. 10.

[20] Bradley, *Charters*, 206; *St. Mary's Par. Reg.* 167; S.R.O., D.1323/E/1, ff. 221B, 222, 259; D.1323/A/1/2, pp. 208–9; W.S.L. 77/45, f. 6.

[21] S.R.O., D.1323/F/1, town-bond loans, 30 Aug. 1613; /E/1, f. 103v.; W.S.L. 49/112/44, acct. of chars. given to burgesses and poor; W.S.L. 7/64/00, list of loan benefactions; Beaven, *Aldermen of London*, i. 13, 37, 346.

[22] W.S.L. 7/64/00, transcript of acquittance 13 July 1640 and of resolution of common council 25 Aug. 1640; S.R.O., D.1323/F/1, town-bond loans, 25 Aug. 1640.

[23] S.R.O., D.1323/E/1, ff. 259, 268v., 274v.

[24] S.R.O., D.1323/A/1/2, p. 208.

[25] S.R.O., D.1323/E/1, ff. 100v., 180v., 183v.; /F/1, town-bond loans, query of 1615; W.S.L. 7/64/00, list of loan benefactions; W.S.L., H.M. 26/2, pp. 1–10.

[26] W.S.L., H.M. uncat. 26, indenture of 8 Aug. 1620; S.R.O., D.(W.) 1721/1/4, ff. 142–3; S.R.O., D.1323/E/1, f. 105v.; D.1323/F/1, town-bond loans, n.d. but apparently Aug. 1620, and 24 Aug. 1622.

[27] W.S.L., M. 527; W.S.L. 77/45, f. 17v., citing deed of 1635; W.S.L., H.M. 26/2, p. 3.

[28] S.R.O., D.1323/A/1/2, pp. 208–9; W.S.L., H.M. uncat. 29, charities bdle.

[29] S.R.O., D.1323/E/1, f. 259; W.S.L. 77/45, f. 17v.

[30] S.R.O., D.1323/E/1, ff. 103v., 105v., 259. W.S.L. 77/45, f. 6 (1736), calls him 'Francis Dorrington', presumably confusing the donor with the Fra. Dorrington who was twice mayor (Bradley, *Charters*, 206); no ref. to Edw. Dorrington other than those cited is known.

[31] S.R.O., D.1323/E/1, ff. 103v., mentioning in 1620 interest of £3 to buy bread, 105v.; W.S.L., H.M. 26/2, p. 9.

[32] S.R.O., D.1323/A/1/2, p. 208.

periods at interest which was to be given to the poor. The corporation stated that to the best of its belief nothing had ever been received, and the money was omitted from a list of corporation obligations made in 1740.[33]

In or before 1622 Richard Astbury gave £10 which provided two £5 loans for burgesses at 5 per cent interest, probably for two-year periods. The interest was still being distributed to the poor in 1631. Of the capital £5 was lost in 1675; the rest remained in 1720.[34]

'Lottery Money', a £10 fund out of which two loans were made to burgesses in 1622, may have been a prize won in the lotteries run by the Virginia Company between 1612 and 1621. It remained intact until at least 1641, but by 1671 it had dwindled to a single £5 lot, then lent interest-free. By 1679 it was only £3, which was last lent in that year at 2s. 6d. interest and was lost thereafter.[35]

Ann Harding (d. 1635), wife of the incumbent of Baswich and widow of John Webb, bequeathed £20 which was lent to burgesses in four lots of £5 for two-year periods at 5 per cent interest. The interest was spent on a yearly bread-dole; the last known distribution was in 1641.[36] Of the capital £7 was lost in 1694 and 1699; the rest remained in 1720.[37]

In or before 1675 Edwin Skrymsher, probably Edwin Skrymsher of Aqualate in Forton (d. 1689), M.P. for Stafford in 1681, gave the town £40 which provided eight £5 lots for burgesses for two-year periods, interest-free; £9 13s. was lost in 1675 and 1689, and the rest remained in 1720.[38]

Before 1677 Oliver Emery, mayor of Stafford 1645–6, gave £20 which provided four £5 loans for burgesses for four-year periods, interest-free; £13 10s. was lost in 1679 and 1689, and the rest remained in 1720.[39]

In or before 1679 Sir Thomas Armstrong, M.P. for Stafford 1679–81 and executed in 1684 for complicity in the Rye House Plot, gave £40 which provided eight £5 lots for burgesses for two-year periods, interest-free. In the 1680s £12 10s. was lost; the rest remained in 1720.[40]

Before 1689 Richard Font gave either £10 or £20 which was lent to burgesses in £5 lots, apparently for two-year periods at 5 per cent. By 1698 the capital seems to have been £10. Apparently £5 was lost in 1689; £5 remained in 1720.[41]

Before 1697 Ann Burgess gave £10 which was lent to burgesses as a single lot at 5 per cent, probably for two-year periods. It was still intact in 1720.[42]

By c. 1700 the Town Bonds were in confusion; separate funds had been divided unsystematically and money lost through loans made on inadequate security.[43] By 1714 the losses were so great that the corporation suspended loans from the Bonds and transferred the remaining capital, then £301 5s. or less out of a nominal capital of at least £593 to an 'old alderman', Henry Walker, who was to restore order. He failed to recover most of the missing money and the corporation decided to leave the remaining capital to accumulate at interest in his hands until the losses had been made good.[44] By 1725 Walker, with the help of grants from the corporation and a gift of 20 guineas in 1722 from a candidate for one of the borough seats in Parliament, had in his possession £590. On the advice of its high steward Lord Macclesfield, the corporation, instead of leaving in Walker's hands the £21 interest received in 1725 on the money originally handed to him, distributed it in 10s. lots to 42 poor burgesses.[45] It was alleged c. 1740 that the distribution had been made 'to prevent a clamour, and was called hush money'.[46] In 1736 the corporation recovered the £590 from Walker's son, but a Chancery decree of 1740 transferred it, with £255 3s. 6d. interest, to the accountant-general of Chancery. The corporation received back £21, the sum distributed in 1725, and the rest was invested in £745 17s. 3d. stock. In 1742 a further decree ordered that the dividend should be distributed yearly among poor burgesses at 40s. a head, in order of their seniority on the burgess roll. None should receive the dole twice until all the poor on the roll had received it once.[47] In the early 19th century the fund consisted of £710 12s. 3d. stock, which produced £21 6s. 4d. a year. In 1808 it was stated that until 1807 the corporation had permitted any burgess who applied to benefit. By the early 1820s 10 poor burgesses received the charity annually; an eleventh was added when the balance allowed. In 1893 it was distributed to twelve.[48] The charity passed into the control of the Stafford Charity Trustees in 1836 and became part of the United Charities in 1922.

Stafford United Charities. In 1836 the Stafford charities formerly administered by the corporation, consisting of the King Edward VI Grammar School, the Queen Elizabeth Grant property, Noell's almshouses (with the subsidiary charities of John Chet-

[33] S.R.O., D.1323/E/1, ff. 103, 111, 116; W.S.L. 77/45, ff. 9v., 26v. King's father-in-law was a Staffs. man: *D.N.B.*
[34] S.R.O., D.(W.) 1721/1/4, f. 163; W.S.L. 77/45, f. 6; W.S.L., H.M. uncat. 29, charities bdle.; S.R.O., D.1323/E/1, ff. 163, 181, 183v.; D.1323/A/1/2, pp. 208–9.
[35] S.R.O., D.1323/F/1, town-bond loans, 23 Aug. 1622, 22 Apr. 1625, 20 Mar. 1627, Whitsun 1641, 1671; D.1323/A/1/2, pp. 208–9; D.(W.) 1721/1/4, f. 162v.; T. Harwood, *Hist. and Antiquities of Church and City of Lichfield* (Gloucester, 1806), 375; C. M. Andrews, *Colonial Period of American Hist.: Settlements* (Yale, 1934), 117, 137; W.S.L., H.M. 26/2, p. 9.
[36] *Berkswich w. Walton Par. Reg.* (Staffs. Par. Reg. Soc. 1905), 20; *S.H.C.* 1915, 25; S.R.O., D.1323/E/1, ff. 221B, 222, 259; W.S.L., H.M. 26/2, p. 9; W.S.L. 77/45, f. 6; above, p. 271.
[37] S.R.O., D.1323/A/1/2, pp. 208–9.
[38] W.S.L. 7/64/00, list of loan benefactions; W.S.L., H.M. 26/2, p. 2; *S.H.C.* 1920 and 1922, 150; S.R.O., D.1323/A/1/2, pp. 208–9.
[39] S.R.O., D.1323/F/1, town-bond loans, Whitsun 1677, 1679; D.1323/A/1/2, pp. 208–9; W.S.L., H.M. 26/2, p. 8;

[40] S.R.O., D.1323/F/1, town-bond loans, 1679; D.1323/A/1/2, pp. 208–9; W.S.L. 7/64/00, list of loan benefactions; W.S.L., H.M. 26/2, p. 4; above, p. 238.
[41] W.S.L. 7/64/00, list of loan benefactions; W.S.L. 77/45, f. 6; W.S.L., H.M. 26/2, p. 9; S.R.O., D.1323/A/1/2, pp. 208–9.
[42] W.S.L., H.M. 26/2, p. 8; W.S.L. 77/45, f. 6; S.R.O., D.1323/A/1/2, p. 208.
[43] S.R.O., D.(W.) 1721/1/4, f. 162; S.R.O., D.1323/A/1/1, pp. 237, 264, 270, 300, 357, 368; W.S.L., H.M. 26/2, pp. 1–10.
[44] W.S.L. 77/45, ff. 15, 42, 57; S.R.O., D.1323/A/1/2, pp. 208–10.
[45] W.S.L. 77/45, f. 15; W.S.L., H.M. Chetwynd 32; S.R.O., D.1323/A/1/2, p. 266.
[46] W.S.L. 49/112(B)/44, 'Relator's Proofs', f. 4.
[47] W.S.L. 77/45, ff. 16v.–17v., 31v.–33v.; *11th Rep. Com. Char.* 604.
[48] *11th Rep. Com. Char.* 603–4; Keen, *Letter to Inhabitants of Stafford*, 55–8; *Staffs. Advertiser*, 23 Dec. 1893.

wynd, Katherine Abnett, Philip and Thomas Foley, and Richard Bynns), the Poor Burgesses Charity, and the charities of Izaak Walton, Simon Fowler, Robert Sutton, John Palmer, Barbara Crompton, Robert Lovett, Richard Startin, William Farmer, Rebecca Crompton, John Webb, and William Fowler, were placed under a body of Stafford Charity Trustees who were also governors of the school and were appointed by the Lord Chancellor.[49]

In 1920 the grammar school became a maintained secondary school,[50] and the other charities were thereafter administered separately. A Scheme of 1922 set up the Stafford United Charities under a new body of trustees. The charities in their hands were Noell's alms-houses with their subsidiary endowments (by then including the Stranaghan Alms-house Trust and the bequest of William Marson), the Poor Burgesses Charity, the charities of John Palmer, Barbara, John and Prudence Crompton, Robert Lovett, and John Rogers, and the charities of Izaak Walton, Robert Sutton, William Farmer, and Rebecca Crompton in so far as they applied to the poor. In 1962 a fresh Scheme was approved under which the United Charities comprised all the last-mentioned charities save Rogers's, together with those of Henry Woodhouse, Olive Jenkinson, and John Shallcross. The trustees were allowed to use the income of the Poor Burgesses Charity and those of John Palmer, Barbara, John and Prudence Crompton, Robert Lovett, Robert Sutton, William Farmer and Rebecca Crompton, and Izaak Walton, after payment of Walton's £5 for maids and of 13s. 8d. to the rector of St. Mary's, for the general benefit of the poor of Stafford. The funds of the remaining charities were to maintain the alms-houses.[51] From 1963 all the income was applied to the alms-houses, except the £5, which was so applied from 1973. Further endowments were received of £2,000 in 1965 under the will of Mrs. M. M. P. Cookson, proved 1959; of £2,000 from an anonymous donor in 1966; of £500 from Mrs. M. E. King by will proved 1967; and of £1,261.52 from Miss W. E. Gaydon by will proved 1970. Land behind the alms-houses was sold to the corporation for £865 in 1965. In 1975 the income was £440 from stock and bank deposits, £1,001 from alms-house rents, £469 from a county council grant, and £50.59 from other sources.[52]

[49] White, *Dir. Staffs.* (1851), 328; Griffith, *Free Schools*, 57–9; C. G. Gilmore, *Hist. of K. Edw. VI Sch., Stafford*, 34; *Accts. of Stafford Public Chars. 1836–42* (copy in W.S.L. Pamphs. *sub* Stafford); Mun. Corp. Act, 5 & 6 Wm. IV, c. 76, s. lxxi. For the Queen Elizabeth Grant see above, pp. 205–6. [50] See p. 166.

[51] Char. Com. Schemes, 19 Dec. 1922 and 20 July 1962.
[52] Ex inf. the sec., Stafford United Chars. (1977).

INDEX